Informatik aktuell

Herausgeber: W. Brauer
im Auftrag der Gesellschaft für Informatik (GI)

T0178364

Springer
Berlin
Heidelberg
New York
Hongkong
London
Mailand
Paris
Tokio

Klaus Irmscher
Klaus-Peter Fähnrich (Hrsg.)

Kommunikation in Verteilten Systemen (KiVS)

13. ITG/GI-Fachtagung
Kommunikation in Verteilten Systemen
(KiVS 2003)
Leipzig, 25.–28. Februar 2003

Eine Veranstaltung der Informationstechnischen
Gesellschaft (ITG/VDE) unter Beteiligung der
Gesellschaft für Informatik (GI)
Ausgerichtet von der Universität Leipzig

ITG INFORMATIONSTECHNISCHE
GESELLSCHAFT IM VDE

Springer

Herausgeber

Klaus Irmscher
LS Rechnernetze und Verteilte Systeme

Klaus-Peter Fähnrich
LS Anwendungsspezifische Informationssysteme

Institut für Informatik, Universität Leipzig
Augustusplatz 10/11, 04109 Leipzig

Unterstützung und Mitwirkende

Universität Leipzig
Informationstechnische Gesellschaft
im VDE
Gesellschaft für Informatik

Sponsoren

adesso AG
Cisco Systems GmbH
DaimlerChrysler AG
Deutsche Telekom AG
(T-Systems)
Deutsche Telekom AG
(T-Systems Multimedia Solutions GmbH)

dpunkt.verlag GmbH
NEC Deutschland GmbH
perdata Gesellschaft für Informations-
verarbeitung mbH
Siemens AG
Universitätsbuchhandlung&Schweitzer OHG

Programmkomitee

S. Abeck, Universität Karlsruhe
H. Baldus, Philips Research Labs Aachen
G. Blakowski, FH Stralsund
T. Braun, Universität Bern
B. Butscher, GMD Fokus Berlin
J. Charzinski, Siemens AG München
R. Eberhardt, DaimlerChrysler AG
W. Effelsberg, Universität Mannheim
W. Erhard, Universität Jena
K.-P. Fähnrich, Universität Leipzig
S. Fischer, TU Braunschweig
K. Froitzheim, TU Bergakademie Freiberg
K. Hänßgen, HTWK Leipzig
K. Geihs, TU Berlin
H.-G. Hegering, LMU München
R. Herrtwich, DaimlerChrysler AG
B. Hohlfeld, DaimlerChrysler AG
U. Hübner, TU Chemnitz
K. Irmscher, Universität Leipzig
P. Kaufmann, DFN e.V.
N. Kalt, Siemens AG München

U. Killat, TU Hamburg-Harburg
H. König, BTU Cottbus
W. Küchlin, Universität Tübingen
P. J. Kühn, Universität Stuttgart
W. Lamersdorf, Universität Hamburg
R. Lehnert, TU Dresden
C. Linnhoff-Popien, LMU München
N. Luttenberger, Universität Kiel
H. de Meer, University College London
J. Niemeier, T-Systems MM Solutions GmbH,
Dresden
D. Reschke, TU Ilmenau
H. Ritter, FU Berlin
K. Rothermel, Universität Stuttgart
A. Schill, TU Dresden
O. Spaniol, RWTH Aachen
R. Steinmetz, TU Darmstadt
H. J. Stüttgen, NEC Europe Heidelberg
L. Wolf, TU Braunschweig
B. Wolfinger, Universität Hamburg
A. Wolisz, TU Berlin
M. Zitterbart, Universität Karlsruhe

Bibliographische Information der Deutschen Bibliothek
Die Deutsche Bibliothek verzeichnet diese Publikation in der Deutschen Nationalbibliografie; detaillierte
bibliografische Daten sind im Internet über http://dnb.ddb.de abrufbar.

CR Subject Classification (2001): C2

ISSN 1431-472-X

ISBN 3-540-00365-7 Springer-Verlag Berlin Heidelberg New York

Springer-Verlag Berlin Heidelberg New York
ein Unternehmen der BertelsmannSpringer Science+Business Media GmbH

http://www.springer.de

© Springer-Verlag Berlin Heidelberg 2003

Printed in Germany

Satz: Reproduktionsfertige Vorlage vom Autor/Herausgeber
Gedruckt auf säurefreiem Papier   SPIN: 10908921   33/3142-543210

Vorwort

Die Fachtagung KiVS (Kommunikation in Verteilten Systemen) kann auf eine sehr erfolgreiche Tradition von Tagungen zurückblicken. Nach den Veranstaltungen in Berlin, Aachen, Mannheim, München, Chemnitz, Braunschweig, Darmstadt und zuletzt in Hamburg wird sie nun in Leipzig, einem Zentrum der Wissenschaft, der Industrie und des Sports im Kreuzungspunkt wichtiger Handelswege Deutschlands durchgeführt. Die Austragungsstelle Universität Leipzig als eine der ältesten Universitäten Deutschlands zeichnet sich durch traditionelle und innovative Lehr- und Forschungsgebiete aus.

Die 13. ITG/GI-Fachtagung KiVS03 befasst sich mit modernen Technologien drahtgebundener und drahtloser Kommunikationsnetzen und darauf basierenden Anwendungslösungen verteilter Systeme. Zu Beginn des 3. Jahrtausends wird mit der KiVS03 ein wissenschaftliches Forum für den erreichten Entwicklungsstand in der Telekommunikation, zur Präsentation aktueller Arbeiten sowie zur Diskussion der Trends für die 'Kommunikation in Verteilten Systemen' für die nächsten Jahre ausgestaltet.

Aus den ca. 100 eingereichten Beiträgen hat der Programmausschuss 29 Arbeiten zur Präsentation ausgewählt. Zusätzlich werden weitere 21 Einreichungen im Rahmen von Kurzbeiträgen und Praxisberichten vorgestellt. Begleitet wird die Fachtagung von Tutorials zu Themen wie Mobile adhoc Netze, Peer-to-Peer-Networking, Web-Services und Sicherheit in mobilen Netzen. In einer Podiumsdiskussion stehen Fragen zur Entwicklung von Netzen und Anwendungen sowie einem Workshop zu E-Learning an. Die Kommunikations-Fachtagung KiVS03 wird zeitgleich mit der Datenbank-Fachtagung BTW03 durchgeführt und gemeinsam eröffnet.

Für die eingeladenen Vorträge konnten namhafte Wissenschaftler aus der Industrie und dem universitären Bereich gewonnen werden, zu Themenstellungen wie Web-Services (F. Leymann, IBM Deutschland), Ubiquitous Computing - Vision und Umsetzung (F. Mattern, ETH Zürich) und Verkehrstelematik – Present & Future (G. Siegle, Robert Bosch GmbH). Die Beiträge sind in 9 Sitzungen gruppiert, die sich mit Themen zu Entwicklungen im Internet, World Wide Web, Mobile Computing, Dienstgüte in Computernetzen, Verteilte Systeme, Sicherheit in Netzen, Telematik-Anwendungen, Management von Netzen und Modellierung von Kommunikationsvorgängen befassen sowie Praxisberichte zu neuen Kommunikationstechnologien.

Die KiVS (Kommunikation in Verteilten Systemen) ist die Fachtagung des gemeinsamen Fachausschusses der ITG (Informationstechnische Gesellschaft im VDE) und der GI (Gesellschaft für Informatik) und wird in einem zweijährigen Turnus durchgeführt. Mit der Universität Leipzig wurde eine traditionsreiche Universität mit einer jungen und aufstrebenden Informatik-Einrichtung zur Ausrichtung beauftragt. Die Universität Leipzig ist eingebettet in ein großes wissenschaftliches und industrielles Umfeld, vertreten durch mehrere Max-Planck-Institute und Innovationszentren sowie durch alteingesessene Firmen als auch Neuansiedlung von Firmen wie BMW oder Porsche. Die im Jahre 2002 wiederhergestellte Universitätsbibliothek ist ein wichtiges Zentrum der wissenschaftlichen Arbeit. Und nicht zuletzt das kulturelle und touristische Leipziger Stadtleben und traditionsreiche Zentren, wie Auerbachs Keller,

Thomaskirche (Wirkungsstätte von J.S. Bach) und Nikolaikirche (Stätte der Montagsgebete) sind eine Bereicherung des begleitenden Konferenzprogramms.

Dem Programmausschuss sei an dieser Stelle für die zeitaufwendige Arbeit im Vorfeld der KiVS03 herzlich gedankt. Unser Dank gilt besonders auch dem lokalen Organisationskomitee, insbesondere Frau I. Dietrich und den Mitarbeitern Herrn J. Hotzky, J.-A. Müller und M. Thränert, die wesentlichen Anteil an der Vorbereitung, Organisation und Planung geleistet haben. Und nicht zuletzt sei auch den Sponsoren gedankt, ohne deren Beitrag die Konferenz nicht in dieser Weise hätte ausgerichtet werden können.

Klaus Irmscher   Klaus-Peter Fähnrich

Leipzig, im Februar 2003

Inhaltsverzeichnis

Session Verteilte Systeme

Session Mobile Computing

Session Telematik

Session Modellierung

Session Security/Management

Session Internet

Preisträger

Eingeladene Vorträge

From Distributed Systems to Ubiquitous Computing – The State of the Art, Trends, and Prospects of Future Networked Systems

Friedemann Mattern

Peter Sturm

Department of Computer Science
ETH Zürich
CH-8092 Zürich, Switzerland
mattern@inf.ethz.ch

Department of Computer Science
University of Trier
D-54286 Trier, Germany
sturm@uni-trier.de

Abstract: We summarize trends in communication paradigms for networked systems, mention well-established as well as innovative software infrastructures for distributed systems (such as COM+, CORBA, .NET and Jini), and give an overview of application domains such as grid computing, peer-to-peer computing, and mobile agents. We then discuss issues in spontaneous networking, and we explain the vision of Ubiquitous Computing and its intriguing prospects.

1. Introduction

Distributed systems techniques have attracted much interest in recent years due to the proliferation of the Web and other Internet-based systems and services. Well-established techniques such as interprocess communication and remote invocation, naming services, cryptographic security, distributed file systems, data replication, and distributed transaction mechanisms provide the run-time infrastructure supporting today's networked applications [CDK 00]. The dominant model is still the traditional client-server architecture. However, application development for distributed systems now relies more and more on middleware support through the use of software frameworks (e.g. CORBA or Web services) that provide higher-level abstractions such as distributed shared objects, and on services including secure communication, authentication, yellow pages, and persistent storage.

In the future, distributed application frameworks may support mobile code, multimedia data streams, user and device mobility, and spontaneous networking [CDK 00]. Scalability, quality of service, and robustness with respect to partial component failures will become key issues.

Clearly, a shift towards large-scale systems has occurred in recent years: not only the pure Internet with its basic protocols, but also the higher-level World Wide Web is becoming a standard platform for distributed applications. Here, the Internet (or an all-encompassing intranet) and its resources are viewed as the global environment in which computations take place. Consequently, high-level protocols and standards, such as XML, enter the focus of distributed system research while low-level issues (such as operating system peculiarities) become less important. The increasing number of computers connected to the Internet has also laid the foundations for new application domains such as grid computing and peer-to-peer computing. Grid computing emphasizes the fact that the Internet can be viewed as a globally distributed computer with an enormous potential for computing power. In contrast to this, peer-to-peer computing underscores the needs of the people behind all these machines. Their desires for immediate and unrestricted information exchange, for anonymity, and for independence from restrictive rules imposed by providers or governments are about to shape the Internet again.

Rapidly evolving network and computer technology, coupled with the exponential growth of the services and information available on the Internet, will soon bring us to the point where hundreds of millions of people have fast, pervasive access to a phenomenal amount of information, through desktop machines at work, school and home, through mobile phones, personal digital assistants (PDA), and car dashboards, from anywhere and everywhere [KG 99]. The challenge of distributed system technology is to provide flexible and reliable infrastructures for such large-scale systems that meet the demands of developers, users, and service providers.

Looking further into the future, essential techniques of distributed systems will be incorporated into an emerging new area, called "Ubiquitous Computing" [Wei 91]. The vision of Ubiquitous Computing (or "pervasive computing", as it is sometimes called) is in some sense a projection of the Internet phenomenon and the mobile phone proliferation phenomenon we observe today into the future, envisioning billions of communicating smart devices forming a world-wide distributed system several orders of magnitude larger than today's Internet.

2. Communication Paradigms

There are many ways in which application software components residing on different machines can communicate with one another over a network. One low-level technique is to directly use the call interfaces of the transport layer, such as the socket mechanism, together with a custom communication protocol. However, programming at this level of abstraction is advisable only in special circumstances since it leaves complex problems such as the guarantee of security, the management of heterogeneity, and concurrency control completely to the application programmer. Instead, developers should choose from a variety of higher level communication protocols and frameworks the one that best suits their needs. Some of these protocols such as the well-known remote procedure call are self-contained and can be used in any application program with almost no additional overhead. Other protocols and frameworks are confined to specific programming languages or execution platforms.

2.1 Remote Procedure Call

One well-established classical communication scheme that fits well with the client-server model is the remote procedure call (RPC). In this model, a component acts as a client when it requests some service from another component; it acts as a server when it responds to a request from a client. RPC makes calling an external procedure that resides in a different network node almost as simple as calling a local procedure. Arguments and return values are automatically packaged in an architecture-neutral format sent between the local and remote procedures.

For each remote procedure, the underlying RPC framework needs a so-called stub procedure on the client side (which acts as a proxy for the remote procedure) and a similar object on the server side. The role of the stub is to take the parameters passed in a regular local procedure call and pass them to the RPC system (which must be resident on both the client and server nodes) [carl b]. Behind the scenes, the RPC system cooperates with the stubs on both sides to transfer the arguments and return values over the network [wash].

To facilitate the creation of stubs, RPC toolkits include special tools. The programmer provides details of an RPC call in the form of specifications encoded in an Interface Definition Language (IDL). An IDL compiler is used to generate the stubs automatically from the IDL specifications [carl]. The stubs can then be linked into clients and servers [carl b].

Several different RPC systems coexist today. On Unix/Linux platforms, an RPC system introduced by Sun Microsystems [ONC] is used for accessing many system services such as the network file system NFS and the network information system NIS. The DCE-RPC [DCE] is used as the basis for Microsoft's COM+ middleware. RPC frameworks have become an established technique, and are typically invisible to application programmers since they merely represent the basic transport mechanism used by more general middleware platforms as presented in section 3.

2.2 XML-based RPC

Although RPC systems explicitly address the issue of interoperability in open systems, client and server programs that make use of this principle are tied to a single RPC framework in order to cooperate successfully. The main reason for this is that every RPC system defines its own encoding for data structures. Despite this difference, the basic semantics of most RPC systems are quite similar since all of them are based on a synchronous procedure call in a C-like syntax format.

Viewing the messages sent between clients and servers in an RPC system as documents with a given syntax was a major breakthrough in RPC technology. Using XML to define the syntax of RPC requests and replies was a simple idea, but it paved the way for interoperability between different RPC systems [BSL 00, McL 01]. As a result, XML-based RPC systems are used today to integrate otherwise incompatible application programs, and they are thus an essential part of solutions in collaborative business which integrate the different legacy applications used by cooperating companies. For legacy software, additional wrapper programs must be implemented that translate a specific set of XML-based RPC requests into proprietary function calls. Some modern database-centric execution platforms are even capable of processing a given XML-based RPC dialect directly.

The essential idea in XML-based RPC frameworks is to use XML to define a type system that can be used to communicate data between clients and servers. These type systems specify primitive types such as integers, floating points, and text strings, and they provide mechanisms for aggregating instances of these primitive types into compound types in order to specify and represent new data types. One of the first XML-based RPC frameworks was the simple object access protocol SOAP [SOAP], defined by a consortium of companies including Microsoft, IBM, and SAP. SOAP is now an integral part of Windows operating systems (as part of the COM+ and .NET middleware). A key advantage of SOAP is its extensibility by use of XML schemas and the fact that the widespread HTTP protocol can be used as the transport mechanism between clients and servers, thus using the Web as a communication infrastructure and a tunnel between cooperating distributed applications. Servers may appear in this scenario as dedicated Web servers with the ability to trigger servlets, scripts, or any other means of program execution.

Other XML-based RPC dialects such as standard XML-RPC have also been specified [McL 01]. Most of them, however, do not incorporate XML schemas and are thus limited to a fixed set of primitive data types, as are traditional RPC systems. Fortunately, having to cope with different dialects of XML-based RPC systems is not as involved as dealing with incompatible classical RPC frameworks, because in many situations simple transformation rules can be defined to convert XML encoded messages between different RPC platforms.

2.3 Remote Method Invocation

Whilst RPC is reasonably well suited to the procedural programming paradigm, it is not directly applicable to the object-oriented programming style that has gained much popularity in recent years. Here, Remote Method Invocation (RMI) – a newer technique for Java-based systems – comes into its own. RMI is similar to RPC, but integrates the distributed object model into the Java language in a natural way [MIT]. With RMI, it is not necessary to describe the methods of remote objects in a separate type definition file. Instead, RMI works directly from existing objects, providing seamless integration [jsol]. Furthermore, remote objects can be passed as parameters in remote method calls, a feature that classical RPC systems usually do not possess.

In classical RPC systems, client-side stub code must be generated and linked into a client before a remote procedure call can be made. RMI is more dynamic in this respect: owing to the Java capability of transferring code, the stubs that are needed for an invocation can be downloaded at runtime (in architecture-neutral bytecode format) from a remote location, for example directly from the server just before the remote method is actually invoked. Internally, RMI makes use of object serialization to transmit arbitrary object types over the network, and because downloaded code can potentially be harmful to the system, it uses a security manager to check this.

RMI seems to fit well with the general trend of distributed systems becoming increasingly dynamic.

2.4 Asynchronous Protocols

RPC and RMI are basically synchronous calls: the client is blocked while the call is processed by the server. Asynchronous variants that require multithreading are difficult to handle and are error prone. However, the trend in distributed systems is towards asynchronous and reactive systems – systems that cannot wait indefinitely for a synchronous call to terminate. Typical examples are user interface systems or real-time systems.

Such reactive and asynchronous systems are better served by a more abstract communication paradigm based on events. Events are simple asynchronous messages, but they are attractive because they represent an intuitive (although somewhat restricted) way of modeling that something has happened that is potentially of interest to some other objects. Distributed infrastructures based on this paradigm are often called "publish and subscribe middleware" or simply "event channel" or "software bus".

The concept of such a software bus is quite simple: all clients (i.e. consumers of events) are connected to a shared medium called a "bus". They announce their interest in a certain topic (i.e. type of events) by subscribing to it. Objects or processes that want to send a message or an event to clients publish it under a certain topic to the bus. If the receiver's topic matches the sender's topic, the message is forwarded to the receiver.

From a software design point of view, the event paradigm offers the benefits of direct notification instead of busy-probing: an object tells the environment to inform it when something happens, and when something happens it reacts accordingly [cal]. It thus eliminates the need for consumers to periodically poll for new events. Furthermore, the concept easily allows the use of adapters that act as programmable middlemen in the event streams. They may for example multiplex, filter, or aggregate events.

However, although the publish/subscribe paradigm is attractive due to its conceptual simplicity and has the benefit of decoupling objects in space and time (while at the same time abstracting from the network topology and the heterogeneity of the components), it requires a powerful brokering mechanism that takes care of event delivery. Furthermore, its use requires the implicit or explicit semantics of the brokering mechanism to be carefully analyzed – a priori it is not clear how quickly events are to be delivered, whether events are to remain on the bus for a certain period of time (for example, so that subscribers who miss anything due to system failure can catch up on missed events) and whether there are any guarantees on the delivery order. It should be noted that the publish/subscribe paradigm is basically a multicast scheme, and it is well known from distributed systems theory that broadcast semantics, in particular for dynamic environments, is a non-trivial issue.

The overall trend in communication paradigms seems to be clear: it is progressing from the simple procedural paradigm requiring relatively little system support, via the object-oriented method invocation principle, towards Web-based infrastructures and more abstract schemes for loosely-coupled asynchronous systems that require complex run-time infrastructures. One can expect platforms supporting such abstract communication paradigms on the global Internet scale to become increasingly important in the future, probably being integrated with the routing and management schemes for general Internet-based messaging services. Scalability and efficient realization of such infrastructures is a real challenge, however.

3. Trends in Infrastructures and Middleware

Middleware and software infrastructures for distributed systems provide basic communication facilities to application components and handle issues such as platform heterogeneity that are due to differing hardware systems, operating systems, or programming languages. Furthermore, they provide a set of standard services that are typically needed by distributed applications such as directory services and cryptographic security.

One of the first commercially available middleware systems was DCE [DCE], which is still being used in many large legacy applications. Communication in DCE is based on RPC, and it essentially provides directory services, security services (based on the well-known Kerberos system), and a distributed file service. Many middleware concepts were initially implemented using DCE and evolved over time as part of more modern middleware systems. Some of today's most prominent candidates are presented in the following sections.

3.1 COM+

The component object model COM and its latest version COM+ have their roots in the basic clipboard mechanisms provided by early Microsoft operating systems to enable the exchange of data between different applications [EE 99]. This simple mechanism was iterated over the years and evolved into a pragmatic component platform. The COM+ platform is widely used in industry and a huge variety of COM+ components are available and can be purchased from specialized vendors.

Components in COM+ are defined through a set of interfaces. The interface definition language MIDL is an extension of the DCE IDL. This IDL allows the definition of common static and dynamic data types (essentially variable-length arrays). It is object-oriented in the sense that single inheritance is possible for interfaces. Unfortunately, there is no implementation inheritance, thus a component defining a derived interface must implement all functions of the base interfaces again, no matter whether the semantics of the method are changed or not. The root of all interface hierarchies is the IUnkown interface with its main method of downcasting to any derived interface if possible. Interfaces are identified by 128-bit random numbers called global unique identifiers (GUID). COM+ allows the representation of meta-information about interfaces by means of type libraries (generated automatically by the IDL compiler). This type information is used in a process called "automation", where the calling application can interrogate implemented interfaces, method signatures, and data types of a component at runtime. Based on this information, the caller can build and issue method calls to a component step by step by using the rather involved IDispatch interface.

Since COM+ is a binary component standard, a component itself ships as a dynamic link library (DLL) with tables holding function pointers to the methods of each interface. Each component is again identified by another 128-bit GUID. The most prominent usage of components is through so-called inproc servers by linking the requested DLL to the virtual address space of the client program and accessing methods using indirect function calls. The mapping between the component identifier (GUID) and the path of the dynamic library is stored in the registry of the Windows operating system. Additionally, components can also be executed within their own virtual address space, for example as dedicated servers or more commonly as a dynamic library linked into a specialized surrogate process. A third possibility is to use a component of a remote server. In this case, RPC requests and replies are generated transparently by the COM+ runtime platform. The required stub and proxy functions, generated automatically by the MIDL compiler, are implemented as additional dynamic libraries. They are again identified by the COM+ runtime system using the Windows registry and the 128 bit interface identifier.

Most of the functionality of Microsoft Windows operating systems has subsequently been converted to COM+ services. Some of these components are rather heavyweight such as Internet Explorer, the office program suite, or DirectX (for efficiently accessing multimedia devices), and most of them are used only locally. But an increasing number of COM+ components form an integral part of standard services in Microsoft Windows networks and may be used remotely, such as directory services (Active Directory), event propagation, file and printer sharing, and even remote desktops.

Despite its widespread use, COM+ middleware has a number of deficiencies and limitations. Most importantly, the implementation of components is quite complex and requires the implementation of an impressive number of additional methods. Integrated development environments such as Visual Studio try to tackle this problem by offering assistance (for example, using so-called wizards) to ease the burden on the component developer. Because of the flat namespace, the COM+ components available on a given system are also difficult to manage and organize. Furthermore, the packing of components into one or more dynamic libraries and the flat identifier namespace for interfaces as well as components within the Windows registry are susceptible to system instability in the event of program installation or updates.

3.2 The .NET Framework

Some of the deficiencies of COM+ middleware are addressed by Microsoft's more recent initiative, the .NET framework [TL 02, Ric 02]. Primarily introduced as a rival product to Sun's Java platform, .NET defines a virtual runtime system CLR (Common Language Runtime) for most components and applications. The CLR is based on a Common Type System (CTS), a single-inheritance object-oriented hierarchy of common built-in types such as integers, floating points, and text strings. Ideally, components and application programs implemented in a given programming language are translated into an intermediate language (IL), comparable to Java bytecode, using the CTS. This so-called "managed code" can be executed by the CLR. Currently, IL compilers are available for Visual Basic, JScript, C++ (with restrictions, of course), and C# as part of Visual Studio .NET. Any IL code is translated into native machine language on a per method base before it is executed within the CLR. In contrast to the Java virtual machine, this intermediate language is never interpreted at the instruction level. The CTS enables the immediate use of built-in types as well as user-defined types within different programming languages, e.g. a class in managed C++ code (C++ code within the restrictions defined by the CTS) can be derived from a Visual Basic super class (something all serious developers have been wanting to do for years).

More interesting with respect to distributed systems are advances in component packaging, so-called assemblies. Assemblies are used to keep track of all the resources required by a single component or application. Each assembly is accompanied by a manifest which stores the assembly name and version, security information, names and versions of other assemblies referenced by this assembly, and type information about the public classes defined in this assembly. Additionally, a code base URL can be defined where all the files of an assembly can be downloaded if necessary. Since all the meta-information making up an assembly is stored in a single manifest file, management of installed assemblies and their interdependencies is substantially improved compared to the classical registry approach. The technique used in .NET resembles the packaging of enterprise beans in Java (see also section 4.1) in a broader sense, although the manifest information itself is not described by a self-descriptive language such as XML. In contrast to enterprise beans which ship as a single jar file, assemblies may still consist of several files in order to allow for the partial download of complex components.

3.3 CORBA

One of the most widely-used infrastructures for distributed systems based on an object-oriented model is still CORBA, the Common Object Request Broker Architecture, which is supported by a large industry consortium. The first CORBA standard was introduced in 1991, and it has undergone continual and significant revisions ever since [wash]. Part of the specification describes an Interface Definition Language (IDL) that all CORBA implementations must support. The CORBA IDL is based on C++ and is used by applications to define the externally visible parts of object methods that can be invoked by other objects. It has a similar function to the IDL of COM+.

The central component of a CORBA system is the object request broker (ORB). The ORB provides a mechanism for transparently communicating client requests to target object implementations. It simplifies distributed programming by decoupling the client from the details of the method invocations: when a client invokes an operation, the ORB is responsible for finding the object implementation, transparently activating it if necessary, delivering the request to the object, and returning any response to the caller [Corba].

In addition to the ORB, CORBA defines what are known as object frameworks: object services (application-independent services at the system level such as naming, trading, or security services), common facilities (application-independent services at the application level such as printing services), and domain facilities (services for specific application fields).

CORBA has gained much momentum in industry and research. Implementations of the standard are available from a large number of vendors and even exist as freeware [PR 01]. CORBA supports all major programming languages, is suited for almost every combination of hardware and operating system, and is also being used to realize mission-critical applications in industries as diverse as health care, telecommunications, banking, and manufacturing.

While in the past almost all additions to the CORBA specification have been integrated by vendors into their products over time, this will probably become increasingly difficult in the future. The recent CORBA-3 specification is huge and includes the following major additions: Internet integration (CORBA through firewalls, URL addressing for CORBA objects), quality of service control (fault tolerance, real-time), and a component model similar to EJB (Enterprise Java Beans). It is questionable whether CORBA and in particular implementations of the standard can, in the long run, adopt all these and other foreseeable developments in the field of distributed systems.

Furthermore, CORBA was conceived for static distributed systems, requires considerable resources at run time, and uses the traditional client-server model as the basic metaphor. It is therefore not well suited for small devices, highly dynamic systems, and services that are spontaneously integrated into a federation. This, however, is a major trend in distributed systems, to which Jini and similar systems are better adapted.

3.4 Jini

Jini is an infrastructure that runs on top of Java and RMI to create a federation of devices and software components implementing services. Jini enables any device that can run a Java Virtual Machine to interoperate with others by offering and using services. A service is defined as an entity that can be used by a person, a program, or another service [darm]. Typical examples of services are printing a document or translating from one data format to another, but functional hardware devices are also considered to be services.

All services are granted as leases. Each service, when in use, is registered as being leased by another service. Leases are time-dependent and have to be renewed upon expiration. If the lease is not renewed, then Jini removes the service from the list of services offered.

A device or a service uses a standard mechanism to register with the federation. First, it polls the local network to locate a so-called lookup service. Then, it registers itself with the lookup service. The lookup service is similar to a bulletin board for all services in the federation. It can store not only pointers to the services, but also the code for these services or proxies representing the service, as well as defining service characteristics and attributes (e.g. a printer may specify whether it supports color printing) [jini].

When a client wants to use a service offered to the community, it can download the required proxy object from the lookup service (after having located and contacted the lookup), including any code such as device drivers or user interfaces. Dynamic code mobility enables clients to take advantage of services without pre-installing or loading drivers. The downloaded proxy object can then be used locally to interact directly with the selected device or service, with any device-specific details being hidden by the proxy.

Jini and similar infrastructures (e.g. Universal Plug and Play or UPnP, which is a service discovery framework at a somewhat lower level than Jini) are thus well-suited for highly dynamic distributed systems where components may be mobile and typically form spontaneous networks – an important trend in distributed systems [Ker 00].

3.5 Bridges Between Different Middleware Systems

Each middleware system presented in the previous sections is supported by strong commercial forces. Together with the inertia of existing legacy software – all closely tied to one of these infrastructures (especially in the case of Microsoft's COM+ platform) – it is unlikely that any one of them will surpass its competitors. For this reason, bridges have been defined and standardized for the most widely used middleware platforms.

One such bridge mediates between the two major middleware parties CORBA and COM+. It is derived from the standard IOP protocol (Inter-ORB protocol) that allows basic interaction between CORBA objects served by ORBs from different vendors. Because CORBA-1 compliant ORBs were not able to talk to ORBs from other vendors, this Inter-ORB protocol was a major improvement in CORBA-2. It still allows proprietary protocols between two or more ORBs to exist, but requires a General Inter-ORB protocol (GIOP) to be understood by any CORBA-2 compliant ORB [GIOP]. This abstract protocol defines the syntax and semantics of messages to allow independently developed ORBs to communicate over any connection-oriented transport protocol. Two instances of this GIOP exist: the IIOP (Internet Inter-ORB protocol) implements GIOP over TCP streams, and the DCE-IOP, which forms the basis for the interaction between COM+ components and CORBA objects [DCE-IOP].

The Java platform tightly integrates CORBA through its org.omg.CORBA package, a library with more than 100 classes that can interact with CORBA ORBs and CORBA objects [j2ee]. These classes represent the mapping between Java and the interface of a CORBA object defined in the CORBA IDL. The package also comprises a Java implementation of an ORB.

Within the Microsoft middleware, bridges are also defined to provide backward compatibility. COM+ components written in languages such as Visual Basic or C# are now compiled to and thus accessible in the .NET environment. Moreover, any managed component (code that is based on the Common Type System) can directly be used as a COM+ component. For COM+ components implemented in unmanaged programming languages such as C++, appropriate .NET wrappers can be generated automatically if type libraries for these components exist. With the aid of these wrappers, unmanaged components are accessible within .NET-compliant applications and vice versa. In the open source community there is also a project called MONO [MONO] which aims at creating a .NET conforming platform for the Linux operating system.

Basic obstacles in bridging middleware systems are substantial performance penalties due to additional marshalling costs, friction losses because of incompatible models, and limitations in the expressiveness of the involved IDLs. The mutual sympathies of the participating companies and their licensing plans as well as their patent politics also have a strong influence on the proliferation of bridges between different middleware platforms. Currently, most of the bridges have been used in simple applications only as a proof of concept, and serious commercial usage seems to be rare.

4. Trends in Distributed Application Structures

Dramatic changes at the application level accompany the evolution of distributed middleware. In e-commerce and cooperative business, the Web and its underlying HTTP protocol are becoming the standard execution platform for distributed and component-based applications. The increasing number of computers and users on the Internet has led to new cooperation structures such as peer-to-peer computing, an interesting exercise in scalability with almost political implications for the networked society. It has also stimulated new developments in the area of computing clusters and so-called grids. Independent of the application domain, the integration of mobile clients into a distributed environment and the ad-hoc networking of dynamic components are becoming ever more important.

4.1 Application Servers

The client-server model is still the prevalent pattern of communication in distributed systems. But programmed client-server systems based on a traditional RPC scheme are losing ground in favor of Web-based communication between clients and servers. Enhanced HTTP servers receive client requests (typically a URL get request) and are capable of performing the necessary computation to satisfy the client request and replying with a dynamically generated HTML document. A variety of technologies are available for servers as well as for clients. Client-side technologies primarily deal with user interface issues. Server-side technologies, on the other hand, define how application code gets executed upon the arrival of a client request. Heavyweight mechanisms such as CGI (Common Gateway Interface) and ASP (Active Server Pages, [ASP]) are widely used where scripts or whole executables are started on receipt of each incoming request. However, besides performance penalties, these mechanisms raise a number of problems regarding security, authentication, and state management.

With respect to application architectures, a shift from 2-tier solutions with front-end clients and back-end servers (legacy programs or database platforms) towards 3-tier structures can be observed. In a 3-tier client-server system, functional issues (what is known as business logic) are separated from the issues concerning data modeling and persistent storage. The latter are still realized by traditional database systems, but the business logic is typically executed on a so-called application server (middle-tier), a specialized platform for the execution and management of application components. Typically, this application server is tightly coupled with a Web server, and client requests are delivered directly to the responsible business object. Two opposing approaches on modeling, deploying, and managing business logic exist today – the Enterprise Java Beans (EJB, [EJB]) standard defined on top of the Java platform, and the COM+ component model extended with the Microsoft Transaction Server (MTS).

The EJB standard defines two types of beans, where a bean is a specialized Java class that conforms to certain rules in order to reflect the class structure. Entity beans represent data objects inside the application server. They are instantiated when they are first referenced by some other component. Two types of instantiation are possible: the data members of the object are retrieved automatically from databases using the Java database connectivity mechanism JDBC (container-managed persistency) or manually by any application-defined mechanism (bean-managed persistency). Container-managed persistency can be used as an automated migration of a database-centric system structure to a more modern object-oriented application architecture. The bean-managed approach may serve as an object-oriented wrapper for legacy applications. The flow of control is modeled in EJB by so-called session beans. Session beans come in a stateless and a stateful flavor. A stateful session bean stores conversational state encompassing successive client requests only inside the application server. It is never stored persistently. A similar architecture is used with COM+ and MTS, the Windows counterpart of the application server. In this environment, COM+ components implementing specific interfaces correspond to entity beans or session beans.

In component-based application architectures, a tendency to distinguish between functional and non-functional aspects can be observed. Entity components and session components are still being developed with traditional programming languages such as C, C++, Java, or even Visual Basic, for implementing the functional part. But non-functional issues such as transactional scope, role-based security mechanisms, connection and object pooling (reusing connection and objects for independent requests), as well as load balancing are not being implemented as part of a component anymore; instead, each component is being augmented by supplementary attributes. In the case of COM+, some of these attributes are defined as part of the source code or the interface definition using a special syntax. In the EJB context, all attributes are defined in a dedicated XML manifest file that is part of the bean's jar file. Attributes are recognized and implemented by the application server together with specific wrappers that surround each component (containers in the context of EJB or so-called interceptors in the Windows environment). By these means, complex applications can be managed on a more abstract and descriptive level without the need for specific programming skills. For this purpose, dedicated management consoles are used by application administrators that provide access to all non-functional aspects of an application.

4.2 Peer-to-Peer Computing

The Internet boom in the late 1990s led to an unexpected explosion in the number of private computers connected to the global network. According to [isc], a rough estimate for the number of hosts connected to the Internet in January 2002 was 147 million (hosts advertised in the DNS). The major technical challenge for the Internet and its protocol suite IPv4 was to keep up with this growing number of hosts and users. One specific risk was that of running out of IP addresses. In particular, a shortage of class B networks and the small size of class C networks have led to a number of competing enhancements to the existing addressing schemes of IPv4.

Besides classless Internet domain routing (CIDR, [CIDR]) and network address translation (NAT, [NAT]), a widely-used approach to remedy this situation is based on the assumption that most private computers are connected to the Internet only sporadically. Therefore, no static IP addresses are assigned to these hosts anymore. Instead, the Internet provider uses a fixed contingent of addresses and assigns a dynamic IP address temporarily whilst one of these private hosts is connected to the Internet. As a consequence, the majority of computers in the Internet cannot be identified by unambiguous IP addresses anymore, since these addresses change frequently over time.

The millions of new users mostly had rather different expectations about the network and its opportunities. This new community did not fit into the traditional client-server scheme where only a minority of servers stored most of the information accessed by the majority of clients. Many of the new users were primarily interested in exchanging information with each other, be it mp3 audio files, movies, or more questionable things such as license keys, operating systems, application programs, and cracked games.

This shift in the perception of the Internet and its functionality has given rise to the peer-to-peer (P2P) movement [P2P 01]. Today, P2P comprises a variety of different application domains, but the above-mentioned exchange of data amongst peers is the most prominent one. Technically, programs for this purpose are complicated due to scalability issues and because of the dynamic IP addresses of most of their clients. Basically, these systems store only meta-information about the documents available in the P2P network, the data itself being kept by the peers and downloaded directly by the client (disregarding the fact that the widespread use of asymmetric DSL modems – a remnant of the earlier client-server structure – leads to weak uplinks when peers act as servers). Due to legal and copyright issues, storing this meta-information in a single place, e.g. by dedicated servers, can be prohibitive. Napster [naps], one of the first P2P networks, implemented this approach and became much less attractive due to several lost lawsuits. Other P2P networks such as Gnutella [gnut] and its clients (e.g. BearShare [bear], Morpheus [morph], and LimeWire [lime]) bypass this single point of storage by circulating the meta-information within the overlay network itself. By these means, however, they introduce a huge additional network load.

The peer-to-peer movement also has a political dimension [P2P 01]. The classical client-server structured Internet can be viewed as a political system where a small number of residents define the rules for the masses. In this respect, peer-to-peer is sometimes interpreted as a process of democratization. This is also one of the reasons why the Open Source community has strong relations with the P2P movement. A number of projects emerged from this political motivation. One driving force behind these projects is the impetus to provide anonymity for clients accessing sensitive information, to protect against governmental supervision, to prohibit censorship, and to protect privacy.

4.3 Grid Computing

The latent computing power of the Internet is vast, and with the ever-increasing quality and bandwidth of network technology it is possible to tap some of this potential. Unlimited computing power is needed in many application domains, especially in research disciplines such as physics, chemistry, bio-chemistry, astronomy, and meteorology, where many simulations are computationally expensive. Many of these simulations have previously been performed on vector supercomputers, but the availability of high-performance networks has led to a shift towards arrays of inexpensive personal computers and workstations [FK 98, grid]. In the Linux environment, there is even a competition for the largest number of Linux boxes connected to form a single virtual supercomputer. Impressive systems are also commercially available – not for everyone's wallet – with more than 8000 processors [top].

Because of the quality of the network connection, computer clusters with an increasing diameter can be deployed successfully, although the vision of a global computer grid comprising most of the hosts available in the Internet is still several years away. The project coming closest to this vision is seti@home [seti]. Technically, seti@home is a client-server based loosely-coupled cluster system, where any client computer can download a set of radio data. Clients perform a Fourier analysis during idle times to look for signals of artificial origin. The results are then sent back to the server system. The total statistics of this project as of March 23, 2002 are quite impressive: more than 3.6 million clients have contributed to seti@home until now, 1.42E+21 floating point operations have been performed, and a total computation time of 921,190 CPU years has been spent so far.

A number of middleware projects such as JXTA [jxta], Globus [glob], and Legion [leg] aim at providing a virtual platform for the execution of distributed applications on such grid computer systems. Most of them are based on early middleware for cluster computers such as PVM [pvm] and MPI [mpi]. In the latest middleware systems, emphasis is put on the establishment and maintenance of a computer grid, the ease of communication between heterogeneous computer systems, and enhanced communication patterns essential to vector-based mathematics.

4.4 Mobility

People have an increasing desire for ubiquitous access to information, anywhere, anyplace, and anytime. For that, they need not only mobile and portable devices, but also adequate communication systems and software infrastructures.

Mobile devices in the form of portable telephones, PDAs, and notebook computers are now commonplace. Technologies such as WAP, imode, GSM, and in particular UMTS and similar so-called third generation cellular communication standards will soon give rise to new mobile devices providing fast and immediate (i.e. "always connected") access to the Internet.

However, mobile devices are currently poorly integrated. One example is data synchronization: since from the mobile worker perspective it is crucial that data (such as phone numbers and calendar information) remains consistent across the various devices, automatic synchronization is a necessity. Current synchronization software consists of proprietary products that only allow synchronizing between specific devices and applications. The trend here is moving towards standards (such as SyncML, propagated by an industry consortium) and more general synchronization middleware [HMNS 00].

Another infrastructure problem is transparent roaming. Although protocols and systems such as mobile IP provide users the freedom to roam beyond their home subnet whilst consistently maintaining their home IP address, this is not as simple as roaming in cellular phone networks and has several drawbacks with respect to efficiency and scalability.

It is not only people and computing devices that can be mobile, but also program code. Mobile code is executable program code that moves from a source machine to a target machine where it is executed. Mobile code may help to support user mobility: personalized environments can follow a user between computers [cam]. Platform independence of mobile code is usually achieved by using scripting languages for which interpreters are available on most systems, or by compiling into some platform-independent representation such as Java bytecode.

Mobile code is an important programming paradigm and opens up new possibilities for structuring distributed software systems in an open and dynamically changing environment. It can improve speed, flexibility, structure, and the ability to handle disconnections, and it is particularly well-suited if adaptability and flexibility are among the main application requirements. It has applications in many areas, such as mobile computing, active networks, network management, resource discovery, software dissemination and configuration, electronic commerce, and information harvesting [KM 00].

Java applets are a prime example of mobile code components. Applets are best known as small Java programs, embedded in a Web page, that can be executed within the Web browser. However, applets together with the ubiquitous availability of the Java Virtual Machine, Java's class loading mechanism, its code serialization feature, and RMI make Java a full mobile code system where arbitrary code can be downloaded over the network and executed locally. Of course, security is a major concern in this context.

A more elaborate form of mobile code, based on the "push principle" as opposed to the "pull principle" of mere code downloading, is that of mobile agents [KM 00].

They consist of self-contained software processes which can autonomously migrate from one host to another during their execution. In contrast to simple mobile code systems, mobile agents have navigational autonomy, they decide on their own (based on their programmed strategy and the current state of the context) whether and when they want to migrate. While roaming the Internet or a proprietary intranet and visiting other machines, they do some useful work on behalf of their owners or originators.

Compared to traditional distributed computing schemes, mobile agents promise, at least in some cases, to cope more efficiently and elegantly with a dynamic, heterogeneous, and open environment which is characteristic of today's Internet. Certainly, electronic commerce is one of the most attractive areas in this respect: a mobile agent may act (on behalf of a user or owner) as a seller, buyer, or trader of goods, services, and information. Accordingly, mobile agents may go on a shopping tour of the Internet – they may locate the best or cheapest offerings on Web servers, and when equipped with a negotiation strategy (i.e. if they are "intelligent agents") they may even carry out business transactions on behalf of their owners [FM 99].

Another general application domain is searching for information on the Internet or information retrieval in large remote databases when queries cannot be anticipated. Other uses of mobile agent technology include monitoring, remote diagnosis, groupware applications, and entertainment.

In general, mobile agents seem to be a promising technology for the emerging open Internet-based service market. They are well-suited for the personalization of services, and dynamic code installation by agents is an elegant means of extending the functionality of existing devices and systems. Agent technology therefore enables the rapid deployment of new and value-added services. Furthermore, mobile code and mobile agents are of interest for future Ubiquitous Computing applications, where small mobile devices may be "spontaneously" updated with new functionality or context-dependent program code.

Some important problems remain to be solved, however. The most important issues are probably security concerns: protecting hosts from malicious agents, but more crucially also protecting agents and agent-based applications from malicious hosts. The second issue is crucial for applications such as electronic commerce in an open world, but unfortunately it is difficult to tackle. The main point is that, as an agent traverses multiple hosts which are trusted to different degrees, its state can be changed by its temporary hosts in ways that adversely impact its functionality [nist]. Transactional semantics for migration (i.e. "exactly-once migration" in the event of communication failures), interoperability with other systems, coordination issues, and the management of large societies of mobile agents also still pose non-trivial challenges. Furthermore, a seamless integration of mobile agents into the Web environment is crucial for the success of mobile agent technology.

4.5 Spontaneous Networking

Device mobility and the emergence of information appliances are spurring on a new form of networking: unmanaged, dynamic networks of devices, especially mobile devices, which spontaneously and unpredictably join and leave the network. Underlying network technologies already exist – for example, Bluetooth. Consumers will expect these ad hoc, peer-to-peer networks to automatically form within the home, in networked vehicles, in office buildings, and in various arbitrary environments [IBM].

In such environments, the ability to dynamically discover devices and services ("service discovery") is a key component for making these networks useful [ibm]. Service discovery protocols provide a standard method for applications, services, and devices to describe and to advertise their capabilities to other applications, services, and devices, and to discover their capabilities. Such protocols also enable them to search other entities for a particular capability, and to request and establish interoperable sessions with these devices to utilize those capabilities [eet].

The most important technologies to date for service discovery are Jini (as described in section 3.4), Salutation, Universal Plug and Play (UPnP) from Microsoft, E-speak from Hewlett-Packard, and the Service Location Protocol (SLP), which has been jointly developed by researchers from both academia and industry as a widely accepted and usable Internet standard for service discovery.

However, a crucial point is service mediation: matching requests for services with service descriptions. This is not as easy as it seems (e.g. does or should a request for a 300 dpi printer match a 600 dpi printer?), and designing a framework for service types is an especially difficult problem for open, dynamic networks, in which the communicating parties may have never encountered each other before, and cannot assume shared code or architectures [ncsa]. Technologies such as XML may provide at least a syntactical basis for that problem. Another technology currently being developed by the World Wide Web Consortium (W3C) is the Resource Description Framework (RDF), which provides interoperability between applications that exchange machine-understandable information. However, none of these technologies addresses the underlying fundamental conceptual and semantic problem of service mediation, which remains an important open issue.

5. Towards Ubiquitous Computing

Given the continuing technical progress in computing and communication, it seems that we are heading towards an all-encompassing use of networks and computing power, a new era commonly termed "Ubiquitous Computing". Its vision is grounded in the firm belief amongst the scientific community that Moore's Law (i.e. the observation that the computer power available on a chip approximately doubles every eighteen months) will hold true for at least another 15 years. This means that in the next few years, microprocessors will become so small and inexpensive that they can be embedded in almost everything – not only electrical devices, cars, household appliances, toys, and tools, but also such mundane things as pencils (e.g. to digitize everything we draw) and clothes. All these devices will be interwoven and connected together by wireless networks. In fact, technology is expected to make further dramatic improvements, which means that eventually billions of tiny and mobile processors will occupy the environment and be incorporated into many objects of the physical world.

Portable and wireless Internet information appliances are already now a hot topic in the computer industry. Soon everything from laptops and palmtops to electronic books, from cars and telephones to pagers, will access Internet services to accomplish user tasks, even though their users may have no idea that such access is taking place

[Kot]. It is clear that today's mobile phones and PDAs, connected to the Internet, are only the first precursors of completely new devices and services that will emerge. This will give rise to many interesting new applications and business opportunities.

5.1 Smart Devices

Progress in technologies for sensors (and thus the ability to sense the environment), together with the expected increase in processing power and memory, will render classical devices or everyday objects "smart" – they may adapt to the environment and provide useful services in addition to their original purpose. Most of these new emerging "smart devices" will be small and therefore highly mobile; some might even be wearable and be worn much as eyeglasses are worn today. They will be equipped with spontaneous network capabilities and thus have access to any information or provide access to any service "on the net". Connected together and exchanging appropriate information, they will form powerful systems.

Future smart devices will come in various shapes and sizes and will be designed for various task-specific purposes. They all have in common the fact that they are equipped with embedded microprocessors and are connected (usually by wireless means) to other smart devices or directly to the Internet. Some of these devices may also be equipped with appropriate task-specific sensors. Others, known as "information appliances", will allow users to gain direct and simple access to both relevant information (e.g. daily news and email) and services [Nor 98] [ibm]. Their user interface may be based on speech recognition, gesture recognition, or some other advanced natural input mode technology that is appropriate for their purpose, size, and shape. Multimodal human-computer interaction techniques will also help to identify people and thus protect access to the device. All these devices will be so highly optimized to particular tasks that they will blend into the world and require little technical knowledge on the part of their users – they will be as simple to use as calculators, telephones or toasters [ibm].

Extremely flat and cheap screens that can be fixed to walls, doors and desks are conceivable. The displays could be configured to present information such as weather, traffic, stock quotes or sports results extracted from the Web. Once configured, users could place these displays wherever they felt it was convenient. As humans, we are accustomed to looking in particular places for particular pieces of information [MIT b]. This way, dynamic information would become much easier to find and assimilate – a user might, for example, place today's weather forecast on the wardrobe door.

Smart toys are another appealing prospect. Compared to an ordinary toy, a networked toy would have access to a huge world of information and could be more responsive to its owner and environment. For example, a toy that teaches spelling could access a large dictionary. It could also invoke a speech recognition process running on a remote computer to convert a child's story into text. Or it might know the current weather and other global or local news and events. A toy (such as a smart teddy bear) might also act as a telecommunication device or even a telepresence device and serve as an avatar for the friends and family of the toy owner [MIT c].

Of course, many other types of smart devices are conceivable. Wearable computing devices will be used to keep people informed, connected, and entertained. Just like the carriage clock of 300 years ago that subsequently became a pocket watch and then a wristwatch, personal electronic devices will become items that can be worn as clothing, jewelry, and accessories [phil]. Wearable electronics may even become a new clothing concept: textiles that are electrically conductive but also soft and warm to touch exist already. As a result, it is relatively easy to move audio, data, and power around a garment. Conductive fibers can be integrated into woven materials, and conductive inks allow electrically active patterns to be printed directly onto fabrics.

One of the unique aspects of mobile devices is that they can have an awareness of the location where they are used. However, location-awareness is only one aspect of context-awareness as the encompassing concept, which describes the ability of a device or program to sense, react to, or adapt to the environment in which it is running. Context-awareness enables new applications based on the special nature of the context, for example interactive guide maps. However, it may also be exploited in determining the form of interaction supported and modifying interface behavior. For example in a car system, unimportant feedback may be limited during periods of rapid maneuvering [RCDD 98].

A dominant constraint for many information appliances will be their power consumption. If we assume a future where many task-specific devices exist instead of few general purpose machines, clearly users will not be interested in charging or replacing dozens of batteries. For mobile and wearable devices, however, only one of the devices (e.g. a mobile phone) that a user carries will need to communicate with wide-area networks. Other, more power-thrifty personal devices may communicate over a link that only covers a person's immediate space [wash b].

Prototypes of such personal area networks already exist. IBM has developed a technology that uses a tiny electrical current to transmit information through the body of a person [IBM b]. In this way, a user's identification and other information can be transmitted from one person to another, or even to a variety of everyday objects such as cars, public telephones and ATMs. The bandwidth is relatively small, but more than enough to carry identification, or medical information [IBM c].

Networked embedded processors, which form the heart of all smart devices, will become an important research and development field. New types of low-power processors will be developed specifically for networked embedded applications. Also of primary interest are advances in networking technology that could allow large numbers of embedded computers to be interconnected so they can share information and work together as part of a larger system. Reliability is crucial in embedded computing systems, since such systems will increasingly control critical functions where safety is a factor (e.g. braking, navigation, driving) and, in some applications, may be given authority to take some actions with little or no human intervention. Ensuring the reliability of networked embedded computing systems could be difficult since large, interconnected information systems are notorious for becoming unstable. Such problems could be magnified by the presence of millions of interconnected embedded systems [NRC].

Progress in material science, chemistry, and physics will eventually change the appearance of information appliances. For example, light emitting polymer (LEP) displays that are now available in first prototypes offer many processing advantages, including the possibility of making flexible large-area or curved displays capable of delivering high-resolution video-rate images at low power consumption, visible in daylight and with wide viewing angles [cdt].

Somewhat speculative are techniques known as "electronic ink" or "electronic paper". Although initial prototypes exist, there is still a long way to go before paper can be replaced by electronic versions. However, the impact of this technology, once it is available, is significant: just imagine carrying your calendar and contact list on a foldable piece of electronic paper, or pulling out a large screen from a mobile phone or a tubular scroll containing the remaining electronics of a PC! Combined with small GPS receivers, maps that display their exact location ("you are here") are a real possibility.

5.2 Remote Identification

One of the major problems in Ubiquitous Computing is the identification of objects [HMNS 00]. For retail-based applications, barcode labels are typically used, but these have a number of drawbacks (such as the visibility of the barcode and the fact that it is a read-only item). So-called smart labels or RFID tags represent a newer and more interesting concept for identifying objects [Fin 99].

A smart label is a small, low-power microchip combined with an antenna, implanted in a physical object. Each label has a unique serial number and can contain other programmable information. The information contained in a label can be transmitted to a nearby reader device by a radio frequency (RF) signal [aim]. Hence, smart labels are contactless, and require neither touch nor line of sight. In particular, they work through plastic, wood, and other materials [MIT d].

Such identification tags can be battery powered or unpowered, and can be manufactured in a variety of sizes and configurations. The simplest give out a single preprogrammed number when placed in the vicinity of a reader [MIT d]. It is also possible to store a limited amount of information on the tags. More elaborate forms of smart labels are contactless smart cards. In addition to storage memory, they contain a processor (with an operating system) and are able to process data (e.g. perform cryptographic functions and thus disclose their state only to authorized entities). Smart card technology is already well-established (smart cards have been used for many years as secure tokens for access control and authentication), but low-power requirements for contactless variants pose new challenges. Research is currently also underway to produce tags that report information about their physical environment, such as temperature or position [MIT d].

Battery-powered labels, known as active tags, can transmit their information over relatively large distances. Their disadvantages are that they have a limited operating life, and are more expensive than passive devices [cwt]. Passive tags, on the other hand, collect the energy they require to operate from the RF field emitted by a reader device, and therefore do not need a battery. They are less expensive (approx. 10 cents to $1), but can only be sensed at distances of up to a few meters. In some of these passive systems, the antenna is replaced by non-metallic, conductive ink. The substrate of the labels is usually paper or plastic, yielding a paper-thin and flexible label, which can be self-adhesive and be printed on. The labels are small enough to be laminated between layers of paper or plastic to produce low-cost, consumable items.

Smart labels are already used to identify packages for express parcel services, airline baggage, and valuable goods in retail. Industry estimates the smart label market will reach 1 billion items in 2003. Future smart labels equipped with sensors and more processing power will be capable of monitoring their environmental conditions, actively sending alerts or messages, and recording a history of status information, location, and measurement data.

Once most products carry an RFID tag (similar to today's ubiquitous barcode labels), scenarios that go beyond the original purpose of those tags are conceivable. For example, an intelligent refrigerator may make use of the labels attached to bottles, which could be useful for minibars in hotel rooms. Even more intriguing are scenarios where prescriptions and drugs talk to a home medicine cabinet, allowing the cabinet to say which of those items should not be taken together, in order to avoid harmful interactions [MIT e]. In a similar manner, packaged food could talk to the microwave, enabling the microwave to automatically follow the preparation instructions.

The underlying idea is that everyday objects can, in some sense, become smart by having RFID labels attached to them and by equipping the environment with sensors for those labels. The information on the label would then not be merely an identity, but a URL-like pointer to an infinite amount of information somewhere on the Internet. This means that each object could acquire an electronic identity in addition to its physical structure [MIT f]. These electronic identities might then interact within a virtual world, independently from the physical world. If more and more of the physical world were to become "smart", and both worlds were more closely linked, they would both be richer [hp].

5.3 The Prospects

The ultimate vision of Ubiquitous Computing, where inanimate everyday objects communicate and cooperate, seems to be realizable in the long term. This would then provide us with an unparalleled level of convenience and productivity [MIT e]. Much remains to be done, however, on the conceptual level and quite a considerable infrastructure would have to be implemented before this vision could become a reality. The long-term consequences of a world in which things "talk" to each other are not yet clear, but the prospects are fascinating.

However, there are many concerns and issues to consider, even on the political, legal, and social level. Privacy is of course a primary concern when devices or smart everyday objects can be localized and traced, and when various objects we use daily report their state and sensor information to other objects. Another issue is information overload. Internet users are already overwhelmed by the sheer volume of information available, and the problem will get worse as the Internet grows and we enter the era of Ubiquitous Computing. Search engines, portals, and email filtering are existing technologies that allow the user to reduce the torrent to a manageable stream, but these technologies are still quite limited [Kot]. New technologies and services are definitely required.

It is clear that we are moving only gradually towards the ultimate vision of Ubiquitous Computing. Much progress in computer science, communication engineering, and material science is necessary to render the vision economically feasible and to overcome current technological hurdles such as energy consumption. However, it is also clear that Ubiquitous Computing will, in the long run, have dramatic economic effects: many new services are possible that could transform the huge amount of information gathered by the smart devices into value for the human user, and an entire industry may be set up to establish and run the infrastructure for the new smart and networked information appliances.

Applications for Ubiquitous Computing will certainly be found in areas where the Internet already plays an important role, such as mobile commerce, telematics, and entertainment, but without doubt many other traditional areas (e.g. healthcare and education) and newly emerging areas will benefit from Ubiquitous Computing technologies.

6. Conclusion

Mark Weiser, the pioneer of Ubiquitous Computing, once said *"in the 21st century the technology revolution will move into the everyday, the small and the invisible"*. And at the turn of the century Randy Katz, Professor at UC Berkeley, succinctly stated *"as we approach 2001, we are in the Information Age, not in the Space Age."* Seen that way, the future of distributed systems and Ubiquitous Computing is indeed promising, fascinating, and challenging at the same time!

7. References

[BSL 00] D. Box, A. Skonnard, J. Lam: Essential XML – Beyond Markup, Addison-Wesley, 2000
[CDK 00] G. Coulouris, J. Dollimore, T. Kindberg: Distributed Systems – Concepts and Design, 3rd Edition, Addison-Wesley, ISBN 0-201-62433-8, 2000
[EE 99] G. Eddon, H. Eddon: Inside COM+ Base Services, Microsoft Press, 1999
[Fin 99] K. Finkenzeller: RFID-Handbook, Wiley, ISBN 0-471-98851-0, 1999
[FK 98] I. Foster, C. Kesselman (Editors): The Grid: Blueprint for a New Computing Infrastructure, Morgan Kaufmann, 1998
[FM 99] S. Fünfrocken, F. Mattern: Mobile Agents as an Architectural Concept for Internet-based Distributed Applications – the WASP Project Approach, in: Steinmetz (ed.) Proc. KiVS'99, Springer, pp. 32-43, 1999
[HMNS 00] U. Hansmann, L. Merk, M.S. Nicklous, T. Stober: Pervasive Computing Handbook, Springer, ISBN 3-540-67122-6, Oct. 2000
[Ker 00] R. Kehr: Spontane Vernetzung, Informatik-Spektrum, Volume 23, Issue 3, pp. 161-172, 2000
[KG 99] D. Kotz, R. Gray: Mobile Code – the Future of the Internet, Third International Conference on Autonomous Agents, Seattle, 1999
[KM 00] D. Kotz, F. Mattern (Eds.): Agent Systems, Mobile Agents, and Applications, Springer-Verlag, ISBN 3-540-41052-X, 2000
[McL 01] B. McLaughlin: Java & XML, O'Reilly, 2nd Edition, 2001
[Nor 98] D.A. Norman: The Invisible Computer, MIT Press, ISBN 0262140659, 1998
[NRC] National Research Council: Study Committee on Networked Embedded Computers
[P2P 01] A. Oram (Editor): Peer-to-Peer – Harnessing the Power of Disruptive Technologies, O'Reilly, 2001
[PR 01] A. Puder, K. Römer: MICO – MICO is CORBA, 2nd Edition, dpunkt Verlag, 2001
[RCDD 98] T. Roden, K. Chervest, N. Davies, A. Dix: Exploiting Context in HCI Design for Mobile Systems, First Workshop on HCI for Mobile Devices, 1998
[Ric 02] J. Richter: Applied Microsoft .NET Framework Programming, Microsoft Press, 2002

[TL 02]   T. Thai, H.Q. Lam: .NET Framework Essentials, O'Reilly, 2nd Edition, 2002
[Wei 91]   M. Weiser: The Computer for the 21st Century, Scientific American, September 1991, pp. 94-10

Quotations and other text fragments come from several Web resources. Although not all of them could be identified in retrospect, the most important are:

[aim]   www.aimglobal.org/technologies/rfid/resources/papers/rfid_basics_primer.htm
[bear]   www.bearshare.com/
[ASP]   msdn.microsoft.com/library/default.asp?URL=/library/psdk/iisref/aspguide.htm
[cal]   www.cs.caltech.edu/~adam/phd/why-events.html
[cam]   www.cl.cam.ac.uk/users/dah28/thesis/thesis.html
[carl]   www.sce.carleton.ca/courses/94587/Introduction-to-open-distributed-computing.html
[carl b]   www.sce.carleton.ca/courses/94580/Introduction-to-open-distributed-computing.html
[cdt]   www.cdtltd.co.uk/
[CIDR]   ftp://ftp.isi.edu/in-notes/rfc1519.txt
[Corba]   www.cs.vu.nl/~eliens/online/tutorials/corba/overview.html
[cwt]   www.cwt.vt.edu/faq/rfid.htm
[darm]   www.kom.e-technik.tu-darmstadt.de/acmmm99/ep/montvay/
[DCE]   www.opengroup.org/dce/
[DCE-IOP]   www.omg.org/docs/formal/01-03-08.pdf
[eet]   www.eet.com/story/OEG20000110S0027
[EJB]   java.sun.com/j2ee/
[GIOP]   www.omg.org/news/whitepapers/iiop.htm
[glob]   www.globus.org/
[gnut]   www.gnutella.com/
[grid]   www.gridcomputing.com/
[hp]   www.cooltown.hp.com/papers/webpres/WebPresence.htm
[IBM]   www-3.ibm.com/pvc/ in particular:
            www-3.ibm.com/pvc/index_noflash.shtml
            www-3.ibm.com/pvc/sitemap.shtml
            www-3.ibm.com/pvc/pervasive.shtml
            www-3.ibm.com/pvc/nethome/
[IBM b]   www.research.ibm.com/journal/sj/384/zimmerman.html
[IBM c]   www.research.ibm.com/resources/magazine/1997/issue_1/pan197.html
[isc]   www.isc.org/ds/
[jini]   www.sun.com/jini/factsheet/
[jsol]   docs.rinet.ru/JSol/ch16.htm
[j2ee]   java.sun.com/j2ee/corba/
[Kot]   www.cs.dartmouth.edu/~dfk/papers/kotz:future/
[leg]   www.cs.virginia.edu/~legion/
[lime]   www.limewire.com/
[MIT]   tns-www.lcs.mit.edu/manuals/java-rmi-alpha2/rmi-spec/rmi-intro.doc.html
[MIT b]   www.media.mit.edu/pia/Research/AnchoredDisplays/
[MIT c]   www.media.mit.edu/~r/academics/PhD/Generals/Hawley.html
[MIT d]   www.media.mit.edu/ci/research/whitepaper/ci13.htm
[MIT e]   auto-id.mit.edu/index2.html
[MIT f]   www.media.mit.edu/~jofish/ieee.paper/ieee.cga.jofish.htm
[MONO]   www.go-mono.com/

[morph]	www.musiccity.com/
[mpi]	www.mpi-forum.org/
[naps]	www.napster.com/
[NAT]	ftp://ftp.isi.edu/in-notes/rfc3022.txt
[ncsa]	www.ncsa.uiuc.edu/People/mcgrath/Discovery/dp.html
[nist]	csrc.nist.gov/nissc/1996/papers/NISSC96/paper033/SWARUP96.PDF
[ONC]	www.ietf.org/rfc/rfc1831.txt
[phil]	www.extra.research.philips.com/password/passw3_4.pdf
[pvm]	www.csm.ornl.gov/pvm/pvm_home.html
[seti]	setiathome.ssl.berkeley.edu/
[SOAP]	www.w3.org/TR/SOAP/
[top]	www.top500.org/
[wash]	www.cs.washington.edu/homes/abj3938/cse588/MotivatingCORBA.htm
[wash b]	portolano.cs.washington.edu/proposal/

Stand und Zukunft der Verkehrstelematik

Prof.Dr.Gert Siegle, Robert Bosch GmbH

Telematische Systeme bieten die Möglichkeit, mit begrenztem Aufwand Verkehrsabläufe zu optimieren und bestehende oder neue Verkehrswege bestmöglich zu nutzen

Bei geregelten Verkehren auf der Schiene, auf dem Wasser oder in der Luft sind Informations- und Steuerungssysteme seit langem eingeführt und Voraussetzung für den zumeist reibungslosen Betrieb.

Straßenverkehre sind komplexer, ungleich mehr individuell handelnde Verkehrsteilnehmer sind betroffen. So sind telematische Systeme dort zwar schwerer einzuführen, haben dafür aber ein großes Potential - und bieten vor allem darstellbaren Nutzen für die vielen Millionen Verkehrsteilnehmer.

Der Vortrag zeigt auf, wie Telematik im Verkehr logisch strukturiert ist - Verkehrserfassung, Interpretation der Daten, Ableitung von Informationen zur Steuerung von Verkehrszeichen und zur Fahrerinformation, Übertragung der Daten, Anzeige/Ansage und Auswirkungen auf den Verkehr.

Nach einem kurzen Abriss der bereits längst eingeführten Systeme wie Verkehrsfunk, Wechselverkehrszeichen und dynamischer Navigation werden die wichtigsten künftigen Systeme und die Pläne zu ihrer Einführung und Umsetzung übersichtlich dargestellt.

Es wird gezeigt, dass die scheinbare Vielfalt gegliedert werden kann in voneinander fast unabhängige Teillösungen zur parallelen und schrittweise Einführung.

Erläutet werden im Einzelnen die Verfahren und konkreten Pläne zur Verkehrserfassung, zu heutigen und künftigen Fahrerinformationssystemen, die Lösungen zur Mauterfassung und die Planungen zur Unfallvermeidung durch vorausschauende Sicherheit (eSafety, ein Schwerpunktthema der Europäischen Kommission), intelligente Verkehrszeichen, Ansätze zu "Intelligent Speed Alert" sowie die Erweiterung der heutigen digitalen Verkehrsdatenübertragung auf innerstädtische Informationen.

Besondere Aufmerksamkeit verdienen zudem Systeme, die den Reisenden unterwegs Informationen zur Nutzung mehrerer Verkehrsträger während einer Reise geben können (multimodaler Verkehr).

Wie in der Vergangenheit auch, werden Einführung und Nutzung dieser Dienste schrittweise und nicht selten auch regional unterschiedlich schnell erfolgen, die derzeit absehbaren Zeitabläufe und nationalen wie auch europäischen Planungen werden dargestellt.

Session WWW

Scone: Ein Framework zur evaluativen Realisierung von Erweiterungen des Webs

Harald Weinreich, Volkert Buchmann, Winfried Lamersdorf

Arbeitsbereich Verteilte Systeme und Informationssysteme (VSIS)
Fachbereich Informatik, Universität Hamburg
Vogt-Kölln-Str. 30, 22527 Hamburg

{weinreich|lamersdorf}@informatik.uni-hamburg.de
volkert@spacecactus.net

Zusammenfassung: Projekte, die sich mit der Entwicklung und Evaluation von Konzepten, Techniken und Werkzeugen zur Verbesserung der Benutzbarkeit des Webs befassen, stehen oft vor dem Problem, dass die Implementation entsprechender Prototypen sehr aufwendig ist. Es stand bisher kein angemessenes Framework zur Verfügung, das solche Entwicklungen vereinfachen könnte. Dieses Paper stellt das Framework „Scone" vor, das die prototypische Entwicklung und Evaluation von unterschiedlichen Arten von Web-Erweiterungen – insbesondere solcher zur Navigation und Orientierung im Web – erleichtert. Das Framework bietet eine Reihe von Komponenten, welche es u.a. erlauben, die Darstellung der Dokumente im Browser zu ändern, auf Benutzeraktionen mit dem Browser zu reagieren, den Browser zu steuern und auch selbsttätig Informationen aus dem Netz zu sammeln. Zusätzlich wird die Evaluation solcher Systeme durch Benutzbarkeitsstudien unterstützt.

1 Die Herausforderungen der Navigation im Web

Das „Surfen" im Web stellt auf den ersten Blick keine großen Anforderungen an die Benutzer. Die notwendigen Bedienkonzepte sind vergleichsweise schnell und leicht zu erlernen. Bei genauerer Betrachtung kann aber eine ganze Reihe von gravierenden Benutzbarkeitsproblemen festgestellt werden. Diese werden nicht nur durch wenig fachgemäß entworfene und realisierte Web-Sites verursacht, sondern sind vielmehr größtenteils systemimmanent. Einige Schwierigkeiten für Benutzer sind in der *Hypertext-Charakteristik* des Webs begründet, andere werden durch die Mängel der inzwischen leider etablierten und daher schwer zu ändernden *User-Interfaces der Browser* hervorgerufen. Weitere Probleme verursachen die teilweise *unzureichenden Sprachen und Protokolle* des Webs, sowie sein globaler und strukturloser *verteilter Aufbau*.

Das Web erfüllt durch die in den Dokumenten enthaltenen Verweise auf andere Objekte das Schlüsselkriterium für *Hypertext-Systeme*. Dies ist wohl zugleich seine größte Stärke als auch Ursache für viele Herausforderungen bei seiner Benutzung. Conklin charakterisierte bereits in [10] die gravierendsten Probleme bei der Navigation im *Hyperspace*:

- *Disorientation* – Benutzer verlieren leicht die Orientierung; es gibt keine globalen "Wegweiser" oder "Landkarten". Die Strukturen des Hyperspace sind zudem viel zu kompliziert um sie zu überschauen oder auswendig zu lernen. Dies führt zu dem so genannten "Lost in Hyperspace"-Problem.

- *Cognitive Overhead* – Um im Hyperspace zum Ziel zu kommen, müssen Benutzer neben den Herausforderungen der Navigation und Orientierung auch ihre Aufgabe im Auge behalten. Daraus ergibt sich eine doppelte Belastung des Kurzzeitgedächtnisses.

Diese bereits vor der Einführung des World Wide Webs erkannten Probleme sind auch für das Web relevant; dennoch berücksichtigen die im Web benutzten Konzepte sie kaum und greifen bewährte Lösungen älterer Hypertextsysteme nicht auf.

Ebenso sind einige gravierende Schwachstellen des Webs in den *User Interfaces heutiger Browser* auszumachen. Sie bieten von sich aus vergleichsweise wenige und unzureichende Werkzeuge, um die Navigation und Orientierung im Web zu erleichtern [4]. Während einerseits die technischen Möglichkeiten der Browser ständig erweitert werden, beispielsweise im Bereich der XML-Sprachfamilie oder bei Programmiersprachen wie ECMA-Script[1], hat sich andererseits bei den Benutzungsschnittstellen seit den ersten Versionen von Mosaic[2] kaum etwas verändert. Andere Hypertext-Systeme leisteten bereits vor langem mehr. Beispielsweise bot der Browser Harmony des Systems Hyper-G grundsätzlich eine Übersicht zur Site-Struktur und Zugriff auf ein integriertes Suchsystem [2]. Bei Web-Browsern führt hingegen schon der Back-Button wegen seines Stack-basierten Charakters zu Problemen [9]. Ebenso ist die History (auch „Verlauf" genannt), die alle in den letzten Wochen besuchten Seiten aufzeigt, immer noch wenig ausgereift. Sie macht das Wiederfinden von früher besuchten Dokumenten aufgrund ihrer schlechten Repräsentation schwierig und wird folglich selten genutzt [24]. Ein drittes Beispiel sind „Bookmarks" (bzw. „Favoriten"), deren Verwaltung vielen Benutzern als zu aufwändig erscheint [1; 16].

Die Schwächen von *HTML und HTTP* wurden bereits in vielen Bereichen angegangen, dennoch sind noch viele Probleme ungelöst. Beispielsweise führen die ins Dokument eingebetteten und semantisch ausdrucksschwachen Links zur so genannten "*Hub and Spoke*"-Navigation, bei der ein Benutzer nacheinander mehreren Verweisen einer Seite folgt, um herauszufinden, welche Informationen sich hinter ihnen verbergen, bis er letztendlich das gewünschte Dokument gefunden hat [24]. Hinzu kommt die mangelhafte Einbindung von semantischen oder Meta-Informationen in HTML-Dokumente, wodurch die Effizienz und Erstellung von Katalogsystemen und integrierenden Diensten erheblich erschwert werden. Diese Schwächen werden durch die *globale Verteilung* der Informationen und Dienste des Webs auf Millionen von Servern noch verstärkt. Das WWW kann als eine sich stets verändernde, inkonsistente Datenbasis angesehen werden, die zudem so umfangreich und dabei ohne einheitliche Struktur ist, dass heutige Suchsysteme auf eine Anfrage in der Regel zu viele ungewünschte oder unpassende Treffer ausgeben. Doch auch für die Betreiber einer Web-Site ist es schwer, die eigenen Daten konsistent zu halten. Innerhalb einer Web-Site können Content-Management-Systeme für konsistente Links sorgen, fehlerhafte externe Verweise lassen sich jedoch mangels standardisierter Konzepte und *Protokolle*[3]

---

[1] ECMA-Script ist ein internationaler Standard für Scriptsprachen im Web und damit der Versuch, Inkompatibilitäten der Ausgangssprache JavaScript zu beseitigen.
[2] Mosaic war der erste Web-Browser mit GUI für X-Windows-Systeme. Mehr Informationen unter http://archive.ncsa.uiuc.edu/SDG/Software/Mosaic/
[3] Es gab hierzu bereits einige Lösungsansätze. Ein Beispiel ist der Atlas Link-Server [22].

bis heute nicht immer vermeiden. So konfrontieren „Broken Links" die Benutzer immer wieder mit wenig hilfreichen Fehlermeldungen. Untersuchungen zeigen, dass im Herbst 2002 durchschnittlich über 5% der Links fehlerhaft sind [17].

Zusammengefasst sind die Simplizität der Grundkonzepte des Webs und die minimalistischen User Interfaces der Browser die größten Schwachpunkte des Webs: Die verwendeten Sprachen und Protokolle werden vielen Problemen von verteilten Hypertextsystemen nur unzureichend gerecht. Konzepte zur Behebung vieler altbekannter Hürden bei der Benutzung verteilter Hypertextsysteme, Dienste und Informationssysteme fehlen oder ließen sich bis heute nicht umsetzen. Zahlreiche Schwierigkeiten wären absehbar und vermeidbar gewesen, wenn für diese Konzepte zuvor eine Entwicklung von Prototypen und deren Evaluation stattgefunden hätte.

2   Strategien für ein besser benutzbares Web

Viele Forschungsprojekte versuchen, die Benutzbarkeit des Webs zu verbessern. Um dies zu erreichen, wird zum einen versucht, auf Basis der existierenden Technologien und Infrastrukturen bessere Interfaces für Benutzer zu entwickeln. Andere Projekte arbeiten daran, die technischen Grundlagen des Webs zu erweitern. Um den tatsächlichen Nutzen solcher Konzepte und Werkzeuge beurteilen zu können, müssen entsprechende Prototypen erstellt und in Anwendungsszenarien evaluiert werden.

Die Ziele von Projekten, die sich mit einer Verbesserung der Benutzbarkeit des Webs beschäftigen, können in der Regel den drei Kernbereichen Orientierung, Navigation und Kollaboration zugeordnet werden.

Um eine einfache *Orientierung* im Web zu gewährleisten, müssen die Fragen "Wo war ich?", "Wo bin ich?" und "Wo kann ich hin?" jederzeit klar beantwortet werden können. Orientierungshilfen können beispielsweise innerhalb des Dokuments, der Site, dem thematischen Kontext oder der topologischen Umgebung geboten werden. Ein Ansatz in dieser Richtung sind graphische Übersichten [11].

Zudem soll zielgerichtete *Navigation* möglich sein. Neue Informationen müssen problemlos gefunden und bereits besuchte Dokumente einfach wieder erreicht werden können. Ein Beispiel einer Erweiterung, die die Navigation im Web vereinfacht, ist der „Google Toolbar"[4]. Er positioniert sich unter der Adressleiste des Internet Explorers und erlaubt mittels neuer Interaktionselemente einen direkten Zugriff auf viele der Funktionen von Google; es lassen sich beispielsweise direkt Suchanfragen stellen oder verwandte Seiten zum aktuellen Dokument ermitteln.

Die *Kollaboration* im Web wird bis heute kaum unterstützt. Antworten auf Fragen wie „Welche Dokumente können mir Benutzer mit ähnlichen Zielen empfehlen?" und „Wie hilfreich fanden andere Benutzer diese Seite?" enthalten wertvolle Hinweise für die Suche nach Informationen. Sowohl durch die synchrone als auch durch die asynchrone Zusammenarbeit können Benutzer von den Erfahrungen anderer profitieren [23]. Eine Reihe solcher Anwendungen finden sich beispielsweise im E-Commerce-Umfeld, jedoch handelt es sich dabei nicht um systemimmanente, server-übergreifende Dienste des Webs.

---

[4] Den Google Toolbar gibt es kostenlos für den Internet Explorer: http://toolbar.google.com/

XLink und die *Semantic Web Initiative* sind Beispiele für Bestrebungen, die mittels Erweiterungen auf technischer Ebene den Umgang mit dem Web vereinfachen und erweitern sollen. XLink ist im Zusammenhang mit XML als Ersatz für die simplen eingebetteten Links von HTML vorgesehen. Beispiele für die erweiterten Navigationsmöglichkeiten von XLink sind bidirektionale Verweise und Verweise mit multiplen Zielen. Des weiteren erlaubt XLink das Speichern von Links außerhalb der Dokumente in so genannten Link-Datenbanken. XLinks können mit semantischen Informationen versehen werden, wodurch beispielsweise die benutzerspezifische Filterung von Verweisen möglich wird [12]. Bisher stehen den XLink-Techniken allerdings nur vage Konzepte für geeignete User Interfaces gegenüber – diese wurden bewusst außen vor gelassen. Probleme bei der Umsetzung werden in [27] beschrieben.

Die Semantic Web Initiative geht einen anderen Weg. Es wird hierbei unter anderem versucht, das Web mittels der Sprache RDF um Meta-Informationen anzureichern und so für Maschinen lesbar zu machen. Dies soll Systeme ermöglichen, die für den Benutzer Informationen zusammensuchen und kombinieren [3]. Die Beschreibungen der User Interfaces hierzu sind jedoch vergleichsweise unbestimmt, und praxisreife technische Realisierungen fehlen. Zu bedenken ist zudem, dass Untersuchungen auf Autorenprobleme mit dem Hinzufügen von Meta-Informationen zu Dokumenten und Verweisen hingewiesen haben [25].

Die Schwächen heutiger User Interfaces und die Probleme bei der Umsetzung neuer technischer Standards des Webs machen deutlich, dass die prototypische Evaluation der technischen Konzepte in den gegebenen Anwendungsszenarien ein integraler Bestandteil der Entwicklung sein sollte. Für viele der technischen Erweiterungen fehlen bisher ausgereifte ergonomische Realisierungen, so auch bei XLink und RDF. Da sich diese Konzepte letztendlich daran messen lassen müssen, ob sie eine echte Verbesserung und eine Vereinfachung für die Benutzer darstellen, sollten sie schon vor ihrem Einsatz prototypisch in Anwendungsszenarien evaluiert und gegebenenfalls angepasst werden [21]. Diese Problematik war ein ausschlaggebender Motivationsfaktor, um ein Framework zu erstellen, das die einfache Erstellung von Prototypen für möglichst viele Konzepte in diesem Themenbereich ermöglicht. Zusätzlich soll die Evaluation der Prototypen unterstützt werden, damit die gewonnenen Daten wieder in den Entwicklungsprozess einfließen und so zu einem qualitativ hochwertigen Ergebnis beitragen können.

3 Anforderungen an das Framework

Die vorherigen Betrachtungen sind Ausgangspunkt für die Konzeption und Umsetzung des Frameworks *Scone*. Im Vordergrund stehen dabei die Flexibilität des Frameworks und die Unterstützung aktueller Sprachen und Technologien. So soll das Framework sowohl Möglichkeiten bieten, schnell experimentelle User Interfaces für neue Basistechnologien zu realisieren, als auch neue Konzepte für die Unterstützung der Orientierung, Navigation und Kollaboration im Web umzusetzen.

Bei der Entwicklung des Frameworks war zu bedenken, dass es recht unterschiedliche Kategorien von Konzepten zur Erweiterung der User Interfaces von Web-Browsern gibt [5; 8]. Einige Konzepte versuchen die *Darstellung der Dokumente im*

Browser zu verändern, andere fügen *dem Browser selbst neue Interface-Elemente* hinzu. Des weiteren gibt es Erweiterungen, die ein *eigenes Fenster* in Ergänzung zum Browser anbieten, oder gar *unabhängig vom Browser* funktionieren, um ihn für bestimmte Aufgaben zu ersetzen.

Auch die Personalisierbarkeit ist je nach Ansatz unterschiedlich ausgeprägt. Einige Konzepte verzichten auf die Unterscheidung von Benutzern und arbeiten aufgaben- oder sitzungsbasiert. Oft ist eine Differenzierung aber notwendig, damit Dienste personalisiert werden können oder Benutzer die Möglichkeit zur Kollaboration erhalten.

Zudem kann die Art der zur verbesserten Orientierung und Navigation zusätzlich benötigten Informationen stark variieren. Einige Werkzeuge benötigen zusätzliche Daten aus dem Netz, andere analysieren oder adaptieren die Informationen, die der Benutzer aus dem Netz abruft. Entsprechend vielseitige Schnittstellen sollten für die Entwickler von neuen Web-Erweiterungen zur Verfügung stehen: so muss das Framework beispielsweise Proxy-, Server- und Robot-Funktionalität bereitstellen.

Diesen unterschiedlichen Anforderungen kann ein Framework am besten mit einem modularen Aufbau gerecht werden; einfach kombinierbare, programmierbare und erweiterbare Komponenten können so die jeweiligen Ansätze abdecken. Zudem fördert eine komponentenorientierte Architektur das Einbinden von anderen Toolkits und Bibliotheken, etwa zur Bearbeitung von XLinks oder RDF.

4 Die Architektur des Scone-Frameworks

Scone ist als objektorientiertes Framework [13, S.26] in Java implementiert worden. Es bietet eine Reihe von Klassen und Interfaces, die je nach nötiger Flexibilität zumeist durch Komposition, zum Teil aber auch durch Subclassing Einsatz finden. Die Klassen und Interfaces des Framework können in vier Kernkomponenten und eine Reihe von Hilfskomponenten zusammengefasst werden (s. Abb. 1).

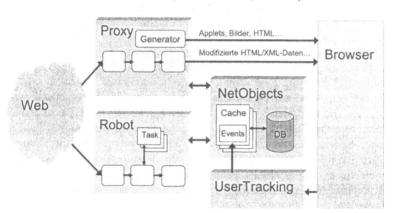

Abbildung 1: Die Kernkomponenten von Scone

Die erste der vier Basiskomponenten ist die Realisierung eines objektorientierten Datenmodells, das die wichtigsten Basiskonzepte des Internets wie URLs, Dokumente und Links als persistierbare Java-Objekte, die *NetObjects*, bereitstellt. Eine weitere

Komponente ist ein programmierbarer *Proxy*, der die zwischen Server und Browser transferierten Daten analysieren und modifizieren kann. Ein einfach zu programmierender, flexibler und nebenläufiger *Robot* ermöglicht das aktive Laden von Informationen aus dem WWW. Die vierte Kernkomponente ist das *UserTracking*, welches es erlaubt, die Aktionen unterschiedlicher Benutzer mit dem Browser zu verfolgen und aufzuzeichnen. Diese vier Komponenten werden von einer Reihe von Hilfskomponenten unterstützt. Die Komponenten sind in eine Architektur eingebunden, die es mittels eines Plugin-Konzepts erlaubt, sie zu einer Vielzahl von Erweiterungen für das Web zu kombinieren.

Die NetObjects
Die *NetObject*-Komponente stellt Möglichkeiten zur Verfügung, die in Bezug auf das WWW elementaren Objekte zu repräsentieren und bei Bedarf auch zu persistieren. Dazu gehören beliebige, durch URLs identifizierte Objekte des Internets, insbesondere aber auch Web-Dokumente mit Meta-Daten und verschiedene topologische Informationen, beispielsweise Links. Zudem lassen sich die Benutzer und ihre Aktionen darstellen. Dieses Modell lässt sich leicht anpassen und erweitern. Da das Speichern auf Sekundärspeicher vergleichsweise langsam ist und Techniken wie CASTOR oder EJBs beim Persistieren von Daten recht schwerfällig sind oder umfangreiche Application-Server voraussetzen, wurde für Scone ein optimiertes, leichtgewichtiges Caching-Konzept entwickelt, dass ein performantes und einfach adaptierbares Mapping von Java-Objekten auf relationale Datenbanken ermöglicht. Scone benutzt das Datenbanksystem MySQL, da es eine außergewöhnlich hohe Performanz aufweist. Es gibt zudem eine weitere Implementation, bei der eine Anbindung an die objektorientierte Datenbank Poet FastObjects t7 umgesetzt wurde[5].

Der Proxy
Eine weitere Komponente ist der programmierbare *HTTP Proxy*. Er wird benutzt, um die zwischen Server und Browser transferierten Daten zu analysieren und zu modifizieren. Scone verwendet und erweitert hierfür das WBI Development Kit[6] vom IBM Almaden Research Center [18]. Scone-Plugins können sich mit Hilfe des Proxys in den Datenstrom zwischen Browser und Server einklinken und haben dadurch Zugriff auf die übertragenen Web-Dokumente. Auf diese Weise kann das im Browser dargestellte Dokument beliebig angepasst und ergänzt werden. WBI wurde für Scone um einige Funktionen erweitert. So wurde zur Effizienzsteigerung die ursprüngliche Byte-basierte Verarbeitung der Web-Dokumente durch eine Token-basierte Verarbeitung ergänzt, wobei ein Token beispielsweise einen HTML-Tag oder einen Text repräsentiert. Die Dokumente werden automatisch in verschiedene Token zerlegt und in dieser Form den Plugins angeboten. Im Zuge einer Kooperation mit IBM wurde das Token-basierte Verarbeitungskonzept in WBI integriert. Durch die Transcoding-Fähigkeiten von WBI ist es Scone möglich, die Transformation und Adaption von unterschiedlichen Datenformaten während der Übertragung vorzunehmen [15]. Hierdurch können beispielsweise User Interfaces für neue technische Konzepte wie XLink erprobt werden.

---

[5] Mehr Informationen zu Poet FastObjects t7 unter: http://www.fastobjects.de/
[6] Das WBI-DK ist für den nicht-kommerziellen Einsatz kostenlos erhältlich unter: http://www.almaden.ibm.com/cs/wbi/

Der Robot
Die dritte Basiskomponente ist ein *Robot*. Er ist ähnlich einem Suchmaschinen-Robot in der Lage, ganze Web-Sites zu indizieren, kann darüber hinaus aber flexibel programmiert werden und wurde für den Einsatz auf Client-Seite optimiert. So kann der Robot je nach Anforderung nebenläufig mehrere Seiten gleichzeitig übertragen, oder auch lastminimierend eingesetzt werden und auf lokale (Netz-)Inaktivität warten. Er stellt ein *Classifier-Filter*-Konzept zur Verfügung, mit dessen Hilfe sowohl Links als auch Dokumente erst aufgrund ihrer Eigenschaften klassifiziert werden und dann entsprechend den Filterbedingungen behandelt werden. Mittels dieses Konzeptes lässt sich unter anderem angeben, welche Links weiterverfolgt und wie mit den Ziel-Dokumenten verfahren werden soll. Der Robot kann dann beispielsweise den Dokumenttyp ermitteln, die Antwortzeiten eines Servers abschätzen oder Titel und Länge eines Dokuments bestimmen. So kann der Scone Robot als ein User Agent agieren, der für den Benutzer hilfreiche Informationen sammelt.

Das UserTracking
Das *UserTracking* erlaubt es, Benutzeraktionen zu verfolgen und zu protokollieren. Es werden Interaktionen des Benutzers mit dem Browser, wie zum Beispiel der Klick auf einen Link, das Drücken des Back-Buttons oder das Ausfüllen eines Formulars berücksichtigt. Solche Aktionen erzeugen unterschiedliche Java-Events, über die ein Scone-Plugin – z.B. eine Browser-Erweiterung – mittels des Observer-Patterns informiert werden kann. Benutzer können bei Bedarf unterschieden werden; hierfür stellt Scone grundlegende Verwaltungsfunktionen wie die Registrierung und das Login zur Verfügung. Scone bietet drei unterschiedliche Varianten des UserTrackings an, die sich in der Detailliertheit der protokollierten Daten unterscheiden. Die einfachste Variante ermittelt mit Hilfe von eingebettetem JavaScript-Code, welche Dokumente wie lange in den Browser-Fenstern dargestellt wurden, nach welcher Zeit der Benutzer eine Seite wieder verlassen hat und welcher Link angeklickt wurde. Die zweite Variante bindet zudem ein unsichtbares Applet in die Seite ein, mittels dessen sich auch beliebige Aktionen auf der Seite (z.B. Tastatureingaben und Mausbewegungen) protokollieren lassen. Die komplexeste Variante verwendet zusätzlich ein Hilfsprogramm in C, das sich direkt in den Internet Explorer integriert und so genau ermitteln kann, welche Bedienelemente im Browser angeklickt wurden.

Hilfskomponenten
Neben diesen vier Basiskomponenten stehen eine Reihe weiterer Hilfskomponenten innerhalb der Scone-Architektur zur Verfügung:
- Scone bietet für die Verwaltung der Plugins ein GUI, das es erlaubt, Plugins zu registrieren und zu konfigurieren. Zur Speicherung der Konfigurationsparameter einzelner Plugins wurde ein XML-Schema definiert, aus dem automatisch ein grafisches Java-Interface zum Modifizieren der Werte generiert wird.
- Zur Analyse von HTML-Dokumenten steht ein *Standard Document Parser* zur Verfügung. Er extrahiert unterschiedliche Meta-Informationen wie die Sprache, Schlüsselwörter oder die Anzahl der Links. Zudem erzeugt er mittels heuristischer Methoden eine Kurzzusammenfassung.
- Eine wichtige Hilfskomponente ist die Browsersteuerung. Die Kommunikation mit dem Browser geschieht zum einen über ein durch den Proxy eingebundenes Applet. So lassen sich beispielsweise weitere Browser-Fenster öffnen, das ange-

zeigte Dokument oder die Position und Größe des Fensters ändern. Einige in C geschriebene Hilfsprogramme erlauben weitere Funktionen, wie das Starten eines neuen Browsers oder das Löschen der Browser-History.

- Eine beliebte Möglichkeit zur Repräsentation von Web-Seiten stellen Thumbnails dar. Scone kann auf Java basierende Komponenten zum Rendern von HTML einbinden[7] und so Web-Dokumente als Grafiken zur Verfügung stellen.
- Das Scone Framework wird durch ein Paket zur Evaluation der entwickelten Prototypen abgerundet. Mit Hilfe dieser Komponente lassen sich einfach GUIs erstellen, die Benutzer in ein Evaluationsszenario einführen und sie mittels interaktiver Fragebögen durch Aufgaben leiten. Die Eingaben und Aktionen der Benutzer können zur späteren Auswertung abgespeichert werden.

Durch die kombinierte Nutzung dieser Komponenten können vergleichsweise schnell und einfach Navigationswerkzeuge unterschiedlichster Art erstellt werden. Dabei werden von den meisten Komponenten je nach Anforderung unterschiedlich hohe Abstraktionsebenen angeboten. Ein Plugin kann beispielsweise mittels des Proxys nicht nur in den Bytestrom vom und zum Browser eingreifen, HTML-Dokumente können auch als eine Folge von Objekten wie HTML-Tags, Links und Text bearbeitet werden. Eine noch höhere Abstraktionsebene wird durch die NetObjects-Komponente erschlossen. Sie stellt Meta-Informationen des Dokuments wie Sprache, Anzahl der Links und eine Zusammenfassung bereit.

5 Möglichkeiten und Grenzen von Scone

Scone wurde als ein Framework entwickelt, das die Realisierung von möglichst vielen Ideen zur besseren Benutzbarkeit des Webs ermöglichen sollte. Dabei gibt es Konzepte, die sich mit Scone schnell und einfach realisieren lassen und andere, bei denen Scone nicht sinnvoll einsetzbar ist.

Scone eignet sich besonders gut, um Erweiterungen an bestehenden Systemen vorzunehmen. So können serverseitige Werkzeuge HTML-Dokumente mit zusätzlichen Navigationselementen anreichern oder neuartige Serverdienste erproben. Werkzeuge auf der Seite des Clients können beispielsweise innovative Navigationsmittel in einem Fenster neben dem Browser darstellen und dabei mit dem Browser interagieren oder auch neue benutzerbezogene Orientierungshilfen in Webseiten einbringen. Auch der Einsatz in Workgroups, um eine breite Evaluationsbasis zu erhalten, oder um Kollaborationskonzepte zu realisieren, ist dank des verwendeten Proxys möglich.

Eine nahtlose Integration in die Bedienelemente des Browsers, wie beim Google Toolbar, ist mit Scone momentan allerdings noch nicht umzusetzen. Dies liegt zum Teil an der eingesetzten Sprache Java, die nicht den Zugriff auf alle System- und Browserfunktionen ermöglicht, dafür aber den Vorteil der Plattformunabhängigkeit bietet. Allerdings gibt es vielversprechende erste Ergebnisse mit dem Browser Mozilla, der eine beliebige Gestaltung aller User-Interface-Elemente mittels der Sprache XUL zulässt. Auch auf Serverseite sind Grenzen erkennbar. Zwar bietet Scone die Möglichkeit, als erweiterte Kopie eines beliebigen Servers eingesetzt zu werden,

---

[7] Beispielsweise kann die *WebWindow-Komponente* von Horst Heistermann eingesetzt werden. Eine Testversion ist unter http://home.earthlink.net/~hheister/ erhältlich.

aber eine Integration, z.B. in Application Server, ist bisher nicht vorgesehen. Bei unseren bisherigen Projekten waren diese Einschränkungen allerdings nicht gravierend, da sich entweder eine gute Annäherung an die optimale Lösung finden ließ oder sie mit kleinen Erweiterungen des Frameworks durch Hilfsprogramme in C gelöst werden konnten.

Strukturelle Probleme bieten Objekte in Binärformaten wie Flash, die bisher von Scone nicht verarbeitet werden können. Ferner lassen sich mittels HTTPS verschlüsselt übertragene Objekte nicht von dem Proxy analysieren oder verändern.

Durch die fehlende direkte Einbindung von Scone in bestehende Browser und Server und die benötigten Komponenten wie WBI und MySQL ist nicht zu erwarten, dass Endprodukte mit Scone gefertigt werden. Die Stärke von Scone liegt in der Möglichkeit, schnell experimentelle Erweiterungen für bestehende Systeme zu implementieren um diese dann zu evaluieren. In kurzer Zeit können so Browser, bestimmte Web-Seiten oder ganze Sites um neue Techniken oder User Interfaces ergänzt werden, ohne die komplizierten und teilweise proprietären APIs heutiger Browser oder Server verwenden zu müssen. Diese bieten zudem zumeist nicht die Möglichkeiten und Werkzeuge von Scone, um neue Hilfsmittel zur Navigation und Orientierung zu realisieren. Und nicht zuletzt lässt sich Scone in *einer* API für Erweiterungen auf Client- und Serverseite einsetzen.

6 Mit Scone entwickelte Prototypen

Es wurde bereits eine ganze Reihe von unterschiedlichen Plugins für Scone realisiert. Die interessantesten sollen hier kurz vorgestellt werden.

Die Browsererweiterung **HyperScout** [26] ist ein Scone-Plugin, das die im Browser dargestellten Dokumente modifiziert. Alle HTML-Dokumente werden bei der Übertragung durch den Scone-Proxy um zusätzliche Funktionen ergänzt, die es erlauben, zu allen Links einer Web-Seite automatisch generierte, ergänzende Informationen in *Popups* darzustellen. Diese Popups erscheinen, sobald der Benutzer die Maus etwas längere Zeit über einen Link hält. So können Benutzern bei Bedarf schon vor Auswahl eines Links mehr Informationen zum Ziel angeboten werden: *Ist das Dokument verfügbar? Welchen Inhalt hat es? Wann war ich bereits auf der Seite?* Diese zusätzliche Funktionalität wurde ermöglicht, indem HyperScout alle Link-Elemente einer Seite um JavaScript-Events erweitert, die mittels LiveConnect ein ebenfalls eingebundenes Java Applet ansteuern. Dieses Applet stellt bei Bedarf ein Popup neben dem Mauszeiger dar. Die angezeigten Informationen werden unter anderem durch den Robot gesammelt und vom Applet bei Bedarf direkt von Scone geladen. HyperScout wurde bereits mehreren Benutzbarkeitstests unterzogen und entsprechend überarbeitet.

Das Projekt **Browsing Icons** von Matthias Mayer stellt eine Navigationshilfe dar, die das Wiederfinden von Web-Seiten auch nach mehreren Tagen oder Wochen vereinfachen soll. Das Tool zeichnet hierfür in einem Fenster neben dem Browser dynamisch einen animierten Graphen der Benutzerpfade während des Surfens im Web auf. Diese Graphen werden mit Attributen der Dokumente angereichert und nach dem Beenden einer Aufgabe oder einer Sitzung als Icons bereitgestellt. Eine am HCI-Lab der University of Maryland durchgeführte Studie hat gezeigt, dass dieses Tool das

Zurückkehren zu früher besuchten Seiten in vielen Fällen vereinfacht [19]. Scone wird in diesem Projekt als Schnittstelle zum Browser verwendet.

Der **Web-Rückspiegel** ist ein Prototyp, der in einem Fenster eine Reihe von Thumbnails der Seiten darstellt, die auf das im Browser angezeigte Dokument verweisen. Hierdurch ist es möglich, im Web „rückwärts" zu navigieren und sich so einen Überblick zu verwandten Dokumenten zu verschaffen. Das Plugin fordert über den Scone-Robot oder die Google SOAP-API [14] eine Liste von „Backlinks" an. Die laut Google relevantesten dieser Seiten werden dann als Thumbnails dargestellt.

In einem weiteren Forschungsprojekt haben wir Scone dazu verwendet, um unterschiedliche **Visualisierungen und Interaktionsformen für erweiterte XLinks** [27] prototypisch umzusetzen und in Benutzbarkeitstests zu evaluieren. Die Ergebnisse der Tests werden demnächst publiziert.

7 Verwandte Arbeiten

Wenn nur Teilaspekte von Scone betrachtet werden, so gibt es eine beträchtliche Anzahl von verwandten Projekten. Proxys sind beispielsweise seit langem bekannt und bewährt, um das Caching von Web-Dokumenten durchzuführen und so die Netzlast zu reduzieren. Sie finden sich zudem in Firewalls oder auch als Filter-Werkzeuge, um Werbung aus dem Web auszublenden. Ebenso sind Robots inzwischen eine etablierte Technik, um den Index von Suchmaschinen zu erstellen oder die Konsistenz von Links zu prüfen. Scone greift auf diese Techniken zurück und erlaubt durch ihre Kombination und Erweiterung die Realisierung von vielen unterschiedlichen Konzepten für das Web.

WBI ist ein Proxy Framework, das im IBM Almaden Research Center entwickelt wurde. WBI implementiert das Konzept der „Intermediaries": aktive Komponenten, die an beliebiger Stelle zwischen Client und Server positioniert sein können. Sie haben die Fähigkeit, Daten zu beobachten, zu verändern oder zu generieren. WBI wurde in Java implementiert und unterstützt ebenfalls ein Plugin-Konzept. Diese Plugins setzen sich aus so genannten MEGs zusammen, die mit unterschiedlichen Aufgaben in den HTTP-Datenstrom eingeklinkt werden können [18]. Scone verwendet WBI als Grundlage für die Proxy-Funktionalität, wobei es aber in entscheidenden Teilen erweitert wurde. Eine dieser Erweiterungen – ObjectStream-basierte Plugins – wurde von IBM im Rahmen eines wissenschaftlichen Austausches übernommen.

Ein mit WBI teilweise vergleichbares Java-Framework ist *Muffin*. Es wurde als Open Source Projekt an der San Diego State University entwickelt. Muffin implementiert ein Filter-System, das Endnutzern mehr Kontrolle über die zum Browser transferierten Daten geben soll. Das Projekt beinhaltet diverse anpassbare Filter, die Web-Seiten nach Bedarf analysieren, speichern und verändern können [7]. Muffin ist flexibel, erreicht aber nicht die Performanz und Funktionalität von WBI.

Arakne, ein Projekt der Universität Aarhus, ist ein offenes kollaboratives Hypermedia-System für das Web. Arakne bietet eine den Browser erweiternde Umgebung, in der eine offene Menge von Hypermedia-Werkzeugen, genannt „Views", existiert. Diese Werkzeuge sind vom Entwickler weitgehend programmierbar und statten den Benutzer mit Navigations-, Guided Tour- und Strukturierungsmechanismen für Web-Dokumente aus. Arakne kommuniziert mit dem Internet-Explorer über eine Java-

COM-Bridge und kann so direkt auf das DOM des angezeigten Dokuments zugreifen, um es zu analysieren und zu manipulieren [6].

WebSphinx von der Carnegie Mellon University unterstützt die Entwicklung von persönlichen Web-Crawlern. WebSphinx erlaubt die einfache Erstellung von Site-spezifischen, persönlichen und migrierbaren Crawlern. Das Java-Framework bietet eine Architektur, die es gestattet, nebenläufig Dokumente zu laden. WebSphinx führt den Begriff der „Classifier" ein. Diese kleinen Programme ermöglichen auf einfache Weise die Analyse und Klassifikation von Web-Dokumenten, um so den Robot zu steuern. Eine interaktive Entwicklungsumgebung, genannt „Crawler Workbench", erlaubt Benutzern, einfache perönliche Crawler zu spezifizieren und aufzurufen, ohne Programme schreiben zu müssen. Sie unterstützt zudem unterschiedliche Visualisierungstechniken für die zusammengesuchten Dokumente [20]. Einige der Konzepte von Scones Robot wurden durch dieses Projekt inspiriert.

8 Resümee

Die vielfältigen Benutzbarkeitsprobleme des Webs sind nicht zuletzt auf die oft fehlende Evaluation von Konzepten und Systemen zurückzuführen. Die wachsende Vielfalt an Anforderungen und Anwendungen im Web macht zudem neue Techniken und Sprachen notwendig, wobei hier häufig ausgereifte Konzepte für ergonomische Benutzungsschnittstellen fehlen.

Das vorgestellte Framework Scone kann als Basis dienen, um neuartige User Interfaces für Erweiterungen des Webs prototypisch zu implementieren. Diese Prototypen bieten dann eine Evaluationsgrundlage, um Konzepte und Techniken schon während der Entwicklung in Anwendungsszenarien mit Benutzern zu testen und zu optimieren.

Scone hat sich bereits in einer Reihe unterschiedlicher Projekte bewährt. Es bietet einen breiten Funktionsumfang und läuft stabil, ist aber nicht für Endprodukte konzipiert. Der Einsatz des Frameworks hat in mehreren Projekten zu einer entscheidenden Zeitersparnis geführt, so dass mehr Aufmerksamkeit den wichtigen – und in der Informatik leider immer noch viel zu oft vernachlässigten – Benutzbarkeitstests gewidmet werden konnte. Das Framework Scone sowie weitere Abbildungen und Informationen sind unter **http://www.scone.de/** verfügbar.

Danksagungen
Wir möchten allen an der Entwicklung von Scone Beteiligten unseren Dank aussprechen, insbesondere Frank Wollenweber, Torsten Haß, Björn Stephan, Hartmut Obendorf und Matthias Mayer.

Literatur

[1] D. Abrams, R. Baecker, M. Chignell: *Information Archiving with Bookmarks: Personal Web Space Construction and Organization.* In: ACM SIGCHI 1998, LA, USA, S. 41-48
[2] Keith Andrews: *Browsing, Building, and Beholding Cyberspace*, Ph.D. Thesis, Graz University of Technology, 1996, ftp://ftp.iicm.tu-graz.ac.at/pub/keith/phd/
[3] Tim Berners-Lee, James Hendler, Ora Lassila: *The Semantic Web.* Scientific American, 284(5), Mai 2001, S. 34-43

[4] M. Bieber, F. Vitali, H. Ashman, V. Balasubramaniam, H. Oinas-Kukkonen: *Forth Generation Hypermedia: Some Missing Links for the World Wide Web*. International Journal of Human Computer Studies, Vol. 47 (1), Academic Press, 1997, S. 31-65

[5] Niels O. Bouvin: *Unifying strategies for Web augmentation*. In: Proc. 10 th ACM Hypertext Conference, Darmstadt, Feb. 1999, S. 91-100

[6] Niels O. Bouvin: *Augmenting the Web through Open Hypermedia*. Ph.D. Thesis, University of Aarhus, Denmark, 2002, http://www.daimi.aau.dk/~bouvin/Arakne/thesis.pdf

[7] Mark Boyns, 1998: *Design and Implementation of a World Wide Web Filtering System*, Masters Thesis, San Diego State University, USA, 1998

[8] Andy Cockburn, Steve Jones: *Design Issues for World Wide Web Navigation Visualisation Tools*. In: Proc. RIAO'97, McGill Univ., Canada, 1997, S. 55-74

[9] A. Cockburn, B. McKenzie, M. Jasonsmith: *Evaluating a Temporal Behaviour for Web Browsers' Back and Forward Buttons*, In: Proc. 11th WWW Conference. Honolulu, 2002

[10] Jeff Conklin: *Hypertext: An Introduction and Survey*. IEEE Computer 20 (9), September 1987, S. 17-40

[11] Martin Dodge, Rob Kitchin: *Atlas of Cyberspace*, Addison Wesley, August 2001, http://www.cybergeography.org/atlas/

[12] Steve DeRose, Eve Maler, David Orchard (eds.): *XML Linking Language (XLink)*. World Wide Web Consortium Recommendation, June 2001, http://w3.org/TR/xlink/

[13] Erich Gamma, Richard Helm, Ralph Johnson, John Vlissides: Design Patterns: Elements of Reusable Object-Oriented Software, Addison Wesley Longman, 1994

[14] Google Inc.: The Google Web APIs, April 2002, http://www.google.com/apis/

[15] S. Ihde, P. Maglio, J. Meyer, R. Barrett: *Intermediary-Based Transcoding Framework*. In: IBM Systems Journal, Vol. 40 (1) 2001, New York, S. 179-192

[16] William Jones, Harry Bruce, Susan Dumais: *Keeping Found Things Found on the Web*. In: 10th Conf. Information and Knowledge Management, Atlanta, 2001, S. 119-126

[17] LinkAlarm Inc.: *Web Integrity Benchmark*. Juni 2002, http://linkquality.com/

[18] Paul Maglio, Rob Barrett: *Intermediaries Personalize Information Streams*. Communications of the ACM, Vol. 43(8), August 2000, S. 96-101

[19] Matthias Mayer, Ben Bederson: *Browsing Icons: A Task-Based Approach for a Visual Web History*. HCIL Technical Report, University of Maryland, 2001

[20] Robert C. Miller, Krishna Bharat. *SPHINX: A Framework for Creating Personal, Site-Specific Web Crawlers*. In: Proc. WWW7, Brisbane, Australia, 1998, S. 119-130

[21] Jakob Nielsen: *Usability Engineering*, Academic Press, San Diego, USA, 1993

[22] James Pitkow, R. Kipp Jones : *Supporting the Web: A Distributed Hyperlink Database System*. In: Computer Networks and ISDN Systems, Vol. 28, 1996, S. 981ff

[23] Gabriel Sidler, Andrew Scott, Heiner Wolf: *Collaborative Browsing in the World Wide Web*. In: 8th Joint European Networking Conference, Edinburgh, 1997

[24] L. Tauscher, S. Greenberg: *How People Revisit Web Pages: Empirical Findings and Implications for the Design of History Systems*. Int. J. Human Computer Studies, 47(1), Academic Press, S. 97-138

[25] Weigang Wang, Roy Rada: *Experiences with Semantic Net Based Hypermedia*. In: International Journal of Human Computer Studies, Vol. 43, 1995, pp. 419-439

[26] Harald Weinreich, Winfried Lamersdorf: *Concepts for Improved Visualization of Web Link Attributes*. Computer Networks, Vol. 33, 2000, S. 403-416

[27] H. Weinreich, H. Obendorf, W. Lamersdorf: *The Look of the Link - Concepts for the User Interface of Extended Hyperlinks*. In: Proc. Hypertext'01 , Aarhus, 2001, S. 19-28

Automated Testing of XML/SOAP Based Web Services

Ina Schieferdecker[1], Bernard Stepien[2]

[1]FOKUS, Berlin, Germany, [2]University of Ottawa, Canada
[1]`schieferdecker@fokus.fhg.de`, [2]`stepien@site.uottawa.ca`

Web services provide seamless connections from one software application to another over private intranets and the Internet. The major communication protocol used is SOAP, which in most cases is XML over HTTP. The exchanged data follow precise format rules in the form of XML Document Type Definitions or more recently the proposed XML Schemas. Web service testing considers functionality and load aspects to check how a Web service performs for single clients and scales as the number of clients accessing it increases. This paper discusses the automated testing of Web services by use of the Testing and Test Control Notation TTCN-3. A mapping between XML data descriptions to TTCN-3 data is presented to enable the automated derivation of test data. This is the basis for functional and load tests of XML interfaces in TTCN-3. The paper describes the mapping rules and prototypical tools for the development and execution of TTCN-3 tests for XML/SOAP based Web services.

Introduction

Web services are more and more used for the realization of distributed applications crossing domain borders. However, the more Web services are used for central and/or business critical applications, their functionality, performance and overall quality become key elements for their acceptance and wide spread use. Consumers of Web services will want assurances that a Web service will not fail to return a response in a certain time period. Even more, systematic testing of Web services is essential as Web services can be very complex and hard to implement: although the syntax of the data formats is described formally with XML, the semantics and possible interactions with the Web service and use scenarios are described textually only. This encompasses the risk of misinterpretation and wrong implementation. Therefore, testing a final implementation within its target environment is essential to assure the correctness and interoperability of a Web service.

Testing a system is performed in order to assess its quality and to find errors if existent. An error is considered to be a discrepancy between observed or measured values provided by the system under test and the specified or theoretically correct values. Testing is the process of exercising or evaluating a system or system component by manual or automated means to check that it satisfies specified requirements. Testing approves a quality level of a tested system. The need for testing approaches arose already within the IT community: so-called interoperability events are used to evaluate and launch certain XML interface technologies and Web services, to validate the specifications and to check various implementations for their functionality and performance. However, the tests used at interoperability events are not uniquely defined, so that one has to question on which basis implementations are evaluated.

On contrary, there are test-engineering methods and a conformance testing methodology within telecommunication, which have evolved over years, are widely spread and successfully applied to assess the correctness of protocol implementations. The standardized test specification language TTCN-3 [7] with its advanced features for test specification is expected to be applied to many testing applications that were not previously open to TTCN. TTCN-3 has been defined to be applicable for protocol testing (including mobile and Internet protocols), service testing (including supplementary services), module testing, testing of CORBA based platforms, API testing etc. TTCN-3 is not restricted to conformance testing and can be used for many other kinds of testing including interoperability, robustness, regression, system and integration testing. The application of TTCN-3 to specific target technologies can be made effective by allowing the direct use of the data definitions of the system to be tested within the TTCN-3 test specification: ASN.1 (Abstract Syntax Notation One) for protocol stacks, IDL (Interface Definition Language) for CORBA (Common Object Request Broker Architecture) and XML (Extended Markup Language) for Web services. TTCN-3 predefines a mapping for ASN.1 to TTCN-3 in the standard itself. A mapping for IDL has been defined in [9]. This paper presents the mapping of XML to TTCN-3 as a basis for automated Web services tests with TTCN-3.

In Section 1, an overview on Web services, XML and SOAP and a discussion on testing Web services are given. Automated testing of Web services with TTCN-3 is presented in Section 2. In particular, the mapping rules for XML Schemas are described. Conclusions finish the paper.

1   Web services, XML and SOAP

A Web service is a URL-addressable resource returning information in response to client requests. Web services are integrated into other applications or Web sites, even though they exist on other servers. So for example, a Web site providing quotes for car insurance could make requests behind the scenes to a Web service to get the estimated value of a particular car model and to another Web service to get the current interest rate. A Web service can be seen as a Web site that provides a programmatic interface using the communication protocol SOAP, the Simple Object Access Protocol: operations are called using HTTP and XML (SOAP) and results are returned using HTTP and XML (SOAP). The operations are described in XML with the Web Service Description Language (WSDL). Web services can be located via the Universal Description, Discovery and Integration (UDDI) based registry of services[1].

XML stands for Extensible Markup Language and as its name indicates, the prime purpose of XML was for the marking up of documents. Marking up a document consist in wrapping specific portions of text in tags that convey a meaning and thus making it easier to locate them and also manipulating a document based on these tags or on their attributes. Attributes are special annotations associated to a tag that can be used to refine a search. An XML document has with its tags and attributes a self-

---

[1] Both, WSDL and UDDI are not considered in this paper.

documenting property that has been rapidly considered for a number of other applications than document markup. This is the case for configuration files of software but also for telecommunication applications to transfer control or application data like for example to Web pages. XML follows a precise syntax and allows for checking well-formedness and conformance to a grammar using a Document Type Description (DTD)[2] or a *Schema*. First of all, XML schemas [2] are defined using the basic XML syntax of tags and end tags. Second, XML schemas are true data types and contain many of the data typing features found in most of the recent high level programming languages.

Embedded schema

```
<schema>
  <element name="weather">
    <complexType>
      <sequence>
        <element name="location">
          <complexType >
            <sequence>
              <simpleType name="city">
                <restriction base="string">
                  <pattern value="[a-zA-Z]"/>
                </restriction>
              </simpleType>
              <element name="country" type="string"/>
            </sequence>
          </complexType>
        </element>
        <element name="temperature" type="integer"/>
        <element name="barometric_pressure" type="integer"/>
        <element name="conditions" type="string"/>
      </sequence>
    </complexType>
  </element>
</schema>
```

Named types

```
<schema>
  <complexType name="weatherType" >
    <sequence>
      <element name="location" type="locationType"/>
      <element name="temperature" type="integer"/>
      <element name="barometric_pressure" type="integer"/>
      <element name="conditions" type="string"/>
    </sequence>
  </complexType>
  <complexType name="locationType" >
    <sequence>
      <element name="city" type="cityType"/>
      <element name="country" type="string"/>
    </sequence>
  </complexType>
  <simpleType name="cityType">
    <restriction base="string">
      <pattern value="[a-zA-Z]"/>
    </restriction>
  </simpleType>
  <element name="weather" type="weatherType"/>
</schema>
```

Flat catalog

```
<schema>
  <element name="temperature" type="integer"/>
  <element name="barometric_pressure" type="integer"/>
  <element name="conditions" type="string"/>
  <element name="country" type="string"/>
  <simpleType name="city">
    <restriction base="string">
      <pattern value="[a-zA-Z]"/>
    </restriction>
  </simpleType>
  <element name="location">
    <complexType >
      <sequence>
        <element ref="city"/>
        <element ref="country"/>
      </sequence>
    </complexType>
  </element>
  <element name="weather">
    <complexType>
      <sequence>
        <element ref="location"/>
        <element ref="temperature"/>
        <element ref="barometric_pressure"/>
        <element ref="conditions"/>
      </sequence>
    </complexType>
  </element>
</schema>
```

Figure 1.   XML Schema for the Weather Service

The central concept of XML schemas is the building block approach by defining components that consist themselves of type definitions and element declarations. However most important is the fact that XML Schemas are very flexible and allow to describe the same rules in many different ways depending on the use of the following structuring concepts: primitive data typing including byte, date, integer, string, etc. ; simple and complex types; type inheritance; restrictions and extensions; global and local definitions; embedded, flat catalog and named type structuring constructs. This paper uses a weather service as an example: the weather is given for a location being a city in a country. It is described in terms of the temperature, the barometric pressure and further, textually described conditions (see Figure 1).

---

[2] DTDs are not considered here due to lack of space.

The *embedded method* derives from the nested tags mechanism of XML itself. In this method, elements are defined where they are used inside the hierarchy. Consequently there is no need to name a local type - it is called an anonymous type. Eventually the leaves of the tree that constitutes an embedded type definition are composed exclusively of either primitive types or already defined types. This implies that a local definition can be used only once and that there is no need for reusability in a specific application. The *flat catalog* approach uses the concept of substitution. Each element is defined by a reference to another element declaration. *Named types* are the closest to traditional computer languages data typing. Each element has a name and a type name and each subtype is defined separately. In addition, XML schemas provide two inheritance mechanisms to restrict and extend types. In Figure 2, weather is extended to EuroWeather with an additional attribute for the EuroLanguage. In the restriction, two fields are implicitly removed by setting their maximal occurrences to zero.

SOAP is a simple mechanism for exchanging structured and typed information between peers in a decentralized distributed environment using XML [2][5][6]. SOAP as a new technology to support server-to-server communication competes with other distributed computing technologies including DCOM, Corba, RMI, and EDI. Its advantages are a light-weight implementation, simplicity, open-standards origins and platform independence. The protocol consists only of a single HTTP request and a corresponding response between a sender and a receiver but that can optionally follow a path of relays called nodes, which each can play a role that is specified in the SOAP envelope. A SOAP request is an HTTP POST request. The data part consists of the SOAP envelope; the SOAP binding framework; the SOAP encoding rules; and the SOAP RPC representation called the body.

```
<complexType name="EuroWeather">
  <simpleContent>
    <extension base="weather">
      <attribute name="language" type="EuroLanguages"/>
    </extension>
  </simpleContent>
</complexType>
<complexType name="locationWeather">
  <complexContent>
    <restriction base="EuroWeather">
      <sequence>
        <element name="city" type="string" maxOccurs="0"/>
        <element name="country" type="string" maxOccurs="0"/>
      </sequence>
    </restriction>
  </complexContent>
</complexType>
```

Figure 2.   Extension and restriction for the Weather Service

Testing of Web services (as for any other technology or system) is useful to prevent late detection of errors (possibly by dissatisfied users), what typically requires complex and costly repairs. Testing enables the detection of errors and the evaluation and approval of system qualities beforehand. An automated test approach helps in particular to efficiently repeat tests whenever needed for new system releases in order to assure the fulfilment of established system features in the new release. First approaches towards automated testing with proprietary test solutions exist [10], however, with such tools one is bound to the specific tool and its features and capabilities. Specification-based automated testing, where abstract test specifications independent of the concrete system to be tested and independent of the test platform are used, are superior to proprietary techniques: they improve the transparency of the test process, increase the objectiveness of the tests, and make test results comparable. This is mainly due to the fact that abstract test specifications are defined in an unambiguous, standardized notation, which is easier to understand, document, communicate and to discuss. However, we go beyond "classical" approaches towards specification-based automated testing, which till now mainly concentrate on the automated test implementation and execution: we consider test generation aspects as well as the efficient reuse of test procedures in a hierarchy of tests.

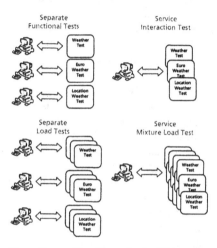

Figure 3.   Test hierarchy for Web services

Testing of Web services has to target three aspects: the discovery of Web services, the data format exchanged, and request/response mechanisms (i.e. SOAP). The data format and request/response mechanisms can be tested within one test approach: by invoking requests and observing responses with test data representing valid and invalid data formats. Since a Web service is a remote application, which will be accessed by multiple users, not only functionality in terms of sequences of request/response and performance in terms of response time, but also scalability in terms of functionality and performance under load conditions matters. Therefore, we have developed a hierarchy of test settings starting with separate functional tests for the individual services of a Web service, to a service interaction test checking the simultaneous request of different services, to a separate load tests for the individual services up to a combined load test for a mixture of requests for different services (see Figure 3). All the tests return not only a test verdict but also the response times for the individual requests.

2   Test automation with TTCN-3

Our means to automate Web service testing is the Testing and Test Control Notation TTCN-3 [7], which has been developed by the European Telecommunication Standards Institute ETSI not only for telecommunication but also for software and data communication systems. Like any other communication-based system, Web services are natural candidates for testing using TTCN-3.

TTCN-3 is a language to define test procedures to be used for black-box testing of distributed systems. Stimuli are given to the system under test (SUT), its reactions are observed and compared with the expected ones. On the basis of this comparison, the subsequent test behaviour is determined or the test verdict is assigned. If expected and observed responses differ, then a fault has been discovered which is indicated by a test verdict fail. A successful test is indicated by a test verdict pass. TTCN-3 allows an easy and efficient description of complex distributed test behaviour in terms of sequences, alternatives, loops and parallel stimuli and responses. Stimuli and responses are exchanged at the interfaces of the system under test, which are defined as a collection of ports. The test system can use a number of test components to perform test procedures in parallel. Likewise to the interfaces of the system under test, the interfaces of the test components are described as ports. TTCN-3 is a modular language and has a similar look and feel to a typical programming language. However, in addition to the typical programming constructs, it contains all the important features necessary to specify test procedures and campaigns for functional, conformance, interoperability, load and scalability tests like test verdicts, matching mechanisms to compare the reactions of the SUT with the expected range of values, timer handling, distributed test components, ability to specify encoding information, synchronous and asynchronous communication, and monitoring. A TTCN-3 test specification consists of four main parts:

– type definitions for test data structures
– templates definitions for concrete test data
– function and test case definitions for test behaviour
– control definitions for the execution of test cases

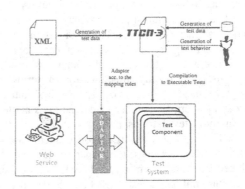

Figure 4. Testing of Web services with TTCN-3

The data type definitions are generated from the corresponding XML schema of the Web service to be tested. The templates are based on the corresponding data types and the behaviour of the service being tested that consist of sequences of requests and responses. An approach towards automated testing of Web services with TTCN-3 requires therefore the following steps (see Figure 4).

1. The structure of the test data is derived from the XML definition.

2. Test data (i.e. the concrete values for test stimuli and observations) is generated.

3. Test behaviour (i.e. the sequences of test stimuli and observations) is generated. The resulting TTCN-3 module is compiled to executable code.

4. The tests are performed using a test adaptor, which follows the mapping rules for test data structure to encode and decode the Web service requests and replies.

Currently, steps 1 and 4 can be automated with the help of tools as described in Section 2.1. The automation for step 2 and 3 requires further work: for this step mainly test synthesis approaches based on finite state machines or labelled transition systems will be used. The test adaptor for step 5 has to be developed only once, so that it can be used for any Web service and TTCN-3 test following the mapping rules from step 1.

2.1   Generating Test Data Structure: Mapping XML to TTCN-3

The target of the mapping of XML to TTCN-3 is the integral type system of TTCN-3, which is similar to ASN.1 in terms of availability of basic and structured types. The type system contains basic types (integer, float, boolean), basic string types (such as bitstring and charstring) and user-defined structured types (such as record, enumerated, and union). XML and TTCN-3 data types are somewhat similar conceptually but because of their differences in purpose and structure the actual mappings require some transformations that are more than pro-forma translations.

XML schemas have a wide variety of *predefined types and subtypes*. For example, Schemas have an integer type but also countless variations about integers such as positive integers and negative integers, etc. These map mainly to TTCN-3 basic types together with additional attributes to reflect the specific variation of a basic type, e.g. an attribute to indicate positive or negative integers. Further, some primitive types such as Time and Date are mapped to TTCN-3 records. *Simple types* are mapped to TTCN-3 basic types with the respective lexical restrictions represented by a range of values. The XML list construct is mapped to a TTCN-3 array and enumerations to enumerated types. Since there is no inheritance mechanism in TTCN-3 data types, XML *extensions and restriction* constructs must be mapped to a duplication of the definition of the inherited type and the potential conversion of its complex kind in the case of choice constructs. This means that if the current type being defined is a sequence and the inherited type is a choice, we need to create a new field with inherited type while if the inherited type is a sequence as well, we merely concatenate the fields of the inherited type with those of the target type. The same situation applies to the case of a defined choice type that inherits a sequence type. The restriction mechanism consists in removing fields in the inheriting type to be mapped.

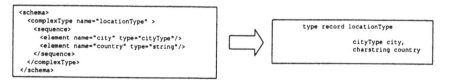

Figure 5.   Mapping for named type XML schema

The *named type* approach has a one to one mapping with TTCN-3 data types since both have the concept of field name and field type name. The element name becomes the field name and the element type becomes the field type name.

The main construct of XML schema *embedded type* approach is the local type definition. There is no corresponding construct in TTCN-3. Consequently, the local definition must be taken out of the type definition to be defined separately with a new generated type name that is also used as a field type name for the element being mapped to.

```
<schema>
  <element name="weather">
    <complexType>
      <sequence>
        <element name="location">
          <complexType >
            <sequence>
              <simpleType name="city">
                <restriction base="string">
                  <pattern value="[a-zA-Z]"/>
                </restriction>
              </simpleType>
              <element name="country" type="string"/>
            </sequence>
          </complexType>
        </element>
        <element name="temperature" type="integer"/>
        <element name="barometric_pressure" type="integer"/>
        <element name="conditions" type="string"/>
      </sequence>
    </complexType>
  </element>
</schema>
```

```
type record weather
{
    location_Type location,
    integer temperature,
    integer barometric_pressure,
    charstring conditions
}
type record location_Type
{
    charstring city ("a".."z","A".."Z"),
    charstring country
}
```

Figure 6.   Mapping for embedded XML schema

The *flat catalogue* approach consists in type substitution. This is different from named types where each name found in the content specification refers to a separate element declaration. The difference is however that the referenced separate element declaration may be further defined using one of the three different approaches. Consequently, if the separate element declaration is using a named type approach we merely use its type for our current field type name, but if the referenced element uses the flat catalogue or the embedded style we need again to generate a type name.

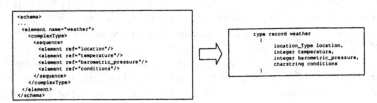

Figure 7.   Mapping for flat catalogue XML schema

2.2   Generating test configuration

In addition to the structure of the test data, the test configuration in terms of test components and ports has to be generated (see Figure 8). We use a message port to access a Web service. This port can transfer request and response messages. Furthermore, we use a varying set of parallel test components (PTC) to represent separate functional tests, service interaction tests, separate load tests and load tests for service mixtures. Every PTC like the SUT has a port to represent the Web service interface. The PTCs use the same basic test functions to stimuli requests and observe responses. The main test component (MTC) controls the dynamic creation of the test components according to the kind of tests. The tests with several components are parameterized, so that the actual number of test components emulating the use of a certain service varies depending on the current value of the parameters.

```
type port WeatherService message (
         out weatherRequest;
         in  weatherResponse;
)

type component SUTType (
         port WeatherService weatherservice_port;
)
type component PTCType (
         port WeatherService weatherservice_port;
         timer T_wait := 1.0;
)
type component MTCType (
)
```

Figure 8.   Test components

For the main kinds of tests shown in Figure 3, a fixed set of test cases being independent of the concrete Web service to be tested can be defined. They follow all the same procedure: the MTC creates PTCs according to the services to be tested and according to the load to be generated. Every PTC gets a concrete test function assigned and is started. Afterwards, the MTC awaits the termination of all PTCs. The overall test verdict is the accumulated test verdict of all the PTCs.

```
testcase ServiceInteractionTest
(intarray Service)
runs on MTCType system SUTType
(
    var integer serviceno:= sizeof(Service);
    var PTCType PTC[serviceno];
    for (var integer j:=1; j<= serviceno; j:= j+1)
    (
        PTC[j]:= PTCType.create;
        PTC[j].start(SeparateFunctional(Service[j]));
    )
    all component.done
)
```

```
testcase SeparateFunctionalTest
(integer Service)
runs on MTCType system SUTType
(
    var PTCType PTC:= PTCType.create;
    PTC.start(SeparateFunctional(Service));
    all component.done
)
```

```
testcase SeparateLoadTest
(integer Service, integer Load)
runs on MTCType system SUTType
(
    var PTCType PTC[Load];
    for (var integer j:=1; j<= Load; j:= j+1)
    (
        PTC[j]:= PTCType.create;
        PTC[j].start(SeparateFunctional(Service));
    )
all component.done
)
```

```
testcase MixedServiceLoadTest
(intarray Service, Load)
runs on MTCType system SUTType
(
    var integer serviceno:= sizeof(Service);
    for (var integer j:=1; j<= serviceno; j:= j+1)
    (
        var PTCType PTC[Load[j]];
        for (var integer k:=1; k<= Load[j]; k:= k+1)
        (
            PTC[k]:= PTCType.create;
            PTC[k].start(SeparateFunctional(Service[j]));
        )
    )
    all component.done
)
```

Figure 9.   Test cases for the different kinds of tests – the Test Framework

The generic test cases can be controlled with a general test case control mechanism like shown in Figure 10. Within the control part at first, the functionality of each service offered by a Web service is tested. Then, load tests for the successfully tested services are performed with an increasing load. Afterwards, service pairs are taken in order to test for service interaction. Finally, the successfully tested service pairs are tested for increasing load. Both, the services to be tested, the maximal load for a service test and the increase for the load tests have to be determined by test execution only – these values are declared as external constants to the TTCN-3 module representing the Test Framework. The control part can be enhanced to reflect other test combinations for e.g. not only tests for service pairs but service sets.

2.3   Generating test data

Templates are used to define the concrete test data to be used for requests to and responses from the Web service. The response template uses patterns to indicate ranges of acceptable values. For example, the temperature should be given in the response, but the concrete value is open.

```
module TestFrameWork {
  type record ServiceLoad {
    integer Service,                              // the service to be tested
    integer Load                                  // the maximal load for the service
  }
  external const ServiceLoad Services[];          // array of services to be tested
  external const integer increase;                // load increase for the load tests
  ...
  control {
    var integer serviceno:= sizeof(Services);

    var verdicttype ServicesResult[serviceno];     // test result per service

    for (var integer j:=1; j<=serviceno; j:=j+1) {   // functional test per service
      ServicesResult[j]:= execute(SeparateFunctionalTest(Services[j].Service));
    }
    for (var integer j:=1; j<=serviceno; j:=j+1) {   // load test per service
      if (ServicesResult[j] == pass) {
        for (var integer k:= increase; k <= Services[j].Load; j:= j+increase) {
                                                    // load tests with increasing load
if (ServicesResult[j] == pass) {
          ServicesResult[j]:= execute(SeparateLoadTest(Services[j].Service, k));
    } } } }


    var verdicttype ServicesMixResult[serviceno][serviceno];   // test result per service pair

    for (var integer j:=1; j<=serviceno; j:=j+1) {   // service interaction test per service pair
      if (ServicesResult[j] == pass) {
        for (var integer k:=1; k<=serviceno; k:=k+1) {
          if (ServicesResult[k] == pass) {
            const integer ServicePair[2]:= {Services[j].Service, Services[k].Service };
            ServicesMixResult[j][k]:= execute(ServiceInteractionTest(ServicePair));
    } } } }

    for (var integer j:=1; j<=serviceno; j:=j+1) {   // mixture load test per service pair
      for (var integer k:=1; k<=serviceno; k:=k+1) {
        if (ServicesMixResult[j][k] == pass) {
          const integer ServicePair[2]:= {Services[j].Service, Services[k].Service };
          for (var integer l:= increase; l <= Services[j].Load; l:= l+increase) {
                                                    // load tests with increasing load
            for (var integer m:= increase; m <= Services[k].Load; m:= m+increase) {
              const integer PairLoad[2]:= { l, m };
              ServicesMixResult[j][k]:= execute(MixedServiceLoadTest(ServicePair, PairLoad));
    } } } } }
}
```

Figure 10.   Execution Control for the Test Framework

We work on approaches towards the automated generation of test data by using the classification tree method [11] being implemented in the CTE tool. This method enables the generation of exhaustive templates for requests, however, needs to be extended to enable the generation of response templates with patterns as well.

2.4 Basic test function for the weather service

The basic test function for the weather service is consists mainly of a pair of request and response to the Weather service. If the expected response is received, a pass is assigned. In addition, unexpected and no response are handled – these cases lead to fail. The log information logs received response or the timeout and the respective time stamp. This basic test function is specific to the Web service to be tested, but has to be developed once and can then be reused for the various types of tests presented above.

2.5 The tool environment for Web service tests with TTCN-3

The tool environment for automated testing of Web services with TTCN-3 uses the TTCN-3 to Java *compiler* TTthree [12], an XML to TTCN-3 *conversion* tool and a test *adaptor* for XML/SOAP interfaces. Since there are both XML DTDs and XML schemas it would appear that we would have to build two separate tools to handle the automated mapping of XML type definitions. However, there are at least three reasons to avoid this duplication: there exist already DTD to Schema conversion tools [4]; most of XML applications where TTCN-3 can be useful as a testing tool use only XML schemas – this is the case for the Simple Object Access Protocol; XML schemas can be parsed directly using off the shelf parsers like DOM because an XML schema is defined with the same principle of tags and attributes of XML documents[3]. We have therefore developed a conversion tool using the XML Document Object Model (DOM). The *adaptor* for XML/SOAP interfaces realizes the functions of the TTCN-3 runtime interface and the TTCN-3 control interfaces, both in [7]. The adaptor performs the adaptation of the compiled TTCN-3 code to the target test device (in our case a Solaris workstation, Windows or Linux PC) and covers the test system user interface, test execution control, test event logging, as well as communication with the SUT and timer implementation. For the communication with the SUT, i.e. the Web service, SOAP request messages are encoded from and SOAP response messages are decoded to TTCN-3 data used in the test specification. The adaptor is generic and enables the testing of any Web service using XML/SOAP interfaces. In order to use this adaptor, the mapping rules provided in Section 2.1 have to be respected by the tests being defined in TTCN-3.

3 Conclusion

Testing Web services presents a variety of new and interesting challenges. In particular, test automation will be essential to a sound and efficient Web service development process, for the assessment of the functionality, performance and scalability of Web services as well as for the approval and acceptance of Web services developed by application providers.

This paper presents a flexible test framework for Web services using the Testing and Test Control Notation TTCN-3. The test framework is developed for Web services with XML/SOAP interfaces and provides functional, service interaction, and load tests with flexible test configurations and varying load. The provided test hierarchy of predefined kinds of tests is generic as it can be used for arbitrary Web services. The specifics of a concrete Web service are handled within basic test functions emulating the use of the services offered by a Web service. These basic test functions are reused by the kinds of tests provided in the test hierarchy. A further key element of the test framework is the automated translation of XML data to TTCN-3, so that test skeletons can be generated directly from the specification of the Web service. For that, XML Schemas have been analyzed and mapping rules have been developed. These rules are realized by a conversion tool from XML to TTCN-3. The conversion tool together with the TTCN-3 compiler and execution environment TTthree provides us a complete tool chain for test data type generation, test development, implementation and execution. A detailed description of the work done is available as technical report.

Future work will further elaborate methods for test data generation. In particular, the classification tree method will be investigated for potential extension towards the generation of templates for SOAP responses. In addition, the test framework will be enhanced to deal with further elements of Web services like the specifics of WSDL and UDDI.

References

[1]   W3C: *Extensible Markup Language (XML) 1.0*, W3C Recommendation, Oct. 2000, http://www.w3.org/TR/2000/REC-xml-20001006
[2]   W3C Recommendations: *XML Schema*, May 2001
       Part 0: *Primer*, http://www.w3.org/TR/2001/REC-xmlschema-0-20010502
       Part 1: *Structures*, http://www.w3.org/TR/2001/REC-xmlschema-1-20010502/
       Part 2: *Datatypes*, http://www.w3.org/TR/2001/REC-xmlschema-2-20010502/
[3]   R. Jeliffe: *The XML Schema Specification in Context* http://www.ascc.net/~ricko/XMLSchemaInContext.html
[4]   W3C: *A Conversion Tool from DTD to XML Schema*, http://www.w3.org/2000/04/schema_hack/, Apr 2000
[5]   W3C: *Simple object Access Protocol (SOAP) 1.1*, May 2000, http://www.w3.org/TR/SOAP
[6]   B. McLaughlin: *Java & XML*, 2nd edition, O'Reilly, Chapter 12: *SOAP*.
[7]   ETSI MTS, http://www.etsi.org: The Testing and Test Control Notation TTCN-3
       Part 1: *TTCN-3 Core Language* - ETSI ES 201873-1 V2.2.1 (2002-10)
       Part 5: *The TTCN-3 Runtime Interface TRI* - ES 201873-5 V2.0.0 (2002-10)
       Part 6: *The TTCN-3 Control Interfaces TCI* - DES 201873-6 V1.0.0 (2002-10)
[8]   Schieferdecker, S. Pietsch, T. Vassiliou-Gioles: *Systematic Testing of Internet Protocols - First Experiences in Using TTCN-3 for SIP*. 5th IFIP Africom Conference on Communication Systems, Cape Town, South Africa, May 2001.
[9]   M. Ebner, A. Yin, M. Li: *Definition and Utilisation of OMG IDL to TTCN-3 Mapping.* – 16th Intern. IFIP Conference on Testing Communicating Systems (TestCom 2002), Berlin, March 2002.
[10]   *ANTS* (Advanced .NET Testing System), Red Gate Software, http://www.red-gate.com/ants.htm.
[11]   Grochtmann, M., J. Wegener and K. Grimm: *Test Case Design Using Classification Trees and the Classification-Tree Editor CTE*. Proc. of 8th International Software Quality Week, SanFrancisco, California, USA, pp. 4-A-4/1-11, 1995.
[12]   *TTthree* (TTCN-3 to Java compiler), Testing Technologies IST GmbH, http://www.testingtech.de.

Adaptation-Aware Web Caching: Caching in the Future Pervasive Web

Sven Buchholz, Alexander Schill

Dresden University of Technology
Department of Computer Science
D-01062 Dresden, Germany
{buchholz, schill}@rn.inf.tu-dresden.de

Abstract. In the upcoming world of Pervasive Computing, content adaptation is an essential concept to meet the heterogeneous requirements of web users using various web access technologies. However, content adaptation interferes with the effectiveness of web caching. Leveraging the advantages of web caching even in the world of Pervasive Computing is the subject of this paper.
We present an approach that joins the concepts of web caching and content adaptation in a uniform scheme. We have conceived an architecture of hierarchical, independent caching proxies that are aware of the heterogeneous capabilities of the client population. Content adaptation is performed by adaptation services on behalf of the proxies. By this means, the proxies merge their local cache management with the composition of a distributed adaptation path and avoid the interference between content adaptation and web caching.

1   Introduction

In the upcoming world of Pervasive Computing, users access information sources in the World Wide Web by a huge variety of mobile devices featuring heterogeneous capabilities (regarding display, data input, computing capacity, etc.). Those mobile devices coexist with fixed workstations, possibly Internet enabled TV sets, or public information terminals resulting in an even broader diversity of device characteristics and capabilities. The miscellaneous devices are attached to the Internet by a variety of communication systems, such as cellular radio networks, local area wireless networks, dial-up connections, or broadband connections. The various communication systems offer different functionality and heterogeneous characteristics (bandwidth, delay, etc.).

The key to meet the demands in this heterogeneous environment is the adaptation of the contents to the capabilities of the devices and communication systems. However, content adaptation interferes with effectiveness of web caching that is applied in the World Wide Web to improve performance by avoiding redundant data transfers. Leveraging the advantages of web caching even in the world of Pervasive Computing is the subject of this paper.

The remainder of the paper is organized as follows. In the next section the concept of content adaptation is introduced and different approaches for performing content adaptation are discussed. Section 3 points out the importance of web caching in the application domain of Pervasive Computing and analyzes the interference of content adaptation with the effectiveness of web caching. Our proposed solution, eliminating the interference between content adaptation and web caching, is presented in section 4. Section 5 discusses related work. Finally, some concluding remarks and future directions are given in section 6.

2 Content Adaptation

The term content adaptation refers to the modification of the representation of web objects in order to meet the media handling capabilities of the device and the transmission restrictions imposed by the network connection. Such modifications may include: format transcoding (e.g. XML to WML, JPEG to WBMP), scaling of images as well as video and audio streams, media conversion (e.g. text-to-speech), omission or substitution of document parts (e.g. images by a textual representation), or document fragmentation. Even semantic conversions, such as language translation, are considered as content adaptation operations.

A lot of effort has been spent in the field of content adaptation. We distinguish three different approaches for performing content adaptation described in previous work: *server-side adaptation*, *proxy-based adaptation*, and *adaptation paths*.

Server-side adaptation (e.g. [1]) means servers serve adapted documents to the clients (cf. fig. 1a). This can be done either by on-demand dynamic adaptation or by having a repository of pre-adapted documents.

With proxy-based adaptation (e.g. [2]), the documents are served by the servers in a generic representation[1]. The adaptation is performed on demand by intermediary proxies, which are placed close to the clients (cf. fig. 1b).

The adaptation paths approach (e.g. [3]) is a refinement of the concept of proxy-based adaptation. It is predicated on the finding that adaptation is often composed of

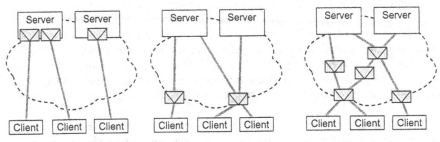

a) Server-side adaptation   b) Proxy-based adaptation   c) Adaptation paths

Fig. 1. Approaches for Performing Content Adaptation

---

[1] A generic representation of a text document will typically be some kind of XML document. Images or other multimedia contents may be generically represented by a loss-free compressed format.

elementary successively applied adaptation steps. Just as with proxy-based adaptation, the server serves the document in a generic representation. On its way to the client the document passes several distributed adaptation proxies performing the adaptation in a step-by-step manner (cf. fig. 1c). By this means a distributed adaptation path is established.

3   Web Caching in the Context of Content Adaptation

The concepts of server-side adaptation or on-demand dynamic adaptation (by a single proxy or an adaptation path) introduced in the previous section have one thing in common: They assume every information access to result in a data flow from the server to the client (if applicable via one or several adaptation proxies). On the other hand, today's Internet providers tend to avoid unnecessary data flows between servers and clients. Therefore, several web caching techniques (cf. [4, 5]) have been developed and deployed. Besides the widely used approach of proxy caching (e.g. [6, 7]), Content Delivery Networks (CDN, cf. [8, 9]) rely on distributed caching of web contents to improve the performance of web accesses.

Web caching exploits sharing effects and temporal locality in client access patterns to satisfy requests by cached copies of the requested objects[2]. By terminating client requests at local caching proxies, the network traffic on the Internet as well as the server load is reduced whereas the response time is improved. Furthermore, the robustness of web services is enhanced as a client may retrieve a document from the proxy cache if the server is unavailable (due to server crash, congestion, or network partitioning). Certainly, significant reductions in response time due to communication costs will be achievable only if there are considerable delays between proxy and server or the bottleneck link is between the proxy and the server. However, this is not always true in Pervasive Computing because often the bottleneck link is the wireless link to the client.

We envision leveraging the advantages of web caching even in the world of Pervasive Computing where content adaptation is necessary. However, the concepts of web caching and content adaptation cannot be considered orthogonal since content adaptation interferes with the effectiveness of web caching. On the other hand, web caching in conjunction with content adaptation may gain even more benefits as adapted contents may be reused, eliminating the cost for re-computing an adapted document. The interferences of web caching and content adaptation are illustrated in the following.

With server-side adaptation servers always serve fully adapted documents. Hence, proxies may cache fully adapted documents only. The drawback of caching fully adapted documents is that sharing benefits are reduced significantly: Though it is likely to have multiple clients requesting the same document, the likelihood of requiring the same representation of the document is considerably smaller.

---

[2] According to [10], 85% of all cache hits are due to sharing whereas 15% account for temporal locality. Nevertheless, in the domain of Pervasive Computing, temporal locality in the users' browsing behavior will result in more locality hits at the proxies because several client devices (such as Smart Phones) do not have a user agent cache.

As opposed to server-side adaptation, proxy-based adaptation allows the caches to be placed between the information sources and the adaptation proxies. Thus the caches store the generic documents that can be adapted to fit all client requests. Whereas this approach fully benefits from sharing, it might undermine the cache memory efficiency. This is due to the fact that generic documents are potentially larger[3] than adapted documents. Accordingly, fewer documents fit in the cache. Cache performance studies [11] suggest that increasing the cache size by a magnitude of 4 may increase the document hit ratio by up to about 25% and the byte hit ratio by up to about 35%. Reducing the size of the documents in the cache by adaptation will gain similar improvements in cache hits. Besides, even higher compression rates than by the magnitude of 4 might be achievable by content adaptation resulting in even higher improvements of the hit ratios. Reduced cache memory efficiency, however, is only an issue in environments with limited cache memory. Experiences with live web proxies teach cache memory is not necessarily a limitative factor today [12]. But the increasing share of streamed multimedia contents will probably turn it into a limitative factor in the future if caches are used for streaming content, too. Besides reduced cache memory efficiency, another problem with proxy-based adaptation in conjunction with web caching is that caching generic documents results in full adaptation costs with every request. Reuse of adapted documents is not possible.

With the adaptation paths approach, caches might be deployed (1) between the server and the first adaptation proxy in the path, (2) between the last adaptation proxy and the client, or (3) between proxies within the adaptation path. The first deployment suffers from reduced sharing benefits as described for server-side adaptation. The second approach may undermine the cache memory efficiency and turns the reuse of adapted contents impossible (cf. proxy-based adaptation). Placing caches within the adaptation path requires coordination between caching and adaptation path composition. However, coordinating caching and content adaptation has not been investigated before. Anyhow, coordination of caching and adaptation path composition may gain optimal benefits from caching. Caches within the adaptation path may always store the representation of an object that is adequately generic to fulfill subsequent requests from heterogeneous clients and sufficiently adapted to be efficient by means of cache memory consumption and adaptation costs.

4   A Unified Approach for Web Caching and Content Adaptation

According to the previous section, web proxy caching must be coordinated with content adaptation to allow maximum cache efficiency. In the following we present an approach that achieves the coordination by joining cache management and adaptation path composition in a uniform scheme.

---

[3] Adapted documents are not necessarily smaller in size than generic ones, e.g. if different compressions are used. However, due to the average information content of the generic representation being greater or equal to the one of the adapted representation, adapted documents can be compacted using loss-free compression to be smaller than the (compacted) generic documents.

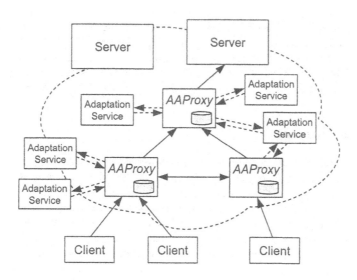

Fig. 2. System Scenario

4.1 System Scenario

Our approach is based on the system scenario presented in figure 2. The architecture consists of a hierarchy of independent caching proxies, having parental and sibling relationships, which cooperate to satisfy client requests. The hierarchy approach is based on the concepts of hierarchical caching, which was first proposed by the Harvest project [6]. In terms of Squid [7], hierarchical caching is the dominant web caching infrastructure on today's Internet.

However, as opposed to Squid and other existing web caching concepts, the caching proxies of the proposed architecture are aware of the heterogeneous capabilities of the clients. The caches store the generic, a partially adapted, or the fully adapted representation of an object depending on which representation seems most appropriate to fulfill subsequent requests. Hence, we call this kind of caching proxy *Adaptation-Aware Proxy (AAProxy)*.

The content adaptation is performed on behalf of the AAProxies by separate adaptation services (cf. fig. 2). They are invoked by a proxy in a client/server manner to perform particular adaptation operations. The concept of separate adaptation services conforms to the intentions of the ICAP Internet Draft [13].

Certainly, in the application scenario of Pervasive Computing clients should always find their nearest proxy without manual configuration by the user. Therefore we propose the application of transparent caching [14]. Transparent caching means the client addresses its request directly to the web server, but the request gets intercepted at the route and is transparently forwarded to a proxy. By intercepting the request on their route to the server, the requests may always be forwarded to the most appropriate proxy.

Even though the architectural description above relies on the terminology "proxy", it is not restricted to the classical approach of proxy caching. The functionality of the AAProxies might also be performed by the Edge Servers (cf. [9]) in a Content Delivery Network. In the context of CDN the effectiveness of adaptation-aware caching might be even more significant because technologies such as Edge Side Includes [15] allow for more dynamic contents to be pre-adapted, cached, and reused.

4.2 Request Handling

The basic operation of the proposed system is illustrated in the following (cf. fig. 3). When a user requests an object, the request is forwarded to a nearby AAProxy. Attached to the request the client device provides a description of its media handling capabilities. The media handling capabilities are expressed by means of the media features of the representation the client can handle. This representation we call the *target representation of the client*. As a client may be capable of handling different representations, it may provide a set of multiple target representations. Preferences of particular representations are expressed by assigning different quality values to the different target representations. We propose the application of IETF Media Feature Sets [16] for the purpose of expressing sets of target representations because they allow a flexible yet compact description.

On receiving a request, a AAProxy checks whether the requested object is available from its cache (or possibly from the cache of a sibling proxy) in a representation that meets the requirements of the client or that can be adapted to the client using the available adaptation services. If so, the AAProxy invokes necessary adaptation operations and eventually delivers the object to the client.

In case the request cannot be fulfilled from the cache contents, it is propagated up the hierarchy to the parent AAProxy. Thereby the media handling capabilities description is altered to include those representations that can be adapted to a target representation of the client using available adaptation services. All representations that may be a basis for fulfilling the client request (by invoking zero, one, or multiple adaptation services) constitute the set of *target representations of the proxy*. The adaptation costs and a measure for the quality of the adapted document (taking the client's preferences for the different target representations into account) are included in the media handling capabilities description. They are used to determine the optimal adaptation path, the path with the best ratio of quality to overall costs.

If the proxy considers the requested object to be popular enough to be cached, target representations that are assumed to fulfill not just the current but even future requests are privileged in the ranking by means of adaptation costs and quality. The ranking is weighted corresponding to the assumed probability that a cached copy can be reused. Assumptions about the reuse probability are gained from predicting the target representations of future requests based on an evaluation of the media handling capabilities descriptions received with the current and previous requests[4].

---

[4] We have not yet conceived the mechanisms for this evaluation. Nevertheless, we assume the proxies to estimate the capabilities of their client population based on an object spanning interpretation of the media handling capabilities descriptions received with previous requests and to infer the static probabilities for requests for certain target representations.

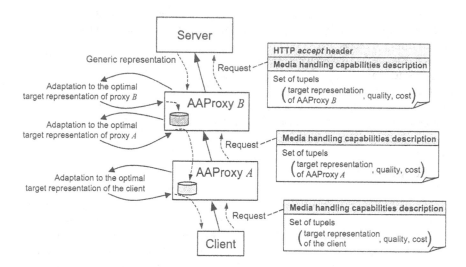

Fig. 3. Request Handling

On receiving a request from a child proxy, the parent AAProxy checks its cache for the requested object. If the request can be fulfilled from the cache, the parent generates its child's target representation that promises the best overall quality-to-costs ratio. Thereby, the costs and quality effects of the adaptations invoked by the parent proxy are also taken into consideration. The target representation promising the best quality-to-costs ratio we call *optimal target representation*.

If the requested object is not available from the cache in an appropriate representation the media handling capabilities description of the request is altered as outlined above and the request is sent to the respective parent. Eventually, the root proxy sends the request to the origin server.

If the origin server understands media handling capabilities descriptions, it determines all target representations of the root proxy that may be fulfilled by a copy of the requested object. The optimal target representation is selected and returned to the root proxy. Thereby the server picks the optimal adaptation path.

Nevertheless, we do not indispensably require the servers to understand media handling capabilities descriptions. By this means legacy servers can be easily integrated. A legacy server may simply return an object that meets the requirements expressed by the HTTP *accept* header in the request. In this case, the selection of the optimal adaptation path is done by the root proxy. To allow for legacy severs to be integrated we require a root proxy to set the HTTP *accept* header field according to its set of target representations.

While the response travels down the hierarchy, the particular AAProxies invoke adaptation services to make the response meet the optimal target representation of their respective child proxies. By means of successively producing the target representations of the AAProxies in the path, step-by-step adaptation is performed. Moreover, intermediary results of the step-by-step adaptation of cache-worthy objects are stored in the caches of the proxies. Possible other representations of the same object that can be generated (by adaptation) from the new cache copy might be evicted from the cache.

Even the cache replacement mechanisms may exploit the awareness of the AAProxy for content adaptation issues. For instance, instead of completely evicting an object from the cache, the representation may be adapted to consume less memory and still meet the capabilities of a majority of the clients[5]. However, the design of an appropriate cache replacement policy is subject to ongoing research.

5 Related Research

Related research to our work actually spans different research areas. On the one hand this is web proxy caching research. This research area has been investigated for quite a long time and many aspects have been deeply examined [6, 7, 10, 11, 14, 17, 18, 19, 20, 21]. The idea of proxy caching goes back to the CERN proxy [17]. It was further developed in the Harvest project [6], which also created the concepts of hierarchical caching, the basis of our system scenario. The subsequent open source project Squid [7] has further developed the Harvest ideas and integrated inter-cache communication [18, 19] to improve caching efficiency. Even though hierarchical caching by means of Squid is today's most dominant web caching infrastructure, there are several drawbacks that have motivated the development of alternative caching architectures, such as distributed caching [20] or Adaptive Web Caching [21].

One of the weak points of hierarchical caching is that web objects are stored redundantly at different levels in the caching hierarchy. This does not generally apply to our approach as we propose to store different representations (different intermediary results in the adaptation process) at the different levels in the hierarchy. Nevertheless, the algorithms presented in section 4 do not guarantee that there are no redundant copies. The adaptation path considered optimal may absolutely comprise redundant copies.

An alternative concept for improving web performance besides proxy caching is the approach of Content Delivery Networks (CDN; [8, 9]). As opposed to proxy caching, CDNs do not improve the general web access. They speed up the access to selected web sites by caching the contents of the CDN provider's customers. Hence, CDNs are deployed on behalf of the web site providers and not on behalf of the users as with proxy caching. The caching is done close to the users in so-called Edge Servers [9] ran by the CDN provider. According to [8], CDNs may use both pre-caching (which is actually push replication) and just-in-time caching, as applied in proxy caching. Unlike proxy caching, CDNs are not necessarily transparent to the content providers but may use proprietary protocols or protocol extensions. They are used, for instance, to distribute invalidation or update messages to ensure freshness of the cached contents.

---

[5] This is illustrated by the following example. A proxy may have cached a high resolution image that has been exceptionally requested from a full scale laptop computer although the vast majority of the client devices are WAP phones. Such a proxy could free cache memory by scaling-down the image to WAP phone resolution instead of evicting it from the cache.

Recent research in Content Delivery Networks deals with increasing the cacheability of dynamic contents by decomposing complex web objects into fragments with different cacheability. With Edge Side Includes (ESI; [9, 15]), endorsed e.g. by Akamai and Oracle, hypertext documents can be described as a composition of a template and multiple document fragments. The resulting hypertext document is assembled at the Edge Servers of the CDN. Hence, the fragments may be cached and updated independent from each other.

As mentioned before, the approach presented in this paper may be applied in CDNs. Technologies such as ESI complement our approach to provide for more dynamic contents to be pre-adapted, cached, and reused. The assembly of the result document can be considered an adaptation step in the adaptation path.

In addition to caching architectures, cache replacement and admittance policies, cache coherency, deployment options, and implementation details have been subject to research. An overview of research issues in web caching is given in [4, 5].

Content adaptation research is another area with relevance to our approach. Early efforts date back to the *DeleGate* Gopher proxy [22] for Kanji transcoding that started in 1994. Leveraging content adaptation to adapt to the capabilities of mobile devices was investigated by the *Daedalus* project at the UC Berkeley. It has proven that on-demand dynamic adaptation of text and images by proxies is feasible and powerful [2]. The concept of proxy-based dynamic adaptation was further refined by the UC Berkeley's Ninja Project [3]. The project proposes a robust, scalable architecture for web access by heterogeneous devices. In the Ninja project, on-demand dynamic adaptation is done in a step-by-step manner by several adaptation proxies establishing an adaptation path, the so-called Ninja Path. The ideas of Ninja Paths are the basis for the step-by-step adaptation used in our approach. Ninja assumes a centralized instance of the path subsystem performing the path composition and implementation [23]. While the Ninja approach guarantees the composition of valid paths, path optimization is not addressed.

Algorithms for composing and optimizing a distributed adaptation path have been dealt with by [24, 25]. Ooi et al. [24] describe an algorithm to distribute the computation of multimedia streams across multiple multimedia gateways. However, the algorithm presented in the paper optimizes the computation with respect to resource consumption only. Aspects such as sharing of intermediary results are not addressed. Likewise, caching is not an issue. Kasim et al. [25] present a more general and more abstract approach. They describe algorithms to determine a valid distributed adaptation path to make a multimedia object in a certain representation available at the client node. The origin object may reside on different nodes in different representations. In [25], the authors describe bottom-up as well as top-down algorithms. Furthermore, they have proven the top-down algorithm to determine the optimal adaptation path. These algorithms, however, do not deal with caching or sharing of intermediary adaptation results. Even though, the bottom-up algorithm is the basis for the algorithm we are developing for the proposed architecture.

A lot of effort has been spent on the adaptation of web documents. Automatic re-authoring of HTML pages to adapt them to the capabilities of mobile devices is done by the *Digestor* system [26] and its successor, the m-link system [27], by Fuji Xerox Palo Alto Laboratory (FXPAL). Those systems use heuristics to understand web documents to enable content adaptation. However, the potentials of such heuristics are limited. In order to overcome those limitations, other work considers generic XML-based representations of documents that are augmented by meta information to allow smarter adaptation (e.g. [28]). The approach presented in this paper does not rely on the one or the other concept for the adaptation of web contents. It is meant to deal with arbitrary means of content adaptation.

In the context of streaming media, caching of quality adaptive streams has been investigated [29, 30]. This is related to our approach as streams may be cached in different representations (qualities). However, as opposed to our ideas they only take the adaptation of multi-media streams by dropping layers or frames into account. Rejaie et al. [29] consider every layer of a multi-layered encoded stream as a separate object by means of the cache replacement algorithm and apply a weighted *LFU-Aging* algorithm to determine a *victim layer*, which is to be evicted from the cache. Yu et al. [30] do not only take multi-media streams but even non-continuous media, such as text and images, into account. They present a media-characteristic-weighted replacement policy that considers single frames of media streams as separate objects just as non-continuous media objects. Media-characteristic-weighted replacement means that dependencies between different objects (e.g. between I, P and B frames of an MPEG stream) are taken into account and different media types may be assigned different priorities. Adaptation, however, is limited to dropping particular frames.

As opposed to our approach, those approaches for proxy caching of quality adaptive multimedia streams only consider simple one-dimensional adaptations (dropping frames or layers of a multi-media stream). Our approach, however, considers arbitrary adaptations as far as they can be performed by an adaptation service. Furthermore, they do not exploit caching hierarchies to benefit from different representation of objects at different hierarchy levels. Accordingly, only our approach describes the negotiation of the optimal target representations for the different proxies and thereby the composition of a distributed adaptation path.

6 Conclusions

This paper discussed the application of web caching in the domain of Pervasive Computing where content adaptation is necessary to adjust to the particularities of the heterogeneous client devices. We pointed out that content adaptation interferes with the effectiveness of web caching. That is why novel schemes that coordinate web caching and content adaptation are necessary.

We presented an approach that joins the concepts of web caching and content adaptation in a uniform scheme. We conceived hierarchical, independent caching proxies that are aware of the heterogeneous capabilities of the client population. Content adaptation is performed by adaptation services on behalf of the proxies. By this means, the proxies merge their local cache management with the composition of a distributed adaptation path.

The presented approach is still subject to ongoing research. Currently, we are investigating the algorithms for negotiating the adaptation path in detail. Open questions include the estimation of adaptation costs and quality effects of operations that enable free scaling of objects. Furthermore, we want to refine the definition of caching costs, as the current algorithm does not take the costs for re-requesting evicted objects into account. Thereby we will also design a media features aware replacement policy for the proxy caches. Moreover, early experiences with our algorithm suggest the proxies might have to maintain a lot of information about the client population and will possibly exchange a significant amount of extra data for target representations. In case this suspicion comes true we will need heuristics to reduce the overhead.

The benefit of the approach presented in the paper shall be evaluated using simulation. Therefore we are working on a flexibly parametrizable trace synthesizer to generate traces that estimate the access patterns of future pervasive web users. First intermediary results have been published in [12].

References

1. Oracle 9i Application Server: Wireless Edition, Technical White Paper, Oracle Corporation, Redwood City, CA, USA (2000).
2. Fox A., Gribble, S.D., Chawathe, Y., Brewer, E.A.: Adapting to Network and Client Variation Using Active Proxies: Lessons and Perspectives. In: A Special Issue of IEEE Personal Communications on Adaptation (1998).
3. Gribble, S.D., Welsh, M., von Behren, R., Brewer, E.A., Culler, D., Borisov, N., Czerwinski, S., Gummadi, R., Hill, J., Joseph, A., Katz, R.H., Mao, Z.M., Ross, S., Zhao, B.: The Ninja architecture for robust Internet-scale systems and services. In: Computer Networks 35(4) (2001).
4. Wang, J.: A survey of web caching schemes for the Internet. In: ACM Computer Communication Review 29(5) (1999).
5. Barish, G., Obraczka, K.: World Wide Web Caching: Trends and Techniques. In: IEEE Communications, Internet Technology Series (2000).
6. Chankhunthod, A., Danzig, P.B., Neerdaels, C., Schwartz, M.F., Worrell, K.J.: A Hierarchical Internet Object Cache. In: Proceedings of the USENIX Technical Conference, San Diego, CA, USA (1996).
7. Wessels, D., Claffy, K.: ICP and the Squid Web Cache. In: IEEE Journal on Selected Areas in Communication 16(3) (1998).
8. Liste, M.: Content Delivery Networks (CDNs) - A Reference Guide. In: Cisco World, White Papers (2001). URL: http://www.ciscoworldmagazine.com/webpapers/2001/03_thrupoint.shtml [2002-10-15]
9. Turbo-Charging Dynamic Web Sites with Akamai EdgeSuite. Akamai White Paper AKAMWP-TCD1201, Akamai Technologies, Inc. Cambridge, MA, USA (2001). URL: http://www.akamai.com/en/resources/pdf/Turbocharging_WP.pdf [2002-10-15].
10. Duska, B., Marwood, D., Freeley, M.J.: The Measured Access Characteristics of World-Wide-Web Client Proxy Caches. In: Proceedings of the USENIX Symposium on Internet Technologies and Systems. Monterey, CA (1997).
11. Mahanti, A.: Web Proxy Workload Characterisation And Modelling. M.Sc. Thesis, Department of Computer Science, University of Saskatchewan (1999).
12. Buchholz, S., Jaensch, S., Schill, A.: Flexible Web Traffic Modeling for New Application Domains. In: Proc. of the IASTED International Conference on Applied Modelling and Simulation (AMS 2002), Cambridge, MA, USA (2002).
13. Elson, J., Cerpa, A.: ICAP the Internet Content Adaptation Protocol. Internet Draft, The ICAP Protocol Group (2001). URL: http://www.i-cap.org/spec/icap_specification.txt [2002-10-17]

14. Cohen, A., Rangarajan, S., Singh, N.: Supporting Transparent Caching with Standard Proxy Caches. In: Proceedings of the 4th International Web Caching Workshop, San Diego (1999).
15. Tsimelzon, M., Weihl, B., Jacobs, L.: ESI Language Specification 1.0. Akamai Technologies, Inc. Cambridge, MA, USA , Oracle Corporation, Redwood City, CA, USA (2001). URL: http://www.esi.org/language_spec_1-0.html [2002-10-16]
16. Klyne, G.: A Syntax for Describing Media Feature Sets. RFC 2533 (1999).
17. Luotonen, A., Altis, K.: World-Wide Web Proxies. In: Computer Networks and ISDN Systems 27(2), Elsevier Science (1994).
18. Wessels, D., Claffy, K.: Internet Cache Protocol (ICP), version 2, RFC 2186 (1997).
19. Rousskov, A., Wessels, D.: Cache Digest. In: Proceedings of the 3rd International WWW Caching Workshop, Manchester, UK (1998).
20. Tewari, R. Dahlin, M., Vin, H.M., Kay, J.S.: Beyond Hierarchies: Design Considerations for Distributed Caching on the Internet. Technical Report TR98-04, University of Texas at Austin (1998).
21. Zhang, L., Floyd, S. Jacobson, V.: Adaptive Web Caching. In: Proceedings of the NLANR Web Cache Workshop, Boulder, CO (1997).
22. Sato, Y.: DeleGate Server. (1994). URL: http://www.delegate.org/y.sato/DeleGate/ [2002-10-17]
23. Chandrasekaran, S., Madden, S., Ionescu, M.: Ninja Paths: An Architecture for Composing Services over Wide Area Networks. CS262 class project writeup, UC Berkeley (2000). URL: http://ninja.cs.berkeley.edu/dist/papers/path.ps.gz [2002-10-17]
24. Ooi, W.; van Renesse, R.: Distributing Media Transformation Over Multiple Media Gateways. In: Proc. Of the 9th ACM International Multimedia Conference, Ottawa, Canada (2001).
25. Candan, K., Subrahmanian, V., Rangan, P.: Collaborative Multimedia Systems: Synthesis of Media Objects. In: IEEE Transactions on Knowledge and Data Engineering 10(3) (1998).
26. Bickmore, T., Girgensohn, A., Sullivan, J.W.: Web Page Filtering and Re-Authoring for Mobile Users. In: The Computer Journal 42 (6) (1999).
27. Schilit, B.N., Trevor, J., Hilbert, D.M., Koh, T.K.: m-Links: An Infrastructure for Very Small Internet Devices. In: Proc. of the 7th Annual Int'l Conference on Mobile Computing and Networking, Rome, Italy (2001).
28. Goebel, S., Buchholz, S., Ziegert, T., Schill, A.: Device Independent Representation of Web-based Dialogs and Contents. In: Proceedings of the IEEE Youth Forum in Computer Science and Engineering (YUFORIC'01), Valencia, Spain (2001).
29. Rejaie, R., Yu, H., Handley, M., Estrin, D.: Multimedia Proxy Caching Mechanism for Quality Adaptive Streaming Applications in the Internet. In: Proc. of IEEE INFOCOM 2000, Tel-Aviv, Israel (2000).
30. Yu, F., Zhang, Q., Zhu, W., Zhang, Y.: Network-Adaptive Cache Management Schemes for Mixed Media. In: Proc. of the 2nd IEEE Pacific-Rim Conference on Multimedia (IEEE-PCM), Beijing (2001).

Session Dienstgüte

A Reflective Server Design to Speedup TCP-friendly Media Transmissions at Start-Up

Jens Schmitt, Michael Zink, Steffen Theiss, Ralf Steinmetz

KOM, Darmstadt University of Technology, Germany
{Jens.Schmitt, Michael.Zink, Steffen.Theiss, Ralf.Steinmetz}@KOM.tu-darmstadt.de

Abstract: The Internet has built its success story to a large degree on the Transmission Control Protocol (TCP). Since TCP still represents the by far most important transport protocol in the current Internet traffic mix, new applications like media streaming need to take into account the social rules implied by TCP's congestion control algorithms, i.e., they need to behave *TCP-friendly*. One problem of this insight is that these new applications are not always well served by inheriting TCP's transmission scheme. In particular, TCP's initial start-up behaviour is a problem for streaming applications. In this paper, we try to address this problem by proposing a *reflective server design* which allows to do inter-session congestion control, i.e., to share network performance experiences between sessions to make informed congestion control decisions. Since our focus is media streaming, we show the design in the framework of a media server, which means in particular not employing TCP itself but a TCP-friendly transmissions scheme.

1 Introduction

1.1 Background: TCP Congestion Control and Media Streaming

Despite its age and known shortcomings, TCP and its reactive congestion control method still dominate today's Internet traffic mix [1], whereas proactive, open-loop congestion control approaches like, e.g., RSVP/IntServ seem still far away. It comes thus as a kind of Internet law of nature that data transmissions have to be compatible to TCP with respect to their handling of congestion situations, i.e., they have to be *TCP-friendly*.

TCP's congestion control involves two basic algorithms: slow start and congestion avoidance [2]. During slow start (SS) a sender exponentially increases its sending window during each round trip time (RTT) starting with a window size of 1 to trial the available bandwidth in the network. It thus makes no assumptions and tries to find out fast what could be its fair share of the available bandwidth. Once it encounters an error, either due to a retransmission time-out or due to 3 consecutive duplicate acknowledgments (fast retransmit), it halves its slow start threshold (sstresh) and does another SS. This repeats until slow start reaches sstresh without any losses, then the congestion avoidance (CA) phase is started. In CA the sender still probes the network for more capacity but now at a linear increase per RTT.

For new multimedia applications like media streaming TCP has several drawbacks:
- *retransmissions* are unnecessary since old (retransmitted) data is usually worthless for streaming applications,
- the *bandwidth* resulting from TCP's window-based congestion control algorithms tends to *oscillate* too much for streaming applications,
- the *initial slow start behaviour* is the exact opposite of what streaming applications would desire, namely an initially high rate that allows to fill the playback buffer such

that later rate variations can be accommodated by the smoothing effects of the buffer.

This is why many of these applications employ UDP (User Datagram Protocol) as a transport protocol. However, UDP does not have a congestion control, based on the assumption that there is little UDP traffic. Yet, this may be not true any more if such UDP-based streaming applications become successful. That is why a number of TCP-friendly congestion control schemes have been devised for UDP transmissions such as media streaming. The definition of TCP-friendliness is informally phrased "achieve fairness with concurrent TCP transmissions, i.e., achieve the same long-term average throughput as a TCP transmission". Of course, it should be mentioned that by *TCP-fairness* the following is meant: if N TCP sessions share a bottleneck link each should get $1/N$-th of the link's capacity (assuming they do not want less, a more formal definition of TCP's max-min fairness captures this case).

1.2 Motivation: Why and How to Avoid TCP Slow Start

If TCP-friendliness is accepted as a MUST in the Internet, it needs to be observed that, while TCP-friendly transmission schemes can avoid the problems of retransmissions and unsteady bandwidth availability to some degree (we will discuss some proposals below), all TCP-friendly protocols inherit TCP's gross start-up behaviour resulting from slow start. Note that TCP's start-up behaviour has for some time been realized as a problem for transfers of short duration as typically seen for HTTP requests [3]. Yet, also for long-term streaming applications in contrast to long-term file transfers the initial transmission performance is of high importance, since they need to present transmitted data (more or less) immediately to the user and it might be especially dissatisfying if the start of a media transmission is badly disturbed or heavily delayed due to a slow filling of the playback buffer (which might make the consumer switch away again). Besides, promising optimizations of media distribution systems like patching may involve short transfers, too [4].

On a higher level of abstraction one could argue that TCP is transiently unfair to new sessions which are still in their probing phase. Ideally, one would wish for a new session to start sending with its fair share and immediately go into a CA-like phase. The question now is how could we make a step towards this ideal behaviour. Since our target application is media streaming, we may assume that we have high-performance servers streaming the media towards a large number of clients. We are thus in a situation where TCP's zero knowledge assumption about the network state at the start of a new transmission towards a client is unnecessarily limiting since such a server could take advantage of the probing of past and concurrent transmissions to the same or "*similar*" clients. The server could thus improve its congestion control decisions by *reflecting* on past decisions / experience and could start the transmission at a higher rate avoiding the SS phase altogether. Of course, care must be taken to back-off from this rate immediately if the estimation of available bandwidth turns out to be erroneous.

In essence, the goal of our investigations is the development of a reflective server design build around TCP-friendly transmission schemes but using statistics from past network experience to achieve a favourable start-up behaviour for media streaming applications. The basic motivation stems from empirical data gathered by [5] which reports on temporal as well spatial stability in throughputs for Web transfers: they already concluded "... this allows for caching and sharing to achieve efficiency ..."

2 Related Work & Own Contribution

We present the related work in three areas: *TCP-friendly transmission protocols* on which we build, but which we do not aim to improve themselves or propose yet another one; *TCP optimizations for short transfers* like HTTP requests as a motivation and basic groundwork for our investigation; *Inter-session congestion control* as directly related work.

2.1 TCP-Friendly Transmission Protocols

The design of TCP-friendly transmission protocols has recently experienced a lot of attention. A nice overview can be found in [6]. Their basic rationale is to avoid retransmissions and to improve TCP's oscillating bandwidth behaviour by smoothing the available bandwidth to a session. There is mainly two flavours:
- window-based schemes like [7, 8] that generalize resp. slightly change TCP's basic AIMD (additive increase, multiplicative decrease) behaviour to allow for a smoother transmission behaviour,
- rate-based schemes like [9, 10, 11] which adapt their sending rate according to a certain rule between experienced loss and estimated available bandwidth. For example, the TCP-friendly Rate Control (TFRC) protocol proposed in [9] is based on the empirical equation in [12] which relates loss to the fair bandwidth share of a session.

While window-based schemes inherit TCP's favourable self-clocking characteristic and can generally be assumed to react faster to dynamic changes in available bandwidth, rate-based schemes usually achieve a smoother transmission scheme which makes them more favourable for streaming applications. Furthermore, the rate-based TFRC has been shown to react relatively fast to changes and has been extended to the multicast case [13]. For these reasons we chose TFRC as the TCP-friendly transmission scheme which shall be integrated into our reflective server design. Yet, note that most of our work is independent of the actual transmission scheme and may even be applied to TCP itself (which from our background is not so interesting due to TCP's bad characteristics for streaming media).

2.2 Short TCP Transfer Optimizations

There has been some work on improving TCP performance for short transfers in particular for Web transfers. [14] experimented with *larger initial window sizes* and found larger initial window sizes particularly helpful for short transfers. *Persistent HTTP* (P-HTTP) [15] is a technique to reuse TCP connections within one HTTP session, thus not loosing the congestion window value. The *TCP Fast Start* technique proposed by [16] enhances P-HTTP to use cached congestion window values for the same HTTP session after an idle period of that session and proposes to send packets during such a fast start phase at a lower priority. Similarly, [17] proposes to differentiate between short and long transfers by assigning *different drop priorities* to the latter and shows by simulations to improve short transfers' performance. As a comment to the latter two approaches, note that they require a form of differentiation within the network a la DiffServ. While this is technically feasible one needs to be aware that it essentially destroys IP's traditional best-effort model and in particular its economic model of access charging.

2.3 Inter-Session Congestion Control

Directly related to our work is what we call inter-session congestion control. These proposals go beyond proposals in the preceding section in the sense that they consider network performance experience from other concurrent or past sessions for their congestion control decisions. To gather data from other sessions one can imagine two different types of inter-session congestion those based on the collection of all sessions of a single host which then typically needs to be a busy server or to accumulate the different sessions' experience at a certain (shared) gateway. While the former type of inter-session congestion control requires the installation of such a gateway and its integration in the routing of sessions as well as a distributed protocol for accessing its information, the latter approach exploits purely local information. This is why we favour inter-session congestion control at a single server since it requires much less changes of existing infrastructure. On the other hand, this means that a server needs to make as optimal use of its experiences as possible because the scope of the available data may be limited. The Congestion Manager concept introduced by [18] focuses on sharing of knowledge between *concurrent* sessions within a host, whereas we concentrate on *past* experiences. Also, [18] is more about mechanisms like an API to exchange congestion control information which makes it complementary to our work, in the sense that it may be a good framework for implementing the mechanisms we propose here. [19] introduces what they call inter-host congestion control and give some nice introductory motivation for the efficiency gains that may be achievable. Their sharing of congestion control information is solely based on what they call *network locality*, i.e., only destinations that have a common 24-bit subnet mask share information. Their proposal is restricted to TCP transmissions. Along the same lines yet more detailed is [20], which proposes the use of a gateway. Again this work is only suited for Web-like traffic since only TCP is considered and they only share information between destinations with common 24-bit subnet masks (network locality). In conclusion, while the above proposals are very interesting, they are specialized for TCP transmissions and may require substantial infrastructure changes due to the gateway approach. Furthermore, they employ a simple rule for sharing congestion control information, which, while it is empirically shown to be a good rule [20], may be too restrictive for the case of a server-based inter-session congestion control for media streaming, which involves compared to a Web server a lesser number of sessions.

2.4 Own Contribution

After the review of related work our contribution can be summarized as follows: we try to make use of information from past experience at a media server to improve the start-up behaviour of TCP-friendly media streaming sessions at a minimum of necessary changes to existing infrastructure. The latter constraint means we only allow for media server-internal changes in contrast to existing work discussed above. Furthermore, we concentrate on TCP-friendly transmission protocols like TFRC instead of TCP itself, since our case is media streaming. Another specific of a media server that must be taken into account is that compared to a Web server it serves only a limited number of sessions over a certain time interval. That means we need to put special care in how good sharing rules between information from sessions to different clients can be achieved. Therefore, we go beyond the simple common 24-bit subnet mask heuristic and try to exploit similarities between different clients as much as possible. In particular, the sharing rules should be defined along common bottlenecks for clients. While network locality is a fairly safe heuristic for that (and much better than just host locality), we try establish more advanced sharing rules in order to be able to use bandwidth availability data from as many sessions as possible.

3 Reflective Server Design for Inter-Session Congestion Control

In this section, we give an overview of the high-level design of our reflective media server. The underlying principles of our reflective media server proposal is to gather past bandwidth availability data, process these data intelligently in order to make more *informed decisions* when starting a new TCP-friendly streaming session. Note that, in principle, a reflective server design could involve more changes of congestion control decisions than just at start-up. However, here we only want to focus on the initial congestion control behaviour.

3.1 Functional Components

Two different, concurrently performed areas of operation can be distinguished for the reflective media server: the actual handling of media requests and the reflection on the corresponding transmission observations. The latter process of reflection is further on called *data management* because it involves the gathering and processing of statistical data for past sessions. The results from the data management operations are then exploited in serving the media requests, i.e., in the congestion-controlled *transmission* of the media objects.

Data Management: The following subtasks for the data management component can be identified:

- *data gathering,* i.e., record the data from sessions on a periodical basis for later use by other sessions,
- *data clustering,* i.e., explore the data on past and concurrent sessions for similarities in order to find maximum sharing rules between the recorded data,
- *data prediction,* i.e., forecast fair bandwidth share for a session based on the sharing rules constructed in the preceding step.

Transmission: As discussed above we focus on the improvement of the start-up behaviour for media streams, i.e., we introduce what we call *informed start* which contrasts to slow start by assuming knowledge when choosing an initial transmission speed (in terms of a rate when a rate-based scheme is used or a window size if a window-based scheme is employed)

Since our case is media servers we employ a TCP-friendly transmission scheme instead of TCP due to its problems with media streaming described above. In Section

2, we have argued for our use of TFRC, although most of our proposal could be easily transferred to other TCP-friendly transmissions schemes.

Design Decisions and Overall Scheme: The major design decisions we have made are to:

- use *passive measurements* from past and existing connections in order not to require substantial changes to existing infrastructure;
- *restrict* our inter-session congestion control scheme *to single servers*, i.e., have no exchange of information between servers, although this could be an interesting extension, yet again we only wanted to introduce local, minimal-invasive changes;
- *sample* the *fair bandwidth share* instead of more algorithm-specific measures like congestion window sizes or loss rates, this is especially motivated by compatibility of the data management component with differing transmission schemes as well as favoring of rate-based transmission protocols for media transmissions;
- put *strong emphasis on the data clustering* step in order to support environments where we have potentially scarce data such that exploitation needs to be done effectively, i.e., we need to maximize sharing of information between sessions to improve upon prediction accuracy;
- target at *rate-based* TCP-friendly transmissions.

The overall scheme of our refective media server design with its two concurrent subcomponents and their subtasks is depicted in Figure 1.

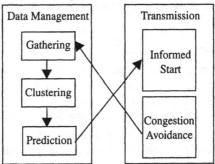

Figure 1: Reflective Media Server Design.

4 Data Management

In this section, we take a more detailed (albeit informal) look at the data management component and its subtasks within our reflective media server design.

4.1 Data Gathering

The major questions for data gathering are which data to gather and when. We decided to gather the available bandwidth values after they have reached a certain equilibrium state (i.e., the rate does not vary too much any more). The available bandwidth of each session (identified by the client's destination address) is tracked on two time-scales, one on the order of RTTs and one on the order of minutes. These serve different purposes. The longer time-scale values are used for identifying similar available bandwidth properties for different clients, i.e., they are input for the data clustering task. A time-scale on the order of minutes seems sufficient for that purpose based on the temporal stability observations reported in [5]. The shorter time-scale values are used within the data prediction step and therefore need to be very recent. During the course of time, the short time-scale data become the longer time-scale data and are therefore aggregated as the mean available bandwidth in a given time interval of a session, in order to save storage space. Of course, data also need to be removed when they become too old, in particular we decided to track session characteristics only for 24 hours.

4.2 Data Clustering

The data clustering subtask is a preparation step for the actual data prediction in order to make as much use as possible from the given data. In particular, we perform a cluster analysis along the available bandwidth samples of different sessions, which promises more comprehensive sharing rules than for a second-order criterion like network locality, since it allows to capture more similarities between clients / sessions, e.g., like the use of the same access technology which might always form a bottleneck or the situation when a transatlantic link is underdimensioned and a certain subset of clients is only reachable via this link. So, clients do neither need to share exactly the same bottleneck but only a structurally similar one, nor does the bottleneck need to be close to them. Both of these insights can be used to increase sharing between sessions. Furthermore, we cluster along available bandwidth trajectories, and not just single values, over relatively large time-scales (24 hours), which also allows to identify temporal similarities. Please note again here that all of this data is only used for clustering while for the prediction we are well aware that such data can be considered stale for congestion control purposes, yet the aim is to make the available data set for prediction as large as possible in order to improve the prediction accuracy.

Since for individual clients the covering of a 24 hour interval by sampled available bandwidth values is likely to be insufficient, we first aggregate the samples of all clients of a network cloud defined by the common 24-bit subnet mask heuristic (network locality). The actual technique we then use for clustering the network clouds is so-called *agglomerative clustering* based on maximizing the inter-cluster distance while minimizing the intra-cluster distance where we use the euclidean distance norm for the bandwidth trajectories [21]. The resulting clusters represent the sharing rules used for data prediction. The alert reader may notice that the bandwidth trajectories for different network clouds may be based on different time reference systems, which is why we first (linearly) interpolate the bandwidth trajectories on a common time reference system. In addition, we eliminate network clouds for which too little data have been sampled. Note that network clouds that have been excluded from the cluster analysis are not excluded further on from the prediction step, but have to cope with less information for the prediction since they form individual clusters.

4.3 Data Prediction

The data prediction step takes as an input the short time-scale samples from the data gathering and uses the sharing rules resulting from the data clustering subtask to obtain a set of samples as large as possible to ensure an accurate prediction. The quantity to predict is the fair share of bandwidth available to a new media stream. Note that for different congestion control schemes this value may have to be transformed in the quantity that is relevant for the respective scheme, i.e., for a window-based scheme this has to be transformed into an initial window size (which would require to also sample the RTT, which for ease of discussion we have left out here since our focus is on rate-based schemes).

The actual prediction technique we use is an optimal linear predictor [22], i.e., we make relatively little assumptions on the underlying stochastic process. This optimal linear predictor uses the existing realization of the stochastic process of the available bandwidth to set its linear coefficients such that the prediction error is minimized. This is only possible if the underlying process is ergodic, however, the results reported in [5] are encouraging with respect to this assumption. The number of linear coefficients that are employed depend on the number of samples that are available, the more samples are available the more linear coefficients are used resulting in a higher prediction accuracy. So, this is exactly the point where the maximization of the sharing rules is exploited.

Note that the choice of an optimal linear predictor is not necessarily the best and final choice, but hopefully a good first step for a prediction technique since it does not make too strong assumptions on the underlying stochastic process to be predicted. Furthermore, it allows for a confidence value to be computed which allows potentially to make use of the performance parameter estimated in a statistically controlled fashion.

5 TFRC Transmission Using *Informed Start*

Concurrently to the data management operations, the actual transmission of media streams takes place. As discussed above we chose TFRC as a (good) example of a TCP-friendly transmission protocol for media streams. Now, we describe how a TFRC-based media streaming can take advantage of the data gathered and evaluated by the data management component to improve a media stream's start-up behaviour by using what we call an *informed start* instead of the normal slow start algorithm. Therefore, we first discuss in a little bit more detail how TFRC works especially at start-up.

At the start-up of a session, TFRC mimics TCP's SS behaviour: it doubles its sending rate every RTT and even tries to emulate TCP's self-clocking characteristic by limiting the sending rate to two times the received bandwidth as reported by the receiver (which sends these reports every RTT). It does so until a loss event occurs. This enables then a receiver-based rough estimation of the loss rate as the corresponding loss rate for half of the current sending rate. This estimated loss rate is returned to the sender and used to compute the allowable sending rate using the TCP rate formula proposed in [12]. Furthermore, the sender then turns into a less aggressive CA-like behaviour which is again determined by the TCP rate formula: if the formula results in a higher value than the current sending rate then the sending rate is increased by one packet per RTT. Assuming we have enough data to make a sensible fair share bandwidth prediction we can avoid the SS-like behaviour and start with the predicted bandwidth, i.e., perform an informed start (IS) and turn to the CA-like phase of TFRC directly. An IS requires, however, special care since the prediction might be wrong. In particular, IS works the following way:

- The transmission starts with the predicted rate. After 1.5 RTT the receiver calculates the corresponding loss rate from the inverse TCP rate formula and sends it towards the sender. It cannot invoke the TCP rate formula before because it requires an estimate of the RTT which is only determined after 1 RTT at the sender and then sent to the receiver (which takes another 0.5 RTT).
- Before the sender receives the first loss rate estimate the sender uses the minimum of predicted rate and received rate as reported by the receiver. This restriction minimizes the negative effect of a wrong prediction for the available fair share of the bandwidth.
- After it got the first loss rate estimation (after 2 RTT), the sender uses TFRC's normal CA-like behaviour further on.
- In case of packet loss two cases must be distinguished:
  1) packet loss *before 2 RTT*: this indicates that the predicted available bandwidth was too optimistic and the sender should backoff immediately in order not to interfere with other TCP sessions. Of course, due to the packet loss we have a first estimate of the loss rate, however it is very likely to be too pessimistic since due to the overestimation of the allowed sending rate losses are probably excessive. Using that loss rate would consequently lead to an underestimation of the actual allowed sending rate. Fortunately, we also have the received rate as reported by the receiver as a further guide. While the received rate itself is obviously too high because we have been overly aggressive at the start-up, we can take a compromise between underestimating and overestimating the allowed sending rate by taking the mean of the fair bandwidth share as computed by the TCP rate formula and the received bandwidth (the mean is the best estimate if we have no further information on which of the two values could be closer to the actual allowed sending rate). When the fair rate eventually becomes higher than the received rate we turn to normal CA-like TFRC behaviour.
  2) packet loss *after 2 RTT*: here we just use normal TFRC behaviour, i.e., the loss rate is reported to the sender and the sender invokes the TCP rate formula to adapt its current sending rate.

A further question that comes up after this discussion is what happens if we underestimate the currently available bandwidth. Here, the problem is that since we do not use a SS-like trialling of the available bandwidth at the start of a new session we may remain in a state of underutilizing the fair share for that media stream. However, at least we are not harming anybody besides that session and probably for the case of media streaming we should actually reject the request for a new stream if the predicted available bandwidth is too low since we cannot expect our estimate to be too low and it is better not to start a session which can anyway not deliver the quality a user would expect. Alternatively, we could decide to use SS for that session to at least attempt to set it up.

6 Simulations

The aim of the following simulation experiments with the ns-2 simulator is to show the basic improvements that can be achieved with an IS over the normal SS-like behaviour of TFRC. They are not about the analysis of the data management component of our reflective media server design, but make extreme assumptions on the outcome of the data management operations: the fair share bandwidth predictions are assumed to be either correct, far too high, or far too low. We are aware that the simulations can only have a partial and simplifying character, yet, they give a basic showcase for a comparison between IS and SS-based media transmissions. The simple simulation setup we used for these experiments is shown in Figure 2.

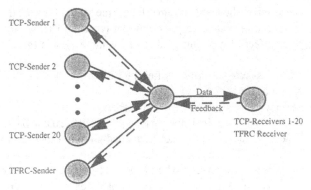

Figure 2: Simulation Setup.

The queue at the bottleneck link uses drop tail, all links are dimensioned at 10 Mb/s (or 1.25 MB/s) with a propagation delay of 10 ms. The TCP senders use TCP Reno (i.e., they employ fast retransmit) and all of them are all started at the beginning of the simulation runs (t = 0s). At approximately t = 4s they achieved an equilibrium state where they shared the available bandwidth at the bottleneck link fairly. Thus at t = 4s we started our different versions of TFRC:

• TFRC with usual SS,
• TFRC with IS and correct prediction (CORR), i.e., the fair share bandwidth prediction is 1/21 of 1.25 MB/s (≈ 60 KB/s)
• TFRC with IS and far too high prediction (HIGH), in particular, the fair share bandwidth prediction is 3 times too high (≈ 180 KB/s)
• TFRC with IS and far too low prediction (LOW), in particular, the fair share bandwidth prediction is 3 times too low (≈ 20 KB/s)

In Figure 3, the simulation outcomes for the different scenarios are given. Here, we have depicted the sending behaviour of one of the TCP senders (TCP-Sender 1 - the others showed the same behaviour, though with some phase shifts) vs. the respective TFRC sending behaviour in the relevant time-scale (from 3s to 15s). It is obvious that with a correct prediction we can substantially improve on TFRC's usual start-up behaviour resulting from SS: TFRC with SS took about 5s (from t = 4s to 9s) until it turns to a stable CA-like behaviour, whereas TFRC with IS(CORR) shows immediate stability from its start. Interestingly, also for a far too high prediction of the fair bandwidth share for the TFRC session, it takes only about 1s until a stable behaviour can be observed. So, we have achieved the goal of a fast reaction of the informed start on an overestimated bandwidth prediction. The case IS(LOW) shows that an underestimation requires a longer start-up phase until the fair bandwidth share is reached than the other cases (including the slow start case), yet it does so in a fairly smooth way which from the perspective of streaming applications should be desirable.

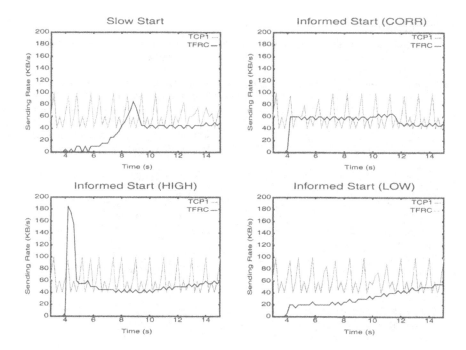

Figure 3: Slow Start vs. Informed Start TFRC with Differing Prediction Scenarios.

7 Conclusions & Outlook

In this paper, we have investigated how TCP-friendly transmission schemes for media streaming could be enhanced to circumvent the inheritance of TCP's disadvantageous start-up behaviour by the use of inter-session congestion control. For that purpose we have introduced a reflective media server design and described its major functional components: data management and transmission. In contrast to previous work, we have focussed on the maximization of sharing rules between sessions by the use of cluster analysis techniques taking into account the specific requirements for media streaming servers. We have shown how TFRC, a special instance of a TCP-friendly transmission protocol can be extended to use an informed start based on the operations performed by the data management component of the reflective media server. By simulations we have shown the benefits of an informed start over the normal slow start-like behaviour of TFRC.

A major open question is how well the data management component performs. This is naturally one of our future goals to investigate. For this we need extensive empirical data, similar to the study performed in [5]. Besides, we are currently integrating TFRC into our publicly available media streaming system KOMSSYS and plan to realize the presented reflective media server design in that framework. A related issue we want to investigate is whether the predictions on available bandwidth from the data management component could also be used as a starting point for a *tentative admission control* of new streams for a media server operating over a best-effort network as the Internet.

80

References

[1] S. McCreary and K. Claffy. Trends in Wide Area IP Traffic Patterns. In *Proceedings of 13th ITC Specialist Seminar on Internet Traffic Measurement and Modeling*, September 2000. http://www.caida.org/outreach/papers/AIX0005.

[2] V. Jacobson. Congestion Avoidance and Control. *ACM Computer Communication Review; Proceedings of the Sigcomm '88 Symposium in Stanford, CA, August, 1988*, 18, 4:314–329, 1988.

[3] R. Braden. RFC 1644 - T/TCP – TCP Extensions for Transactions Functional Specification. Standards Track RFC, July 1994.

[4] K. A. Hua, Y. Cai, and S. Sheu. Patching: A Multicast Technique for True Video-on-Demand Services. In *Proceedings of the ACM Multimedia Conference 1998, Bristol, England*, pages 191–200, September 1998.

[5] H. Balakrishnan, M. Stemm, S. Seshan, and R. H. Katz. Analyzing Stability in Wide-Area Network Performance. In *Proc. of the ACM SIGMETRICS, Seattle, WA*, pages 2–12, 1997.

[6] J. Widmer, R. Denda, and M. Mauve. A Survey on TCP-Friendly Congestion Control. *Special Issue of the IEEE Network Magazine "Control of Best Effort Traffic"*, 15(3):28–37, May 2001.

[7] D. Bansal and H. Balakrishnan. TCP-friendly Congestion Control for Real-time Streaming Applications. In *Proceedings of the 20th Annual Joint Conference of the IEEE Computer and Communications Societies (INFOCOM'01)*. IEEE Computer Society Press, Anchorage, April 2001.

[8] S. Jin, L. Guo, I. Matta, and A. Bestavros. TCP-friendly SIMD Congestion Control and Its Convergence Behavior. In *Proceedings of ICNP'2001: The 9th IEEE International Conference on Network Protocols, Riverside, CA*, 2001.

[9] R. Rejaie, M. Handley, and D. Estrin. RAP: An End-to-End Rate-based Congestion Control Mechanism for Realtime Streams in the Internet. In *Proceedings of the Eighteenth Annual Joint Conference of the IEEE Computer and Communications Societies 1999, New York, NY, USA*, pages 395–399, March 1999.

[10] S. Floyd, M. Handley, J. Padhye, and J. Widmer. Equation-Based Congestion Control for Unicast Applications. In *Proceedings of the ACM SIGCOMM '00 Conference on Applications, Technologies, Architectures, and Protocols for Computer Communication 2000, Stockholm*, pages 43–56, August 2000.

[11] I. Rhee, V. Ozdemir, and Y. Yi. TEAR: TCP emulation at receivers - flow control for multimedia streaming. Technical report, North Carolina State University, April 2000.

[12] J. Padhye, V. Firoiu, D. Towsley, and J. Kurose. Modeling TCP Throughput: A Simple Model and its Empirical Validation. In *ACM SIGCOMM '98 Conference on Applications, Technologies, Architectures, and Protocols for Computer Communication*, pages 303–314, Vancouver, CA, 1998.

[13] J. Widmer and M. Handley. Extending Equation-Based Congestion Control to Multicast Applications . In *Proceedings of the ACM SIGCOMM '01 Conference on Applications, Technologies, Architectures, and Protocols for Computer Communication 2001, San Diego, CA*, pages 275–285, August 2001.

[14] M. Allman, C. Hayes, and S. Ostermann. An evaluation of TCP with larger initial windows. *ACM Computer Communication Review*, 28, 3:41–52, 1998.

[15] R. Fielding, J. Gettys, J. Mogul, H. Frystyk, L. Masinter, P. Leach, and T. BernersLee. RFC 2616 - Hypertext Transfer Protocol – HTTP/1.1. Standards Track RFC, 1999.

[16] V. Padmanabhan and R. Katz. TCP fast start: a technique for speeding up web transfers. In *Proc. IEEE Globecom '98 Internet Mini-Conference, Sydney, Australia*, 1998.

[17] L. Guo and I. Matta. The War Between Mice and Elephants. In *Proceedings of ICNP'2001: The 9th IEEE International Conference on Network Protocols, Riverside, CA*, 2001.

[18] H. Balakrishnan, H. Rahul, and S. Seshan. An Integrated Congestion Management Architecture for Internet Hosts. In *Proceedings of the ACM SIGCOMM '99 Conference on Applications, Technologies, Architectures, and Protocols for Computer Communication 1999, New York, NY, USA*, pages 175–187, August 1999.

[19] S. Savage, N. Cardwell, and T. Anderson. The Case for Informed Transport Protocols. In *Proceedings of the Seventh Workshop on Hot Topics in Operating Systems, Rio Rico, AZ*, March 1999.

[20] Y. Zhang, L. Qiu, and S. Keshav. Speeding Up Short Data Transfers: Theory, Architecture Support, and Simulation Results. In *Proceedings of NOSSDAV 2000*, June 2000.

[21] A. Gordon. *Classification*. Chapman-Hall, 1999.

[22] A. Papoulis. *Probability, Random Variables, and Stochastic Processes*. McGraw-Hill, 1991.

Leistungsbewertung von Algorithmen zur dynamischen Ressourcenverwaltung in lokalen "Broadcast"-Netzen

Jürgen Wolf[1], Bernd E. Wolfinger[1], Gwendal Le Grand[2] und Pascal Anelli[3]

[1] Universität Hamburg, TKRN; {jwolf|wolfinger}@informatik.uni-hamburg.de
[2] ENST-INFRES, Paris; gwendal.legrand@enst.fr
[3] LIP6, Université P. et M. Curie, Paris; Pascal.Anelli@lip6.fr

Zusammenfassung. Dienstgütegarantien in Kommunikationsnetzen, wie sie insbesondere bei Echtzeitkommunikation erforderlich sind, lassen sich durch Betriebsmittelreservierung beim Aufbau von Kommunikationsverbindungen realisieren. Durch dynamische Schwankungen des tatsächlichen Betriebsmittelbedarfs während der Verbindungsdauer können indes reservierte Betriebsmittel (z.B. Übertragungskapazität) ungenutzt bleiben. Eine effizientere Ressourcennutzung ist möglich durch ein temporäres Ausleihen unbenötigter Betriebsmittel, z.B. zwischen Stationen eines "Broadcast"-Netzes.

Der vorliegende Beitrag beschäftigt sich mit zwei zentralen Problemen eines derartigen Ausleihverfahrens von Ressourcen: einerseits Abschätzung des Momentanbedarfs an Betriebsmitteln basierend auf Lastmessungen sowie andererseits Bereitstellung von Algorithmen zur dynamischen Weitergabe reservierter, jedoch temporär unbenötigter, Übertragungsressourcen. Für die vorgeschlagenen Algorithmen zur Lastcharakterisierung sowie zum Weiterreichen von Übertragungsbetriebsmitteln erfolgt eine detaillierte Bewertung ihrer Effizienz mittels elementarer mathematischer Modelle mit Fokus auf das Endsystemverhalten und unter Berücksichtigung von Echtzeitverkehren.

Schlagworte: Dienstgüte, Ressourcenmanagement, Verkehrsmanagement, Echtzeitkommunikation, Leistungsbewertung

1 Einleitung und Problemstellung

Das verstärkte Interesse an Audio-/Videoübertragung in Echtzeit betrifft in besonderem Maße lokale Rechnernetze, da in diesen Netzen Übertragungsressourcen relativ preisgünstig bereitgestellt werden können. Gleichwohl sind auch lokale Netze ohne Erweiterungen ihrer Netzarchitektur bzw. ihrer Protokolle in der Regel nicht in der Lage, die Kommunikationsdienste dauerhaft mit der für eine Echtzeitkommunikation erforderlichen Qualität zu erbringen. Eine Garantie von Dienstqualität/Dienstgüte (QoS) in lokalen Rechnernetzen kann indes durch Maßnahmen wie Betriebsmittelreservierungen, Verkehrspriorisierung oder aber einer absichtlichen Überdimensionierung der Netzressourcen erreicht werden.

Das Aufteilen von Bandbreite in konventionellen Kommunikationsnetzen ohne Echtzeitbedingungen ist bereits relativ gut verstanden [7]. Bei Kommunikationsnetzen mit zu garantierenden Maximalverzögerungen der zu übertragenden Dateneinheiten zwischen Endsystemen ("end-to-end delay") sind dynamische Bandbreitevergabe-Algorithmen noch Gegenstand intensiver Forschung [1, 2, 6]. Dies gilt insbesondere für "Broadcast"-Netze, wie sie bei Mobilkommunikation typisch sind, die Dienstgütegarantien hinsichtlich maximaler Ende-zu-Ende-Verzögerungen zu erbringen haben [3].

In diesem Beitrag betrachten wir den Ansatz der Betriebsmittelreservierung (primär bezogen auf Übertragungskapazität) sowie seine Nutzung in (o.B.d.A. lokalen) "Broadcast"-Netzen. Insbesondere wollen wir untersuchen, auf welche Weise Betriebsmittel, die bereits reserviert und kommunizierenden Endbenutzern fest zugeordnet sind, zeitweise "verliehen" werden können. Das Verleihen erfolgt dabei in Phasen, zu denen der "Besitzer" der Betriebsmittel diese nicht benötigt. Selbstverständlich muss sichergestellt werden, dass der Besitzer im Bedarfsfall verliehene Betriebsmittel umgehend zurück erhält, um Echtzeitanforderungen bzw. QoS-Garantien nicht zu verletzen.

Die durch uns vorgeschlagenen Algorithmen zur dynamischen Ressourcenverwaltung gehen von der Voraussetzung aus, dass das Problem der Reservierung und statischen Betriebsmittelzuweisung bereits gelöst ist (vgl. [4]), und dass die Betriebsmittelreservierung für ein relativ großes Zeitintervall vorgenommen wird (z.B. für die Dauer eines Audio-/Videostroms, typischerweise im *min*-Bereich). In unserem Ansatz überprüft jeder Besitzer (B) von Betriebsmitteln periodisch, ob die lokal anstehende Kommunikationslast die fortgesetzte Reservierung sämtlicher Betriebsmittel rechtfertigt. Sofern eine hinreichend große Menge von Betriebsmitteln von B als temporär unbenötigt erachtet wird, so wird B diese an seine "Nachbarn" verleihen. Um die Echtzeitbedingungen für seine abzusendenden Daten zu respektieren, wird B die Ankünfte bezogen auf seine Übertragungswarteschlange beobachten und seine Betriebsmittel zurückholen, sobald die lokale Belastung wieder zunimmt. Diese Freigabe und Rückforderung von Betriebsmitteln könnte zu Oszillationen in der Ressourcenverwaltung führen. Daher verwenden wir bei der Ermittlung der Momentanbelastung und des daraus resultierenden Betriebsmittelbedarfs Schätzfunktionen, die eine Glättung für die in B generierte Last erzielen (vgl. hierzu auch [5, 8]). Überdies führen wir ein System von (Last-)Schwellwerten ein, welches das Versenden von Kontrollnachrichten beträchtlich reduziert, da diese nur noch beim Überqueren der Schwellwerte seitens des Lastschätzers verschickt werden.

Der Beitrag ist wie folgt strukturiert: Abschnitt 2 führt Schätzfunktionen zur Charakterisierung von Momentanbelastungen auf Basis von Lastmessungen und unter Nutzung verschiedenartiger Gewichtsfunktionen ein und bewertet diese bezüglich ihrer Eignung zur effizienten Realisierung einer dynamischen, bedarfsorientierten Betriebsmittelverwaltung. Der dritte Abschnitt führt Schwellwertsysteme mit unterschiedlicher Reaktionsfähigkeit auf Lastschwankungen ein, um das Versenden von Kontrollnachrichten zu steuern, und bewertet diese detailliert. Abschnitt 4 schließt mit einem Überblick über die bisherigen Erkenntnisse.

2 Schätzfunktionen für Momentanbelastungen und ihre Bewertung

2.1 Ein Modell für die leihweise Bereitstellung von Übertragungsressourcen

Wir stellen nunmehr das grundsätzliche Procedere vor, das wir in der Folge für die Reservierung und Umverteilung von Betriebsmitteln zwischen den Stationen eines lokalen "Broadcast"-Netzes annehmen:

– Betriebsmittel-(BM-)Reservierung:
  Wir setzen voraus:
  - $n + 1$ Stationen $S_0, S_1, \ldots, S_n$, die über ein lokales Netz mit gemeinsamem Übertragungsmedium miteinander kommunizieren können (z.B. WLAN, Ethernet, Token Ring [9]); nota bene: die durch uns entwickelten Algorithmen lassen sich indes auch direkt auf irreguläre Netztopologien übertragen;
  - eine Last in den Stationen, die aus zeitkritischen und nicht-zeitkritischen ("best effort") Datenübertragungsaufträgen besteht, vgl. Warteschlangen RT_Q (real-time queue) und nRT_Q (non real-time queue) in Abb. 1;
  - in jeder Station existieren ≥ 1 Besitzer von Betriebsmitteln, wobei die reservierte Datenrate ("Bandbreite") das in der Folge exemplarisch betrachtete Betriebsmittel darstelle;
  - die für zeitkritische Übertragungen einer Station S benötigten Betriebsmittel werden stets vor Beginn eines neuen (Video-)Stroms mit Echtzeitanforderungen reserviert und stehen dem Besitzer bis zum Abbau der Verbindung zur Verfügung; die reservierte Bandbreite ist dabei so, dass die QoS-Anforderungen auch dann noch erfüllt werden können, wenn die Quelle mit der maximal zulässigen Senderate Daten generiert.
– Temporäre Betriebsmittelumverteilung:
  Wir setzen voraus, dass ein Besitzer von BM (hier Station S) eine Teil der reservierten Bandbreite temporär an andere Stationen weiterreichen kann. Dazu führen wir zwei Typen von Kontrollnachrichten ein:
  - FREE_BW$(S, \Delta d)$, mit der S eine Bandbreite (bzw. Datenrate) von Δd bit/s an andere Stationen weiterreicht, und
  - RECALL_BW$(S, \Delta d)$, um Bandbreite im Umfang von Δd zurückzufordern.
  Die Art der Aufteilung der freien verliehenen Bandbreite unter den Nachbarstationen ist nicht Gegenstand dieses Beitrags (in Abb. 1 ist eine elementare Lösung gewählt). Bei Empfang einer RECALL_BW Nachricht muss der Empfänger sofort die Nutzung der rückgeforderten Bandbreite einstellen.
– Ansatz zur Schätzung des Niveaus der Momentanbelastung (durch zeitkritische Übertragungsaufträge):
  Wir setzen periodische Lastmessungen (mit vernachlässigbaren Messfehlern) voraus zu Zeitpunkten $t_i \equiv t_0 + i \cdot \Delta t$, wobei die gemessenen Stichprobenwerte ρ_i die gesamte im Intervall $T_i \equiv [t_{i-1}, t_i)$ seitens der Quelle generierte Last

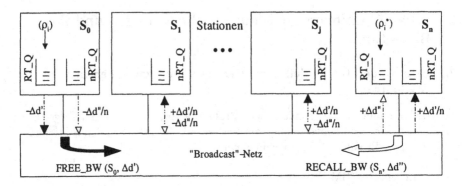

Abb. 1. Umverteilung von Bandbreite: Abgabe von $\Delta d'$ seitens Station S_0 und Rückforderung im Umfang von $\Delta d''$ seitens S_n

(nur zeitkritische Aufträge) charakterisiert. Offensichtlich ist $\rho_i = d_i/(r \cdot \Delta t)$, wobei d_i die Menge der während T_i generierten zeitkritischen Daten (in bit) bezeichnet und r die Datenrate (in bit/s), die beim Verbindungsaufbau reserviert und dem Besitzer fest zugewiesen wurde. Die Sequenz der Stichprobenwerte (ρ_i) wird zum Zeitpunkt t_i genutzt, um den Schätzer $\hat{\rho}(t_i)$ der Momentanbelastung zu berechnen. Somit ist $\hat{\rho}(t_i)$ eine Funktion von $\rho_0, \rho_1, \ldots, \rho_i$. Bei der Generierung der ρ_i handelt es sich um eine Sekundärlastmessung, im Sinne von [10], für eine Primärlast mit Echtzeitanforderungen.

Die generierte Echtzeitlast (z.B. durch Videoquelle) einer Station ist in ihrem Umfang dynamisch abzuschätzen, um die reservierte Übertragungskapazität dem tatsächlichen Bedarf anzupassen. Reservierte, aber ungenutzte Bandbreite führt zu Verschwendung und sollte daher vermieden werden. Andererseits droht bei zu geringer verfügbarer Datenrate die Verletzung von QoS-Anforderungen. So ist es wichtig einen Schätzer zu finden, der auf Lastschwankungen adäquat reagiert.

Der Schätzer sollte einerseits kleinere Lastschwankungen glätten, größere Schwankungen der Datenrate indes hinreichend schnell entdecken. Letzteres gilt besonders dann, wenn es darum geht, ausgeliehene Bandbreite bei erneuter Lasterhöhung so schnell zurückzufordern, dass keine Echtzeitbedingungen verletzt werden. Wir wollen nun derartige Schätzer einführen und bewerten.

2.2 Algorithmen zur Charakterisierung von Momentanbelastungen

Basierend auf den periodischen Lastmessungen ρ_i für die Beobachtungsintervalle T_i schlagen wir hier zwei grundsätzlich verschiedene Typen einfach parametrisierter Schätzer vor, wahlweise mit *geometrischer* oder *arithmetischer* Gewichtung.

Definition 1 (Geometrische Gewichtung)

$$\hat{\rho}(t_i) = \alpha \rho_i + (1 - \alpha) \cdot \hat{\rho}(t_{i-1}), \quad i \geq 1, \ \alpha \in (0,1], \ \hat{\rho}(t_0) := \rho_0.$$

Der Faktor α deutet an wie schnell die Schätzfunktion auf deutlich veränderte Werte der Lastmessung reagiert (genauer untersucht in Abschnitt 2.4). Die geometrische Gewichtung ist auch als *exponential weighted moving average* (EW-MA) bekannt [8]. Als Abkürzung bezeichnen wir im Folgenden mit G_α die geometrische Gewichtung mit Parameter α.

Definition 2 (Arithmetische Gewichtung)

$$\hat{\rho}(t_i) = C_0 \cdot \sum_{j=0}^{w-1} \frac{w-j}{w} \rho_{i-j}, \quad i \geq 1,$$

wobei $w \in \{1, 2, \ldots\}$ *mit* ρ_k *zu initialisieren für alle* $2 - w \leq k \leq 0$ *und* C_0 *bezeichne eine Normalisierungskonstante.*

Diese Schätzfunktion ist gleichbedeutend mit einem Schiebefenster der Größe w und linear wachsendem Gewicht. Bei der arithmetischen Gewichtung wird jedem der w herangezogenen Messwerte das Gewicht $\frac{k}{w}$ zugeordnet, wobei k die Position innerhalb des Fensters ist und der jüngste Messwert die Position $k = w$ einnimmt. Der Faktor C_0 normalisiert die Summe der Gewichte auf 1 und beträgt somit $C_0 = \frac{2}{w+1}$. Für die arithmetische Gewichtung mit Fenstergröße w benutzen wir im Folgenden die Abkürzung A_w.

2.3 Bewertung der Schätzfunktionen für Momentanbelastungen

In der Folge wollen wir die Schätzfunktionen mit geometrischer und arithmetischer Gewichtung bewerten. Die angestrebten Ziele unserer Bewertung sind:

Z1: Ein Beweis, dass der Schätzer jeweils der gesamten entstehenden Last genau einmal Rechnung trägt.

Z2: Untersuchung wieviel Arbeitsrückstand ("backlog") im ungünstigsten Fall entsteht, dadurch dass der Schätzer entstehende Last verspätet berücksichtigt.

Z3: Untersuchung der zusätzlichen Verzögerungszeit, die aus der Abarbeitung des maximalen Arbeitsrückstandes entstehen kann.

ad Z1: Sei l_0 die im Intervall T_i entstehende Last
(a) Fall "*geometrische Gewichtung*":
Im j-ten Intervall, $j \geq 1$, nach dem Auftreten von l_0 geht der Anteil $\alpha \cdot (1-\alpha)^{j-1} \cdot l_0$ in den Lastschätzer ein. Demnach wird von l_0 langfristig

$$l_0 \cdot \alpha \cdot \sum_{j=0}^{\infty} (1-\alpha)^j = l_0$$

berücksichtigt, d.h. die gesamte entstandene Last geht ein.
(b) Fall "*arithmetische Gewichtung*":
Im j-ten Intervall, $1 \leq j \leq w$, nach dem Auftreten von l_0 geht $\frac{2}{w+1} \cdot \frac{w-(j-1)}{w} \cdot l_0$ in den Lastschätzer ein. Insgesamt wird von l_0 der Anteil

$$l_0 \cdot \frac{2}{w+1} \cdot \sum_{j=0}^{w-1} \frac{w-j}{w} = l_0$$

berücksichtigt, d.h. auch im Falle der arithmetischen Gewichtung wird die gesamte generierte Last langfristig exakt berücksichtigt.

ad Z2: Da wir $\rho_i \leq 1$ für alle Beobachtungsintervalle annehmen, liegt der Extremfall einer Lasterhöhung vor, falls $\rho_i = 1 \; \forall i \geq i'$ und $\rho_i = 0$ für $i < i'$. Wir ermitteln hierfür (mit $i' = 1$) den maximalen Arbeitsrückstand.

(a) Fall *"geometrische Gewichtung"*:

Für den Schätzer $\hat{\rho}(t_i)$ zum Zeitpunkt t_i ergibt sich für $\hat{\rho}(t_0) = 0$:

$$\hat{\rho}(t_i) = \alpha\rho_i + \alpha(1-\alpha)\rho_{i-1} + \alpha(1-\alpha)^2\rho_{i-2}$$
$$+\ldots+ \alpha(1-\alpha)^{i-1}\rho_1 + \alpha(1-\alpha)^i\rho_0 = 1 - (1-\alpha)^i, \quad i \geq 1.$$

Somit ergibt sich als BL ("backlog"), der im Intervall T_i durch Unterschätzung der entstandenen Last entsteht

$$BL(i) = \begin{cases} 1 - (1 - (1-\alpha)^i) = (1-\alpha)^i & \text{für } i \geq 1 \\ 0 & \text{für } i = 0. \end{cases}$$

Dies führt zu einer Gesamtsumme der seit t_0 unterschätzten Last direkt nach dem Intervall T_i, d.h. zu $t = t_i$:

$$BL_i = \sum_{j=1}^{i} BL(j) = \sum_{j=1}^{i}(1-\alpha)^j = \frac{1 - \alpha - (1-\alpha)^{i+1}}{\alpha}$$

Die unterschätzte Last ist damit nach oben beschränkt durch

$$BL_i \leq BL_\infty = \lim_{k\to\infty} \frac{1 - \alpha - (1-\alpha)^{k+1}}{\alpha} = \frac{1-\alpha}{\alpha} \quad \forall \alpha \in (0,1], \; \forall i$$

(b) Fall *"arithmetische Gewichtung"*:

Für den Schätzer $\hat{\rho}(t_i)$ zum Zeitpunkt t_i ergibt sich:

$$\hat{\rho}(t_i) = \begin{cases} 0 & \text{für } i \leq 0 \\ \frac{2}{w+1}\sum_{j=0}^{i-1}\frac{w-j}{w} = \frac{2wi+i-i^2}{(w+1)w} & \text{für } 1 \leq i \leq w \\ 1 & \text{sonst.} \end{cases} \quad (1)$$

Dies impliziert einen BL durch Lastunterschätzung im Intervall T_i von

$$BL(i) = \begin{cases} 1 - \frac{2wi+i-i^2}{(w+1)w} & \text{für } 1 \leq i \leq w \\ 0 & \text{sonst} \end{cases}$$

und damit als Gesamtsumme der seit t_0 unterschätzten Last zu $t = t_i$:

$$BL_i = \sum_{j=1}^{i} BL(j) = \sum_{j=1}^{i}(1 - \frac{2wj+j-j^2}{(w+1)w}) \;, 1 \leq i \leq w, \quad (2)$$

sowie $BL_i = BL_w$ für $i > w$.

Für die unterschätzte Last stellt BL_w eine obere Schranke dar, d.h.

$$BL_i \leq BL_w = \sum_{j=1}^{w}(1 - \frac{2wj+j-j^2}{(w+1)w}) = \frac{w-1}{3} \quad \text{für alle } w \geq 1, \; \forall i$$

ad Z3: Wir wollen nun die zusätzliche Verzögerungszeit $\tau_z(i)$ berechnen, die aus der Unterschätzung der angebotenen Last ungünstigstenfalls resultiert unter der Annahme, dass der akkumulierte BL im Intervall T_{i+1} mit der Rate $\hat{\rho}(t_i) \cdot r$ abgearbeitet wird. Diese Verzögerung besitzt drei Zeitanteile:

1. die maximale Wartezeit $\tau_w(i)$, die die Dateneinheiten des zum Zeitpunkt t_i vorhandenen BL bereits in der Sendewarteschlange verbracht haben:

$$\tau_w(i) = (BL_i \cdot \Delta t \cdot r)/r = BL_i \cdot \Delta t$$

2. die Bediendauer $\tau_b(i)$ für den gesamten BL ab Beginn einer Bedienung zum Zeitpunkt t_i:

$$\tau_b(i) = \frac{BL_i \cdot \Delta t \cdot r}{\hat{\rho}(t_i) \cdot r} = \frac{BL_i \cdot \Delta t}{\hat{\rho}(t_i)}$$

3. die Verzögerung τ_s durch die nur periodische Erfassung der dynamisch generierten Last mit Periodendauer Δt: $\tau_s = \Delta t$

Zusammenfassend lässt sich $\tau_z(i)$ somit zu

$$\tau_z(i) = \tau_w(i) + \tau_b(i) + \tau_s = BL_i \cdot \Delta t + (BL_i \cdot \Delta t)/\hat{\rho}(t_i) + \Delta t$$

berechnen. Es ist offensichtlich, dass auch eine Definition von $\tau_z(i)$ ohne den Verzögerungsanteil τ_s vertretbar wäre, da τ_s im engeren Sinne nicht aus dem Verleihen von Übertragungskapazität resultiert.

Wenn wir nun $\varphi(i) \equiv BL_i + \frac{BL_i}{\hat{\rho}(t_i)}$ definieren, so ist $\tau_z(i) = \varphi(i) \cdot \Delta t + \Delta t$. Wir suchen – bei Ermittlung der maximalen Zusatzverzögerung τ_{max} – den Wert $i = i_0$, der $\tau_z(i)$ maximiert. Da Δt konstant ist, ist dies gleichbedeutend mit der Suche des Maximums von $\varphi(i)$ und es ist $\tau_{max} = \tau_z(i_0)$.

(a) Bestimmung von τ_{max} für den Fall einer *geometrischen Gewichtung*

$$\varphi(i) = \frac{(1-\alpha) - (1-\alpha)^{i+1}}{\alpha} + \frac{(1-\alpha) - (1-\alpha)^{i+1}}{\alpha \cdot (1 - (1-\alpha)^i)} = \frac{1-\alpha}{\alpha} \left(2 - (1-\alpha)^i\right)$$

Dies führt für das gesuchte Maximum zu der Lösung $i_0 = \infty$ und zu

$$\tau_{max} = \tau_z(\infty) = \varphi(\infty) \cdot \Delta t + \Delta t = \Delta t \cdot (2/\alpha - 1). \qquad (3)$$

Gleichung (3) ergibt für $\alpha = 1$ das a priori offensichtliche Resultat $\tau_{max} = \Delta t$. Grafisch ist τ_{max} im linken Diagramm von Abb. 2 illustriert.

(b) Bestimmung von τ_{max} für den Fall einer *arithmetischen Gewichtung*

Aus Komplexitätsgründen begnügen wir uns hier mit einer oberen Schranke für τ_{max}. Wir schätzen $\varphi(i)$ für $w \geq 3$ wie folgt ab:

$$\varphi(i) \leq \max\left(BL_1 + \frac{BL_1}{\hat{\rho}(t_1)}, BL_2 + \frac{BL_2}{\hat{\rho}(t_2)}, \max_{i \geq 3}\left(BL_i + \frac{BL_i}{\hat{\rho}(t_i)},\right)\right)$$

$$\leq \max\left(BL_1 + \frac{BL_1}{\hat{\rho}(t_1)}, BL_2 + \frac{BL_2}{\hat{\rho}(t_2)}, BL_w + \frac{BL_w}{\hat{\rho}(t_3)}\right).$$

Als obere Schranke ergibt sich somit (vgl. Gleichungen (1) und (2)):

$$\tau_{max} = \varphi(i) \cdot \Delta t + \Delta t$$

$$\leq \Delta t \cdot \max\left(\frac{w^2 + 4w - 1}{2(w+1)}, \frac{w^4 + 5w^3 - 10w^2 + 8w - 2}{(w^2 + w)(2w - 1)}, \frac{w^3 + 6w^2 + 5w - 12}{18w - 18}\right) \qquad (4)$$

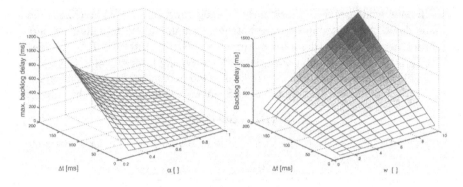

Abb. 2. Maximale Zusatzverzögerung τ_{max} bei geometrischer (links) bzw. arithmetischer Gewichtung in Abhängigkeit von den Parametern α bzw. w und Δt.

Für $w = 2$ beschränkt sich die Maximumbildung selbstverständlich auf die ersten beiden Terme und $w = 1$ führt wiederum zu dem trivialen Resultat $\tau_{max} = \Delta t$, vgl. auch Abb. 2.

2.4 Reaktionsfähigkeit der verschiedenen Schätzfunktionen auf Lastschwankungen

In der Folge untersuchen wir die Auswirkungen der Wahl des Schätzers und der Parametrisierung auf die Reaktionsfähigkeit bei Änderungen der Lastmessungen. Entscheidend für die Auswahl der Schätzfunktion ist neben der maximalen zusätzlichen Verzögerung (vgl. Gl. (3) und (4)) aber auch deren qualitatives Verhalten. In Abbildung 3 wird hierzu beispielhaft das Reaktionsverhalten der beiden Schätzer mit je zwei unterschiedlichen Parametrisierungen illustriert. Dazu betrachten wir das Verhalten der Schätzer, wenn die Lastmessungen ρ_i einmalig der größtmöglichen Veränderung ausgesetzt sind (vgl. Abschnitt 2.3 - Z2).

Wir erkennen, dass die Funktionen A_{10} und $G_{0.3}$ schneller auf die Änderungen der Messung reagieren, als die Funktionen A_{20} und $G_{0.1}$ (Abk. in 2.2 eingeführt). Dies liegt daran, dass die geometrische Gewichtung mit α nahe bei 1 und die arithmetische Gewichtung mit kleinem w die aktuellen Messungen stärker gewichtet und die älteren Werte deswegen schneller "ausgeblendet" werden. Mit anderen Worten kann man sagen, dass A_{20} die Lastmessungen besser glättet, aber dafür weniger schnell reagiert. Desweiteren kann man erkennen, dass $G_{0.3}$ schneller auf die Änderung reagiert als A_{10}, aber trotzdem deutlich mehr Messwerte benötigt, um die Auslastung von exakt 100% hinreichend gut zu approximieren.

3 Schwellwertsysteme zur Steuerung der Betriebsmittelfreigabe

In diesem Abschnitt stellen wir stellvertretend drei verschiedene Schwellwertsysteme unterschiedlicher Granularität vor und schätzen die ungenutzte Übertragungskapazität im schlechtesten und einem mittleren Fall ab.

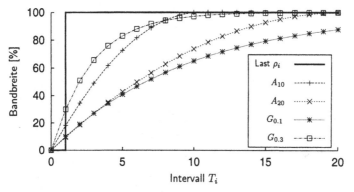

Abb. 3. Reaktionszeit des Schätzers im "worst case"

Schwellwertsysteme sollen bei der Steuerung von Betriebsmittelfreigabe bzw. -rückforderung unter Zuhilfenahme von Schätzern der Momentanbelastung folgende Eigenschaften erfüllen:

- Verhinderung von Oszillationen beim Versenden der Nachrichten zur Betriebsmittelfreigabe bzw. -rückforderung,
- rechtzeitige Zurückforderung von Bandbreite, bevor sie benötigt wird und
- Glättung der Schätzung der Momentanbelastung.

Insbesondere ist jeder "Besitzer" von Übertragungskapazität selbst für das evtl. Bereitstellen an andere Stationen zuständig, d.h. nach unserem Ansatz benutzt jede Station zur Steuerung der Betriebsmittelfreigabe/-reservierung ein individuelles Schwellwertsystem.

Wir repräsentieren Schwellwertsysteme je durch ein Zustandsmodell (Abb. 4). Dabei bezeichnen die Namen der Zustände, im Bereich von 0-100, den Anteil der vorab reservierten Kapazität in Prozent, der aktuell dem Besitzer zur Verfügung steht. Die Zustandsübergänge finden statt, wenn obere bzw. untere Schwellwerte für den Schätzer der Momentanbelastung über- bzw. unterschritten werden. In dem Drei-Zustands-Modell (linke Grafik in Abb. 4) findet also ein Übergang von Zustand 100 statt, genau dann wenn der Schätzer $\hat{\rho}(t_i)$ zum aktuellen Zeitpunkt t_i einen Wert ≤ 55 annimmt. Ist $20 < \hat{\rho}(t_i) \leq 55$, so findet ein Übergang in Zustand 70, ansonsten in Zustand 35 statt. Dies bedeutet hier, dass vom Zustand 100 ausgehend 30% der Bandbreite "verliehen" wird, sobald die Momentanbelastung vom Schätzer zwischen 20 und 55 Prozent eingestuft wird.

Um einfach strukturierte und gegen Oszillationen möglichst robuste Schwellwertsysteme zu erhalten, haben wir die Werte in den Modellen so gewählt, dass

- der Abstand zwischen oberem und unterem Schwellwert ≥ 10 beträgt,
- der Zustand sich immer $\geq 5\%$ über dem Wert des Schätzers befindet, und
- die Abstände zwischen den benachbarten Zuständen konstant sind (Ausnahme: Rundungen $33\frac{1}{3} \rightarrow 35$ und $66\frac{2}{3} \rightarrow 70$ im Drei-Zustandsmodell).

3.1 Obere Schranke der Überreservierung durch Schwellwerte im "worst case"

Die Übertragungskapazität, die im schlechtesten Fall durch den Einsatz der unterschiedlichen Schwellwertsysteme für andere Stationen ungenutzt bleibt, kann

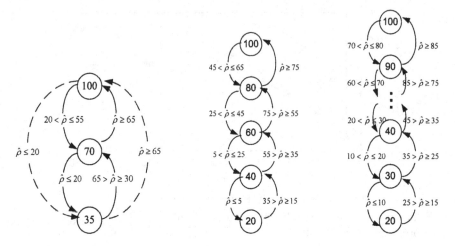

Abb. 4. Schwellwertmodelle mit drei, fünf und neun verschiedenen Zuständen – aus Gründen der Übersichtlichkeit wurde bei den beiden rechten Modellen auf die vollständige Darstellung der Übergänge verzichtet.

einfach aus den Zustandsmodellen abgelesen werden (maximaler Abstand zwischen Schätzer $\hat{\rho}$ und korrespondierendem Zustand). Es ergeben sich für die vorgestellten Modelle mit drei, fünf, bzw. neun Zuständen die Werte 50%, 35%, bzw. 20%. Nota bene: Zur Ermittlung der ungenutzten Übertragungskapazität reicht es, den Schätzer $\hat{\rho}$ zu betrachten, da – wie in Abschnitt 2.3 (Z1) gezeigt – die gesamte entstehende Last genau einmal im Schätzer berücksichtigt wird.

Die Abschätzung im schlechtesten Fall scheint allerdings nur bedingt realistisch zu sein, z.B. für einen Strom mit konstanter Datenrate. Trotzdem kann hier abgelesen werden, dass sogar mithilfe eines Schwellwertsystems grober Granularität, wie z.B. des Fünf-Zustands-Modells aus Abb. 4, selbst im schlechtesten Fall noch 65% der Gesamtkapazität genutzt werden kann.

3.2 Abschätzung der Überreservierung durch Schwellwerte

Wir wollen nun die "mittlere" Überreservierung ermitteln, die durch die von uns vorgeschlagenen Schwellwertesysteme besteht. Dazu nehmen wir an – da wir keine weiteren Annahmen über die Charakteristik der Aufträge und deren zeitliche Abfolge treffen – dass die durch den Schätzer $\hat{\rho}(t_i)$ ermittelte Momentanbelastung im Intervall [0, 1] gleichverteilt sei.

Wir illustrieren die Vorgehensweise zur Abschätzung an dem Drei-Zustands-Modell aus Abbildung 4. Zur Analyse bestimmen wir je die Überreservierung zu den einzelnen Bereichen möglicher Werte des Schätzers $\hat{\rho}(t_i)$. Diese kann wie folgt ermittelt werden: Im Fall $0 \leq \hat{\rho}(t_i) \leq 20$ (dargestellt in der ersten Zeile von Tabelle 1) befindet sich die Station in Zustand 35, hat also 65% der a-priori reservierten Kapazität "verliehen". Als Überreservierung für diesen Bereich ergibt sich demnach im Mittel 25%.

In der nächsten Zeile der Tabelle ist der Bereich $20 < \hat{\rho}(t_i) \leq 30$ beschrieben. In diesem Fall kann der Zustand der Station nicht eindeutig vorhergesagt werden, da dieser von dem vorausgehenden Zustand abhängt. Die Station könnte sich entweder in Zustand 35 oder in Zustand 70 befinden. Falls wir davon ausgehen, dass sich die Station ständig in Zustand 35 bzw. Zustand 70 befindet, so mittelt sich die ungenutzte (aber reservierte) Kapazität zu 10% bzw. 45%, ansonsten zu einem Wert dazwischen.

$\hat{\rho}(t_i)$ [%]	Zustand (reserviert [%])	überreserviert [%]
0-20	35	25
20-30	35 ∨ 70	10-45
30-55	70	27.5
55-65	70 ∨ 100	10-40
65-100	100	17.5

Tabelle 1: Zustände und Überreservierung einer Station für unterschiedliche Bereiche des Schätzers $\hat{\rho}(t_i)$.

Aus Tabelle 1 können wir nun zwei Werte σ_o bzw. σ_p ableiten, welche mit der optimistischen bzw. pessimistischen Annahme korrespondieren, dass sich die Station ständig (in Bezug auf die Überreservierung) im günstigen bzw. ungünstigen Zustand befindet. Die Annahme der Gleichverteilung von $\hat{\rho}(t_i)$ führt zu den Abschätzungen $\sigma_o = 20\%$ und $\sigma_p = 26.5\%$.

In Tabelle 2 sind abschließend die Abschätzungen angegeben, die sich für alle hier vorgestellten Modelle ergeben. Es ist die Abhängigkeit der, durch Überreservierung, ungenutzt bleibenden Kapazität von der Granularität der Modelle erkennbar. Insbesondere liegt aber die Überrervierung für alle Modelle – unter der hier vorgestellten Annahme – *deutlich* unter der Kapazität, die im statischen Fall im Mittel verschwendet wird (50%): Selbst mit dem einfachen Drei-Zustands-Modell aus Abb. 4 wird die verschwendete Bandbreite um 23.5% bis 30% der a priori reservierten Kapazität vermindert, bei dem vorgeschlagenen Neun-Zustands-Modell sogar um 36% bis 40%.

	optimistisch [%]	pessimistisch [%]
3-Zustands-Modell	20	26.5
5-Zustands-Modell	14	22
9-Zustands-Modell	10	14

Tabelle 2: Abschätzung der Überreservierung der vorgestellten Schwellwertsysteme

4 Resümee und Ausblick

Wie wir in diesem Beitrag durch analytische Bewertungen zeigen konnten, ist die vorgeschlagene Methode zum dynamischen Weiterreichen temporär unbenötigter Übertragungsressourcen – bei geeigneter Auswahl und Parametrisierung von Lastabschätzungs- und Bandbreitenweitergabealgorithmen – durch eine Reihe von Vorteilen gekennzeichnet, wie

– eine gegenüber nicht-lastadaptiven Verfahren deutlich bessere Auslastung des Betriebsmittels "Bandbreite" (des gemeinsam genutzten "Broadcast"-Netzes) bei gleichzeitiger Gewährleistung von Echtzeitschranken für die maximale Übertragungsverzögerung;

– dem Vermeiden von Oszillationen beim Versenden der Freigabe- bzw. Rück-
forderungsnachrichten für Betriebsmittel (bei Einsatz der glättenden Lastschätzer in Kombination mit Schwellwertsystemen für die dynamische Band-
breitenvergabe);
– eine dem Netzbenutzer ermöglichte gezielte Prioritätensetzung zwischen hoher Netzauslastung einerseits oder aber der Einhaltung niedriger Echtzeit-
Verzögerungsschranken.

Eine relativ geringfügige Überreservierung (z.B. 5%) auch in Zeiten niedriger geschätzter Momentanbelastung kann den maximalen Arbeitsrückstand einer Station durch verspätete Rückforderung verliehener Bandbreite – auch in
ungünstigsten Fällen – für eine garantierte Echtzeitfähigkeit hinreichend gering
halten.

Die bisherigen analytischen Bewertungen sind indes noch auf das Verhalten
der Endsysteme fokussiert und werden deshalb in weiteren Forschungsarbeiten
gegenwärtig durch Simulationsexperimente komplettiert, die auch das Verhalten
des Kommunikationsnetzes im Detail reflektieren (u.a. durch Berücksichtigung
der evtl. erhöhten Übertragungsverzögerungen bei sehr großen Mengen auszu-
tauschender Kontrollinformationen). Durch geeignete Simulationsexperimente
lässt sich auch die interessante Frage der Reaktionsgeschwindigkeit in Echtzeit-
Anwendungen beantworten. Wenn auch diese simulativen Studien die bislang
gewonnenen Erkenntnisse bestätigen, so wird sich durch unseren neuen Ansatz
zur dynamischen Betriebsmittelweitergabe in "Broadcast"-Netzen die mittlere
Netzauslastung bei vertretbarem Zusatzaufwand (Momentanlastbeobachtung,
Versenden von Kontroll-Nachrichten) trotz zu erfüllender Echtzeitanforderungen signifikant erhöhen lassen.

Literatur

[1] Pascal Anelli and Gwendal Le Grand. Differentiated Services over Shared Media.
In *IWQoS*, pages 288–293, Karlsruhe, Germany, 2001.
[2] Manuel Bouyer and Eric Horlait. Bandwidth Management and Reservation over
Shared Media. In *SFBSID'97*, Fortaleza, Brasil, November 1997.
[3] D. Chalmers and M. Sloman. A Survey of Quality of Service in Mobile Computing
Environments. 2(2), 1999.
[4] H. Jonathan Chao and Xiaolei Guo. *Quality of Service Control in High-Speed
Networks*. J. Wiley, 2002.
[5] David D. Clark and Wenjia Fang. Explicit Allocation of Best-Effort Packet Delivery Service. *IEEE/ACM Transactions on Networking*, 1998.
[6] Gwendal Le Grand. *Qualité de service dans des environments Internet mobile*.
PhD thesis, Université P. et M. Curie, LIP 6, Paris, July 2001.
[7] L. Massoulié and J. Roberts. Bandwidth Sharing: Objectives and Algorithms.
IEEE/ACM Transactions on Networking, 10(3):320–328, 2002.
[8] Erwin P. Rathgeb. Modelling and Performance Comparison of Policing Mechanisms for ATM Networks. *IEEE Selected Areas In Commun.*, 9(3):325–334, 1991.
[9] Andrew S. Tanenbaum. *Computer Networks*. Prentice-Hall, 3rd edition, 1996.
[10] Bernd E. Wolfinger, Martin Zaddach, Klaus Dieter Heidtmann, and Guangwei
Bai. Analytical Modeling of Primary and Secondory Load as Induced by Video
Applications using UDP/IP. *Computer Commun.*, 25(11/12):1094–1102, 2002.

Performance of a Bandwidth Broker for DiffServ Networks

Günther Stattenberger and Torsten Braun

Institute of Computer Science and Applied Mathematics,
University of Bern,
Neubrückstr. 10,
3012 Bern,
Switzerland
{stattenb, braun}@iam.unibe.ch
http://www.unibe.ch/~rvs

Abstract. The need of a powerful tool for the management of large backbone networks is growing. Furthermore, new applications and user behavior require the ability to quickly adapt the network configuration to a dynamically changing environment. We present an architecture and an implementation of a bandwidth broker for DiffServ network management. The performance evaluation shows, that our implementation is able to serve as the central management station for a network containing several hundred nodes while still providing a short flow setup time. Further improvements of the current implementation are discussed, too.

1   Introduction

Managing a backbone network of even a medium size Internet Service Provider (ISP) is a difficult and time-consuming task. The sheer number of routers and the heterogeneity of the network (i.e. the routers are bought from different vendors and therefore have different command line interfaces for configuration) complicate the configuration of the network and this often results in a rather static configuration of the backbone routers. However, in modern communication networks dynamic and frequent changes in the settings of some of the backbone routers are necessary to fulfill the requirements (e.g. bandwidth reservations) of customers (e.g. mobile users). A bandwidth broker (BB) can support the network administrator of an ISP network in various ways: first the heterogeneity of the network can be hidden behind a uniform configuration interface. Furthermore, the configuration of the routers can be automated and completely delegated to the broker. The BB offers a small set of possible contracts to the customers (so-called Service Level Agreements, SLAs) and takes care of the correct completion of those contracts. The users can therefore dynamically set up and release resource reservations at high rates, which is very convenient and satisfactory for the customer.

The difficulties of deploying an interdomain service in the internet are listed and discussed in [11]. For example, a big barrier are the necessary upgrades for providers, since *all* ingress interfaces of the whole domain must police. In addition, the current lack of router support poses a big problem. Serious concerns about operational cost and complexity have to be considered, too. Some of those problems are addressed by existing architectures of bandwidth brokers [9, 10]. All of them try to reduce the complexity of the configuration procedure. The different approaches mainly follow the design of the two-tiers managment architecture presented in [8].

In this paper we present an architecture and an implementation of a bandwidth broker capable to manage and configure even large-scale networks with an acceptable speed. This broker introduces a novel object-oriented way of interconnecting the management and configuration layer of the common bandwidth broker architecture. This interconnection is built on top of a QoS Management API [15], that can be used to build a virtual network representation that combines a topology database and the knowledge of the amount of traffic reserved at each router interface. The features of the broker include a generic communication interface for user - broker communication as well as for broker - broker communication and a policy database providing methods for subnet-based admission control. Altogether we are able to show the ability of our architecture to perform the necessary actions in several separated ISP networks in order to provide end-to-end service guarantees for the user.

The rest of this paper is organized as follows: Section 2 discusses some bandwidth broker implementations of other authors, in Section 3 we explain our bandwidth broker architecture using a single-ISP broker as an example. Section 4 evaluates the memory consumption and the reservation setup speed of this architecture. Section 5 discusses several enhancements of the basic architecture and their possible effects on the overall performance.

2   Related Work

Several bandwidth brokers have been designed and developed through the last years since having been introduced in [8]. This section will focus on the differences of some of the most referenced bandwidth broker implementations [4, 6, 7, 10, 17], and discuss some of their characteristics and drawbacks. While not presenting a broker implementation for DiffServ [6] is included in this discussion for more general aspects of network management.

When developing a bandwidth broker several design choices are quite canonical, therefore the different architectures and implementations differ in several details only: A flow database that contains the flow requests from the users is available in each implementation, only the interface to this database is different. For example, [4] uses a set of configuration commands usable by a client host, while [17] uses a web interface to the database that only a network administrator is allowed to use. The second database which occurs in all implementations is a policy database. This is the database deciding whether a flow request can be served or not. COPS (Common Open Policy Server) is chosen in several implementations [7, 17] to handle the communication between the bandwidth broker (Policy Decision Point (PDP)) and the routers (Policy Enforcement Point (PEP)) but also alternative approaches are being proposed, such as SNMP in [10] or TCP sockets and telnet in [6, 4]. If a detailed flow description is documented, this also contains the same entries throughout several different implementations: source and destination addresses as well as ports, protocol ID, start time, duration and service level information (such as bandwidth etc.).

One point that is missing in many documentations about implementations is the discussion about topology knowledge. One implementation [10] proposes to introduce special route discovery signaling using the IP record route option, but other implementations neglect this topic. A topology database is used in [6], but the authors fail to mention, how this database is built and kept up to date.

Regarding the performance of the different implementations the evaluation tests that are presented in the publications merely represent a functionality test not exceeding the setup of DiffServ reservations at one single router. No tests are shown how many routers can be configured by the implementation simultaneousely, and how much time it takes for a flow reservation request to be processed.

3   The Bandwidth Broker Architecture and Implementation

Our bandwidth broker implementation is based on the implementation of the QoS Management framework [15] for a Linux DiffServ (DS) router. The framework roughly consists of three abstract C++ classes, that define a generic interface for the three basic building blocks of a DiffServ network: a router, an interface at a router and a traffic conditioner at the interface. The implementation of this framework for the Linux DS router implements specific C++ classes derived from those abstract base classes to support the specific needs of the Linux Router (e.g. command line syntax, routing table format ...). Different router hardware is supported by deriving special child classes for each type of router.

The BB uses those three classes to build a representation of the underlying network topology. It can configure the router hardware by using common configuration commands (such as add_flow). Those generic commands are translated into the configuration scripts by the corresponding Router instance. This solves the problem of supporting various kinds of router hardware by adding a software layer flexible enough to deal with various routers by using different derivations of a common base class. The base class provides an interface identical to all routers thus hiding the differences from the user.

The API additionally provides the necessary functionality to keep track of the amount of bandwidth reserved for a specific DiffServ class at each interface of each router. Figure 1 shows the architecture in more detail: Our bandwidth broker contains a flow database, that holds all registered flows. This is one of the two databases that are always present in a broker implementation. The second one, the policy database is not used in this simple scenario but will be added in the multi-ISP scenario (see Figure5). As a new feature, our architecture has a virtual representation of the network to be managed. This representation contains all routing tables of the routers from the network, thus providing a topology database. This database will use a large amount of memory, but the forwarding path of a flow can be obtained very quickly without additional signaling. In addition, this virtual network offers the common router configuration interface of the management framework to the broker's management software, making it easier for new management implementations to be deployed. Our implementation keeps track of the link utilisation as well as the reserved bandwidth per link. Those parameters are stored in two tables, enabling the broker to perform basic admission control based on the link utilisation. Finally a user interface offers a set of generic flow management commands (add_flow, delete_flow, change_flow, list_flows) to the customer.

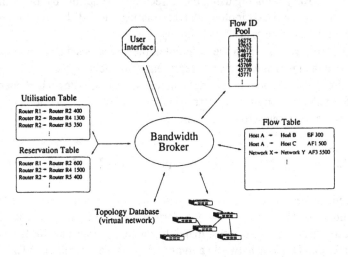

Fig. 1. The bandwidth broker architecture for an isolated network

During the initialization the broker automatically generates a network representation. This can be done either by reading a local topology database from the hard disk, or by broadcasting a broker advertisement message. Each router has to reply to this advertisement message giving its host name and its router type. We chose this approach because of its stability against changes in the topology, although we had to accept the resulting need of a router daemon running on each router. Since we anyhow depend on a router daemon to perform the configuration commands from the bandwidth broker, this is not a big drawback.

After this step the bandwidth broker fetches all routing tables from the network. It now has the full knowledge of the topology on the IP layer, which is sufficient for our task (i.e. configuring DiffServ flows). In addition, all necessary traffic conditioners needed to support DiffServ are already set up and a default configuration is loaded. This default configuration simply consists of empty DiffServ reservations at each interface.

The bandwidth broker can now load an initial DiffServ configuration to the network. This is perhaps necessary, if there are contracts with adjacent bandwidth brokers concerning DiffServ traffic entering or leaving the domain from outside. Additionally a network administrator can choose to reserve a certain amount of bandwidth for DiffServ traffic in advance in order to reduce the total configuration overhead in the backbone. The programmer of a bandwidth broker should generally take care of reducing the amount of reconfigurations of a backbone router. Overprovisioning, i.e. reserving more bandwidth than it is actually needed by the running applications is one way to relieve the backbone routers [2].

Finally, the bandwidth broker is ready to accept incoming reservation requests from the customers. The protocol that is used for the communication between the bandwidth broker and the user is described in [14]. This protocol allows the user to specify a flow (i.e. source and destination) together with the required bandwidth and excess bandwidth as well as some flags indicating the additional requirements of the flow (e.g. realtime traffic). For each request the BB sequentially queries the routing tables from the source to the destination and thus finds all routers that potentially might need to be reconfigured (the result is equivalent to a `traceroute` from source to destination). This approach results in a delay thet is proportional to the diameter of the topology (i.e. the average number of hops between two arbitrary nodes). As an alternative, [10] proposes to use the IP *record route* option and ICMP messages to discover the route of a given flow. This has the advantage of providing up-to-date information, but adds an additional delay to the setup procedure. Furthermore, the problem of route breakdowns and the resulting reconfigurations in order to provide guaranteed QoS to all registered flows is not addressed. This topic is addressen in Section 5.3, where we show, how a central topology database could be kept up to date quite easily.

Following this, an appropriate DiffServ Codepoint (DSCP) based on the requirements of the user is chosen. Now the ingress router can be configured. Note that in a DiffServ network the ingress router has always to be reconfigured, since it is responsible for shaping the traffic based on the exact flow description. The bandwidth broker can check, if it is necessary to perform reconfigurations at the core and egress routers (e.g. adjust the EF rate limiter in a core router [1]). This is based on the brokers values of the total amount of traffic and the reservations at each interface. Usually there is more bandwidth reserved than actually used due to over-provisioning, and no reconfigurations have to be done. The broker only has to update its bandwidth usage variables for the interfaces. This approach speeds up the flow setup significantly.

In this rather simple scenario of an isolated network only a very basic form of admission control is performed: at each router we check, if the newly allocated amount of bandwidth for the service classes does not exceed a pre-configured threshold. If so the flow is rejected. It is guaranteed, that a certain amount of bandwidth is avaliable for best effort traffic in every case. A more elaborate form of admission control based on a subnet-indexed policy database will briefly be discussed in Section 5.1.

Finally the BB stores the flow request in its global flow database. This database assigns a unique flow ID to each new flow and passes this flow ID to the user. All future operations depending on this specific flow setup are referenced by this ID.

4 Performance Evaluation

The performance evaluation of our architecture shows, how fast the bandwidth broker can handle flow requests when managing a reasonable large network. In addition, we were interested in the memory consumption of the bandwidth broker, which we expect to be quite large because of the central topology and flow databases. All measurements were performed on a dual-processor AMD Athlon MP 2000+ Linux PC with 2 GB main memory. For the evaluation several test topologies have been created using the tiers [3] program. This program randomly generates a topology consisting of a single WAN with several MANs and several LANs per MAN. The number of routers per network can be chosen freely. We generated topologies containing 157, 208 305, 535, 710, 928, and 1010 nodes.

For the evaluation it is necessary to run a very large number of configuration daemons in parallel. Using a dedicated Linux router per daemon would be too much a financial and organisational overhead, since the load (in terms of CPU time) such a daemon creates on a PC is minimal — its only job is the execution of configuration commands, that are not computationally intensive. Therefore, we were able to run a number of router configuration daemons (about 200) on a single PC without creating too much load on the CPU. This does not at all diminish the amount of work to be done by the bandwidth broker since the access link is by far fast enough to handle all flow requests. Most likely, the bandwidth broker would be even faster than shown in our results, since the configuration requests are handled one after another on a single machine and are not processed in parallel on multiple machines. The only restriction we had to make was to disable the changes in the routers forwarding path: one can understand easily that a large amount of configuration daemons changing the settings of the Linux router simultaneously would result in a huge confusion and cause the router to crash. However each router configuration daemon program still parses each flow request and creates the necessary configuration scripts that would be needed to configure the router. Thus as much as possible of the computation expense is preserved.

The load on the bandwidth broker is created by requesting many flow reservations in a short period of time. Those reservation requests are generated by a small application that sends a request to the bandwidth broker, waits for the acknowledgement from the broker and immediately afterwards sends another request. By sending several hundreds of reservation requests from this program we can easily calculate the time the bandwidth broker needs for setting up a flow.

4.1 Results

For calculating the memory consumption, we used 7 tiers topologies. Using the Bellman - Ford distance vector (DV) algorithm [16] routing tables have been generated for each node in the networks and saved to the harddisk. With this algorithm each router has a routing table containing an entry for each router in the network. For each node of those topologies a router configuration daemon program has been executed. This daemon reads the routing table from the harddisk and passes it to the BB. The broker collects all routing tables from the daemons and builds the topology database.

The memory consumption of a centralized application is always a critical issue. Our bandwidth broker relies on two large databases — the topology database containing the routing tables and the flow database. The flow database is not very critical because only a very small amount of data has to be stored per flow (ca. 50 - 60 byte), and the memory consumption of this database grows linear with the number of established flows requests. However, in our scenarios the total size of all routing tables will grow quadratically with the number of nodes in the topology. This is an effect of the DV algorithm, that creates an routing table entry for each router of the network. Nevertheless we can estimate, how much memory a router instance consumes when its routing table contains a reasonable number of entries (ca. 10000 - 30000). This is approximately the size of the routing table of a backbone router in a large ISP network. A simple quadratic interpolation shows, that the amount of memory per routing table containing 30000 entries is about 15 MB. This means that with our workstation equipped with 2 GB memory we could manage more than 100 backbone routers.

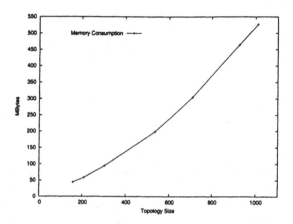

Fig. 2. Memory consumption of the bandwidth broker

Figures 3 and 4 show the flow reservation speed of the bandwidth broker. Each flow request reserved an amount of 100 kbit/s bandwidth between randomly chosen source and destination nodes. However, the amount of bandwidth reserved has absolutely no influence on the setup speed of the bandwidth broker. The time measurements were performed using the UNIX t ime command. This command measures the total (wall-clock) time a command needs for execution, as well as the "user time", i.e. the time that is spent in the program code, and the "system time", the time that was spent by the system, e.g. for performing I/O calls. The results show the total time the client application spent performing a given number of flow requests.

Topology Size	Best Case Speed (Flows/s)	Worst Case Speed (Flows/s)
710	1546.3	970.9
928	1836.2	1280.4
1010	1490.9	930.2

Table 1. Flow setup speed

In Figure 3 the performance of the bandwidth broker under optimal circumstances is presented. This is, when the bandwitdh broker has already allocated enough bandwidth on the whole forwarding path (by overprovisioning) so that only the ingress router has

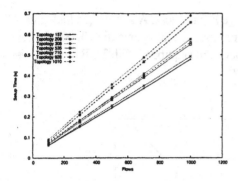 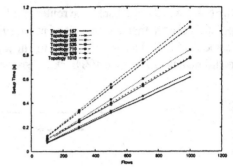

Fig. 3. Flow reservation time of the bandwidth broker (best case)

Fig. 4. Flow reservation time of the bandwidth broker (worst case)

to be reconfigured. Each graph represents one topology and shows the time that was needed to set up 0 – 1000 flows in seconds. In Table 1 we show the speed of the bandwidth broker measured in flow setups per seconds, measured over 10000 Flows setups.

In both results we can see, that the speed (i.e. the slope of the graph) does not directly depend on the topology size. The important parameter is in fact the diameter of the topology. Due to the randomness of the topology generation the diameters differ from e.g. 20.5 hops for the 710 nodes topology to 12.2 hops for the 928 nodes topology.

Figure 4 and Table 1 show the performance of the bandwidth broker under worst conditions: now the bandwidth broker had to reconfigure every router along the path. We had to force this situation by disabling the overprovisioning algorithm in the bandwidth broker. Again we can see the aforementioned dependency on the diameter of the topology. The total performance of the broker is however not bad considering the fact that compared to the best case scenario we have to reconfigure in average 12 – 20 routers per flow. But reconfiguring a core router is much easier than an ingress router, since only a single variable has to be changed (the limit of the aggregated bandwidth), while at the ingress router a new traffic conditioner has to be inserted and configured.

5 Further Improvements

The results presented in the previous section show, that our architecture is capable of configuring a backbone network at a reasonable high speed. Nevertheless, there are still some possibilities for optimization. First of all, the computing power (CPU speed and I/O bandwidth) of the bandwidth broker host has a big impact on the overall performance. Further results on this topic can be found in [13].

5.1 Hierarchical Bandwidth Brokers

Dividing an ISP domain into independently managed subnetworks will distribute the requests of the users to different bandwidth brokers, each capable of performing a certain amount of flow setup procedures per second. Therefore the overall capacity of manageable user requests can be extended. Such a hierarchy of bandwidth brokers has already been presented in [18]. The authors can show, that this can reduce the processing over-head for a flow reservation.

Such an enhanced version of the bandwidth broker can also be used for a multi-ISP scenario, when we cannot assume, that all routers belong to the same domain. This is a much more realistic scenario, and has multiple applications, e.g. in Mobile IP management.

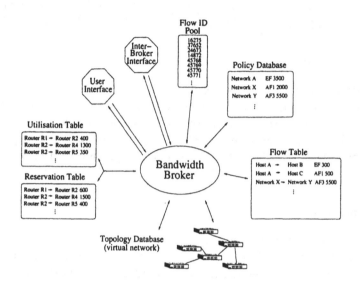

Fig. 5. The bandwidth broker architecture for multi-ISP scenarios

In [9] a hierarchy of brokers (called Resource Control Points) is presented, too. The authors mention, that dividing the network into parts, each managed by a single broker is not trivial and needs the knowledge of the topology as well as information about the expected SLAs. Therefore this topic is still under development.

Figure 5 shows the necessary extensions for a BB capable to communicate with other brokers: The protocol between the brokers as used by the inter-broker communication interface can be the same as in the user-broker communication, as it has been described in [14]. Using this protocol the brokers can reserve aggregations of flows by masking the source / destination address just like any user can reserve a flow at the broker. In addition, a policy database for restricting the amount of traffic from / to other domains is necessary. This policy database contains the information about the amount of traffic the specific subnets are allowed to send. This rather coarse access restriction can surely be improved, but it is e.g. sufficient to limit the number of users on a limited access network (e.g. a wireless access point). Based on this policy database we can provide admission control on the subnet of sender / receiver address of a flow.

If an ISP wants to split its network into several independent management domains, the separation will most likely be done on a IP subnet basis: Usually nodes with the same subnet mask are topologically close and therefore aggregation can be performed

much easier. In addition, the separation of the ISP network into several IP subnets automatically uniquely maps a bandwidth broker to the nodes of the subnet: As mentioned
in Section 3 each broker can send a broadcast message for detecting the network topology. Due to the correlation of broadcast addresses and subnet masks each broker only
gets a reply from nodes within its management domain. Any flow reservation request
containing a source or destination IP address unknown to the broker denotes a flow
involving several domains. The broker will then forward the flow request to the bandwidth broker the flow will cross next. For getting the IP address of the bandwidth broker
of a foreign network, an additional service has to be established at the border routers.

5.2 Parallelizing the Broker

As already mentioned in Section 4 the flow requests are currently handled sequentially. Since configuring the network implies the bandwidth broker waiting a significant
amount of time, it would be better to handle the user requests in parallel threads. Since
it is not very likely, that many consecutive flow requests require the reconfiguration of
one single backbone router, the probability of decoupling is quite high and a significant
performance boost will result.

5.3 Topology Changes

Throughout this paper we assumed the topology to remain static after the startup of
the bandwidth broker. This allowed us to simplify the design of the topology and the
reservation databases. However, this assumption may not be valid in a large network
over a longer time interval. Although the routes to popular destinations seem to be
reasonable stable — despite the large number of BGP updates [12] — it might happen
that a route changes while a reservation is still relying on the forwarding given by this
route. We now want to shortly discuss possible solutions for this problem, which is still
not solved in any bandwidth broker implementation.

The problem of routing changes is the aggregation of flows in the core routers:
the core routers do not store per-flow information because of scalability reasons but
only the overall sum of bandwidth is kept. If a link goes down, the underlying routing
protocol might change the routing in a way, that one part of the flows is now routed via
a interface, but another part via another interface of this router (and / or might not cross
this router at all). Since the core router only has information about the aggregate sum of
bandwidth we cannot know how to divide this sum into parts needed for the new routes.

One possible solution would be the allocation of the total sum of bandwidth on the
new outgoing interfaces. This of course would result in a large overprovisioning and
waste of bandwidth and is therefore not desirable. We propose another solution that
breaks the rule of only storing aggregate information in the core routers in a way, that
the bandwidth broker maintains a reservation value not only for each interface of a core
router but for each routing table entry (see Table 2).

With this additional information we can correctly change the topology and reservation database in case of routing changes: Let us assume, the link of Interface 1 breaks,
and the routing protocol provides us with the following new routes: destinations $Dest_1$
and $Dest_2$ are now routed via interface Ifc_2, while $Dest_4$ is routed via Ifc_3. The new

Destination	Gateway	Interface	Reservation
$Dest_1$	$Gatew_1$	Ifc_1	500
$Dest_2$	$Gatew_1$	Ifc_1	300
$Dest_3$	$Gatew_2$	Ifc_2	700
$Dest_4$	$Gatew_1$	Ifc_1	700
$Dest_5$	$Gatew_3$	Ifc_3	500
$Dest_6$	$Gatew_2$	Ifc_2	200

Table 2. Example for the new routing table format

Destination	Gateway	Interface	Reservation
$Dest_1$	$Gatew_2$	Ifc_2	500
$Dest_2$	$Gatew_2$	Ifc_2	300
$Dest_3$	$Gatew_2$	Ifc_2	700
$Dest_4$	$Gatew_3$	Ifc_3	700
$Dest_5$	$Gatew_3$	Ifc_3	500
$Dest_6$	$Gatew_2$	Ifc_2	200

Table 3. The routing table after the topology changes

routing table now looks like Table 3. The bandwidth newly to be configured at the interfaces can easily be computed from the routing table: Ifc_2 needs 1700 units, while Ifc_3 will be configured 1200 units.

Deletion of a routing table entry is also quite simple: we will only have to check the new routing table, over which gateway the addresses of the deleted subnetwork will now be routed. The only thing we have to do now is to add the bandwitdh used for the deleted network to the reservation entry of this gateway.

6 Summary and Conclusion

In this paper we have presented the design of a centralised bandwidth broker for Differentiated Services networks. Our implementation is based on a generic QoS management framework providing the necessary functionality. The performance evaluations of our implementation focused on two critical factors of possible bottlenecks: the memory consumption and the flow processing time of the central bandwidth broker. We could show, that the amount of main memory nowadays available at a workstation is sufficient to hold a large topology database. The flow setup time presented here was limited by the CPU speed and memory bandwidth of the hardware used during the measurements. Besides using faster hardware additional enhancements of the current architecture have been proposed, such as a hierarchical bandwidth broker architecture or parallelising of the flow request processing. Hierarchical architectures have already proven successful in increasing the performance of a bandwidth broker and also a parallel processing will help to make the broker perform even better.

7 Acknowledgement

The work described in this paper is part of the work done in the project Mobile IP Telephony (MIPTel) funded by the Swiss National Science Foundation (Project No. 2100-057077.99/1).

References

1. B. Davie, A. Charny, J.C.R. Bennet, K. Benson, J.Y. Le Boudec, W. Courtney, S. Davari, V. Firoiu, and D. Stiliadis. RFC 3246: An Expedited Forwarding PHB (Per-Hop Behavior), March 2002. Obsoletes RFC2598 [5].

2. G. Dermler, M. Günter, T. Braun, and B. Stiller. Towards a Scalable System for Per-Flow Charging in the Internet. In B. Bodnar, editor, *Applied Telecommunication Symposium*, volume 32 of *Ariel Sharon Simulation Series*, 2000.
3. Matthew Doar. Tiers topology generator. http://www.geocities.com/ ResearchTriangle/ 3867/ sourcecode.html.
4. Bandwidth Broker Implementation. www.ittc.ukans.edu/ ~ kdrao/ BB/ bbreport.html.
5. V. Jacobson, K. Nichols, and K. Poduri. RFC 2598: An Expedited Forwarding PHB, June 1999. Obsoleted by RFC3246 [1].
6. I. Khalil and T. Braun. Implementation of a Bandwidth Broker for Dynamic End-to-End Resource Reservation in Outsourced Virtual Private Networks. In *The Conference on Leading Edge and Practical Computer Networking*, November 2000.
7. P. Kivimäki. Policy Based Networks & Bandwidth Broker. www.atm.tut.fi/ workshop01/ workshop01-bb.pdf.
8. K. Nichols, V. Jacobson, and L. Zhang. RFC 2638: A Two-bit Differentiated Services Architecture for the Internet, July 1999.
9. G. Politis, P. Sampatakos, and I. Venieris. Design of a Multi-Layer Bandwidth Broker Architecture. In Sathya Rao and Kaare Ingar Sletta, editors, *Next Generation Networks — Networks and Services for the Information Society*, volume 1938 of *Lecture Notes in Computer Science*, October 2000.
10. O. Pop, T. Mahr, T. Dreilinger, and R. Szabo. Vendor-Independent Bandwidth Broker Architecture for DiffServ Networks. In *Proceedings of the IEEE International Conference on Telecommunications*, 2001.
11. QBone Premium Service. http://qbone.internet2.edu/premium/, March 2002.
12. J. Rexford, J. Wang, Z. Xiao, and Y. Zhang. BGP Routing Stability of Popular Destinations. In *Proceedings of the Internet Measurement Workshop 2002*, November 2002.
13. G. Stattenberger. *Scalable Quality of Service Support for Mobile IP Users*. PhD thesis, University of Bern, December 2002.
14. G. Stattenberger and T. Braun. QoS Provisioning for Mobile IP Users. In H. Afifi and D. Zeghlache, editors, *Conference on Applications and Services in Wireless Networks, ASW 2001*, Paris, July 2001.
15. G. Stattenberger, T. Braun, and M. Brunner. A Platform - Independent API for Quality of Service Management. In *Proceedings of the IEEE Workshop on High Performance Switching and Routing*, May 2001.
16. A. S. Tanenbaum. *Computer Networks*. Prentice Hall, 3rd edition, 1996.
17. A. Terzis, J. Ogawa, S. Tsui, L. Wang, and L. Zhang. A Prototype Implementation of the Two-Tier Architecture for Differentiated Services. In *Proceedings of the Fifth IEEE Real-Time Technology and Applications Symposium*, June 1999.
18. Zhi-Li Zhang, Z. Duan, and Y. T. Hou. On Scalable Network Resource Management Using Bandwidth Brokers. In *Proceedings of the Network Operations and Management Symposium*, April 2002.

Deterministische Dienste für Echtzeitanwendungen in DiffServ-Domains mit prioritätsgesteuerten Warteschlangen

Jean-Alexander Müller, Klaus Irmscher

Universität Leipzig
Institut für Informatik
Rechnernetze und Verteilte Systeme
Augustusplatz 10-11, 04109 Leipzig
(jeanm,irmscher)@informatik.uni-leipzig.de

Zusammenfassung. Eine große Anzahl der existierenden Netze unterstützt Mechanismen zur statischen Zuordnung aggregierter Datenströme zu prioritätsgesteuerten Warteschlangen. Unser Beitrag stellt ein Modell zur Bereitstellung höherwertiger Dienste auf der Basis solcher Netze vor. Diese Dienste lassen eine deterministische Beschreibung der maximalen Verweilzeit in den Warteschlangen des Netzes zu. Das Modell fußt auf der Berechnung der effektiv benötigten Bandbreite zur Bedienung eines Aggregats innerhalb einer vorgegebenen Zeit. Durch eine Abbildung der Ende-zu-Ende-Datenströme auf Kanäle mit konstanter Paketrate und Paketgröße erreichen wir eine deutliche Reduktion der im Netz benötigten Statusinformationen. Die Effizienz des Modells ist abhängig von den definierten Diensten und der Pfadlänge des Netzwerkes. Anhand eines konkreten Beispiels zeigen wir, dass die Effizienz hinreichend groß ist, um den Anforderungen eines Telephonieszenarios zu genügen.

1 Einführung

1.1 Motivation

Echtzeitanwendungen benötigen zugesicherte Übertragungseigenschaften (Dienstgüte, QoS), um den Bedürfnissen der Benutzer gerecht zu werden. Es ist das Ziel dieser Arbeit diese Eigenschaften auf der Basis aggregierter Datenströme bereitzustellen. Die Spannweite der davon profitierenden Anwendungen reicht von Telephonieanwendungen über Transaktionssysteme bis hin zu kooperativen multimedialen Einsatzszenarien. Gemeinsam ist diesen Anwendungen die Forderung nach einer möglichst geringen minimalen Übertragungsverzögerung und vorbestimmter Varianz selbiger. Weiterhin sind Paketverluste auszuschließen.

Die minimale Übertragungsverzögerung kann durch die Regelung der Bedienrate des Transportnetzes beeinflusst werden. Wichtiger als die minimale Übertragungsverzögerung ist die Varianz der Übertragungsverzögerung, die von der veränderlichen Last des Netzwerkes abhängt. Sie bestimmt wesentlich die Interaktivität von Echtzeitanwendungen und soll nach oben beschränkt sein.

Es muss aus unserer Sicht zwischen statistischen und exakten Zusicherungen unterschieden werden. Ein statistischer Ansatz erlaubt im Vergleich oft eine höhere Auslastung zum Preis eines teilweise instabilen Dienstes. In Ausnahmesituationen variiert die Übertragungsverzögerung stärker als zugesichert (siehe [4]). Diese Ausnahmen müssen von der Anwendung ausgeglichen werden. Dies geschieht durch sog. *playout buffer*, deren Größe durch die maximale Varianz der Übertragungsverzögerung bestimmt wird. Dies ist nur mit exakten Zusicherungen möglich. Als Resultat dieser Überlegung muss die Länge der Warteschlangen, auf die die Pakete eines Datenstroms im Netz treffen, nach oben beschränkt sein.

Aus der Sicht der Netzwerke darf ein dafür geeignetes Berechnungssystem nicht auf Basis von Einzeldatenströmen agieren. Einerseits wird dies durch die gegenwärtig allgemein akzeptierte Annahme begründet, dass ein auf Einzeldatenströmen basiertes System nicht skaliert. Andererseits benötigen Ansätze wie Integrated Services (IntServ)[1] oder Stateless Core[10] Schedulingmechanismen, die kurz- bis mittelfristig nicht in jedem Netzwerk verfügbar sind. Einen Ausweg bieten Systeme, die ob der aggregierten Behandlung einzelner Datenströme in der Lage sind, den Anforderungen der Einzeldatenströme gerecht zu werden. Solche Systeme müssen zwei grundlegende Anforderungen erfüllen. Die Dienste müssen stabil und vorhersagbar erbracht werden. Gleichzeitig muss die Anzahl der zu haltenden Statusinformationen sinnvoll reduziert werden (vgl. [5]), um Problemen der Skalierbarkeit aus dem Weg zu gehen.

Das Differentiated Services Modell[7] ist eine mögliche Basis für solche Systeme. Das Modell eignet sich ursprünglich nur für die relative Zusicherung von Übertragungseigenschaften (kurz: Dienstgarantien). Die absoluten Differentiated Services stellen eine Erweiterung des Modells um Zugangskontrollmechanismen dar. Mit Hilfe dieser soll die Überlastung von Warteschlangen vermieden werden, so dass statt relativer absolute Dienstgarantien gegeben werden können. Die Problematik liegt in der Wahl geeigneter Dienstbeschreibungen. Einerseits müssen diese für das skizzierte Anwendungsfeld zutreffen. Andererseits muss die Beschreibung eine Reduktion der Statusinformationen erlauben.

Als Lösung dieser Problematik schlagen wir eine Modellierung von Datenströmen durch Einzeldatenströme mit konstanter Paketrate und Paketgröße vor. Dies sind Eigenschaften, die insbesondere für Telephonieanwendungen exakt zutreffen. In Anlehnung an das Telefonsystem werden diese Einzeldatenströme als Kanäle bezeichnet. Diese Modellierung erlaubt eine Reduktion der Statusinformationen auf die Anzahl der zwischen zwei Zugangsroutern eines Netzwerkes genutzten Kanäle. Die Zugangskontrolle zur Begrenzung der Wartezeiten basiert auf einer *worse case*-Berechnung der effektiv benötigten Bandbreite.

1.2 Outline

Der nächste Abschnitt führt in das zu Grunde liegende Modell sowie die Notation ein. Wir beschränken uns dabei auf die Betrachtung von strikt prioritätsgesteuerten Warteschlangensystemen. Die Idee des Kanalkonzeptes wird in Abschnitt 3 zu einem zur Zugangskontrolle geeigneten Verfahren entwickelt. Diese stützt sich im wesentlichen Maße auf die Berechnung der effektiv benötigten Bandbreiten, um eine Bedienung aller Kanäle innerhalb einer nach oben beschränkten Wartezeit zu garantieren. Im Anschluss wird das Modell bezüglich seiner Einsetzbarkeit sowie seiner Vor- und Nachteile bewertet. Der zunächst allgemein geführten Bewertung folgt in diesem Abschnitt eine Diskussion anhand konkreter Dienste. Abschnitt 5 schließt diesen Beitrag ab und bietet einen Ausblick auf weitere Arbeiten.

2 Modell, Annahmen und Terminologie

Wir nehmen an, dass alle Knoten im Netzwerk über strikt prioritätsgesteuerte, gepufferte Ausgangswarteschlangen verfügen. Die Anzahl der Ausgangswarteschlangen pro Link sei nicht kleiner als drei. Der Best Effort Dienst werde in jedem Knoten über die Warteschlange mit der geringsten Priorität erbracht und im folgenden nicht weiter beachtet.

Im gesamten Netzwerk seien zwei höherwertige Dienste s_p ($p = 1 \dots 2$) definiert. Ein höherwertiger Dienst s_p garantiert die Weiterleitung von Paketen mit einer maximalen Verweilzeit in den Warteschlangen des gesamten Netzes von $\tau(s_p)$. Der Dienst s_2 wird durch die Warteschlangen höchster Priorität erbracht und s_1 von den Warteschlangen einer mittleren Priorität.

Als Kanal wird ein Datenfluss von Paketen mit maximaler Paketgröße $M(s_p)$ und konstanter Paketrate $r(s_p)$ bezeichnet. Er beschreibt den Datenfluss von einem Eingangsknoten des Netzwerkes bis zu einem Ausgangsknoten. Jeder Kanal ist genau einem höherwertigen Dienst zugeordnet. Er kann als Leaky Bucket Datenstrom aufgefasst werden. Die maximale Paketgröße sei gleichzeitig auch die minimal in der Berechnung berücksichtigte Paketgröße (*Minumum Policed Unit, MPU*). Ein Ende-zu-Ende-Datenstrom von einem Eingangsknoten des Netzwerkes zu einem Ausgangsknoten des Netzwerkes lässt sich als Bündel von Kanälen gleichen Dienstes beschreiben. Es ist erlaubt, bis zu $f(s_p)$ Kanäle zu bündeln, um Ende-Zu-Ende-Datenströme mit einer Paketgröße von bis zu $U(s_p) = f(s_p) * M(s_p)$ auf diese abbilden zu können.

Die maximale Verweilzeit $\tau(s_p)$ im gesamten Netzwerk sei für die beiden höherwertigen Dienste auf die Warteschlangen im Netzwerk verteilt. Für alle Pfade durch das Netzwerk übersteige die Summe der maximalen Verweilzeiten in den einzelnen Warteschlangen $\tau(s_p)$ nicht. Die maximale Verweilzeit in einer Warteschlange von einem Knoten x zu einem Knoten y für einen höherwertigen Dienst s_p wird mit $\tau_{(x,y)}(s_p)$ beschrieben.

Die von den vorhergehenden Warteschlangen in eine Warteschlange einfließenden Kanäle werden als Aggregat bezeichnet. Es wird definiert als eine Menge $I_{(x,y)}(s_p)$ von Kanalbündeln die in das Aggregat eingehen. Für jede vorhergehende Warteschlange existiert in dieser mit n indexierten Menge genau ein Element $i_n(s_p) \in I_{(x,y)}(s_p)$, welches die Anzahl der gebündelten Kanäle angibt. Die in eine Warteschlange einfließenden Kanalbündel werden durch eine TSpec (r, M, p, b) beschrieben(vgl. [1]). Als Spitzendatenrate wird die Bedienrate $(C_n(s_p))$ der vorhergehenden Warteschlange angenommen. Die durchschnittliche Datenrate sowie die Burstgröße berechnen sich aus der Anzahl der gebündelten Kanäle, multipliziert mit der durchschnittlichen Rate eines Kanals bzw. der MPU.

3 Effektiv benötigte Bandbreite von Kanalbündeln in prioritätsgesteuerten Warteschlangen

Unser Ansatz basiert auf der Berechnung der effektiv benötigten Bandbreite zur Bedienung der Pakete eines Kanals innerhalb einer vorgegebenen maximalen Verteilzeit τ. Wir verwenden das Berechnungsmodell in [3] für die Aggregation von TSpec-konformen Datenströmen in FIFO-Warteschlangen. Weiterhin stützen wir uns auf die Aussagen in [2]. Demnach kann für jedes Netzwerk mit einer Prioritätsklasse eine obere Schranke der Wartezeiten als Funktion von Auslastung und Durchmesser des Netzwerkes berechnet werden. Wir verbinden beide Arbeiten zu einem Modell, welches die eingangs aufgestellten Forderungen erfüllt.

Als Ausgangsbasis nutzen wir eine auf unsere Notation angepasste und in Formel 1 dargestellte Form des in [3] vorgestellten Calculus zur Berechnung der effektiv benötigten Bandbreite R für mehrere in einer FIFO-Warteschlange aggregierte Kanalbündel. Die Formel vernachlässigt zunächst die Existenz weiterer Warteschlangen. In die Berechnung geht die maximale Burstzeit $\theta_i(s_p) = \frac{b_{i(s_p)} - U_{i(s_p)}}{p_{i(s_p)} - r_{i(s_p)}}$ eines Kanalbündels als Indexfunktion ein.

$$R(I(s_p)) = \max \begin{cases} \frac{M*|I(s_p)|}{\tau(s_p)} \\ r * \sum_{n=1}^{|I(s_p)|} i_n(s_p) \text{ mit } i_n(s_p) \in I(s_p) \\ \max_{n=1...|I(s_p)|} \frac{b_n^* + r_n^* * \theta_{i_n}(s_p)}{\tau(s_p) + \theta_{i_n}(s_p)} \end{cases} \quad (1)$$

$$\nu_k^l(x,y) = \begin{cases} x, \text{ falls } k \neq l \wedge \theta_{i_k}(s_p) \leq \theta_{i_l}(s_p) \\ y \text{ sonst} \end{cases}$$

$$b_n^* = \sum_{k=1}^{|I(s_p)|} \left(\nu_k^n \left(U(s_p), M(s_p) * i_k(s_p) \right) \right)$$

$$r_n^* = \sum_{k=1}^{|I(s_p)|} \nu_k^n \left(i_k(s_p) * r(s_p), C_k(s_p) \right)$$

Die in die Berechnung eingehenden Parameter der durchschnittlichen Datenrate $r_{i(s_p)}$ sowie der maximalen Paketgröße $U_{i(s_p)}$ sind in unserem Modell trivial. Die tatsächliche Spitzendatenrate $p_{i(s_p)}$ mit der ein Kanalbündel eingeht, ist in jedem Fall nach oben begrenzt durch die Bedienrate der vorhergehenden Warteschlange. Die maximale Anzahl der Pakete eines Kanalbündels, die als Burst $b_{i(s_p)}$ eingehen, wird gegeben durch die Anzahl der gebündelten Kanäle. Wir liefern die Begründung hierfür im folgenden.

Die maximale Verweilzeit $\tau(s_p)$ in den Warteschlangen des gesamten Netzwerkes sei für alle dem Dienst s_p zugeordneten Kanäle kleiner als das sog. Inter Packet Delay (IPD, $\Delta(s_p) = \frac{U(s_p)}{r(s_p)}$) dieser Kanäle. Um einen Zusammenschluss zweier aufeinanderfolgender Pakete eines Kanals zu vermeiden, muss $\tau(s_p)$ kleiner sein als $\Delta(s_p)$ reduziert um die maximale Bedienzeit $\delta(s_p)$ eines Paketes der Größe $M(s_p)$ in den Links des Netzwerkes. [1] Innerhalb von $\Delta(s_p)$ empfängt ein Ausgangsknoten des Netzwerkes

---

[1] Wir gehen im folgenden davon aus, dass die maximale Bedienzeit im Vergleich zu $\tau(s_p)$ vernachlässigbar klein ist. Siehe auch [8] zu typischen Bedienzeiten in Netzen.

pro Kanal maximal zwei Pakete. In einem beliebigen Zeitraum $(\Delta(s_p) - \tau(s_p))$ trifft aber höchstens ein Paket ein. Aus diesem Grund wählen $\tau(s_p) \leq \frac{\Delta(s_p)}{2} - \delta(s_p)$. Daraus folgt, dass sich in den Warteschlangen der Knoten im Inneren des Netzwerkes für ein beliebiges Intervall der Größe $\tau(s_p)$ pro Kanal höchstens ein Paket befindet. Zu jedem Kanalbündel kann somit die Anzahl der Pakete, die im schlechtesten Fall in einem Burst, auftreten bestimmt werden. Sie entspricht der Anzahl der zu dem Kanalbündel zusammengefassten Kanäle.

Verteilt man die maximale Verweilzeit $\tau(s_p)$ in den Warteschlangen des gesamten Netzwerkes gemäß unseres Modells auf die einzelnen Warteschlangen, kann die Berechnung der effektiv benötigten Bandbreite für jede Warteschlange unabhängig von den bisher erfahrenen Wartezeiten erfolgen. Begründet wird dies durch das *Pay bursts only once* Phänomen, nach dem bisher erfahrene Wartezeiten nur einmal in die gesamte Wartezeit eingehen. Es ist gleichzeitig offensichtlich, dass innerhalb jedes Intervalls kleiner als $\tau(s_p)$ höchstens ein Paket pro Kanal in die Warteschlange einfließen kann. Die Berechnung der effektiv benötigten Bandbreite ist damit nur von der Bedienrate der vorangestellten Knoten bzw. der Datenrate der Links am Eingang des betrachteten Knotens und der Auslastung der Kanalbündel abhängig. Alle anderen Werte gehen als Konstanten in die Berechnung ein.

Die Formel 1 eignet sich bisher nicht zur Anwendung auf prioritätsgesteuerte Warteschlangen, da sie deren Abhängigkeiten nicht berücksichtigt. Einerseits müssen alle Warteschlangen auf die Bedienung des aktuell bedienten Paketes warten (unabhängig von dessen Priorität). Grund dafür ist das non-preemptive Scheduling in Paketvermittlungsnetzen. Die Größe dieses Paketes sei als maximal angenommen und mit m bezeichnet. Andererseits erfolgt die Bedienung einer Warteschlange nur dann, wenn alle Warteschlangen höherer Priorität leer sind. Für ein gegebenes Intervall $\tau(s_p)$ lässt sich die maximale Anzahl der in Warteschlangen höherer Priorität auftretenden Pakete berechnen. Diese Anzahl von Paketen geht in die Berechnung als zusätzlicher ebenfalls nicht unterbrechbarer Burst $B_{I(s_p)}$ ein. In unserem Fall berechnet sich $B_{I(s_1)}$ aus der Anzahl der Intervalle $\Delta(s_2)$, welche die Wartezeit $\tau(s_1)$ teilweise oder vollständig überdecken, multipliziert mit der Anzahl der von s_2 zugeordneten Kanäle (bezogen auf die aktuell betrachtete Warteschlange). Formel 2 liefert eine verallgemeinerte Form zur Berechnung von $B_{I(s_p)}$ für $N \geq 2$ Warteschlangen höherer Priorität (respektive Dienste) an, die zusätzlich m berücksichtigt.

$$B_{I(s_p)} = \begin{cases} m, \text{ falls } p = N \\ m + \sum_{k=p+1}^{N} \left(\left\lceil \frac{\Delta(s_p)}{\Delta(s_k)} \right\rceil * M(s_k) * \sum_{l=1}^{|I(s_k)|} i_l(s_k) \right), \text{ falls } p < N \end{cases} \quad (2)$$

Dies erlaubt nun die Formulierung der Formel 3 zur Berechnung der effektiv benötigten Bandbreite R^{prio} für eine prioritätsgesteuerte Warteschlange[2]. In Erweiterung zu Formel 1 geht $B_{I(s_p)}$ als zusätzlicher Burst in die Berechnung ein.

---

[2] Unser Modell lässt sich leicht für CBQ-Warteschlangen erweitern. In diesem Fall erfolgt die Berechnung der effektiv benötigten Bandbreite unabhängig von den anderen Warteschlangen. Des weiteren geht anstatt der Linkrate, die Bedienrate der jeweiligen Warteschlange im vorherigen Knoten ein.

$$R^{prio}(I(s_p)) = \max \begin{cases} \frac{M*|I(s_p)|+B_{I(s_p)}}{\tau(s_p)} \\ \sum_{k=p}^{N} r(s_k) * \sum_{n=1}^{|I(s_k)|} i_n(s_k) \text{ mit } i_n(s_k) \in I(s_k) \\ \max_{n=1\ldots|I(s_p)|} \left(\frac{B_{I(s_p)}+b_n^*+r_n^**\theta_{i_n}(s_p)}{\tau(s_p)+\theta_{i_n}(s_p)} \right) \end{cases} \quad (3)$$

Der Erhöhung der Auslastung eines Kanalbündels kann zugestimmt werden, wenn das Maximum der effektiv benötigten Bandbreite über alle Warteschlangen höherer Priorität kleiner ist als die zur Verfügung stehende Linkrate μ (siehe Formel 4).

$$\mu \geq \max_{k=1\ldots N} R^{prio}(I(s_k)) \quad (4)$$

4 Bewertung

Dieser Abschnitt dient der Bewertung des Modells bezüglich seiner Einsetzbarkeit sowie seiner Vor- und Nachteile. Wir führen zunächst eine allgemeine Diskussion, die im Anschluss auf Basis eines Anwendungsbeispiels vertieft wird.

4.1 Allgemeine Bewertung

Unser Modell erlaubt die Bereitstellung von Übertragungsdiensten mit oberen Schranken für die maximal zu erwartenden Wartezeiten. Durch Kanalbündelung lassen sich so höherwertige Dienste mit garantierten Datenraten und nach oben beschränkten Wartezeiten realisieren. Im Unterschied zum Ansatz der Integrated Services sind die Anforderungen an die Router des Netzwerkes stark reduziert. Der Preis dieser Reduktion ist ein beschränkter Einsatzbereich. Die maximale Verweilzeit ist eine Funktion der Auslastung und des Durchmessers eines Netzwerkes[2]. Sie ist in unserem Modell bezüglich eines bestimmten Dienstes als unveränderlich anzusehen. Dementsprechend kann der jeweilige Dienst mit wachsendem Durchmesser weniger Dienstnutzern bereitgestellt werden. Die Umkehrung der Aussage trifft ebenfalls zu.

Die Aussagen in [2] wurden für ein Modell mit nur zwei unterschiedlichen Prioritätsklassen getroffen. Da unser Modell prinzipiell beliebig viele Prioritätsklassen (bzw. Dienste) erlaubt, muss zudem die Auslastung höherer Dienste (relativ zum aktuell betrachteten) berücksichtigt werden. Wie aus Formel 3 leicht zu erkennen ist, reduziert sich die Anzahl der bedienbaren Kanäle mit steigender Zahl der mit höherer Priorität bedienten Kanäle. Wie im folgenden Abschnitt 4.2 dargestellt wird, ist der Einsatzbereich für die beispielhaft ausgewählten Dienste dennoch ausreichend groß.

Die Effizienz des Kanalmodells, also der Abbildung realer Datenströme auf Kanäle konstanter Paketrate, ist von den Einsatzgebieten abhängig. Es ist offensichtlich, dass Datenströme mit stark variierender Datenrate eine geringere Effizienz erreichen[3]. Einige Kanäle des anzufordernden Kanalbündels dienen in solchen Fällen nur zur Bedienung von sog. Daten-Spikes. Diese treten aber oftmals nicht mit der Paketrate des Kanals auf, so dass hier Leerlaufzeiten entstehen, die nicht explizit anderen Diensten

---

[3] Der Vergleich bezieht sich auf Datenströme mit konstanter Datenrate.

zur Verfügung gestellt werden können. Leerlaufzeiten können auch bei der Abbildung von Datenströmen auftreten, die mit konstanter Paketrate senden. Sie treten auf, wenn die abzubildende Paketrate kleiner ist als die des Kanals (bzw. Kanalbündels) oder die maximale Paketgröße unter der angenommenen minimalen Paketgröße des Kanals liegt. Die Tabelle 1 zeigt dies examplarisch für ausgewählte Sprach-Codecs.

Ähnliche Probleme treten bei der Übertragung von beliebigen Datenströmen über ISDN-Kanäle bzw. ATM CBR-Kanäle auf. Umgekehrt gilt, dass Datenströme bzw. Anwendungen, die für solche Übertragungskanäle entworfen wurden, sich gut in unser Modell integrieren. Telephonieanwendungen sind ein Beispiel.

Wir gehen in unserem Modell vom sog. *worse case* aus. Einerseits nehmen wir an, dass innerhalb eines Intervalls der Länge $\tau_{(x,y)}(s_p)$ alle Pakete der gebündelten Kanäle als Burst eingehen. Zudem müssen wir annehmen, dass dieser Burst mit der Linkrate des Eingangsports empfangen wird, da über den bisherigen Verlauf der Aggregation keine Informationen vorliegen. Mit anwachsender Linkrate verkürzt sich die Burstzeit $\theta_i(s_p) = \frac{b_i(s_p) - U_i(s_p)}{p_i(s_p) - r_i(s_p)}$ eines Kanalbündels (siehe Abschnitt 2). Die effektiv benötigte Bandbreite verhält sich zu $\theta_i(s_p)$ indirekt proportional. Mit steigender Linkrate an den Eingängen wächst die effektiv benötigte Bandbreite bei gleicher Auslastung der Warteschlangen. Wünschenswert erscheint eine Entkopplung der maximalen Spitzendatenrate von der Linkrate. Aufgrund der getroffenen Annahmen ist dies nicht möglich. Erst durch eine Erweiterung des Warteschlangenmodells auf ratenlimitierte Warteschlangen (beispielsweise Class Based Queueing), kann ein solches Verhalten realisiert werden.

Abschließend soll noch auf die Auswirkung der beschriebenen höherwertigen Dienste auf den Best Effort Dienst eingegangen werden. Aufgrund des Einsatzes von prioritätsgesteuerten Warteschlangen ist die Entstehung von Bursts in den höheren Warteschlangen unvermeidbar. Die maximale Dauer der Blockierungen durch diese Bursts kann mit Hilfe von Formel 2 berechnet werden. Die Häufigkeit deren Auftretens wird, in unserem Modell, durch die Paketraten der höherwertigen Dienste bestimmt. Die maximale Unterbrechung des Best Effort Dienstes lässt sich somit in Abhängigkeit von diesen Diensten und deren Auslastung berechnen. Durch eine geeignete Wahl der maximalen Kanalauslastung in einem Knoten kann die Benachteiligung des Best Effort Verkehrs gesteuert werden.

4.2 Bewertung anhand eines konkreten Szenarios

Zur weiteren Bewertung definieren wir zunächst zwei Dienste, die für Telephonieanwendungen geeignet sind. Der höherwertige Dienst s_2 sei zugeschnitten auf die Bedürfnisse des Standards G.726(24kbps)[12]. Er garantiere eine maximale Verweilzeit[4] von 10ms im Netzwerk bei einer angenommenen Paketrate von 50 Paketen pro Sekunde und einer Paketgröße von $M(s_2) = 100 Byte$ (800Bit). $f(s_2)$ sei nicht größer als zwei. Der zweite höherwertige Dienst s_1 soll für den Transport von Videodaten mit einer maximalen Rate von 10 Bildern pro Sekunde geeignet sein. Wir setzen die Bildrate gleich der Paketrate. Als Paketgröße wird $M(s_1) = 1500 Byte$ (12000Bit) angenommen. Größere Pakete sind nicht erlaubt ($f(s_1) = 1$). Durch den Zusammenschluss zweier Kanäle

---

[4] Zur Vereinfachung wählen wir einen runden Wert und vernachlässigen die Reduktion um die Bedienzeit δ.

wird eine Datenrate von 240kbps erreicht. Dies entspricht ungefähr der maximal zulässigen Rate für Videokonferenzen im Mbone. Die für den Best Effort Dienst maximal zulässige Paketgröße (MTU) betrage ebenfalls $m = 1500Byte$.

Die Wahl der Paketraten und Paketgrößen für höherwertige Dienste muss in Abhängigkeit von den Hauptanwendungen gewählt werden. Wie aus Tabelle 1 ersichtlich ist, eignet sich die Definition von s_2 für Audiodatenströme, die nach G.726(24kbps) oder G.711 codiert wurden. Die dabei entstehenden Paketgrößen sind jeweils ganzzahlige Vielfache von $M(s_2)$. Andere Codecs, wie beispielsweise G.729 oder G.726(32kbps), können die Kanäle nicht vollständig auslasten, da sie mit Paketgrößen arbeiten, die Vielfache von 60Byte bzw. 80Byte sind. Ähnlich verhält sich dies mit Codecs, die Datenströme geringerer Paketrate generieren.

Codec	Paylod plus Paketkopf in Byte	anzufordernde Kanäle	Verlust
G.729	$20 + 40 = 60$	1	16kbps
G.728	$40 + 40 = 80$	1	8kbps
G.726(24kbps)	$60 + 40 = 100$	1	0kbps
G.729(32kbps)	$80 + 40 = 120$	2	32kbps
G.711	$160 + 40 = 200$	2	0kbps

Tabelle 1. Die Wahl der Paketgröße bestimmt die Effizienz der Abbildung realer Datenströme auf die Kanäle. Hier wird dies exemplarisch anhand der Abbildung für verschiedener Sprach-Codecs auf eine Paketgröße von 100Byte bei 50pps dargestellt.

Im folgenden soll ein beliebiger Knoten eines Netzes mit ein, zwei, vier oder fünf Eingangslinks pro Dienst betrachtet werden. Ziel der Betrachtungen ist die Bewertung des Modells in Abhängigkeit von der Anzahl der Eingangslinks und deren Kapazität bei konstanter Auslastung der Dienste. s_2 sind 500 Kanäle und s_1 sind 200 Kanäle zugeordnet, die gleichmäßig auf die Eingänge verteilt werden. Die Betrachtungen werden für die im G-WiN typischen Linkraten von 34, 100, 155, 622, 1000 und 2440 (alle in Mbps) durchgeführt(siehe [10]). Die Linkraten sind für die Eingangslinks jeweils identisch.

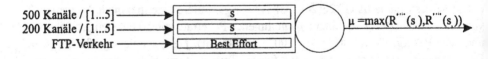

Abb. 1. Der für die Bewertung herangezogene Knoten verfügt über 1,2,4 oder 5 Eingangslinks pro Dienst (s_2, s_1 und Best Effort). Die Linkrate ist für alle eingehenden Links gleich groß. Bedienrate des Warteschlangensystems ist gleich der berechneten effektiv benötigten Bandbreite.

Zur Bewertung ziehen wir die von einem Integrated Services Ansatz benötigte Bandbreite zur Bedienung der 500 Kanäle des Dienstes s_2 heran. Wir stützen uns dabei auf das Berechnungsmodell für *Guaranteed Service* (siehe [1,9]). Tabelle 2 zeigt die in der Summe benötigte Bandbreite für maximale Verweilzeiten von 10ms, 20ms und 50ms. Um eine maximale Verweilzeit von 10ms zu erreichen, wird eine Bedienrate von mindestens 640 Mbps benötigt. Der Grund liegt in der separierten Bedienung der einzelnen Kanäle, die vernachlässigt, dass in den Knoten tatsächlich maximal 5 Kanalbündel parallel einströmen[5].

Tabelle 3 zeigt die effektiv benötigte Bandbreite für verschiedene Kanalauslastungen an einem Knoten mit fünf Eingangslinks für beide Dienste, wobei der jeweils andere Dienst (entweder s_1 oder s_2) unbelastet bleibt. Als maximale Verweilzeiten wurden 5ms für s_1 und 1ms für s_2 angenommen. Es wird deutlich, dass die effektiv benötigte Bandbreite für ein Netzwerk des Durchmessers 10, also einer maximalen Verweilzeit von 10ms, im Vergleich des Dienstes s_2 mit der von einer IntServ-Lösung benötigten Bandbreite geringer ist. Soll eine größere Verweilzeit von 20ms oder gar 50 ms gewählt werden, so steht die Lösung einem IntServ-Ansatz allerdings nach (vgl. Tabelle 2 und Tabelle 3), da dies in unserem Modell nicht möglich ist. Die Aussagen treffen gleichfalls für s_1 zu. Anhand von Tabelle 5 kann man die Abhängigkeit der effektiv benötigten Bandbreite von der Spitzendatenrate und der Anzahl der eingehenden Kanalbündel erkennen. Sie wird nach unten durch die Summe der durchschnittlichen Datenraten der einzelnen Kanäle beschränkt. Nach oben wird sie durch die Anzahl der innerhalb der maximalen Verweilzeit bedienbaren Kanäle beschränkt. Diese Schranke wird durch die Bedienrate des Warteschlangensystems gegeben[6].

Die effektiv benötigte Bandbreite wächst sehr schnell auf ein hohes Niveau zwischen 260Mbps und 365Mbps (nur s_2) bzw. 310Mbps bis 480Mbps (beide Dienste). Grund dafür ist die starke Verkürzung der Burstzeit durch ein Anwachsen der Spitzendatenraten bzw. durch eine Erhöhung der Anzahl eingehender Kanalbündel, jeweils bei gleicher Auslastung. Beide Parameter sollten daher nur langsam anwachsen. Die Anzahl der eingehenden Kanalbündel ist nur begrenzt beeinflussbar. Sie wird durch die Topologie des Netzes und der Wegewahl in diesem Netz bestimmt. In unserem Modell lässt sich dies nicht berücksichtigen. Wie bereits angedeutet könnte eine Ratenlimitierung der einzelnen Warteschlangen im Modell berücksichtigt werden. Aufgrund des schnellen Anwachsens der effektiv benötigten Bandbreite ist zu vermuten, dass dadurch eine Verdoppelung der maximal bedienbaren Kanäle nicht erreicht werden kann.

Tabelle 5 zeigt abschließend noch einen interessanten Effekt unseres Modells. Die vollständige Auslastung des Dienstes s_2 verbietet den Dienst s_1 nicht. In Abhängigkeit von der zur Verfügung stehenden Bedienrate und der Spitzendatenraten kann die Auslastung der Dienste geringerer Priorität, in diesem Fall s_1 und Best Effort, bis zu der von s_2 effektiv benötigten Bandbreite erhöht werden.

---

[5] Prinzipiell lässt sich dies bereits mit Formel 1 (siehe [3]) begründen. Mit [9] sei an dieser Stelle einer der Ansätze benannt, die eine entsprechende Verbessung des Berechnungsmodells für IntServ erreichen.

[6] Vorausgesetzt, dass bei dem Erreichen der oberen Schranke keine weitere Kanäle akzeptiert werden.

	34Mbps	100Mbps	155Mbps	622Mbps	1Gbps	2,44Gbps
10ms	652	644	643	641	640	640
20ms	323	321	321	320	320	320
50ms	128	128	128	128	128	128

Tabelle 2. Die Tabelle zeigt die in der Summe benötigte Bandbreite (in Mbps) zur Bedienung von 500 Kanälen des Typs s_2 innerhalb von 10ms, 20ms und 50ms in Abhängigkeit von der Bedienrate basierend auf dem IntServ-Modell für Guaranteed Service.

Linkate	s_2 5x10	s_2 5x20	s_2 5x50	s_2 5x100	s_1 5x10	s_1 5x20	s_1 5x30	s_1 5x40
34Mbps	43	64	101	127	77	107	123	133
100Mbps	49	80	154	235	103	170	219	256
155Mbps	50	84	171	277	110	191	255	307
622Mbps	51	90	200	368	120	228	329	424
1000Mbps	52	91	204	383	122	234	342	445
2440Mbps	50	91	209	399	123	240	354	467

Tabelle 3. Dargestellt wird die effektiv benötigte Bandbreite (in Mbps) für die Dienste s_2 (links) und s_1 (rechts) in Abhängigkeit von der Spitzendatenrate und der Auslastung der jeweils 5 eingehenden Kanalbündel. Die maximale Bedienzeit beträgt 1ms für s_2 und 5ms für s_1. Für den jeweils anderen Dienst wurde eine Auslastung von 0 Kanälen angenommen.

Linkate	s_2 1x500	s_2 2x250	s_2 4x125	s_2 5x100	s_1 1x200	s_1 2x100	s_1 4x50	s_1 5x40
34Mbps	33	62	108	127	n.m.	89	128	152
100Mbps	85	142	212	235	98	170	264	296
155Mbps	119	185	256	277	140	227	326	357
622Mbps	255	316	358	368	324	413	478	493
1000Mbps	298	346	376	383	387	459	507	518
2440Mbps	354	381	395	399	475	516	539	544

Tabelle 4. Angegeben werden die effektiv benötigten Bandbreiten (in Mbps) für die beiden höherwertigen Dienste in Abhängigkeit von den Spitzendatenraten und der Verteilung der Auslastung von 500 Kanälen (s_2) bzw. 200 Kanälen (s_1).

34Mbps	100Mbps	155Mbps	622Mbps	1Gbps	2,44Gbps
55	110	120	130	130	135

Tabelle 5. Bei einer Auslastung von s_2 mit 5x100 Kanälen kann die Auslastung des Dienstes s_1 bis zu dem angegebenen Niveau ohne Veränderung der aktuell benötigten Bedienrate angehoben werden.

4.3 Bewertung der Reichweitenbeschränkung

Das vorgestellte Modell lässt sich nicht ohne weiteres auf beliebig große Netze anwenden. Mit wachsendem Durchmesser des Netzes verringert sich die maximale Auslastung der Dienste oder die Qualität der Dienste bezogen auf die maximale Verweilzeit. Andererseits erscheint die Anzahl der bedienbaren Kanäle für Netze mit einem relativ geringen Durchmesser von 10 Hops, wie beispielsweise das G-WiN (siehe [10]) als ausreichend, um höherwertige Dienste einzuführen. Voraussetzung dafür ist eine Verkehrsanpassung auf Basis von Ende-zu-Ende-Datenströmen an den Übergängen zu den angeschlossenen Kundennetzen. Eine solche Anpassung erfolgt implizit, wenn in den Kundennetzen höhere Dienste basierend auf dem IntServ-Ansatz bereitgestellt werden. Die Aufgabe der Anpassung könnte ein Router übernehmen, der beide Netze miteinander verbindet. In letzterem Fall ließe sich im Inneren des Kundennetzes wiederum eine Lösung auf der Basis unseres Modells realisieren. In einer solchen Umgebung kann die Reichweitenbeschränkung zum Teil aufgehoben werden. Als Seiteneffekt erlaubt dies die Bereitstellung von Diensten mit größeren maximalen Verweilzeiten im Netz aus G-WiN und Kundennetzen, da die Summe der maximalen Verweilzeit in den Teilnetzen die maximale Verweilzeit im gesamten Netzwerk bestimmt. Dient unser Modell als Verbindungsnetz zweier IntServ-Netze, so geht es in die Berechnung als ein Knoten mit der Verzögerung[7] $\tau(s_p)$ ein.

4.4 Simulation

Die in den Tabellen 3 und 5 angegebenen Werte der effektiv benötigten Bandbreite wurden mit Hilfe des Netzwerksimulators *ns2*[11] geprüft. Beobachtet wurde die Verweilzeit in den Warteschlangen eines Knotens (siehe Abbildung 1), in die Bursts maximaler Länge eingehen. Die Länge der Warteschlangen höherer Priorität wurde auf die Länge des maximal zu erwartenden Bursts angepasst. Das Datenaufkommen im Bereich des Best Effort Dienstes wurde mit FTP-Datenquellen erzeugt.

Unser Berechnungsmodell konnte für die angegebenen Werte durch die Simulationen, bestätigt werden. Zu keinem Zeitpunkt wurde die maximale Verweilzeit eines Paketes überschritten. Es wurden keine Paketverluste beobachtet.

5 Zusammenfassung

Die Bedienung von ratenlimitierten Ende-zu-Ende-Datenströmen innerhalb maximaler Verweilzeiten bedingt nicht notwendig eine separierte Behandlung der einzelnen Ende-zu-Ende-Datenströme in jedem Knoten eines Netzwerkes. Unser Modell erlaubt diese Zusicherungen für Netzwerke in denen nur prioritätsgesteuerte Warteschlangen zur Verfügung stehen. Wir erreichen dies durch eine Abbildung der Ende-zu-Ende-Datenströme auf Kanäle konstanter Paketrate und Paketgröße. Die Wahl der Eigenschaften dieser Kanäle bestimmt in Abhängigkeit von den Anwendungen die Effizienz dieser Abbildung. Ende-zu-Ende-Datenströme von Echtzeitanwendungen lassen sich sehr gut auf solche Kanäle abbilden. Die Einführung der Kanäle erlaubt eine Reduktion

---

[7] Die Übertragungszeit wurde hier vernachlässigt.

des notwendigen Wissens über das Netzwerk und die Parameter der Ende-zu-Ende-Datenströme auf eine kleine Anzahl von Dienstbeschreibungen und die Auslastung der über einen Knoten laufenden Kanäle. Die Effizienz unseres Modells ist abhängig von der maximalen Pfadlänge des Netzwerkes und der Auslastung. Für eine maximale Ausdehnung von 10 Knoten erreichen wir eine Effizienz die mit anderen Ansätzen vergleichbar ist. Die Reichweitenbegrenzung kann teilweise aufgehoben werden, wenn an den Übergängen zu benachbarten Netzen eine Verknüpfung mit geeigneten Mechanismen zur Verkehrsanpassung vorgenommen wird.

In folgenden Arbeiten sollte die Implementierung des Modells für reale Netze durchgeführt werden. Hier erscheint insbesondere die Beobachtung des mittleren und maximalen Burstverhaltens realer Ende-zu-Ende-Datenströme interessant. Weiterhin ist die Eignung des Modells für adaptive Datenströme mit relativ großen maximalen Verweilzeiten (z.B. 200ms) zu untersuchen. Interessant ist zudem, ob eine Überbuchung des Dienstes bis zu einem gewissen Grad ohne Auswirkungen auf die maximale Verweilzeit bleibt. Nicht zuletzt bietet unser Modell eine deutliche Reduktion der zur Zugangskontrolle benötigten Statusinformationen. Daraus ergeben sich Möglichkeiten zur Vereinfachung existierender Reservierungsprotokolle, die zu untersuchen sind.

Literatur

1. R. Guérin, V. Peris, *Quality-of-service in packet networks: basic mechanisms and directions*, IEEE Journal on Computer Networks 31 (1999) 169-189
2. A. Charny, J.-Y. Le Boudec *Delay Bounds in a Network With Aggregate Scheduling*, Proceedings of Quality of Future Internet Services (QofIS 2000), Berlin, Sept. 2000
3. J-Y. Le Boudec, P. Thiran, *NETWORK CALCULUS: A Theorie of Deterministic Queueing Systems for the Internet*, Springer Verlag, LNCS 2050, 2001
4. M. Andrews, *Instability of fifo in session-oriented networks*, Proceedings of the Eleventh Annual ACM-SIAM Symposium on Discrete Algorithms, 2000
5. Steven Berson, *Aggregation of Internet Integrated Services State*, Proceedings of the 7th IEEE/IFIP International Workshop on Quality of Service (IWQoS'99), London, 1999
6. J.-A. Müller, *Deterministische Dienste für IP-Telefonie auf Basis von DiffServ*, 2. MMB-Arbeitsgespräch, Hamburg, Sept. 2002
7. S. Blake, D. Black, M. Carlson, E. Davies, Z. Wang, W. Weiss, *An Architecture for Differentiated Services*, RFC 2474, Dec. 1998
8. J. Micheel, I. Graham and S. Donnelly *Precision Timestamping of Network Packets* Proceedings of the ACM SIGCOMM Internet Measurement Workshop, San Francisco, Nov. 2001
9. J. Schmitt, M. Karsten, L. Wolf, R. Steinmetz *Aggregation of Guaranteed Service Flows*, Proceedings of the 7th IEEE/IFIP International Workshop on Quality of Service (IWQoS'99), London, UK
10. J. Schmitt, O. Heckmann, K. Pandit, M. Hoffmann, M. Jobmann *LETSQoS Milestone 1* Technischer Bericht der TU-Darmstadt, Darmstadt, Jun. 2002
11. K. Fall and K. Varadhan (editors) *ns Notes and Documentation* The VINT Project, UC Berkeley, LBL, USC/ISI, and Xerox PARC, Apr. 2002, http://www.isi.edu/nsnam/ns/
12. CISCO TechNotes, *Voice Over IP - Per Call Bandwidth Consumption*, http://www.cisco.com/warp/public/788/pkt-voice-general/bwidth_consume.html

Session Verteilte Systeme

Modellierung und Zusicherung nicht-funktionaler Eigenschaften bei Entwurf, Implementierung und zur Laufzeit verteilter Anwendungen

Torben Weis, Andreas Ulbrich und Kurt Geihs

TU Berlin, Fakultät für Elektrotechnik und Informatik, Intelligente Netze und Management verteilter Systeme, Einsteinufer 17, 10587 Berlin
{weis,ulbi,geihs}@ivs.tu-berlin.de

Zusammenfassung Wir stellen einen Software-Entwicklungsprozess für komponenten-basierte verteilte Anwendungen vor, der Mehrkategorie-Dienstgüte während des Designs, der Implementierung und zur Laufzeit berücksichtigt. Für das Design haben wir die UML um Konzepte zur Dienstgüte-Modellierung erweitert. Das Modell wird für die Implementierung weitgehend automatisch auf unser .NET Remoting-basiertes Dienstgüte-Rahmenwerk abgebildet. Zur Laufzeit unterstützt das Rahmenwerk die Erbringung und Überwachung der Dienstgüte. Desweiteren unterstützt unser Prozess eine mehrstufige Abbildung von anwendungsspezifischen Dienstgüten auf Betriebsmittel, um für eine konkrete Dienstgüte die nötigen Betriebsmittel zu bestimmen.

1 Einleitung

Ziel unserer Arbeit ist die Entwicklung eines Software-Entwicklungsprozesses und den dazugehörigen Werkzeugen samt Rahmenwerk, welche die Zusicherung und Erbringung nicht-funktionaler Eigenschaften durchgehend, das heißt vom Entwurf, über die Implementierung bis hin zum praktischen Einsatz und der Laufzeit einer verteilten Anwendung, unterstützen. Dabei sind in erster Linie die möglichst einfache Anwendung durch den Softwareentwickler und die saubere Trennung funktionaler und nicht-funktionaler Aspekte von Interesse. Angestrebt wird außerdem eine durchgehende Unterstützung von Mehrkategorie-Dienstgüten, d.h. die gleichzeitige Unterstützung mehrerer unterschiedlicher Dienstgüte-Kategorien.

Unser Entwicklungsprozess beruht auf der komponenten-basierten Software Entwicklung (component based software engineering, oder kurz CBSE). Der wesentliche Vorteil im Vergleich zum klassischen objekt-orientierten Design ist, dass Komponenten nicht nur Schnittstellen anbieten, sondern auch explizit darstellen, welche Schnittstellen sie benötigen. Daher kann man modellieren, welche Dienste und Dienstgüten eine Komponente anbietet und welche sie ihrerseits in Anspruch

---
* Die hier vorgestellte Arbeit wird unterstützt durch das europäische QCCS-Projekt www.qccs.org, IST-1999-20122, das DFG-Projekt GE 776/4 und das Discourse-Projekt www.discourse.de

nehmen wird. Eine Verbindung (connector) zwischen zwei Komponenten (beziehungsweise zwischen den Ports zweier Komponenten) ist dementsprechend nur dann erlaubt, wenn der angebotene (provided) Port mindestens die Schnittstelle und Dienstgüte zur Verfügung stellt, die der konsumierende (required) Port fordert. Insbesondere kann man auch modellieren, dass angebotene Dienstgüten davon abhängen, welche Dienstgüten die Umgebung zur Verfügung stellt. Im Endeffekt erhält man so ein Design, das angebotene und benötigte Dienstgüten und deren Abhängigkeiten ausdrückt. Das ist wesentlich übersichtlicher, als diese Information jedes Mal aus dem Code zu extrahieren.

Laufzeitumgebungen für Komponenten wie CCM [16], EJB [5] oder auch .NET bilden Komponenten allerdings durch klassische Objekte und Vererbungshierarchien nach. Daher benutzen wir den reinen komponenten-basierten Ansatz zur Modellierung und ein Werkzeug, das ein Modell automatisch in die entsprechende Klassenstruktur umwandelt.

2 Beispiel

Wir benutzen nachfolgend beschriebenes Beispiel zur Illustration unseres Ansatzes. Eine Komponente zur wiederholten Suche von komplexen Formen in Bilddaten stellt zwei Ports (provided ports) zur Verfügung. Die Schnittstelle des ersten Ports (Such-Port) bietet eine Methode zum Finden einer bestimmten Form in einem Bild. Sie erhält die Bilddaten als Eingabe und liefert Größe, Ausrichtung und Position der gesuchten Form als Ergebnis. Die Schnittstelle des zweiten Ports (Konfigurations-Port) erlaubt es, die gesuchte Form mit Hilfe von Vektordaten zu konfigurieren.

Für den Such-Ports sind Genauigkeit und Durchsatz als Dienstgüten definiert. Die Umsetzung des Durchsatzes durch den Dienstgütemechanismus soll durch Lastverteilung auf mehrere Bediener erfolgen. Dabei existieren verschiedene Bediener für die unterschiedlichen Genauigkeiten der Suche. Die nichtfunktionale Eigenschaft des Konfigurations-Ports ist Zugriffskontrolle. Die dazu notwendige Authentifikation kann durch Nutzername und Passwort bzw. Zertifikate erfolgen. Der Dienstgütemechanismus benutzt zur Zugriffskontrolle dementsprechende Authentifikationsverfahren.

In diesem Beispiel wird davon ausgegangen, dass die Berechnung im Vergleich zur Kodierung und Übertragung der Bilddaten sehr komplex ist. Deshalb sollen Kodierungszeit und Bandbreite hier nicht betrachtet werden, um das Beispiel kompakt zu halten.

3 Dienstgüte-Modellierung

Im Folgenden stellen wir unser Meta-Modell zur Dienstgüte-Modellierung vor. Die von uns genutzten Begriffe Modell, Meta-Modell und die Meta-Ebenen M0, M1, M2 entsprechen den Definition der UML (Unified Modelling Language) [17].

Abb. 1 zeigt den Teil des Meta-Modells, der die Konzepte zur Modellierung von Dienstgüte-Kategorien enthält. Solche Kategorien sind zum Beispiel

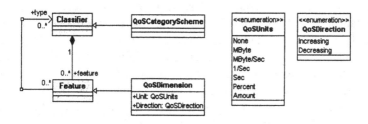

Abb. 1. Meta-Modell für Dienstgüte Kategorien

Verfügbarkeit, Antwortzeit oder Durchsatz. Allerdings kann man eine Kategorie nur bedingt modellieren, denn Semantik lässt sich nur schwer in Modellen erfassen. Daher modellieren wir die Dimensionen der Kategorie. Um klar zu machen, dass eine Aggregation von Dimensionen wegen der fehlenden Semantik eine Kategorie nicht vollständig beschreibt, haben wir die entsprechende Meta-Klasse QoSCategoryScheme genannt (Dienstgüte-Kategorieschema).

Dem Meta-Modell ist zu entnehmen, dass das Verhältnis zwischen einem QoSCategoryScheme und seinen aggregierten QoSDimensions dem Verhältnis zwischen einem Classifier und seinen Attributen ähnelt. Letztgenannte Meta-Klassen haben wir aus der UML Spezifikation [17] übernommen. Eine QoSDimension hat zwei Felder. Zum einen die QoSDirection, welche angibt, ob größere oder kleinere Werte besser sind. Das Feld Unit hingegen gibt die physikalische Maßeinheit für die Dimension an. Da QoSCategoryScheme von Classifier abgeleitet ist, kann man ein solches Schema zur Laufzeit auch instanziieren.

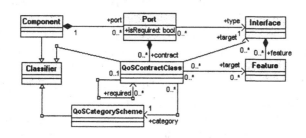

Abb. 2. Meta-Modell für Komponenten mit Dienstgüte

Abb. 2 zeigt das Meta-Modell für Komponenten. Gemäß des Meta-Modells des aktuellen UML2-Entwurfs [21] kommuniziert eine Komponente mit ihrer Umgebung mittels Ports. Jedem Port ist genau eine Schnittstelle zugeordnet. Das Attribut isRequired bestimmt, ob ein Port angeboten wird oder ob es ein Port ist, der die Dienste einer anderen Komponente konsumiert.

Es soll möglich sein, dass an einem Port mehrere Vereinbarungen über nichtfunktionale Eigenschaften existieren. Beispielsweise kann die Kommunikation über den gesamten Port verschlüsselt sein, aber für die Antwortzeit einer besonderen Methode gilt zudem eine spezielle obere Schranke. An einen Port kann man daher mehrere Kontrakte binden. Das Konzept von Kontrakten wird durch die Meta-Klasse `QoSContractClass` eingeführt. Gemäß dem alltäglichen Verständnis des Wortes Kontrakt muss ein solcher festlegen, wer die Vertrags-Parteien sind, was Vertrags-Gegenstand ist und was die Vertrags-Bedingungen sind. Der Vertrags-Gegenstand ist entweder die gesamte Schnittstelle des Ports oder ausgewählte `Features`. Ein solches `Feature` [17] ist entweder eine Methode oder ein Attribut. Die Vertrags-Bedingungen werden durch ein assoziiertes `QoSCategoryScheme` festgelegt. Die Vertrags-Parteien sind die zwei Komponenten, deren `Ports` durch einen Connector (die gestrichelten Linien in Abb. 3 und 4) verbunden sind.

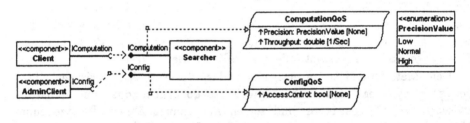

Abb. 3. Modell für das Beispiel

Meta-Modelle sind nötig, um die zur Verfügung stehenden Konzepte präzise zu formulieren. Der Anwender hingegen will sich damit nicht abgeben müssen. Daher nimmt ein UML-Tool ihm dies ab. Der Anwender konstruiert ein Modell (M1). Jedes Element eines solchen Modells ist Instanz einer Meta-Klasse (M2). Die Art der graphischen Notation drückt dabei für jedes Element die zu Grunde liegende Meta-Klasse aus. Ein Kategorieschema zeichnen wir beispielsweise mit geschwungenen Seitenrändern und die Dimensionen stehen unter dem Kategorienamen. Dementsprechend haben wir die Notation für Komponenten, wie sie im UML2-Entwurf vorgesehen ist, in unser UML-Tool *Kase* [12] eingebaut und es um Notationen für die neuen Meta-Klassen erweitert.

Abb. 3 zeigt die Komponenten unseres Beispiels. Die `Searcher` Komponente stellt ihre Dienste mittels zweier Ports zwei anderen Komponenten zur Verfügung. Um Platz zu sparen haben wir die Definition der jeweiligen Schnittstellen ausgelassen. Der gestrichelte Pfeil zwischen dem Port und dem Dienstgüte-Kategorieschema zeigt an, dass der jeweilige Port einen Vertrag anbietet, der für die gesamte Schnittstelle gilt. Jedes Dienstgüte-Kategorieschema zeigt den Namen der Dienstgüte und die einzelnen Dimensionen. Der Pfeil vor jeder Dimension zeigt an, ob größere oder kleinere Werte besser sind. Jede Dimension hat außerdem einen Typ, der hinter dem Doppelpunkt steht. Die physikalische Maßeinheit steht in eckigen Klammern dahinter.

In unserem Beispiel realisiert der `Searcher` seine Dienstgüte-Kategorie, indem er mehrere Instanzen seiner Bediener einsetzt und darauf Load-Balancing

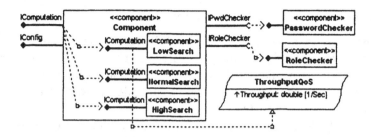

Abb. 4. Verfeinerung des Beispiels

betreibt. Abb. 4 zeigt eine Verfeinerung des Modells aus Abb. 3. Das Diagramm enthält drei Versionen von Bedienern, jeweils eine für die geforderte Suchgenauigkeit. Jede dieser Versionen arbeitet intern mit einem anderen Such-Algorithmus. Die Bediener offerieren für ihre Schnittstellen ihrerseits einen Dienstgüte-Vertrag, der einen gewissen Durchsatz garantiert. Die Idee dabei ist, dass der Searcher die geforderten Durchsatzraten liefert, indem er geeignet viele Bediener allokiert, die ihrerseits nur einen schwächeren Durchsatz bieten. Diese Abbildung von einer Dienstgüte-Kategorie auf andere ist ein zentraler Bestandteil unseres Ansatzes. Dieses Konzept ist nicht nur im Design nützlich, um schrittweise Verfeinerungen des Designs durchzuführen. Dieses Konzept findet sich auch in unserem Rahmenwerk - also auf Implementationsebene - bei der Vertragsaushandlung und der Betriebsmittelallokation wieder.

Die geforderte Präzision bei der Suche (Dimension Precision) wird realisiert, indem der Searcher auf den richtigen Bediener zurückgreift. Um die Zugriffsrechte auf das IConfig Interface regeln zu können, benötigt die Komponente einen PasswordChecker und einen RoleChecker. Hier existiert demnach eine weitere Abhängigkeit zwischen Kontrakten. Um den Kontrakt ConfigQoS erfüllen zu können, müssen zwei andere (rein funktionale) Kontrakte erfüllt sein. In diesem Fall müssen die geeigneten Checker-Komponenten existieren. Ein rein funktionaler Kontrakt ist ein Spezialfall, bei dem das Kategorieschema leer ist, daher hat er auch keine explizite visuelle Repräsentation im Diagramm.

4 Dienstgüte-Spezifikation im Rahmenwerk

Unser Dienstgüte-Rahmenwerk basiert auf dem Remoting-Framework von Microsoft .NET. Die modulare Architektur dieses Frameworks sowie verschiedene Merkmale des Common Type Systems [7] und der Programmiersprache C# [6], speziell Reflexion und der Umgang mit Meta-Information, erleichtern die Implementierung eines Dienstgüte-Rahmenwerkes. Die gezeigten Prinzipien lassen sich in abgewandelter Form aber auch auf andere Middleware-Architekturen, z.B. CORBA, übertragen. Einige Grundtechniken wurden aus MAQS [2] übernommen, das auf dem freien ORB MICO [15] basiert.

4.1 Spezifikation von Kategorieschemata

Um Dienstgütemechanismen generisch in Middleware-Architekturen integrieren zu können, ist es notwendig, Dienstgüte-Kategorieschemata und deren Instanzen spezifizieren bzw. darstellen zu können. Existierende Ansätze erweitern dazu Schnittstellenbeschreibungssprachen (QIDL [1]) oder entwickeln entsprechende Beschreibungssprachen neu (QML [8]).

Beim Einsatz des .NET Frameworks zusammen mit der Programmiersprache C# sind solche Erweiterungen nicht notwendig. Vielmehr können durch so genannte Custom Attributes [7] Klassen, Methoden und Felder dekoriert werden. Innerhalb unseres Rahmenwerkes werden Schemata durch Klassen modelliert. Kategorieparameter sind demzufolge eine Instanz dieser Klasse. Kategoriedimensionen sind Properties [6] eines einfachen Datentyps, die mit einem speziellen Attribut dekoriert wurden. Dieses Attribut spezifiziert dabei auch Richtung und Maßeinheit. Nachfolgend sind die beiden Schemata für das Beispiel aufgeführt.

```
public class ComputationQoS : QoSCategorySchemeBase {
    public enum PrecisionValue { Low, Normal, High }
    [QoSDimension]
    public PrecisionValue Precision { get {...} set {...}}
    [QoSDimension(QoSDirection.Increasing, QoSUnit.PerSec)]
    public double Throughput { get {...} set {...}}
}
public class ConfigQoS : QoSCategorySchemeBase {
    public enum AuthenticationKind { Password, Certificate }
    [QoSDimension]
    public AuthenticationKind AccessControl { get {...} set {...}}
}
```

Die Ausdruckskraft dieser Art der Spezifikation von Dienstgüte-Kategorieschemata entspricht in etwa der von QIDL bzw. QML.

4.2 Bindung von Kategorieschemata an Schnittstellen und Klassen

Neben der Spezifikation von QoS-Kategorieschemata muss es auch möglich sein zu deklarieren, welche Dienstgüte eine Komponente erbringen kann. Wie bereits in Abschnitt 1 erwähnt, werden Komponenten durch eine Hierarchie von Klassen und Schnittstellen implementiert. Deshalb ist es nötig, Kategorieschemata an Klassen und Schnittstellen zu binden. Auch dazu werden Attribute benutzt.

```
[QoSContractClass(typeof(ComputationQoS))]
public interface IComputation {
    void search(double[,] image, out Coords[] position,
        out double[] orientation, out double[] size);
}
[QoSContractClass(typeof(ConfigQoS))]
public interface IConfig {
```

```
    void SetShape(Shape s);
    Shape GetShape();
}
```

Das Beispiel zeigt die Bindung des Dienstgüte-Kategorieschemas ComputationQoS an die Schnittstelle IComputation, die den Such-Port der Komponente definiert. Das Schema ConfigQoS wird an die Schnittstelle IConfig gebunden.

Die Bindung eines Dienstgüte-Kategorieschemas an eine Klasse oder Schnittstelle stellt eine Kontraktklasse im Sinne des M1 Modells dar. Es sei ausdrücklich darauf hingewiesen, dass das Binden von Kategorieschemata an Schnittstellen- und Klassendefinitionen nichts über den eingesetzten Dienstgütemechanismus aussagt. Es ist Aufgabe des Entwicklers, einen Dienstgüte-Mechanismus festzulegen. Der Mechanismus wird vom Rahmenwerk zur Laufzeit zu aktiviert und umgesetzt (siehe Abschnitt 5). Durch das Binden mehrerer Kategorieschemata an eine Schnittstellen- oder Klassendeklaration kann die Unterstützung von Mehrkategorie-Dienstgüten einfach modelliert werden.

5 Dienstgüte-Erbringung zur Laufzeit

Ein Dienstgüte-Mechanismus setzt den Dienstgüte-Kontrakt zwischen Komponenten zur Laufzeit um. Die Umsetzung wird erreicht, indem der Dienstgüte-Mechanismus die für die Erfüllung eines Vertrages notwendigen Betriebsmittel allokiert und entsprechend nutzt.

5.1 Komponenten und Betriebsmittel

Wir benutzen die Begriffe Betriebsmittel, Dienst eines Betriebsmittels, logische und virtuelle Betriebsmittel entsprechend der einschlägigen Literatur [13].

Neben ihren funktionalen Eigenschaften, dem Dienst des Betriebsmittels, besitzen Betriebsmittel auch nicht-funktionale Eigenschaften, die die Dienstgüte angeben, welche das Betriebsmittel in der Lage ist zu leisten. Die Allokation eines Betriebsmittels entspricht dabei dem Abschluss eines Dienstgütevertrages mit dem Betriebsmittel. In unserem Rahmenwerk werden die Betriebsmitteltypen daher als Komponenten mit Dienstgütezusicherung dargestellt. Umgekehrt kann jede Komponente als spezielles Betriebsmittel aufgefasst werden.

Ein Nachrichtenkanal hat als Dienstgüte zum Beispiel Bandbreite und Verzögerung mit der Informationen übertragen werden. Die Funktionen dieses Betriebsmittels das Senden und Empfangen von Nachrichten.

5.2 Dekomposition von Dienstgütemechanismen

Um die für die Erfüllung eines speziellen Dienstgüte-Kontraktes notwendigen Betriebsmittel-Allokationen bestimmen zu können ist es nötig, die vom

Dienstgütemechanismus durchgeführte Dekomposition der Komponente in andere Komponenten mit anderen Dienstgütezusicherungen zu kennen. Die Dekomposition einer Komponente in andere Komponenten kann rekursiv fortgeführt werden. Für die Betrachtung der Dienstgüte kann die Dekompostion spätestens dann abgebrochen werden, wenn die Komponenten keine Dienstgüte-Zusicherungen mehr machen.

Diese Dekomposition kann im Model M1 beschrieben werden. Abb. 4 zeigt dies für die Beispielkomponente und den in Abschnitt 2 beschriebenen Dienstgütemechanismus. So benutzt die Searcher-Komponente zur Laufzeit je nach zugesicherter Genauigkeit mehrere Bediener, Instanzen einer der Komponenten LowSearch, NormalSearch bzw. HighSearch, wobei zur Laufzeit ein Bediener mittels eines Lastverteilungsverfahrens ausgewählt wird. Der von dem Bediener zu erbringende Durchsatz wird mit einem Kontrakt, der die ThroughputQoS-Kategorie enthält, vereinbart. Die Abhängigkeiten dieser ThroughputQoS-Zusicherung von konkreten ComputationQoS-Parametern sind dabei vom Dienstgüte-Entwickler zu implementieren. Damit ist es dem Betriebsmittelsteuerungs-Rahmenwerk möglich, verschiedene Bediener für die Erfüllung des Kontrakts zu allokieren.

Ein Bediener selbst kann wiederum in andere Komponenten zerlegt werden. Für die Zusicherung eines bestimmten Durchsatzes ist zum Beispiel ein Thread mit einer bestimmten Priorität - die Dienstgüte des Threads - notwendig. Dabei muss sichergestellt werden, dass eine bestimmte Anzahl von Threads nicht überschritten wird, damit jeder Thread die für den zugesicherten Durchsatz notwendige Rechenzeit erhält. Die Allokation eines Bedieners schlägt fehl, wenn die maximale Anzahl der Threads überschritten wird.

Analog erfolgt die Umsetzung der Zugriffskontrolle durch Allokierung der Komponenten PasswordChecker und RoleChecker. Allerdings handelt es sich dabei lediglich um eine Instanziierung der entsprechenden Objekte, da diese Komponenten keine Dienstgüte erbringen müssen. Die entsprechenden Komponenten beim Einsatz von Zertifikaten sind nicht dargestellt.

In unserem konkreten Dienstgüte-Rahmenwerk ist außerdem die Allokation einiger weiterer Betriebsmittel notwendig, die aber wiederum selbst keine Dienstgüte erbringen müssen. So ist z.B. in der Client-Komponente ein Lastverteiler zu instanziieren. Er wird mit den allokierten Bedienern konfiguriert. Diese Konfiguration kann von der Betriebsmittelsteuerung nach erfolgter Allokation vorgenommen werden. Das Betriebsmittelsteuerungs-Rahmenwerk basiert auf dem bereits in MAQS vorhandenen. Übernommen wurden dabei weitgehend die Konzepte für die Betriebsmittelverwaltung, also das Ein-und Austragen von Betriebsmitteln und deren Zuordnung zu Dienstgüte-Kontrakt. Die Betriebsmittelvergabe wurde so reimplementiert, dass Betriebsmittel auf Basis einer Dienstgüte-Zusicherung reserviert werden können.

5.3 Integration von Dienstgüte in .NET Remoting

Das .NET Remoting Framework [20] ist Bestandteil des .NET Rahmenwerks von Microsoft und bildet dessen objekt-orientierte Verteilungs-Plattform. Die

Funktionalität dieser Middleware ist in etwa mit der von CORBA vergleichbar, wobei .NET Remoting über einige zusätzliche Leistungsmerkmale verfügt. Eine Besonderheit von .NET Remoting ist allerdings die modulare Architektur der Middleware und deren Konfigurierbarkeit. Abb. 5 (links) zeigt den allgemeinen Aufbau des Remoting-Nachrichtenpfades durch weitgehend austauschbare Komponenten (im Bild grau). Zum Transport einer Nachricht vom Proxy (Transparent- und RealProxy) eines entfernten Objektes zum StackBuilder* wird ein Kanal (Channel) genutzt. Eine Nachricht kann auf ihrem Pfad durch so genannte Sinks verändert werden bzw. weitere Aktionen auslösen. Dabei wird zwischen kanalspezifischen (im Bild unterhalb der Trennlinie) und nicht-kanalspezifischen Sinks unterschieden. Damit existieren sowohl client- als auch server-seitige Sink Chains die von einer Nachricht durchwandert werden. Durch das Einfügen neuer Sinks bzw. den Austausch existierender Sinks kann das Remoting Framework an die eigenen Bedürfnisse angepasst werden.

Insbesondere bietet sich diese modulare und konfigurierbare Architektur aber an, um damit Dientsgüte-Mechanismen zu implementieren und in Remoting zu integrieren. Die Remoting-Architektur kann damit auch als konsequente Fortführung und Generalisierung des in MAQS eingesetzten Mediator-Konzeptes verstanden werden.

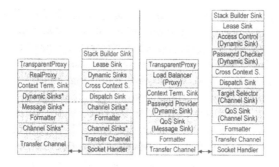

Abb. 5. originaler (l.) und angepasster (r.) Nachrichtenpfad

Durch den Austausch des Real Proxy kann direkt in die Nachrichtenerzeugung und Nachrichtenemission eingegriffen werden. Damit ist es zum Beispiel möglich, je nach geforderter Dienstgüte den für die Übertragung am Besten geeigneten Kanal auszuwählen. In einer client-seitigen Dynamic Sink können einer Nachricht je nach Kontext weitere Informationen, z.B. Nutzerdaten für die Authentifizierung, hinzugefügt werden.

Die client-seitigen Message Sinks bearbeiten Nachrichten vor ihrer Formatierung. Message Sinks können auch die Weiterverarbeitung einer Nachricht

---

* Der StackBuilder entspricht in seiner Funktionalität dem Skeleton in CORBA ist aber vollständig generisch.

beeinflussen oder weitere Nachrichten erzeugen. Der Formatter setzt ein spezifisches Nachrichtenprotokoll (z.B. SOAP) um. Auch dieses kann entsprechend den Anforderungen an die Dienstgüte ausgetauscht werden. Nach der Formatierung findet eine weitere Bearbeitung der Nachricht in den client-seitigen Channel Sinks statt. Damit lassen sich unter anderem Ver- und Entschlüsselungsmechanismen oder Komprimierungs- und Dekomprimierungsverfahren in den Nachrichtenpfad integrieren. In der server-seitigen Sink Chain finden sich die Gegenstücke zu den Sinks in der Client Sink Chain. Auch hier kann von Verschlüsselung in den Channel Sinks bis hin zur Zugriffskontrolle in einer Dynamic Sink beliebig in die Nachrichtenverarbeitung eingegriffen werden. In Abb. 5 (rechts) sind die Anpassungen (im Bild grau) der Remoting-Architektur für den Dienstgütemechanismus der Beispielkomponente dargestellt. Ein angepasster Proxy (Load Balancer) übernimmt die Lastverteilung und benutzt für jeden Aufruf den Channel, der zum ausgewählten Bediener führt. Der Password Provider fügt Nutzername und Passwort in die Nachricht ein. Im Server werden diese Information vom Password Checker überprüft. Tritt hier ein Fehler auf, wird eine Exception-Nachricht an den Client zurückgesandt. Ähnlich arbeitet die Sink für Access Control. Entsprechend des ausgehandelten Dienstgüte-Niveaus für die Suchgenauigkeit wählt der Target Selector eine Instanz LowSearch, NormalSearch oder HighSearch aus. Dazu wird lediglich die Ziel-URI der Nachricht überschrieben.

Zusätzlich dazu gibt es sowohl auf Client- als auch auf Server-Seite eine generische QoS Sink, die Teil unseres Rahmenwerkes ist. Hier werden Informationen über den Dienstgüte-Kontrakt in die Nachricht integriert bzw. ausgewertet. So muss die QoS Sink im Server jede Nachricht zuverlässig einem ausgehandeltem Kontrakt zuordnen bzw. die Vertragsverhandlung anstoßen. Dazu ermittelt die Sink per Reflexion, die von der Zielkomponente unterstützte Dienstgüte-Kategorie und initiiert die Reservierung der Betriebsmittel durch die Betriebsmittelsteuerung. Schlägt diese fehl, kommt der vom Client gewünschte Vertrag nicht zustande. Anderenfalls liefert die server-seitige QoS Sink Informationen über allokierte Betriebsmittel (z.B. die Bediener) an die QoS Sink im Client. Damit kann dann unter anderem der Lastverteiler konfiguriert werden.

6 Verwandte Arbeiten

Die OMG schlägt die MDA (Model Driven Architecture) [3] vor, um den Übergang von plattformunabhängigen Modellen (PIM) hin zu plattformabhängigen (PSM) Modellen und schließlich einer Implementierung zu machen. Zentraler Punkt dabei ist, dass Werkzeuge den Übergang weitestgehend automatisieren sollen. Die OMG beschreibt die MDA in [19] als eine Erweiterung der OMA (Object Management Architecture), zu deren Referenzmodell auch CORBA gehört. Unser Ansatz verfolgt ähnliche Prinzipien wie die MDA. Die Komponenten-Diagramme können als PIM und die Realisierung auf Basis unseres Rahmenwerks als PSM angesehen werden.

Neben unserem Vorschlag für die QoS-Integration in die UML [22] existieren
weitere Vorschläge [10] [11]. Die Meta-Modell Erweiterung von [11] umfasst etwa 20 neue Klassen. Wir haben hingegen versucht, die Änderungen an der UML
möglichst klein zu halten, um anstatt einer Meta-Modell Erweiterung später
ein reines UML-Profil anbieten zu können. Weder [10] noch [11] nutzt die neu-
en Konzepte zur Modellierung von Komponenten wie sie der aktuelle UML2-
Entwurf [21] bietet. Die OMG hat einen RfP zum Thema "UML Profile for
Modeling QoS and FT Characteristics and Mechanisms RFP" [18] herausgege-
ben. Zur Zeit liegt aber noch keine Initial Submission vor.

In [4] beschreiben Duran-Limon und Blair die Dekomposition von Betriebsmitteln, ohne dabei die Abhängigkeiten der Dienstgüte-Zusicherung zu betrachten. Zur Rekonfiguration der Anwendung bei wechselnder Betriebsmittel-
verfügbarkeit wird eine Beschreibungssprache eingeführt, die feste Dienstgüte-
Niveaus auf Betriebsmittel abbildet. Diese Arbeit basiert auf OpenORB [9],
einem rekonfigurierbaren Object Request Broker. Der ORB wurde um Reflexi-
onsmechanismen, sogenannte MetaSpaces [14], erweitert. Die in .NET vorhanden
Reflexionsfunktionalität und dessen Custom Attributes machen MetaSpaces zu-
mindest für Dienstgütespezifikation und Rekonfiguration überflüssig.

7 Zusammenfassung und Ausblick

Wir haben gezeigt, wie Dienstgüte bei der Modellierung, Implementierung
und Laufzeit einer verteilten Anwendung durchgehend und zusammenhängend
betrachtet werden kann. Dazu haben wir die UML durch eine Metamodell-
Erweiterung um Konzepte zur Dienstgüte-Modellierung erweitert. Insbesondere erlaubt unsere UML-Erweiterung, auch die nicht-funktionalen Eigenschaften
der Ports von Komponenten zu beschreiben. Durch Verfeinerung der Modelle
kann die Dekomposition komplexer Dienstgüte-Kategorien in einfachere Kategorien bzw. Betriebsmittel modelliert werden. Unsere Modelle lassen sich durch
ein Tool auf ein geeignetes Rahmenwerk abbilden. Unser auf MAQS basieren-
des Rahmenwerk unterstützt die Spezifikation, Laufzeitrepräsentation sowie die
Allokation von Betriebsmitteln auf Basis von Dienstgüte-Verträgen.

Der hier vorgestellte Entwicklungsprozess und das Dienstgüte-Rahmenwerk
führen Entwurf und Implementierung verteilter Anwendungen zusammen. Sie
sind damit die logische Ergänzung und Weiterentwicklung der Management Architecture for Quality of Service (MAQS). Geplant ist die Erweiterung unseres
Entwicklungsprozesses und der dazugehörenden Werkzeuge um weitere Elemen-
te. Zur Zeit ist die Vertragsaushandlung noch optional. In einigen Anwendungsszenarien kann es aber notwendig sein, ein Mindestdienstgüteniveau für alle Interaktionen mit einem Port zu erzwingen. Dazu ist es notwendig, diese Konzepte
sowohl bei der Modellierung als auch im Rahmenwerk zu berücksichtigen.

Außerdem werden wir die in MAQS vorhandenen Aushandlungsmechanis-
men in unser .NET basiertes Rahmenwerk integrieren und entsprechenden Code
zu deren Steuerung bei der Generierung aus dem Modell erzeugen. Neben der
einmaligen Aushandlung eines Vertrages muss sich bei wechselnder Betriebs-

mittelverfügbarkeit das System, wenn möglich, selbständig adaptieren oder eine
Neuverhandlung anstoßen.

Literatur

1. C. Becker and K. Geihs. Generic QoS Specification for CORBA. In *Proceedings of KiVS'99*, Mar. 1999.
2. C. Becker and K. Geihs. Generic QoS-Support for CORBA. In *Proceedings of ISCC'00*, Antibes, France, July 2000.
3. D. Dsouza. Model-Driven Architecture and Integration, http://www.omg.org/mda/presentations.htm, 2002.
4. H. A. Duran-Limon and G. S. Blair. The Importance of Resource Management in Engineering Distributed Objects. *Lecture Notes in Computer Science*, 1999:44–60, 2001.
5. B. S. (editor). Java 2 Platform - Enterprise Edition Specification, v1.3. Technical Report 7/27/01, Sun Microsystems, Inc., 2001.
6. European Computer Manufacturers Association. C# Language Specification. Technical Report 334, ECMA, Genf, Schweiz, 2001.
7. European Computer Manufacturers Association. Common Language Infrastructure. Technical Report 335, ECMA, Genf, Schweiz, 2001.
8. S. Frolund and J. Koistinen. Quality-of-Service Specification in Distributed Object Systems. *IOP/BCS Distributed Systems Engineering Journal*, Dec. 1998.
9. G. S. Blair and G. Coulson and A. Andersen, L. Blair and M. Clarke and F. Costa and H. Duran-Limon and T. Fitzpatrick and L. Johnston, R. Moraira and N. Parlavantzas and K. Saikoski. The Design and Implementation of Open ORB 2. *Distributed Systems online*, Vol. 2, No. 6, Sept. 2001.
10. J. Aagedal and E. Ecklund. Modelling QoS: Towards a UML Profile. In *UML 2002*, volume 2460, pages 275–289. Springer, Oct. 2002.
11. Juan I. Asensio and Víctor A. Villagrá and Jorge E. López de Vergara and Julio Berrocal. UML Profiles for the Specification and Instrumentation of QoS Management Information in Distributed Object-based Applications, 2001.
12. J.-M. Jézéquel, N. Plouzeau, T. Weis, and K. Geihs. From Contracts to Aspects in UML Designs. In *AOSD Workshop on Aspect-Oriented Modeling with UML http://lglwww.epfl.ch/workshops/aosd-uml/Allsubs/jean.pdf*, Enschede, The Netherlands, Apr. 2002.
13. W. Kalfa. *Betriebssysteme*. Akademie Verlag Berlin, 1988.
14. F. Kon, F. Costa, G. S. Blair, and R. H. Campbell. The Case for Reflective Middleware. In *Communications of the ACM* [9], pages 33–38.
15. MICO Team. MICO is CORBA, http://www.mico.org.
16. Object Management Group. CCM Specification. Technical Report ptc/01-11-03, OMG, Framingham, MA, 2001.
17. Object Management Group. Unified Modeling Language Specification 1.4. Technical Report 01-09-67, OMG, Framingham, MA, 2001.
18. Object Management Group. UML Profile for Modeling QoS and FT Characteristics and Mechanisms RFP. Technical Report 02-01-07, OMG, Framingham, MA, 2002.
19. OMG. OMA: http://www.omg.org/oma, 2002.
20. I. Rammer. *Advanced .NET Remoting*. Apress, 2002.
21. U2Partners. UML 2.0 Proposal v0.671: http://www.u2-partners.org, 2002.
22. T. Weis, C. Becker, K.Geihs, and N. Plouzeau. A UML Meta-model for Contract Aware Components. *Springer LNCS*, 2185, 2001.

Durchgängige Entwicklung großer verteilter Systeme – Die SILICON-Fallstudie

R. Gotzhein, C. Peper, P. Schaible, J. Thees

Arbeitsgruppe Rechnernetze
Fachbereich Informatik
Universität Kaiserslautern
67663 Kaiserslautern

Kurzfassung

Dieser Beitrag befasst sich mit der durchgängigen Entwicklung großer verteilter Systeme, insbesondere mit der Verfolgbarkeit zwischen Produkten aufeinanderfolgender Entwicklungsphasen. In den einzelnen Phasen kommen wiederverwendungsorientierte Ansätze zur Anwendung, die erstmals in einer umfassenden Fallstudie syntaktisch und semantisch integriert werden. Aufgrund des sehr umfangreichen Materials ist die Darstellung in diesem Beitrag auf die Systemarchitektur der einzelnen Phasen beschränkt.

1 Einleitung

Die ingenieurmäßige Entwicklung großer, qualitativ hochwertiger verteilter Systeme birgt eine Reihe besonderer Schwierigkeiten, wie etwa die Beherrschung der Komplexität, die Durchgängigkeit des Entwicklungsprozesses, die Verfolgbarkeit der Produkte über alle Entwicklungsphasen sowie die Integration unterschiedlicher Beschreibungssprachen und Entwicklungsmethoden. Methoden wie z.B. SOMT [17], SDL+ [15] oder TIMe [5] liefern hier zwar ein gewisses Grundgerüst sowie Richtlinien zur Entwicklung von verteilten Systemen und decken dabei den gesamten Entwicklungsprozess von der Anforderungsanalyse bis zur Implementierung ab. Individuelle Prozessschritte werden jedoch nur sehr grob behandelt, so dass der Nutzen insgesamt hinter den Erwartungen und Möglichkeiten zurückbleibt.

Große Systeme sind heute in der Regel nebenläufig und verteilt. Aus diesem Grund sind Kommunikationssysteme meist zur Realisierung der Anwendungsfunktionalität erforderlich und daher ein integraler Bestandteil großer Systeme. Bedingt durch verschiedenartige Anwendungen und Technologien sind die Anforderungen an Kommunikationssysteme sehr vielfältig, so dass sie nicht immer durch wenige typische, möglichst viele Erfordernisse abdeckende Protokollstapel befriedigt werden können. Daraus ergibt sich ein Bedarf an anwendungsangepassten, maßgeschneiderten Kommunikationssystemen mit exakt abgestimmten Protokollfunktionalitäten.

Zur Reduzierung des durch die Maßschneiderung entstehenden Entwicklungs-
aufwandes untersucht und entwickelt die Arbeitsgruppe Rechnernetze im Rahmen des Sonderforschungsbereichs 501 „Entwicklung großer Systeme mit generischen Methoden" [1] verschiedene Wiederverwendungsansätze. Dabei haben sich
bislang drei neuartige Ansätze herausgebildet: der FoReST-Ansatz zur musterbasierten Anforderungsanalyse [12], der SDL-Pattern-Ansatz zum musterbasierten
Entwurf von verteilten Anwendungen und Kommunikationsprotokollen [7, 9] sowie der komponentenbasierte Ansatz zum Entwurf von Mikroprotokollen [8]. Diese Ansätze verfeinern jeweils eine bestimmte Entwicklungsphase und haben sich
in zahlreichen Fallstudien (z.B. [12, 9, 16, 8]) bewährt. Vor diesem Hintergrund
hatte die Arbeitsgruppe Rechnernetze sich die Aufgabe gestellt, diese Ansätze
syntaktisch und semantisch zu integrieren und dies anhand einer durchgängigen
Fallstudie zu erproben. Für eine erfolgreiche Integration war insbesondere zu
zeigen, dass die Durchgängigkeit des gesamten Entwicklungsprozesses sowie die
Verfolgbarkeit der Produkte über sämtliche Entwicklungsphasen hinweg gegeben
sind.

Dieser Beitrag gibt einen Überblick über die Fallstudie SILICON (System
Development for an Interactive LIght CONtrol), in der eine verteilte Lichtsteuerung für ein Gebäudemodell - ausgehend von der informellen Anforderungsbeschreibung - ingenieurmäßig entwickelt wurde. Die Lösung beinhaltet neben den
Anwendungskomponenten insbesondere die maßgeschneiderte Kommunikations-
middleware, die neue Kommunikationsbasistechnologie UART/TP (Universal
Asynchronous Receiver Transmitter / Token Passing) sowie die erforderliche
Hardware zur Ansteuerung der Sensoren und Aktuatoren. Der Schwerpunkt dieses Beitrags liegt auf der Darstellung der Durchgängigkeit des Entwicklungsprozesses sowie der Verfolgbarkeit der Produkte auf der Ebene der Systemarchitektur. Das Gebäudemodell wurde auf mehreren Industriemessen, darunter die
Embedded Systems 2001 und die CeBIT 2001, ausgestellt.

Die vorgestellte Fallstudie weist eine Reihe von Bezügen zu anderen Arbeiten auf. Ein zentraler Aspekt ist dabei die vertikale Verfolgbarkeit, bei der eine explizite Dokumentation der Relation zwischen den Elementen verschiedener
Abstraktionsebenen gefordert ist [10]. Dieser Gedanke wird in verschiedenen Ver-
feinerungstheorien aufgegriffen [2] und präzisiert. Ein weiterer wichtiger Aspekt
ist die Kombination mehrerer Entwicklungssprachen innerhalb eines Projekts,
wie dies beispielsweise in der UML-Suite [3], der SDL-Suite [15] und in Fusion
[6] der Fall ist. Schließlich sei an dieser Stelle auf eine weitere umfangreiche Fallstudie verwiesen, die dem Nachweis der Praktikabilität formaler Entwicklungs-
ansätze dient [13]. Im Unterschied zu den aufgeführten Arbeiten, die stellvertretend für eine sehr reichhaltige Literatur zu jedem der genannten Aspekte stehen,
stand bei der Fallstudie SILICON die ganzheitliche Systementwicklung im Mit-
telpunkt. Dies erfordert die integrierte Betrachtung aller genannten Aspekte.
Eine Besonderheit der Fallstudie besteht darüberhinaus in der Maßschneiderung
von Systemkomponenten bis hin zu Hardware-Bausteinen und Kommunikationstechnologien.

2 Die SILICON-Fallstudie

2.1 Das Referenzprozessmodell des SFB 501

Zur Steuerung des Gesamtentwicklungsprozesses dient das Referenzprozessmodell des SFB 501 (s. Abb. 1). Dieses Modell ist auf Maßschneiderung ausgelegt, was sich u.a. in den Prozessschritten Kontrollsystem-, Kommunikationssystem-, Betriebssystem- und Hardwareentwicklung äußert. Einige dieser Prozessschritte werden nachfolgend genauer erläutert.

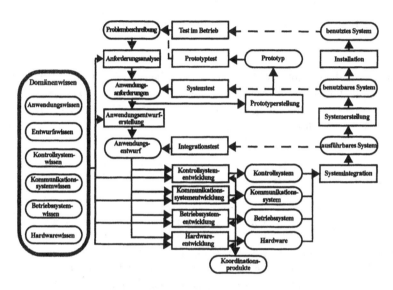

Abbildung 1. Referenzprozessmodell des SFB 501

2.2 Die Problembeschreibung

In der Fallstudie wird ein Ausschnitt eines Gebäudes der Universität Kaiserslautern zugrunde gelegt (s. Abb. 2). Darin sind zwei Büroräume („office") *o415* und *o417* sowie der Flurabschnitt („hallway") *hw2* dargestellt. Die Büroräume verfügen über je zwei Lichtgruppen, die separat über Schalter betätigt werden können. Weiterhin gibt es je zwei Fenster, die sich mit Sonnenblenden einzeln abdunkeln lassen. Bewegungsmelder und Türkontakte ergänzen die Basisinstrumentierung.

Als Zusatzausstattung ist ein User Control Panel vorgesehen, über das sämtliche Grundfunktionen des Raums zugänglich sind; zusätzlich sollen Lichtszenarien frei definierbar und abrufbar sein. Für das Gesamtmodell ist weiterhin ein Facility Manager Control Panel zu realisieren, über das sämtliche Einzelfunktionen der Gebäudeteile sowie zusätzlich Sammelfunktionen (z.B. Ein-/Ausschalten aller Lichter, Schließen aller Sonnenblenden) bereitzustellen sind.

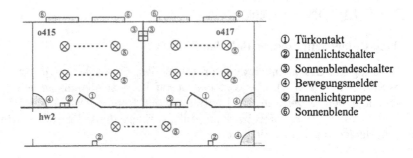

Abbildung 2. Grundriss des Gebäudemodells mit Installationen

Die zugrunde gelegte Problembeschreibung basiert auf einer vorangegangenen, ebenfalls im SFB 501 entwickelten Fallstudie [4], in der zusätzliche Anforderungen an die Lichtsteuerung sowie an die Temperatursteuerung der gesamten Etage gestellt werden.

2.3 Anforderungsanalyse

Zur formalen Spezifikation von Systemanforderungen wurde die auf die Anwendungsdomäne „Gebäudeautomation" zugeschnittene *Formal Requirements Specification Technique (FoReST)* [12], die objektorientierte Konzepte mit der Realzeit-Logik tRTTL (tailored Real Time Temporal Logic) integriert, eingesetzt. FoReST-Spezifikationen bestehen aus einer Sammlung von Klassendefinitionen, wobei die aus der objektorientierten Modellierung bekannten Assoziationen wie Aggregation, Komposition und Spezialisierung direkt unterstützt werden. Abweichend von den bekannten Techniken werden die Objekte einer Klasse jedoch nicht durch Operationen näher charakterisiert, sondern durch ihre Eigenschaften, die mit tRTTL formal spezifiziert werden. Ferner existiert eine Sammlung von FoReST-Requirement Patterns, die die wiederverwendungsorientierte Formalisierung von Anforderungen unterstützt.

Die Struktur der SILICON-Anwendungsanforderungen ist eng an die Gebäudetopologie, die in der Problembeschreibung (s. Abb. 2) enthalten ist, angelehnt. Dies unterstützt die *Verfolgbarkeit auf Architekturebene*, da ein 1:1-Bezug vorhanden ist. Die Verfolgbarkeit des Systemverhaltens wird durch die Verwendung eigenschaftsorientierter Beschreibungsmittel und eine uniforme Rückübersetzung in eine kundenlesbare Form erreicht.

Ein Ausschnitt der Struktur der Anwendungsanforderungen ist in Abb. 3 als UML-Objektdiagramm repräsentiert. Das UML-Diagramm dient hier lediglich der Übersicht, es ist nicht Bestandteil der FoReST-Spezifikation, kann aber als abstrakte Sicht verstanden werden. Details zur vollständigen FoReST-Spezifikation sind in [12] zu finden.

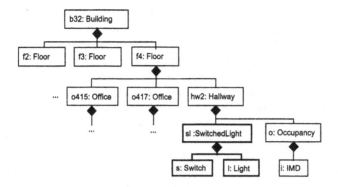

Abbildung 3. Anwendungsanforderungen: Auszug aus der Systemarchitektur

2.4 Anwendungsentwurf

Im nun folgenden Anwendungsentwurf (s. Abb. 1) wird die Systemarchitektur verfeinert, und es findet ein Übergang von der eigenschaftsorientierten Spezifikation des Systemverhaltens zu einer operationalen Darstellung statt. Dies bedingt einen Wechsel der Modellierungssprache. Als Konsequenz der Entwurfsentscheidung, das System verteilt zu realisieren, wird im folgenden die von der ITU-T genormte formale Beschreibungssprache *SDL (Specification and Description Language)* [11] verwendet. SDL eignet sich zur Spezifikation der Architektur und des Verhaltens verteilter Systeme sowie von Kommunikationsprotokollen, was für den Kommunikationssystementwurf (s. Kap. 2.5) von Nutzen ist. Ferner existiert eine Sammlung von SDL-Patterns [7,9], die den wiederverwendungsorientierten Anwendungsentwurf unterstützt.

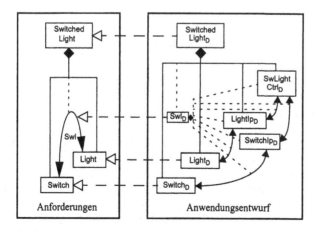

Abbildung 4. Übergang von den Anforderungen zum Anwendungsentwurf

Abb. 4 illustriert den Übergang von den Anwendungsanforderungen zum Anwendungsentwurf für die Klasse SwitchedLight, hier zunächst in Anlehnung an UML. Um die *Verfolgbarkeit* zu gewährleisten, wird für jede Klasse und für jede Relation (Eigenschaft) aus den Anforderungen eine korrespondierende Klasse im Entwurf eingeführt. Für jede Instanz von *SwitchedLight*, die ein Licht- und ein Schalterobjekt aggregiert, gibt es also im Entwurf eine Instanz der Entwurfsklasse *SwitchedLight$_D$*, welche (gemäß den Anwendungsanforderungen) Verfeinerungen von Light bzw. Switch aggregiert. Darüberhinaus enthält der Entwurf für *SwitchedLight* noch eine Kontrollkomponente *SwLightCtrl$_D$* zur Umsetzung der Schalter-Licht-Funktionalität, sowie explizite Interaktionspunkte *LightIp$_D$* und *SwitchIp$_D$*, die die verteilte Realisierung vorbereiten. Die ursprüngliche Eigenschaft *Swl* gilt immer noch, aber in ihre verteilte Realisierung *Swl$_D$* ist jetzt eine Reihe weiterer Klassen und Relationen involviert.

Ein Auszug aus der Systemarchitektur des Anwendungsentwurfs, repräsentiert als expandierte SDL-Spezifikation, ist in Abb. 5 dargestellt. Die Komponenten aus Abb. 4 werden übernommen und durch SDL-Blöcke repräsentiert. Ferner werden SDL-Kanäle aus der Anforderungsarchitektur abgeleitet. Die Verbindungsstruktur ist eine direkte Konsequenz der Kompositionshierarchie der Anforderungsspezifikation. Die spätere Topologie des Kommunikationssystems (s. Abb. 8) wird hierdurch nicht vorweggenommen.

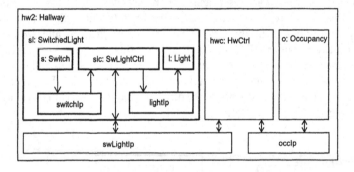

Abbildung 5. Anwendungsentwurf: Auszug aus der Systemarchitektur

2.5 Kommunikationssystementwicklung

In der nun folgenden Kommunikationssystementwicklung (s. Abb. 1) werden die Interaktionspunkte des Anwendungsentwurfs verfeinert, der Entwurf der Anwendungskomponenten bleibt unverändert. Wie im Prozessschritt zuvor wird die Beschreibungssprache SDL verwendet. Ziel ist die Maßschneiderung von Kommunikationssubsystemen, die exakt auf die Kommunikationsanforderungen der Anwendungskomponenten abgestimmt sind. Die methodischen Grundlagen für diese Verfeinerung sowie die musterbasierten Entwurfsschritte werden in [7,9] dargestellt. Wie zuvor wird dadurch die *Verfolgbarkeit* sowohl bzgl. der Architektur als auch des Komponentenverhaltens gewährleistet. Ein Ausschnitt der Struktur des Kommunikationssystementwurfs ist in Abb. 6 dargestellt, wie bereits zuvor durch expandierte SDL-Blöcke. Jeder Interaktionspunkt wird in zwei Protokollinstanzen, die über eine Basistechnologie kommunizieren, verfeinert. Dies ist konform mit der im Protocol Engineering üblichen Verfeinerung der Dienstarchitektur in die Protokollarchitektur. Die *Verfolgbarkeit* ist durch die strukturerhaltende Verfeinerung (vgl. Abb. 5) unmittelbar gewährleistet. Die aus der Verfeinerung resultierende verteilte Realisierung des Interaktionspunktverhaltens wird mit Hilfe der in [9] dargestellten Methodik unter Anwendung von SDL-Patterns synthetisiert, so dass die Verfolgbarkeit auch hier gegeben ist. Ferner wird in diesem Prozessschritt die Anpassung an die Basistechnologie - i.d.R. eine MAC-Schicht - und das jeweilige Fehlermodell vorgenommen.

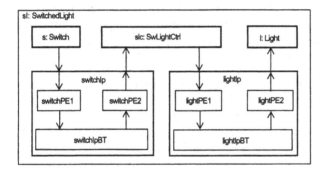

Abbildung 6. Kommunikationssystementwurf: Auszug aus der Systemarchitektur

2.6 Kodegenerierung

Zur Vorbereitung der Kodegenerierung werden die Komponenten des Anwendungs- und Kommunikationssystementwurfs nun einzelnen Rechnerknoten zugeordnet, abgestimmt auf die spätere Netztopologie. Bei der Planung der Netztopologie spielen sehr unterschiedliche Faktoren wie Leitungs- und Knotenkosten, Gebäudedimensionen, Performanz (Übertragungsraten, Verzögerungen) Echtzeitgarantien eine Rolle. Dies kann Rückwirkungen auf die Funktionalitäten der Protokollinstanzen (z.B. Fehlerkontrolle, Leitwegvermittlung) haben.

In Abb. 7 ist der Kommunikationssystementwurf in einen ersten Implementierungsentwurf umstrukturiert. Anwendungskomponenten und Protokollinstanzen werden knotenweise zusammengefasst, die Basistechnologie wird entfernt. Dadurch entstehen syntaktisch vollständige offene SDL-Systeme, die im nächsten Schritt separat übersetzt und in der Zielumgebung installiert werden. Zur automatischen Kodeerzeugung dient ein kommerzieller Kodegenerator in Verbindung

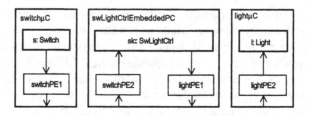

Abbildung 7. Implementierungsentwurf: Auszug aus der Systemarchitektur

mit dem in der AG Rechnernetze entwickelten Werkzeug *EnvGen (Environment Generator)*, das die Anbindung offener SDL-Spezifikationen an Kommunikationsbasistechnologien (u.a. CAN, UART/TP, Bluetooth) unterstützt.

Ausgehend vom Entwurf wurde eine vollständige, maßgeschneiderte Implementierung, bestehend aus einem physischen Gebäudemodell, einer neuartigen Kommunikationstechnologie, Applikationshardware, Kommunikationssoftware und Anwendungssoftware entwickelt. Die Topologie der Gebäudemodellimplementierung ist in Abb. 8 dargestellt, in Ergänzung des Grundrisses aus Abb. 2. Die Kommunikationstopologie ist hierarchisch:

- Auf Raumebene sind mehrere Mikrocontroller, die die Schalter, Lichtgruppen, Sonnenblenden, Bewegungsmelder und User Control Panel implementieren, sowie Embedded PCs zur Implementierung der Büro- und Flurkontrollzellen vernetzt. Als Technologie wird der echtzeitfähige UART/TP-Bus, eine Eigenentwicklung, eingesetzt, und zwar jeweils ein eigener Bus pro Raum.
- Auf Etagenebene sind zusätzlich die Embedded PCs vernetzt, als Technologie dient der CAN-Bus (Controller Area Network).
- Auf Gebäudeebene ist beabsichtigt, Embedded PCs unterschiedlicher Etagen via Ethernet zu vernetzen. In dieser Fallstudie wird diese Option für andere Zwecke genutzt, z.B. zum Download von Kode und zur Visualisierung der Kommunikation. Außerdem kann das Facility Manager Control Panel über diese Technologie vernetzt werden.
- Unabhängig von dieser hierarchischen Struktur ist eine drahtlose Bluetooth-Vernetzung zwischen dem Facilitiy Manager Control Panel und den Bürokontrollzellen realisiert.

2.7 Kommunikationsbasistechnologien

Die Auswahl bzw. Maßschneiderung der Basistechnologien des hierarchisch strukturierten Kommunikationssystems und der einzelnen aktiven Komponenten erfolgte in erster Linie anhand verschiedener technischer Anforderungen, wie z. B. Kommunikationsaufkommen, Echtzeitanforderungen, Reichweite und Zuverlässigkeit. Daneben wurden jedoch auch wirtschaftliche Aspekte wie Leitungs- und Knotenkosten, Erweiterbarkeit und Entwicklungsaufwand berücksichtigt. Dabei zeigte sich, dass sich speziell bei den in großer Zahl vorhandenen aktiven

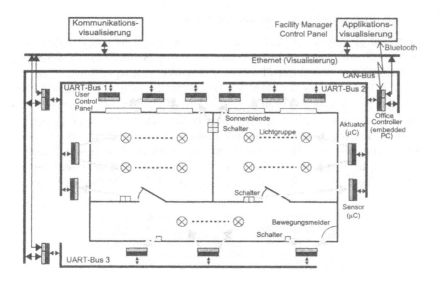

Abbildung 8. Topologie der Gebäudemodellimplementierung

Sensoren und Aktuatoren der untersten Hierarchiestufe des Gebäudeautomationssystems die niedrigsten Anforderungen technischer Art (Übertragungsrate, Rechenleistung) mit dem höchsten Kostendruck bezüglich Leitungs- und Knotenkosten verbinden.

Da die verfügbaren Basistechnologien (wie z.B. CAN) zur Vernetzung von Microcontrollern unter den technischen Randbedingungen dieser untersten Hierarchiestufe des Kommunikationssystems kein optimales Ergebnis bezüglich der o. g. wirtschaftlichen Anforderungen boten, wurde mit dem UART/TP-Bus eine völlig neue Kommunikationsbasistechnologie für diese Anwendung maßgeschneidert. Der UART/TP-Bus nutzt die in praktisch allen Microcontrollern als Hardwarekomponente vorhandene serielle Schnittstelle (UART) zusammen mit einem einfachen Interface zur Ankopplung an einen seriellen Bus, über den gleichzeitig auch die Stromversorgung der einzelnen Knoten erfolgt. Zur Busarbitrierung wird ein auf den Microcontrollern per Software implementiertes Token-Passing-Verfahren eingesetzt, über das eine feingranulare Modellierung der Echtzeiteigenschaften des Kommunikationssystems möglich ist.

Auf Grund der geringen Hardwareanforderungen erlaubt UART/TP dabei die Implementierung der einzelnen Kommunikationsknoten auf sehr preisgünstigen Microcontrollern (z.B. 80c51: 8-Bit-Design, 128 Byte RAM). Aber auch eine direkte Ankopplung von PCs über deren serielle Schnittstelle ist möglich, und wird in der Fallstudie zur Ankopplung der Office- und Hallway-Controller eingesetzt.

2.8 Das funktionsfähige Gebäudemodell

Ein Foto des physischen Gebäudemodells wird in Abb. 9 gezeigt. Das Gebäudemodell wurde auf mehreren Industriemessen, darunter die Embedded Systems 2001 in Nürnberg und die CeBIT 2001 in Hannover, in Kooperation mit der Fa. Telelogic präsentiert. Im vorderen Teil des Gebäudemodells sind die mit Sonnenblenden ausgestatteten Fenster zu erkennen. Am Sockel sind mehrere Mikrocontroller zur Implementierung der Schalter-, Sonnenblenden- und Lichtgruppenfunktionalitäten montiert. Die User Control Panels sind vor dem Gebäude angebracht und erlauben die separate Kontrolle sämtlicher Aktuatoren. Darüberhinaus kann der Benutzer mit Hilfe der User Control Panels Lichtszenarien definieren und abrufen. Die Embedded PCs sind unter dem Gebäude installiert.

Abbildung 9. Gebäudemodell „Verteilte Lichtsteuerung"

Links vom Gebäudemodell sind zwei Computerbildschirme zu erkennen. Der vordere Bildschirm gehört zu einem Laptop, der als Facility Manager Control Panel fungiert. Das Display oberhalb dient der Visualisierung der Kommunikationsereignisse.

3 Ergebnisse und Erfahrungen

In der vorgestellten SILICON-Fallstudie wurde die syntaktische und semantische Integration verschiedener generischer Ansätze zur Systementwicklung demonstriert. Diese Ansätze dienen zur Bewältigung der inhärenten Schwierigkeiten bei der Entwicklung großer verteilter Systeme, wie die Beherrschung der Komplexität, die Verfolgbarkeit der Produkte über alle Entwicklungsphasen sowie die Integration unterschiedlicher Beschreibungssprachen und Entwicklungsmethoden. Es hat sich dabei gezeigt, dass gerade durch diese Integration jeweils genau passende Beschreibungsmittel in den verschiedenen Entwicklungsschritten eingesetzt werden konnten: Die eigenschaftsorientiert in tRTTL formulierten Anwendungsanforderungen formalisieren ausschließlich Eigenschaften der externen Systemschnittstelle, ohne Design-Entscheidungen vorwegzunehmen; der

struktur- und kommunikationsorientiert in SDL entwickelte Anwendungsentwurf
stellt dagegen die Steuerungs- und Kommunikationsaspekte des Systems in den
Vordergrund und dient dabei insbesondere durch seine operationale Formalisierung als Ausgangspunkt für die teilautomatische Implementierung; diese wiederum wurde auf unterschiedlichen Plattformen imperativ und zustandsorientiert
in Sprachen wie z.b. C entwickelt.

Der Vorteil des Einsatzes derartiger, auf die jeweiligen Entwicklungsschritte zugeschnittener Beschreibungssprachen und Entwicklungsmethoden wird jedoch erkauft durch inhärente Brüche bei dem damit unweigerlich verbundenen
Paradigmenwechsel zwischen den einzelnen Prozessschritten. So zeigten sich in
der Fallstudie z.b. beim Wechsel von der eigenschaftsorientierten Anforderungsbeschreibung zum operationalen Anwendungsentwurf mehrmals Schwierigkeiten bei der semantikerhaltenden Abbildung. Analog zeigten sich bei der Abbildung der nachrichtenorientierten Aspekte der Anforderungsbeschreibung auf
die zustandsorientierten Implementierungen (speziell auf Ebene der ressourcen-
beschränkten Microcontrollersysteme) Probleme bei der Entwicklung effizienter
Implementierungen.

Ein wichtiges Ergebnis der Fallstudie in dieser Hinsicht war, dass bereits in
einer möglichst frühen Phase des Projekts eine enge Abstimmung der in den einzelnen Prozessschritten eingesetzten Techniken und Methoden erfolgen muss, um
so Brüche in der Durchgängigkeit und Verfolgbarkeit effektiv zu vermeiden und
die Skalierbarkeit über die Systemgröße sicherzustellen. Dazu zählt insbesondere eine Ausrichtung bei der Beschreibung einer Ebene auf die Anforderungen
und Möglichkeiten darauffolgender Entwicklungsschritte. Eine wirksame Realisierung scheint hier auf Basis der eingesetzten musterbasierten Techniken (z.b.
FoReST, SDL-Patterns) möglich, da hier die Umsetzbarkeit auf nachfolgenden
Ebenen bereits integraler Bestandteil der Mustersammlungen sein kann. Dies
ist insbesondere vor dem Hintergrund der Formalisierung und des Werkzeugein-
satzes innerhalb des gesamten Enwicklungsprozesses zu sehen: Hier ist neben
der Verfolgbarkeit im Entwicklungsprozess auch eine effektive Unterstützung bei
Rückgriffen in diesem Prozess gefordert, um einen durchgängigen und möglichst
nahtlosen Übergang zwischen den Entwicklungsschritten zu erreichen.

Danksagungen

Die hier vorgestellten Arbeiten sind unter Mitwirkung der weiteren folgenden
Personen entstanden (in alphabetischer Reihenfolge): Barbara Erlewein (Organisation), Birgit Geppert (SDL-Pattern-Ansatz), Erhard Kintzel (Gebäudemodell), Marc Müller (UART-Basistechnologie), Frank Rößler (SDL-Pattern-
Ansatz). Allen sei an dieser Stelle für ihren Einsatz gedankt. Ferner danken wir
der Deutschen Forschungsgemeinschaft für die Förderung des Teilprojekts B4
„Generische Entwicklung von Kommunikationssystemen", in dem diese Fallstudie durchgeführt wurde, sowie der Fa. Telelogic für die Finanzierung des Modells
und seiner Präsentation auf der Embedded Systems 2001 und der CeBIT 2001.

Literatur

1. Avenhaus, J., Gotzhein, R., Härder, T., Litz, L., Madlener, K., Nehmer, J., Richter, M., Ritter, N., Rombach, D., Schürmann, B., Zimmermann, G.: *Entwicklung großer Systeme mit generischen Methoden - Eine Übersicht über den Sonderforschungsbereich 501, Informatik, Forschung und Entwicklung*, 13(4):227-234, Dezember 1998
2. Back, R. J. R.: *A Calculus of Refinements for Program Derivations*, Acta Informatica, 25:593-624, 1988
3. Booch, G., Rumbaugh, J. and Jacobson, I.: *The Unified Modelling Language User Guide*, Addison Wesley, Reading, Massachusetts, 1999
4. Börger, E., Gotzhein, R. (Guest Editors): *Requirements Engineering: The Light Control Case Study*, Special Issue of the Journal of Universal Computer Science, Springer, July 2000
5. Braek, R., Haugen, O.: *Engineering Real Time Systems*, Prentice Hall, 1993
6. Coleman, D. et al.: *Object-Oriented Development - The Fusion Method*, Prentice Hall, 1994
7. Geppert, B.: *The SDL-Pattern Approach - A Reuse-Driven SDL Methodology for Designing Communication Software Systems*, Ph.D. Thesis, University of Kaiserslautern, 2000
8. Gotzhein, R., Khendek, F., Schaible, P.: *Micro Protocol Design: The SNMP Case Study*, SDL and MSC Workshop (SAM'2002), Aberystwyth, UK, June 24-26, 2002
9. Gotzhein, R.: *Consolidating and Applying the SDL-Pattern Approach: A Detailed Case Study*, Information and Software Technology, Elsevier Sciences (in print)
10. Haumer, P., Pohl, K., Weidenhaupt, K., Jarke, M.: *Improving Reviews by Extending Traceability*, Proceedings of the 32nd Annual Hawaii International Conference on System Sciences (HICSS), 1999
11. *ITU-T Recommendation Z.100 (11/99): Specification and Description Language (SDL)*, International Telecommunication Union (ITU), 1999
12. Kronenburg, M., Peper, C.: *Application of the FOREST Approach to the Light Control Case Study*, Journal of Universal Computer Science (J.UCS), Special Issue on „Requirements Engineering: The Light Control Case Study", Springer, 2000
13. Lewerentz, C., Lindner, T.: *Formal Development of Reactive Systems:Case Study Production Cell*, LNCS 891, Springer-Verlag, January 1995
14. Peper, C.: *Transformations in Pattern-based System Specifications*, 9th GI/ITG-Fachgespräch „Formale Beschreibungstechniken für verteilte Systeme" (FBT'99), München, 1999, Herbert-Utz-Verlag, ISBN 3-89675-918-3, pp. 165-173
15. R. Reed: *Methodology for Real Time Systems, Computer Networks and ISDN Systems*, Special Issue on SDL and MSC, 28 (1996), pp. 1685-1701
16. Rößler, F., Geppert, B., Schaible, P.: *Re-Engineering of the Internet Stream Protocol ST2+ with Formalized Design Patterns*, Proceedings of the 5th International Conference on Software Reuse (ICSR.5), Victoria, British Columbia, Canada, 1998
17. Telelogic: *Tau 3.4 SDT Methodology Guidelines - Part 1: The SOMT Method*, 1998

Modeling a Mobile Memory Aid System

Hendrik Schulze, Thomas Hoffmann, Andrei Voinikonis, Klaus Irmscher

Leipzig University, Institute of Computer Science
Chair of Computer Networks and Distributed Systems
Augustusplatz 10-11, D-04109 Leipzig, Germany
[hendrik,thoff,voinikon,irmscher]@informatik.uni-leipzig.de
http://rnvs.informatik.uni-leipzig.de/memos

Keywords

Electronic memory aid, mobile computing, telemedicine, distributed computing, XML, componentware

Abstract. The electronic memory aid system MEMOS was developed at Leipzig University to support patients with memory disturbances. Starting from this application background MEMOS is designed as a distributed system where a central server component controls a special handheld computer, the Personal Memory Assistant (PMA), over a GSM or a GPRS cellular phone network. To guarantee a wide flexibility and adaptability of the system to concrete deployment scenario the structuring of the information which is generated by the system and processed by the PMA is an essential component of MEMOS. This paper describes the modeling of the central data structures and the consequences to the system architecture.

1 Introduction

The combination of information and communication technologies with medical and psychological knowledge gives us the possibility to solve a new quality of problems in the treatment of patients.

This paper describes the architecture, implementation and use of the distributed neuropsychological care system MEMOS (Mobile Extensible MemOry Aid System). Textual focus is put on modeling the information structures and the transformation of the data during the treatment process. These data structures are developed to ensure an wide adaptability to the special application scenario without changing the system.

MEMOS is build on an Enterprise Java Beans (EJB) based application server communicating with a special mobile handheld computer, called Personal Memory Assistant (PMA). The PMA supports head injured persons solving real life tasks by reminding them of essential facts and due dates and by providing them additional information which the patient needs to finish tasks successfully. It is the first time in clinical neuropsychology that bi-directional cellular phone based communication devices are used. The care system enables the therapist with the assistance of the patient's family to supervise and manage the actions of brain damaged people even outside the clinical setting. On one side, the time and costs of treatment could be reduced. On the other side, the patients autonomy and quality of life will increase. Integrating the heterogeneous group of involved caregivers in the MEMOS-System, a cooperative treatment of the patient is possible and the administrative overhead for the caregivers is reduced. Last but not least, a major aim of MEMOS is to moderate the social strains in the families of head injured persons, unburdening the family members of the care for their loved ones.

Using EJB's as the platform for the server part (base system) of our care system, we were able to implement an extensible, scalable and fault tolerant software product. As MEMOS is not a rigid system with fixed neuropsychological guidelines but rather an adaptive framework to give therapists the possibility to find the best way in treatment, central component of MEMOS is a control and data structure which ensures adaptability to a broad class of operation scenarios without any modifications to the source code. EJB's guarantee an efficient software development process on various hardware systems without any dependencies on proprietary software or special hardware. MEMOS can be extended easily by adding new beans or user interfaces for different caregiver classes, who support the patient.

The patients are furnished with the PMA. To save battery power and connection costs the PMA works offline most of the time. It connects to the care system for only a few minutes a day to send its state and get new information for the patient. Most of the time the PMA works autonomously, but can call the base system in critical situations. The patient can establish a voice connection to the therapist if he is disoriented or needs help. The PMA can also connect to the base system if the patient didn't confirm a due task within a time frame or reacted in the wrong way[1]. The graphical interface of the PMA is adapted to the patients' restricted abilities. To implement it to their needs and to enable the palmtop to work autonomously, a specialized markup language "M2"[2] based on XML is developed. With the help of a M2-based tiny browser, the PMA can edit all information it needs to guide a patient through a complex task.

To implement this mobile care system the interdisciplinary project MOB-TEL[1] was founded in 1998. In spring 2002 the follow-up project MOBREGIO was granted by the German Ministry of Education and Research as a cooperation of different partners at Leipzig University (Department of Computer Science / Chair of Computer Networks and Distributed Systems and the Day-care Clinic for Cognitive Neurology) together with "RBM electronic automation", an electronics company in Leipzig.

---

[1] E.g. if the patient has to take a medicine, like insulin, in a strict time slot, he/she has to confirm the task in time.

[2] Mobtel Markup Language v2

2 Neuropsychological Requirements

2.1 Memory Disturbances

Memory problems are one of the most common complaints after a brain injury. Such memory deficits may affect the ability to recall both past events (retrospective memory) and future events and intentions (prospective memory).

While the scientific focus was on the retrospective memory in the past, impairments affecting prospective memory are more disabling and significantly decrease the patients' autonomy. Without the ability to recall intended tasks, the patient is unable to make a reliable plan of future tasks and appointments. The patient loses his/her autonomy and depends on other people, mostly family members, because he/she needs an external impulse to start an intended action. One consequence is a strongly burdened family environment, full of social strains. So a brain injury causes not only restrictions to the quality of the patient's life but also to the life of his/her family members.

The most promising approach of neuropsychological treatment for memory disorders is to use conventional external memory aids[3] or electronic devices to compensate their memory deficits.

However, the use of external aids has often failed due to several difficulties inherent to patients' functional deficits. The patient may forget to write down an appointment or to look things up in the right time. On the other hand, modern electronic hand-held computers or organizers are too complex in design and handling, so the patients are not able to learn the use of such an external electronic device.

Studies showed that patients can benefit from external memory aids or from electronic memory aid systems but all existing therapy approaches using external memory aids also have a couple of disadvantages because of functional limitations of those devices[2].

2.2 Requirements of a comprehensive memory aid

The drawbacks of the existing neuropsychological treatments for memory disorders suggest the development of a specialized memory aid system that considers the special needs of all persons involved in the treatment process[4].

An ideal memory aid system has to help the patient compensate the deficits in his/her prospective memory and has to be adaptable to the individual occurrence of the memory disturbances[13].

Therefore, the memory aid system has to support the patient encoding the information. All caregivers have to contribute to this process and the memory aid system has to coordinate the input of all persons. To plan the intended tasks, it is important to consider all relevant information stored in the system.

Of importance for the reminder-process is monitoring the actions being performed. In the case of a failure the memory aid system has to decide whether to

---

[3] such as diaries, calendars, memory books, "Post-It's"
[4] patients, physicians, therapists, family members and other persons

cancel the task, restart the reminder, or contact a caregiver. Thus the memory aid system needs the possibility to get feedback from the patient.

Furthermore, a useful memory aid system has to consider the requirements for a cognitive prosthesis summarized by Cole[12]. The cognitive prosthesis needs to address a wide range of the individual's priority functional activities to be valuable. So the prosthesis has to be adaptable due to a number of factors:

1. patient priorities for activities,
2. abilities in context of the environment where the target activity is performed,
3. functional deficits which require support,
4. features that make the system "userfriendly" for the patient, who may also have physical impairments.

The memory system has to ensure the user can use it without becoming confused. For example, the user must be able to continue after making an error. And the training to use the system successfully has to be minimal.

3 The Information Model

3.1 Target Requirements of MEMOS

As consequence of the requirements of a comprehensive memory aid, described in section 2.2, the major objective during the realization of MEMOS was to build a fault tolerant, reliable memory aid system on restricted mobile resources which is userfriendly and integrates a heterogeneous group of caregivers in the treatment process. Furthermore MEMOS has to provide the possibility for adaptions with respect to the individual patient and it also has to give the therapists the possibility to develop and test new treatment methods without touching the PMA or confusing the patient.

The architectural consequence of the outlined requirements is that the memory aid system has to consist of two components, the PMA as mobile component supporting the patient, and a base system as centralized component coordinating the caregiver's actions and controlling the PMA. PMA and base system have to communicate using a cellular telephone network[5] since only this technology provides an acceptable coverage and reliability at moderate costs. A further consequence is that the most important features which have to be realized in MEMOS are a wide adaptability and a great flexibility.

3.2 Technical Requirements of MEMOS

To support the memory process as smooth as possible, the memory aid system has to ensure the following features:

1. Complex tasks or information must be splited into atomic pieces of information which have to be provided to the patient one at a time.

---
[5] GSM,GPRS or UMTS

2. Information which belongs together must not be mixed up with other information.
3. The patient has the possibility to react to the data given. Depending on his reaction the PMA will process and display different information.
4. Since there is no 100% reliability to establish a connection between the PMA and the base system, the PMA must be able to work autonomously for longer time intervals.

To assure this features and to accomplish the adaptability and flexibility, a major element of the MEMOS system is a convenient data structure. This data structure has not only to allow the correct modeling of information pieces for the patient, but also has to assure an efficient generation, management and transfer of the data. Moreover the data has to be parsed and interpreted on a mobile device with limited computing resources. To ensure an autonomous work of the PMA, the units of information transmitted to the PMA must be coarse enough. Last but not least the modeled data structure must allow a monitoring of the patients reactions.

3.3   Modeling the Fundamental Data Structures

Based on the criteria given above we developed a data model which distinguishes between 3 components: **task, deck** and **card**.

Card: A card is an atomic information which is shown to the patient. Every card contains additional control data to indicate how the PMA has to react on the patient's actions[6]. A card should fit into a screen.

Deck: A deck is a set of cards which belong logically together. Besides the cards, a deck contains deck-wide control information about execution time, deck-wide timers and so on. A deck is not interruptible by another deck.

Task: A task is a set of at least one deck and contains all information necessary to guide a person to fulfill a certain intention. A task is a management unit of the base system. It is not known by the PMA[7], which only knows decks and cards.

Encoding the task may be done straightforward as Java object which contains the decks and the additional management information. The deck can be considered as a graph, were the nodes are the cards (states) and the edges the events which lead from one card to another. Figure 1 illustrates the correlations between the 3 components.

---

[6] E.g. how often a card has to be refreshed, or what the next card is after a button has been pressed.
[7] The PMA only knows decks and cards.

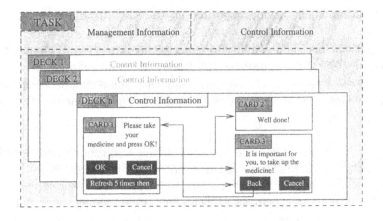

Fig. 1. The correlation between tasks, decks and cards.

3.4 Including XML in the Design Process

Since the data format to exchange information between base system and PMA is based on XML (see section 4.3) it is important to consider the generation of XML during the design of the central data structures. As the components have to be implemented as an object hierarchy and there exists a couple of mature software products which can realize this on top of XML based structures it is suggesting to design the base system by using such a XML processing software.

Integrating XML [4] in the own software product can be done in several ways. Each way has its own advantages and disadvantages. In general it could be distinguished between software that accesses and handles XML in a proprietary way and software which supports a standardized API to access and handle XML documents and XML oriented data structures.

The biggest disadvantage of proprietary software is the dependence on the future development of the certain product.

It was important for the decision regarding the used XML software for MEMOS to choose a technology which is based on an open standard and/or which is open source itselfs. So we could choose between SAX[8] based XML parser, software which supports DOM[9], JDOM and JAXP[10]. While SAX and DOM are programming language independent API's, JDOM and JAXP are developed for Java.

SAX is an API for event based parsing and generation of XML documents. Generating a software intern representation of the XML document must additionally be done by the programmer. SAX is fast and efficient.

Similar to SAX, DOM provides methods for reading and writing XML documents. In contrast to SAX, however, it generates an object model of the docu-

---

[8] Simple API for Parsing XML
[9] Document Object Model
[10] Java API for XML parsing

ment and methods to manipulate the object model. DOM is powerful but since the document has to be parsed and stored in the memory at once, DOM is quite slow and needs a lot of resources.

JAXP could be described as a Java based abstraction layer for DOM and SAX. It is an extra layer and is a little bit slower than accessing SAX or DOM directly, but it provides a greater flexibility and independence from the parser. At the time of decision for a technology it was not finally specified, thus we don't took it into our considerations yet.

JDOM is a independent Java based approach, which bridges the gap between SAX and DOM. It integrates itself into both DOM and SAX by adapter classes, so it needs SAX or DOM for reading and writing a XML document. The difference between JDOM and DOM is a document object model which is especially developed for Java. JDOM is faster and much more efficient than DOM. JDOM is no open standard but an open source product with a transparent perspective and a very good documentation of the interfaces.

As MEMOS uses J2EE as basic software and distribution platform, JDOM is chosen for handling XML documents.

4 MEMOS Architecture

As already described in section 3.1, MEMOS consists of two parts, the stationary base system and the mobile device for the patient, the PMA.

4.1 The MEMOS Base System

A major requirement influencing the architecture of the base system is the integration of existing hardware[11] and a software architecture, which facilitates a fast and efficient development process. Furthermore, the system must be scalable and extensible to future needs. The most important requirement is the reliability of the base system and all used technologies.

We chose a web-based architecture where the user interfaces for the caregivers are designed as web clients. The caregiver can access the base system over a web-server[7]. All critical information is processed by the business logic in a EJB-server, the web sites are created dynamically by the JSP engine[8].

This approach has several advantages. The business logic is implemented only once in the EJB server and has to be maintained only at a single point[6]. Adaptions on the business logic can be done without changing the user interface. The user interfaces are implemented as JSP's and connect the base system over IIOP. The caregivers need only a computer with an Internet connection and a standard browser like "Netscape Navigator" or "Internet Explorer". Therefore the caregiver is not tied to a specific workstation and can work with MEMOS from different places.

---

[11] Particulary existing workstations in the clinics and private personal computers of patients' family members have to be integrated, as a terminal for exapmle.

To hide unimportant functionalities and restricted data from unauthorized caregivers, different classes of caregivers are assigned different user interfaces. New interfaces can be implemented easily without changing the business logic.

J2EE provides with EJB's a comprehensive framework with a couple of services we otherwise would have implemented ourselves[12].

Most of the business logic is implemented as an Enterprise Java Bean. Since EJB's cannot create a socket connection, the connection to the mobile patient devices are established by a special server object (PMA gateway). This gateway is a CORBA object for the base system as well as a SOAP server for the PMA. When the PMA connects to the gateway, it asks the gateway for a list of new or updated decks and loads down all XML files for these decks.

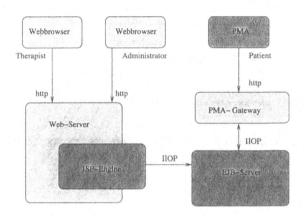

Fig. 2. The simpliefied architecture of the distributed care system.

4.2 The Personal Memory Assistant (PMA)

The PMA should be usable for patients with cognitive deficits, so it must be fault tolerant and very easy to handle. Currently we pursue two policies. The first one is realizing a PMA on a J2ME (Java 2 Micro Edition) based device[5]. The second way is to use a more complex Java based smart phone. For both alternatives we need devices with an integrated mobile communication unit.

The Motorola Accompli 008 is a suitable smart phone which supports J2ME. Unfortunately it has a slow processor and very limited memory. The virtual java machine, however, is very much prone to maloperation up to turning off the GPRS module. Due to this major disadvantage the Accompli is only useable by patients with little memory problems.

---

[12] Especially the scalability, reliability and transactional aspects influenced our decision.

Better chances to control the whole device give the PocketPC or LINUX based smart phones (like Siemens SX 45, Compaq IPAQ H3860 or Sharp Zaurus). We also use Java on these devices to profit from its platform independence. Both of the two hardware sets communicate with the base system in the same way.

4.3 The Data Exchange between Base System and PMA

The real communication is realized over a TCP/IP network using the http protocol. The data exchange between the both major components of MEMOS is based on XML. The main reason to use XML is the availability of stable software, providing the functionality which otherwise had to be implemented by ourselves. It is obvious that an own protocol could be better optimized to the special needs and has less overhead than a generic document format like XML but developing a protocol and implementing the protocol stack is time expensive and fault-prone. Since XML is a thoughtful standard and there exists a great variety of high quality XML tools, there is no need for an other protocol design and implementation.

The use of DTD's (Document Type Definition) or XML Schemas allows a flexible restriction of XML to the special problem. Thus a problem specific DTD, called M2, was specified for MEMOS. The focus of the specification is on a simple conversion between the modeled data structures and the XML structures.

4.4 Processing Task Information for the Patient

Designing every new task from scratch is very time expensive, fault-prone and not reasonable concerning the exoneration of therapists and family members. Therefore MEMOS has task templates which are skeletons of often used tasks. These templates are stored as XML documents and contain meta information about possible parameters. With help of the parameter a template task can be adapted to the patients' needs.

Typical parameters are e.g. the name of a medicine or the time when the medicine should be taken. Control information like start time or the maximal allowed delay are also possible parameter.

Template tasks are generated and managed by a graphical designer tool. Once stored in the system, every template can be chosen for a new task. The base system loads the XML document using the SAXBuilderclass and generates a JDOM object model.

Once the task is parameterized, checked for consistency and confirmed by the therapist, the system generates a XML document for the task which is stored on a gateway. The next time the PMA connects the gateway the XML document is transmitted to the PMA. Of course, the XML document contains only data which is relevant for the PMA. So, it holds only decks and cards, but no task information.

The only problem which has to be solved for the XML generation is that XML represents a tree whereas a deck is a graph but no a tree. Thus the edges between the nodes (cards) are resolved as references in XML (ref. figure 3).

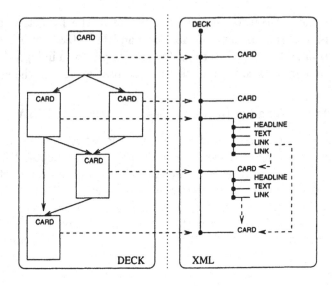

Fig. 3. The transformation of a deck to a XML representation.

On the Motorola Accompli the XML document is parsed by a special XML parser named "kxml"[11] which is optimized to the restricted ressources and works together with J2ME.

The data is interpreted and all decks and cards will be generated and the actual card will be displayed at the right moment. After an event (the patient presses a button or after a time out) the PMA will display the next card. Furthermore the PMA records the action into a log file. If a deck comes into a critical state[13] or after a dedicated time, the PMA connects to the base system and transmits the log data and requests new data. The base system analyzes the log data and decides about further actions[14].

5 Actual State and Practical Use

The described base system is realized and running at Leipzig University. In a predecessor project [1] a special PMA was developed. Due to technical problems and economic considerations, we decided to use comercial PDA's which are 5 times cheaper than the first used PMAs. In winter 2002/2003 the PMA based on the motorola Accompli will be finished. After some first evaluations at the daycare clinic for cognitive neurology at Leipzig University the new know-how will help us to finish the PocketPC based PMAs.

Both types of PMA connect to the base system using the services of an internet service provider. The base system is hosted on a dual Intel PIII/ 800MHz server with 1 GB memory running LINUX. We use the Inprise Application Server

---

[13] every card could be marked as critical by the therapist

[14] E.g. in critical situations a SMS could be sent to the therapist or the task will be restarted later

4.5 as EJB-server, Visibroker 4 as CORBA ORB and Oracle 8.1.7. At the moment all components run on the same computer, but the Application Server can be clustered easily by installing multiple instances on differnt computers using a consistent naming service. The same installation works on a Windows 2000 server or a SUN Solaris server, but the maintainability and the costs of the hard- and software influenced the decision towards LINUX.

6 Conclusions and Outlook

MEMOS is the first mobile electronic memory aid system which uses a bidirectional communication to the PMA. Besides the common features of systems for telemedical use, like reliability, scalability and fault-tolerance, to name a few, the strenght of MEMOS is its flexibility and adaptability. The approach to use a XML-browser on the PMA and the communication based of the data structures, described in this paper, was successfully realized with MEMOS.

MEMOS is successfully utilized as MEMORY aid system at the Day-care clinic for Cognitive Neurology at Leipzig University, were it is not only used as MEMORY aid system but also as platform for further neuropsychological research.

The generality of the MEMOS architecture opens the possibility to apply the system to other fields also. With the MOBREGIO project, MEMOS will be adapted to support people with deficits in accessing and processing information.

References

1. Schulze, H. and Irmscher,K., *Mobtel - A Mobile Distributed Telemedical System*, Lecture Notes in Computer Science Vol.1890, Springer, 2000
2. Schulze, H., *MEMOS - A Mobile Extensible Memory Aid System*, Proceedings of Healtcom2001 - Enterprise Networking and Computing in Health Care Industry, Third International IEEE Workshop,SSGRR, 2001, pp. 179
3. Irmscher, K., *Mobile Access to Care Services in a Web and Enterprise Computing based Distributed Area* Proceedings of 6th Annual World Conference on the WWW and Internet (WebNet 2001), Oct. 23 - 27, 2001; Orlando, Florida, USA.
4. Ahmed, K. et.al., *Professional JAVA XML*, Wrox Press, 2001
5. Riggs, R. et.al., *Programming Wireless Devices with the Java 2 Platform, Micro Edition*, Sun Microsystems, 2001
6. Monson-Haefel, R., *Enterprise Java Beans*, O'Reilly, 2000
7. Flanagan, D., *Enterprise Java in a Nutshell*, O'Reilly, 1999
8. Avedal, K. et.al., *JSP Professional*, Wrox Press, 2001
9. Alur, D. et.al., *core J2EE Patterns*, Sun Microsystems, 2001
10. Website W3C, http://www.w3c.org
11. Website KXML, http://www.kxml.org
12. Cole, E., *Cognitive Prosthetics: an overview to a method of treatment*, Neurorehabilitation,12,1999,pp.39
13. Kvavilashvili, L., Ellis, J., *Varieties of Intention: Some Distinctions and Classifications*, in Prospective Memory. Theory and Applications, Mahwah, NJ, Lawrence Erlbaum Associates, 1996, pp. 23-51

Ein CORBA-basiertes, geschichtetes Unified Messaging System

Frank Köhler, Reinhold Kröger, Holger Machens

Labor für Verteilte Systeme
Fachhochschule Wiesbaden - University of Applied Sciences
{koehler, kroeger, machens}@informatik.fh-wiesbaden.de
http://wwwvs.informatik.fh-wiesbaden.de/

Zusammenfassung Der Bereich der Unified Messaging Anwendungen gewinnt in den letzten Jahren immer mehr an Bedeutung. Die zentralen Forderung ist hierbei, Informationen zu jeder Zeit, an jedem Ort und in beliebiger Form empfangen zu können. Hierfür ist es notwendig, Systeme bereit zu stellen, die alle notwendigen Ein- bzw. Ausgabeformaten unterstützen und über entsprechende Konverter für die Nachrichtentransformation verfügen. Da in der Regel eine große Nutzeranzahl auf diese Systeme zugreift, werden besondere Anforderungen in Hinblick auf Verfügbarkeit und Skalierbarkeit gestellt. Dieser Beitrag stellt eine Architektur für solche Systeme vor, die sich in eine unterliegende, generische CORBA-basierte Schicht, bestehend aus einem Object Request Broker und einem CORBA Notification Service, sowie eine darauf basierende Unified Messaging Schicht gliedert. Während die unterliegende Schicht als skalierbare Integrationsplattform dient, werden durch die darüberliegende Unified Messaging Schicht die notwendigen Systemkomponenten eines Unified Messaging Systems realisiert.

1 Einleitung

Die wachsende Konvergenz zwischen Telefonnetzen, Datennetzen und mobilen Netzen führt zu der zentralen Vision, Informationen zu jeder Zeit, an jedem Ort und in beliebiger Form senden und empfangen zu können. Diese Vision bildet die Grundlage für Forschungs- und Entwicklungsaktivitäten mit dem Problem der nahtlosen Integration einzelner Kommunikationssysteme in eine vom Trägermedium abstrahierenden Kommunikationsumgebung für mobile Nutzer.

Ein Teilbereich dieser Forschungsaktivitäten wird heute unter dem Begriff "Unified Messaging" zusammengefaßt. Ein Unified Messaging System (UMS) soll die Produktivität eines Nutzers dadurch steigern, dass die bisherige, in der Regel aus verschiedenen Applikationen bestehende Infrastruktur des Nutzers durch eine Kommunikationsumgebung ersetzt wird, die alle Nachrichtentypen empfängt und diese an einem logisch zentralen Ort zur Verfügung hält. Eine solche, in der Regel auf Internet-Protokollen basierende Umgebung soll es dem Nutzer ermöglichen, unabhängig von seinem Aufenthaltsort und dem gerade zur Verfügung stehenden Kommunikationsendgerät auf seine Nachrichten zugreifen zu können.

Die bestehenden Forschungsaktivitäten im Bereich der UMS-Lösungen konzentrieren sich auf entsprechende Architekturansätze für die Realisierung von Unified Messaging Systemen. In [VDM99] werden hierzu einzelne Entwicklungsstufen von Nachrichtensystemen vorgestellt. Darauf basierend werden die Anforderungen an ein Unified Messaging System spezifiziert und eine komponentenbasierte Systemarchitektur vorgestellt. Ein weiterer Architekturansatz für ein Unified Messaging System wird in [GMD00] diskutiert. Dieser Ansatz beschreibt die einzelnen Funktionsgruppen eines UMS, zeigt aber keine konkreten Implementierungsmöglichkeiten auf.

Eine notwendige Voraussetzung für die Integration verschiedener Kommunikationssysteme ist die Modularität der Komponenten in Hinblick auf Austauschbarkeit und Erweiterbarkeit. Hierfür wird eine Integrationsplattform benötigt, die ein hohes Maß an Verfügbarkeit und Skalierbarkeit gewährleistet und möglichst eine plattformunabhängige Implementierung des Systems sowohl auf einem einzelnen Rechner als auch in einer verteilten heterogenen Umgebung ermöglicht. Eine weitere Kernforderung liegt in der Gewährleistung von Zustellgarantien für alle empfangenen Nachrichten, da diese für die Realisierung eines Unified Messaging Systems von essentieller Bedeutung sind.

Im Bereich Unified Messaging gibt es am Markt bereits eine Reihe kommerzieller Systeme. Die Produkte *cycos mrs* [CYC02] und *TOPCALL Unified Messaging* [TOP02] erweiterten kommerzielle Groupware Lösungen um die Eigenschaften eines Unified Messaging Systems. Bei dem Produkt *space2go enterprise2go* [S2G02] handelt es sich um eine externe Unified Messaging Lösung, die den Zugriff auf die notwendigen Unternehmensdaten über eine gesicherte Internet-Verbindung oder ein Virtual Private Network (VPN) realisiert. Als Datenquelle werden auch hier nur kommerzielle Groupware-Lösungen unterstützt. Durch die Abhängigkeit dieser kommerziellen Unified Messaging Lösungen von Fremdprodukten ergeben sich sowohl Einschränkungen bei der späteren Erweiterbarkeit als auch Beschränkungen bei der Auswahl der Betriebssystemplattform.

Die bestehenden Einschränkungen der existierenden Systeme führen zu einem neuen Architekturansatz eines Unified Messaging Systems, der im Rahmen dieses Beitrags vorgestellt wird und die zuvor genannten Forderungen wie Modularität, Verfügbarkeit, Skalierbarkeit und die Gewährleistung von Zustellgarantien für alle empfangenen Nachrichten erfüllt. Er basiert auf der Common Object Request Broker Architecture (CORBA) [OMG02] der Object Management Group (OMG) und einem CORBA Notification Service [OMG00] und kann somit plattformunabhängig realisiert werden.

Nach einer kurzen Einführung in die Grundlagen und Anforderungen von Unified Messaging Systemen (Kap. 2) erfolgt die Vorstellung der im Labor für Verteilte Systeme der Fachhochschule Wiesbaden entwickelten Systemarchitektur (Kap. 3) und des implementierten Prototyps (Kap. 4).

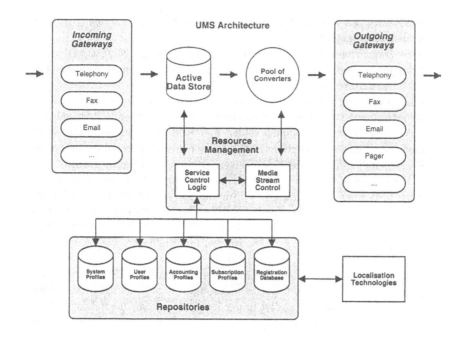

Abbildung 1. Unified Messaging Architektur nach [GMD00]

2 Grundlagen des Unified Messaging

Die Realisierung von Unified Messaging Systemen kann grundsätzlich nach zwei verschiedenen Architekturansätzen erfolgen, wobei teilweise auch Mischformen zum Einsatz kommen, die aus einzelnen Elementen der beiden Architekturen bestehen. *Client-basierte* Unified Messaging Systeme speichern alle empfangenen Nachrichten in ihrem Ursprungsformat, d.h. die Konvertierung in ein anderes Format erfolgt außerhalb des UMS. Hierzu ist auf dem UMS-Client eine spezielle Software erforderlich, die entsprechende Zugriffsmodule für alle unterstützten Ein- und Ausgabeformate enthält. Im Gegensatz dazu erfolgt bei *Server-basierten* Unified Messaging Systemen die Konvertierung der empfangenen Nachrichten direkt innerhalb des UMS, d.h. für die spätere Betrachtung von Nachrichten in einem Web-Browser oder einem E-Mail Client ist keine zusätzliche Software erforderlich. Aus diesem Grund konzentrieren sich die aktuellen Forschungsaktivitäten (z.B. [VDM99], [GMD00]) weitgehend auf Server-basierte Unified Messaging Lösungen.

Eine Referenzarchitektur für ein Server-basiertes System wird in [GMD00] vorgestellt. Diese in Abbildung 1 dargestellte Architektur besteht aus den folgenden Funktionsgruppen:

– *Gateways:* Gateways versetzen das Unified Messaging System in die Lage, Nachrichten in verschiedenen Formaten und über verschiedene Kommunikationsendgeräte empfangen und versenden zu können. Diese Gateways werden in die Kategorien *Incoming* (Nachrichtenempfang) bzw. *Outgoing* (Nachrichtenversand) eingeteilt.

- *Active Data Store:* Alle Nachrichten, die vom Unified Messaging System empfangen werden, werden vor der weiteren Verarbeitung innerhalb eines Active Data Store zwischengespeichert.
- *Pool of Converters:* Im Idealfall sollte das System alle technisch möglichen Konvertierungen von Eingabeformaten in die entsprechenden Ausgabeformate unterstützen. Ausnahmen bilden hier Konvertierungen, die zwar auf technischer Ebene realisierbar wären, deren Unterstützung aber nicht sinnvoll erscheint (zum Beispiel eine Konvertierung von Fax nach SMS).
- *Repositories:* Für den Betrieb des Unified Messaging Systems ist es für die Authentifizierung von Sendern bzw. Empfängern gegenüber dem UMS erforderlich, Informationen über Sender und Empfänger zu speichern. Zusätzlich ist es erforderlich Listen über die abonnierten Ereignisse der verschiedenen Empfänger zu führen. Diese Daten werden innerhalb verschiedener Repositories abgelegt.
- *Resource Management:* Die innerhalb der einzelnen Repositories abgelegten Einstellungen werden vom Unified Messaging System miteinander verknüpft und ausgewertet. Diese Logik ist in der Resource Management Komponente gekapselt, die auch für die Speicherung und Modifikation der Systemeinstellungen zuständig ist.
- *Localisation Technologies:* Soll der wahrscheinliche Aufenthaltsort eines Empfängers automatisch ermittelt werden, so ist es erforderlich, innerhalb des UMS sogenannte Localisation Technologies zu implementieren.

Zusätzlich zu den beschriebenen Komponenten in der Architekturansicht besteht eine Kernforderung an ein Unified Messaging System in der garantierten Zustellung aller Nachrichten. Kommt es im Bereich der zentralen Datenhaltung (Active Data Store) zu Störungen, führen diese unter Umständen zu einem kompletten Ausfall der Gateways. Der weitere Empfang bzw. Versand von Nachrichten ist in diesem Fall nicht mehr möglich. Aus diesem Grund ist es erforderlich, alle Nachrichten innerhalb des Systems so lange zwischenzuspeichern, bis sie an alle interessierten Empfänger zugestellt wurden oder aber ihre zeitliche Relevanz verloren haben. Zusätzlich werden Mechanismen benötigt, die garantieren, daß das Unified Messaging System nach einem Programm- oder Systemfehler wieder in einen konsistenten Zustand versetzt werden kann und ein Nachrichtenverlust ausgeschlossen wird.

3 Systemarchitektur

Ausgehend von der in Kapitel 2 vorgestellten Referenzarchitektur eines Unified Messaging Systems und den Anforderungen hinsichtlich Verfügbarkeit, Skalierbarkeit und Plattformunabhängigkeit wird im folgenden eine geschichtete Systemarchitektur für die Realisierung eines Unified Messaging Systems vorgestellt. Diese in Abbildung 2 dargestellte Architektur besteht aus einer unterliegenden

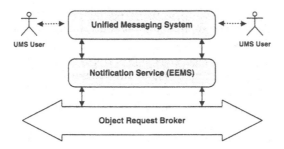

Abbildung 2. Geschichtete Systemarchitektur

generischen CORBA-basierten Schicht, bestehend aus einem Object Request Broker und einem CORBA Notification Service, sowie einer darauf basierenden Unified Messaging Schicht. Die CORBA-basierte Schicht dient innerhalb der Architektur als Integrationsplattform für die einzelnen Komponenten des Unified Messaging Systems. Auf die CORBA-basierte Schicht wird anschließend eine Unified Messaging Schicht aufgesetzt, welche die einzelnen Komponenten der beschriebenen Referenzarchitektur enthält. Hierauf wird in Abschnitt 3.2 eingegangen.

3.1 Extended Event Management Service

Der im Labor für Verteilte Systeme der Fachhochschule Wiesbaden entwickelte Extended Event Management Service (EEMS) ist parallel zur Spezifikation des Notification Service der OMG entstanden. Er besitzt neben den für das UMS notwendigen Eigenschaften des Notification Service, die im folgenden geschildert werden, einige wichtige Erweiterungen. Konzeptuell unterstützt der von der OMG spezifizierte Notification Service als Integrationsplattform aus vielerlei Hinsicht die Einhaltung der für das UMS definierten Anforderungen. Die Plattformunabhängigkeit ist bereits grundlegender Bestandteil von CORBA. Darauf aufbauend stellt der Notification Service eine Integrationsplattform, die ideal zur Entwicklung modularer, entkoppelter und skalierbarer Systeme ist. Allein die asynchrone, ereignisorientierte Kommunikation ermöglicht die Entkopplung interagierender Komponenten eines Systems, ohne sie in ihrer Funktion zu beeinträchtigen. Insbesondere eignen sich die Gateways und die Konverter des UMS hervorragend für eine solche Modularisierung, da sie ausschließlich asynchron agieren. Darüber hinaus lassen sich Instanzen von Notification Services miteinander verbinden und dadurch ganze Netzwerke aus Diensten bilden, was eine Verteilung des Dienstes selbst darstellt. Durch Filterung können die in einem solchermaßen verteilten Dienst auftretenden Ereignisströme nach beliebigen Kriterien gelenkt werden. Hierdurch kann z.B. ein intelligentes load-balancing realisiert werden. Die in Frage kommenden Filterkriterien sind vielfältig und könnten beispielsweise medien-, empfänger- oder ortsbezogen sein. Die Verfügbarkeit des Notification Service ist insbesondere in den Konsistenzeigenschaften des

Dienstes verankert, da sie eine rasche Wiederaufnahme des Betriebs im Fehlerfalle ermöglichen. Persistente Verbindungen und persistente Ereignisse erlauben die Unterbrechung von Verbindungen und den Ausfall von Teilen des Dienstes ohne Verlust eingegangener Ereignismeldungen. Durch die Möglichkeit, Erzeuger oder Konsumenten dynamisch miteinander zu verbinden, lassen sich zusätzlich Ersatz-Server einrichten, die im Betrieb hinzugeschaltet werden können, um ausgefallene Teilsysteme zu ersetzen, ohne noch aktive Teile des Systems negativ zu beeinflussen.

Über die bereits genannten grundlegenden Eigenschaften des CORBA Notification Service hinaus verfügt der EEMS zusätzlich über Mechanismen zur Authentifizierung von Benutzern, über eine Verschlüsselung von Ereignismeldungen nach dem Secure Socket Layer-Verfahren (SSL) sowie über eine Service Monitoring Schnittstelle.

Die Authentifizierung und Verschlüsselung ist insbesondere dann unverzichtbar, wenn Verbindungen zu Klienten über ungesicherte Netze hergestellt werden müssen. Weiterhin spielen beide Mechanismen eine wichtige Rolle bei der Verteilung des Dienstes, die sich ebenfalls über ungesicherte Netze hinweg erstrecken kann (Abbildung 3).

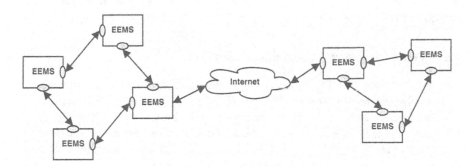

Abbildung 3. EEMS Netzwerk

Ein EEMS kennt drei unterschiedliche Sicherheitsanforderungen:

- *SSL MANDATORY:* Ein EEMS dieser Sicherheitstufe läßt ausschließlich verschlüsselte SSL-Verbindungen mit authentisierten Clients zu und ist dadurch auch für Verbindungen über öffentliche Netzwerke geeignet.
- *SSL OPTIONAL:* Diese Sicherheitsstufe erlaubt verschlüsselte und unverschlüsselte Ereigniskommunikation. Der Client bestimmt hier beim Verbindungsaufbau, ob die Kommunikation verschlüsselt erfolgen soll oder nicht.
- *SSL NO:* In Intranets, die als sicher vor unerlaubten Zugriffen angenommen werden, ist der Einsatz von Verschlüsselungs- und Authorisierungsverfahren meist nicht erforderlich. Für solche Systeme existiert diese Sicherheitsstufe, in der weder Authentisierung noch Verschlüsselung aktiv sind.

Um verschlüsselte Verbindungen zwischen Ereignisdiensten über öffentliche Netzwerke zu realisieren, ist es erforderlich, EEMS-Dienste der Sicherheitstufen "SSL NO" (privates Netzwerk) und "SSL MANDATORY" (öffentliches Netzwerk) zu verknüpfen. Dieses ist jedoch nur durch den Einsatz ein für den EEMS entwickelter EEMS Transceiver möglich, der verschlüsselte und unverschlüsselte Kommunikation beherrscht und eingehende Ereignisnachrichten an einen anderen EEMS weiterleiten kann. Er kann sich als EMS-Klient an zwei Ereignisdiensten unterschiedlicher Sicherheitsstufen anmelden und Ereignisse zwischen ihnen vermitteln. Er ermöglicht damit auch die Verbindung zwischen einem ungesicherten EEMS im privaten Netzwerk und einem gesicherten EEMS im öffentlichen Netzwerk.

Die vom Extended Event Management Service angebotenen Monitoring-Schnittstellen ermöglichen es, den EEMS als Ressource in das integrierte Management eines verteilten Systems einzubeziehen und durch proaktives Management die Systemverfügbarkeit weiter zu verbessern.

3.2 Unified Messaging Schicht

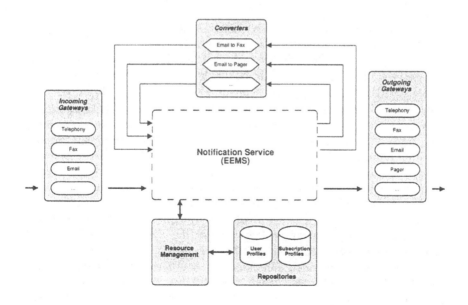

Abbildung 4. UMS Schicht auf Basis des Extended Event Management Service

Die Unified Messaging Schicht setzt auf dem in Abschnitt 3.1 beschriebenen Extended Event Management Service auf und verwendet diesen als Integrationsplattform für die einzelnen Funktionsgruppen des UMS (Abbildung 4). Die Funktionsgruppen des Systems werden abhängig von ihren Aufgaben (Versand bzw. Empfang von Ereignisnachrichten) als Erzeuger (Supplier) bzw. Verbraucher (Consumer) des Extended Event Management Service realisiert.

Hierdurch kann ein hohes Maß an Verfügbarkeit und Skalierbarkeit erreicht werden, da das System zur Laufzeit um neue Funktionsgruppen erweitert werden kann bzw. einzelne Funktionsgruppen auf andere Rechner innerhalb einer verteilten heterogenen Umgebung verlagert werden können (Rekonfiguration im laufenden Betrieb). Durch die im Extended Event Management Service bereitgestellten Persistenzeigenschaften wird sichergestellt, daß das Unified Messaging System bei einem Programm- oder Systemfehler wieder in einen konsistenten Zustand versetzt werden kann (d.h. alle Verbindungen innerhalb des Systems sind funktionsfähig, alle Objekte besitzen ihre ursprünglichen Signaturen, etc.) und ein Nachrichtenverlust ausgeschlossen wird. Hierbei kann es sich sowohl um Fehler außerhalb des UMS (z.B. Hardware, Betriebssystem, etc.), als auch um Fehler innerhalb des UMS (z.B. Verbindungsverluste) handeln.

Alle UMS-Nachrichten innerhalb des Systems werden über die im Extended Event Management Service verfügbaren Filterfunktionen selektiert.

Die Zuordnung eines Gateways kann entweder zu einem bestimmten Unified Messaging Sender bzw. Empfänger (zum Beispiel bei Sprach- oder Faxnachrichten) oder aber zu einer Gruppe von Sendern bzw. Empfängern erfolgen(zum Beispiel bei E-Mail-Nachrichten). Jedes Gateway besitzt zusätzlich zur Erzeuger- bzw. Verbraucherschnittstelle zum Extended Event Management Service noch eine Schnittstelle zum Resource Management. Über diese Schnittstelle ist es einerseits möglich, eine Authentifizierung der UMS-Nutzer durchzuführen und andererseits die für den Versand von Nachrichten notwendigen Informationen (zum Beispiel E-Mail Adresse, Telefonnumer, Faxnummer, etc.) abzufragen.

Abweichend von der in Kapitel 2 beschriebenen Referenzarchitektur, erfolgt die Konvertierung der empfangenen Nachrichten nicht innerhalb einer einzelnen Komponente (Pool of Converters). In dem hier vorgestellten Architekturansatz werden die Konverter in Form von einzelnen Modulen realisiert. Diese Konvertermodule besitzen sowohl eine Verbraucher- als auch eine Erzeugerschnittstelle. Hierdurch ist es möglich, Ereignisnachrichten vom Extendend Event Management Service zu empfangen bzw. an diesen zurück zu senden. Ist es erforderlich, eine Nachricht in ein bestimmten Format zu konvertieren, wird diese Nachricht vom Extended Event Management Service über die Konsumentenschnittstelle an den entsprechenden Konverter zugestellt, innerhalb des Konverters in das neue Ausgabeformat gewandelt und dann über die Erzeugerschnittstelle erneut an den EEMS gesendet. Dieser Ansatz ermöglicht es, Nachrichten in verschiedenen Formaten innerhalb des Extended Event Management Service abzulegen, und bietet eine enge Integration mit der bestehenden Infrastruktur. Eine spätere Erweiterung des EEMS um weitere Konverter ist jederzeit möglich.

Alle für den Betrieb des Unified Messaging Systems notwendigen Zusatzinformationen werden analog der Referenzarchitektur innerhalb eines *Repositories* abgelegt und von einer *Resource Management* Komponente verwaltet. Darüber hinaus besitzt die sie Informationen über alle innerhalb des Unified Messaging Systems existierenden Ein- bzw. Ausgabe-Gateways. Diese Informationen werden benötigt, damit an den einzelnen Gateways während der Laufzeit dynamisch alle notwendigen Filter Constraint gesetzt werden können (abhängig von den Benutzerdaten innerhalb des Repositories). Die Benutzerdaten des Unified Messaging Systems befinden sich entweder in einer lokalen Datenbank oder aber in einem Verzeichnisdienst (wie zum Beispiel LDAP [NWG95]).

4 Prototyp

Den Ausgangspunkt für die Implementierung der Extended Event Management Service Schicht bildete der ebenfalls im Labor für Verteilte System der Fachhochschule Wiesbaden entstandene Event Management Service, der derzeit auf der CORBA-Plattform ORBacus [ION02] aufsetzt. Er verfügt bereits über die grundlegenden Schnittstellen und Funktionen einer am Notification Service angelehnten ereignisorientierten Kommunikationsplattform und erlaubt eine fein granulierte Ereignisfilterung. Ein Monitoring und die Verwendung des SSL-Protokolls werden ebenso unterstützt wie der Einsatz von EEMS Transceivern.

In Hinblick auf eine Nutzung für ein Unified Messaging System war es erforderlich, die bestehende Version des Event Management Service um Ereignispersistenz und Verbindungspersistenz zu erweitern. Dazu werden alle für die Wiederherstellung der empfangenen Ereignisse und für Objektverbindungen benötigte Informationen persistent gespeichert. Hierzu wurde die Datenbankbibliothek Berkeley DB [SPC01] gewählt. Über eine spezielle Datenbankklasse werden alle Ereignisse und die aktuelle Konfiguration des Extended Event Management Service in entsprechenden Datenbanktabellen unter Verwendung der Transaktionsschnittstelle des Berkeley DB abgelegt. Nach einem Programm- oder Systemfehler erfolgt eine automatische Wiederherstellung der gesicherten Konfiguration und die Wiederaufnahme der unterbrochenen Ereigniszustellung.

Im Rahmen der prototypischen Implementierung der Unified Messaging Schicht auf Basis des Extended Event Management Service wurden Gateways für den Empfang von Faxnachrichten, Sprachnachrichten und E-Mail entwickelt. Zusätzlich wurden Ausgabegateways für Faxnachrichten, Short Messages (SMS), Sprachnachrichten und die Druckausgabe implementiert. Diese Gateways basieren auf frei verfügbaren Software-Komponenten, die für verschiedene Betriebssystemplattformen verfügbar sind (z.B. mgetty + sendfax [DOE02], vgetty [EBE98] und Festival Speech Synthesis System [UOE02]). Entsprechend ihren Funktionen (Nachrichtenempfang bzw. Nachrichtenversand) sind die Gateways in der Rolle eines Erzeugers bzw. Konsumenten mit dem Extended Event Management Service verbunden. Die vom UMS verarbeiteten Nachrichten werden in Form von Ereignismeldungen zwischen den einzelnen Komponenten des Systems vermittelt.

Die vom System unterstützten Ein- und Ausgabeformate des Unified Messaging Systems machen es erforderlich, bestimmte Nachrichtentypen vor der weiteren Verarbeitung durch einen EMS-Konsumenten zu konvertieren. Eine Sonderstellung nimmt hierbei die Ausgabe einer E-Mail als E-Mail, Sprache oder SMS ein. Für diese Gruppe von Ausgabeformaten ist eine Konvertierung der empfangenen Nachricht vor der weiteren Verarbeitung nicht notwendig. Der Text der E-Mail Nachricht kann von den einzelnen Ausgabe-Gateways direkt weiterverarbeitet und als E-Mail, in Form von Sprache oder als SMS ausgegeben werden.

Im Rahmen des Prototyps wurden die Repositories für Benutzer- und Abonnementprofile als einfache Datenstrukturen realisiert, die auf Datenbanktabellen abgebildet wurden. In einer Produktivumgebung sollte für die Speicherung und Verwaltung der notwendigen Profile ein Verzeichnisdienst wie zum Beispiel LDAP [NWG95] genutzt werden.

In Hinsicht auf eine leistungsorientierte Bewertung liegen erste Ergebnisse vor. Analog zur geschichteten Architektur wurde zunächst der Ereignisdurchsatz der EEMS-Schicht gemessen. Auf einem gering ausgestatteten PC mit einem 233 MHz getakteten AMD K6-2 Prozessor und 128 MB RAM wurden dabei für die in einem UMS zu erwartenden Ereignistypen Durchsatzraten zwischen 200 und 300 Ereignissen pro Sekunde festgestellt (s. [MAC00]). Dieses wird bei aktueller Hardware als ausreichend angesehen. Zum Beispiel beträgt das SMS-Verkehrsaufkommen aller vier Provider in England nach Schätzung anhand der Statistiken der Mobile Data Association etwa 1400 SMS pro Sekunde. Die Durchsatzrate bei aktivierter Ereignispersistenz fiel mit etwa 100 Ereignissen pro Sekunde nicht zufriedenstellend aus (s. [KOE01]). Dieses Ergebnis ist auf das synchrone Speichern der Ereignisse zurückzuführen und kann durch eine asynchrone Transaktionsvorbereitung verbessert werden (s. [KOE01]). Die Leistungsmessungen auf Anwendungsebene stehen noch aus.

Der Testbetrieb des Prototypen innerhalb einer verteilten Umgebung hat gezeigt, daß ein geschichteter Architekturansatz für die Implementation eines Unifed Messaging Systems sehr geeignet ist. Durch die Verwendung des CORBA-basierten Extended Event Management Service als Kommunikationsplattform wurde eine Systemarchitektur geschaffen, die die Integration verschiedener Unified Messaging Komponenten (Gateways, Konverter, etc.) auf einem einzelnen System oder aber innerhalb einer verteilten Systemumgebung ermöglicht und damit in hohem Maße skalierbar ist.

5 Zusammenfassung

Im Rahmen dieses Beitrags wurde ein zweischichtiger Architekturansatz zur Realisierung eines Server-basierten Unified Messaging Systems beschrieben, der auf CORBA als unterliegende Middlewareplattform aufsetzt. Für die unterliegende Schicht wurde der im Labor für Verteilte Systeme entwickelte Extended Event Management Service verwendet. Innerhalb der Unified Messaging Schicht wurden die für den Betrieb des Systems notwendigen Komponenten (Gateways, Konverter und Resource Mangement) realisiert. Daran anschließend wurde der Prototyp dieser Architektur vorgestellt.

Es ist abzusehen, daß der Bereich der Unified Messaging Anwendungen in den nächsten Jahren stark an Bedeutung gewinnen wird. Durch die steigende Flexibilität und Mobilität der Benutzer nimmt die Forderung, Informationen zu jeder Zeit, an jedem Ort und in beliebiger Form empfangen zu können, einen immer größeren Stellenwert ein. Die absehbare Bereitstellung neuer moderner Kommunikationsnetze (z. B. UMTS), die eine schnelle Übertragung großer Datenmengen zu einem mobilen Endgerät ermöglichen, wird diese Entwicklung weiter fördern.

Literatur

[BRO98] Broßler, E.: Ein verteilter offener Event Management Service auf der Basis von CORBA. Diplomarbeit, Fachhochschule Wiesbaden, FB Informatik, 1998.

[CYC02] Cycos AG: mrs - Advanced Unified Messaging, http://www.cycos.de/.

[DOE02] Döring, G.: mgetty + sendfax, a collection of programs to send and receive faxes in a unix environment. http://alpha.greenie.net/mgetty/.

[EBE98] Eberhardt, M.: vgetty, a collection of programs to add voice capabilities to mgetty. http://alpha.greenie.net/vgetty/.

[GMD00] GMD FOKUS: Technology PACER, The Technology Newsletter of GMD FOKUS for the PACE Project, No. 3, July 2000.

[ION02] IONA Technologies: ORBacus 4.1, http://www.orbacus.com/

[KOE01] Köhler, F.: Erweiterung eines CORBA-basierten Event Management Dienstes zur Realisierung eines Unified Messaging Systems. Diplomarbeit, Fachhochschule Wiesbaden, FB Informatik, 2001.

[MAC00] Machens, H.: Redesign eines CORBA-basierten Event Management Dienstes zur Kooperation intelligenter Automatisierungsgeräte. Diplomarbeit, Fachhochschule Wiesbaden, FB Informatik, 2000.

[NAN97] Nanneman, D.: Unified Messaging: A Progress Report. Telecommunications Magazine, March 1997.

[NWG95] Network Working Group: Lightweight Directory Access Protocol, RFC-1777, 1995.

[OMG00] Object Management Group: Notification Service Specification. Version 1.0, 2000.

[OMG01] Object Management Group: Event Service Specification. Version 1.1, 2001.

[OMG02] Object Management Group: CORBA/IIOP Specification. Version 2.6.1, 2002.

[PIK98] Magedanz T., Pfeifer T.: Unified Messaging + Medienflexibilität = Allgegenwärtige Erreichbarkeit. PIK - Praxis der Informationsverarbeitung und Kommunikation, 21. Jahrgang 3/1998.

[S2G02] space2go.com GmbH & Co. KG: enterprise2go - Mobile E-Mail- und Intranetlösungen, http://www.space2go.com/

[SPC01] Sleepycat Software Inc.: Berkeley DB. New Riders Publishing, 2001.

[TOP02] TOPCALL International AG: TOPCALL Unified Messaging, http://www.topcall.com/

[UOE02] University of Edinburgh: The Festival Speech Synthesis System. http://www.cstr.ed.ac.uk/projects/festival/.

[VDM99] v.d. Meer, S., Arbanowski, St., Magedanz, T.: An Approach for a 4th Generation Messaging System. The Fourth International Symposium on Autonomous Decentralized Systems, ISADS'99, Tokyo, March 1999.

Session Mobile Computing

Interaktionsmuster zur dynamischen Personalisierung von Dienstendpunkten in Ubiquitous Computing Umgebungen

Michael Samulowitz, Claudia Linnhoff-Popien

Institut für Informatik, Ludwig-Maximilians-Universität München, Oettingenstr. 67
D-80538 München, Tel: 089 / 2180-9149, Fax: 089 / 2180-9147
{samulo | linnhoff}@informatik.uni-muenchen.de

Zusammenfassung

Künftige Computerumgebungen sollen dem Nutzer kaum Aufmerksamkeit für die eigentliche Technik abverlangen. Dabei ist die kontextadaptive Dienstbereitstellung zentrales Anliegen für ein nutzerfreundliche Systemverhalten. Als Schritt in diese Richtung soll ein Konzept zur Personalisierung von Endgeräten in einer Ubiquitous Computing Umgebung vorgestellt werden.

Dabei werden individuellen Geräten sogenannte Interaktionsmuster zugewiesen. Diese spezifizieren das Verhalten der Endgeräte, indem sie die Interaktionen zwischen den Geräten bzgl. kontextueller Bedingungen einschränken. Zugewiesene Interaktionsmuster können zu jeder Zeit manipuliert oder auch gelöscht werden. Auf diese Weise ist es möglich, das Systemverhalten anzupassen, ohne unterliegende Softwarekomponenten modifizieren zu müssen. Ein entwickeltes Tool unterstützt den Benutzer bei der Erstellung von Interaction Templates und deren Verbreitung auf die Endgeräte.

1 Einleitung

Die Entwicklung von Ubiquitous Computing Systemen geht einher mit dem Konzept der Smart Spaces [KLST 96, AS 00]. Der Computer wird omnipräsent, d.h. Teil unseres Alltags zur Ausführung privater und geschäftlicher Aufgaben. Neben diesen technischen Aspekten steht das Ubiquitous Computing Paradigma auch für den Anspruch der einfachen Benutzbarkeit von computerbasierten Diensten, so beispielsweise dafür, die Anzahl der Nutzer/System-Interaktionen zu reduzieren.

Ein Smart Space ist ein Raum, der von einer Menge sogenannter Smart Nodes aufgespannt wird. Dies sind Endgeräte oder eingebettete Systeme [BW 00] mit einer autonomen Energieversorgung und einem drahtlosen Netzzugang, sowie ggf. Sensoren, um die Implementierung situationsadaptiver Applikationen zu begünstigen [Dey 00, DeyAb 00]. Beispiele für Smart Nodes sind PDAs, Drucker, Kameras, Head-up Displays und Mikrofone. Smart Nodes werden anwendungsbezogen in dynamischen Föderationen organisiert, die direkt vernetzt sind oder auch indirekt über Backbones wie z.B. das Internet.

Smart Nodes bilden einen Dienstraum, der sich aus dem Dienstangebot der einzelnen Knoten zusammensetzt. Diesbezüglich werden diensterbringende Smart Nodes als *Dienstendpunkte* bezeichnet. Im folgenden soll ein Konzept vorgeschlagen werden, welches es erlaubt, das Prozeßverhalten von Dienstendpunkten zu personalisieren. Ziel ist dabei eine Vereinfachung des Umgangs mit Endgeräten. Während klassische Methoden sich insbesondere auf die Personalisierung von einzelnen Anwendungssystemen beziehen – z.B. auf den personalisierten Web-Zugriff –, soll hier ein Konzept vorgeschlagen werden, welches die Personalisierung der Interaktionen zwischen Dienstendpunkten ermöglicht. Dieses Konzept basiert auf einem System zur kontextadaptiven Dienstnutzung [SMLP 01a, SMLP 01b], welches die situationsbezogene Selektion und Ausführung von Diensten in einer Ubiquitous Computing Umgebung erlaubt. Diese Basis ist Gegenstand von Kapitel 3.

Darauf basierend präsentiert Kapitel 4 das Konzept des *Interaktionsmusters*. Damit ist es möglich, die Dienstinteraktionen zwischen individuellen Dienstendpunkten dynamisch anzupassen, um so dem Ziel der Personalisierung innerhalb eines Dienstraumes gerecht zu werden. Kapitel 5 vermittelt eine Übersicht über die prototypische Implementierung, und Kapitel 6 schließt mit einem Ausblick ab.

2 Technische Grundlagen einer Ubiquitous Computing Umgebung

Ubiquitous Computing Umgebungen zeichnen sich durch einfache Bedienbarkeit intelligenter Endgeräte, Diversifikation und damit einhergehende Heterogenität sowie Möglichkeiten der spontanen Vernetzung aus. Diese Techniken sollen im folgenden detaillierter betrachtet werden.

Abb. 1: Kommunikationshierarchie der Spontanen Vernetzung

Spontane Vernetzung

Spontane Vernetzung dient der dynamischen Kooperation von Endgeräten. Sie erstreckt sich über die Ebenen der Kommunikationshierarchie eines Systems [Kur 00], vgl. Abbildung 1.

Die *Netzwerkebene* ist für die Kommunikation zwischen Dienstendpunkten zuständig, wobei eine automatische Verhandlung von Kommunikationsparametern gefordert wird. Dies können bei TCP/IP-Netzen [Stev 94] bspw. IP-Adressen sein, welche den einzelnen Dienstendpunkten mittels DHCP [DL 02] zugewiesen werden. Spontane Kommunikation wird dabei im allgemeinen durch sogenannte Zero-Configuration-Netze [ZERO 02] realisiert, bei denen keine dedizierte Instanz für die Konfiguration und Administration erforderlich ist.

Bluetooth [Blue] ist das Beispiel eines typischen Ad-Hoc-Netzes zur spontanen Kommunikation zwischen Endgeräten wie Handys, PDAs, Note- und Subnotebooks. Die Kommunikation erfolgt über drahtlose Piconetze. Bluetooth-Geräte, die aktuell keinem Piconetz angehören, horchen dabei laufend nach anderen Bluetooth-Geräten. Kommen diese genügend nahe, so identifizieren sich die neuen Geräte und werden selbst Mitglied des Pico-Netzes. Dadurch können bei Bedarf auch andere Geräte mit ihnen kommunizieren.

Die *Infrastrukturebene* realisiert den Austausch von Informationen, welche eine Kooperation von multiplen Ressourcen unterstützen. Dieser Vorgang dient der Kommunikation von Diensteigenschaften zwischen Ressourcen und wird auch als Dienstvermittlung bezeichnet.

Die *Dienstebene* behandelt schließlich die eigentliche Nutzung eines durch die Infrastrukturebene vermittelten Dienstes, wobei Vorgaben der Infrastrukturebene den Prozeß der Dienstnutzung mitbestimmen können.

Dienstvermittlung

Ausgangspunkt für die Dienstvermittlung ist eine Dienstbeschreibung, welche die Funktionalität und Schnittstelle eines Dienstes spezifiziert und dessen Format vom zugrundeliegenden Dienstvermittlungsprotokoll abhängig ist. Nachdem ein Dienstanbieter seinen Dienst angeboten hat, kann durch eine anfragende Instanz über einen Lookup-Prozeß die Vermittlung eines Dienstes erfolgen, indem ein Name, eine Adresse oder ein bestimmtes Matchingkriterium ausgewertet werden. Eine derartige Implementierung ist z.b. im CORBA Naming Service [OMG 99] oder LDAP [WHK 97] realisiert.

Im Gegensatz zu einem Lookup-Dienst erlaubt ein Discovery-Dienst das Auffinden von Objekten unabhängig von einem dedizierten Verzeichnisdienst. Objekte können ihre Verfügbarkeit anderer Objekten unmittelbar mitteilen, und auch das Auffinden von Objekten kann durch direkte Kommunikation zwischen Objekten geschehen. Besondere Merkmale eines Discovery-Dienstes sind die spontane Lokalisierung und Konfiguration von Diensten und Netzelementen und die automatische Anpassung an eine sporadische Verfügbarkeit von Objekten, z.b. auf Grund von Mobilität [McG 00]. Diese Form der Dienstvermittlung wird von folgenden Entwicklungen unterstützt.

Jini [JINI] ist eine Java-basierte Entwicklung der Firma Sun Microsystems. Alle Jini einsetzenden Systeme müssen vollständig konfiguriert sein und über eine Java Virtual Machine verfügen. Jini-Systeme bestehen aus dienstanfragenden Clients, anzubietenden Dienstinstanzen und einem über einen Service Discovery Mechanismus zu lokalisierenden Lookup Service. Zur Beschreibung von Diensten werden Service Templates eingesetzt, ein Dienst-Proxy-Objekt ist Gegenstand der eigentlichen Vermittlung. Das Problem der Aktualität wird über Leasings realisiert, d.h. Objektreferenzen sind nur endliche Zeit gültig.

Im Gegensatz zu Jini unterstützt Universal Plug and Play (UPnP) [UPnP] die spontane Vernetzung von Komponenten in einem Ad-Hoc-Netz. Zur Lokalisierung eines Dienstes initiiert der Discovery Client eine Anfrage mittels des Simple Service Discovery Protocols (SSDP), einem HTTP-basieren Dienstvermittlungsprotokoll. Geeignete Geräte reagieren durch Rücksendung ihrer URL. Weitere Ansätze der Dienstvermittlung sind das Service Location Protocol (SLP) der Internet Engineering Task Force und das in Bluetooth verwendete Service Discovery Protocol (SDP).

Kontextadaptivität

Nach [DeyAb 00] wird unter *Kontext* jegliche Information verstanden, die zwecks Charakterisierung der Situation einer Entität benutzt werden kann. Eine Entität ist dabei eine Person, ein Ort oder ein – bzgl. der Interaktion zwischen Nutzer und Anwendung – relevantes Objekt.

Die Nutzung und anwendungsspezifische Interpretation solcher Kontextinformationen ermöglicht Dienste, die sich der jeweilige Situation anpassen. Entsprechend ihrer Relevanz unterscheidet man primäre und sekundäre, d.h. abgeleitete Kontexttypen. Zu ersteren gehören die Identität einer Entität, Ortsinformationen und Aktivitäten. Sekundär könnten Zeitinformationen, Umgebungsvariablen und Ressourcen in der Nähe des Benutzers sein.

Ein *kontextadaptives System* interpretiert diese Informationen, um sich einer Situation anzupassen. Dazu ist eine z.B. über Sensoren erzielte Konstruktion [SDA 99, SL 01], eine Repräsentation und die situationsadaptive Verarbeitung von Kontextinformationen erforderlich [Pas 98b]. Basis von Austausch und Verarbeitung auf verteilten Komponenten ist ein einheitliches Repräsentationsformat [Sch 00].

Charakteristisch für kontextadaptive Systeme sind das Lokalitätsprinzip und die Zeitnähe. Unter dem Lokalitätsprinzip versteht man, dass Kontextinformationen in ihrer Bedeutung örtlich eingeschränkt sind. Am Ort der Gewinnung ist eine Kontextinformation am höchsten, und mit zunehmendem Abstand davon nimmt ihre Bedeutung in der Regel ab. Diesen Anforderungen soll im folgenden mittels eines ortsspezifischen Domänenmodells entsprochen werden.

Komplementär ist das Prinzip der Zeitnähe zu verstehen. Mit zunehmender zeitlicher Verzögerung nimmt die Relevanz von Messdaten ab. Optimal wäre eine Gleichzeitigkeit von Erfassung und Auswertung der Messdaten, wodurch systemtechnisch Echtzeiteigenschaften eines kontextadaptiven Systems gefordert wären.

3 Ein System zur kontextadaptiven Dienstnutzung

Die vorgestellten Techniken der Dienstvermittlung sollen nun zu einer kontextadaptiven Selektion in dem Sinne erweitert werden, dass die Vermittlung nicht ausschließlich durch die Spezifikation von gewünschten Dienstattributen erfolgt, sondern auch Kontextinformationen Berücksichtigung finden. In gleichem Sinne kann auch die Ausführung eines Dienstes kontextabhängig erfolgen. Die Kombination von kontextadaptiver Selektion und Ausführung ermöglicht so eine personalisierte und situationsbezogene Bereitstellung von Diensten.

Zunächst soll ein Szenario vorgestellt werden.

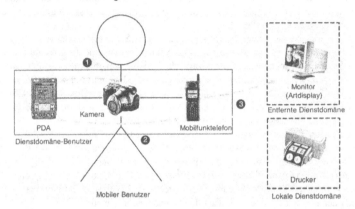

Abb. 2: Szenario der Bildverarbeitung eines digitalen Nutzers

Drei Endgeräte eines mobilen Nutzers, d.h. Digitalkamera, PDA und Handy, seien innerhalb eines Peronal Aera Networks (PANs) wie etwa Bluetooth organisiert. Das PAN bilde dabei eine abgeschlossene Dienstdomäne, so dass die angeschlossenen Geräte wechselseitig genutzt werden können. In zwei weiteren entfernten Dienstdomänen außerhalb des PAN seien ein sogenanntes Artdisplay zur dauerhaften Anzeige von digitalem Bildmaterial bzw. ein Drucker verfügbar. Die vom Nutzer geschossenen Fotos können nun auf dem PDA angezeigt und ggf. weiterverarbeitet werden. Entsprechend dem Dienstangebot der Umgebung – z.B. Existenz eines Druckers – könnte alternativ auch ein Ausdruck auf einem lokal verfügbaren Drucker erfolgen. Steht dieser nicht zur Verfügung, so soll die Anzeige des Bildes auf dem heimatlichen Artdisplay erfolgen. Die Daten werden dann zunächst an das Mobiltelefon übertragen. Dieses Telefon agiert als Kommunikationsserver. Zu einem früheren Zeitpunkt hatte der Benutzer bereits verfügt, dass Daten, die ein bestimmtes Volumen überschreiten, aus Kostengründen i.a. nicht über Weitverkehrsnetze übertragen werden dürfen. Da diese Daten nicht zeitkritisch sind, soll ein Datentransport erst in Reichweite des Heimatnetzes erfolgen, so dass das Bild dann auf dem Artdisplay angezeigt werden kann.

Zur Realisierung eines solchen Systemverhaltens soll im folgenden eine Architektur vorgestellt werden, welche die Vermittlung von Daten inhaltsbezogen und basierend kontextueller Restriktionen zu gestalten.

Datenzentrisches Protokoll

Zwecks Realisierung einer kontextadaptiven Dienstvermittlung in Ubiquitous Computing Umgebungen soll ein Datenzentrisches Protokoll [EHAS 99] genutzt werden, das der Kommunikation von Anwendungsdaten zwischen verteilten, autonomen Netzwerkknoten dient. Dieses zeichnet sich aus durch

- Uniforme Datenformate für Applikationsdaten
- Applikationsspezifische Metadaten

- Contentbased Routing
- Mechanismen zur Daten- und Dienstkomposition

Der Weg einer Nachricht vom Sender über intermediäre Knoten bis zum Empfänger wird durch Datenpfade beschrieben, die durch Context Constraints festgelegt werden [SMLP 01a]. Metadaten erlauben die Unterstützung von Weak Connectivity und Ad-Hoc-Netzen. So können Daten z.b. auch dann zu ihrem Empfänger geschickt werden, wenn die Netzverbindung zum Sender nicht mehr vorhanden ist, da der assoziierte Netzpfad die Verarbeitung der versandten Daten vollständig beschreibt.

Dienstmodell

Basierend auf dem Lokalitätsprinzip und dem Einsatz lokaler Netze wie bspw. Bluetooth wird eine Einteilung in Domänen vorgenommen, die über einen sogenannten Service Interaction Proxy (SIP) zwecks Verwaltung der enthaltenen Dienste und Sensoren verfügen. SIPs sind über ein Backbonenetz miteinander verbunden, so dass eine indirekte Kommunikation zugehöriger Ressourcen möglich ist, vgl. Abbildung 3.
Der Vorteil dieser Herangehensweise liegt in einer möglichen Standardisierung der Kommunikation zwischen Domänenkontrollern. Damit lässt sich auch in einer heterogenen Dienst- oder Sensorumgebung ein einheitliches Datenformat für die Kommunikation einsetzen.

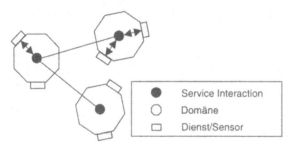

Abb. 3: Dienstmodell für die kontextadaptive Dienstnutzung

Context Aware Packets (CAPs)

Das Endgerät eines Benutzers soll nun als Portal in den umgebenden Dienstraum fungieren. Damit erhält es die Rolle eines Mediators, d.h., es vermittelt Dienstanforderungen zwischen einem Nutzer und der umgebenden Infrastruktur.
Aufbauend auf dem Datenzentrischen Protokoll soll nun von einer *Assoziativen Adressierung* ausgegangen werden. Da sich Adressen aufgrund dynamischer Adresszuweisungen in Ubiquitous Computing Umgebungen ändern können, wird unter der Assoziativen Adressierung eine dynamische Determinierung von empfangenden Netzwerkknoten verstanden, die mit der Spezifikation des Empfängers über Context Contstraints zusammenwirken.
Zentral ist ferner ein uniformes Datenformat, welches zur Repräsentation und Vermittlung von Dienstanforderungen zwischen den Komponenten eines Systems eingesetzt wird. Dieses Datenformat wird als Context-Aware Packet (CAP) bezeichnet.
CAPs werden vom Endgerät des Nutzers erzeugt und in den umgebenden Dienstraum „injiziert" und dort evaluiert, so dass eine Selektion und Ausführung von einem oder mehreren Diensten kommt. Dabei gestatten sie die Darstellung von Dienstanforderungen mit hohem Abstraktionsgrad. Ein Nutzer sendet ein CAP zu einem SIP, der das eingehende CAP evaluiert und es ggf. mittels eines durch Context Constraints gesteuerten Routingprozesses an eine andere zuständige Domäne weitersendet.
CAPs lassen sich in drei Teile gliedern, siehe Abbildung 4: *Context Constraints* repräsentieren Nutzeranforderungen, *Meta Constraints* definieren Regeln zur Evaluierung assoziierter

Context Constraints. Dabei können sie einfach (One shot) oder mehrfach (Multiple shot) eingesetzt werden bzw. mit (Interactive mode) oder ohne Bestätigung (Non Interactive Mode) eines Nutzers zur Ausführung kommen. Ferner kann die Fehlerbehandlung über Meta Constraints beeinflusst werden und eine Abspeicherung von Zwischenergebnissen einer CAP-Evaluierung erfolgen. Ein *Datenteil* enthält schließlich die zur Ausführung einer Interaktion beim Empfänger benötigten Daten. Dabei können sowohl die Anzahl der Dateneinträge als auch deren Formate variieren.

Context Constraints: $(cc_1, ..., cc_N)$
Meta Constraints: $(mc_1, ..., mc_M)$
Data: $(part_1, ..., part_N)$

Abb. 4: Struktur eines CAPs

Die CAPEUS-Architektur

Die beschriebenen Konzepte werden nun innerhalb einer Architektur zusammengefasst, die als *Context Aware Packets Enabling Ubiquitous Computing (CAPEUS)* [SMLP 01b] bezeichnet wird. Dabei definiert ein mehrstufiges CAP eine Folge von Dienstinteraktionen über eine Menge von verteilten Domänen hinweg. In Abbildung 5 wird ein solcher Prozeß beschrieben.

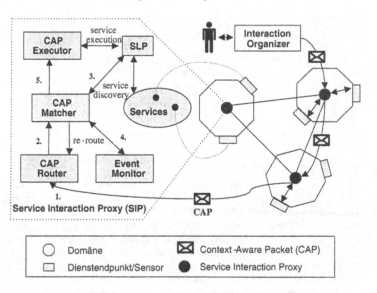

Abb. 5: Die CAPEUS-Architektur

Ein Benutzer tritt über einen als Benutzeragenten fungierenden Interaction Organizer in Interaktion mit der Umgebung. Nutzer- bzw. aufgabenbezogen erzeugt der Interaction Organizer CAPs, die an eine Menge vernetzer Dienstdomänen gesendet werden. Ein CAP-Router empfängt das Paket (1) und leitet es an einen Matcher weiter (2). Angenommen, es liegt die richtige Domäne vor und alle CAP-Relationen können erfolgreich ausgewertet werden (3), so kann ein Dienst lokalisiert werden und das CAP verbleibt im SIP (4). Der Event-Monitor beobachtet dann die Umgebung, bis eine Situation entsteht, die den in den Context Constraints angegebenen Events entspricht (5). Schließlich wird der Dienst ausgeführt, indem der Datenteil des CAPs und eine Dienstreferenz zum Executor gesendet werden.

4 Das Konzept der Interaktionsmuster

Die kontextadaptive Dienstintegration basiert auf dem Konzept des Interaktionsmusters. Interaktionsmuster ordnen einem Endgerät bzw. Dienstendpunkt ein bestimmtes Prozessverhalten zu. Dazu werden folgende Attribute verwendet: *Name, Location, Iteration, SessionID, Trigger* und eine Menge von assoziierten Interaktionen. Analog zur Spezifikation der CAPs können die Operationen als Iteration im Modus One shot oder Multi shot ausgeführt werden. Der Trigger definiert – ausgehend vom internen Status einer Entität – mittels eines logischen Ausdrucks, unter welchen Bedingungen das System ein Interaktionsmuster aktiviert.

Die erfolgreiche Evaluierung eines Interaktionsmusters mündet in der kontextadaptiven Generierung eines oder mehrerer CAPs oder einem lokalen Methodenaufruf bzw. der rekursiven Erzeugung eines weiteren Interaktionsmusters, vgl. Abbildung 6.

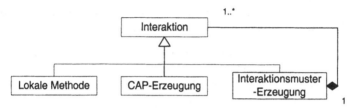

Abb. 6: Rekursive Komposition von Interaktionen

Lokale Methode bezeichnen dabei gerätespezifische Dienste eines Dienstendpunktes, z.B. einen Bildauslösemechanismus bei einer Digitalkamera. Zwecks CAP-Erzeugung muß eine Entität ein entsprechendes API zur Verfügung stellen. Ein Constraint und ein Data Constructor definieren in Übereinstimmung mit dem Interaktionsmuster, mit Applikationsdaten und Statusinformationen eine Menge von Entitätsbeschreibungen und Relationen, die in einem CAP angelegt werden, siehe Abbildung 7. Das generierte CAP kann dann entweder lokal oder über einen SIP versendet werden.

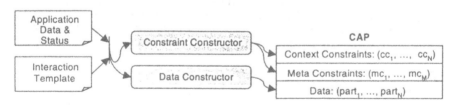

Abb. 7: Konstruktion eines CAPs

Schließlich kann die Auswertung eines Interaktionsmusters auch in der Erzeugung neuer Interaktionsmuster resultieren.

Komposition von Interaktionsmustern

Als Gegenstück kann im Falle ein und derselben Entität auch eine Kombination von Interaktionsmustern erfolgen, um eine komplexere Aufgabe geschlossen abzubilden. Als dadurch induzierte Kommunikationsmuster (Communication Patterns) sollen Sequenz, Verzweigung und Zyklus unterschieden werden. Das Prinzip wird in Abbildung 9 und 10 anhand zweier Szenarien veranschaulicht.

Das Übertragen des Fotos zum Handy und das Speichern im Albumdienst beziehen sich im einführenden Szenario auf dieselben Daten, d.h. das erstellte Foto. Aus diesem Grund muß ein Interaktionsmuster mit Bedingung „Foto erstellt" als spezifizierten Trigger definiert werden.

Bei Erfüllung der Triggerfunktion konstruiert die Digitalkamera das CAP, welches das Mobiltelefon beauftragt, das Foto zum Anzeigedienst zu senden und dann der Zielentität den Befehl „Anzeige des Fotos" erteilt. Diese Sequenz wird automatisch ausgeführt.

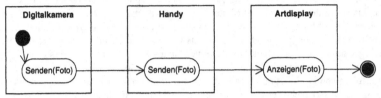

Abb. 9: Datenbasierte Sequenz

Komplementär zu diesem Konzept der *datenbasierten Sequenz* können sich Sequenzen auch auf einen einzigen Dienstendpunkt beziehen, dieser Sachverhalt soll als *dienstendpunktbasierte Sequenz* bezeichnet werden.

In einem Interaktionsmuster kann auch ein Auslöser definiert werden, der sich auf die Bedingung einer Verzweigung bezieht. Als Beispiel soll die Lautstärke einer Stereoanlage beim Telefonieren reduziert werden und nach Beendigung des Telefonats in den Ursprungszustand zurückversetzt werden.

Abb. 10: Verzweigung

Dazu wird am Telefon ein Multi-shot Interaktionsmuster definiert, das durch das Abheben des Telefonhörers ausgelöst wird und aus zwei Interaktionen besteht. Die erste Interaktion konstruiert ein CAP, um die Lautstärke zu verringern, dann generiert das Interaktionsmuster ein weiteres One-shot Interaktionsmuster, um die Lautstärke am Ende des Telefonats wieder zu erhöhen.

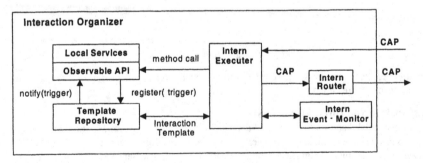

Abb. 11: Architektur des Interaction Organizers

Evaluierung von Interaktionsmustern

Die CAPEUS-Architektur soll nun hinsichtlich einer automatischen Generierung von CAPs erweitert werden. Dazu wird die Komponente des Interaction Organizers in dem Sinne erweitert, dass basierend auf der Evaluation von Interaktionsmustern CAPs automatisch generiert werden können. Ferner wird eine sitzungsabhängige Adressierung für CAPs unterstützt. Die resultierende Architektur ist in Abbildung 11 dargestellt. Oft ist es von Interesse, bestimmte Komponenten über einen Statuswechsel einer anderen Komponente zu benachrichtigen. Das Observable API erlaubt es analog zu [Woo 96], Interaktionstypen zur Laufzeit eines Systems zu parametrisieren. Insbesondere bei der spontanen Vernetzung kann dieses Konzept gewinnbringend eingesetzt werden. Observable APIs erlauben die Inspektion einer Schnittstelle (Examination), die Beeinflussung des Status einer Komponente (Manipulation) sowie die Überwachung von Statusinformationen (Observation). Die Registrierung von interessierenden Komponenten erfolgt dabei nicht über a priori gegebene Definitionen sondern über einen logischen Ausdruck, der festlegt, bei welchem Zustand eine Benachrichtigung erfolgt. Wird eine Trigger-Bedingung erfüllt, so wird das Template Repository benachrichtigt – ein Datenbankmanagementsystem, das den Primärschlüssel *Name* verwendet. Mit dem Template Repository können Interaktionsmuster hinzugefügt, gelöscht, aufgelistet und ausgewählt werden, um an den Intern Executer weitergegeben zu werden. Der Intern Executer ist die zentrale Komponente für die Ausführung von Interaktionen und die Evaluierung von Interaktionsmustern und CAPs, siehe Abbildung 12.

---

1. Falls die Interaktion kein Event enthält, gehe zu Schritt 2; anderenfalls liefert der Intern Executer die Event Bedingung an den Intern Event Monitor. Wenn die Auswertung des Events positiv ist, gehe zu Schritt 2, anderenfalls wird die Auswertung der Interaktion abgebrochen.

2. Wenn die Interaktion eine lokale Methode bezeichnet, wird sie bei der *Observable API* aufgerufen.

3. Falls es sich bei der Interaktion um eine CAP-Erzeugung oder Interaktionsmuster-Erzeugung handelt, wird sie direkt beim *Intern Executer* bearbeitet, als Resultat wird das konstruierte CAP bzw. Interaktionsmuster zurückgeliefert.

4. Das konstruierte CAP wird an den *Router* und das Interaktionsmuster an das *Template Repository* weitergeleitet.

Abb. 12: Algorithmus des Intern Executers für die Interaktionsaußführung

Der Intern Event-Monitor bezieht Umgebungsdaten mittels Sensoren und implementiert zwecks Abgleich von Sensordaten sowohl ein Push- als auch ein Pullmodell.

Das Konzept des Intern Routers erweitert schließlich die von CAPEUS implementierten Routingprozesse. Basierend auf der Auswertung von Interaktionsmustern kann ein Teil der Routingfunktionalität unmittelbar in Dienstendpunkte verlagert werden. Während CAPEUS die assoziative Zustellung von CAPs über Subnetze hinweg erlaubt, kann das Routing des Intern Routers innerhalb eines Subnetzes angewandt werden. Diese Kombination bietet sich insbesondere in Personal Area Networks an, in denen individuelle Dienstendpunkte mittels einer drahtlosen Netztechnologie miteinander verbunden werden, z.B. mittels Bluetooth. Der sich ergebende Routing-Algorithmus ist in Abbildung 13 für sogenannte abstrakte Entitäten dargestellt, bei denen die Zieladresse durch die in den Context Constraints angegebenen Dienstanforderungen bestimmt wird.

Toolkit zur Konstruktion von Interaktionsmustern

Mittels eines Mediators wird die Konstruktion neuer sowie die Modifikation bereits bestehender Interaktionsmuster ermöglicht. Dabei wird der Nutzer durch ein Toolkit mit einer graphischen Nutzeroberfläche unterstützt. Zunächst wird die Menge der an einem Prozeß beteiligten Dienstendpunkte bestimmt, von denen die Dienstschnittstelle angefordert wird. Dann erfolgt die Definition der Interaktionsmuster und ggf. eine Zerlegung und Verteilung.

1. Service Discovery initiieren (vgl. Abschnitt Dienstvermittlung).

2. Evaluieren der Ergebnisse aus Schritt 1 bzgl. Relationen des CAPs.

3. Ausgabe von Schritt 2 nach einen vordefinierten Kriterium sortieren (z.B. räumlicher Abstand). Das erste Ergebnis wird dann als Ziel selektiert, die verbleibenden Kandidaten werden im Meta Constraint des CAPs zwischengespeichert.

4. Zieladresse uns SessionID in die Routing-Tabelle eintragen.Falls die Ziel-Entität nicht ansprechbar ist oder das CAP wegen anderer Gründe (z.B. Netzfehler) nicht zustellbar ist, wird der nächste Kandidat den Meta Constraints entnommen; die Routing-Tabelle wird entsprechend modifiziert. Dieser Prozeß wird solange wiederholt, bis keine weiteren Kandidaten mehr verfügbar sind.

Abb. 13: Routing-Algorithmus des Intern Executers am Beispiel abstrakter Entitäten

5 Prototypische Implementierung

Der Interaction Organizer zur Handhabung der Interaktionsmuster erweitert die in Java implementierte CAPEUS-Architektur um die kontextadaptive Dienstintegration in Ubiquitous Computing Umgebungen. Zur Implementierung dieser Komponente wurden die entsprechenden Komponenten in der Programmiersprache Phyton [Ph] implementiert.

Phyton ist eine objektorientierte, interpretierte Sprache, die als freie Software für nahezu alle gängigen Systemumgebungen (u.a. UNIX, Microsoft Windows, Apple Macintosh, Palm OS) verfügbar ist. Neben der Plattformunabhängigkeit und Ausnahmebehandlung bietet Phyton eine direkte Realisierung der Mehrfachvererbung, gut integrierte XML-Anbindung sowie dynamische Generierung und Interpretation von Quelltext.

So ist es möglich, zur Laufzeit die Objektstruktur zu modifizieren, so dass Objekte dynamisch aufgebaut werden können. Mittels der Funktionen eval und exec besteht die Möglichkeit, Codefragmente zur Laufzeit auszuwerten. Innerhalb des Interaction Organizers kann eval in hervorragender Weise zur dynamischen Auswertung von Trigger-Bedingungen eingesetzt werden, die mittels Phyton Codefragmenten repräsentiert werden.

Im folgenden insbesondere die Implementierung der Observable API erläutert werden.

Implementierungsaspekte Observable API

Zur Realisierung der Observable API wurden die Software-Techniken Mehrfachvererbung und das erweiterte Observer Designmuster [GHJV 95] angewandt. Die Erläuterung der Implementierung erfolg bzgl. des Szenarios aus Kapitel 4, Abbildung 10. Folgende Klassen dienen zur Realisierung der Observable API: Telephone, ObservableService und ObservableAPI. Die Telephone Klasse spezifiziert die native Dienstschnittstelle des Telefons. Telephone unterscheidet die folgenden Attribute zur Spezifikation des internen Zustandes: isRinging, isWaiting und isTalking. Neben den Attributen definiert die Klasse noch folgende Methoden: ring(self), pickUp(), ringOff(), activateSpeaker() und getService-Description(), welche die entsprechenden Dienste implementieren. Der Aufruf der Methode getServiceDescription() liefert die Dienstbeschreibung des Telefonapparates als XML-Dokument.

Die ObservableService-Klasse realisiert das erweiterte Observer-Designmuster, welches es erlaubt, den Status einer Komponente bzgl. registrierbarer Kriterien zu überwachen und die erfüllten Kriterien bekannt gibt. Die ObservableService-Klasse ist nicht dienst- oder gerätespezifisch. Sie kann bei allen zu überwachenden Dienstendpunkten eingesetzt werden. Sie enthält zwei Attribute: criterList, templateManager. Das Attribut citerList ist eine Liste, die alle registrierten Kriterien zusammenfaßt. Das Attribut templateManager verweist auf den Interessenten für ein bestimmtes Kriterium. Zur Verwaltung der zu überwachenden Kriterien definiert ObservableService die folgenden Methoden:

- __init__() : der Konstruktor erzeugt ein neues Objekt des beobachtbaren Dienstes
- addCriterion(criter) : registriert das übergebene Kriterium criter, indem es in die Liste criterList hinzugefügt wird
- deleteCriterion(criter) : löschen eines registrierten Kriteriums
- getCriterions() : gibt alle registrierten Kriterien aus
- Notify(criter) : teilt dem templateManager das erfüllte Kriterium mittels self.templateManager.fire(criter) mit
- checkAll() : überprüft alle registrierten Kriterien und meldet erfüllte Kriterien an templateManager
- check(criter) : überprüft mittels eval(criter) das angegebene Kriterium criter und liefert das Ergebnis zurück

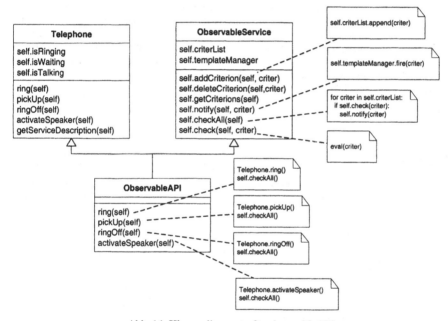

Abb. 14: Klassendiagramm für observableAPI

Die Observable API ist die erweiterte API und vereinigt die Funktion der nativen Dienstschnittstelle eines Dienstendpunktes mit Überwachungsfunktionen. Das heißt, die Klasse ObservableAPI erhält die Funktionalitäten der beiden oben beschriebenen Klassen; sie wird daher mittels Mehrfachvererbung der beiden Klassen realisiert, siehe Abbildung 14.

Die abgeleitete Klasse ObservableAPI besitzt nun alle Attribute und Methoden der beiden Oberklassen. Die Überwachung der registrierten Kriterien wird dadurch realisiert, daß nach jedem Aufruf jeder Methode, die eine Änderung des internen Zustandes verursachen kann - ring(), pickUp(), ringOff() und activateSpeaker() – alle registrierten Kriterien überprüft werden. Die Methoden, die in der ObservableAPI implementiert werden, sind also die Methoden die den internen Zustand des Dienstendpunktes alternieren können. Davon ausgeschlossen ist beispielsweise getServiceDescription(), welche eine Lese-Operation durchführt. Es ist zu bemerken, daß auch nicht öffentliche Methoden Bestandteil der ObservableAPI sein können. Die Implementierung der ObservableAPI ist offensichtlich abhängig von dem in Frage kommenden Dienstendpunkt. Sie muß deshalb zum Einsatz bei anderen Dienstendpunkten entsprechend angepaßt werden.

Neben dem Interaction Organizer wurde auch ein Tool entwickelt, welches die Konstruktion und Distribution von Interaktionsmustern basierend auf einer grafischen Oberfläche erlaubt.

6 Ausblick

Die toolgestützte Modellierung von Prozessen innerhalb von Ubiquitous Computing Umgebungen bildet einen noch jungen Forschungsbereich. Daher lassen sich eine Reihe von weiteren Forschungsgebieten ableiten. Mit dem Observer Mechanismus können Objekte innerhalb eines Prozessen miteinander kommunizieren, während der sogenannte Conference Bus [Rom 98] die Kommunikation zwischen Objekten, die in separaten Prozessen ausgeführt werden, und damit die Korrelation multipler Objekte ermöglicht. Dieser Ansatz bietet grundlegend neue Möglichkeiten für weiterführende Arbeiten.

Künftige Arbeiten sollten die Erstellung und Verteilung von Interaktionsmustern noch einfacher bedienbar machen und in noch stärkerer Weise automatisieren. Dazu wäre es denkbar, die von einem Benutzer ausgelösten Aktionen in einer Ubiquitous Computing Umgebung bei Zustimmung eines Nutzers aufzuzeichnen. Dadurch wäre es denkbar, automatisch Interaktionsmuster und Codefragmente zu identifizieren, die nachfolgend in Abhängigkeit kontextueller Restriktionen zur Ausführung gebracht werden.

Ferner wäre neben der qualitativen auch eine quantitative Analyse wünschenswert. Insbesondere eine Variation der vorgestellten Mechanismen würde so Aufschluß über die Effizienz der eingesetzten Methoden geben.

Literatur

[AS 00]   G. Abowd, J.P.G. Strebenz. *Final Report on the Inter-Agency Workshop on Research Issues for Smart Environments. IEEE Personal Communications*, October 2000.

[Blue]   Bluetooth. http://www.bluetooth.com

[BW 00]   G. Borriello, R. Want. Embedded computation meets the world wide web. *CACM*. May 2000.

[Dey 00]   Anind K. Dey. Providing Architectural Support for Building Context-Aware Applications. PhD thesis, *College of Computing, Georgia Institute of Technology*, December 2000.

[DeyAb 00]   A. K. Dey and G. D. Abowd. Towards a Better Understanding of Context and Context-Awareness *In the Workshop on The What, Who, Where, When, and How of Context-Awareness, as part of the 2000 Conference on Human Factors in Computing Systems (CHI 2000)*, The Hague, The Netherlands, April 2000.

[DL 02]   R. Droms, T. Lemon. The DHCP Handbook. *Macmillan Technical Publishing*, Indianapolis, IN. 2002

[EHAB 99]   M. Esler, J. Hightower, T. Anderson, and G. Borriello. Next century challenges:data-centric networking for invisible computing. the portolano project at the university of washington. In *Proc. of the Fifth ACM/IEEE Intl. Conf. on Mobile Networking and Computing*, August 1999.

[GHJV 95]   Erich Gamma, Richard Helm, Ralph Johnson, and John Vlissides. Design Patterns: Elements of Reusable Object-Oriented Software. *Addison-Wesley, Reading*, MA, 1995.

[JINI]   JINI, http://java.sun.com/products/jini.

[KLST 96]   R. H. Katz, D. Long, M. Satyanarayanan, S. Tripathi. Workspaces in the Information Age. In *Report of the NSF Workshop on Workspaces in the Information Age.* Leesburg, VA. October 1996

[Kur 00]   Roland Kurmann .Spontane Vernetzung, Dienstbeschreibung, service discovery. Fachseminar 2000. ETH Zürich. 2000.

[McG 00]   R. E. McGrath. Discovery and Its Discontents: Discovery Protocols for Ubiquitous Computing. 2000

[OMG 99]   Object Management Group. CORBAServices: Common Object Services Specification. Object Management Group (OMG). 1999

[Pas 98]   J. Pascoe. The Stick-e Note Architecture: Extending the Interface Beyond the User. Technical Report, *University of Kent*, Canterbury, 1998.

[Ph]   http://www.python.org

[Rom 98]   C. Romer. A Composable Architecture for Scripting Multimedia Network Applications. Technical report. *University of California*, Berkley, July 1998.

[Sch 00]   A. Schmidt. Implicit Human Computer Interaction Through Context. *Personal Technologies* Volume 4(2&3), June 2000.

[SDA 99]   D. Salber, A. K. Dey , G. D. Abowd. The context toolkit: Aiding the Development of Context-Enabled Applications *Proceeding of the CHI 99 conference on Human factors in computing systems : the CHI is the limit,* May 1999

[SL 01]   M. Samulowitz, Y. Lin. Interaction Templates for Pervasive Service Chains. In *Proceedings ICII 2001*, Beijing, China, October 2001

[SMLP 01a]   M. Samulowitz, F. Michahelles, C. Linnhoff-Popien. Adaptive Interaction for Enabling Pervasive Computing Services. In: *2nd ACM International Workshop on Data Engineering for Wireless and Mobile Access (MobiDE'01) in cooperation with ACM SIGMOD*, Santa Barbara, California, USA, May 20, 2001

[SMLP 01b]   M. Samulowitz, F. Michahelles, C. Linnhoff-Popien. CAPEUS: An Architecture for Context-Aware Selection and Execution of Services. *Third IFIP WG 6.1 International Conference on Distributed Applications and Interoperable Systems (DAIS'2001)*, Krakow, Poland, September 17-19, 2001

[Stev 94]   W. Richard Stevens. The Protocols (TCP/IP Illustrated, Volume 1). *Addison-Wesley*. January 1994.

[UpnP]   Universal Plug and Play (UPnP). http://www.upnp.org

[WHK 97]   M. Wahl, T. Howes, S. Kille. Lightweight Directory Access Protocol (v3). *IETF RFC 2251*. December 1997.

[Woo 96]   A. Wood. CAMEO: Supporting Observable APIs. *Position Paper for the WWW5 Programming the Web Workshop.* April 1996.

[ZERO 02]   Zero Configuration Networking (zeroconf). http://www.ietf.org/html.charters/ zeroconf-charter.html. 2002

Marketplaces as Communication Patterns in Mobile Ad-Hoc Networks*

Daniel Görgen, Hannes Frey, Johannes K. Lehnert, and Peter Sturm

University of Trier
Department of Computer Science
54286 Trier, Germany
E-mail: {goergen|frey|lehnert|sturm}@syssoft.uni-trier.de

Abstract. This paper proposes a novel communication pattern for mobile multihop ad-hoc networks which is based on a marketplace metaphor. In order to substantially increase the probability that negotiating peers sucessfully reach an agreement, communication is focused on a static geographic area, called the marketplace. Users are not constrained to be at the marketplace physically, but are allowed to utilize other ones mobile devices located at the marketplace to let a software agent or a service installed on each device negotiate with others on their behalf. The forwarding and negotiation protocols needed to implement the marketplace solution are described in this work. Additionally, a prototypical implementation of the protocols is evaluated in a simulation environment. Since simulation results strongly depend on the mobility model, three realistic models based on an extension of the random waypoint model are used. Their movement patterns are resulting from persons on a music festival, a university campus, and an exhibition.

1 Introduction

Mobile distributed systems are formed by PDAs, Pocket PCs, and even smaller systems that communicate with nearby devices using wireless transmission technologies such as IEEE 802.11 or Bluetooth. Wireless communication is characterized by low bandwidth, a high probability for packet loss due to interference, short interaction periods with generally yet unknown neighbors (ad-hoc), and the additional constraint to conserve energy in low powered devices. It is state of the art to realize so-called single-hop mobile systems, where wireless communication is only used in order to utilize an otherwise traditional network infrastructure such as IPv4 – and any middleware on top of it – via a stationary access point. In contrast, multi-hop networks are characterized by the absence of such a stable and dependable backbone network. In order to manage these networks successfully and to execute mobile applications efficiently, self-organization techniques have to be deployed instead. The underlying principle of this kind of

---

* This work is funded in part by DFG, Schwerpunktprogramm SPP1140 "Basissoftware für selbstorganisierende Infrastrukturen für vernetzte mobile Systeme".

self-organization is to base all decisions of a mobile device on its local knowledge, to cooperate (sometimes altruistically) with immediate neighbors only, and to achieve the overall goals primarily through synergy.

A fundamental communication pattern for many self-organizing distributed applications is to identify one or more mobile peers satisfying a given set of requirements as defined by some client. This general pattern can be used e.g., to implement a mobile auction system in which one or more bidders have to be found for offered goods. Other examples are digital ride boards to arrange possible lifts among drivers and travelers or electronic blackboards where students seek for tutors assisting in exercises. The simple solution for a client to just wait until a matching peer device comes into communication range has to fail, since the probability to find such a peer by random might be too low. In contrast, flooding the entire ad-hoc network with all active client requests is doomed to fail as well because of the immediate network saturation arising from broadcast storms [16].

A working solution for this communication pattern is based on a marketplace metaphor. A marketplace is a fixed geographical location where information is traded at given times. Marketplaces should be located were high device density could be expected. Information about time and location of marketplaces is assumed to be distributed within the network by means of an underlying basic information dissemination protocol[6]. Client requests or agents acting on behalf of the client travel to the marketplace by infecting promising nearby devices. This decision to infect another device within communication range is based primarily on the relative geographical positions of the device actually carrying the request resp. the agent, the candidate device, and the marketplace itself. When arriving at the marketplace, the device actually hosting the request or agent is searching for matching peers by periodically announcing the set of requirements. These infrequent broadcasts are limited to a given perimeter around the geographical center of the marketplace. Hosting devices are changed if they are going to leave the marketplace. When the market is closed, any data and agents involved in the marketplace stick to their actual host device and travel back at the next opening time. At a given deadline or if a sufficient number of matching peers is found, the response resp. the successful agent will travel back to the coordinates of the home zone, defined by the initiator. Depending on the application, some condensed data may remain at the marketplace for a limited time to identify and eliminate duplicates that are likely to occur in this highly dynamic environment.

By assigning a marketplace to a specific geographical location and by requiring the client requests or agents to move to this place, the probability to identify matching peer devices can be increased substantially. Devices within the marketplace perimeter may even host more than one request or agent at a time and may broadcast accumulated data periodically. The number of devices at the marketplace and the number of active requests impose a communication load within the marketplace. This load is observed locally by special caretaker agents that may decide to split the place into two separate markets if the load exceeds a given threshold or to join two independent marketplaces in case of low utilization. How to partition the problem space for two separate markets is defined by the application, e.g. in case of a digital ride board the zip codes of the destinations can be subdivided or in case of the auction system categories for goods can be introduced and distributed among the marketplaces.

In the following section, the required protocols to implement marketplaces are presented in detail. Due to space limitations, protocols to balance the load among several marketplaces and further issues concerning the caretaker agents are not presented. Section 3 discusses simulation results with respect to agent mobility and negotiation. These simulations have been evaluated with three realistic mobility models: (a) the festival model with a single big hotspot of mobile devices, (b) the campus model as defined by populated buildings with well-defined paths in between, and (c) the exhibition model where mobile devices randomly move from booth to booth. Section 4 discusses related work. In the last section, the conclusion that marketplaces are well-suited communication patterns for certain application domains in the area of self-organized mobile systems is drawn and work in progress is pointed out.

2 Protocol description

This section describes the protocols used to implement the marketplace-based communication patterns. The first subsection outlines the protocol used to move to and from the marketplace. The second subsection describes the protocol used to negotiate at the marketplace.

2.1 Moving to and from the marketplace

Agents are required to be location-aware in order to use location information to reach the marketplace resp. their home zone. By using trajectory information of its current host and the hosts in its direct neighborhood, the agent *jumps* on that host, which makes it most likely reach the destination. The trajectory information of adjacent devices could be gathered by periodical broadcasts or requests after the discovery of a new neighbor. This work proposes three strategies for moving to a desired geographic coordinate.

- *D-method* is the easiest way to reach the geographic destination by using the greedy method as proposed in [14]. By using this method, the neighbor having the least distance to the desired geographical position is chosen.
- By using *DC-method*, first a set of best devices regarding distance to destination is determined. From this set the device with the best course to the destination is selected.
- *CD-method* is analogous to *DC-method* but the other way round.

Due to frequent topology changes in a mobile ad-hoc network, there is no guarantee for two devices remaining connected during an agent transmission. In particular, there is no guarantee that disconnected devices will subsequently be reconnected, so that an error recovery can take place in case of a link failure during agent transmission. Thus, agents might get lost during transmission. To

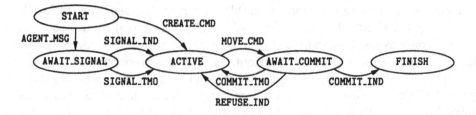

Fig. 1. Life cycle of an agent on a particular device.

cope with this problem, an agent remains on the sending device until it is sure, that its copy arrived at the receiving device. This prevents agent losses but might lead to agent duplicates.

An agent is tagged with a duplicate flag indicating that duplicates of itself may exist. This flag is examined upon arrival at the marketplace. The following algorithm uses such a flag. It can easily be proved, that the algorithm assures that if duplicates exist of a particular agent, each incarnation of this agent is tagged with the duplicate flag. The opposite does not hold. That is, if an agent incarnation is tagged with the duplicate flag, it does not always hold that there really exists a second incarnation of itself. As a consequence, a recovery procedure has to be started at the marketplace to delete possible additional instances of an agent.

The finite state machine of figure 1 depicts the lifecycle of a particular agent and its possible duplicates on the agent platform of a mobile device.

The initial state START denotes that the agent is not yet existing on that device. There are two possible events leading to an incarnation of an agent on a device, creation of a new agent (CREATE_CMD) and receipt of an agent (AGENT_MSG) which has to be transmitted to this platform. The first state of a newly created agent is ACTIVE.

An agent in state ACTIVE is allowed to change its hosting device by the MOVE_CMD. This decision might follow one of the strategies described above. Once a MOVE_CMD occurs, an agent sends a copy of itself to the new device and switches into state AWAIT_COMMIT. Additionally, a timeout COMMIT_TMO is set, which is noticed in state AWAIT_COMMIT.

State AWAIT_COMMIT means, that the agent still remains on its old platform, since it is not sure, whether its transmission was successful. There are three possible events noticed in this state. The event COMMIT_IND occurs if agent transmission was successful and a notification from the receiving platform was received on the sending platform and thus the agent can be deleted there. The sender switches to state FINISH and notifies the receiving device with a SIGNAL_IND message. The REFUSE_IND will occur if the receiving device is not capable to host an additional agent due to memory or processor limitations. The third event COMMIT_TMO is noticed if the time to wait for a COMMIT_IND or REFUSE_IND expired. In this case it is not certain, whether during the transmission to the new platform the agent itself or the notification from the receiving platform was lost. Thus, the agent is not removed from the sending device and is tagged with a duplicate flag and switched back to state ACTIVE. From now on the agent and its possible duplicates will remain tagged as duplicated.

When a mobile device receives an agent in an AGENT_MSG and there are enough resources, the agent is placed on the agent platform in state AWAIT_SIGNAL and the SIGNAL_TMO timeout is set. Subsequently, it replies with a COMMIT_IND message. If there are not enough resources to host the new agent, a REFUSE_IND message is sent instead. An agent will remain in AWAIT_SIGNAL state until a timeout SIGNAL_TMO expires or SIGNAL_IND is received from the sending device. If the timeout SIGNAL_TMO occurs in this state it is not certain, whether the reply message COMMIT_IND from the receiving device or the reply message SIGNAL_IND from the sending device got lost during the agent transmission protocol. Thus, it is not clear if an agent copy remains on the sending device. As a consequence, the agent switches into state ACTIVE but is tagged with the duplicate flag and remains tagged as described above. If an agent receives a SIGNAL_IND in state AWAIT_SIGNAL, it knows that its former incarnation on the sending device was removed. Hence, it can switch into state ACTIVE without being tagged.

2.2 Negotiating at the marketplace

Agents that arrive at the marketplace can negotiate with other agents. An agent may have two roles in such a negotiation. Either it announces its own offer or it looks for suitable offers.

Marketplaces may be bigger than half of the sending radius of the devices. Therefore RegionCast, a geographically limited form of flooding, is used to distribute offers and responses over the whole marketplace. Here RegionCast is used to address agents. Each device receiving a RegionCast message must decide if the addressed agent is locally available and then forward the message to it. Thus, even agents moving away from the center of a marketplace or changing between agent platforms can be reached.

The basic negotiation protocol as depicted in figure 2 works as follows. All agents start in state IDLE. An agent switches to state AWAIT_RPL and starts a new offer when it reaches the marketplace. The agent repeatedly sends DEAL_REQ messages to the marketplace and waits for DEAL_RPL messages from other agents interested in its offer. As soon as the agent accepts one DEAL_RPL message by sending a DEAL_S_COMMIT message to its originator, it switches to state AWAIT_C_COMMIT, waiting for the final DEAL_C_COMMIT message from its negotiating party. Any DEAL_RPL messages arriving from other agents are refused by sending a DEAL_REFUSED message. When the agent receives the DEAL_C_COMMIT message, it switches to state DEAL_OK, accepts the deal and starts to move to its home zone. An agent looking for new and suitable offers listens to DEAL_REQ messages from other agents. If it is interested it sends back a DEAL_RPL message and switches to state AWAIT_S_COMMIT. In the AWAIT_S_COMMIT state it waits for an acknowledgement by the other agent; when it receives the DEAL_S_COMMIT message it responds with a DEAL_C_COMMIT message, switches to state DEAL_OK, accepts the deal and starts to move back to its home zone.

Since this negotiation protocol is used in a multihop ad-hoc network, the additional DEAL_C_COMMIT message is necessary: both DEAL_S_COMMIT and DEAL_RPL

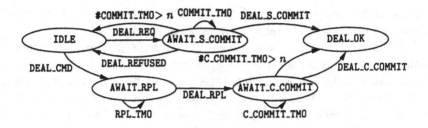

Fig. 2. Negotiation between offerer and bidder.

messages may be lost. Without the DEAL_C_COMMIT message the offering agent could already be on its way home and the responding agent would have no information about its state if the DEAL_S_COMMIT message was lost. A lost DEAL_RPL message would force the offering agent to negotiate with other agents, while the corresponding agent would accept the deal. The introduction of the DEAL_C_COMMIT message does not completely solve the problem since it may be lost, too, but the resulting undefined status is more easily resolvable.

An offering agent registers a timeout C_COMMIT_TMO when it switches to state AWAIT_C_COMMIT. Whenever this timeout occurs, it sends the DEAL_S_COMMIT message and registers the timeout again. This is repeated until the timeout has occured more than n times (e.g. $n = 10$ was used in the simulations). The repeated retransmission will fix the problem of lost DEAL_S_COMMIT messages, but will not help for lost DEAL_C_COMMIT messages. If the timeout has occured more than n times, the agent switches to DEAL_OK state and accepts the deal because it can assume that the DEAL_C_COMMIT message was lost.

An agent responding to an offer uses the same technique. It registers a timeout COMMIT_TMO when it enters state AWAIT_S_COMMIT. If this timeout occurs, it resends the DEAL_RPL message and registers the timeout again. This repeated sending of the DEAL_RPL message helps if either the DEAL_RPL message or DEAL_S_COMMIT message are lost. If nonetheless the timeout occurs more than n times, the probability of a lost DEAL_REFUSED message is high and the agent may safely switch back to state IDLE and wait for new offers.

All these additional measures cannot guarantee that no incorrect negotiations take place, but they minimize the probability a lot.

3   Simulation

The simulation environment and the simulation results are presented in this section. The first subsection describes the mobility models and common simulation parameters. The two following subsections present the simulation results regarding the mobility and negotiation protocols.

3.1   Simulation environment

Three different mobility patterns extending the random waypoint model [3] as shown in figure 3 are used to model the movement of devices. The mobility

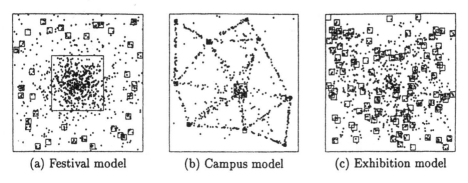

| (a) Festival model | (b) Campus model | (c) Exhibition model |

Fig. 3. Screenshots of the mobility models.

patterns use hotspots to influence the movement of devices. Hotspots have a higher probability of being a destination than the surrounding area. The figures show hotspots as rectangles and devices as dots.

The festival model (3a) imitates the movement pattern of people at a music festival. Most people move to a central place and stay for a while to listen to the music. This central place is surrounded by lots of smaller places where people relax. The campus model (3b) simulates the movement of students at a university campus with a set of hotspots (buildings). In order to model the use of paths, devices are only allowed to choose nearby destinations. The exhibition model (3c) represents the movement of people at an exhibition. People randomly move from booth to booth with short pauses to look at the displayed products. This pattern is modeled with 100 small hotspots representing the booths.

Common parameters for evaluating the mobility strategies are the size of the simulated area (500m × 500m), a wireless communication facility with a sending radius of 25 meters, a transmission rate of 100 kBytes/s, and a simulation duration of five hours. The negotiation protocol is evaluated with a smaller festival model (200m × 200m) and a duration of two hours. All measured values are averaged over 10 simulation runs using independently chosen seed values.

3.2 Evaluation of the mobility strategies

The evaluation of agent mobility is primarily focused on the time needed to move to the marketplace and return back to the home zone. Additionally, the number of hops and the number of duplicates are examined. All values are investigated depending on the movement strategy and the mobility model. During one simulation run 100 agents are produced on the first 100 devices, all of them targeting the marketplace and thereafter a dedicated home zone. Agents use one of the three moving methods mentioned in section 2.1. Furthermore, the number of devices (250, 500, 1000, 2000) and the device speed (1, 2, 4 and 8 m/s) are varied.

Mobility models have less effect on movement strategies, when simulating with a high device population (figure 4). This is not limited to the depicted example, but is observed in all performed simulation runs with a high device population. An increasing number of mobile devices leads to a less partitioned

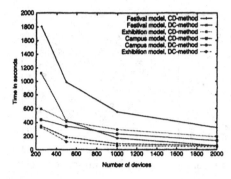
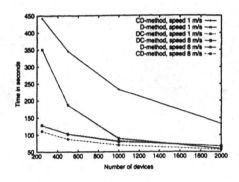

Fig. 4. Mobility models: time for varying device numbers (speed 1 m/s).

Fig. 5. Campus model: movement strategies for varying device numbers.

network. Thus, selecting a device with the best course to the destination is less significant, as there exists a possible path from source to destination. Due to space limitations only a part of the results and only the campus model is imaged.

Concerning duration and hops, D- and DC-method produce nearly the same results. Both are fast strategies but increasing speed, particularly in campus and exhibition model, causes better results for CD-method (figure 5). This is substantiated with a higher device mobility than in festival model, which is strengthened by increasing speed. Due to longer pause times the mobility in the festival model is lower and so the network is quasi static. Thus, increasing speed has barely no effects on strategy quality because of a quasi static network [3].

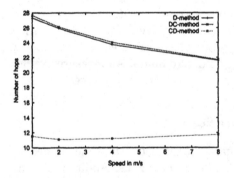
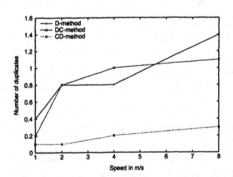

Fig. 6. Campus model, 250 devices: number of hops for varying device speeds.

Fig. 7. Campus model, 250 devices: number of duplicates for varying device speeds.

The number of hops needed directly affects the number of messages needed and thus the network load. D- and DC-method need much more hops to reach a destination than the CD-method (figure 6). This is distinctly observable with campus and exhibition models; the festival model results show a smaller gap. Increasing speed leads to improvement in campus, caused by devices walking on paths, but to deterioration in exhibition model, caused by the fact that nearly every device in range has another direction. The more devices are in the simulation, the less hops are needed by D- and DC-method in all models, so the differences to CD-method gets smaller.

Regarding agent duplication (figure 7) CD-method performs best in all models. This is due to the fact that with D- and also DC-method an agent tries to get as far as possible in each jump and so the receiving devices are near the maximum range of the sending device so that message losses are likely.

3.3 Evaluation of the negotiation protocol

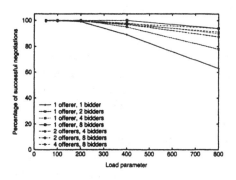 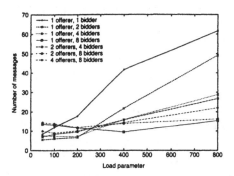

Fig. 8. Percentage of successful negotiations under varying loads.

Fig. 9. Number of messages necessary for each potential negotiation.

In order to examine the negotiation protocol, two classes of agents are used, one to generate load, the other to negotiate under load. Load in the simulation is varied over an average number of 50, 100, 200, 400 and 800 negotiating agents per minute. Protocol and negotiation duration as well as successful, failed and incorrect negotiations are measured. Measurement agents consist of m offerers and n bidders with $m \in \{1, 2, 4\}$, $n \in \{1, 2, 4, 8\}$ and $m \leq n$.

The number of agents per device is restricted to 16 so that the marketplace is saturated at about 260 agents in this model. Since there are more agents wanting to reach the marketplace the measure agents are not able to enter the marketplace and are deleted after waiting up to 6 minutes. That explains the decreasing number of successful negotiations in figure 8. As described in 2.2 incorrect negotiations are possible as well but this never occurred during the simulations. The protocol after receiving a DEAL_REQ message takes about 1,3 msec at load 50 up to about 1,5 msec at highest load. The duration measurement starts after both agents are on the marketplace and ends when the last negotiation message is received. This takes about 5-11 secs up to 63-101 secs.

Figure 9 depicts the number of messages needed for every potential negotiation ($\hat{=}$ number of offerers) and as supposed the number of messages increases with increasing load. The order of the results at load parameter 50 is as expected: as the amount of bidders per offerer increases, the number of messages increases. But at high load the order is rolled over. This can be explained as follows: finding only one partner is more difficult under high load than finding one out of many possible partners.

4 Related work

A lot of work in the area of mobile ad-hoc networks concentrates on the special case of a dense population of mobile devices, i.e. algorithms cope with the problem of frequent link failures resulting from mobile nodes, on the condition that sometimes there is a path from source to destination over one or more wireless links. In particular, adaptions and extensions [9, 19, 18, 17] of existing routing protocols known from static networks, will not deliver any packet when facing permanent network partitions. This also applies to routing protocols based on location information specially designed for ad-hoc networks [15, 11, 10, 12]. In an area with sparse device population, link failures are likely to happen and in particular there permanently might not exist a direct communication path from source to destination node. The communication paradigm proposed in this paper works well even if there are permanent network partitions. This is due to the fact that there might be intermediate nodes moving towards the location of the destination node and thus, by using the node mobility, messages can be transmitted to a not directly reachable host.

If location based routing is used to deliver packets to a certain mobile device whose position is not generally known, an additional location service is needed for tracking device positions. Proposals for location services can for example be found in [1, 13]. These proposals have in common that they put additional load on the underlying mobile network which increases the faster the network topology changes, since they have to update position information dynamically due to node mobility. It is advantageous to allow execution state migration and to define a marketplace as a well known geographic area with fixed position, since there is no additional overhead to track device positions, which increases scalability compared to existing solutions.

Since the choice of the mobility model can have significant effects on the performance investigation of an ad-hoc network protocol [3, 7, 20], the simulation environment uses a more complex model tailored to the usage scenarios where the proposed framework may be utilized. Thus, the simulation results have regarding these scenarios a more practical relevance than other performance simulations [8, 2, 5, 4] based on a general random waypoint model [3]. In paper [20], this model is restricted to positions covered by vertices and edges of a graph to achieve more realistic movement patterns. The definition of hot spots as proposed in this paper, is less restrictive for scenarios like music festival, university campus and exhibition, since devices are allowed to walk outside of such predefined paths.

5 Conclusions and future work

This paper introduces a novel communication paradigm for ad-hoc networks. It is based on a marketplace metaphor, which organizes offers and bids by using software agents or an already installed service running on each mobile device. Negotiations done on behalf of their originators are restricted to a fixed geographic area, the marketplace. The solution consists of three main parts, message delivery to and from the marketplace, negotiation at the marketplace and load balancing at the marketplace. The proposed solution scales well and is independent of a sparse device population as long as there are devices moving towards the marketplace.

Three strategies for packet forwarding to the marketplace are presented: D-method, DC-method, and CD-method. D-method is known as greedy packet forwarding [14], the others are extensions of it, additionally using information about the course of a device. Simulation results show for devices moving with walking speed that the following holds: The higher the device population the less the marketplace approach depends on the movement strategy. At a lower density there exists a tradeoff between the proposed strategies. D- and DC-method deliver packets substantially faster than CD-method, whereas CD-method needs only a fraction of messages. If device speed is increased this tradeoff between time and message complexity disappears. That is, in a highly dynamic network CD-method is the best strategy with the least time and messages complexity to deliver a packet to the marketplace. Also, the number of duplicates produced during message delivery due to link failures are least with CD-method.

No incorrect deal occurs during the negotiation protocol simulations due to a restricted number of agents per device and the introduction of a second commit message.

Furthermore, the negotiation time, when a negotiation among offerer and bidder is started is negligible even if the marketplace is under higher load. Restricting the maximum number of agents on a device avoids network congestions and leaves bandwith for other applications using the ad-hoc network. If the rate of agents moving to the marketplace is higher than the rate these agents are served on the marketplace, this solution will lead to an increasing queue of agents willing to enter the marketplace. Under this condition, the marketplace has to be split in geographically disjoint parts all serving a portion of the negotiation classes.

The next step within the scope of this work is a prototypical implementation of a marketplace solution for a distributed ride board using PDAs with a IEEE 802.11 communication facility. Since there is the need to determine the position of a device, these will additionally be equipped with a GPS receiver. In a further step this prototype will be extended to an indoor solution using an GPS-free form of triangulation technique.

References

1. S. Basagni, I. Chalamtac, and V. R. Syrotiuk. A distance routing effect algorithm for mobility (dream). In *Proc. of the 4th ACM/IEEE Int. Conf. on Mobile Computing and Networking (MobiCom'98)*, pages 76–84, 1998.
2. J. Broch, D.A. Maltz, D.B. Johnson, Y.-C. Hu, and J. Jetcheva. A performance comparison of multi-hop wireless ad hoc network routing protocols. In *Proc. of the 4th ACM/IEEE Int. Conf. on Mobile Computing and Networking (MobiCom'98)*, pages 85–97, 1998.
3. T. Camp, J. Boleng, and V. Davies. Mobility models for ad hoc network simulations. *Wireless Communication & Mobile Computing (WCMC): Special issue on Mobile Ad Hoc Networking: Research, Trends and Applications*, 2002.

4. S. Das, R. Castañeda, and J. Yan. Simulation based performance evaluation of mobile, ad hoc network routing protocols. *ACM/Baltzer Mobile Networks and Applications (MONET) Journal*, pages 179–189, 2000.

5. S. Das, C. Perkins, and E. Royer. Performance comparison of two on-demand routing protocols for ad hoc networks. In *Proc. of the 2000 IEEE Computer and Communications Societies Conference on Computer Communications (INFOCOM-00)*, pages 3–12, 2000.

6. H. Frey, J.K. Lehnert, and P. Sturm. Ubibay: An auction system for mobile multihop ad-hoc networks. *Workshop on Ad hoc Communications and Collaboration in Ubiquitous Computing Environments (AdHocCCUCE'02)*, 2002.

7. X. Hong, M. Gerla, G. Pei, and C. Chiang. A group mobility model for ad hoc wireless networks. In *Proc. of the 2nd ACM/IEEE Int. Workshop on Modeling and Simulation of Wireless and Mobile Systems (MSWiM'99)*, pages 53–60, 1999.

8. P. Johansson, T. Larsson, N. Hedman, B. Mielczarek, and M. Degermark. Scenario-based performance analysis of routing protocols for mobile ad-hoc networks. In *Proc. of the 5th ACM/IEEE Int. Conf. on Mobile Computing and Networking (MobiCom'99)*, pages 195–206, 1999.

9. D.B. Johnson and D.A. Maltz. Dynamic source routing in ad hoc wireless networks. In *Mobile Computing*, volume 353 of *The Kluwer International Series in Engineering and Computer Science*. Kluwer Academic Publishers, 1996.

10. Y.-B. Ko and N.H. Vaidya. Geocasting in mobile ad hoc networks: Location-based multicast algorithms. Technical report, TR-98-018, Texas A&M University, 1998.

11. Y.-B. Ko and N.H. Vaidya. Location-aided routing (LAR) in mobile ad hoc networks. In *Proc. of the 4th ACM/IEEE Int. Conf. on Mobile Computing and Networking (MobiCom'98)*, pages 66–75, 1998.

12. Y.-B. Ko and N.H. Vaidya. Geotora: A protocol for geocasting in mobile ad hoc networks. Technical report, TR-00-010, Texas A&M University, 2000.

13. J. Li, J. Jannotti, D. De Couto, D. Karger, and R. Morris. A scalable location service for geographic ad-hoc routing. In *Proc. of the 6th ACM Int. Conf. on Mobile Computing and Networking (MobiCom'00)*, pages 120–130, 2000.

14. M. Mauve, J. Widemer, and H. Hartenstein. A survey on position-based routing in mobile ad-hoc networks. *IEEE Network Magazine*, 15(6):30–39, 2001.

15. J.C. Navas and T. Imielinski. Geocast - geographic addressing and routing. In *In Proc. of the 3rd ACM/IEEE Int. Conf. on Mobile Computing and Networking (MobiCom'97)*, pages 66–76, 1997.

16. S.-Y. Ni, Y.-C. Tseng, Y.-S. Chen, and J.-P. Sheu. The broadcast storm problem in a mobile ad hoc network. *Proc. of the 5th ACM/IEEE Int. Conf. on Mobile Computing and Networking*, pages 151–162, 1999.

17. V.D. Park and M.S. Corson. A highly adaptive distributed routing algorithm for mobile wireless networks. In *Proc. of the Conf. on Computer Communications (IEEE INFOCOM'97)*, pages 1405–1413, 1997.

18. C. Perkins and P. Bhagwat. Highly dynamic destination-sequenced distance-vector routing (DSDV) for mobile computers. In *ACM SIGCOMM'94 Conference on Communications Architectures, Protocols and Applications*, pages 234–244, 1994.

19. C.E. Perkins. Ad-hoc on-demand distance vector routing. In *MILCOM '97 panel on Ad Hoc Networks*, 1997.

20. J. Tian, J. Hähner, C. Becker, I. Stepanov, and K. Rothermel. Graph-based mobility model for mobile ad hoc network simulation. In *Proc. of the 35th Simulation Symposium, in cooperation with the IEEE Computer Society and ACM*, 2002.

Applying Ad-Hoc Relaying
to Improve Capacity, Energy Efficiency,
and Immission in Infrastructure-Based WLANs

Martin Kubisch, Seble Mengesha, Daniel Hollos, Holger Karl, Adam Wolisz*

Fachgebiet Telekommunikationsnetze
Sekr. FT 5-2, Einsteinufer 25, 10587 Berlin Technische Universität Berlin
kubisch|mengesha|hollos|karl|wolisz@ee.tu-berlin.de

Abstract. In classical infrastructure-based wireless systems such as access point-equipped wireless LANs, all mobile terminals communicate directly with the access point. In order to improve the capacity or energy efficiency of such systems, the use of mobile terminals as intermediate relays has been proposed. The rationale is that intermediate relays reduce the communication distance and hence the emitted power. Therefore, relaying could also reduce electromagnetic immission. To assess these potential benefits, we study the effectiveness of various relaying algorithms in a uniform, HiperLAN/2-based system model that has been amended by relaying functionality. These algorithms jointly select intermediate relay terminals and assign transmission power as well as modulation to mobile terminals. The energy efficiency of a point-to-point communication is indeed improved by relaying, however, this effect only marginally transfers to scenarios taking into account several terminals. Nevertheless, it is still possible to extend the lifetime of a network by taking into account available battery capacities.

For a discussion of capacity improvements, two different modes of conceiving system fairness are identified. For both system modes, we present relaying algorithms. Moreover, adding an additional frequency to a cell is beneficial: Using two frequencies can almost double the cell capacity, and for one fairness mode, even relaying with one frequency can improve capacity by up to 30 %.

In addition, all these algorithms reduce the immitted power averaged over the area of a cell. All algorithms show improvements, an additional algorithm specialized to reduce immission power can cut the average power almost in half.

Keywords: Relaying, capacity, energy efficiency, immission, WLAN, HiperLAN/2

1 Introduction

The use of multi-hop wireless communication systems has been advocated where a sender communicates with its destination with the help of intermediate relay stations. Relaying is a necessary ingredient in realizing ad-hoc, spontaneously formed networks

---

* Part of this work has been supported by the BMBF under HyperNET/IBMS[2] and the MiniWatt projects.

with no infrastructure support where not all the mobile terminals are in direct radio contact with each other. But relaying can also be applied in infrastructure-based, cellular communication systems in order to improve different aspects of their operation. Figure 1 shows such a scenario consisting of a far terminal A relaying via B to an access point.

Fig. 1. Example scenario for choosing relaying terminals

The expectation why relaying could actually be beneficial in an infrastructure-based environment is the reduction of distances over which communication takes place: No longer do all terminals have to communicate with a potentially far-away access point, but rather could communicate with an intermediate relay that is perhaps halfway towards the access point. Relaying allows the mobile terminal to reduce the power it uses for transmission. This power reduction can be leveraged to improve three key properties of a wireless communication system: energy efficiency, capacity, and electromagnetic immission.

Energy efficiency can be improved by the non-linear relationship of distance and transmission power: Communicating twice over short distances requires a smaller total radiated power than just once over a long distance. This could lead to a more efficient use of energy stored in a mobile terminal's batteries, but also requires to account for the additional overheads in receiving transmission, powering amplifiers, etc.

Capacity can be improved because smaller radiated power also means smaller interference. Shorter distances also allow the use of faster modulations. In addition, relaying could also open the way to add additional resources, i.e., frequencies, to a cell and thus increase cell capacity.

Electromagnetic immission can be improved because of the immediate benefits of using smaller transmission power levels, resulting in smaller average or peak immission values, depending on the distance from the access point.

Yet another aspect of relaying is the extension of the coverage of an access point by means of relaying. This paper focuses on relaying *within* a single cell, complementing other research focusing on coverage extension (e.g., [13]). While this restriction limits the problem scope, it allows to pursue simpler solutions for the relaying entities.

Such a relaying entity could be part of a fixed infrastructure (and connected to a fixed power supply), or the mobile terminals themselves could act as relaying entities whenever this is necessary and beneficial for the entire system. In the former case, much of the design decisions are quite simple and it is straightforward to see improvements with regard to these three aspects. The later case is much more challenging as the system is much more dynamic and as a relaying terminal, unlike a fixed relaying entity, also has its own traffic requirements and user needs that it has to support. We concentrate in this paper on the second case of purely using mobile terminals as relaying entities.

The contribution of this paper is to show how ad-hoc relaying via mobile entities can be integrated into a cellular system and to evaluate these three aspects in a uniform, mobile system environment. For each aspect we describe algorithms that determine which terminal is relaying data for which relayed terminal (essentially, solving a routing problem) and how these communication relationships are organized in time (in essence, a scheduling and modulation selection problem). In addition, assigning appropriate transmission power levels to mobile terminals is a crucial issue. As it will turn out, jointly optimizing transmission power and modulation schemes used for each communication is the key technique to leverage the potential benefits of relaying.

The remainder of this paper is organized as follows. Section 2 describes the model assumptions used here. Sections 3, 4, and 5 describe our algorithms for optimizing energy efficiency, capacity, and electromagnetic immissions, along with simulation-based evaluations of their performance.Finally, Section 6 concludes the paper.

2 System model

While extending infrastructure-based systems by relaying can be researched in the context of classical cellular systems like GSM or UMTS, this paper concentrates on access point-based wireless LANs as basic technology. Currently, there are two viable candidates for WLAN systems: IEEE 802.11 a/b as well as HiperLAN/2. While IEEE 802.11 is more popular at the moment, HiperLAN/2 will be able to provide comparable bandwidth and a superior QoS support. In addition, its centralized system structure allows to easier experiment with different routing and scheduling algorithms: In HiperLAN/2, the access point is responsible for computing a communication schedule for a MAC frame 2 ms long. In a frame, each mobile terminal is assigned time slots in which it is allowed to send or receive data to or from the access point or other mobile terminals; moreover, this schedule also stipulates the transmission power a mobile uses and which one out of seven different, standardized modulation types is used within a time slot.[1]

We extended this frame structure by a relaying protocol that allows traffic to travel from a mobile terminal to the access point via an intermediate relaying terminal (and vice versa) [10]. This extension is very lightweight but, unlike other extensions [13], does not result in an extended coverage of the access point. Using this protocol, the access point can use different algorithms to compute transmission schedules for a MAC frame, depending on which performance metric is to be optimized. The algorithms work on the basis of the current channel gains between access point and mobile terminals (which are available with a certain precision using HiperLAN/2's radio map). In the following, we identify the channel gains with the relative positions of the terminals. As we do not consider any obstacles in our evaluation, this is an acceptable simplification.

The next three sections will present algorithms that are optimizing energy efficiency, capacity, and electromagnetic immission. These sections also present performance results, based on a uniform simulation model [9]: A single cell is considered, mobile

---

[1] Nevertheless, we expect our results in principle to carry over to IEEE 802.11-based systems as well since a similar physical layer is used, albeit a practical implementation is going to be somewhat quite from an HiperLAN/2 system. The main difference is the lack of a central control, necessitating a distributed version of our algorithms.

terminals are randomly placed on a square area of 70 m x 70 m, the access point is in the middle. The path loss coefficient α for most of the simulations is set to 3.2; all confidence levels are 95 %.

3 Optimizing energy efficiency

In order to use relaying to optimize energy efficiency, first an appropriate model of energy consumption must be developed. In recent publications [3, 6] energy models for relaying with adaptive transmission power have been developed, but either energy necessary to receive data has been neglected or power consumption not relevant to energy efficiency (e.g., power consumption in the AP) has been considered.

The first step for such a model is to define the power consumed in a single terminal. The following model is based on measurements [2, 4] which indicate a transmission power consumption behavior that can be approximated as follows:

$$P_{tx} = a \cdot P_{radiated} + P_{txFix}$$

where P_{tx} is the total power consumed while transmitting data, a is a proportionality factor representing the amplifier's power consumption, $P_{radiated}$ is the network card's actual power output and P_{txFix} is the power needed for amplifier-unrelated parts, e.g., baseband processing. Both power required to receive data P_{rx} and idle power P_{idle} are assumed to be constant.

Choosing values for these constants is in principle straightforward, except for P_{idle}: "idle" could refer to a network card neither sending nor receiving, or it could mean a network card that is actually powered down to a sleep mode [14]. On the one hand, idle power in the first sense is not much different from P_{rx}; on the other hand, the tightly scheduled HiperLAN/2 structure easily allows to assume sleep modes for inactive wireless terminals. Hence, in the following evaluation, the P_{idle} value is chosen considerably smaller than P_{rx}. While this neglects energy necessary to switch between idle and sleep modes, this can be assumed to be a minor source of energy dissipation.

Sending a fixed amount of data can be done by using different modulations, requiring different amounts of time. In order to determine the modulation with the highest energy efficiency to be used between two terminals, a target packet error rate (PER) has to be set. Based on this target PER, the optimal radiated power can be computed as a function of the distance [12], and the average energy per *correct* bit can be computed. Hence, a mapping from target PER and distance to the optimal modulation and radiated power can be derived.

Using this mapping, the total energy required to transmit a fixed amount of data either by direct communication of a far source terminal MT_{FAR} with the AP or by relaying via a relay candidate MT_{REL} can be computed.[2] Here, the frame structure of HiperLAN/2 and the resulting idle times have to be taken into account. The equations for these cases are:

$$E_{direct} = P_{tx,FAR \rightarrow AP,i} \cdot T_i + P_{idle} \cdot (T_{frame} - T_i) + \qquad (1)$$
$$P_{tx,REL \rightarrow AP,k} \cdot T_k + P_{idle} \cdot (T_{frame} - T_k)$$

---

[2] The target PER for the relay case is smaller than for the direct case in order to result in the same end-to-end PER.

$$E_{\text{relay}} = (P_{\text{tx,FAR}\rightarrow\text{REL},k} + P_{\text{rx}}) \cdot T_k + P_{\text{idle}} \cdot (T_{\text{frame}} - T_k) +$$
$$2 \cdot P_{\text{tx,REL}\rightarrow\text{AP},k} \cdot T_k + P_{\text{idle}} \cdot (T_{\text{frame}} - (2 \cdot T_k)) \tag{2}$$

where E_{direct} and E_{relay} are the total energy for either case, $P_{\text{tx},X\rightarrow Y,i}$ is the power necessary for transmitting at modulation i and T is the time for sending or receiving the number of used information units at modulation i. Equation (2) describes the case of a relay terminal which also has data of its own to transmit; it has to be modified for an idle relay or a relay terminal that already is relaying data for some other terminal.

As an example, Figure 2[3] shows the ratio between total energy consumed in the direct and relaying case when the relay terminal is placed halfway between far terminal and AP. Relaying can considerably improve energy efficiency, but only for rather large distances of relayed terminal and access point (already approaching coverage limits) and optimal relay position; a combination that does only rarely happen in practice. As expected, reducing the fixed power offset P_{txFix} offers more possibilities for relaying and improves the relaying gain.

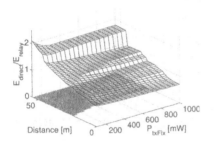

Fig. 2. Ratio between E_{direct} and E_{relay} **Fig. 3.** Lifetime extension, a function of G

3.1 Energy efficient relay selection

Based on these calculations, a relay algorithm is simple to derive. The terminal with the lowest E_{relay} is used as a relay for a relayed terminal, if this energy is lower than E_{direct}. In addition, communication in HiperLAN/2 requires the distribution of the schedule from the AP, causing some small additional overhead [10] for the relaying case, and also causing an additional term in Equation (2).

Evaluating this algorithm in a scenario as described in Section 2 at a total load of about 3.8 MBit/s (two packets per frame and terminal) shows that energy efficiency increases (averaged over 55 different terminal placements) by only about 0.6 percent even though, in some placements, the gain is up to 10.8%. In fact, relaying is only effective in 16 out of 55 scenarios. The reason for this effect is the comparably large distance required for relaying to be beneficial—a condition that is only rarely met in

---

[3] Parameters: $\alpha = 3.2$, target PER = 1%, $P_{\text{rx}} = 100$ mW, $a \approx 3.45$, two packets per frame. Gray area in the bottom plane indicates $E_{\text{direct}} > E_{\text{relay}}$.

scenarios with a maximum distance of about 50 m. Also, as all terminals have to be able to receive from the AP, larger distances are not feasible at the given α and target PER.

3.2 Relay selection considering battery capacity

Energy per bit is a system perspective, not immediately evident to the user. From a user's perspective, energy consumption is relevant as it reduces the time the terminal is functional. This "lifetime" of a terminal depends on the consumed energy, but also on the battery capacity. As some terminals have a large amount of battery capacity (e.g., terminals installed in cars), these could help out other users to improve the lifetime of their terminals.

Technically, this means that the relaying algorithm should not solely be based on the energy efficiency as such, but should also take into account the available battery capacity when choosing a relay terminal. More specifically: a terminal is considered to be a relay candidate for a far terminal if the following inequality holds:

$$\frac{C_{\text{REL}}}{C_{\text{FAR}}} > G \cdot \frac{E_{\text{relay}}}{E_{\text{direct}}} \tag{3}$$

where C_{FAR} and C_{REL} are the battery capacities of the far and the candidate relay terminal, respectively. G is a scaling factor and can be interpreted as the willingness of the algorithm to use non-optimally placed relay terminals when they have a large battery available. Among all candidates, the terminal with the smallest required energy to communicate with the far terminal is chosen as relay. This way, far terminals have a higher chance of using small transmission power and the load on relay terminals is spread according to their battery capacities.

To evaluate this algorithm, the smallest lifetime of all terminals in a cell using either direct communication or battery-aware relaying are compared. Figure 3 shows the lifetime extension achievable with different values of G where lifetimes are again averaged over 55 different scenarios and 9 MT's transmitting to the AP with a fixed data rate. Even though in this scenario, the energy efficiency can only be marginally improved, it is indeed possible to extend the lifetime of the network as a whole by more than 18% (the precise value depends on parameters like covered area, PER, and α).

4 Optimizing capacity

The reduced distances made possible by relaying can improve the capacity of a wireless cell—here defined as the total amount of data that can be successfully handled by the access point per unit time—in two different ways: one is the reduced interference in neighboring cells (because of smaller transmission power), the other is the possibility of using faster modulations over these shorter distances.

Here, we are not focusing on the interference reduction resulting from relaying (this effect has been investigated in [11] and, for CDMA-based systems, in [1]), but here we are rather interested in the possibility to improve capacity by optimizing transmission schedules and modulations and by adding additional wireless resources. Relaying problems akin to this one have been studied in a number of publications (e.g., [5, 7, 8]), but the goals and system models are usually somewhat different: In particular, the combination of ad-hoc relaying as a means to amend a fixed network with a joint optimization of routing, modulation, and scheduling has—to our knowledge—not been studied before. In general, though, we corroborate the overall tendency of all papers that relaying can improve wireless capacity, but only up to a point.

4.1 System modes

Assuming a TDMA-like system, terminals like those in Figure 1 need to send their traffic in a given time slot. How to fairly divide the system resources (i.e, the time the AP can receive) between terminals—even in the direct case—gives raise to two different ways of contemplating the system. Fairness among terminals can be maintained by scheduling the communication such that either all terminals obtain an equal share of the total frame time (the "uniform slot size" scheme) or all terminals are allowed to send a constant amount of data in slots of varying length depending on their modulation and, basically, their distance from the access point (the "uniform traffic size" scheme); see Figure 4a. While the first scheme will result in a higher total goodput (as far terminals are given a relatively smaller weight), the second scheme corresponds better to user expectations. These two fairness schemes also extend to the relaying case: either all slots have the same length, or time slots are arranged such that all terminals receive the same effective goodput, no matter whether they are relayed or not.

In simple relaying, terminal A waits for an exclusive time slot to send data to B. A second time slot is then needed to communicate A's data from B to the AP (where a faster modulation can be used in these time slots). However, C's sending to the AP and A's sending to B involve different entities and could—in principle—be scheduled concurrently. Doing so on the same frequency might be possible in large cells, but in order to avoid interference within a cell, another frequency could be used for the relaying step. Switching between two frequencies is indeed feasible as it is possible to have frequency switching times in ranges of few microseconds; also, no additional synchronization is necessary as switching happens within a frame. Figure 4b and c show the different fairness schemes for both one- and two-frequency relaying cases. Using an additional frequency might be inconvenient when this frequency is used in neighboring cells. When there are sufficiently many frequencies available, this is not necessarily a problem: HiperLAN/2, e.g., specifies 19 frequencies, which should be sufficient for most reuse patterns. Moreover, the use of the second frequency can be confined to the communication of the AP with nearby terminals, which takes place at small transmission power values—from the outside, such a cell would indeed not disturb a frequency assignment too much.

4.2 Routing

The potential benefit of relaying depends on the data rates that can be realized between relayed terminal, relaying terminal, and access point. Hence, a joint optimization of routing and scheduling is necessary that decides which terminal to use for relaying and

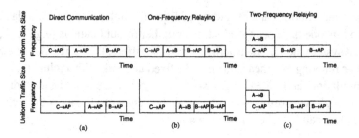

Fig. 4. Time-freqency representation of the example scenario

that selects modulation and transmission power. Currently, the algorithm optimizes only the uplink case and considers a single intermediate relay.

The effective data rate between two terminals can be determined based on their distance and a target packet error rate, allowing to compute, for each modulation, the required transmission power (based on results in [12]). Any modulation that requires more than a maximum allowable power or that does not match receiver sensitivity is ruled out, resulting in the optimum modulation for this pair of terminals; the transmission power is then adjusted to the smallest value that still meets the target PER for this modulation. This determines the modulation to be used in the scheduling decisions.

The routing then proceeds as follows: for a mobile terminal X, its data rate in the direct and relaying case is computed for all possible relaying terminals; the effective data rate for a relayed terminal is the minimum rate of both involved links. X selects that terminal as a relayer that results in the largest data rate for X and that exceeds the direct case data rate. This is a local routing decision only, global optimizations are left for further work; also, relaying terminals always communicate directly with the AP.

4.3 Scheduling mechanism

For both uniform slot size and uniform traffic size fairness schemes, relaying schedules are computed on the basis of the routing decisions. Let us first consider the uniform slot size case. In direct communication, all terminals are assigned an equal share of transmission time. In one-frequency relaying, additional time slots are needed for communication from the relayed to the relaying terminals, from the relaying terminals to the AP for their own traffic and from the relaying terminals to the AP for the relayed traffic. Each of these communications is assigned an equal share of time. For the two-frequency relaying, as communication from the relayed terminals to the relaying terminals can overlap with other communication, the total number of time slots depend on this overlap; and again, all slots are of uniform length.

In the case of uniform traffic size schedules, the optimal traffic size per slot depends on the modulations chosen in the routing phase. The schedule construction is in principle similar to the uniform slot size case, but here the slot length is individually varied for each terminal such that all terminals' goodput at the AP results in the same value, taking into account the need to relay traffic in two slots.

4.4 Results

For the model described in Section 2, the goodput achieved by capacity-oriented schedules for direct, one-frequency, and two-frequency relaying are averaged over 55 different placements of terminals. The resulting average total goodputs are shown, for ten entities and varying pathloss coefficient α, for both uniform slot size (Figure 5) and uniform traffic size schedules (Figure 6). For small α, all approaches are capable of fully utilizing the access point's maximum goodput. As α increases, the range of communication over which the 1% PER condition can be met at a fixed modulation and limited transmission power decreases. Hence, the observed goodput at the access point also goes down. When α exceeds 3.2, the 1% PER can no longer be met even with the slowest modulation, therefore, no values for larger α are shown.

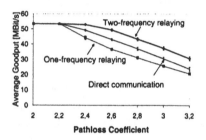 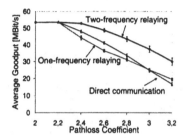

Fig. 5. Average goodput as a function of α for uniform slot size fairness

Fig. 6. Average goodput as a function of α for uniform traffic size fairness

For both scheduling types, the goodput achieved by one-frequency relaying is (for this number of terminals) smaller than that of direct communication. This is due to the additional time slot requirement to send the relayed traffic to the access point. As α increases, one-frequency relaying approaches direct communication and actually surpasses it for uniform traffic size schedules (this tendency continues to larger α when the PER requirement is relaxed). In either case, two-frequency relaying considerably improves the total performance.

This somewhat ambivalent result is partially due to the number of terminals used in this example. Figure 7 and 8 study the impact of varying the number of terminals. While in the uniform slot size case, one-frequency relaying still does not compare favorably with the direct case, uniform traffic size scheduling results in an improvement already for a modest number of terminals. Again, in both cases, two-frequency relaying results in considerable improvements, almost doubling the direct case's goodput in extreme examples. This dependency on the number of terminals is essentially a stochastic effect: the far terminals have a higher probability of finding a relay terminal, more often enabling faster modulations. Hence, relaying does generate more capacity when it is most sourly needed. Of course, relaying is not capable of improving the goodput per terminal as the AP is the bottleneck, in accordance with theoretical results.

The performance results for one-frequency relaying also show that the local heuristic used to determine relaying terminals needs to be extended for the uniform slot size

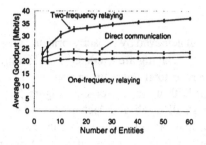

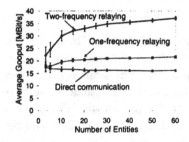

Fig. 7. Average goodput as a function of entities for uniform slot size ($\alpha = 3.2$)

Fig. 8. Average goodput as a function of entities for uniform traffic size ($\alpha = 3.2$)

scheduling case in order to also result in a *global* improvement of goodput. This is a challenging issue for future work.

5 Electromagnetic field immission

As relaying reduces transmission power, it should also be a viable technique to lower electromagnetic field (EMF) immissions, which is currently often considered a health hazard. We examined the electromagnetic immission (received power) when using our energy- and capacity-optimized algorithms; moreover, we also developed a relaying algorithm that minimizes the radiated energy (power multiplied by time) while keeping the target PER.

While executing the simulations described in Sections 3 and 4, the EMF immission power is recorded by a regular grid of "sensors", placed 10 m apart. Relaying-based immission power is then compared to the direct case using two different metrics: First, the time-weighted average of the immitted power is calculated for all sensors (averaged over all topologies). Second, the sum of the time during which the immitted power exceeds a threshold is calculated (averaged over all topologies for each sensor).

Regarding the first metric, in Figure 9 the EMF immission ratio of the radiated-energy-optimized algorithm to the direct case is shown. The dark surface shows the region at which the immitted EMF is reduced (ratio < 1). This algorithm reduces the immitted power value by about 45%, averaged over all sensors and topologies. The curves for other algorithms (with respect to direct communication) are similar and they all do reduce the average immission power between 1.4 % (for the battery-optimizing algorithm) and 11 % (for the energy-optimizing algorithm). The loads used in these evaluations were the same as in the capacity and energy-efficiency evaluations, respectively.

The second metric's purpose is to reflect the current debate about the precise medical relevance of immitted power levels. As so far no safe threshold is established, we show the amount of time that a sensor is exposed to power levels exceeding an arbitrary threshold. To compare different algorithms, the resulting times are normalized to a single MAC frame length (2 ms). The results are shown in Figure 10; as an example, an average sensor is exposed to immitted power larger than 50 nW for 50 μs in every MAC frame when using the emission-optimized relaying.

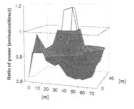 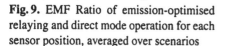

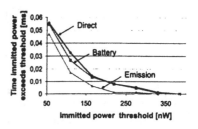

Fig. 9. EMF Ratio of emission-optimised relaying and direct mode operation for each sensor position, averaged over scenarios

Fig. 10. Amount of time during a MAC frame for which the threshold is exceeded, averaged over all sensors and scenarios

One conclusion is that the characteristics of the curves are not changed by relaying, yet there is an improvement for all thresholds and algorithms. As an outcome we can improve capacity or energy efficiency while simultaneously reducing both average and peak immitted power. In most cases, immission power values at the edges are smaller (thus also reducing the inter-cell interference) and somewhat increased inside, near to the AP.

Note that these measurements are only for uplink data transmissions. In the downlink case, we expect a decrease in immitted power since the AP itself transmits for a longer time such that power reduction should have a considerable effect.

6 Conclusions and outlook

The concepts and algorithms presented in this paper show that relaying is a viable means to improve the operations of an infrastructure-based wireless communication system: it is possible to extend the lifetime of the network, considerably increase the cell capacity or reduce the electromagnetic immission. Moreover, the algorithms are practical as they are not computationally intensive, they can be implemented as online algorithms iteratively improving intermediate solutions, and are based on information (in particular, channel gain between terminals) that can be provided by real systems with acceptable overhead (e.g., HiperLAN/2's radio map). We are currently implementing (together with partners from the HyperNET/IBMS2 project) relaying in a real Hiper-LAN/2 testbed and will study its performance.

A number of questions remain open: foremost, the impact of mobility should be investigated. Preliminary studies show that the algorithm performance is robust up to medium speed and that the update interval for channel gain measurements is acceptable. Also, the possibilities of relaying-based immission reduction warrant additional investigations. Furthermore, the effects of interference reduction and usage of multiple frequencies will be studied in a multi-cell context. An issue of larger magnitude is the integration of directed (smart) antennas, which should bring additional benefits to all aspects of the relaying problem.

206

Bibliography

[1] M. Bronzel, W. Rave, P. Herhold, and G. Fettweis. Interference Reduction in Single Hop Relay Networks. In *Proc. of 11th Virginia Tech Symposium on Wireless Personal Communications (to appear)*, Blacksburg, VA, June 2001.

[2] B. Burns and J.-P. Ebert. Power Consumption, Throughput and Packet Error Measurements of an IEEE 802.11 WLAN Interface. Technical Report TKN-01-007, Telecommunication Networks Group, Technische Universität Berlin, August 2001.

[3] T. A. ElBatt, S. V. Krishnamurthy, D. Connors, and S. Dao. Power Management for Throughput Enhancement in Wireless Ad-Hoc Networks. In *ICC 2000*, New Orleans, LA, June 2000. IEEE.

[4] L. M. Feeney and M. Nilsson. Investigating the Energy Consumption of a Wireless Network Interface in an Ad Hoc Networking Environment. In *INFOCOM*, Anchorage, AK, US, April 2001. IEEE.

[5] M. Gastpar and M. Vetterli. On the Capacity of Wireless Networks: The Relay Case. In *Proc. INFOCOM*, New York, NY, June 2002.

[6] J. Gomez, A. T. Campbell, M. Naghshineh, and C. Bisdikian. Conserving Transmission Power in Wireless Ad Hoc Networks. In *9th International Conference on Network Protocols*, Riverside, California, November 2001. IEEE.

[7] M. Grossglauser and D. Tse. Mobility Increases the Capacity of Wireless Adhoc Networks. In *Proc. Infocom*, 2001.

[8] P. Gupta and P. R. Kumar. The Capacity of Wireless Networks. *IEEE Trans. on Information Theory*, November 1998. http://black.csl.uiuc.edu/~prkumar/ps_files/capacity_final.ps.

[9] D. Hollos and H. Karl. A HiperLAN/2 simulation model in OMNeT++. In *Proc. 2nd Intl. OMNeT++ Workshop*, pages 61–70, Berlin, Germany, January 2002.

[10] D. Hollos and H. Karl. A protocol extension to HiperLAN/2 to support single-relay networks. In *Proc. of 1st German Workshop on Ad-Hoc Networks*, pages 91–108, Ulm, Germany, March 2002. http://www-tkn.ee.tu-berlin.de/publications/papers/frame2.pdf.

[11] H. Karl and S. Mengesha. Analyzing Capacity Improvements in Wireless Networks by Relaying. In *Proc. IEEE Intl. Conf. Wireless LANs and Home Networks*, pages 339–348, Singapore, December 2001.

[12] J. Khun-Jush, G. Malmgren, P. Schramm, and J. Torsner. HIPERLAN type 2 for broadband wireless communication. *Ericsson Review*, 2:108–119, 2000. http://www.ericsson.com/review/2000_02/files/2000026.pdf.

[13] J. Peetz. HiperLAN/2 Multihop Ad Hoc Communication by Multiple-Frequency Forwarding. In *Proc. of Vehicular Technology Conference (VTC) Spring 2001*, Rhodes, Greece, May 2001.

[14] Y. Xu, J. Heidemann, and D. Estrin. Geography-Informed Energy Conservation for Ad Hoc Routing. In *Seventh Annual ACM/IEEE International Conference on Mobile Computing and Networking*. ACM, July 2001.

Increasing Connectivity of Ad-Hoc Networks

Horst Hellbrück[1] and Stefan Fischer[2]

[1] International University - School of IT, Campus 2, D-76646 Bruchsal
[2] TU Braunschweig - IBR, Mühlenpfordtstr. 23, D-38106 Braunschweig

Abstract. Mobile Ad-Hoc networks are built spontaneously from mobile devices communicating via wireless interfaces. The idea is that some of the devices act as relay stations in such a way that two stations, which are not in direct range, can communicate with each other over this new multi-hop connection. However, the nature of Ad-Hoc networks and especially the mobility of nodes makes it difficult to achieve a certain minimum connectivity, which is an indispensable property for reliable communication. With our simulation tool ANSim (Ad-Hoc Network Simulator), we have already shown that with randomly moving nodes (a realistic assumption) one needs many mobile devices to achieve an acceptable connectivity. In this paper, we therefore investigate the idea of introducing *mobile robots* to such a network, whose only function is to act as a relay station thus not to fulfil any application-specific task. The robots have to find out the optimal position in the network, i.e., the place where they can best support application-oriented devices in their work. In this first approach we assume that the robots have full knowledge of the positions of all other devices. We simulate their behaviour in this situation. The results indicate that further work on this idea will be worthwhile.

1 Introduction and Background

Recent years have seen a tremendous growth in the usage of devices equipped with communication interfaces for Wireless LAN, Bluetooth or GSM. This has opened the possibility of building Ad-Hoc networks. The idea consists of forming a network of mobile stations in proximity to each other, where some of the devices act as relay stations. The desired result is that two stations, which are not in direct range, can communicate with each other, by forming longer routes using available intermediate stations.

However, the nature of Ad-Hoc networks and especially the mobility of the nodes makes it difficult to achieve a certain minimum connectivity, which is an indispensable property for reliable communication. It is obvious that there is little point in forming a long-lasting communication connection, if the probability for the successful set-up is very small, and if established connections can be constantly interrupted by the mobility of the intermediate stations. Pre-estimations are useful for certain applications in a specific geographical surrounding. For an Ad-Hoc network operator the service availability is the key point of success. In addition to difficulties like denial of service attacks or various technical problems, the lack of wireless nodes itself is a serious threat to service availability.

Our idea is to introduce autonomous mobile robots in the network that act as maintainers of the network by moving to broken links. They place themselves between the nodes and close the gap between isolated node groups with the help of a positioning algorithm. We assume that the robots have full knowledge of the positions of all other devices. We will study their behaviour in this situation and compare the result to alternative solutions like fixed nodes.

To provide a simple way for pre-estimations we developed the simulation tool "ANSim" (Ad-hoc Network Simulation). It serves as a tool for statistical simulation for practice-oriented Ad-Hoc scenarios. The user can determine the boundary conditions of the simulation by the input of some base parameters. These include size and shape of the geographical area, range of the stations, etc. The user receives results like the probability that two selected stations are connected. This tool was extended to introduce mobile robots to the Ad-Hoc network.

The rest of the paper is organised as follows: Section 2 presents the basic communication model used throughout the paper. Before the main part, which covers the positioning algorithm and the simulation results of the robots-enhanced Ad-Hoc networks, we will briefly introduce the problem domain and present our new idea. Section 3 shows the current version of the simulation tool developed at the International University and describes the positioning algorithm of the robots. Section 4 presents first results including interpretations. This paper concludes with a presentation of related work (Section 5), as well as a conclusion and future extensions (Section 6).

2 Connectivity in Ad-Hoc Networks

In previous papers ([5], [6]) we have investigated the connectivity between two arbitrarily placed nodes in static and mobile scenarios including various mobility models. Especially the average number of neighbouring nodes *neighbours* in direct range necessary to achieve connectivity ($p_{ges} \approx 95\%$ and higher) was of interest. The basic findings are given here without further explanation after presentation of the underlying model. The last subsection introduces some more details about the idea of the robots and illustrates their operation.

2.1 Ad-Hoc Network Model

For the analysis of the system behaviour we use a simple model in the geometry of two dimensions $\Re^2$, as illustrated in Figure 1.

We select as illustration a rectangular area A in the geometry of two dimensions $\Re^2$ (Figure 1) for possible positions of N nodes numbered N_0 to N_{N-1}. The transmission range is indicated as a circle with radius r.

Edge effects, such as shading, reflection, dispersion and diffraction, are left out, and only the free-space loss is taken into account. This model, as also used in [4], uses a simple decision algorithm:

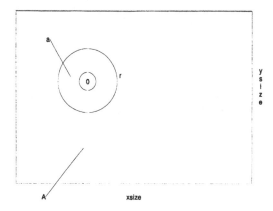

Fig. 1. Illustration of the basic communication model

- if the distance d between two nodes is smaller than the transmission radius r, communication is possible.
- no transmitting can take place outside the transmission range.

We distribute nodes with thes digital transmitting characteristics within the area A. The positions $P_A = (x_a; y_a)$ and P_B of two arbitrary nodes N_A and N_B are uncorrelated and independent of each other, i.e., $P_B \neq f(P_A)$.

All the following investigations, if not marked otherwise, are based on the **MANET** standard scenario as used in [10], [9], and [2], with $N = 50$ Nodes randomly placed or moving in a $1000m \cdot 1000m$ square area having a transmission radius of $r = 250m$

2.2 Connectivity Basic Findings

In previous investigations [5] and [6]) we concluded that

- only a very small increase in connection probability can be achieved by bringing in single intermediate random placed or moving nodes,
- an unexpectedly large number of nodes are necessary in order to form a completely interconnected network structure.

For example Figure 2 shows the average number of direct neighbours for differently shaped areas versus the mean distance between sender and receiver divided by the range r of the nodes necessary for a connection probability of $95\% \pm 2\%$.

For the MANET Scenario, for example 50 Nodes are needed to get a fully connected Ad-Hoc network $p_{ges} = 99,5\%$, equivalent to 12 direct neighbours (using a Random Waypoint model where the nodes do not stop). The node distribution and hereby the connectivity is very much influenced by the mobility model and the ratio between moving time and stop time. For more details see [6].

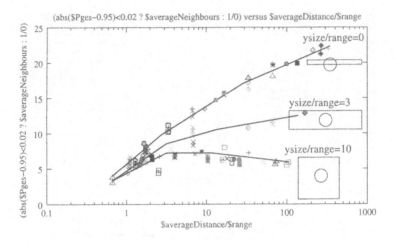

Fig. 2. average Number of direct neighbours for various shapes of *A* and uniformly distributed nodes.

2.3 A possible Solution

Since Ad-Hoc networks need high connectivity to be applicable we investigate ways to improve the connectivity for such networks that lack enough nodes. In this article we present the idea of introducing a small number of mobile nodes called *robots* into the Ad-Hoc network that act as "Maintainers" of the network in case of poor connectivity. The robots task is to connect as many nodes as possible by acting as relay stations between broken links as illustrated in Figure 3.

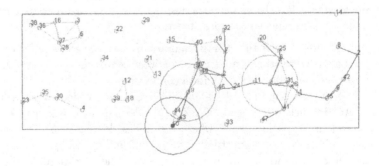

Fig. 3. Robot N_{49} enabling connection between N_0 and N_{50}

The challenge is to locate the optimal destination for a robot, as there might be many broken links that need to be fixed. The robot must take into account its own current position, as it needs some time to reach the destination, and the benefit for the whole network when healing an interrupted link. Last but not least the robot must coordinate with other robots in order to avoid several robots moving to the same destination. In Subsection 3.1 we deduce the implementation of the positioning algorithm and provide some more details.

3 Simulation Tool ANSim

As analytic approaches are limited to a small number of nodes as shown in [5] the "ANSim" (**A**d hoc **N**etwork **Sim**ulation)[3] tool has been developed, and implemented in the programming language Java. The graphical version uses AWT, and is available as standalone application or applet. The simulations can also be performed by command line calls in combination with shell scripts.

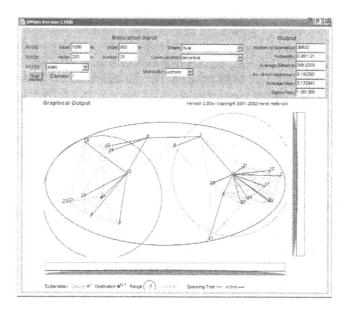

Fig. 4. Graphical User Interface of the simulation tool ANSim

The input parameters of ANSim are: *xsize, ysize, shape* - description of the area; r - range of stations; N - number of nodes distributed within the area; n - number of scenarios to examine (*only in command line version*); e - extension of

[3] www.i-u.de/schools/hellbrueck/ansim/start.htm

the area to a multiple of the original area; c - communication mode (peripheral or central); *mode* - operation mode of ANSim (static, mobile).

The additional input parameters of the *static* mode are: *distr* - distribution of the nodes;

The additional input parameters of the *mobile* mode are: *model* - the mobility model of the nodes; *robots* - the number and positioning model of the robots; *vmax* - the maximum speed of the nodes (uniformly distributed between 0 and max); *max. stop* - the maximum time the nodes stop when finished movements (uniformly distributed between 0 and max); *max. move* - the maximum time the nodes move until the stop (uniformly distributed between 0 and max);

The output parameters are: p_{ges} - total probability that two arbitrarily chosen nodes are connected; *dist* - average distance between two nodes; *neighbours* - average number of directly attainable nodes; mean value of the hops to reach the target and appropriate variance; p_n - portions of probabilities that connection consists of n hops (only in command line version); *logs* - various distributions of locations and connectivity parameters (available in GUI version).

p_{ges} is calculated statistically as the quotient of the successful scenarios with connectivity and the total number of examined scenarios.

$$p_{ges} = \frac{\{\text{Scenarios} \mid (\text{Sender \& Receiver connected})\}}{\text{Number of examined Scenarios}} \qquad (1)$$

Figure 4 illustrates some parameters and introduces the user interface of the graphical simulation tool. On the left side one finds an input block with the simulation parameters to be entered. On the right side the textual output block displays the numeric results calculated by the simulation. Within the lower region (graphical output block) individually analysed scenarios plus some statistics are visualized. The figure shows a screen shot with the input parameters xsize=1000m, ysize=500m, shape=oval, range=150m, N=30, extension=1, communication=decentral, mode=static, distribution=uniform. The sending and receiving nodes are highlighted in the graphical output. The transmitting node N_0 (in green) tries to establish the shortest possible connection (Spanning Tree according to Dijkstra [1]) to N_{29} (in blue). The algorithm ends as soon as the receiving node is reached (connectivity achieved), or the tree cannot be further extended (no connectivity). The black lines show the spanning tree (the connections found on the way from green to blue). All the existing connections between the nodes are marked in grey. In Figure 4 the connection is established via 4 hops. The two circles of the transmitting and receiving node indicate the transmission range. The left bar diagram (in green) shows the distribution of the y positions. The lower bar diagram illustrates the distribution of the x positions.

3.1 ANSim Extensions for Robots

Having introduced the input and output parameters of the simulation in the previous section, we perform simulations with and without robots and investigate the results according to the set of parameters in Table 1. Within this set of scenarios we decrease the number of Nodes $N = 50, 30, 20, 15, 10, 5$ to see if the

Parameter	Value
Area A	rectangle $1000m \cdot 1000m$
Transmission range r	$250m$
Mobility Model $model$	Random Waypoint
max. velocity $vmax$	$5m/s$
max. stop time $max.\ stop$	$0s$
communication c	decentral

Table 1. Scenarios under investigation

robots are able to maintain connectivity. The robots include the same transmission characteristics and especially the same range as the standard Nodes that move randomly.

The detailed subsequent steps of investigation are scenarios where

1. Robots move according to a random pattern equivalent than the standard nodes (Reference)
2. Robots follow a positioning algorithm & move with $v = infinite$ (Reference)
3. Robots follow a positioning algorithm and move with the maximum velocity of the standard nodes
4. Stationary robots according to the results of the previous steps

The positioning algorithm applies a modified nearest neighbour clustering algorithm to find the isolated node groups G_k $(k = 0 \cdots M)$ with M as the number of node groups. It is a distributed algorithm that is based on the assumption that a robot knows every position of the nodes including the other robots. This exchange of locations uses another small band network like GSM.

Description of the positioning algorithm

1. **Begin**
2.   create robots list
3.   **Do**
4.   cluster analysis of nodes without elements of the robots list
5.   find a robot and a position with maximum Cost-/Benefit Relationship
6.   send the robot to that position and remove it from robots list
7.   **until** robots list == empty **or** Number of Clusters == 1
8. **End**

The benefit function reflects the overall goal: Connectivity. We define the benefit function $b(G_j, G_k)$ for two node groups G_j and G_k as the number of additional connections that are established, when connecting these two node groups. That is simply the multiplication of the number of nodes in a group G_j and G_k.

$$b(G_j, G_k) = N(G_j) \cdot N(G_k) \tag{2}$$

Cluster	G_1	G_2	G_3	G_4	Total
Number of nodes in Cluster $N(G_j)$	80	30	50	50	210
Probability of connection $(N(G_j)/N)^2$	0,145	0,02	0,057	0,057	**0,279**

Table 2. Example Node Clusters

where $N(G_j)$ is the number of nodes in node group G_j.

A small example serves as reasoning for the above algorithm. Imagine we have four node clusters as given in Table 2. One single robot can either connect G_1 and G_2 (results in a cluster of 110 nodes) or G_3 and G_4 (results in a cluster of 100 nodes).

As we are interested in the overall connectivity we calculate the probability that an arbitrary connection between two randomly chosen nodes can be established. The final result for unconnected clusters gives $p_{ges} = 0,279$. The results for the two solutions can be compared in Table 3 and Table 4.

Cluster	$G_1 + G_2$	G_3	G_4	Total
Number of nodes in Cluster $N(G_j)$	110	50	50	210
Probability of connection $(N(G_j)/N)^2$	0,274	0,057	0,057	**0,388**

Table 3. Example Node Clusters connect G_1 and G_2

Cluster	G_1	G_2	$G_3 + G_4$	Total
Number of nodes in Cluster	80	30	100	210
Probability of connection $(N(G_j)/N)^2$	0,145	0,020	0,227	**0,392**

Table 4. Example Node Clusters connect G_3 and G_4

This small calculation shows that connecting $G_3 + G_4$ is better as this allows for more additional connections instead of building the largest possible node group $(G_1 + G_2)$.

The cost function $c(G_j, G_k, N_r)$ is defined between two node groups G_j, G_k and the robot N_r as

$$c(G_j, G_k, N_r) = \frac{d(G_j, G_k)}{r}(1 + \frac{d(P(j,k), N_r)^2}{r^2})$$ (3)

where $d(G_j, G_k)$ is the distance between the node groups calculated as the minimum distance between two nodes of G_j and G_k. $P(j,k)$ is the intermediate point between the two nearest nodes and $d(P(j,k), N_r)$ the distance between a robot N_r and the intermediate point.

The positioning algorithm finds the maximum of $b(G_j, G_k)/c(G_j, G_k, N_r)$ considering all node groups and all available robots.

4   Results and Interpretations

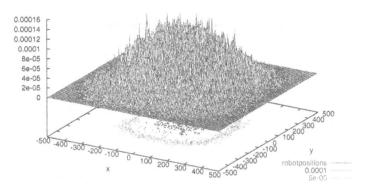

Fig. 5. statistical distribution of the locations of mobile robot nodes with infinite velocity as a base for the fixed location of robots

The statistical distribution of the mobile robot nodes with infinite velocity serves as information base for the fixed locations in Figure 5. The distribution has its maximum in the center and decreases rapidly at the edges. So the optimum position for one robot with fixed positions is the central point of A. The second up to the fifth robot with fixed position extends that range towards the edges of A.

Figure 6 shows a comparison of all approaches of the test scenario. We clearly see that improvement in connectivity varies with the strategy of the robots. One additional robot improves the connectivity p_{ges} from 48% up to max. 67%, using the above positioning algorithm compared to 51% for a random movement of the robot. In other words one "intelligent" robot is as good as 5 robots with randomly moving pattern. The linear increase of the connectivity for static robots is a consequence of the increasing coverage area of the robots. e.g. 5 robots cover $5 \cdot a \approx 0.8 \cdot A$ so that $\approx 80\%$ of the possible node positions are already covered. So infrastructure mode is a worthwhile alternative for Ad-Hoc networks that lack nodes.

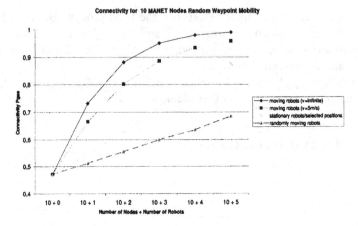

Fig. 6. MANET Scenario with 10 standard Nodes (*Random Waypoint* Mobility) including robots

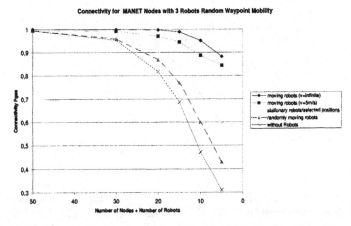

Fig. 7. MANET Scenario with decreasing Number of Nodes (*Random Waypoint* Mobility) including three robots

Figure 7 presents another view of the effect. The effort of three robots with various strategies to maintain connectivity when decreasing the number of nodes is displayed. The mobile strategy clearly outperforms the other solutions. Even a decrease to just 10 nodes can be improved to 90% connection probability with this simple positioning algorithm.

The positioning algorithm is not optimal. It does not cover the case that one single robot might connect up to five node groups instead of connecting just the two largest. The improved algorithm to find the optimal position falls into the category of NP problems and is therefore not suited to run in a resource-limited environment. The actual implementation of the algorithm is further limited in that way that robots act individually. The algorithm does not yet cover the case that two robots together can fill the gap between two large node groups but this functionality can easily be implemented.

5 Related Work

The discrete event network simulator *ns-2* [7] serves primarily as an evaluation tool. Its purpose is the analysis of protocols focusing on MAC and network layer based on concrete scenarios of nodes either wired or as combination of wireless and wired LAN connections. The simulation model covers in detail the transmission channels, delay times, datagram header etc. up to the application itself. The script language Tcl serves as interface to the users. Due to the detailed model, the simulation times are long compared to ANSim, and therefore allow for a precise analysis of protocols. ANSim, however, abstracts from the details of the transmission. It benefits from the reduced run time of the investigation of a single scenario to examine as many scenarios as possible, and calculates statistical mean values of the obtained individual results.

Based on the theoretical investigations in [4], diverse simulations were performed with the help of the network simulator *ns-2* [7] under 802.11 in order to acknowledge the results of the throughput estimation. Here we present briefly one exemplary simulation result from MIT [8]: with the limitation of only one transmitting couple and long chains of nodes (in ideal distance d somewhat smaller than r), just approximately a quarter of the entire bandwidth of the wireless channel is usable as throughput. In particular the throughput calculation and optimisation of wireless Ad-Hoc networks remains an interesting research area. New approaches like the one of S. Toumpis [11] are some examples to be mentioned.

The approach of M. Grossglauser [3] exploits mobility to improve the throughput in Ad-Hoc networks by delivering packets that are not time critical at the receiver instead of relaying them across the network. The work focuses on the increase of throughput in an Ad-Hoc network whereas we concentrate on the connectivity part. A combination of the two approaches is a promising option for the future.

6 Conclusion and Future Work

Based on a simple theoretical model, we simulated connection probabilities of Ad-Hoc networks. A basic finding is that only a small increase in connection probability can be achieved by bringing in intermediate nodes. An unexpectedly large number of nodes are necessary in order to form a completely interconnected network structure. In order to reach connection probabilities of approx. 100% in Ad-Hoc networks each node needs between 10 and 20 direct neighbours on average.

218

A tool "ANSim" performing statistical simulations was previously developed in Java. With the help of a graphical user interface, the most important parameters of an Ad-Hoc network can be entered and statistical output was produced. Extensions of the tool enable the investigation of autonomous robots introduced into the network and running a distributed positioning algorithm. We showed that mobile robots significantly improve the connectivity of mobile Ad-Hoc networks and help to maintain links between nodes in the case of decreasing number of nodes. An important future project is a modification of the positioning algorithm to cope with the fact that the robots just know the locations of the connected nodes and do not have an overall picture of the network. A further improvement already planned is the proactive movement of the robots towards links at high risk of breaking soon. These extensions are in development.

Designers of Ad-Hoc networks as well as researchers can benefit from this tool by deriving scenarios for detailed investigations of protocols e.g. by means of *ns-2*.

References

1. E. Dijkstra. A note on two problems in connection with graphs, 1959.
2. T.D. Dyer and R.V. Boppana. A comparison of tcp performance over three routing protocols for mobile ad hoc networks. ACM Mobihoc, October 2001.
3. M. Grossglauser and D. Tse. Mobility increases the capacity of ad-hoc wireless networks. IEEE INFOCOM, April 2001.
4. P. Gupta. *Design and Performance Analysis of Wireless Networks*. PhD thesis, Coordinated Science Labatory, University of Illinois, 2000.
5. Horst Hellbrück and Stefan Fischer. Basic analysis and simulation of ad-hoc networks. Technical Report TR01, International University Bruchsal, December 2000.
6. Horst Hellbrück and Stefan Fischer. Towards analysis and simulation of ad-hoc networks. In *Proceedings of the 2002 International Conference on Wireless Networks (ICWN02)*, pages 69–75, Las Vegas, Nevada, USA, June 2002.
7. Kannan Varadhan Kevin Fall. *The ns Manual*. The VINT Project - a collaboration between researchers, 1989-2001.
8. Jinyang Li, Charles Blake, Douglas S. J. De Couto, Hu Imm Lee, and Robert Morris. Capacity of ad hoc wireless networks. In *Proceedings of the 7th ACM International Conference on Mobile Computing and Networking*, pages 61–69, Rome, Italy, July 2001.
9. Elizabeth M. Royer and Charles E. Perkins. Transmission range effects on aodv multicast communication. Swedish Workshop on wireless Ad-Hoc Networks, March 2001.
10. J. Macker S. Corson. Routing protocol performance issues and evaulatin considerations. Technical Report RFC2501, MANET Working Group, January 1999.
11. S. Toumpis and A. Goldsmith. Capacity regions for wireless ad hoc networks. IEEE Transactions on Wireless Communications, Sept. 2001.

Session Telematik

Parallel Rendering von Portlets

Performance-Optimierung bei der Integration weit verteilter Anwendungen

Prof. Dr. Klaus-Peter Fähnrich[1], Gerhard Stark[2], Dirk Köhler[1]

[1] Universität Leipzig, Institut für Informatik,
Augustusplatz 10–11, 04109 Leipzig, Germany
`faehnrich@informatik.uni-leipzig.de`
[2] IBM Deutschland Entwicklung GmbH, ADS Pervasive Computing,
Schönaicher Straße 220, 71032 Böblingen, Germany
`gstark@de.ibm.com`

Zusammenfassung Portal-Server erlauben die Erstellung und den Betrieb von domainspezifischen Portalen im geschäftskritischen Bereich des E-Business. Sie stellen eine Informations- und Kommunikationsplattform unter Einsatz von Techniken der Telematik dar, die eine zentralisierte Nutzung weitverteilter Datenbestände, Inhalte und Anwendungen und in Form eines Portaldienstes gestatten. In einigen von ihnen kommt das auf der J2EE-Technologie basierende Portlet-Konzept zum Einsatz.[3] Portlets stellen die Informationskomponenten von Portalseiten dar, die Inhalte und Anwendungen dem Nutzer zur Verfügung stellen. Sie werden innerhalb des Portal-Servers ausgeführt und erzeugen während des Rendering-Vorgangs Markup, der zur Aggregation von Portalseiten verwendet wird. Der Begriff Rendering ist in der Literatur für den Bereich von Portlet-Servern eingeführt [6, 1]. Er bezeichnet – in Anlehnung der entsprechenden Begrifflichkeit im Grafikbereich – den gesamten Prozess der Datenbeschaffung, Transformation und Darstellung durch Portlets. Das Ziel dieses Beitrags ist es, die Vorteile des Parallel Rendering von Portlets durch den effizienten Aufbau von Portalseiten aufzuzeigen. Darüber hinaus werden adaptive Verfahren vorgestellt, die es erlauben, das Parallel Rendering von Portlets an die Veränderungen der Laufzeitumgebungen anzupassen. Abschließend werden aufbauend auf einer prototypischen Implementierung am Beispiel IBM WebSphere Portal Server die Ergebnisse einer Evaluation vorgestellt und signifikante Steigerungsraten bezüglich der Performance beim Seitenaufbau durch Parallel Rendering von Portlets belegt.

1 Einleitung

1.1 Portale, Portal-Server und Portlets

Portale stellen spezielle Webseiten dar, die heterogene und verteilte Informationen und Applikationen in aggregierter Form einer Portalseite zentralisiert nutzbar machen.

---

[3] z. B. IBM WebSphere Portal Server

Die durch Portal-Server generierte Benutzeroberfläche nutzt dabei zumeist das auf J2EE basierte Portlet-Konzept [6], wodurch nahezu in Echtzeit Informationen und Dienste tausenden von Portalnutzern personalisiert und aktuell zugänglich gemacht werden können.

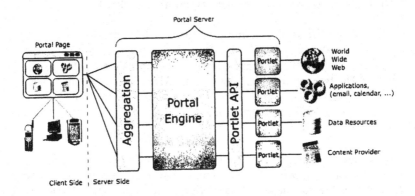

Abbildung 1. Integration weit verteilter Anwendungen auf der Präsentationsebene

Portlets sind dynamische, wiederverwendbare Informationskomponenten eines Portaldienstes, die in Portal-Seiten eingebettet werden (vgl. Abb. 1). Die durch sie bereitgestellte Funktionalität kann von der Darstellung statischer Informationen über dynamisch erzeugte Inhalte bis zu komplexen und interaktiven Anwendungen variieren.

Sie entsprechen einer speziellen Art von Java-Servlets, die jedoch gegenüber der Servlet-Spezifikation über spezielle Erweiterungen und Einschränkungen verfügen [1]. So darf ein Portlet nur Markup-Fragmente generieren, die mithilfe des Aggregationsmoduls des Portal-Servers und weiterem Portlet-Markup zu einer vollständigen Portalseite zusammengefasst werden.

Die Portal-Engine löst Anfragen auf, bietet Verwaltungsfunktionen und Ablaufsteuerungen.

Die Koordination und Einbindung in die Portalseiten wird durch den Portal-Server übernommen. Er stellt die Funktionalität bereit, die notwendig ist, Markup-Fragmente in einen einheitlichen Rahmen einzubetten, zu konfigurieren und zu verwalten.

1.2 Parallel Rendering von Portlets

Das primäre Anliegen dieses Verfahrens zielt nicht auf die direkte Nutzung von Multiprocessing-Fähigkeiten der darunter liegenden Plattform zur Abarbeitung eines Portal-Requests bzw. zur parallelen Ausführung der darin enthaltenen Portlets ab, vielmehr auf die Nutzung sogenannter externer Parallelität.

Der Rendering-Vorgang beinhaltet die Abarbeitung der folgenden fünf Kommunikationsschritte, die jeweils mit Verzögerungen behaftet sein können:

1. Aufbau der Verbindung zwischen dem Portlet und der Datenquelle;
2. Anforderung der Daten durch das Portlet;
3. Generierung/Aufbereitung der angeforderten Daten durch die Datenquelle;
4. Übertragung der Daten von der Datenquelle zum Portlet;
5. Abbau der Verbindung zwischen Datenquelle und Portlet.

Im Falle des sequenziellen Portlet-Rendering können signifikante Verzögerungen zwischen der ersten und letzten Teilphase entstehen, wodurch CPU-Zyklen ungenutzt bleiben. Die Antwortzeit einer Portal-Seite ergibt sich demnach in diesem Fall unmittelbar aus der Summe der einzelnen Portlet-Antwortzeiten.

Durch den Einsatz von Multithreading beim Parallel Rendering können weitere Portlets einer Portalseite Systemressourcen nutzen und die Anforderung benötigter Daten bereits initiieren, obwohl der Rendering-Vorgang des zuvor gestarteten Portlets noch nicht vollständig beendet wurde. Dadurch ist es möglich, potenzielle Verzögerungen optimal für die parallele Ausführung weiterer Portlets zu nutzen. Das Antwortzeitverhalten einer Portalseite verändert sich und wird im günstigsten Fall nur noch direkt von dem Portlet abhängen, für das die längste Renderingzeit beansprucht wird. [4]

Beim sequenziellen Rendering von Portlets besteht ein weiteres Problem: die mögliche temporäre Nichtverfügbarkeit bestimmter Portlet-Ressourcen. Wird von einem Portlet der Zugang zu einer Ressource benötigt, die zeitweise nicht zur Verfügung steht, kann die umgebende Portalseite nicht vollständig aufgebaut werden. Die Abarbeitung des Portal-Requests steht bis zu einer einer spezifizierten Zeit (Timeout) still, falls die Portlet-Antwort ausbleibt.

Im Gegensatz dazu ermöglicht das Parallel Rendering die unabhängige Bearbeitung einzelner Portlets. Da hierdurch das Portlet-Rendering in separaten Threads eines Threadpools[5] ausgelagert wird, kann in dem Fall der Nichtverfügbarkeit einer Ressource nach Ablauf des Timeout das Portal (Portal-Thread) reagieren und eine entsprechende Meldung ausgeben. Dies bedeutet, dass das Portal-System reaktiv bleibt, auch wenn Ressourcen zeitweise nicht zur Verfügung stehen. Dadurch kann die Antwortzeit einer Portalseite zugesichert werden, die in diesem Fall direkt von der Anzahl der darin eingebetteten Portlets und dem jeweiligen Timeout abhängig ist.

Die maximale Antwortzeit einer Portalseite unter dem ausschließlichen Einsatz des Parallel Portlet Rendering entspricht somit:

$$\max \text{Antwortzeit}_{Portalseite} \geq \sum_{i=0}^{n} \text{Auszeit}_{Portlet_i} \gg \sum_{i=0}^{n\cdot} \text{Antwortzeit}_{Portlet_i} \quad (1)$$

---

[4] Ein Beispiel dafür wird in [3] aufgeführt.
[5] Die Verwendung eines Threadpools ist laut [3] aus Gründen des Speichermanagements bzw. aus Sicht des Stabilität des Portal-Server-Systems essenziell.

Die Verwendung von Threads für das Parallel Rendering von Portlets impliziert aus Gründen der Performance und Effizienz die initiale Klassifikation von Portlets in:

- sinnvoll parallelisierbar und
- nicht sinnvoll parallelisierbar.

Die „Sinnhaftigkeit" erstreckt sich dabei auf die mögliche Effizienzsteigerung durch die Verwendung von Threads. [3]

1.3 State of the Art

Im Bereich der Unternehmensapplikationen haben die Performance und die Effizienz von Softwarekomponenten einen sehr hohen Stellenwert. Dies haben bereits Anbieter wie Plumtree[6] und Oracle[7] erkannt und Funktionalitäten für das konsequente Parallel Rendering von Portlets entwickelt [7, 4].

Mithilfe der im Folgenden vorgestellten Rendering-Strategien wird darüber hinaus versucht, den Prozess des Parallel Rendering von Portlets in restringierten, d. h. ressourcenknappen, Laufzeitumgebungen weiter zu optimieren und es dabei adaptiv an Laufzeitveränderungen anzupassen. Dabei hat die Nutzung dieser Verfahren direkten Einfluss auf die Effizienz bei der Aggregation von Portalseiten.

2 Parallel Rendering – Strategien

2.1 Aggressive Parallel Rendering

Aggressive Parallel Rendering ist ein statisches Verfahren, welches keine äußeren Einflüsse,wie Systemressource oder Netzlast, berücksichtigt. Hier werden alle als parallelisierbar deklarierten Portlets tatsächlich parallel gerendert.

Dieses Verfahrens lässt sich laut [3] wie folgt bewerten:

Vorteile:

- Maximierung der Threadpool-Auslastung und damit Minimierung der Antwortzeiten- bzw. Renderingzeiten des Portals;
- triviale Entscheidungsfindung durch geringe Komplexität.

Nachteile:

- Exzessives Threading erhöht die Gefahr des „Leerwerdens" des Threadpools (Abweisung von Portlets);
- aus der notwendig werdenden Überdimensionierung des Threadpools resultiert erhöhter Verwaltungsaufwand und ungenutzte Kapazität;

---

[6] http://www.plumtree.com/
[7] http://www.oracle.com/

- Gleichbehandlung von Portlets unterschiedlicher Laufzeiten;
- Charakteristik der Portalseiten bzw. die Renderingzeiten der Portlets haben keinen Einfluss auf die Rendering-Entscheidungsfindung.

Dieses Verfahren sollte hauptsächlich in hochverfügbaren Einsatzumgebungen Anwendung finden, in denen das Portal nie unter Volllast gerät. Wie aus den Nachteilen des Aggressive Parallel Rendering hervorgeht, bedarf es gerade in restringierten Laufzeitumgebungen eines dynamischen Verfahren, das zur Laufzeit anhand bestimmter Kriterien kontrollierte Entscheidungen trifft, um so ein Ausbalancieren von Lastspitzen zu ermöglichen. Dies ermöglicht das reaktive Verfahren Defensive Parallel Rendering.

2.2 Defensive Parallel Rendering

Auf der einen Seite versucht dieses Verfahren den Threadpool möglichst ressourcensparend zu nutzen, wobei eine Priorisierung von Portlets vorgenommen wird. Es wird hierbei anhand definierter Kriterien zur Laufzeit entschieden, ob ein Portlet durch einen eigenen Thread parallel oder sequenziell gerendert wird. Die Entscheidung hängt von den Veränderungen der Systemumgebung, wie im Folgenden erläutert ab.

Auf der anderen Seite ist es aber Ziel, den Threadpool so optimal wie möglich zu nutzen, wobei dies ein Trade-Off zu dem zuvor genannten darstellt.

Grundsätzlich ist die wichtigste Einflussgröße die Renderingzeit eines Portlets. Über diese kann vorab keine Aussage getroffen werden, da sie von äußeren Faktoren stark beeinflusst wird. Diese Verzögerungen können verschiedenste Ursachen, wie z. B. die Auslastung der Ressource, die aktuelle Netzlast, die Art und Güte der Verbindung zu einer Datenquelle u. s. w. haben.

Es ist ein Verfahren zu nutzen, das Aussagen über das zukünftige Verhalten der Renderingzeiten von Portlets liefern kann. Ein solches Verfahren stellt das Shortest Job First-Verfahren [5] dar. Die Anwendung dieser Berechnungsvorschrift für die geschätzte Renderingzeit T_{n+1} eines Portlets zum Zeitpunkt $n+1$ lautet:

$$T_{n+1} = at_n + (1-a)T_n \quad \text{mit } n \in [0, \infty) \text{ und } a \in [0,1] \quad (2)$$

Dabei entspricht t_n der tatsächlichen Renderingzeit des Portlets zum Zeitpunkt n. Der Faktor a wichtet den tatsächlich ermittelten Wert des letzten Aufrufs für die neu zu schätzende Renderingzeit. Dieses Verfahren ermöglicht eine zuverlässige Schätzung der Renderingzeiten, die auf Erfahrungswerten basiert.[8]

Nachdem nun ein Berechnungsverfahren gefunden wurde, um zukünftige Portlet-Antwortzeiten zu berechnen bzw. zu schätzen, liefert dies die Ausgangsbasis für die Rendering-Entscheidung, die sich in zwei Phasen gliedert – die Vorentscheidung und das Auslastungskriterium.

---

[8] In [3] wird zur Bestimmung der Unbekannten T_0 und t_0 Stellung genommen.

2.2.1 Entscheidungsphase I – Die Vorentscheidung

Das Ziel dieser ersten Entscheidungsphase ist, für die als parallelisierbar gekennzeichneten Portlets einer Portalsseite, im Vorfeld eine Entscheidung zu treffen, ob es notwendig ist, diese parallel zu rendern. Hierfür lassen sich nach [3] zwei verschiedene Ansätze anwenden, die auf unterschiedlichen Kriterien aufbauen.

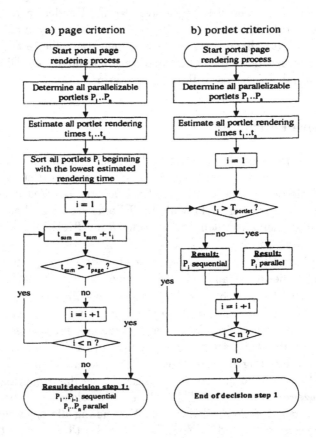

Abbildung 2. Flussdiagramme für Entscheidungsphase I - a) Page-Kriterium, b) Portlet-Kriterium

Das Page-Kriterium macht die Entscheidungsfindung von der individuelle Charakteristik der darzustellenden Portalseite (vgl. Abb. 2a) abhängig. Es berücksichtigt, wie viele und welche Art von Portlets sich auf einer Portalseite befinden. Ausgangspunkt stellt eine portalweit spezifizierte Zeitmarke T_{page} dar, die festlegt, wie lang das Rendering einer Portalseite maximal benötigen sollte. Anhand dieser Zeit wird das Verfahren entscheiden, welche Portlets parallel bzw. sequenziell gerendert werden müssen, um diese Zeitmarke während des Renderings der Portalseite nicht zu überschreiten. Ziel des Page-Kriterium soll es sein, möglichst die Portlets parallel zu rendern, die die längste Zeit benötigen.

Nach dem Portlet-Kriterium (vgl. Abb. 2b) wird explizit für jedes Portlet entschieden, ob dieses parallel gerendert werden soll. Hierzu steht diesem Kriterium ein Parameter in Form einer Zeitmarke $T_{portlet}$ zur Verfügung, die bestimmt, wann genau ein Portlet parallel gerendert werden soll.

Diese, auf unterschiedlichen Annahmen, basierenden Kriterien resultieren oft in unterschiedlichen Rendering-Entscheidungen. Man kann grundsätzlich nicht auf die Vorteilhaftigkeit einer von beiden schließen, da sie vgl. [3] auf unterschiedlichen Annahmen und Absichten aufbauen. Ziel beider Ansätze ist, den Threadpool vor Überlast zu schützen. Die Effizienz des Parallel Rendering von Portlets sinkt, wenn der Threadpool nicht voll ausgelastet wird. Die nun folgende Entscheidungsphase wirkt dem entgegen.

2.2.2 Entscheidungsphase II – Das Auslastungskriterium

Für alle in Entscheidungsphase I gefundenen sequenzielle zu rendernden Portlets wird neu entschieden, ob sie dennoch parallel gerendert werden sollen. Die Orientierung erfolgt dabei an der aktuellen Auslastung des Threadpools, durch einen zusätzlich spezifizierten Parameter. Dieser gibt an, bis zu welcher Auslastung der Threadpool auch durch Portlets genutzt werden soll, die laut Entscheidungsphase I ursprünglich sequenziell gerendert werden.

Es wird für jedes sequenziell zu renderndes Portlet neu entschieden, ob es dennoch parallel gerendert werden soll, falls genügend freie Ressourcen zur Verfügung stehen.

Das Ziel dieser Phase ist es, den Vorteil des Aggressive Parallel Rendering, d. h. eine weitestgehende Auslastung des Threadpools zu erreichen. nicht einzubüßen. Im Fall einer hohen Auslastung des Pools kommt eine sensitiven Entscheidungsfindung zum Tragen, die Threads für das Rendering von Portlets aufspart, deren Prioritäten nach den Kriterien höher eingestuft werden.

3 Implementierung

Um die Einsetzbarkeit des Parallel Rendering von Portlets und die damit potenziell nutzbaren Performance-Vorteile zu untersuchen, wurde es für den Einsatz im IBM WebSphere Portal Server prototypisch implementiert.

Die bisherige Funktionalität der Portlet-Engine reicht zur Realisierung eines Parallel Rendering nicht aus. Diese musste durch eine neue Komponente, den sogenannten Threadpool, erweitert werden. Die Interaktion zwischen Aggregation und Portlet-Invoker wurden (vgl. Abb. 3) definiert. Die unmodifizierte Portal-Engine ist in [3] detailliert spezifiziert und das erweiterte Systemdesign ebenda dokumentiert. Im folgenden wird das Sequenzdiagramm in Abb. 3 näher erläutert.

Der PortletInvoker wird nach der Modifikationen durch die Aggregationskomponente benutzt, um Portlets aufzurufen. Dabei findet bei einer Portal-Anfrage der Aufruf seiner initPage()-Methode zur Initialisierung der angeforderten Portalseite statt, wobei dem PortletInvoker an dieser Stelle bereits bekannt ist, welche Portlets sich auf der jeweiligen Seite befinden. Ohne die Modifikation wurden die einzelnen Portlet-Rendering-Prozesse durch Aufruf seiner `portletService()`-Methode sequenziell angestoßen.

Es war zwischen diesen Aufrufen notwendig, diese Portlets-Rendering-Prozesse vorab parallel unter Nutzung von Threads des `Threadpools` (`addJob()`-Methode) zu initiieren und bei dem eigentlichen Rendering-Aufruf (`portletService()`) den Markup der zuvor parallel initiierten Rendering-Prozesse einzusammeln (vgl. Abb. 3).

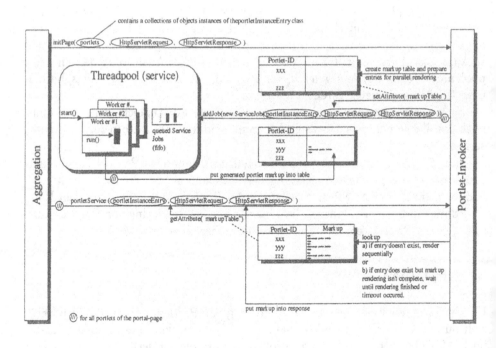

Abbildung 3. Interaktion zwischen `Aggregation` und `PortletInvoker` bei dem Parallel Rendering von Portlets

Sowohl der `PortletInvoker` als auch der `Threadpool` wurden so konzipiert, dass eine Konfiguration und Anpassung an die jeweilige Laufzeitumgebung und Einsatzbedingung möglich wird. Folgende Übersicht zeigt die Möglichkeiten der Konfiguration des `Threadpools`:

Parameter	Auswirkungen	Wertebereich
minThreads	Mindestanzahl von Threads im Pool, zum Initialisierungs-zeitpunt vorab erzeugt	[0,..,maxThreads] default=64
maxThreads	Maximalanzahl von Threads im Pool, bis zu welcher zur Laufzeit dynamisch Threads erzeugt werden können	[minThreads,..,∞) default=128
maxWorkingTime	Maximale Arbeitszeit eines Threads, für das Rendering eines Portlets	default=5(s)
watcherInterval	Thread-Validierungsintervall	default=1(min)
debug	Aktiviert Logging der Threadpool-Aktionen	[true,false] default=false

Ergänzend dazu die neu hinzugefügten Parameter des `PortletInvokers`, die so z. B. die Auswahl der Rendering-Strategie und die Konfiguration der entsprechenden Parameter ermöglicht:

Parameter	Auswirkungen	Wertebereich
useParallelRendering	(De-)Aktivierung des Parallel Rendering	[true,false] default=true
parallelRenderingMode	Auswahl des Rendering-Verfahrens	[0,1,2] 0-aggressiv 1-defensiv/Portlet 2-defensiv/Page
maxWorkingTime	Maximale Arbeitszeit eines Threads, für das Rendering eines Portlets	default=5(s)
portletRenderTimeMark	Portlet-Zeitmarke für die defensive Rendering-Strategie unter Verwendung des Portlet-Kriteriums	default=0.5(s)
pageResponseTimeMark	Page-Zeitmarke für die defensive Rendering-Strategie unter Verwendung des Page-Kriteriums	default=1(s)
threadpoolWorkloadMark	Auslastungsgrenze für die defensive Rendering-Strategie	[0,..,100](%) default=75

4 Evaluation

Nachdem das Parallel Rendering von Portlets prototypisch für den Einsatz im IBM WebSphere Portal Server implementiert wurde, konnten die vorausgegangenen Überlegungen hinsichtlich der zu erwarteten Performance-Steigerung untersucht werden.

Die wichtigsten Einflussgrößen, die hierbei betrachtet wurden, werden vgl. [3] dem Portal-Szenario zugeordnet. Hierzu zählen:

- die Anzahl der Portal-Clients;
- die Anzahl der Portlets je Portalseite;
- und die Portlet-Charakteristik.

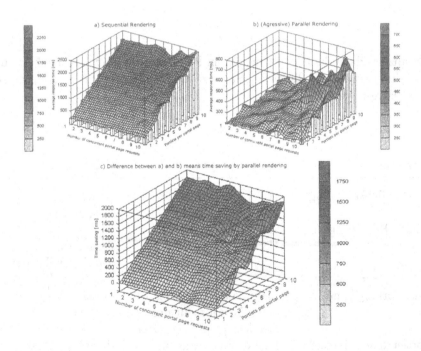

Abbildung 4. Nachweis der Performancesteigerung anhand der durchschnittlichen Antwortzeit pro Portal-Seite [3]

Es wurden zwei umfangreiche Testreihen durchgeführt, die zum einen Aussagen über den durch Parallel Rendering von Portlets erzeugten Overhead machen und zum anderen die Vorteilhaftigkeit des Einsatzes nachweisen (vgl. [3]). Dabei konzentrierten sich die Untersuchung auf den Vergleich des sequenziellen gegenüber dem Parallel Rendering unter Anwendung der Aggressive Parallel

Rendering-Strategie. Sequenzielles Rendering und Aggressive Parallel Rendering stellen Extrempunkte in einem Kontinuum möglicher Strategien dar. Sequenzielles Rendering ist einfach und ineffizient bei mit potenziellen Verzögerungen behafteten verteilten Systemen. Aggressive Parallel Rendering ist zeitoptimal, aber ressourcenintensiv und würde bei Ressourcenknappheit oft unkontrolliert reagieren.

Ein Mittelweg wird durch das Defensive Parallel Rendering gegangen. Dabei kann durch Parametrisierung bestimmt werden, wie nah das Verfahren an den beiden Extrema liegt. Die Optimierungsergebnisse, die für die beiden Extrema nachgewiesen wurden (vgl. Abb. 4), lassen sich wie folgt auf das Defensive Parallel Rendering übertragen.

– Der zusätzliche Overhead durch den Algorithmus bei Defensive Parallel Rendering, der sehr schwer empirisch nachweisbar ist, kann aber aufgrund des Quellcodes abgeschätzt werden und steht dem weitaus deterministischen Gesamtverhalten des Systems gegenüber.
– In den überwiegenden Anwendungsfällen zeigt er – wie das Aggressive Parallel Rendering – ein wesentlich besseres Zeitverhalten.

5 Ausblick

Im Bereich der Unternehmensapplikationen haben die Performance und die Effizienz von Softwarekomponenten einen sehr hohen Stellenwert. Vor allem in dem noch recht jungen Portal-Markt hängen die Akzeptanz und der Erfolg einer Portal-Server-Software nicht zuletzt von deren effizientem Entwurf ab, der sich unmittelbar auf die Nutzbarkeit der Anwendung auswirkt.

Wie wirksam die in diesem Beitrag vorgestellten Strategien für das Parallel Rendering (speziell das Defensive Parallel Rendering) sein werden, und welche Effizienzsteigerungen durch sie in restringierten Laufzeitumgebungen erzielt werden können, konnte bisher noch nicht untersucht werden. Die relativ große Distanz beim Aufbau von Testszenarien zu „realen" Portalen ist ein Grund, warum keine qualitativen Maße für die Effizienzsteigerung angegeben wurden. Dennoch zeigten die verschiedenen Testreihen, welches qualitative Potenzial das neue Verfahren bietet.

In weiteren Untersuchungen sollten die Konfigurationsparameter der Implementierung auf ihre optimale und zumeist interdependenten Einstellungen hin untersucht werden. Die in diesem Schritt gewonnen Informationen können dann direkt von Portal-Administratoren genutzt werden, die darauf bedacht sind, ihr spezifisches Portal-Szenario weitestgehend zu optimieren.

Zusammenfassend kann man prognostizieren, dass der Einsatz des Parallel Rendering von Portlets sowie der Einsatz der hier vorgestellten Rendering-Strategien für die nächste Generation von Portal-Servern von hoher Bedeutung sein wird.

232

Anmerkungen. Die vorliegende Veröffentlichung entstammt einer Kooperation zwischen dem Lehrstuhl für Anwendungsspezifische Informationssysteme an der Universität Leipzig[9] in Zusammenarbeit mit der IBM Entwicklung GmbH Böblingen[10] zum Thema: *„Parallel Rendering von Portlets im IBM WebSphere Portal Server".*

Der dabei entwickelte Prototyp hat aufgrund seiner Stabilität und der verbesserten Effizienz, bei dem Rendering von Portlets, Eingang in das aktuelle Release IBM WebSphere Portal 4.1 gefunden. Darüber hinaus wurden die in diesem Beitrag angeschnittenen Rendering-Strategien in Zusammenarbeit mit IBM in eine Patentschrift aufgenommen.

Literatur

1. Abdelnur, A., Hepper, S.: *JSR 168: Portlet Specification*, Java Specification Requests, http://www.jcp.org/jsr/detail/168.jsp, Februar 2002.
2. Burns, S.: *The Portal Buzz*, Artikel in Executive Update,
   http://www.gwsae.org/ ExecutiveUpdate/1999/December/PortalBuzz.htm, Dezember 1999.
3. Köhler, D.: *Parallel Rendering von Portlets im IBM WebSphere Portal Server*, Diplomarbeit, http://dol.uni-leipzig.de/pub/2002-9, April 2002.
4. Plumtree: *The Massively Parallel Portal Engine*, Plumtree Corporate Portal 4.0 Fact Sheet,
   http://www.plumtree.com/pdf/mppe_fact_sheet.pdf,
   Oktober 2000.
5. Tanenbaum, A. S.: *Modern Operating Systems*, 2nd Edition, Prentice-Hall, ISBN: 0-13-021358-0, Februar 2001.
6. Schaeck, T. , Hepper, S.: *Portal Standards*,
   http://www.theserverside.com/resources/article.jsp?l=Portlet_API,
   Februar 2002.
7. Siva, K.: *Building Web Portlets with Oracle9IAS and the Oracle Portal Development Kit (PDK)*, http://www.its.qut.edu.au/cis/portal/pdf/howtopdk.pdf, Juni 2001.

---

[9] http://ais.informatik.uni-leipzig.de
[10] http://www.ibm.com/de/entwicklung/

Classification and Evaluation of Multicast-Based Mobility Support in All-IP Cellular Networks

Andreas Festag, Holger Karl, Adam Wolisz

TKN, Technical University of Berlin
festag|karl|wolisz@ee.tu-berlin.de
Sekr. FT5-2, Einsteinufer 25, 10587 Berlin, Germany

Abstract. To solve the IP mobility problem, the use of multicast has been proposed in a number of different approaches, applying multicast in different characteristic ways. In this paper, we provide a framework to classify such approaches by analyzing requirements, options for using multicast protocols, and mobility functionalities augmenting the multicast. Within this framework, we identify promising combinations of mechanisms and derive four classes of multicast protocols. These classes include both the standard any-source IP multicast model as well as non-standard multicast models. In particular, the use of source-specific multicast is a new approach to support mobility and turns out to be especially beneficial. The paper describes a corresponding network architecture and a flexible software environment that allows to easily implement these and other classes of mobility-supporting multicast protocols. Based on this software environment, an implemented prototype and measurements quantify handover-specific metrics, namely, handover and paging latency and packet loss and duplication rates, showing that a multicast-based mobility solution has comparable performance to standard Mobile IP/hierarchical Mobile IP. Moreover, it is shown that a non-standard multicast model has reduced implementation and deployment complexity and security risks than a standard multicast model.[1]

1 Introduction

The growing importance of mobile communication deserves support for host mobility in IP-based cellular networks. A common architectural approach is to assign a mobile node, at every wireless access point with which it associates, a new IP address that is topologically correct. Such an address assignment allows to use standard IP routing, the disadvantage is that existing sessions are interrupted as a session is associated with the previous, now invalid IP address. This dichotomy—an IP address represents both node identification and location—is the fundamental problem of mobile IP-based networks and needs to be overcome by mobility concepts.

The mobility concept currently considered to be the most likely candidate for short-term deployment is Mobile IP (1), along with a number of improvements

---

[1] This work was partly supported by a research contract with SIEMENS.

and variations. Mobile IP uses additional agents to separate node identification from current location and ensures that arbitrary nodes can communicate with a mobile node in an uninterrupted way even while the node moves around. Despite this achievement, Mobile IP has been criticized for its performance problems and for not matching all possible requirements for a mobility concept. Hence, other mobility concepts have been proposed to separate a node's identity and location. One approach that inherently uses such a separation is multicasting and has already been considered in several related works: here the identity of a node is the identifier of a multicast group to which a message is destined, the location is a set of conventional addresses. This set of conventional addresses could represent the address(es) under which the mobile node is currently reachable, and as this set can be modified, multicast provides a natural mapping from a fixed identity (equating a mobile node with a multicast group) to a changing set of locations.

The utilization of multicast for mobility support poses a number of challenges. i) Today's IP multicast faces some problems which have prevented its commercial deployment until today (necessity for global address allocation, lack of receiver and transmission authorization, complexity). ii) New challenges arise from the use of multicast for mobility support (dynamic join and leave operations, scalability with respect to number of multicast groups, etc.). iii) Multicast does not offer all functionalities which are required or useful for mobility-related performance.

It is widely accepted that multicast has some attractive features for mobility support, particularly in highly mobile environments with very small cells. Nevertheless, a systematic effort for investigating multicast-based mobility support is still missing. Hence, a number of interesting proposals exist which mostly have different motivations and requirements and are based on different assumptions about the networking architecture. A variety of solutions have been proposed (2) – (10) each providing certain mobility-related functionalities under particular assumptions. The next two sections will derive both the requirements under which to judge such solutions as well as a common framework to classify them and to derive new classes of solutions. In particular, a source-specific multicast approach is a consequence of the application of our framework and has not yet been described in the literature. The before mentioned challenges can be overcome in several different ways, and hence, considerable freedom remains in choosing multicast options to solve the mobility problem. The first main contribution of this paper is an attempt to structure these protocol options and functionalities in an abstract framework. This framework serves as a template from which new concrete solutions can be derived. On the basis of the requirements, we will make our second contribution, a set of preferable instantiations of this template. One of these instantiations is a new multicast-based mobility concept: It relies on modifying the standard *any source* IP service model (ASM) by using the *source-specific* service model (SSM) for mobility support in access networks. Its main benefits lie in reduced implementation and deployment complexity and improved security while achieving a performance that is comparable with that of more complicated multicast models. In order to substantiate this claim we have developed a software environment that turns our abstract framework into a practical platform. While this platform is fixed in some architectural assumptions, it augments a number of different multicast concepts by mobility functionalities in a flexible and extendable manner. Based on this software environment we have evaluated – as the third contribution of this paper – the performance of different multicast schemes demonstrating that the performance is comparable to the classical mobility solution Mobile IP and its hierarchical variant.

The remainder of this paper is organized as follows: The requirements are listed in Section 2 and the abstract framework is introduced in Section 3. Section 4 contains the performance evaluation and Section 5 concludes the paper.

2 Requirements

Identifying the requirements of mobility support is essential for selecting appropriate functionalities for mobility support and for choosing among multicast protocol options. Most of the requirements are evident for mobility support in general (11), therefore, we emphasize requirements that have consequences for the design of a multicast-based mobility solution.

- *Low-end, light-weight end systems* will have only limited memory and processing power, ruling out solutions that have substantial requirements.
- In *heterogeneous access networks*, mobiles will switch between wireless networks with different characteristics regarding bandwidth, etc. (vertical handover). Hence, a multicast scheme cannot assume that network parameters or even organizations remains constant before and after a handover.
- Handovers with *short latency and small packet loss* require a fast execution of multicast join operations, i.e. an unsolicited re-join to the multicast group after a handover.
- In order to support a very high number of mobile hosts, a multicast that is *scalable* with the number of groups with typically a few members is required.
- A full-scale communication network requires *reliable services*, in particular, TCP or a reliable multicast transport protocol should be supported.
- Besides general security concerns for multicast (especially, denial of service and eavesdropping), *location privacy* is important in mobile networks yet constantly violated by today's mobility schemes as temporary IP addresses are tracked and communicated to correspondent nodes.
- *Signaling load* by location updates and handover should be low. Most IP multicast routing protocols provide soft state maintenance where the routing state needs to be refreshed and expires otherwise. Hard state maintenance reduces the signaling overhead, but is less robust for stale states which are likely to occur in error-prone wireless and mobile environments.
- *Redundant data transmissions* caused by delays in maintaining the multicast tree (branches not being removed immediately) should be kept low.

3 Framework Description

Supporting the requirements outlined in Section 2 with multicast requires answers to two questions: The first question is the choice among a number of different multicast protocol options, the second question pertains to different functionalities that are required to support mobility and that can be efficiently implemented using multicast protocols.

3.1 Protocol Options for Multicast-Based Mobility

Multicast protocols can be used in a number of different ways in order to support mobility. The main alternative options are the following:

Multicast endpoint. Selecting the mobile host as multicast endpoint enables multicast protocols to work across the wireless link. This requires multicast protocols which are optimized for small groups and for economical usage of the scarce wireless resources. Alternatively, the access point might be selected as the multicast endpoint and act as a multicast proxy. This option facilitates the usage of optimized signaling protocols on the wireless link.

Micro vs. macro mobility. Using multicast for macro-mobility allows a uniform solution but requires global scalability of the multicast scheme. If, on the other hand, multicast is only used for micro-mobility, an additional solution for handover between access networks is necessary but the scalability requirements are reduced. However, coupling two different mobility solutions will (in general) necessitate some form of address translating (between unicast and multicast).

Multicast tree directionality. A multicast scheme can provide either unidirectional or bidirectional trees. A unidirectional tree is setup to transport downlink packets from a correspondent node/gateway as the root of the tree towards the mobile node while uplink packets use unicast.

X+Multicast. Multicast based on location-independent addressing and routing can be applied as a sole mechanism for mobility support, but not all multicast schemes enjoy this property (e.g. SGM/XCast (12; 13)). Nevertheless, these schemes might be utilized for augmenting specific functionalities in other mobility approaches, e.g. Mobile IP.

Multicast type. Main options are network layer (including IP multicast and unicast-based solutions) and link-layer multicast (especially, ATM multicast). The multicast type determines the service model, such as the receiver-oriented model of IP, the sender-oriented model of ATM, or the call-model in (14).

Dynamic tree. The multicast tree can be static or dynamic. In the first case, the access points belonging to a pre-established multicast tree cover a geographical area. In the second case, the tree follows the current location (i.e. footprint) of the mobile.

Multicast adaptation. Existing multicast protocols can be used "as is," without modifications. However, the protocols might be adapted to better meet the requirements of mobility support.

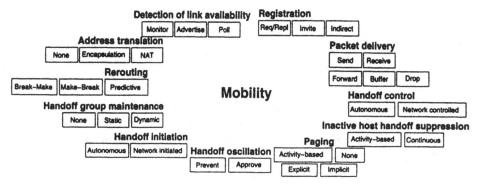

Fig. 1. Functional categories for mobility support.

3.2 Mobility Support Functionalities

The functionalities associated with mobility support can be classified into several categories, each providing a basis for constructing a variant for a multicast-based mobility protocol. The most relevant functionalities are discussed here, additional ones are shown in Fig. 1.

Detection of link availability. Access points may advertise their availability on their local links. A multicast management protocol can directly provide this functionality (e.g. IGMP membership query/report scheme). Optionally, a mobile node may also solicit advertisements from access points.

Registration. On top of existing link-layer connectivity, a mobile node registers with an access point to update its current location information, enabling tracking. Registration can be based on a request/reply scheme initiated by the mobile host or on an invitation by the access point. Alternatively, a mobile node can also be indirectly registered by another access point. Again, the multicast group management protocol can be used for implicit registration.

Rerouting. A rerouting operation changes the network path of packets for a mobile node in a certain access point. A rerouting operation is based on adding and pruning branches of an existing multicast tree. The appropriate multicast operations can be executed in a *break-make* and *make-break* order: new branches are added before old ones are deleted or vice-versa. Additionally, access points can be added to a multicast tree in advance, implementing predictive handover.

Handover initiation and control. Both the network or the mobile host could initiate and control a handover from old to new access point. Controlling a handover means orchestrating the sequence of multicast group manipulation functions. A related issue is the prevention of handover oscillation.

Paging. Inactive mobile nodes reduce their frequency of handover registration and location updates, saving wireless resources. Paging locates such mobile nodes and multicast can be used to efficiently distribute paging requests to a paging area identified by a multicast group. Paging can be done explicitly by sending paging requests to the access points in the paging area or implicitly when data packets are distributed to access points of the paging area.

3.3 Candidate Selections

This framework allows to put together a mobility concept as a combination of various multicast options and supporting functionalities. The application of traditional IP multicast is an evident solution. We follow the approach in (8) in its basic protocol option choices (e.g., placing the multicast endpoint in the access point) and extend it by some additional functionalities (especially support for inactive nodes) resulting in case study MB-ASM (Tab. 1)[2]. We consider this extended version as a base case against which to compare other protocols in a unified experimental environment.

Inspecting this approach reveals that it does not exploit all capabilities of its underlying multicast service model. In particular, all actually necessary multicast functionalities can also be provided by a simplified multicast service model, e.g., source-specific IP multicast resulting in case study MB-SSM. In fact, for fixed networks a trend to a source-specific service model (SSM) can be identified (e.g. by driven by the *EXPRESS* (15) proposal and by availability in commercial products like Cisco IOS-based routers). The benefits of MB-SSM in comparison to MB-ASM are: a) Less protocol complexity and easy deployment, b) inhibits denial of service attacks from unwanted sources and c) averts the problem of address allocation. In this way, SSM alleviates some of the main problems associated with ASM-style multicast as a prerequisite for its utilization for host mobility. Moreover, there are other reasons which endorse the support of SSM: It is ideally suited for tree-like topologies of access networks with a gateway as the root. Since SSM sets up source-based forwarding trees, there is no need for a shared infrastructure with core routers. Finally, the problem of security is aggravated in mobile networks and SSM fairly solves the source access control problem by itself. Additionally, it provides the same actual protocol actions as would result from the use of case study MB-ASM. Hence, the mere performance of both these case studies is expected to be practically identical.

To easily support advanced functionalities such as *make-break* rerouting (in order to implement predictive handover), additional protocol mechanisms such as third-party registration, resource reservation in advance, sub-casting, and others are useful and may eventually improve performance. Such mechanisms provide a larger design space and increased possibilities for the design of multicast-based mobility concepts, but are not available in current IP-based multicast protocols. Yet these mechanisms do exist in some multicast protocols for connection-oriented backbones. In order to investigate such mechanisms, the case study MB-CMAP uses such a connection-oriented, link-layer type multicast protocol. This case study is not investigated in detail in this paper but described in (16).

One of the main objections to multicast is the scalability problem with the number of groups. With a multicast protocol that is to support mobility, a high number of multicast groups exists rather with only very few participants belong to a single group, namely either only the mobile node itself or the access points

---

[2] Abbreviations: MC = Multicast, MIP = Mobile IP, HMIP = Hierarchical Mobile IP, NWL = Network Layer, LL = Link layer, SBT = Source-based tree, NA = Not applicable.

with which the mobile node is currently associated (or immediately neighboring access points in case of predictive handover), depending on where the multicast tree is terminated. But the number of multicast groups is going to be very large. Therefore, a multicast protocol for mobility support should much rather scale with the number of groups, where scalability with the number of group participants is only a secondary concern. One example for multicast protocol optimized in this way is small-group multicast. However, this protocol does not separate location and identity and must hence be supplemented by a mobility mechanism. Choosing mobile IP or hierarchical mobile IP results in case the case study MIP-SGM.

	MB-ASM	MB-SSM	MB-CMAP	MIP-SGM
Micro vs. macro	Micro	Micro	Micro	Micro/Macro
Tree directionality	Uni	Uni	Bi	Uni
X+Multicast	Only MC	Only MC	Only MC	MIP/HMIP
Type	NWL	NWL	LL	NWL
	Shared	SBT	Shared	NA
Registration	Req/Reply & Indirect	Req/Reply & Indirect	Req/Reply & by surrogate reg.	Req/Reply
Address translation	Yes	Yes	Yes	Yes/No
Paging		Activity-based, explicite		None

Table 1. Protocol options and functionalities (different values)

Protocol options	
Multicast endpoint	Access point
Dynamic tree	Yes
Adaptation	No
Functionality	
Detecting link availability	Advertise/solicitate
Packet delivery	Send, receive, forward, buffer, drop
Handover initiation	Autonomous
Handover control	Autonomous
Rerouting	Break-make, predictive

Table 2. Protocol options and functionalities (common to all case studies)

Considering the most important common protocol options in Tab. 2, we assume that the multicast terminates in the access point. Thereby, the mobile host does not need to have any knowledge about multicast. Additional advantages are that this approach better integrates with existing IP-based protocols such as TCP or ARP (3) and that it facilitates the deployment of performance-enabling proxies in the access point improving the protocol performance over wireless links.

4   Evaluation

In order to investigate the selected case studies, we have set up a testbed, designed a set of protocols, implemented a prototype and conducted experiments to quantitatively evaluate mobility-related performance metrics and to compare selected policies. The presented results comprise the case studies MB-ASM, MB-SSM and MB-CMAP including a comparison with basic Mobile IP and hierarchical Mobile IP.[3] The protocols for the three case studies are based on a common protocol design. The full description and specification can be found in (17); a description of the prototype in (18). The software is implemented for Linux systems as daemons running in user space and is based on IPv4. It is worth noting that the prototype provides a generic interface to the multicast that facilitates the utilization of different multicast types. Moreover, the prototype provides hooks for policy handlers to control certain system behavior, such as time and destination of handover, buffering and flushing of packets, retrieving signal quality indicators for handover trigger and paging strategies.[4]

We investigate a network topology depicted in Fig. 2(a). The core components are mobile hosts, access points, multicast nodes and gateways running a mobile agent (MA), mobility-enabling proxy (MEP), multicast routing daemon (MRD) and a gateway proxy (GW-P), respectively. These components comprise an access network, which is a network under the control of a single authority. The gateway interconnects the access network with the global Internet.

The testbed setup is illustrated in Fig. 2(b). In addition to the prototype components MA, MEP and GW-P common to all case studies, for the case study MB-ASM the gateway and multicast node execute a multicast router daemon PIM-SMv2 and the access points use IGMPv2. For the case study MB-CMAP the multicast node is represented by a multicast-capable switch with a switch controller[5] and the MEP and GW use CMAP as a multicast management protocol. In the testbed we replace the wireless link by standard Ethernet. The benefit is that the mobility-specific performance characteristics of various protocols can be studied in a controlled manner in isolation of the error-prone wireless link. Based on the protocol mechanisms, we do not expect any of the protocols to be overly sensitive to wireless errors, so this impact can be safely ignored.

In order to investigate the SSM-style multicast case study, we in fact used an ASM-style multicast implementation. This is indeed feasible and the measurement results are valid as the additional ASM functionality is not used and hence incurs no additional overhead; the differences between the usage of IGMPv2/PIM-SM and IGMPv3/PIM-SSM only marginally affect the performance. Moreover, we are able to corroborate the initial measurements for the handover latency published in (8) of the approach using also IGMPv2/PIM-SM with the same protocol options, but in an extended setup and with enhanced functionalities.

---

[3] Results for MIP-SGM will be published separately due to space limitations.

[4] The prototype is open software (www-tkn.ee.tu-berlin.de/research/mse.html)

[5] These components belong to the WashU Gigabit Switch Kit, an open, nonproprietary networking equipment. http://www.arl.wustl.edu/gigabitkits.

We have also repeated the same set of experiments for basic and hierarchical Mobile IP (MIP and HMIP) using the Dynamics Mobile IP implementation (www.cs.hut.fi/Research/Dynamics) in a comparable testbed setup with MIP agents replacing the corresponding components of our prototype.

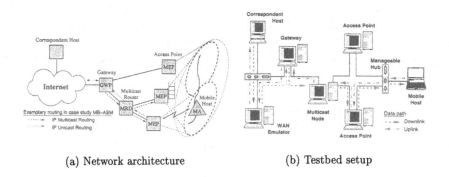

(a) Network architecture   (b) Testbed setup

Fig. 2. Investigated scenario

The handover performance is evaluated in terms of handover latency, TCP throughput, and UDP packet loss and duplications.

Handover latency. The handover latency is measured in the mobile host at the IP layer. A continuous packet stream is sent downlink from the correspondent host to the mobile host. During the receive process, the mobile host executes periodic handovers between both access points. The duration between two subsequent handovers (cell dwell time of a mobile in a particular cell) is exponentially distributed with a mean duration of 10s plus an offset of 5s.

In Fig. 3(a), the mean handover latency is independent of the round-trip time between the correspondent host and the mobile host, except for Mobile IP. We examine three handover types: *Hard* means that the old AP is removed from the multicast tree before the new AP is added. *Soft* inverts this order. With *predictive handover* the neighboring AP are added in advance of a handover and buffer packets. In all cases, the handover latency is comprised of the handover detection time and the handover execution time. The handover detection time is determined by the advertisement lifetime of 300 ms sent with an interval of 100 ms and can be regarded as a constant offset of 250 ms. Both the predictive scheme of MB-ASM and all variants of MB-CMAP are superior to MIP/HMIP. In soft handover with MB-ASM the join operation contributes significantly to the handover latency resulting in a handover latency of about 600 ms.

TCP. In this experiment we study the impact of handover on the throughput of TCP Reno. In order to observe the impact of multiple handovers on TCP where the handover events impact each other, we examine a single long-lived TCP connection with subsequently executed handover events. For an advertisement interval of 100 ms we have observed that the TCP throughput decreases only moderately, since the service interruption is relatively small. However, also for TCP the throughput for predictive handover is larger than for soft handover. Unlike the UDP experiment, this is not an evident result, since the duplication of TCP segments trigger the mobile host to send duplicated acknowledgements, which in turn forces the correspondent host to retransmit TCP segments. However, in our scheme the mobile receives at most two copies of a TCP segment during the handover phase and the TCP retransmission mechanism is not activated. With an advertisement interval of 1 s (Fig. 3(b) the throughput degrades as the handover frequency grows. Since the duration to detect the handover is relatively long, the TCP sender is forced into TCP's slow-start phase and with a high handover rate TCP has less time to recover from loss. Again, with predictive handover the TCP goodput can be improved even with very frequent handover.

UDP. In this experiment we examine the number of lost and duplicated packets due to handover (Fig. 4(a)). The correspondent host shown in Fig. 2(b) continuously generates 1024 byte UDP packets. We vary the inter-packet times to change the offered load; other parameters are set to the same value as in the handover latency experiment. We obtain the number of lost and duplicated packets by comparing the sent and received trace and marking lost and duplicated packets. For hard (MB-ASM) and soft handover (MB-ASM, MB-CMAP) packet loss increases constantly and reaches 25 lost packets per handover while it can be neglected for MB-ASM and MB-CMAP predictive handover. Hence, except MB-ASM (soft), all multicast schemes have less packet loss than MIP/HMIP. However, the reliability of predictive handover causes some costs in terms of duplications 4(b). For predictive handover the duplications grow with the offered load up to a certain point at 25 kBps with 75/90 (MB-ASM/MB-CMAP) duplicated packets per handover. Beyond a load of 25 kBps the number of duplicated packets decreases slowly. The reason for the shape of the curve is the limitation of the buffer size (set to 100 kByte per mobile) and the buffering policy that forwards only new (not older than 5 s) packets and drops outdated ones.

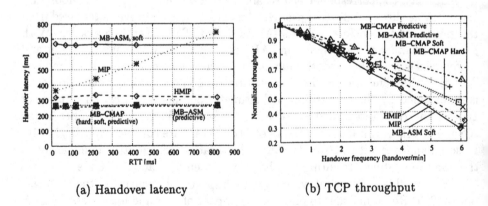

(a) Handover latency   (b) TCP throughput

Fig. 3. Handover latency versus round trip time between CH and MH and TCP throughput versus handover frequency ($\approx$ 230 handovers)

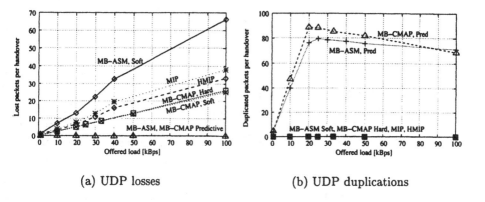

(a) UDP losses   (b) UDP duplications

Fig. 4. UDP losses/duplications versus round trip time between CH and MH for horizontal handover ($\approx$ 230 handovers)

5 Conclusions

The large amount of possible approaches to use multicast in order to solve the mobility problem in IP networks made it necessary to structure all these options. Based on a list of requirements for a mobility concept, we developed a list of possible options how to deploy multicast for mobility and a number of possible support functionalities for mobility that can be implemented using multicast. Requirements, options, and functionalities constitute a framework in which existing approaches can be classified and new approaches can be derived by sensible combinations of decisions for each individual aspect.

In particular, we have derived four classes of mobility support protocols, focusing on micro mobility. As a main result, the newly suggested source-specific multicast is superior to multicast based on the standard service model in a micro-mobility context. The multicast protocols themselves were unchanged but augmented with support functionalities for multicast.

In order to quantify relevant performance metrics for multicast-based mobility protocols, we developed a software environment that allows to easily implement a variety of multicast protocols and to experiment with them. Experiments showed that our protocols provide efficient micro mobility and location management along with smooth, fast handovers.

Applying multicast for mobility raises some common objections. We believe that with a judicious choice of protocol options, most of them are unfounded: Scalability problems with the number of multicast groups can be solved by single-source multicast and the application of paging. The (advocated) use of source-specific multicast simplifies the design of sender authentication and authorization; the small number of group members enables the use of key management protocols for securing multicast even in mobile environments.

Bibliography

[1] Perkins, C.: IPv4 Mobility Support. RFC 2002 (1996)

[2] Keeton, K., Mah, B., Seshan, S., Katz, R., Ferrari, D.: Providing Connection-oriented Network Services to Mobile Hosts. In: Proc. of the USENIX Symposium on Mobile and Location-Idependent Computing. (1993)

[3] Mysore, J., Bharghavan, V.: A New Multicast-based Architecture for Internet Mobility. In: ACM MOBICOM 97. (1997)

[4] Ghai, R., Singh, S.: An Architecture and Communication Protocol for Picocellular Networks. IEEE Personal Communications 1 (1994) 36–46

[5] Acampora, A., Naghshineh, M.: An Architecture and Methodology for Mobile-Executed Handoff in Cellular ATM Networks. IEEE JSAC 12 (1994) 1365–1375

[6] Seshan, S.: Low-latency Handoffs for Cellular Data Networks. PhD thesis, University of Berkeley at California (1996)

[7] Stemm, M., Katz, R.: Vertical Handoffs in Wireless Overlay Networks. ACM MONET, Special Issue on Mobile Networking in the Internet (1998)

[8] Wu, J., Maguire, G.: Agent Based Seamless IP Multicast Receiver Handover. In: Proc. of PWC 2000. (2000) 213–225

[9] Helmy, A.: A Multicast-based Protocol for IP Mobility Support. In: Proc. of ACM NGC 2000). (2000)

[10] Mihailovic, A., Shabeer, M., Aghvami, A.: Multicast for Mobility Protocol (MMP) for Emerging Internet Networks. In: Proc. of PIMRC 2000. (2000)

[11] Festag, A., Karl, H., Schaefer, G.: Current Developments and Trends in Handover Design for ALL-IP Wireless Networks. Technical Report TKN-00-007, TKN, TU Berlin (2000)

[12] Boivie, R.: A New Multicast Scheme for Small Groups. Research Report RC21512(97046)29Juni1999, IBM T.J.Wwatson Research Center (1999)

[13] Boivie, R.e.a.: Explicit Multicast (Xcast) Basic Specification. Internet Draft (2000)

[14] Gaddis, E., Bubenik, R., DeHart, J.: A Call Model for Multipoint Communication in Switched Networks. In: Proc. of IEEE ICC'92. (1992) 609–615

[15] Holbrook, H., Cheriton, D.: IP Multicast Channels: EXPRESS Support for Large-scale Single-source Applications. In: Proc. of ACM SIGCOMM 1999. (1999) 65–78

[16] Festag, A., Westerhoff, L., Assimakopoulos, A., Wolisz, A.: Rerouting for Handover in Mobile Networks with Connection-Oriented backbones – An Experimental Testbed. In: Proc. of ICATM'2000. (2000) 491–499

[17] Festag, A., Westerhoff, L.: Protocol Specification of the MOMBASA Software Environment. Technical Report TKN-01-014, TKN, TU Berlin (2001)

[18] Festag, A., Westerhoff, L., Wolisz, A.: The MOMBASA Software Environment – A Toolkit for Performance Evaluation of Multicast-Based Mobility Support. In: Proc. of Performance Tools 2002, London, GB (2002)

Evaluation of Mobility Management Approaches for IPv6 Based Mobile Car Networks[1]

Michael Wolf, Michael Scharf, Reinhold Eberhardt

DaimlerChrysler AG, Telematics Research, P.O.Box 2360, 89013 Ulm, Germany
michael.m.wolf@daimlerchrysler.com
mscharf@student.ei.uni-stuttgart.de
reinhold.eberhardt@daimlerchrysler.com

Mobile information services are one of the key issues in the upcoming Information Society. Ubiquitous access to Internet has to be provided to mobile devices, such as intelligent cellular phones, personal digital assistants (PDAs) or mobile computers. In conjunction with the convergence of telecommunication networks towards the Internet Protocol (IP), mobility at network layer seems to be very promising. Most of the work done so far in this area considered mobile hosts rather than mobile networks. Future vehicular networks can be regarded as such moving IP based networks allowing seamless IP mobility for users and built-in devices while being attached to different access systems. In this paper existing mobility management approaches are evaluated with respect to their application for mobile networks and as a basis to develop new proposals. An outlook is given to the work that will be done in the EU IST project OverDRiVE.

1 Introduction

Most of the work realized so far in the field of IP based mobility management was dedicated to the mobility of single hosts or terminals. Soon, there will be IP networks that are mobile as a whole, and because of this the restriction to hosts hardly can be upheld. There are many application fields for mobile networks. One of the most important ones are vehicles. For example, [1] includes the following vision of vehicular networks:

"Cases of mobile networks include networks attached to people (Personal Area Network or PAN, i.e. a network composed by all Internet appliances carried by people, like a PDA, a mobile phone, a digital camera, a laptop, etc.) and networks of sensors deployed in aircrafts, boats, busses, cars, trains, etc. An airline company that provides permanent on-board Internet access is an example of a mobile network. This allows passengers to use their laptops [...], PDA, or mobile phone to connect to remote hosts, download music or video, browse the web.[...]. For a number of reasons (network management, security, perform-

---

[1] This work is performed in the framework of the IST project IST-2001-35125 OverDRiVE, which is partly funded by the European Union.

ance, ...), it is desirable to interconnect the Internet appliances deployed in cars, trains, busses by means of, for instance, an Ethernet cable, instead of connecting them individually and directly to the Internet, therefore exhibiting the need to displace an entire network."

Due to the heterogeneous world of access systems, the connection to Internet will not be limited to a single access system. Instead, several different communication networks will be used, having different characteristics and providing different services. For example, in some years a vehicle might be connected to the following types of communication networks:

- cellular telephone networks (GSM or UMTS) for voice communication
- cellular, packet based networks (GPRS or UMTS) for data communication, interactive services, Internet access etc.
- Wireless Local Area Networks (WLAN) for hot spot access e.g. in petrol stations or parking garages
- DAB (Digital Audio Broadcast) and DVB-T (Digital Video Broadcast Terrestrial) for multicast distribution of multimedia streams, and maybe also for point-to-point unidirectional communication
- satellite networks in geographical regions where other networks are not available
- ad-hoc networks, i.e. vehicle-to-vehicle communication

In future, networks in passenger cars and larger vehicles will form a local area network, called Intra-Vehicular Area Network (IVAN)[2], to which built-in and visiting nodes attach. Of course, an IVAN will have Internet access by one or more wireless communication systems. Figure 1 shows a possible IVAN scenario. In some of today's and even more in future vehicles a high speed telematics multimedia bus is deployed, for instance using the optical network architecture MOST (Media Oriented System Transport) [2]. All important built-in multimedia and communication devices are connected to this bus system. They can range from quite simple and low-cost passive devices (like speakers) to very complex terminals with an own control and a sophisticated man-machine-interface. The central entity connecting the vehicle to the outside world is a communication platform implementing a mobile router (MR). For simplicity, a standard passenger car hardly will have installed more than one mobile router. This MR, probably manufactured by a supplier, must be more or less a "black-box" with a defined interface to the rest of the car.

Beside the telematics multimedia bus, several other networks will be deployed in vehicles: First, this holds for control networks, which e.g. have very stringent real-time requirements. One network architecture will hardly be able to meet the divergent requirements of multimedia and control networks. Second, passenger-owned mobile devices like notebooks, personal digital assistants (PDA) and personal area networks (PAN) can connect to a so called "consumer convenience point" e.g. by Bluetooth, WLAN, USB, or IEEE 1394, and the vehicle should provide Internet connectivity to these terminals. And finally, it cannot be excluded that in vehicles further sub-networks with completely different characteristics will exist.

---

[2] Intra-Vehicular Area Network (IVAN) is a special case of a "mobile network" (MONET), a term defined by IETF. In this paper, the term IVAN is used when referring to vehicular networks, whereas MONET is utilized when all types of networks are considered.

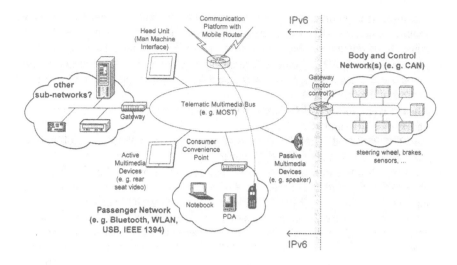

Fig. 1. Scenario for an Intra-Vehicular Area Network

2 Terminology

The movement of IP networks, i.e. "situations where an entire network changes its point of attachment to the Internet and thus its reachability in the topology" [1], is a quite new research topic. So far, there is not even a common terminology for mobile IP networks available. The IETF NEMO Working Group wants to agree on a terminology in the second half of 2002, but currently there are different, inconsistent proposals.

First, it should be noted that "mobility" has in the context of IP a special meaning, i.e. mobility at network layer. Obviously, mobility can also be handled in other protocol layers: For instance, some wireless LAN protocols handle mobility at link layer, and in cellular networks, as far as they use the Internet Protocol, mobility is solved in lower protocol layers, too.

In general, IP mobility includes the notion that a node is able to change its link. [3] states that "mobility in the Internet has traditionally meant movement of hosts or routers away from their topologically correct places". But in the context of Mobile IP, in general the purpose of mobility is to maintain session continuity.

Furthermore, often a distinction is made between "macro mobility" and "micro mobility" dependent on the scope of mobility [3]. The current definition of other entities in this context are as follows:

- **Mobile Network (MONET):** An entire network, moving as a unit, which dynamically changes its point of attachment to the Internet and thus its reachability in the topology. The mobile network is connected to the global Internet via one or more mobile router(s) (MR). The internal configuration of the mobile network is assumed to be relatively stable with respect to the MR and is not a matter of concern.

- **Mobile Router (MR)**: a router which changes its point of attachment to the Internet and which acts as a gateway to route packets between the mobile network and the rest of the Internet [1].
- **Local Fixed Nodes (LFN)**: Node that belongs to the mobile network and which has no mobility support.
- **Local Mobile Node (LMN)**: Node that belongs to the MONET has mobility support (MIPv6) and may be "NEMO enabled".
- **Visiting Mobile Nodes (VMN)**: A VMN does not belong to the MONET but is attached to it (i.e. its home link is not within the mobile network) and obtains an address on that link. It is MIPv6-enabled and may be NEMO-enabled.

Two further controversial concepts related to mobile networks are "nested mobility" and "multi-homing". A typical example for a nested network is a passenger's personal area network inside of a bus, i.e. the MONET of the bus compromises another MONET. In such cases it is not absolutely clear if there is one (large) MONET, or several MONETs, with or without a hierarchy. Some authors e.g. use the term "root MONET" for a MONET directly connected to an access system. [1] proposes the terms "sub-MONET" and "parent-MONET", but a common terminology has not evolved so far.

A single mobile router may have two or more egress interfaces simultaneously connected to the Internet, or a MONET may compromise more than one mobile router, all being attached to Internet. In both cases, a MONET is often referred to as "multi-homed".

3 Mobility Management Approaches

In the following sections the 3 major proposals that are currently discussed in the IETF NEMO group will be presented and analyzed. This analysis is used for a comparison and discussion of open points and future work.

3.1 Prefix Scope Binding Updates

The utilization of Prefix Scope Binding Updates has been proposed by MOTOROLA Labs Paris and INRIA. It is specified in an Internet-Draft [4], but there are also some related presentations available at an INRIA webpage [5]. Basically, a Prefix Scope Binding Update is an enhanced Mobile IPv6 Binding Update associating a care-of address with a prefix instead of a single address. It is assumed that all nodes in a MONET share a common prefix, and MR's ingress interface is configured with this MONET prefix. As in MIPv6, MR's egress interface is configured with the home prefix (when the MR is at home). The modified Mobile IPv6 Binding Update and has a new sub-option, containing the MONET prefix field[3]. The binding cache management in MR's home agent as well as in the correspondent nodes is changed slightly compared to MIPv6, in particular the searching for entries, so that the address comparison considers prefixes:

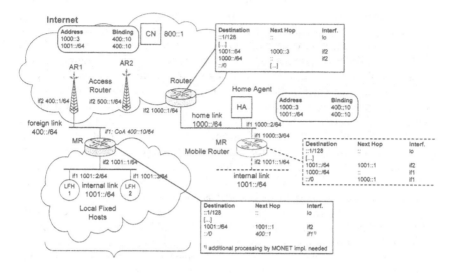

Fig. 2. Example for Prefix Scope Binding Update solution

If the destination address of an IP packet in the correspondent node matches this prefix, it is sent to the care-of address including a routing header similar to MIPv6. The home agent intercepts all packets sent to the MONET prefix by means of proxy neighborhood advertisements and forwards them to the MR. As a consequence, by registering one care-of address for an entire IP sub-network, all packets to nodes in the MONET are forwarded to the care-of address of the MR. The MR obtains a new CoA on each subsequent link using either stateless or stateful address configuration.

Analysis

The Prefix Scope Binding Update approach is explicitly designed for a limited scenario:

- The MONET is not multi-homed, i.e. it attaches to the Internet through only one MR, and the MR has only one egress interface.
- Only local fixed nodes in the MONET are considered. The Internet-Draft does not address problems related to "mobile" nodes.
- Nesting of MONETs is prohibited.

---

[3] The message format used in [4] is not compatible with the latest mobile IP draft [7]

These restrictions result in a very simple MONET, consisting only of one mobile router, and having only one direct connection to Internet. It is commonly agreed that there are application fields for such a MONET, but a more general approach would be very desirable. In principle, the approach could be extended to multi-homed networks, and support for visiting mobile nodes could be added, etc., but for this further research is necessary.

In the Prefix Scope Binding Update solution, the MR is a modified MIPv6 mobile node. As already mentioned, changes in MR's home agent and in correspondent nodes are required. The latter point is quite important, because routing optimization is only available if the correspondent node explicitly supports Prefix Scope Binding Updates. If so, this approach could reduce the so-called "Binding Update storm" problem of MIPv6: If a mobile node, or a MONET, communicates with a large number of correspondent nodes, during the handoff process a large number of Binding Updates has to be sent. With Prefix Scope Binding Updates, only one Binding Update has to be sent to every correspondent node. Hence, signaling is reduced considerably when several nodes in a MONET communicate with the same correspondent node. In contrast, no improvement can be achieved if the correspondent nodes are "scattered", i.e. the communication of the nodes in the MONET is not very correlated.

The main problem with this solution, however, is security: An authentication of the MR is possible, based on its home address, as in MIPv6. But a MR needs to be authorized to register a binding between the MONET prefix and its care-of address, because malicious attackers could claim the ownership of arbitrary prefixes. For correspondent nodes, which do not "know" the MR, this authorization is an unsolved question. One possible solution could consist of a modification of the "return routability"-mechanism used by MIPv6 to certify that the MR actually owns and serves the MONET Prefix. However, it is not possible to check return routability for every possible address behind the claimed prefix. [4] proposes to limit the check to a number of carefully selected addresses, but, of course, this does not provide absolute security. Another possibility could be authorization by some kind of a certificate, but certificates are not used in Mobile IP so far. Because of the lack of security, the existing specification of Prefix Scope Binding Updates cannot be deployed in Internet, in particular not the routing optimization function.

3.2 Hierarchical Mobile IP

The main focus of Hierarchical Mobile IPv6 (HMIPv6) are not mobile networks, but a hierarchical mobility management model for MIPv6, which reduces the amount of signaling to correspondent nodes and the Home Agent (HA) and may improve handoff speed. HMIPv6 has been developed by Ericsson and INRIA and is specified in an Internet-Draft [6].

A new Mobile IPv6 node, called mobility anchor point (MAP), is introduced, which can be located at any level in a hierarchical network of routers. In HMIPv6, two different types of care-of addresses are distinguished: Beside the topologically correct care-of address, called "local care-of address" (LCoA) in this context, a mobile node also obtains an address from a MAP referred to as the "regional care-of address" (RCoA). The RCoA is an address on the MAP's subnet. If there is more than one hierarchy level, a mobile node may even have several RCoAs.

A mobile node uses its (highest-level) regional care-of address for the bindings in its home agent and correspondent nodes. Then, the MAP receives all packets on behalf of the mobile node it is serving and encapsulates and forwards them directly to the MN's current local address. If the Mobile Node (MN) changes its LCoA within a local MAP domain, it only needs to register the new address with the MAP. In contrast, the RcoA registered with Correspondent Nodes (CNs) and the HA does not change, and MN's mobility within a MAP domain is transparent to CNs and the HA.

In HMIPv6, a new MAP option in the router advertisements informs MNs about the presence of a MAP (MAP discovery). Thus, MAP's domain boundaries are defined by the access router advertising MAP information to the attached mobile nodes. A preference value and a distance field is introduced to enable a mobile node to select among different MAPs. Furthermore, HMIPv6 adds a new flag (M flag) to the BU message[4].

Dependent on the assignment of regional care-of addresses, HMIPv6 distinguishes two different modes:

- In "basic mode", the RCoA is formed in a stateless manner (auto-configuration) by combining the MAP's subnet prefix received in the MAP option with the MN's interface identifier. The basic mode is quite simple: The MAP merely is a kind of home agent that binds MN's RCoA to the LCoA, intercepts all packets and tunnels them to the corresponding LCoA.

- In "extended mode", the MN is configured with a regional care-of address that is assigned to one of MAP's interfaces (i.e. no duplicate address detection is necessary). Unlike in basic mode, the mobile node uses its home address in the MAP binding. Packets from the home agent are tunneled to the mobility anchor point and decapsulated there. Based on the home address the MAP routes the packet and encapsulate it again. For routing optimized packets from correspondent nodes, the MAP has to check the routing header for the home address. As in extended mode routing in a MAP is based on the (global) home address of a mobile node, a slight change of the home agent is needed: When the HA tunnels packets with a site-local scope home address, it has to include a routing header in the outer packet with MN's home address as final destination. This is necessary because the MAP does not know home addresses for which it received no binding update, like e.g. site-local home addresses. The extended mode of operation can support both mobile nodes and mobile networks.

Figure 3 illustrates how mobile networks could be realized with Hierarchical Mobile IP. For this, a hierarchy of mobility anchor points is needed, at least consisting of the mobile router (first MAP) and a higher-level MAP (second MAP). The mobile router must be configured in HMIPv6 extended mode, while the higher-level MAP may use either basic or extended mode. Because of the hierarchy, nodes in the MONET have three care-of addresses: A local care-of address (called "CoA1" in Figure 3) and two regional care-of addresses ("CoA2" and "CoA3"). Nodes in the MONET learn the presence of the different MAPs by MAP announcements and are individually responsible for keeping the binding caches up to date. As a consequence, in a HMIPv6-

---

[4] The message format used in [6] is not compatible with the latest Mobile IP draft [7]

based network mobility solution, all nodes in a MONET are aware of the mobility of the MR.

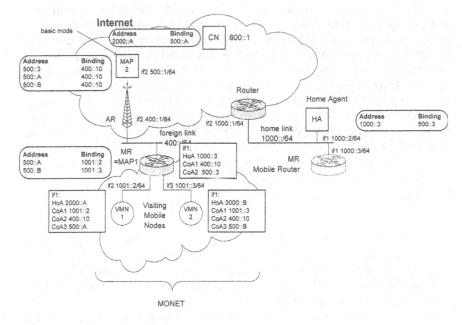

Fig. 3. Example of HMIPv6

Analysis

Hierarchical Mobile IPv6 introduces some extensions to MIPv6 and neighbor discovery and requires minor extensions to the mobile nodes and the home agent (only in extended mode). In theory, the correspondent nodes are not affected. The mobile anchor point essentially acts as a local home agent, limiting the signaling outside a local domain and supporting fast handovers as well as certain network scenarios. The more hierarchical a network topology, the larger the benefits from HMIPv6.

As already outlined, the Internet-Draft proposing HMIPv6 mentions mobile networks, but the support for MONETs does not seem to be the main design goal of HMIPv6, and important questions are still left to be answered. In general, this solution only works for "mobile" nodes being aware of mobility, and every node has to handle its own mobility. "Fixed" nodes are not at all supported. With HMIPv6, in principle even very complex topologies are possible, including nested MONETs, if a hierarchy of several (mobile) MAPs is used. But this is more a theoretical option, since many detail questions are not solved so far. The approach might not scale well to a large number of hierarchies.

But the most important problem again is security. [6] declares, without proof: "HMIPv6 does not introduce more security problems than MIPv6." However, a MAP offers additional possibilities for malicious attacks, and HMIPv6 does not provide any security mechanism to protect Binding Updates. In some configurations the source addresses of packets are topologically not correct, and it is not clear how HMIPv6 can deal with ingress filtering, in particular by access routers. Even worse, the HMIPv6 design is based on outdated Internet-Drafts and is not adapted to recent changes in MIPv6 related to security (for example the return routability test). Nevertheless, the future development of this proposal has to be reviewed since HMIP might be an important solution to structure access networks.

3.3 "Standard" Mobile IP

The third Internet-Draft on mobile networks [8] describes how to support MONETs with Mobile IP, not even restricted to MIPv6, without any mandatory modifications to Mobile IP or routing protocol signaling. The MONET support is just realized by a bi-directional tunnel between the mobile router and its home agent. Both the mobile router and the home agent use unmodified Mobile IPv6, except that there are minor implications to the packet forwarding implementations.

Dependent on the question whether the mobile router is allowed to run a dynamic routing protocol on its home link ("fully enabled" mobile router) or not (″consumer″ mobile router), two different modes are distinguished. In the former case, the MR behaves like a normal fixed router in Internet, and redirects traffic towards its home agent by means of a dynamic routing protocol. The dynamic routing protocol updates the routing state between home agent, mobile router, and gateways to Internet, so that next hop entries now point to the home agent. In the latter scenario, MR's home agent injects static routes for a restricted set of links behind the MR, when the MR is not at home, using MR's home address as the next hop. These static routes are pre-configured. In both cases, MR's home agent captures packets forwarded to the mobile router, and does a route and binding lookup. If the packet is designed for the MONET, i.e. if the next hop is MR's home address, then the packet is tunneled to the care-of address of the MR. For the reverse direction, mobile router's default route points to-wards the tunnel to its home agent, so that all packets from the MONET are reverse tunneled to the home agent.

The mobile router and its home agent must know that a tunnel is to be established, and that packets for the mobile networks must be routed through that tunnel. For this, some signaling in the tunnel is necessary. According to [8] this signaling can be either implicit (meaning that no changes to the Mobile IP messages are used) or explicit. For explicit signaling, an optional "mobile network option" is defined in order to specify prefix mappings, which may be included in Binding Updates and Binding Acknowledgments. This option is not mandatory because the information from the routing protocol should include the prefixes served by the mobile router, i.e. the home agent gets to know them anyway.

Analysis

With respect to the home link, the scenario shown in Figure 1 adapts pretty well to this solution. The only difference would be that a dynamic routing protocol "fully enabled" mode) would change the next hop entry in the gateway router from *1000::3* (home address of the MR) to *1000::2* (address of the home agent). As the already mentioned network prefix option includes also a prefix information, this approach is very similar to Prefix Scope Binding Updates. But, of course, there are also differences: First, this approach does not support any routing optimization to and from the MONET, i.e. all traffic passes the home agent of the mobile router. Therefore, no binding updates are sent to correspondent nodes. Second, this approach supports "mobile" nodes, which can attach to the MONET by means of Mobile IP and can get a care-of address of the link inside of the MONET. And finally, nested MONETs are possible, because a mobile router can inject several prefixes on the home link. This at least holds for "fully-enabled" mobile routers, which can support arbitrary links behind them, both stub- and transit networks. For "consumer" mobile routers, the prefixes are statically configured, i.e. only such MONETs can be nested that use these pre-configured prefixes. However, nested mobile networks result in various, reciprocal tunnels from the mobile routers to the corresponding home agents, i.e. a very inefficient routing.

The multi-homing issue is not considered in [8]. Since dynamic routing protocols can not only be used on the home link, but also inside the MONET, multi-homing would be possible if there was an appropriate dynamic routing protocol. As routing optimization is not used, security in this approach is less critical than in other ones. Of course, the messages exchanged between a mobile router and its home agent must be secured when the mobile router is not on its home link, which can be fulfilled by a static security association between the mobile router and its home agent, like in all other cases. Furthermore, neither Mobile IP nor routing protocols must be changed, and therefore no additional security problems occur. In this approach, a considerable part of the problem is shifted from Mobile IP to the used routing protocol: It is up to the routing protocol to decide whether a route may be injected in the home link, and up to existing Authentication, Authorization and Accounting (AAA) mechanisms to decide whether a mobile node may attach to a MONET.

Thus, the main problem with this concept is that Mobile IP is only used to establish the tunnel between the mobile router and its home agent. In reality, mobility is handled by the chosen routing protocol, on the home link, and to some extend also internally in the MONET. This may be a quite challenging issue when fast topology changes happen. The approach is able to support movement to the same extent as the chosen routing protocol can do so. In other words, if the routing protocol converges slowly, frequent handoffs cannot be handled. But, all in all, this approach is certainly simpler to implement than the other ones presented in this chapter and therefore quite interesting.

3.4 Comparison

The approaches for network mobility presented in this chapter are more basic concepts than final solutions. All of them are restricted to a particular problem, while other issues are left for further study. And, in particular with respect to security, always a lot of work is still needed to make these ideas feasible on a global scale. Table 1 gives a short summary over the characteristics of the three presented proposals, and also identifies the open points.

Name of approach	Address issues	Unsolved issues
Prefix Scope Binding Updates	Local fixed nodes Routing optimization	Authorization of binding updates Visiting mobile nodes Multiple MRs and multi-homing Nesting
HMIPv6	Visiting mobile nodes Routing optimization Nesting	Local fixed nodes Compatibility to Mobile IPv6 Security, ingress filtering Multiple MRs and multi-homing
"Standard" Mobile IPv6	Local fixed nodes Visiting mobile nodes Nesting	Routing optimization Multiple MRs and multi-homing Frequent changes of topology

Table 1. Comparison of IETF approaches

3.5 Related work

The Reverse Routing Header approach, proposed in [9], does not intend to solve the whole mobile network problem, but only defines a new mechanism to handle very complex mobile network topologies, consisting of highly nested mobile networks. The overhead of nested tunnels is avoided by a single bi-directional tunnel between the first mobile router to forward a packet and its home agent. This is accomplished by a new routing header called the "reverse routing header".

Besides the work in the NEMO group the work done in the IETF MANET [10] group has to be carefully studied. Up to now it is the opinion of the NEMO group that MANET's work scope and scenarios (MANET is dealing with more dynamic ad-hoc networking issues whereas the mobile network as such is more static) are different and requires different approaches and solutions.

4 Outlook to OverDRiVE

The project EU IST DRiVE successfully explored and described an IPv6 overlay network that allows mobile users to use the best suited access system for a given application [11,12]. The mobility management is realized by means of an extended Hierarchical Mobile IPv6 (HMIPv6). Moreover, DRiVE defined AAA mechanisms to be applicable in such a heterogeneous environment.

In work package 3 ("Mobile Router and IVAN") of the OverDRiVE [13] project the DRIVE approach with a single mobile entity is extended towards mobile networks in a vehicular environment The work package further investigates the support of access to the Internet by an Internet appliance from within a vehicle. Application scenarios are also including seamless roaming into and out of an IVAN with a mobile Internet device. The main focus is on a car environment but "public" vehicles like busses and trains are also considered especially with respect to IVAN management and AAA.

The main tasks to enable the delivery of IP to vehicular subnets are:

- Definition of a multi-access capable mobile router that connects the IVAN with the OverDRiVE infrastructure
- Definition of efficient IPv6 based solution to support mobile networks with input to IETF
- Extension for DRiVE AAA architecture to support mobile networks
- Mechanisms for dynamic IVAN Management including AAA, i.e. roaming into (or out of) the IVAN
- Support for mapping between cellular and IVAN multicast

OverDRiVE will develop and realize a demonstrator system to show and prove the vehicular router and mobile multicast concepts. The project runs from April 2002 till March 2004.

References

[1] T. Ernst and H.Y. Lach. Network Mobility Support Terminology. Internet-Draft, work in progress, draft-ernst-monet-terminology-01.txt, July 2002

[2] MOST Specification. http://www.mostnet.de/downloads/Specifications/.

[3] J .T. Malinen, C.Williams, and A.Yegin. Micromobility Taxonomy. Internet-Draft, work in progress, draft-irtf-mm-terminology-00.txt

[4] T. Ernst, et.al. Mobile Network Support in Mobile IPv6 (Prefix Scope Binding Updates), Internet-Draft, work in progress, draft-erst-mobileipv6-network-03.txt, March 2002

[5] PLANETE Project at INRIA. http://www.inrialpes.fr/planet/pub/MobiNet/mobinet.html

[6] H. Soliman, et.al. Hierarchical MIPv6 mobility management (HMIPv6). Internet-Draft, work in progress, draft-ietf-mobileip-hmipv6-06.txt, July 2002

[7] D. Johnson and C.Perkins. Mobility Support in IPv6. Internet-Draft, work in progress, draft-ietf-mobileip-v6-18.txt, July 2002

[8] T. J. Kniveton, et.al. Mobile Router Support with Mobile IP. Internet-Draft, work in progress, draft-kniveton-mobrtr-02.txt, July 2002

[9] P. Thubert and M. Molteni. IPv6 Reverse Routing Header and its application to Mobile Networks. Internet-Draft, work in progress, draft-thubert-nemo-reverse-routing-header-00.txt, June 2002

[10] Ad Hoc Networks MANET. http://www.ietf.org/html.charters/manet-charter.

[11] T. Göransson et. al. Roaming and Handover for Inter System Mobility. DRiVE D04, available from http://www.ist-drive.org/, Jan. 2002.

[12] M. Frank et. al. Mobility management in a hybrid radio system. RSRCP Journal - Réseaux et systèmes répartis, calculateurs parallèles, Special Issue on Mobility and Internet, Hermes Science Publications, Volume 13, 2001

[13] OverDRiVE, http://www.ist-overdrive.org/

Stored Geocast

Christian Maihöfer, Walter Franz, Reinhold Eberhardt

DaimlerChrysler Research And Technology,
Communication Technology (RIC/TC)
P.O. Box 2360, 89013 Ulm, Germany
{christian.maihoefer|walter.franz|reinhold.eberhardt}@daimlerchrysler.com

Abstract. For many location based services like location based advertising, location based information services, or in particular, realizing a virtual traffic sign, which is bound to a location over time, we need a stored geocast solution. A stored geocast is a time stable geocast, which is delivered to all nodes that are inside a destination region within a certain period of time. The period of time starts at the time of sending plus network propagation delay and ends at a user defined time or is boundless.
This paper discusses the design space, the semantics, and three reasonable solutions for stored geocast in an ad hoc network. The first approach is an infrastructure-based server solution to store the messages. The second is an infrastructure-less approach that may be more suitable for an ad hoc network. A node inside the geocast destination region is elected to act temporarily as a server for geocast messages. The last approach works infrastructure-less, too, by complementing the exchange of neighbor information necessary for many geographic unicast routing protocols with geocast information.

1 Introduction

Geocast, i.e. the transmission of a message to some or all nodes within a geographical area, allows promising new services and applications. Of particular interest is geocast in the automotive domain. For example in the FleetNet project an ad hoc multi-hop radio network for inter-vehicle communications is developed [1]. Such a vehicle network allows safety-related and information-related applications like collection of traffic states, accident warning, wrong-way driver warning, icy road warning and so forth. Since these applications naturally address all (anonymous) vehicles in an area rather than a single vehicle by its fixed and known address, geocast is necessary to transmit the messages to the corresponding area.

Although the literature proposes several geocast approaches for infrastructure as well as ad hoc networks (see next section for details), we miss one important service for our applications, which we call stored geocast. The following example tries to clarify this. Assume that we want to inform following vehicles about an accident in front of them to avoid rear-end collisions. Currently, warning other vehicles is possible either by traffic signs or police presence or by a warning message over the radio, respectively. A radio warning message has the disadvantage that it is not limited to the vehicles of the area in which the danger spot is located and possibly forgotten by a driver when he actually enters this area. Therefore, we aim at realizing a warning function which is similar to a conventional traffic sign or police presence, i.e. bound to a geographic location or area. All vehicles which enters such an area, possibly by additional considering their driving direction and other parameters, should receive the warning message.

Currently, geocast solutions for ad hoc networks provide only a means to sent a message once, instead of periodically or on-demand every time a mobile node enters the geocast's message destination region. In this paper we discuss the design space, the semantics, and three approaches how such a stored geocast can be realized.

The remainder of this paper is structured as follows. In the next section background of geocast and related work is introduced. Section 3 discusses the semantics of stored geocast. In Section 4 the design space is defined before in Section 5 three approaches are described. Finally, the paper is concluded with a brief summary.

2 Background and Related Work

Mobile ad hoc routing protocols can be classified into topology- and position-based or geographic approaches [2]. Topology-based approaches use only information about existing neighborhood links rather than additional physical (geographical) position information of the participating nodes. Topology-based approaches can be further divided into table driven and source-initiated on-demand driven protocols [3]. Basically, table driven protocols attempt to maintain consistent and up-to-date routing information among all nodes, while source-initiated on-demand driven protocols create routes only when necessary to deliver a packet. Therefore, the former approach is also known as a proactive routing approach and the latter as a reactive approach.

In this paper, only geographic routing approaches are of interest since first, position information for vehicles are available by their navigation system, which promises more efficient routing schemes, and second, many applications explicitly address their (anonymous) communication peers by their position rather than by their identifier.

In contrast to topology-based routing protocols, geographic routing protocols usually refrain from setting up routes to forward packets, which decreases overhead. Instead, the forwarding decision of a node is based on the destination's position and the position of the forwarding node's neighbors (i.e. nodes with a one hop distance).

For geographical unicast routing protocols, three basic forwarding strategies can be identified: 1) greedy forwarding, 2) restricted directional flooding, and 3) hierarchical forwarding. With greedy forwarding a node forwards a packet to a neighbor that is located closer to the destination. If this forwarding strategy fails, since there may be situations in which there is no closer node to the destination than the forwarding node, recovery strategies have to deal with it. Nearest with Forward Progress (NFP) [4] is an example protocol using a greedy forwarding scheme.

The second approach, exemplified by the DREAM protocol [5], is similar to the first approach with the modification that a packet is forwarded to some neighbors rather than to just one neighbor. The third approach tries to improve scalability by forming a hierarchy of non-equal nodes. The Grid protocol [6] uses such a hierarchy for message forwarding.

Besides the unicast delivery described so far, the following approaches allow geocast addressing and routing. We refer to the *destination region* of a geocast packet as the geographical area to which a packet has to be delivered. Geocast protocols belong to one of the classes: 1) directed flooding, or 2) explicit route setup approaches without flooding.

Geocast directed flooding approaches are quite similar to the unicast directed flooding approaches. They define a forwarding zone, which comprises a subset of all network nodes. The forwarding zone includes at least the target area and a path between the sender and the target area. An intermediate node forwards a packet only if it belongs to the forwarding zone. If the target area is reached, they differ from unicast approaches, since they apply a flooding of the whole target area. A node broadcasts a received packet to all neighbors provided that this packet was not already received before and that the node belongs to the target area. Finally, a node accepts a packet and delivers it to its application if the own location is within the specified target area. Examples of geocast directed flooding protocols are Location Based Multicast (LBM) [7] and GeoGRID [8].

The second geocast scheme, explicit route setup without flooding, requires either a fixed network like the Internet, which is exemplified by the GeoNode approach [9]. Or, in the GeoTORA approach [10], for each geocast group a directed acyclic graph comprising all network nodes is maintained, which shows the routing direction to the destination. These acyclic graphs are initially created with a flooding scheme, too. However, their maintenance is achieved without flooding.

GeoNode is the only geocast approach that store messages for periodical delivery such that a stored geocast can be realized. Their assumption is that the network has a fixed cellular architecture with a GeoNode assigned to each cell. Routing is done in two steps, the first between sender and GeoNode and the second between GeoNode and destination region. GeoNodes are able to store the packets they receive for periodical delivery.

3 Semantics of Stored Geocast

Before we present approaches to realize stored geocast, we briefly discuss how to define the semantics, which is especially important if safety-related services have to be realized with a stored geocast solution.

We see two possible approaches to define the semantics. First we can consider the application side, define the semantics necessary for our intended applications and then try to find solutions for this semantics. Or we can define solutions for a broad range of geocast approaches and then analyze the solutions and define their semantics. As we believe that we cannot find all possible applications with their semantics and that likely their intended semantics would be too rich and restricting and would result in fat solution approaches, we follow the second approach. This means, that the detailed semantics of stored geocast is defined together with the approaches in Section 5. Note that this is similar to many other research areas, for example reliable multicast. However, some of the characteristics are identical for all solutions.

First we have to dissociate stored geocast from reliability mechanisms. Although a stored geocast is bound to an area over time, our proposed solutions do not try to achieve reliability. For some applications, in particular safety-related applications, reliable stored geocast is desirable or even mandatory. However, this is a difficult task especially in ad hoc networks, where message transmission failures and network partitions are quite normal rather than unusual. Furthermore, in many cases reliability can be achieved simply by building on a reliable geocast protocol or using general reliability mechanisms on top of an unreliable stored geocast. Though this might not be the most efficient solution, it results in better structured and more modular mechanisms. Therefore, reliability mechanisms are not discussed in this paper.

An inherent question of the stored geocast semantics is the duration of storage and delivery availability. As discussed above, we provide an best effort service without guarantees, which means that we cannot provide guarantees about the duration availability, i.e. we cannot guarantee to reach the full lifetime. However, we assume that we have a mechanism in place to limit the lifetime to a user defined time.

Besides the natural definition of lifetime corresponding to physical clock time, it is possible to define lifetime based on some sort of hop count, similar to the IP approach or some sort of delivery count. For stored geocast it would make sense to limit the number of deliveries or the total number of hops (we will see that for some approaches a stored geocast has to hop in order to keep stored). Another approach would be to limit the lifetime by an opposing event, e.g. in our traffic scenario from the introduction a discard operation after a traffic jam has disappeared. As the exact definition lies outside the scope of this paper, we generically assume that a lifetime of some sort is added to a stored geocast message before it is sent. If this lifetime exceeds, the stored geocast message is discarded.

4   Design Space of Stored Geocast

In this section we discuss and structure the design space of stored geocast before we present geocast approaches in the following section. For a stored geocast solution we identify four building blocks: 1) the underlying geocast routing protocol, 2) the storage of geocast messages within their lifetime, 3) the hand over of stored geocast messages to other nodes, and 4) the delivery of geocast messages to their intended destination nodes.

The underlying geocast routing protocol is necessary for most approaches to deliver the first geocast message to its destination region and possibly for the delivery of all following geocast messages to new nodes entering the destination region later.

The second building block is the storage of geocast messages, which can be done either infrastructure-based by a central server or infrastructure-less, which means distributed on some or all nodes participating in the network.

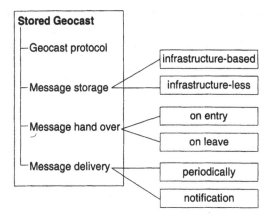

Fig. 1. Design space of stored geocast

With the third building block, the hand over of stored geocast messages, we refer to the problem that a node used for message storage may change its state so that it is no longer considered a suitable node and transfer the message to another, suitable node. For example, the principle of locality may make it desirable to store a geocast message only on nodes inside the destination region. If a storing node leaves the destination region, the stored message is then transfered to another node which is inside the destination region. Transfering a message to another node can be triggered when a new node enters the destination region or when a node inside the destination region is going to leave it.

Finally, the last building block is the delivery of a stored geocast message to new nodes inside the destination region. This can be done either by blind periodical resending of stored geocast messages or on demand, by a notification scheme, when a new node enters the destination region. Figure 1 summarizes the design space. Basically, these four building blocks have to be combined to realize stored geocast. In the next section we will discuss three reasonable combinations.

5 Stored Geocast Approaches

5.1 Infrastructure Approach

Overview: A server is used to store geocast messages. Hand over of messages is not necessary. Message delivery is done periodically or by notification.

Description: The geocast message is first unicasted to the geocast server provided by the infrastructure. Then the geocast server uses a geocast routing protocol to deliver the message to the destination region. After the first delivery, further deliveries can be done either periodically by the geocast server or by notification from moving nodes. Note that this approach has some similarities to the geocast proposal of [11].

If the server periodically delivers the geocast message, the delivery frequency has to depend on the maximum or average velocity of the network's nodes. For example, in a vehicular scenario with a maximum velocity of 200 km/h (= 55 m/s) and a circular destination region of a geocast message with a diameter of 1 km a message frequency of 1000 m / 55 m/s = 18 seconds is required. With this message frequency, based on the maximum velocity, it can be ensured that every node is able to receive a geocast message, provided that no message loss occurs and provided that the nodes cross the region through the center of the stored geocast message's destination region.

If the message frequency is increased further, a certain number of message losses can be tolerated since the probability for receiving at least one of the messages increases. A second advantage of increased message frequency is that nodes receive the geocast message even if they do not cross the full diameter range of the geocast destination region. Assume that the message frequency is denoted as f, the maximum velocity as v and that the shortest crossing distance within the geocast region a node has to cover in order to receive the stored geocast message is denoted as c, the following holds:

$$f \geq \frac{c}{v} \quad , 0 < c \leq s.d \tag{1}$$

s denotes the stored geocast message and $s.d$ the diameter of the destination region. If the message frequency is decreased below the obtained f, fast moving nodes and nodes crossing less than the assumed distance c within the geocast destination region may cross it without receiving a geocast message. Note that besides configuring a quite high message frequency it is possible to increase the destination region of a geocast message beyond its actually intended region. This is necessary if $c = 0$ is required, i.e. the delivery of a geocast message to a node which only touches the geocast destination region (see Figure 2). Assume that the increased destination diameter of the geocast message is denoted as $i.d$, then the following holds:

$$f \geq \frac{i.d - s.d + c}{v} \quad , i.d > s.d, 0 \leq c \leq s.d \tag{2}$$

Besides the periodic delivery a notification from moving nodes can trigger the message delivery. However, as a moving node does not know about the defined destination region of geocast messages stored on the server, this requires moving nodes to periodically send their position to the geocast server. To realize an efficient location notification approach, it should depend on the distance between the current position and the position of the last report to the server rather than on time. The distance between two reports d has to be not greater than the minimum required crossing distance c within a geocast's destination region (which has to be not greater than the minimum diameter of geocast destination regions):

$$d \leq c \quad , 0 < c \leq s.d \tag{3}$$

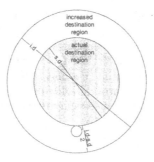

Fig. 2. Increased geocast destination diameter

Like in the periodic delivery scheme from above, increasing the destination region of geocast messages beyond their actually intended region can help to decrease the required message frequency:

$$d \leq i.d - s.d + c \quad , i.d > s.d, 0 \leq c \leq s.d \tag{4}$$

A consequence of the location notification approach is that the geocast server cannot be implemented stateless, since it has to remember requesting nodes and already delivered geocast messages to these nodes.

Coming back to our vehicular scenario from above, the notification approach requires that all vehicles report their location while moving. Assuming an average velocity of 60 km/h (≈ 17 m/s) and a minimum geocast crossing distance of 1 km, the location notification frequency of a random vehicle has to be one message every 1000 m or 1000 m / 17 m/s $\approx$ 60 s. Note that this message frequency may result in a significant overall network load, since all moving nodes have to send location notifications.

A reasonable optimization of the notification approach would be to suppress location notifications if a stored geocast message for the current location is received before, which means that another node has recently reported its presence in the same region. Another optimization would be to synchronize several nodes with similar movement patterns and to send just a single location notification for the synchronized group. Finally, the location information of a node could be sent to the server and additionally as a geocast message to the surrounding of the current location in order to suppress further location notifications of other nodes in the same region.

The decision about the most adequate scheme depends on the frequency of node movements. If nodes move frequently, the node penetration is high, or only few stored geocast messages with small destination regions are active, the periodic sending scheme may be more efficient, otherwise, the notification scheme. Note that with position calculations of dead reckoning approaches [12], especially in vehicular environments with its predefined routes, overhead of too frequent message delivery may be further decreased.

In summary, the infrastructure approach offers a simple and robust mechanism for stored geocast. One disadvantage, the large communication distance between the server and the destination region of geocast messages can be relaxed by distributed geocast servers close to the destination region of their stored messages. Note that a large distance results not only in high overhead but also in low robustness, especially in ad hoc networks where network partitioning and message loss may occur frequently and successful delivery of messages incorporating too many hops become unlikely.

Semantics: We assume that the server is replicated. In the absence of communication failures this approach guarantees that the geocast message is not lost and delivered to all intended nodes. However, note that communication failures are likely to occur due to the usually large distance between server and destination region. This can be relaxed by distributed geocast servers close to their destination regions.

5.2 Election Approach

Overview: A node in the destination region of a geocast message is elected to store geocast messages. Hand over of messages is done when this node leaves the destination region. Message delivery is done periodically or by notification.

Description: Instead of relying on a fixed server infrastructure, a dynamically elected node within the destination region of the geocast message is responsible for storing and delivering the message.

Basically, each node in the destination region is a candidate for the election process. However, to avoid frequent hand over, it is desirable to choose one that stays as long as possible in the destination region. Such a node is characterized by low velocity and closeness to the center of the destination region. For example, the unique tuple <velocity * center distance, nodeid> can be used in the election process. A suitable election algorithm is for example described in the GeoGRID approach [8].

Geocast message delivery is done as follows. The initial sender of a geocast message uses a geocast routing protocol to deliver the message for the first time. Inside the destination region, all nodes receive the geocast message and start the election process. The elected node stores the message and periodically or on request delivers the message as in the previous infrastructure-based approach. In case of periodical delivery, our calculations from the previous approach are effective for the election approach, too. In case of on request delivery, the location notification report is sent as a geocast message to a circular destination region with the actual position as the center.[1] In Figure 3 an example for the message request and delivery is given.

. The configuration of important parameters like diameter of the location notification geocast and frequency of location notifications requires consideration.

---

[1] Note that this is feasible for a random walk scenario. In case of a directed walk like in a vehicular scenario, optimizations by sending a geocast location notification to the region in front of the vehicle may be worthwhile.

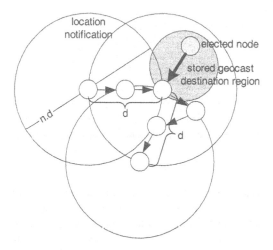

Fig. 3. Example of on request stored geocast delivery with the election approach

A basic observation is that the diameter of the location notification $n.d$ must be no smaller than the doubled maximum diameter of the geocast messages $s.d$:

$$n.d \geq 2 \cdot max(\forall s \in \{\text{stored geocasts}\} : s.d) \tag{5}$$

With $n.d$ smaller than $2 \cdot s.d$ it would be possible to miss the elected node as depicted in Figure 4.

Besides the destination region's diameter of location notifications, the frequency of location notifications is of interest. The distance between two reports d has to be not greater than the minimum required crossing distance c within a geocast's destination region similar to the infrastructure approach possibly relaxed by an increased geocast destination region $i.d$:

$$d \leq c \quad , 0 < c \leq s.d \tag{6}$$
$$d \leq i.d - s.d + c \quad , i.d > s.d, 0 \leq c \leq s.d \tag{7}$$

Location notification suppression schemes as briefly discussed in the infrastructure approach are feasible, too. The geocast based location notification makes it quite simple to suppress an own location notification if another one for the same region has been received before.

Finally, if the elected node leaves the destination region, a new election round is started and the message is handed over to the new elected node. Fault tolerance can be increased by electing not only a single node but several ones which keep message replicas.

Semantics: In the absence of node and communication failures and given that at any time at least one node is within the destination region and that there

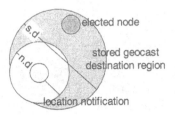

elected node

stored geocast
destination region

location notification

Fig. 4. Small notification diameter misses the elected node

are no network partitions inside the destination region, the election approach guarantees that the geocast message is not lost and delivered to all intended nodes. If there is not always at least one node within the geocast region, only the periodic sending scheme can give the same guarantee provided that a leaving elected node keeps sending geocast messages until another node is elected. The notification scheme fails, since the notification report addressed to the geocast region may fail to reach the elected node which is now outside the destination region. In the presence of a node failure of the elected node, the geocast message may get lost. However, robustness can be increased by replicated elected nodes.

5.3 Neighbor Approach

Overview: Each node stores all geocast packets destined for its location and keeps a table of all neighbor nodes and their location. If a node within a geocast destination region detects a new neighbor it delivers the geocast packet to it, i.e. hand over is done on entry and message delivery is done by notification.

Description: The initial stored geocast message is sent using a regular geocast routing protocol to the destination region. After the first delivery, geocast information is exchanged between neighbors inside the destination region.

Many location-based unicast routing protocols like NFP [4] or DREAM [5] proactively and periodically exchange neighbor information containing their location in order to forward a packet to a neighbor closer to the destination. The neighbor approach simply extends the exchanged neighbor information for the unicast routing with stored geocast information. The following alternative schemes to extend the exchanged neighbor information are reasonable: 1) with neighbor information all stored geocast messages relevant for this location are exchanged, 2) with neighbor information a list of already received stored geocast identifiers relevant for this location is exchanged, or 3) with neighbor information not only the current location but also the last (or some last) reported location information is exchanged.

The first scheme, blindly exchanging stored geocasts with all neighbors, is the most simple but also most bandwidth wasteful one. After receiving a stored geocast, a node has to check whether its location intersects with the geocast destination region. If so, the geocast is delivered to the higher protocol layer and stored for later exchange with neighbors. Otherwise, the geocast is discarded.

With the second scheme, filtering of geocast messages is done before they are exchanged. The exchanged list of geocast identifiers contains unique tuples, for example <initial geocast sender, sequence number> to identify a geocast message. If a node detects that it has stored a geocast message relevant for a neighbor node's location but unknown to the neighbor, the stored geocast is sent to it.

Instead of exchanging geocast messages or their unique identifiers, the third scheme derives a necessary geocast forwarding from the route a node has taken. If the route shows, that the neighbor has 'just recently' entered a geocast destination region, then the geocast message is delivered to the neighbor node. Note that it is difficult to define 'just recently' in more detail. Of course, if this is the first neighbor information exchange inside the destination region, the geocast packet has to be delivered. However, for a second or later neighbor information exchange there is no guarantee that the geocast was already delivered, since it is possible that all former neighbors were located outside the destination region or that two neighbors have entered the destination region simultaneously and hence both have no knowledge about existing stored geocasts. As a consequence, the concrete definition of 'just recently' is a compromise between robustness and overhead and lies outside the scope of our description.

As an optimization of all three schemes, a two round protocol can be introduced. In the first round, only information necessary for most location based unicast routing protocols is exchanged with neighbors. This includes the own identifier and location. If this results in detecting a new neighbor inside a geocast's destination region, a second information exchange round is triggered including the stored geocast information according to one of the three schemes from above.

Semantics: We assume the absence of node and communication failures. Given that at any time at least one node is within the destination region and that there are no network partitions inside the destination region possibly preventing a node from having neighbors, a stored geocast message is not lost and delivered to all intended nodes. Note that the frequency of exchanging neighbor information of the complemented unicast protocol must be adapted according to the obtained distance d from the previous approaches with notification schemes.

6 Summary

Stored geocast is a time stable geocast delivered to all nodes which are inside a destination region within a certain period of time. The period of time starts at the time of sending plus network propagation delay and ends at a defined time or is boundless. We have motivated the need for stored geocast solutions in ad hoc networks with a vehicular scenario, in which a stored geocast is able to realize a virtual traffic sign.

The design space of stored geocast comprises the four dimensions: geocast protocol, geocast storage, geocast hand over and geocast delivery. From the many possible solutions we have selected and described three reasonable ones.

The first approach is an infrastructure-based server solution to store the messages. The second is an infrastructure-less approach which elects a node inside the geocast destination region to act temporarily as a server. The last approach works infrastructure-less, too, by complementing the exchange of neighbor information necessary for many geographic unicast routing protocols with geocast information.

Future work of stored geocast will include performance evaluations of the protocols. Note that as usual for ad hoc protocols, we do not expect to identify an always superior protocol. Instead, the scenario will decide the comparison.

References

1. Franz, W., Eberhardt, R.: Fleetnet - internet on the road. In: Eight World Congress on Intelligent Transport Systems, Sydney, Australia (2001)
2. Mauve, M., Widmer, J., Hartenstein, H.: A survey on position-based routing in mobile ad hoc networks. IEEE Network 15 (2001) 30–39
3. Royer, E., Toh, C.: A review of current routing protocols for ad-hoc mobile wireless networks. IEEE Personal Communications 6 (1999) 46–55
4. Hou, T., Li, V.: Transmission range control in multihop packet radio networks. IEEE Transactions on Communication 34 (1986) 38–44
5. Basagni, S., Chlamtac, I., Syrotiuk, V.R., Woodward, B.A.: A distance routing effect algorithm for mobility (DREAM). In: Proceedings of the ACM/IEEE International Conference on Mobile Computing and Networking (MobiCom), Dallas, USA, ACM Press (1998) 76–84
6. Liao, W.H., Tseng, Y.C., Sheu, J.P.: GRID: A fully location-aware routing protocol for mobile ad hoc networks. Telecommunication Systems 18 (2001) 37–60
7. Ko, Y.B., Vaidya, N.H.: Geocasting in mobile ad hoc networks: Location-based multicast algorithms. In: Proceedings of the 2nd Workshop on Mobile Computing Systems and Applications (WMCSA 99). (1999)
8. Liao, W.H., Tseng, Y.C., Lo, K.L., Sheu, J.P.: GeoGRID: A geocasting protocol for mobile ad hoc networks based on GRID. Journal of Internet Technology 1 (2000) 23–32
9. Imielinski, T., Navas, J.: GPS-based addressing and routing. Internet Engineering Task Force, Network Working Group, Request for Comments, RFC 2009 URL: ftp://ftp.isi.edu/in-notes/rfc2009.txt (1996)
10. Ko, Y.B., H.Vaidya, N.: GeoTORA: A protocol for geocasting in mobile ad hoc networks. In: Proceedings of the 8th International Conference on Network Protocols (ICNP), Osaka, Japan (2000) 240–250
11. Imielinski, T., Navas, J.C.: GPS-based geographic addressing, routing, and resource discovery. Communications of the ACM 42 (1999) 86–92
12. Wolfson, O., Sistla, A.P., Chamberlain, S., Yesha, Y.: Updating and querying databases that track mobile units. Distributed and Parallel Databases Journal 7 (1999) 1–31

Session Modellierung

A Delay Comparison of Reliable Multicast Protocols: Analysis and Simulation Results

Christian Maihöfer**, Reinhold Eberhardt

DaimlerChrysler Research And Technology,
Communication Technology (RIC/TC)
P.O. Box 2360, 89013 Ulm, Germany
{christian.maihoefer|reinhold.eberhardt}@daimlerchrysler.com

Abstract. We compare packet delivery delays from a probabilistic analysis of a flat and two tree-based reliable multicast protocols with simulation results of SRM, RMTP and TMTP variations. Analytical and simulation results show identical behavior with varying packet loss probabilities, number of receivers, and transmission rates. Even the absolute delays of the analytical and simulation results are almost identical which shows that carefully mathematical modelling can provide results of the same quality as simulation does.
A second focus of our work is to identify an optimal branching factor of the control tree established by tree-based reliable multicast protocols. Our analytical and simulation results show that a branching factor which is too small can significantly increase delay.

1 Introduction

The performance of protocols can be analyzed by mathematical analysis, simulation, or measurement either in the Internet or with the help of large testbeds. Measurement in the target environment shows the actual performance of a protocol and its available implementation, however, especially for multicast groups, measurements are difficult to perform since they usually require coordination of many multicast sites. This is why most multicast protocols are analyzed with mathematical analysis or with simulation.

Mathematical analysis requires a well understood and usually simplified model of the environment and the considered protocol. If this is successful, mathematical analysis allows to change parameters and monitor their effect on a protocol's behavior in a quite easy way. Another advantage of mathematical analysis is their usually complete publication, allowing other persons to check the correctness and the assumed system model.

With simulations, the environment and the considered protocols can become more complex and hence, more realistic. However, large simulation systems like NS-2 [1] allow to change a lot of parameters, possibly influencing the results to a great extend. Moreover, it is difficult the check the correctness of simulations, since the implementations are often extensive and in many cases, the simulation

---

** Part of this work was done during the author's stay at the University of Stuttgart, Institute of Parallel and Distributed High Performance Systems (IPVR)

code is not public. This is why we believe that both mathematical analysis and simulation are useful.

In this paper we compare analytical delay results of reliable multicast protocols with NS-2 simulation studies of SRM [2], RMTP [3] and TMTP [4] variations. The packet delivery delay is an important issue for multimedia applications. For example real time applications like interactive distributed simulations, distributed games, or the delivery of MPEG I-frames [5] benefit from guaranteed reliability and low delays. Besides analyzing the delay between sender and receiver we determine the round trip delay between sending a data packet and receiving the last corresponding control packet at the sender. The round trip delay determines the time after a data packet can be removed from memory and influences the sending rate and throughput if the sender uses a window based sending scheme [6]. Furthermore, knowledge about this delay is important to adjust the retransmission timeout at the sender.

For the analytical model as well as for the simulation model we tried to describe the reality as good as possible. This includes data packet and control packet loss, asynchronous local clocks, TTL scoping for retransmissions and spatial loss correlation. Our results show that analytical delays and simulation delays are almost identical and show identical behavior with varying number of receivers, transmission rates, and packet loss probabilities. Besides comparing analytical and simulation results, an important focus of our work was to determine an optimal branching factor of the control tree in tree-based reliable multicast protocols. The optimal branching factor depends on several parameters like packet loss probability, protocol class and whether average delivery delay, or round trip delay is of interest. We can conclude, though, that a tuned branching factor can significantly reduce delay.

The remainder of this paper is structured as follows. In the next section related work is discussed. In Section 3 we discuss the analyzed and simulated protocol classes. In Section 4 we introduce our assumed system model followed by an overview of the delay analysis. Numerical and simulation results are presented in Section 5. Finally, we conclude with a brief summary.

2   Background and Related Work

The first comparative delay analysis of sender- (ACK) and receiver-initiated (NACK) approaches was presented by Yamamoto et al. [7] and DeCleene [8]. Yamamoto et al. have analyzed the expected average delivery delay and showed that receiver-initiated protocols with NACK suppression provide best scalability. However, their analytical model for this class was simplified in assuming that all receivers are perfectly synchronized and thus only one NACK is sent back to the sender in case of packet loss. While the analysis in [7] is independent of the network topology, in [8] a delay analysis of generic ACK- and NACK-based protocols operating over star and linear topologies was presented. In [9] the effect of local recovery and retransmission of parity packets on bandwidth and delay of NACK-based protocols is examined. While the bandwidth analysis is made in detail, the delay analysis is rather brief and comparatively simple. For example, they do not consider queuing delay in detail and neglect feedback processing.

They concluded that local recovery techniques and parity packets outperform other approaches.

Our analysis is based on the delay analysis of Yamamoto et al. [7] and on the basic analytical work of Pingali et al. [10] and Levine et al. [11]. Pingali et al. have done the first comparative analysis of reliable multicast protocols. They have compared the processing requirements of flat protocol classes. Levine et al. have extended this work to the class of ring- and tree-based approaches.

To our knowledge, our work is the first comparative delay analysis of generic classes of tree-based reliable multicast protocols, which considers feedback traffic and queuing delays. Furthermore, this is the first work that compares analysis results with simulation results. In our previous work in [12] we have analyzed two tree-based reliable multicast protocols but without considering aggregated acknowledgements (see next section) and without comparing the analytical results with simulation studies.

3 Protocol Classification and Description

In this section we briefly describe and classify the reliable multicast protocols analyzed and simulated in this paper. A more detailed and more general description for some of these classes can be found in [10], [11] and [9].

The first considered protocol class is a receiver-initiated protocol. Receiver-initiated protocols return only negative acknowledgments (NACKs) from receivers to the sender instead of positive acknowledgements (ACKs). When a receiver detects an error, e.g. by a wrong checksum, a skip in the sequence number or a timeout while waiting for a data packet, a NACK is returned to the sender. A returned NACK asks for a packet retransmission from the sender. We assume that retransmissions are sent using multicast. Our considered protocol class uses multicast NACKs, which is known as NACK-avoidance scheme. A receiver that detects an error sends a multicast NACK provided that it has not already received a NACK for this data packet from another receiver. Thus, in optimum case, only one NACK is received by the sender for each lost data packet. In conformance with [11] we denote this protocol class as N2. An example for such a protocol is the scalable reliable multicasting protocol (SRM) [2].

The next two protocol classes are tree-based protocols. In tree-based protocols, the members of a multicast group are organized in a so-called control tree to overcome the well-known acknowledgment implosion problem of flat approaches, i.e. overwhelming of the sender by a large number of acknowledgments. Since acknowledgments are propagated along the edges of the control tree in a leaf-to-root direction, the implosion problem can be avoided by limiting the branching factor of a node and thus the number of acknowledgment packets.

The first considered scheme is denoted as H3 in conformance with [13]. For both tree-based protocol classes we assume that the initial sender is the root of the control tree and that the initial transmission is multicasted to the global group. Global group denotes the whole multicast group in contrast to a local group, which is described below. H3 uses ACKs sent by receivers to their parent in the control tree, called group leader, in order to indicate correctly received packets. Each group leader that is not the root node also sends an ACK to its parent as soon as a data packet has been received. If a timeout for an ACK occurs at a group leader, a multicast retransmission is invoked for this local group. A local group encompasses a group leader and its directly attached children. Such a retransmission can be sent to a separate multicast address for this local group or sent to the global group address and limited in scope by the TTL value.

Additionally to normal ACKs, H3 uses aggregated ACKs, so called AACKs. In contrast to normal ACKs, they are sent to confirm the correct message delivery for a whole subhierarchy of the control tree. A group leader sends an AACK to its parent not before it has received an AACK from *each* child node. Lead nodes in the control tree send AACKs immediately after correct packet reception. AACKs are necessary to guarantee reliable delivery even in case of node failures, since group leaders remove a packet from memory and thus preventing retransmissions not before their complete subhierarchy in the control tree has acknowledged correct message reception (see [13] for more details). An example of a protocol similar to our definition of H3 but without AACKs is RMTP [3]. RMTP uses subtree multicasting to limit the retransmission scope, which is an extension to regular routers and protocol class H3.

The second tree-based scheme H4 is based on NACKs with NACK suppression similar to N2 and on AACKs. NACKs are used to start a retransmission. Aggregated ACKs are used to announce the receivers' state and allow group leaders to remove data from memory. TMTP [4] is an example for class H4 but without AACKs. For the protocol simulations of RMTP and TMTP we have implemented AACKs to allow a fair comparison between the mathematical analysis and the simulation.

4 Delay Analysis

In this section we present an overview of the delay analysis exemplified by protocol H3, since the analysis of all three protocols is quite lengthy. The other protocols are analyzed in a technical report [14].

4.1 System Model

We assume the following system model for our analytical evaluations. A single sender multicasts a data packet to a set of R identical receivers. With probability q_D the multicast packet is corrupted or lost during the transmission to a single receiver. With probability p_A for ACKs and p_{AA} for AACKs, a control packet is corrupted or lost. According to measurements in the MBone [15] we assume spatially dependent losses in our analysis.

Finally, we assume that nodes do not fail and that the network is not partitioned, i.e. retransmissions are eventually successful. All nodes work exclusively for the multicast protocol and no background load is considered.

4.2 Analytical Approach

Our goal is to determine the delays between the initial generation of a packet at the sender and correct reception at a receiver as well as the reception of the last control packet at the sender. These delays are determined by the necessary processing times for a packet at the sender and receivers, transmission delays, timeout delays to wait for a data or control packet and finally the number of necessary transmissions for correct reception of data and control packets.

The processing time at a node is determined by the load of such a node, i.e. the processing of data and control packets. We first determine the rates for initial sending and arrival of packets. Arrival times are modelled as a poisson distribution, which results in exponentially distributed inter-arrival times. As we assume general distributed service times this queue type is defined as $M|G|1$ queue [16].

The number of necessary data packet transmissions M is determined by the packet loss probabilities q_D and p_A. M has already been obtained for the various protocol classes in our processing and bandwidth requirements analysis [13].

Given the average processing times and the number of transmissions we can determine the delay experienced by a single data packet.

4.3 Analysis

For a delay analysis of tree-based protocols we distinguish among sender, leaf node receivers and group leaders. Although the sender is a group leader as well, here and in the following we will denote only inner nodes as group leaders.

Mean Waiting Times at the Sender (Root Node) First, we have to determine the mean waiting time for a packet between generation and completion of processing or sending. The mean waiting time is determined by the load of a node, i.e. the processing of incoming and outgoing packet flows. The sender has to process the following five arriving packet flows:

1. Data packets from the higher protocol layer that are transmitted for the first time. This packet flow is referred to as λ_t^S and has an assumed rate of λ. The processing time for a data packet is assumed to be X.
2. Data packets that are retransmitted due to packet loss. This packet flow is referred to as λ_r^S and has rate $\lambda(E(M^{H3}) - 1)$, since every packet is on average $(E(M^{H3}) - 1)$-times retransmitted. $E(M^{H3})$ is the expected total number of transmissions per packet until all multicast group members have received it correctly.
3. ACK control packet flow λ_a^S received by the sender with rate $\lambda E(\widetilde{L}_a^{H3})$. The processing time for an ACK packet is assumed to be Y.
4. The AACK flow λ_{aa}^S with rate $\lambda E(\widetilde{L}_{aa}^{H3})$ and processing time Y.
5. Finally, the AACK query flow λ_q^S to ask for AACK retransmissions in case of AACK packet loss with rate $\lambda E(L_{aaq}^{H3})$ and processing time Y.

The expected total number of necessary transmissions $E(M^{H3})$ to receive the data packet correctly at all receivers, the number of received ACK packets $E(\widetilde{L}_a^{H3})$, and received AACK packets, $E(\widetilde{L}_{aa}^{H3})$, and finally the number of sent AACK query packets, $E(L_{aaq}^{H3})$, are given in [13] and not repeated here.

The load on the sender is given by the traffic intensity ϱ, which is generally the product of the traffic rate λ and mean processing time for a request (data transmission, retransmission or request) $E(S)$:

$$\varrho = \lambda E(S). \tag{1}$$

$$\varrho_S^{H3} = (\lambda_t^S + \lambda_r^S)E(X) + (\lambda_a^S + \lambda_{aa}^S + \lambda_q^S)E(Y). \tag{2}$$

As explained in Section 4.2, the system can be modeled as a $M|G|1$ queue. The Pollaczek-Chintchine formula gives the mean number of requests to be processed $E(L)$ [16]:

$$E(L) = \varrho + \frac{\varrho^2 + \lambda^2 Var(S)}{2(1 - \varrho)}. \tag{3}$$

With the formula of Little [16]:

$$E(L) = \lambda E(T), \tag{4}$$

the mean waiting time of a request in the system $E(T)$ is (see Eq. 1, 3, 4):

$$E(T) = E(S) + \frac{\varrho^2 + \lambda^2 Var(S)}{2\lambda(1 - \varrho)}. \tag{5}$$

The mean waiting time for a packet until processing starts is:

$$E(W) = E(T) - E(S) = \frac{\varrho^2 + \lambda^2 Var(S)}{2\lambda(1 - \varrho)}. \tag{6}$$

With Eq. 1 and $Var(X) = E(X^2) - (E(X))^2$ [16]:

$$E(W) = \frac{\lambda E(S^2)}{2(1 - \varrho)} \tag{7}$$

$$E(W_S^{H3}) = \frac{(\lambda_t^S + \lambda_r^S)E(X^2) + (\lambda_a^S + \lambda_{aa}^S + \lambda_q^S)E(Y^2)}{2(1 - \varrho_S^{H3})}. \tag{8}$$

Mean Waiting Times at a Receiver (Leaf Node) A receiver has to process the following two flows. There is the data reception flow λ^R with rate $\lambda E(M^{H3})(1 - q_D)$ which automatically triggers an ACK or AACK flow and therefore results in processing time of $X + Y$. The flow of AACK queries λ_q^R with rate $\lambda E(\widetilde{L}_{aaq}^{H3})$ triggers the replying of AACKs, which results in total processing time $Y + Y$. $E(\widetilde{L}_{aaq}^{H3})$ is given in [13]. The load on a receiver is then:

$$\varrho_R^{H3} = \lambda^R E(X + Y) + \lambda_q^R E(Y + Y). \tag{9}$$

The expectation of the waiting time at the receiver until processing starts is (see Eq. 7):

$$E(W_R^{H3}) = \frac{\lambda^R E((X + Y)^2) + \lambda_q^R E((Y + Y)^2)}{2(1 - \varrho_R^{H3})}. \tag{10}$$

Mean Waiting Times at a Group Leader (Inner Node) The load on an inner node is the sum of the sender's load without the initial transmission and a receiver's load:

$$\varrho_G^{H3} = \lambda_r^S E(X) + (\lambda_a^S + \lambda_{aa}^S + \lambda_q^S)E(Y) + \lambda^R E(X+Y) + \lambda_q^R E(Y+Y). \tag{11}$$

The mean waiting time of a packet at an inner node follows to:

$$E(W_G^{H3}) = \frac{\lambda_r^S E(X^2) + \left(\lambda_a^S + \lambda_{aa}^S + \lambda_q^S\right)E(Y^2) + \lambda^R E((X+Y)^2) + \lambda_q^R E((Y+Y)^2)}{2(1 - \varrho_G^{H3})}. \tag{12}$$

Overall Delay We assume that T is the group leader timeout delay, τ is the network propagation delay, h is the maximum and $\bar{h}$ is the average number of hierarchy levels of the control tree and B is the branching factor of the control tree, i.e. the maximum number of child nodes per group leader. If no retransmission is necessary, the delay from the initial transmission $E(I)$ is:

$$E(I) = E(W_S^{H3}) + E(X) + \tau + E(W_G^{H3}) + E(X). \tag{13}$$

Note that a simplifying pessimistic assumption we made is that the receiver is always a group leader and therefore take $E(W_G^{H3})$ in the above equation.

Now we want to determine the delay for a hierarchical retransmission on condition that the parent node has received the packet correctly. The time for a hierarchical retransmission $E(H)$ is:

$$E(H) = \left(E(M_r^{H3}|M_r^{H3} > 1) - 1\right)\left(T + E(W_G^{H3}) + E(X)\right) + \tau_H + E(W_G^{H3}) + E(X). \tag{14}$$

M_r^{H3} is the number of necessary transmissions for a single receiver r until correct reception (M_r^{H3} is calculated [13]) and τ_H is the network propagation delay for a hierarchical retransmission. For obtaining the overall delay, we determine the probabilities that no data loss occurs, that a node misses a packet but the parent node is able to retransmit it, that a node and its parent misses that packet and the next parent retransmits it and so forth and multiply these probabilities with the expected delays. The overall delay is then:

$$E(S_\phi^{H3}) = \left[\sum_{i=0}^{\bar{h}-2} q_D^i(1 - q_D)\left(E(I) + iE(H)\right)\right] + q_D^{\bar{h}-1}\left(E(W_S^{H3}) + E(X) + (\bar{h} - 1)E(H)\right). \tag{15}$$

Besides the delay for delivering data packets we examine the round trip delay of AACKs, i.e. the mean time between sending a packet and receiving the corresponding AACKs at the sender. Note that this delay is used to manage the sending window and release buffer space. Furthermore, it limits the throughput if a window based sending scheme is used [6]. Before a receiver sends an AACK it must receive the data packet before. The mean waiting time between sending a packet and receiving the last AACK at the sender is given by:

$$E(S_{RTD}^{H3}) =$$
$$\underbrace{\left(E(M^{H3}) - 1\right)\left(T + E(W_G^{H3}) + E(X)\right)}_{\text{sending transmissions}} + \underbrace{E(X) + E(W_G^{H3}) + \tau_H + E(W_G^{H3}) + E(X)}_{\text{receiving last successful retransmission}}$$
$$+ (h - 1)\big[\underbrace{E(\widetilde{L}_{aaq}^{H3})\left(T + E(W_G^{H3}) + E(Y)\right)}_{\text{send AACK queries}} + \underbrace{E(Y) + \tau_H + E(W_G^{H3}) + E(Y)}_{\text{send and receive successful AACK}}\big]. \tag{16}$$

5   Comparison of Analysis and Simulation Results

We have implemented the SRM [2], RMTP [3] and TMTP [4] reliable multi-cast protocols in the NS2 [1] network simulator environment to compare them with the analysis. Recall that SRM is a receiver-initiated protocol, RMTP is a tree-based sender-initiated protocol and TMTP is a tree-based receiver-initiated protocol with NACK suppression.

In contrast to the specification of RMTP we have implemented no subcast mechanism, as this is not available with general routers. Instead we used TTL-limited multicast to send retransmissions. A further significant difference is that we send acknowledgments as soon as a data packet is received rather than periodically. Besides normal ACKs we have additionally implemented aggregated ACKs. As a consequence of the aggregated ACKs, this protocol is of class H3.

In contrast to the specification of TMTP we have implemented AACKs rather than so-called early ACKs. TMTP uses early ACKs to advance the flow control window. An early ACK is sent after the corresponding data packet has been received. This means, a group leader does not need to wait for ACKs from all its children in order to send an early ACK to its parent. While this specification allows to loose data in case of node failures, we have implemented AACKs to cope with such situations. As a consequence of the NACK with NACK suppression and AACK scheme, this protocol is of class H4.

In conformance with the specifications we use a rate and window based sending scheme for flow and congestion control. TMTP defines a periodic interval at which each receiver unicasts an ACK (here AACK) to its parent and suggests to set it on the round trip time to the farthest receiver. In our analysis we have determined the round trip time between sending a data packet and receiving the last corresponding control packet at the sender under the assumption that the control packets are sent immediately. Therefore, our TMTP implementation sends AACKs immediately after receiving a data packet rather than periodically.

Note that our intention is to compare analytical with simulation results and to determine an optimal branching factor rather than to compare SRM, RMTP and TMTP, which makes only limited sense due to the modifications described above and due to the limited simulated group sizes.

For our simulations we have used two networks generated by Tiers [17] with 250 and 1000 nodes. All nodes in the network use DVMRP routing. Each link in the network is configured with probability 0.02 for packet loss. We have measured an average end-to-end packet loss probability for data packets of about 12% for the 250 node network and 15% for the 1000 node network. The average propagation delay was measured to be about 70ms for the 250 node network and 130ms for the 1000 node network. These measured values were used to configure the analysis parameters. While we have varied the sending rate for our simulations, the flow control window size was always 10.

Figures 1-3 show the results of our simulations in comparison with the numerical results of the analysis. The solid lines display the results from the simulation whereas the dotted lines display the numerical results from our analysis. The sending rate for results with varying group size is $1\frac{1}{s}$, the network consists of 250 nodes and the branching factor is 10. For results with varying sending rate, the group size is 100 receivers. For results with varying branching factors,

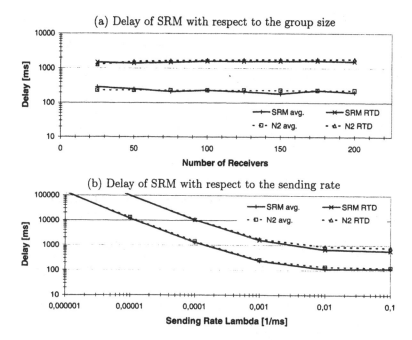

Fig. 1. Analytical vs. simulated delays of SRM

the network consists of 1000 nodes, the multicast group of 200 receivers and the sending rate is $1\frac{1}{s}$.

All results show that the average delivery delay is almost independent of the group size within the simulated range, even for the non-tree based SRM approach.[1] The round trip delay increases only moderately with increasing group size. Although the simulation results show some fluctuations caused by the random packet loss probabilities it is notable that even the absolute delays of the simulations are very close to the predicted results of the analysis.

With respect to varying sending rates we can see that while the average delivery delay and round trip delay of RMTP are independent of the sending rate, the results for SRM and TMTP show high delays with low sending rates. This is caused by the receiver initiated loss detection, i.e. a packet loss is detected not before the first packet with higher sequence number is successfully received. With low sending rates, this delay becomes rather high. This is why in most cases sender-initiated protocols like RMTP result in lower delays.

The last results in Figure 2.c and 3.c show the results with a varying branching factor. As predicted by the analytical results, average delay is hardly influenced by the branching factor. For the round trip delay, though, we see that both the analytical as well as simulation results for RMTP and TMTP show a decrease with increasing local group size due to the decreased height of the

---

[1] However, we know from analytical results that SRM is earlier saturated from feedback implosion and hence cannot support very large group sizes (e.g. see [12]).

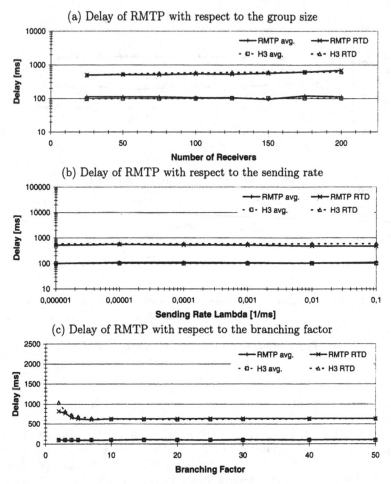

Fig. 2. Analytical vs. simulated delays of RMTP

control tree. This means, a larger branching factor allow higher throughput if a window-based sending scheme is used.

In further simulation runs we have varied the packet loss probability. For example, we have decreased link loss probability to 0.002, resulting in an average end-to-end packet loss probability for data packets of about 1.5% in the simulated network, which has decreased packet delay of RMTP's analysis and simulation results by approximately 25%. More important than the absolute results, though, all protocols show again the same results for both analysis and simulation.

6 Summary

We have presented a probabilistic approach to analyze the average packet delivery delay as well as the round trip delay for reliable multicast protocols. A major

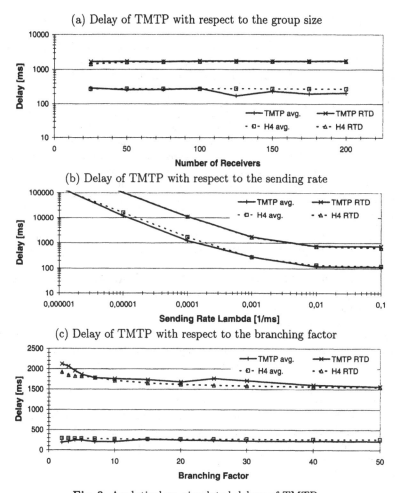

Fig. 3. Analytical vs. simulated delays of TMTP

focus of our work was to compare the gained analytical results with simulation results to prove their correctness. The comparison of a flat and two tree-based reliable multicast protocols has shown identical behavior of analysis and simulation results with varying packet loss probabilities, number of receivers, and transmission rates. Even the absolute delays of the analytical and simulation results are almost identical which shows that carefully mathematical modelling can provide results of the same quality as simulation does.

An important second focus of our work was to determine an optimal branching factor of the control tree established by tree-based reliable multicast protocols. The optimal branching factor depends on several parameters like protocol class and whether average delivery delay or round trip delay is of interest. We can conclude, though, that a branching factor which is too small can significantly increase round trip delay which limits a protocol's throughput.

282

References

1. Bajaj, S., Breslau, L., Estrin, D., Fall, K., Floyd, S., P. Haldar, M.H., Helmy, A., Heidemann, J., Huang, P., Kumar, S., McCanne, S., Rejaie, R., Sharma, P., Varadhan, K., Xu, Y., Yu, H., Zappala, D.: Improving simulation for network research. Technical Report 99-702, University of Southern California, USA (1999)
2. Floyd, S., Jacobson, V., Liu, C., McCanne, S., Zhang, L.: A reliable multicast framework for light-weight sessions and application level framing. IEEE/ACM Transactions on Networking 5 (1997) 784–803
3. Paul, S., Sabnani, K., Lin, J., Bhattacharyya, S.: Reliable multicast transport protocol (RMTP). IEEE Journal on Selected Areas in Communications, special issue on Network Support for Multipoint Communication 15 (1997) 407–421
4. Yavatkar, R., Griffioen, J., Sudan, M.: A reliable dissemination protocol for interactive collaborative applications. In: The Third ACM International Multimedia Conference and Exhibition (MULTIMEDIA '95), New York, USA, ACM Press (1995) 333–344
5. Pejhan, S., Schwartz, M., Anastassiou, D.: Error control using retransmission schemes in multicast transport protocols for real-time media. IEEE/ACM Transactions on Networking 4 (1996) 413–427
6. Allman, M., Glover, D., Sanchez, L.: Enhancing TCP over satellite channels using standard mechanisms. Internet Engineering Task Force, Network Working Group, Request for Comments, RFC 2488
URL: ftp://ftp.isi.edu/in-notes/rfc2488.txt (1999)
7. Yamamoto, M., Kurose, J., Towsley, D., Ikeda, H.: A delay analysis of sender-initiated and receiver-initiated reliable multicast protocols. In: Proceedings of IEEE INFOCOM Conference on Computer Communications, Los Alamitos, IEEE Press (1997) 480–488
8. DeCleene, B.: Delay characteristics of generic reliable multicast protocols. Technical Report TR-08150-3, Logicon TASC (1996)
9. Nonnenmacher, J., Lacher, M., Jung, M., Carl, G., Biersack, E.: How bad is reliable multicast without local recovery. In: Proceedings of IEEE INFOCOM Conference on Computer Communications, New York, USA, IEEE Press (1998) 972–979
10. Pingali, S., Towsley, D., Kurose, J.F.: A comparison of sender-initiated and receiver-initiated reliable multicast protocols. In: Proceedings of the Sigmetrics Conference on Measurement and Modeling of Computer Systems, New York, USA, ACM Press (1994) 221–230
11. Levine, B., Garcia-Luna-Aceves, J.: A comparison of reliable multicast protocols. Multimedia Systems 6 (1998) 334–348
12. Maihöfer, C., Rothermel, K.: A delay analysis of tree-based reliable multicast protocols. In: Proceedings of the Tenth International Conference on Computer Communications and Networks, Scottsdale, USA, IEEE Press (2001) 274–281
13. Maihöfer, C., Rothermel, K.: Optimal branching factor for tree-based reliable multicast protocols. Computer Communications 25 (2002) 1018–1027
14. Maihöfer, C., Rothermel, K.: A delay analysis of tree-based reliable multicast protocols. Technical Report TR 2001/03, University of Stuttgart (2001)
15. Yajnik, M., Kurose, J., Towsley, D.: Packet loss correlation in the MBone multicast network. In: Proceedings of IEEE Global Internet, London, UK, IEEE Press (1996) 94–99
16. Kleinrock, L.: Queueing Systems, Volume II: Computer Applications. Wiley Interscience, New York, USA (1976)
17. Calvert, K., Doar, M., Zegura, E.: Modeling internet topology. IEEE Communications Magazine 35 (1997) 160–163

Generating Prescribed Traffic with HTTP/TCP Sources for Large Simulation Models

Kai Below and Ulrich Killat[1]

Department of Communication Networks
Technical University Hamburg-Harburg (TUHH)
Denickestr. 17, D-21071 Hamburg, Germany
{below,killat}tu-harburg.de, http://www.tuhh.de/et6/

Abstract The computer simulation of realistic networks is an important tool for the development of new protocols or algorithms for communication networks as well as for the optimization of existing technologies. The traditional approach for network simulations is to connect a certain amount of sources to a some network nodes and to measure the traffic intensities, end-to-end delay and further performance parameters.

Network providers have a different view of the problem: The traffic intensities in their network is known, and their target is to optimize the current network. So the first step is to configure the simulation model to generate approximately the same traffic that was measured in the real network.

We discuss the problem of generating a traffic with known characteristics in this paper. We propose a method for dimensioning the number of HTTP/TCP source models for each flow so that the difference between traffic matrix values observed in the real network and in the simulation model is minimized. We show an improved version of our model presented already in [1,2,3] that performs better for the case of large HTTP downloads and small off-times (where the average off time is not much larger than the average download time).

The new aspect in this paper is the discussion of the important aspect for modeling the burstiness of the traffic. We show with a simulation study in this paper that the Hurst parameter, one measure for the burstiness, can be adjusted by the shape parameter α of the truncated power-tail distribution of the HTTP object sizes. We discuss one interesting effect of high Hurst parameter values for link load values bigger than 90 %.

1 Introduction

The classical paradigm of simulating computer networks consists of models for network nodes which are interconnected and together with a routing table form a certain network model. The number of sources and the bandwidth of the links is usually chosen more or less arbitrarily. The traffic intensities on the links and the delays for the flows are measured and are subject to different parameter settings like protocol variants used, buffer management and service disciplines of routers.

Network operators have the inverse problem: they know the traffic on their links and would like to know how this situation changes when parameter settings are changed. To answer this question it is a necessary prerequisite to find a configuration for the simulation model so that the traffic generated by the model sources matches the prescribed (i.e. measured) traffic by the network provider. The number of sources for each node and flow has to be determined in order to solve this problem, which produce the known, observed traffic. This is not a trivial problem since the steady state formulas for the TCP throughput [4] are not applicable for short-lived connections that are characteristic for WWW traffic. We investigate this problem for HTTP applications and thus face the problem of the reactive behavior of TCP.

The intrinsic features of the WWW traffic within the last years are the user behavior and the use of the HTTP/TCP protocols and therefore it is important to use source models that reflect this behavior as opposed to generating aggregated traffic [5]. The traffic measured in the Internet is known to be self-similar [6,7,8], which is generated in simulations with power-tail distributed random variables for the file size distribution [7]. The source model used here (see Sec. 2) generates self-similar traffic, the Hurst parameter can be adjusted with the α parameter of the file size distribution (see Sec. 5.2).

The rest of the paper is organized as follows. The source model is discussed in Section 2. The proposed strategy for determining the number of sources per flow is described in Section 3. The three simulation scenarios used for the validation are illustrated in Section 4. The simulation results are shown in Section 5. We conclude the paper with a summary of the findings in Section 6.

2 Source Model

The target of a realistic simulation can only be reached using a realistic model for the user behavior, therefore we use a HTTP/TCP client model similar to the one described in [9]. We use the simulation software Ptolemy [10] for which we implemented TCP "NewReno" and HTTP 1.1 with pipelining, that is, the full HTTP transfer volume is transmitted in one TCP connection which is being closed at the end of the transfer, see Fig. 1. We do not model the usage of parallel connections here. The TCP implementation was validated with ns-2 [11].

The HTTP request of a client opens a TCP connection via the three way handshake. Some requests for the embedded objects (includes) are sent from HTTP client to server after receiving the main HTTP object. The TCP connection is closed by the client after receiving all requested objects. After successful transmission the user spends a certain amount of time reading. This on / off behavior is the key for being able to derive a simple estimation of the average rate of such a traffic source, especially since the off-time (reading time) is in general larger than the on-time [9]. Further discussion of the distributions and their parameter fittings for the generation of self-similar traffic can be found in [12,13].

The HTTP object size is drawn from a truncated power-tail distribution (TPT) with a truncation level $T = 20$ [14]. We limited the maximum file size to 100 MB additionally to ensure convergence of the simulation. The major contribution to the self-similarity of the traffic comes from the distribution of the file-size [12,13]. Therefore we deviate from [9] in using a geometric distribution for the number of HTTP inline objects and a negative exponentially distributed off-time.

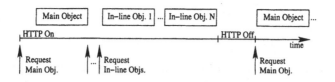

Figure1. HTTP/TCP behavior, no parallel connections.

3 Determining the Number of Sources per Flow

We develop an algorithm which determines the number of sources for each flow of the traffic matrix necessary to create the traffic intensities observed in the network. Due to the granularity of integer values used for the number of sources, the resulting accuracy is limited and depends on the specified off-time and traffic matrix: increasing the value of the off-time reduces the average rate per source so that more sources are needed to generate the same amount of traffic. Therefore the problem of dimensioning the number of sources per flow has a finer granularity such that the accuracy of the method increases. Very small off-times, on the other hand, produce a coarse granularity. If the values of the traffic matrix cover a broad range of traffic intensities it is clear that the flows with the smallest traffic values encounter the largest problem with the granularity.

If the accuracy of the results of the simulation is not sufficient further iterative simulations can be performed, where the respective previous simulation results are taken into account. We have presented an early states of this algorithm in [1,2,3]. The modeling of the congestion avoidance of TCP described in the following section was improved as compared to [1,2,3].

3.1 Estimation of the Required Number of Sources

We consider the traffic matrix TP as given; the elements tp_{ij} denote the throughput of the flow between node i and node j in Mbit/s. The target is to estimate a source allocation S that results in a traffic as described by TP. We derive an estimation of the average rate of a single HTTP/TCP source that can be applied to all flows. Based on this result the number of sources that have to be assigned to a given flow can be calculated. The average rate of a single HTTP/TCP source in Mbit/s in the flow from node i to node j is

$$r_{src_{ij}} = \frac{v}{t_{on_{ij}} + t_{off}},\tag{1}$$

where v represents the average HTTP transfer volume in Mbit $v = b \cdot 8 / 10^6$ and b is the average HTTP transfer volume in Bytes. The quantities $t_{on_{ij}}$ and t_{off} are the average HTTP on- and off-times in seconds, respectively (download time and reading time). The value of $t_{on_{ij}}$ depends on v and it is in general hard to estimate accurate values of $t_{on_{ij}}$ due to the reactivity of the TCP protocol.

A simple estimate of the mean on-time is

$$t_{on_{ij}} = (1 + n_{RTT_{ss}} + n_{RTT_{ca}}) \cdot rtt_{ij}, \tag{2}$$

where rtt_{ij} is the average RTT and $n_{RTT_{ss}}$ and $n_{RTT_{ca}}$ represent the number of RTTs that TCP requires to transmit b Bytes in slow-start and congestion avoidance phase, respectively. The minimum RTT, which is the sum of the propagation delays, is used here as a first-order approximation for the average RTT.

The number of RTTs in slow-start can be expressed as a function of the number of packets to be transmitted n_P and the maximum number of packets that can be transmitted in slow-start phase of TCP $n_{P_{ss,max}}$

$$n_{RTT_{ss}} = \begin{cases} \lceil log_2(n_P) \rceil & n_P \leq n_{P_{ss,max}} \\ n_{RTT_{ss,max}} & n_P > n_{P_{ss,max}}. \end{cases} \tag{3}$$

The improved estimation of the number of RTTs in congestion-avoidance in (4) leads to better results compared to the definition in an earlier work [1,2,3]. The number of RTTs in congestion-avoidance phase can be determined by dividing remaining number of packets after slow-start phase by the average average number of packets that can be transmitted per RTT in congestion avoidance. With the steady state assumption as an approximation, the average congestion window is $CWND_{ca,avg} = 0.75 \cdot CWND_{max}$. Therefore the resulting number of RTTs can be calculated with the Maximum Transfer Unit (MTU) as follows:

$$n_{RTT_{ca}} = \left\lceil \frac{\max\{0, n_p - n_{P_{ss,max}}\}}{\lfloor 0.75 \cdot CWND_{max}/MTU \rfloor} \right\rceil. \tag{4}$$

The source matrix S with the elements s_{ij} representing the number of sources for the flow from node i to node j can finally be calculated with (1) and (2) by dividing the observed throughput tp_{ij} by the average source rate $r_{src,ij}$ for each flow and rounding the resulting numbers:

$$\begin{aligned} s_{ij} &= round\left(\frac{tp_{ij}}{r_{src_{ij}}}\right) \\ &= round\left(\frac{tp_{ij}}{v} \cdot [(1 + n_{RTT_{ss}} + n_{RTT_{ca}}) \cdot rtt_{ij} + t_{off}]\right). \end{aligned} \tag{5}$$

4 Simulation Scenarios

We use three simulation scenarios in this study: the well-known bottleneck scenario (Fig. 2), a so called parking-lot model with four main links and different RTTs and hop-counts for the flows (Fig. 3) and the B-WiN model, a large network model that is representative of an existing backbone (Fig. 4, see also the technical report [15]). The IP-routers are modeled as output buffered systems with FIFO queues.

In the bottleneck scenario all flows share the same link between two routers. We installed different link delays so that the flows experience different minimum RTTs: the bottleneck link between R1 and R2 has a capacity of 50 Mbit/s and a delay of 8 ms. The nodes S1 – S6 are connected via 100 Mbit/s links to R1 and R2, respectively. The propagation delay is 1 ms for S1 and S4, is 5 ms for S2 and S5 and is 10 ms for S3 and S6. The installed flows are depicted as dashed arcs (both directions). The target traffic matrix is set to 11 Mbit/s for each flow resulting in an average link utilization of 66%.

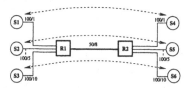

Figure 2. Topology of the bottleneck simulation model (link capacities in Mbit/s and propagation delay in ms).

The parking-lot scenario has the advantage of being already complex enough to show the effect of different round-trip times and loss rates but still being simple enough to provide fast simulations and an easy interpretation of the results. All links between the source nodes S1 – S12 and the router nodes R1 – R5 are configured with a rate of 1 Gbit/s and a propagation delay of 1 ms so that there is no bottleneck there. The core routers are connected via links with 50 Mbit/s. The links from R1 to R2 and R4 to R5 have a propagation delay of 8 ms, the remaining two links have a delay of 24 ms.

The specified traffic matrix for the parking-lot scenario is again very simple: all flows should achieve a throughput of 8.5 Mbit/s which results in a maximum average link load of 68% (between R2 and R4). Although this traffic matrix is simple, it is nevertheless hard to find a source allocation: due to TCP's sensitivity to different round-trip times and packet losses the six-hop connections can not achieve the same rate as the shorter connections so that relatively more sources are needed for longer flows.

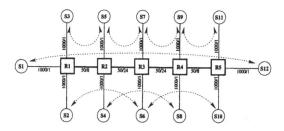

Figure 3. Topology of the parking lot simulation model (link capacities in Mbit/s and propagation delay in ms).

The B-WiN scenario (Fig. 4, left) is very complex, takes a long time to simulate and it is harder to understand the results. Nevertheless, it is a model (of an early state) of the network that connects all German universities and research institutes and for which a complete traffic matrix has been measured. The results of simulations with this model can be regarded as a test case to evaluate real network behavior. The model consists of 11 nodes connected via 18 bi-directional links with a total capacity of 3.9 Gbit/s. The link capacities range from 53 Mbit/s to 167 Mbit/s and the link delays from 0.5 ms to 18.5 ms. Flows from all nodes to all other nodes resulting in 110 flows in total. The routing was optimized by the providers in order to keep the traffic load below 70 % on all links except for those coming from the USA (node "US/11") which were allowed to have a load over 90 % (max. 98.4 %).

The measured traffic matrix (throughput per flow in Mbit/s) is depicted in Fig. 4 (right). The range of values is very large, the minimum value is 0.44 Mbit/s and the maximum value is 126.78 Mbit/s. It can be expected that the relative error for the flows with a very small throughput value will be large due to the fact that we can only select integer values for the number of sources per flow. The impact of these large relative errors is negligible for the total load state of the network which is dominated by the flows with large throughput. Therefore we will measure the performance of the allocation of the sources with the maximum absolute error expressed in percent: we search for the flow with the maximum absolute error in Mbit/s and express this value as a percentage of the given throughput value of this flow.

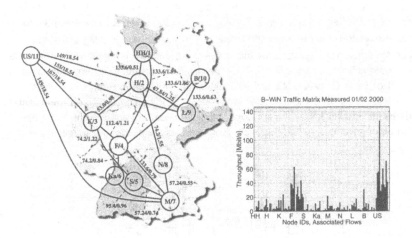

Figure4. Topology of the B-WiN simulation model (link capacities in Mbit/s and propagation delay in ms, left), measured throughput matrix of the B-WiN, Jan/Feb 2000 (right).

5 Simulation Results

The target is to drive simulations with a network traffic that is as close as possible to the real world network traffic. The problem of establishing the target traffic matrix (Sec. 5.1) as well as the Hurst parameter of the traffic (Sec. 5.2) is treated. We try to derive some general insight into this problem that can be helpful for other network scenarios which are not treated here.

We discuss the evaluation of the model for estimating the number of sources per flow (from Sec. 3.1) in Sec. 5.1. The measure for the accuracy is the deviation from the prescribed traffic in terms of the maximum of the absolute error in percent of the target value of the traffic matrix tp_{ij}:

$$\Delta tp_{ij,max,\%} = 100 \cdot \max_{i,j} \{\Delta tp_{ij}\}/tp_{ij}. \qquad (6)$$

Positive error values mean a throughput larger than specified in the prescribed traffic matrix and negative values mean throughput smaller than specified.

Another interesting question is whether the same network traffic can be generated with a reduced number of sources. The B-WiN scenario would require approximately a total of 120000 sources with realistic parameter settings of $b = 60$ KB and $t_{off} = 40$ s [9] according to our model in Sec. 3.1. We perform the evaluation of the B-WiN scenario with smaller values for t_{off} so that the total number of sources is between 1058 and 15435 in order to find out whether it is possible to produce the given traffic with the reduced set of sources.

Tuning the correlation properties of the traffic, as expressed by the Hurst parameter, via the shape parameter α of the power-tail distribution is discussed in Sec. 5.2. Adjusting the Hurst parameter for a new network model can be a tedious task since several simulations with $\alpha = \alpha_1$ (but with different seeds) are needed to produce a good estimate of the Hurst parameter. Another set of simulations must be performed with a new value of $\alpha = \alpha_2$ if the first set of simulations (with $\alpha = \alpha_1$) results in a Hurst parameter that is far away from the target value. Therefore it is important to know a good start value for α to reduce the number of simulations that is required to adjust the Hurst parameter.

5.1 Adjusting the Load State of the Network

The modeling of the congestion avoidance of TCP was improved as compared to [1,2,3], therefore we show a short summary of the new evaluation here. The simulation time was chosen to be 800 s for the bottleneck and parking-lot scenario and 200 s for the B-WiN scenario. We have chosen a constant buffer capacity of the IP router $B = 5000$ packets for all simulation scenarios.

We performed the simulations with the scenarios bottleneck and parking-lot with the parameter sets $b = \{60, 100, 150, 200\}$ KB and $t_{off} = \{10, 20, 40\}$ s; the results are depicted in Fig. 5, left and middle, respectively. The maximum error $\Delta tp_{ij,max,\%}$ is smaller than 10% for all combinations of parameters and for the both scenarios. The parameter sets $b = \{60, 100, 150, 200\}$ KB and $t_{off} = \{1, 2, 5\}$ s were used for the

B-WiN. The deviations from the prescribed traffic matrix for the B-WiN scenario are shown in Fig. 5 (right).The errors are in general much larger than in the bottleneck and parking-lot scenario which can be explained by the larger complexity of this exercise as described in Section 4. The maximum error of most simulations was still less than 10%, only 4 of the 36 cases exceeded this limit.

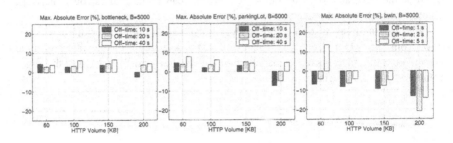

Figure5. Max. deviation from given traffic matrix, bottleneck (left), parking-lot (middle) and B-WiN (right).

5.2 Adjusting the Hurst Parameter

It was shown in [7] that the Hurst parameter H depends mainly on the shape parameter α of the HTTP object size distribution. We evaluate this with five different values for $\alpha = \{1.1, 1.25, 1.5, 1.75, 2.0\}$. We drive ten simulations with different seeds of the random number generator for each value of α and show the average, minimum and maximum of the estimated Hurst parameters in the following figures. We use here values of $b = 60$ KB and relatively small values for the off-time: $t_{off} = 1$ s for the B-WiN scenario and $b = 60$ KB and $t_{off} = 40$ s for the bottleneck scenario in order to keep the simulation duration tolerable.

We have used the Abry/Veitch estimator [16,17] that is based on the wavelet transform to estimate the scaling properties of the process. We have used a counting process for the number of bytes per time frame of 10 ms as the base for the Hurst parameter estimation.

The estimated Hurst parameter H versus the shape parameter α of the truncated power-tail distribution is shown Figure 6 (left) for the B-WiN scenario (mean, minimum and maximum values for 10 seeds). The straight line is the theoretical reference for fractional Gaussian noise (FGN) $H = (3 - \alpha)/2$. The Hurst parameter decreases monotonously with increasing α as expected [7] and differs slightly from the FGN line. The bars show that the estimates can differ for some seed values of the random number generator. The results with the bottleneck scenario in Fig. 6 (right) are very similar.

The Hurst parameter estimations for the B-WiN show an interesting behavior for one link with a high traffic load ($\rho = 91$ %), see Fig. 7: the estimated values for the Hurst parameter are generally larger than those for the low load case; especially large

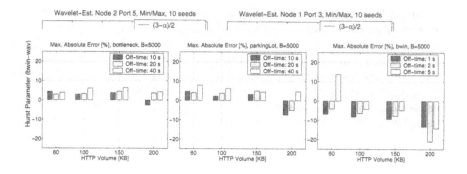

Figure6. Hurst parameter H versus shape parameter α, B-WiN at $\rho = 31$ % (left), bottleneck at $\rho = 28$ % (right).

values of α still result in a high Hurst parameter. This result was completely different from what we expected. We expected the Hurst parameter to decrease for high load since our impression was that the variability of the counting process is reduced if the link is nearly fully utilized.

We tried to validate this phenomenon with the bottleneck scenario under high load, as can be seen in Fig. 7 (right, we used here $b = 60$ KB and $t_{off} = 10$ s). The estimated Hurst parameter values are lower for the bottleneck than for the B-WiN for low values of α. The Hurst parameters in the region $\alpha > 1.5$ are much larger in the B-WiN scenario than in the bottleneck. It seems that the topology of the B-WiN plays a role here such that decreasing α does not reduce the long-range dependence of the counting process anymore.

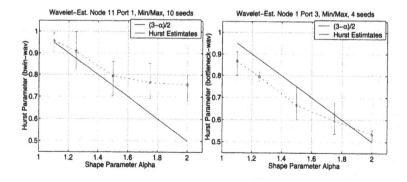

Figure7. Hurst parameter H versus shape parameter α, B-WiN at $\rho = 91$ % (left), bottleneck at $\rho = 91$ % (right).

We try to develop an intuitive understanding of the phenomenon of high Hurst parameter values for high utilization (and low values of α). The counting process of the B-WiN scenario (bytes per 10 ms, scaled to Mbit/s) for $\alpha = 1.1$ is shown in Fig. 8 (left). The link utilization is high, but there are also some very deep dips in the curve which are responsible for the high variability of the process, which is responsible for the high Hurst parameter values. In order to explain this phenomenon intuitively we define the inverse of the counting process by addition of a constant ($\max(P_{count})$) and multiplication by -1:

$$P_{inv,count} = \max(P_{count}) - P_{count}. \tag{7}$$

It is clear that the higher order statistics (like variance or Hurst parameter) are the same for both processes, therefore it is not surprising that the Hurst parameter estimation results in the same value. The example of the inverse process is depicted in Fig. 8 (right).

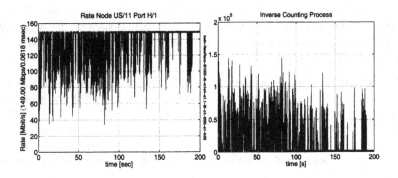

Figure8. Counting process (left) and inverse counting process (right), bottleneck.

One cutout is shown in Fig. 9 where the high variance of the process is obvious. The "visual inspection" shows a very bursty process, similar to e.g. traces in [6] where it is easy to believe that this process is self-similar with a high Hurst parameter value.

We can learn from this experiment that high Hurst parameter values are possible for a very high link utilization of above 90 %; the variability of those processes lie in the depth and frequency of the dips, not in the peaks. The inverse of the counting process, as defined in (7), can help to understand this phenomenon.

We can summarize that it is rather easy to start value for α for the first set of simulations to achieve a certain Hurst parameter on a network link for a low link utilization (see Sec. 5): the equation for FGN, $H = (3 - \alpha)/2$, can be used as a first order approximation. Using the FGN model for the start value of α might not be a good proposal for high link utilization, as the Hurst parameter depends also on the network topology in this case (Fig. 7).

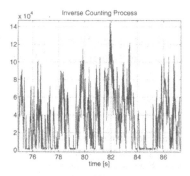

Figure9. Cutout from inverse counting process, bottleneck.

6 Conclusion

We have considered two problems with the target to find configurations for a HTTP/TCP source model that allow the generation of traffic with realistic parameters: the establishment of the average traffic volume in the network and the adjustment of the Hurst parameter of the traffic. We derived some general insight into these problems that could be helpful also for other network scenarios.

We have considered the problem of calibrating the number of HTTP/TCP traffic sources for large simulation models of TCP/IP networks. The target was to minimize the difference between a prescribed traffic matrix (i.e. measured in the real network) and the traffic matrix measured in the simulation model.

We have measured the performance of the proposed algorithm with the maximum absolute deviation from the prescribed traffic matrix. We have shown with various simulations that the proposed method performs reasonably well for all three simulation scenarios. Only 4 of the 36 simulations resulted in absolute deviations of more than $\pm 10\%$ from their respective prescribed throughput values. An error threshold of 10% was used in the discussion since the traffic matrix is not static: the network provider measures fluctuations in his traffic matrix so that a smaller error threshold seems not to be reasonable.

Our evaluations have shown that the Hurst parameter is directly tunable via the shape parameter α of the power-tail distribution, see also [13]. We discussed an interesting phenomenon where we measured high Hurst parameters ($H \geq 0.85$) at a high link utilization ($\rho \geq 90\%$) and derived an intuitive understanding. Further studies will focus on understanding the role of the network topology that is responsible for the high Hurst parameter values that we have measured even for low values of α.

We have treated the problem of reducing the total number of sources generating the described traffic in order to keep the requirements on CPU time and RAM on an acceptable level. Reducing the number of sources by using smaller values for the off-time (as compared to realistic values) was possible for both parameters in question: the traffic matrix and the Hurst parameter could be established also with the reduced number of sources.

Acknowledgment

This work was partially supported by the DFN-Verein and Deutsche Telekom. We would like to thank G. Hoffmann, R. Habermann and T. Pluemer for valuable discussions.

References

1. K. Below and U. Killat, "On the configuration of simulations of large network models with HTTP/TCP sources," in *15th ITC Specialist Seminar, Internet Traffic Engineering and Traffic Management*, P. Tran-Gia and J. Roberts, Eds., Würzburg, July 2002, pp. 143–149.
2. K. Below and U. Killat, "Allocation of HTTP/TCP sources for traffic generation in large network simulations," in *2nd Polish-German Teletraffic Symposium (PGTS 2002)*, Gdansk, Poland, Sept. 2002, pp. 175–182.
3. K. Below and U. Killat, "Internet traffic generation for large simulations scenarios with a target traffic matrix," in *2nd WSEAS International Conference on Simulation, Modelling and Optimization (WSEAS ICOSMO 2002)*, Skiathos, Greece, Sept. 2002, pp. 2901–2906.
4. Robert Morris, "Scalable TCP congestion control," in *IEEE INFOCOM 2000, Tel Aviv*, Mar. 2000, pp. 1176–1183.
5. Sally Floyd and Vern Paxson, "Difficulties in simulating the internet," *IEEE/ACM Transactions on Networking*, vol. 9, no. 4, pp. 392–403, Aug. 2001.
6. Will E. Leland, Murad S. Taqqu, Walter Willinger, and Daniel V. Wilson, "On the self-similar nature of ethernet traffic," Tech. Rep., Bellcore, Boston University, Mar. 1993.
7. Mark E. Crovella and Azer Bestavros, "Self-similarity in World Wide Web traffic: Evidence and possible causes," *IEEE/ACM Transactions on networking*, vol. 5, no. 6, pp. 835–846, Dec. 1997.
8. Vern Paxson and Sally Floyd, "Wide-area traffic: The failure of poisson modeling," *IEEE/ACM Transactions on Networking*, vol. 3, no. 3, pp. 226–244, June 1995.
9. Hyoung-Kee Choi and John O. Limb, "A behavioral model of web traffic," in *Proceedings of the Seventh Annual International Conference on Network Protocols, Toronto, Canada*, Nov. 1999.
10. University of California at Berkeley, "Ptolemy classic," http://ptolemy.eecs.berkeley.edu/ptolemyclassic/body.htm.
11. UCB/USC/LBNL/VINT, "Network simulator ns (version 2)," Avaliable from http://www.isi.edu/nsnam/ns/.
12. Mark E. Crovella and Azer Bestavros, "Explaining World Wide Web traffic self-similarity," Tech. Rep., Boston University, Oct. 1995.
13. Kihong Park, Gitae Kim, and Mark Crovella, "On the relationship between file sizes, transport protocols, and self-similar network traffic," Tech. Rep., Boston University, July 1996.
14. Michael Greiner, Manfred Jobmann, and Lester Lipsky, "The importance of power-tail distributions for modeling queueing systems," *Operations Research*, vol. 47, no. 2, 1999.
15. K. Below, C. Schwill, and U. Killat, "Erhöhung des Nutzungsgrades eines ATM Netzes für den Wissenschaftsbereich (ERNANI)," Tech. Rep., Dept. Communication Networks, Technical University Hamburg-Harburg, Sept. 2001, http://www.tu-harburg.de/et6/papers/documents/Below_Kai/Abschlussbericht-ERNANI.pdf.
16. P. Abry and D. Veitch, "Wavelet analysis of long-range-dependent traffic," *IEEE Transactions on Information Theory*, vol. 44, no. 1, pp. 2–15, 1998.
17. Darryl Veitch and Patrice Abry, "A wavelet based joint estimator of the parameters of long-range dependence," *IEEE Transactions on Information Theory*, vol. 45, no. 3, pp. 878–897, 1999.

A Measurement Study on Signaling in Gnutella Overlay Networks

K. Tutschku[1] and H. deMeer[2]

[1] Institute of Computer Science, University of Würzburg, Am Hubland, 97074 Würzburg, Germany. Tel.: +49-931-888-6641. FAX: +49-931-888-6632. E-mail: tutschku@informatik.uni-wuerzburg.de
[2] Department of Electronic & Electrical Engineering, University College London, Torrington Place, London WC1E 7JE, United Kingdom. Tel.: +44-20-7679-7308. FAX: +44-20-7388-9325. E-mail: H.DeMeer@ee.ucl.ac.uk

Abstract. In this paper we present a measurement study on signaling in Gnutella overlay networks. Both signaling load and the scale of variability in the existence of p2p overlay connections are investigated. The purpose of the study is to identify and understand characteristic scales of variability and stability of peer-to-peer overlay networks. The identified, typical scales should ultimately provide a basis for a dynamic management of peer-to-peer services. Unmanaged peer-to-peer service have often enough incubated a prohibitively large signaling traffic load.

1 Introduction

At first, the Internet was hailed for its capability of providing world-wide remote access to networked resources and its simple and powerful protocols for exchanging data, like SMTP, NNTP, FTP, or Telnet. The second generation Internet was marked by the introduction of the World Wide Web. It effectively and efficiently interconnected distributed information sources by using hyperlinks. The architecture of the Second Generation Internet, however, retained the traditional client/server concept. A relatively small number of fixed servers provide the vast majority of information and resources. A static placement of heavily used servers allows for traffic aggregation techniques to be applied.

The next, or Third Generation, Internet (TGI) could be dominated by loosely connected applications which would be located at network edges. TGI services are expected to be highly dynamic. Variable connectivity, variable addresses, and mobility are considered as the norm. Nodes will be highly autonomous and nodes participating in a group relationship will be characterized by symmetric roles. A node can have the role of a client, a server, or a router, all at the same time. In addition, future high-speed wire-line and wireless access technologies will provide instant high-bandwidth connectivity. These features may lead to dispersion of traffic sources throughout the network and may cause difficulties in controlling traffic flows on relatively small time scales. More traditional traffic engineering techniques, such as Traffic Load Flow Optimization or Multi-Hour dimensioning (see Annex 6 of [1]) may prove inadequate. It is anticipated that new planning and management principles are needed to address topics like reliability, security, or self-organized load-balancing. To compound matters, new methods will have to be robust with respect to dynamic environments.

In this paper we examine the dynamics of the Gnutella filesharing service as a typical representative of peer-to-peer (p2p) services. Both signalling overhead and the scale of variability in the existence of p2p overlay connections are investigated. The variability is characterized by two factors: a) the number of simultaneous overlay connections maintained by a peer and b) the duration of maintaining these connections. We present a first simple statistical model of the process of maintaining overlay connections and provide estimates on some model parameters.

The reminder of this paper is organized as follows. Section 2 briefly outlines the main features of a Gnutella filesharing service. Section 3 then describes the set-up of our measurement environment, discusses the measurement results, and presents a first statistical model of the variability of Gnutella overlays. Section 4 discusses the anticipated impact of TGI services on traffic engineering in future networks. Section 5 is the related work section. Section 6, finally, summarizes the paper.

2 The Gnutella Filesharing Service

The Gnutella service is a fully distributed, information sharing technology. It is based on a peer-to-peer model [2] and applies a distributed, open group membership and search protocol [3] [4]. The Gnutella service forms an application-specific overlay of Internet accessible hosts running Gnutella-speaking applications like LimeWire [5] or Gnut [6]. The Gnutella hosts may have multiple, simultaneous roles. As a client they provide user interfaces for issuing queries, viewing search results, and initiation of downloads. In server mode they accept in parallel queries from other nodes, check for matches against their local data set, respond with results, and manage the file transmission. In Gnutella context, a node is called a *servent (SERver + cliENT)*. The servents are also responsible for routing the *signaling traffic*. This traffic spreads information used to preserve network integrity and is needed to locate information. File downloads are performed outside of the overlay by a direct peer-to-peer connection between servents using HTTP protocol. Since the overlay is reserved for transmitting Gnutella control information it can be denoted as a *signaling overlay*.

The Gnutella protocol defines two categories of signaling messages: *A) Overlay Membership:* To discover additional hosts on the Gnutella network, servents use a "Ping/Pong" protocol. A servent issues a "Ping" message[1] to actively probe the network. A servent receiving a "Ping" is supposed to respond with a "Pong" message, containing the IP address and the amount of data it is sharing on the network. A "Ping" message can be answered with multiple "Pong" messages from multiple servents.

---

[1] The Gnutella "Ping" message should not be mistaken for the ICMP echo request message often colloquially also denoted as "Ping".

B) Searching Information: A piece of information is located in Gntutella via "Query" and "QueryHit" messages. A "Query" contains mainly the search criteria. A servent receiving a "Query" descriptor responds with a "QueryHit" message if a local match is found. A "QueryHit" message contains information to identify the replying servent in the IP address space as well as in the Gnutella domain. In addition, it contains file information such as local identifier, file size and file name.

Once a servent receives a "QueryHit" response, a user may trigger a download. A HTTP connection containing a GET request is directly established between the servents.

In order to join the Gnutella signaling overlay, a new servent connects (i.e. opens a TCP connection) to one of numerous well-known hosts that are always available, e.g. router.limewire.com. After having been connected successfully, servents send messages to interact with each other. The membership in the Gnutella overlay is granted to any servents sending the correct greeting string. Gnutella servents know only about servents which are directly connected to them. Other nodes are invisible unless they announce themselves. A node may maintain multiple simultaneous connections to other servents in the overlay. The maximal number of simultaneous connections can usually be configured by the user.

Signaling messages are routed in the overlay by using two simple principles: *a)* they are *broadcasted* to all neighbors, i.e. sent to all nodes with which the sender has open TCP connections, and *b)* responses are *back-propagated* in the overlay along the path taken by the triggering message.

An important feature of the Gnutella p2p filesharing services is that peers may join or leave the signaling overlay arbitrarily. To preserve network integrity, servents have to maintain multiple simultaneous connections. New overlay connections have to be initiated as soon as old ones terminate. Peers acquire new candidates for its overlay connections by sending periodically "Ping" messages to neighbors and inspecting "Pong" responses. Nodes base their decision where to connect to in the network on their local information. The Gnutella protocol doesn't provide any support for a coordinated organization of the signaling overlay. The Gnutella service forms an randomly structured overlay network.

3 Overlay Measurements

While qualitative justification is straightforward, little is known of quantitative results on the scale of dynamics in overlays and p2p applications. In particular, time scale and variability of the number of virtual overlay connection have to be characterized.

3.1 Measurement Set-Up

To analyze the signaling traffic in the Gnutella overlay, we modified a publicly available Gnutella command line application Gnut [6] to record all signaling

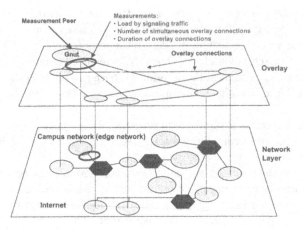

Fig. 1. Overlay measurements

packets with time stamp, payload size, and IP address where a packet was sent to or received from. The Gnut application was executed on an Linux-based PC. The PC was located inside the campus network of the University of Würzburg and was connected to the departmental network via FastEthernet. The measurement campaign was carried out in March 2002. The measurement duration was 60h. Figure 1 shows the position of the measurements in a simplified manner. The measurements have been performed on the edge network connection of the peer at overlay level.

3.2 Traffic Load

Figure 2 shows the sum of all signaling traffic load observed by the measurement peer. The depicted load is the total load of all simultaneous overlay connections. Figure 2 depicts solely traffic load generated by Gnutella search requests ("Query"), search replies ("QueryHit"), host queries ("Pings"), and host announcements ("Pongs"). No download traffic has contributed to the load shown in Figure 2. The load is averaged on 10sec intervals.

The observed average of signaling load was 0.274Mbps in the 10sec-intervals. The maximum was 50.9Mbps. Figure 2 has been prune to the range of 10Mbps in order to focus on the most relevant part of the graph. The figure depicts also the 95% percentile of the load, which is 1.03Mbps. In total, more than 7.06Gbyte of signaling traffic has been transmitted through the measurement peer during the 60h. That data volume, which is equivalent to ten Video-CDs with 700Mbyte each and without any immediate benefit to the user. The high overhead is due to the use of broadcast mechanisms in the Gnutella protocol. The Gnutella overlay network is flooded with signaling information. Moreover, the better the peer's connection to the overlay, the faster messages are forwarded to it. A control of the traffic load is difficult. With the exception of a TTL (Time-To-Life) field, the Gnutella protocol doesn't contain any mechanisms to control the signaling. Traffic control has to be implemented locally and independently on each peer.

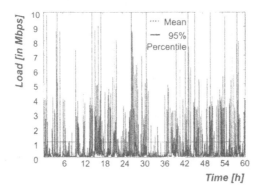

Fig. 2. Sum of signaling traffic load

3.3 Overlay Variability

The variability in the p2p overlay can be characterized by two factors: a) the number of simultaneous overlay relations maintained by a peer and b) the duration of maintaining these relations. The term "relation duration" as used in this paper denotes the time between the first and the last instance of information exchange between the measurement peer and a particular other peer. A peer is identified by its IP address and the TCP port number used by the Gnutella application running on this peer. A peer-to-peer relation may therefore last several physical connections between some peers. The term "connection", however, is not fully appropriate in the context of p2p services. Many signaling messages may be exchanged between some peers, while the same peers may repeatedly join or leave the overlay.

Number of simultaneous overlay relations: A peer tries to maintain a given number of relations. The number can be configured by the user and has been fixed here at 20 relations for the measurement peer. If, for instance, a peer maintains less relations than configured, it picks out an arbitrary host announcement and tries to establish a new relation to this host.

Figure 3 depicts the number of simultaneous p2p relations maintained by the measurement peer during the measurement period. Although the peer was configured to keep up with 20 relations, it maintained only an average of 9.86 relations. Most importantly, however, the connectivity process reveals a very high variability and is far from being constant.[2]

If the connectivity of a peer is high, i.e., a peer maintains high number of simultaneous overlay relations, many signaling messages will be forwarded to it. If bandwidth is not sufficiently available an overload situation is caused in the physical network. If the connectivity of a peer is low, i.e., a peer maintains a small number of relations, then a peer might not receive enough signaling information

---

[2] Figure 3 shows also that the measurement peer occasionally maintained more than 20 connections. This is an implementation feature of the Gnut client.

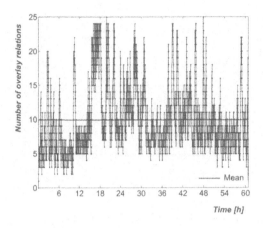

Fig. 3. Number of simultaneous overlay relations

to discover new hosts and new resources. In an extreme case, a peer might drop out of the overlay network and has to be re-connected to a well-known peer. That may cause a severe disruption of the service. This characteristic suggests the existence of an optimal level of connectivity. But rather than consistently maintaining an optimal level of connectivity, connectivity fluctuates widely in unmanaged p2p environments.

The high variability in number of simultaneous overlay relations indicates that management might be needed in order to maintain the optimal point of operation for a peer under given performance and reliability constrains.

Distribution of the relation time: The distribution of the relation times of peers is the second factor in the variability of the overlay.

The measurement peer has exchanged signaling messages with 5320 distinct peers and has monitored the duration of the relation times. Figure 4 a) depicts the histogram of the relation durations observed by the measurement peer. The mean relation holding time is $4.05 \cdot 10^2$sec. The histogram shows also the 90%-percentile, which is between $1.28 \cdot 10^{-1}$sec and $1.28 \cdot 10^3$sec and which reaches over four orders of magnitudes in the time scale. The median is at $6.88 \cdot 10^1$sec. In addition, Figure 4 a) reveals clearly a distribution with two modes. The separating minimum is located at about 10sec. The characteristic indicates that the p2p relation is governed by multiple states.

From user's point of view, the participation in a p2p overlay is fruitful when peers receive sufficient content information. That way, peers might use and contribute resources to the p2p community in a valuable way. Hence the volume of *incoming signaling traffic* was examined in greater detail. The traffic was correlated with the relation times.

Figure 5 and Figure 6 show the correlation of the relation times for the complete amount of incoming signaling data transmitted during existence of a p2p relation. Each point in the diagrams stand for a single relation. The abscissa

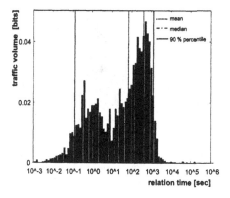

(a) all relations

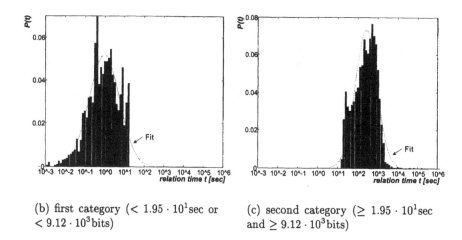

(b) first category ($< 1.95 \cdot 10^1$sec or $< 9.12 \cdot 10^3$bits)

(c) second category ($\geq 1.95 \cdot 10^1$sec and $\geq 9.12 \cdot 10^3$bits)

Fig. 4. Relation times observed by the measurement peer

axis denotes the relation duration and the ordinate represents the transmitted amount of signaling data in this relation.

Figure 5 depicts the 90% percentile for the relation duration (vertical lines) and the traffic volume (horizontal lines). The average and the median are indicated by dotted and dashed lines. The figure allows the identification of two discriminating values which correspond to the lower bound of the percentile. For the relation times a separating value of $3.90 \cdot 10^{-1}$sec and for the signaling traffic volume a total of $1.54 \cdot 10^4$ bits are indicated. The lower bounds of the 90% percentile on the time axis and the 90% percentile on volume axis describe the range of beneficial overlay relation. During this relations either sufficient host or search information is exchanged between peers. The separating values become even more evident when the correlation is performed for the individual Gnutella protocol entities. Figure 6(a) depicts the correlation for "Query" packets, i.e.,

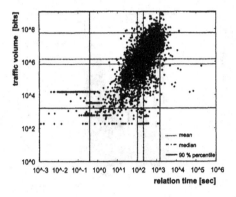

Fig. 5. Correlation of relation times and amount of incoming signaling data: all information (content and host)

for file search requests only. The lower bounds of the 90% percentiles for relation duration and signaling volume are at $1.95 \cdot 10^1$sec and $9.12 \cdot 10^3$ bits. A similar behavior is also visible for "QueryHit" packets, cf. Figure 6(b).

In contrast to the behavior of "Query" and "QueryHit" packets, the correlation analysis for "Ping" packets, i.e., host query packets, shows that a considerable number p2p relations exist which have a duration of less than 10sec. In this case the transmitted amount of signaling information is small, see Figure 6(c), and typically less than 10^4 bits. This is also the case for "Pong" packets, i.e. host announcement information, see Figure 6(d).

3.4 Statistical Model

Based on the correlation analysis the histogram of relation times was re-assessed. The p2p relation times are filtered and divided into two disjoint categories. The categories are determined by the lower bounds of the 90% percentiles of the relation times and traffic volume for queries (see Figure 6(a)). The first category contains overlay relations which last less then $1.95 \cdot 10^1$sec and have less than $9.12 \cdot 10^3$ bits signaling volume, see Figure 4(b), and contains 39.0% of the relations (2077 relations out of the total of 5320). The second category has relation times greater than $1.95 \cdot 10^1$sec and traffic volume of more than $9.12 \cdot 10^3$ bits, see Figure 4(c). The category comprises 61.0% of the relations (3243 out of 5320). In both categories the shape of the histogram of relation times may be approximated by a normal probability distribution. Since the abscissa axis in Figure 4 is of logarithmic scale, it is indicated that relation duration in the two classes are distributed according to *log-normal* distribution function:

$$f(x) = \frac{1}{x\sqrt{2\pi\sigma^2}}e^{\frac{-(\ln x - \mu)^2}{2\sigma^2}}. \tag{1}$$

The fitted distributions are added to the histograms of Figures 4(b) and 4(c). Visual inspection of these figures shows that the fit is remarkably well.

303

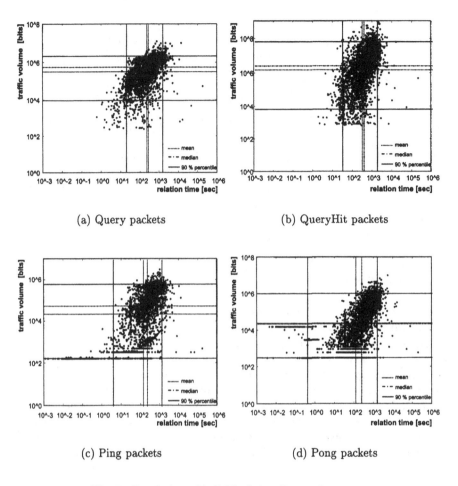

(a) Query packets   (b) QueryHit packets

(c) Ping packets   (d) Pong packets

Fig. 6. Correlation of individual signaling packet types

This indicates in this case that the log-normal distribution appears as a valid statistical model for states which conduct the set-up of overlay relations. Table 1 provides the values (measured and fitted) for the mean and the variance of the relation durations in the two categories.

Significance for P2P Overlays: The correlation analysis leads to a two-state model for Gnutella p2p overlay relations. In the first state, which is called the "short" state, a peer establishes only short-lived connections to other peers. The involved peers exchange some signaling information, typically only host information, and the relation is terminated immediately. In the other state a peer establishes a long-duration relation and exchanges continuously signaling messages, mostly search requests. From the perspective of a user, this state can

	Mean		Variance	
Category / State	Measurement	Fit	Measurement	Fit
1 / "short"	3.01 sec	1.85 sec	$1.98 \cdot 10^1$ sec^2	9.99 sec^2
2 / "stable"	$5.93 \cdot 10^2$ sec	$3.63 \cdot 10^2$ sec	$1.24 \cdot 10^7$ sec^2	$1.29 \cdot 10^5$ sec^2

Table 1. Measured and fitted parameters for relation duration

be called "stable" state, since it permits uninterrupted operation of the p2p service.

The characteristic of log-normal distributed p2p relations indicates that the majority of peers in the stable phase reside in the system for the same average amount of time. A significant number of peers, however, may stay longer than the average. This result supports the view that few peers are more powerful and durable than other peers [7].

4 Possible Impact of Scale of Dynamics on Traffic Management

The observed scales in Gnutella signaling overlay, i.e., signaling volume, number of simultaneous relations, and duration, indicate that traffic management and traffic engineering for future generation Internet will require new approaches. Future applications allow for a permanent coming and going of service requests, resources offerings, and service consumption. In this way they permit an easy forming and dissolving of groups. Reed's findings on *Group Forming Networks (GFN)* [8] demonstrate that the value of GFN networks, which is defined as the number of possible communication relationships, scales exponentially with the number N of participants. Abbreviated, the number of non-trivial subsets that can be formed from a set of N members is $2^N - N - 1$, which grows as 2^N. Even when its participants transmit with probability significantly smaller than one, that relationship still indicates that signaling traffic will grow dramatically. As the measurements on p2p services reveal , that characteristics is already visible in today's networks. Application, protocol, and network design for tomorrow's Internet has to provide mechanisms to reduce the effect.

The group communication support by future applications will additionally lead to the dispersion of traffic sources throughout the network and may also cause difficulties in estimating traffic flows on small time scales. The *scale of dynamics* of future application-specific service overlays might be in the range of the variability of today's p2p overlays. As the measurements of the variability of the Gnutella overlay have shown, cf. Section 3.3, this will be on a time-scale in the order of 10s of minutes. This characteristic prevents the future use today's traffic engineering techniques, such as Traffic Load Flow Optimization or Multi-Hour dimensioning (see Annex 6 of [1]).

The new services offered by future Internet will be built on node autonomy and on symmetric roles of networked nodes. The applications specific overlays may contest for network capacities [9]. In contrast, current IP Quality-of-Service (QoS) design favours the differentiation of traffic, e.g., by explicit use of ToS

(Type-of-Service) bits to select QoS, and avoids congestion. To provide attractive overlay services, future services will have to include self-organization mechanisms on application layer. The mechanisms should be able to observe overlay load and be adaptive on small timescales.

An absence of any traffic engineering, as currently observed with many p2p overlays, will lead to a reduction of the service quality of these services. The service performs well for users with high bandwidth access, i.e., they perceive high throughput for downloads. On the down side, a large amount of signaling traffic is also forwarded to these peers and has to be handled. Considerable bandwidth is consumed without getting immediate benefit. It is anticipated that a management architecture will be needed that can handle specific granularities in time as well as in space to enable dynamic and adaptive operation of future virtual overlay networks.

5 Related Work

Various measurement studies of Gnutella have been performed recently. The first analysis was carried out by E. Adar et al. [7]. Their measurements have shown that there is a strong asymmetry between content providers and content consumers. Nearly 70% of the Gnutella users share no files, and nearly 50% of all responses are returned by the top 1% of sharing hosts. The main results of the measurement done by S. Saroiu et al. [10] was the characterization of end-user hosts participating in Gnutella. The characterization provided numbers and distributions for bottleneck bandwidth, IP-level latencies, how often hosts connect and disconnect from the overlay, and the degree of cooperation between the peers. Jovanovic et al. [11] investigated the connectivity and the degree of cooperation between peers. Their results evidence that degree distribution of the Gnutella network topology follows a *Power-law*. Similar measurements were accomplished by M. Ripeanu et al. [4]. These measurements acknowledged that Power-law in the degree distribution was present in an early stage of the Gnutella overlay, however this characteristics has declined recently. A recent measurement study was performed by J. Vaucher et al. [12]. Their measurements and experiments have shown that the composition of the community changes quite rapidly.

The measurements presented in this paper complement the ones reported in previous publications. The focus of the investigations discussed here, is on the variability in the overlay of the Gnutella service. This aspect was not yet properly addressed in previous research, but is expected to have significant impact on traffic engineering in future networks.

6 Conclusions

In this paper we have presented a measurement study on signaling in Gnutella overlay networks. Both signaling load and the scale of variability in the existence of p2p overlay connections have been investigated. The variability was characterized by two factors: a) the number of simultaneous overlay connections maintained by a peer and b) the duration of maintaining these connections. We presented a first simple statistical model of the process of maintaining overlay connections and provided estimates on some model parameters. It has been validated by measurements that P2P services are prone to highly variable connectivity patterns and traffic load profiles.

Today's peer-to-peer networks exhibit signaling characteristics that are anticipated to be typical for the future services of the Third Generation Internet. We expect a new management architecture to be needed for TGI that can handle specific granularities in time as well as in space to enable dynamic and adaptive operation of future virtual overlay networks. Highly flexible resource and network management methods are required. The upcoming challenges caused by introducing new networking services on demand with significantly reduced provisioning cycles brings that even more into focus.

References

1. G. Ash, "Traffic Engineering & QoS Methods for IP-, ATM-, & TDM-Based Multiservice Networks," Internet draft: <draft-ietf-tewg-qos-routing-04.txt> available at www.ietf.org, IETF, 2001.
2. D. Barkai, *Peer-to-Peer Computing*, Intel Press, Hillsborow, OR, 2001.
3. Anonymous, "The Gnutella protocol," available at http://gnutelladev.wego.com, GnutellaDev, 2001.
4. M. Ripeanu and I. Foster, "Mapping gnutella network," in *1st International Workshop on Peer-to-Peer Systems (IPTPS02), Cambridge, Massachusetts, March 2002.*
5. Anonymous, "LimeWire Version 2.4," available at http://www.limewire.com/, Lime Wire LCC, 2002.
6. Anonymous, "Gnut - console Gnutella client for Linux and Windows," available at http://www.gnutelliums.com/linux_unix/gnut/, 2001.
7. Eytan Adar and Bernardo A. Huberman, "Free riding on gnutella," Research report, Xerox Palo Alto Research Center, October 2000.
8. D. Reed, "The law of the pack," *Havard Business Review*, February 1st 2001.
9. D. Clark, K. Sollins, J. Wroclawski, and R. Braden, "Tussle in cyberspace: Defining tomorrow's internet," in *Proceedings of the ACM SIGCOMM Conference 2002, Pittsburgh, 19-23 August, 2002.*
10. S. Saroiu, P. Gummadi, and S. Gribble, "A measurement study of peer-to-peer file sharing systems," in *SPIE Multimedia Computing and Networking (MMCN2002), San Jose, CA, Jan 18-25, 2002.*
11. M. Jovanovic, F. Annexstein, and K. Berman, "Scalability issues in large peer-to-peer networks - a case study of gnutella," Technical report, University of Cincinnati, 2001.
12. J. Vaucher, P. Kropf, G. Babin, and T. Jouve, "Experimenting with gnutella communities," in *Distributed Communities on the Web (DCW 2002), Sydney, Australia, Apr. 2002.*

Simulationsbasierte Konnektivitätsanalyse von gleich– und normalverteilten drahtlosen Sensornetzen

Christian Bettstetter und Clemens Moser

Technische Universität München (TUM)
Lehrstuhl für Kommunikationsnetze (Prof. Eberspächer)
D–80290 München, Germany, www.lkn.ei.tum.de

Zusammenfassung Diese Arbeit untersucht die Konnektivität in draht-losen Sensornetzen. Insbesondere wird ermittelt, wie viele Sensoren n mit bekannter Funkreichweite r_0 auf einer gegebenen Fläche mindestens nötig sind, um mit einer hohen Wahrscheinlichkeit p ein k–fach zusam-menhängendes Netz zu erhalten. Verglichen werden die Ergebnisse auf einer quadratischen und kreisförmigen Fläche mit gleichverteilten Sen-soren. Ein weiterer Beitrag ist die Untersuchung der Konnektivität von normalverteilten Sensoren mit verschiedener Varianz.

1 Einleitung

Drahtlose Sensornetze sind dezentrale, selbstorganisierende Funknetze, in de-nen elektromechanische Sensoren, ausgestattet mit kostengünstigen Transcei-vern, miteinander kommunizieren. Zwei Sensoren müssen dabei nicht notwen-digerweise in direktem Funkkontakt zueinander stehen, sondern können über bestehende Verbindungen anderer Sensoren hinweg, also über mehrere Hops, miteinander in Kontakt treten. Es gibt im Allgemeinen keine zentrale Instanz, die das so gebildete Multihop–Netz steuert oder kontrolliert. Jeder Sensor ent-scheidet selbstständig, ob und wie eine erhaltene Nachricht weiterzuleiten ist.

Solche verteilten Systeme finden vielseitige Anwendungsmöglichkeiten. Im mi-litärischen Bereich entwickelt man den so genannten „Sensorstaub". Eine Viel-zahl von Sensoren, z. B. Photosensoren, wird von einem Flugzeug aus abgewor-fen, und am Boden bilden diese Sensoren ein drahtloses Multihop–Netz [1][2]. Aus den aufgenommenen Einzelinformationen der Sensoren können Bilder der Umgebung zusammengesetzt oder Bewegungen erkannt werden. Aber auch zi-vile Anwendungen sind von hohem Interesse, beispielsweise zur Vernetzung von Biosensoren im medizinischen Bereich oder von Messgeräten und Robotern in In-dustrieanlagen und in der Luft– und Raumfahrt [3]. In den letzten Jahren wurde, insbesondere in den USA, die Forschung und Entwicklung im Bereich drahtloser Sensornetze intensiviert. Einen Überblick über aktuelle Forschungsthemen findet man in [2], [4] und [5].

308

Diese Arbeit untersucht eine fundamentale Eigenschaft eines solchen Netzes: seine *Konnektivität*. Während es in „konventionellen" Mobilfunknetzen ausreicht, dass eine Mobilstation eine direkte Funkverbindung zur Basisstation besitzt, ist die Situation in verteilten Multihop–Systemen komplexer: Um ein zusammenhängendes Netz zu erhalten, muss jeder Netzknoten zu jedem anderen Netzknoten einen drahtlosen Multihop–Pfad besitzen.

Grundsätzliche Fragen zur Ausbreitung von Nachrichten und zur Konnektivität in verteilten Multihop–Systemen wurden bereits in [6], [7] und [8] diskutiert. Im Jahr 1998 haben Gupta und Kumar dieses Thema in dem mathematischen Artikel [9] wieder aufgegriffen, und kürzlich lieferten Santi und Blough [10][11], Bettstetter [12], Dousse *et al.* [13] und Hellbrück [14] neue Beiträge.

In dem Artikel [12] wurde die Konnektivität eines drahtlosen Multihop–Netzes per Simulation und mit analytischen Methoden aus der Zufallsgraphentheorie untersucht. Hierbei wurde davon ausgegangen, dass die Sensoren zufällig gleichverteilt positioniert werden und alle Sensoren die gleiche Funkreichweite haben. Der vorliegende Artikel ist eine Fortsetzung unserer Arbeit in diesem Gebiet. Nach der Beschreibung der Modellierungsannahmen, einigen graphentheoretischen Grundlagen und der Beschreibung unserer Simulationsmethodik (Kapitel 2), vertiefen wir in Kapitel 3 unsere Erkenntnisse und Ergebnisse zur Konnektivität mit gleichverteilten Sensoren. Wir untersuchen die minimale Funkreichweite, die eine definierte Zahl gleichverteilter Sensoren auf einer definierten Fläche besitzen müssen, so dass das resultierende Sensornetz mit sehr hoher Wahrscheinlichkeit ($p = 95\%$, $p = 99\%$) verbunden ist. Wie auch schon in [12] betrachten wir zusätzlich fehlertolerante Sensornetze, bei denen ein oder zwei beliebige Sensoren ausfallen können aber das Netz immer noch verbunden bleibt. Auch für diesen Fall geben wir die nötigen Parameterpaare für Funkreichweite und Anzahl der Sensoren an. Wir vergleichen die Ergebnisse auf einer quadratischen und kreisförmigen Fläche und zeigen exemplarisch eine Näherungsformel für die minimale Funkreichweite bei gegebener Anzahl an Sensoren. In Kapitel 4 betrachten wir normalverteilte örtliche Sensorverteilungen und untersuchen, wie sich die Varianz dieser Normalverteilung auf die Konnektivität des Sensornetzes auswirkt. Die Annahme einer Normalverteilung der Sensoren ist insbesondere für den Anwendungsfall „Sensorstaub" brauchbar. Abschließend fasst Kapitel 5 die wichtigsten Erkenntnisse zusammen.

2 Modellierung, Problemstellung & Simulationsmethodik

Die Topologie eines drahtlosen Sensornetzes, d. h. die Positionen der einzelnen Sensoren (Knoten) und deren Verbindungen (Links), ist geprägt von der örtlichen Sensorverteilung über einem wohldefinierten Gebiet der Fläche A. Zwei bedeutsame Parameter sind die Sensorzahl n (engl.: *number of nodes*) sowie die Sende– und Empfangsreichweite r_0 (engl.: *range*) eines Sensors. Die Sendereichweite ist eine Funktion der Sendeleistung eines Sensors und der Ausbreitungsbedingungen der Umgebung. In der Praxis ist man bestrebt, die Sendereichweiten aus mehreren Gründen möglichst gering zu halten. Zum einen spielt die Größe und Lebensdauer von Batterien eine wichtige Rolle, zum anderen wird durch große Sendereichweiten die Interferenz erhöht und die räumliche Mehrfachnutzung von Kanälen erschwert. In dieser Arbeit werden die Sende- und Empfangsreichweiten von allen n Sensoren als gleich angenommen. Diese Annahme ist zum Beispiel gerechtfertigt, wenn Sensoren eines einzigen Typs im freien Raum eingesetzt werden und keine Leistungsregelung verwendet wird. Nun hat jeder Sensor die Möglichkeit, mit anderen Sensoren innerhalb eines Kreises mit Radius r_0 um seine Koordinaten direkt zu kommunizieren. Modelliert man dieses Sensornetz als Graph G, so entstehen ungerichtete Kanten (Links) zwischen den Knoten (Sensoren), deren Abstand kleiner als r_0 ist.

Im Folgenden verwenden wir Standardbegriffe aus der Graphentheorie [15]. Grundsätzlich wird dort zwischen Knoten- und Kantenkonnektivität unterschieden. In dieser Arbeit wird jedoch nur die Knotenkonnektivität betrachtet. Im Weiteren wird daher — wie auch in der Graphentheorie üblich — nur noch von Konnektivität an Stelle von Knotenkonnektivität gesprochen. Ein Graph G ist zusammenhängend (engl.: *connected*), wenn zwischen jedem Knotenpaar ein Pfad existiert. Ein Graph G heißt k-fach zusammenhängend (engl.: *k-connected*), wenn nach Entfernen von $k' < k$ beliebigen Knoten der verbleibende Graph G' immer noch zusammenhängend ist. Demzufolge ist es erforderlich, mindestens k Knoten — und alle von ihnen ausgehenden Kanten — zu entfernen, um den Zusammenhang von G zu zerstören. Äquivalent zu dieser Definition ist nach Menger's Theorem ein Graph k-fach zusammenhängend dann, und nur dann, wenn es wenigstens k knotendisjunkte Pfade gibt, die jedes Paar von Knoten verbinden. Diese Analogie zwischen der minimalen Anzahl unabhängiger Wege und der maximalen Zahl von Knotenausfällen, die ein Netz verkraftet, ist auch in Sensornetzen von elementarer Bedeutung.

In dieser Arbeit werden quantitative Aussagen über die Konnektivität in Sensornetzen gewonnen. Dabei bezeichnen wir die Wahrscheinlichkeit, dass ein Netz mit den Parametern (r_0, n) auf einer Fläche A verbunden ist mit P_{con}. Die Wahrscheinlichkeiten für 2- und 3-fach verbundene Netze sind mit P_{2-con} bzw. P_{3-con} bezeichnet. Zur Abschätzung dieser Wahrscheinlichkeiten werden rechnergestützte Simulationen verwendet. Dabei berechnen wir über eine große Zahl von Pseudo-Zufallstopologien die relativen Häufigkeiten

$$h_{k-con} = \frac{\# \ k\text{-fach verbunde Zufallstopologien}}{\# \ \text{Zufallstopologien}}, \quad k = 1, 2, 3,$$

die gemäß der statistischen Definition der Wahrscheinlichkeit gegen die gesuchten Wahrscheinlichkeiten P_{con}, P_{2-con} und P_{3-con} konvergieren. Alle durchgeführten Simulationen basieren auf 10 000 Zufallstopologien. Die Knotenverteilung wird mit einem Zufallsgenerator hoher Güte namens „Mersenne Twister" [16] erzeugt.

Kleine Parameterpaare (r_0, n) liefern $P_{con} = 0$. Erhöht man einen oder beide Parameter, so steigt P_{con} an, bis schließlich $P_{con} \to 100\%$ für große r_0 bzw. n

erreicht wird. Gesucht wird nun nach der nötigen minimalen Sendereichweite r_0 der Sensoren, um bei gegebener Anzahl n und gefordertem k eine vorgegebene Konnektivitätswahrscheinlichkeit P_{k-con} zu erhalten. Ein äquivalentes Problem stellt die Suche nach der notwendigen Knotenzahl n bei gegebener Reichweite r_0 und gegebener Wahrscheinlichkeit P_{k-con} dar. Dies entspricht den Funktionen $r_0 = f(n, P_{k-con})$ bzw. $n = f(r_0, P_{k-con})$. Der einzige Unterschied besteht in der Natur der gesuchten Größen: während die Knotenzahl n einen diskreten Charakter aufweist, lässt sich die Reichweite r_0 als kontinuierliche Größe im Prinzip beliebig genau bestimmen. Zusammenfassend werden also die kleinstmöglichen (r_0, n)-Paare gesucht, bei denen das resultierende Sensornetz zum ersten Mal mit einer Wahrscheinlichkeit P_{k-con} k-fach verbunden ist. Da wir primär an hohen Konnektivitätswahrscheinlichkeiten interessiert sind, fordern wir $P_{k-con} = 95\%$ bzw. in einer zweiten Simulationsreihe $P_{k-con} = 99\%$. Außerdem interessieren uns die (r_0, n)-Paare für Netze, die mit hoher Wahrscheinlichkeit *nicht* verbunden sind ($P_{con} = 5\%$).

Zur Bestimmung der (r_0, n)-Werte wurde ein Simulationstool in C++ geschrieben. Dieses enthält Methoden und Datenstrukturen zur Generierung von Zufallstopologien, zur Überprüfung der Konnektivität für $k = 1, 2, 3$ und zur Generierung eines minimalen Spannbaums (engl:. *minimum spanning tree*) zwischen gegebenen Knoten. Grundsätzlich steigt die Komplexität der Konnektivitätsüberprüfung mit der Knotenzahl n, der Sendereichweite r_0 und der Anzahl der Zufallstopologien an. Speziell bei hohem n ist die Bestimmung der 95% und 99%–Konnektivität ein rechenintensives Problem. Ein wahlloses „Ausprobieren", welche (r_0, n)-Paare der geforderten Konnektivitätswahrscheinlichkeit nahe kommen ist also nicht sinnvoll. Deshalb wurde eine „Regelschleife" implementiert, die sich bei gegebenem n an den gesuchten Parameter r_0 von kleinen Werten her „intelligent" annähert und die Genauigkeit der Ergebnisse, d. h. die Anzahl der Zufallstopologien schrittweise erhöht. Betrachten wir eine Simulation mit $n = 100$ Sensoren für $k = 2$ und $P_{2-con} = 99\%$: Zu Beginn wird r_0 schrittweise inkrementiert, bis zum ersten Mal 99 von 100 Zufallstopologien zweifach verbunden sind. Diese Funkreichweite wird nun mit 1 000 Zufallstopologien simuliert, und aufgrund der Ergebnisse wird entschieden, ob r_0 erhöht oder erniedrigt wird. Der Wert für r_0 wird so lange verändert, bis in einer Simulationsreihe von 1 000 Topologien mindestens 985 und höchstens 995 Topologien zweifach zusammenhängend sind. Auf ähnliche Weise wird der Regelalgorithmus fortgesetzt. Am Ende ist garantiert, dass 10 000 Zufallstopologien mit einem Wertepaar (r_0, n) simuliert werden und die relative Häufigkeit h_{2-con} mit einer maximalen absoluten Abweichung von ± 0.005 erfüllt wird. Der erhaltene Wert für r_0 kann nun als Startwert für die Simulation mit reduzierter Sensoranzahl (z. B. $n = 90$) dienen, und die Regelschleife kann wieder mit 100 Zufallstopologien beginnen.

Zusätzlich zu dieser Regelschleife wurde eine alternative Methode für einfache Konnektivität ($k = 1$) implementiert: Es werden n Sensoren gleichverteilt zufällig platziert, zwischen denen ein minimaler Spannbaum konstruiert wird. Die längste Kante dieses Spannbaums repräsentiert die minimale Funkreichweite, die nötig ist, um den Graphen zusammenhängend zu halten. Die Länge dieser Kante wird anschließend diskretisiert und die Häufigkeit der Längen von 10 000 Spannbäumen in einem Histogramm aufgetragen. Nach einer Normierung und Aufsummierung erhält man daraus eine Schätzung der Verteilungsfunktion der kritischen Kantenlängen, aus der $r_0 = f(n, P_{con})$ abgelesen wird.

3 Gleichverteilung der Sensoren

3.1 Quadratische Fläche

Zunächst werden auf einer Fläche der Größe $A = 1000 \times 1000$ m^2 für gewünschtes P_{con} die notwendigen Sendereichweiten r_0 in Abhängigkeit von der Sensorzahl n ermittelt. Die drei Kurven in Abb. 1a kennzeichnen diejenigen Wertepaare (r_0, n), bei denen von 10 000 Zufallsgraphen gerade 500, 9 500 bzw. 9 900 mindestens einfach zusammenhängend sind. Statistisch gesehen sind das die Kurven, auf denen alle Graphen liegen, die mit einer Wahrscheinlichkeit von 5%, 95% bzw. 99% verbunden sind. Diese Kurven können auch als Höhenlinien der zweidimensionalen Wahrscheinlichkeitsdichtefunktion $f_{con}(r_0, n)$ über der r_0/n–Ebene interpretiert werden.

Wählt man ein Parameterpaar (r_0, n) unter der 5%–Linie, so trifft man mit großer Sicherheit kein zusammenhängendes Sensornetz an. Werte auf oder oberhalb der Linie „95%–connected" führen mit hoher Wahrscheinlichkeit zu einem zusammenhängenden Netz. Wählt man ein Parameterpaar (r_0, n) auf oder oberhalb der Linie „99%–connected", sind mit an Sicherheit grenzender Wahrscheinlichkeit (engl.: *almost surely*) alle Knotenpaare über einen Pfad verbunden. Bei $n = 200$ Sensoren führen beispielsweise alle Sendereichweiten $r_0 \leq 100$ m zu einem unzusammenhängenden Netz. Ab dem Wert $r_0 \approx 150$ m bzw. $r_0 \approx 170$ m ist das Netz dann mit einer Wahrscheinlichkeit von 95% bzw. 99% zusammenhängend. Man erkennt außerdem, dass erst Knotenzahlen $n \geq 600$ auf dieser Fläche für $P_{con} = 0.99$ zu Reichweiten unter 100 m führen.

Wichtig dabei ist, dass sich die in Abb. 1 angegebenen kritischen Werte für r_0 für quadratische Flächen beliebiger Größe $A = a \times a$ skalieren lassen, d. h. $r_0(a) = \frac{r_0(1000 \text{ m})}{1000 \text{ m}} \cdot a$, wobei $r_0(1000 \text{ m})$ die Werte aus Abb. 1 repräsentiert.

Abbildung 1b zeigt schließlich die 99%–Linien für zweifach und dreifach zusammenhängende Sensornetze. In diesem Fall sind klarerweise erhöhte Sendereichweiten (bzw. mehr Sensoren) nötig. Zum Beispiel benötigt man nun $n = 260$ statt 200 Sensoren mit der Reichweite $r_0 = 170$ m, um mit einer Wahrscheinlichkeit von 99% das Netz zweifach zusammenhängend zu bekommen. Zusätzlich zu der Tatsache, dass jetzt ein bzw. zwei beliebige Sensoren ausfallen können, ohne die Konnektivität des Netzes zu gefährden, entstehen alternative Pfade zwischen jedem Sensorpaar, die unter anderem zur Lastteilung bei der Verkehrslenkung verwendet werden können (*multipath routing*). Zwei unabhängige Pfade in einem Sensornetz sind sowohl knoten- also auch kantendisjunkt.

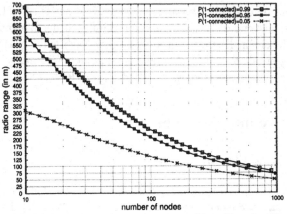

a) Kritische (r_0, n)–Paare für $P_{con} = 5\%$, 95% und 99%

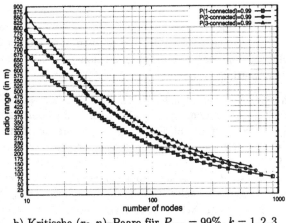

b) Kritische (r_0, n)–Paare für $P_{con} = 99\%$, $k = 1, 2, 3$

Abbildung 1. Konnektivität von gleichverteilten Sensoren auf $A = 1000 \times 1000 \text{ m}^2$.

3.2 Kreisförmige Fläche

Weitere Simulationen wurden auf einer kreisförmigen Fläche mit dem Radius $R = \frac{1}{\sqrt{\pi}} 1000$ m gemacht, d. h. mit einem Flächeninhalt von wiederum $A = 1000^2 \text{ m}^2$. Wie auch schon im letzten Abschnitt kann man die Ergebnisse auf Kreisflächen durch eine Normierung mit dem Radius der Simulationsfläche verallgemeinern. Trotz des gleichen Flächeninhalts verlaufen die $r_0(n)$–Kurven deutlich tiefer, d. h. eine geringere Reichweite bzw. geringere Knotenzahlen als auf dem Quadrat sind ausreichend um die gleiche Konnektivität zu erhalten.

Es lässt sich leicht einsehen, dass neben der Größe auch die Form der Fläche Einfluss auf die Konnektivität hat. Um der Definition der Konnektivität zu

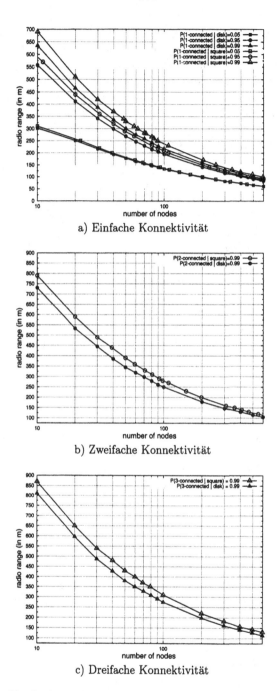

a) Einfache Konnektivität

b) Zweifache Konnektivität

c) Dreifache Konnektivität

Abbildung 2. Vergleich der Konnektivität auf einer Kreisscheibe (engl.: *disk*) und einem Quadrat (engl.: *square*), $A = 1000^2$ m^2

genügen, muss jeder Sensor erreichbar sein. Die Nichtexistenz von isolierten Sensoren ist also eine notwendige, jedoch nicht hinreichende Bedingung, um ein verbundenes Sensornetz zu erhalten. Bezeichnen wir mit $P_{noiso}(r_0, n)$ die Wahrscheinlichkeit, dass kein Sensor im Netz isoliert ist. Diese Wahrscheinlichkeit ist im Allgemeinen eine obere Grenze für $P_{con}(r_0, n)$. In [12] haben wir jedoch — mit Hilfe eines Theorems aus der Zufallsgraphentheorie — erörtert, dass $P_{con}(r_0, n) \approx P_{noiso}(r_0, n)$ für Werte nahe 100% gilt. Und gerade an diesen hohen Konnektivitätswerten sind wir interessiert.

Generell entstehen isolierte Sensoren bei hohen Konnektivitätswahrscheinlichkeiten bevorzugt im Randgebiet der Fläche. Die Verbesserung der Konnektivität auf einem Kreis gegenüber einem Quadrat ist zu erklären, da ein Quadrat in den Ecken einen besonders ausgeprägten Randeffekt (engl.: *border effect, edge effect*, siehe z. B. [17][18]) aufweist. Ein Sensor in der Ecke eines Quadrats hat im Mittel nur ein Viertel so viele Nachbarsensoren als ein Sensor in der Mitte. Deshalb ist seine Wahrscheinlichkeit, isoliert (d. h. ohne Nachbarn) zu sein besonders hoch. Auf einer Kreisfläche hingegen ist die Anzahl der zu erwartenden Nachbarn eines Sensors am Rand nur etwa halb so groß als die eines Sensors ohne Randeffekt (für $r_0 \ll R$). Tatsächlich liegt die Schlussfolgerung nahe, dass auf einer kreisförmigen Fläche im Vergleich zu anderen Flächenformen die höchsten Konnektivitätswahrscheinlichkeiten erzielt werden, da die Randeffekte minimiert sind.

3.3 Regression

Für die simulierte r_0/n–Kurve mit $P_{con} = 0.99$ auf einer quadratischen Fläche der Kantenlänge 1 m wird nun beispielhaft eine Regressionsformel angegeben. Ein Polynom mit 10 Koeffizienten liefert bereits eine sehr genaue Wiedergabe der aus der Simulation gewonnenen Kurve. Mit Hilfe der „Gaußschen Methode der kleinsten Fehlerquadratsumme" wurden die Koeffizienten c_i, $0 \leq i \leq 9$, des Ausgleichspolynoms

$$r_0(n) = c_0 + c_1 \frac{1}{n} + c_2 \frac{1}{n^2} + \ldots + c_9 \frac{1}{n^9}$$

bestimmt. Diese sind in Tabelle 1 dargestellt. Um die Werte für ein Quadrat beliebiger Größe $a \times a$ zu erhalten, multipliziert man $r_0(n)$ mit der Kantenlänge a.

Tabelle 1. Regressionskoeffizienten ($Ej = 10^j$)

c_0	c_1	c_2	c_3	c_4	c_5	c_6	c_7	c_8	c_9
0.07	21.5	−616	1.259E4	−1.569E5	1.195E6	−5.544E6	1.516E7	−2.225E7	1.337E7

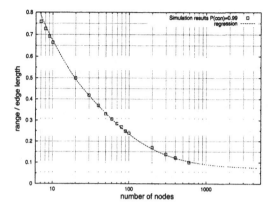

Abbildung 3. Simulation und Regression auf dem Einheitsquadrat

4 Normalverteilung der Sensoren

In diesem Kapitel soll nun eine Normalverteilung der Sensoren auf einer Fläche von wiederum 1000 × 1000 m² betrachtet werden. Eine zweidimensionale symmetrische Gaußsche Wahrscheinlichkeitsdichtefunktion mit den Zufallsvariablen X und Y, dem Mittelwert $\mu = E\{X\} = E\{Y\}$ und der Varianz $\sigma^2 = Var\{X\} = Var\{Y\}$ ist im Allgemeinen gegeben durch

$$f_{XY}(x,y) = \frac{1}{2\pi\sigma^2}\,\exp\left(-\frac{(x-\mu)^2 + (y-\mu)^2}{2\sigma^2}\right), \quad x,\, y \in \mathbb{R}.$$

Um eine Normalverteilung auf einer begrenzten Fläche $0 \le x \le 1000\,\mathrm{m}$ und $0 \le y \le 1000\,\mathrm{m}$ mit dem Mittelwert $\mu = 500\,\mathrm{m}$ zu erreichen, haben wir die *Box-Müller-Transformation* [19] verwendet. Auf Basis zweier unabhängiger, zwischen 0 und 1 gleichverteilter Zufallszahlen X_u und Y_u werden mit

$$X_n = \sqrt{-2\ln Y_u} \cdot \cos(2\pi X_u)$$

$$Y_n = \sqrt{-2\ln Y_u} \cdot \sin(2\pi X_u)$$

zwei statistisch unabhängige Zufallszahlen X_n und Y_n erzeugt, die normalverteilt sind. Mittelwert und Varianz der Normalverteilung mit $\mu = 0$ und $\sigma = \sigma^2 = 1$ werden anschließend unter Beachtung von $E\{X + c\} = E\{X\} + c$ und $Var\{cX\} = c^2 Var\{X\}$ auf die erforderlichen Werte eingestellt. Eine solche Transformation von Zufallsgrößen hat den Vorteil, dass die Zuverlässigkeit des so konstruierten Zufallsgenerators der des bereits erwähnten Mersenne Twisters entspricht. Die Güte der Zufallszahlen ist nur von der verwendeten Gleichverteilung zwischen 0 und 1 abhängig.

Exemplarisch wurde die Konnektivität für die Varianzen $\sigma^2 = 30\,000\,\mathrm{m}^2$ (geringe Varianz), $\sigma^2 = 100\,000\,\mathrm{m}^2$ (mittlere Varianz) und $\sigma^2 = 500\,000\,\mathrm{m}^2$ (hohe

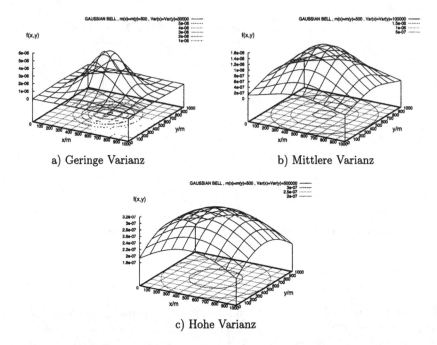

a) Geringe Varianz   b) Mittlere Varianz

c) Hohe Varianz

Abbildung 4. Zweidimensionale symmetrische Normalverteilungen

Varianz) untersucht. Die so entstehenden Dichtefunktionen sind in Abb. 4 veranschaulicht. Eine Gleichverteilung stellt den Grenzfall für $\sigma^2 \to \infty$ dar.

Im Vergleich zur Gleichverteilung haben nun Sensoren im Randgebiet der Fläche im Mittel noch weniger Nachbarsensoren und sind deshalb sehr häufig isoliert. Je niedriger die Varianz, desto geringer ist die zu erwartende Anzahl der Nachbarn eines Sensors im Randgebiet. Die Konnektivität sollte daher mit abnehmender Varianz sinken. Diese Vermutung bestätigt sich in den Simulationsergebnissen (siehe Abb. 5a). Betrachten wir zum Beispiel Sensoren mit $r_0 = 240$ m. Werden diese Sensoren gleichverteilt positioniert, so benötigt man weniger als $n = 100$ Stück um mit einer Wahrscheinlichkeit von 99% ein zusammenhängendes Netz zu erhalten. Bei einer Normalverteilung mit mittlerer Varianz benötigt man schon $n \approx 160$ und bei niedriger Varianz sogar $n \approx 480$ Sensoren.

Bei genauerer Betrachtung erkennt man jedoch ein inverses Verhalten bei geringen Sensorzahlen, weswegen die $n(r_0)$-Kurve in Abb. 5b nochmals im logarithmischen Maßstab aufgetragen wurde. Der Schnittpunkt aller Kennlinien liegt bei circa $(r_0, n) = (340$ m$, 50)$. Die Isolationswahrscheinlichkeit eines Sensors am Rand steigt zwar mit abnehmendem σ^2, jedoch ist die Wahrscheinlichkeit, dass überhaupt mindestens ein Sensor im Randgebiet positioniert wird für kleine Werte von σ^2 und n sehr gering. Kleine Netze profitieren also von dem bevorzugtem Aufenthalt der Sensoren im Zentrum der Fläche.

317

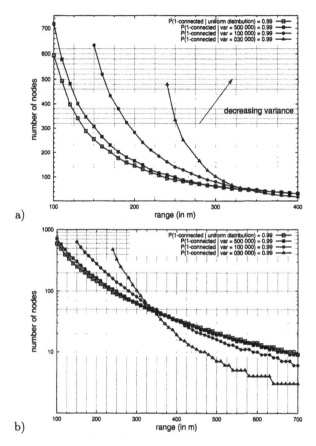

a)

b)

Abbildung 5. Konnektivität von normalverteilten Sensoren auf $A = 1000 \times 1000$ m^2

5 Zusammenfassung

Die Ergebnisse dieser Arbeit ermöglichen die „Dimensionierung" von drahtlosen Sensornetzen im freien Raum. Für eine gegebene Funkreichweite r_0 kann die Anzahl der benötigten Sensoren ermittelt werden, mit der das resultierende Sensornetz mit sehr hoher Wahrscheinlichkeit verbunden ist. Verglichen wurden die Ergebnisse auf einer quadratischen und kreisförmigen Fläche und zwischen Gleich- und Normalverteilung der Sensoren. Außerdem wurde eine Näherungsformel für $r_0(n, P_{con} = 99\%)$ angegeben. Analytische Betrachtungen zur exakten Berechnung dieser Kurven wurden in [20] publiziert.

Literatur

1. H. O. Marcy, J. R. Agre, C. Chien, L. Clare, N. Romanov, and A. Twarowski, "Wireless sensor networks for area monitoring and integrated vehicle health ma-

nagement applications," in *AIAA Guidance, Navigation, and Control Conference and Exhibit,* (Portland, OR), Aug. 1999.

2. J. M. Kahn, R. H. Katz, and K. S. J. Pister, "Next century challenges: Mobile networking for Smart Dust," in *Proc. ACM Intern. Conf. on Mobile Computing and Networking (MobiCom),* (Seattle, WA), Aug. 1999.

3. X. Hong, M. Gerla, T. Kwon, P. Estabrook, G. Pei, and R. Bagrodia, "The Mars sensor network: Efficient, energy aware communications," in *Proc. IEEE Milcom,* (McLean, VA), Oct. 2001.

4. G. J. Pottie and W. J. Kaiser, "Wireless integrated network sensors," *Communications of the ACM,* vol. 43, May 2000.

5. C. S. Raghavendra and K. M. Sivalingam, eds., *Proc. ACM Intern. Wrkshp. on Wireless Sensor Networks and Applications (WSNA).* Sept. 2002.

6. Y.-C. Cheng and T. G. Robertazzi, "Critical connectivity phenomena in multihop radio models," *IEEE Trans. Comm.,* vol. 37, July 1989.

7. T. K. Philips, S. S. Panwar, and A. N. Tantawi, "Connectivity properties of a packet radio network model," *IEEE Tr. Inf. Th.,* vol. 35, Sept. 1989.

8. P. Piret, "On the connectivity of radio networks," *IEEE Tr. Inf. Th.,* Sept. 1991.

9. P. Gupta and P. R. Kumar, "Critical power for asymptotic connectivity in wireless networks," in *Stoch. Analysis, Control, Optim. and Appl.,* Birkhäuser, 1998.

10. P. Santi, D. M. Blough, and F. Vainstein, "A probabilistic analysis for the radio range assignment problem in ad hoc networks," in *Proc. ACM Symp. on Mobile Ad Hoc Netw. and Comp. (MobiHoc),* (Long Beach, CA), Oct. 2001.

11. P. Santi and D. M. Blough, "An evaluation of connectivity in mobile wireless ad hoc networks," in *Proc. IEEE Intern. Conf. on Dependable Systems and Networks (DSN),* (Washington, DC), June 2002.

12. C. Bettstetter, "On the minimum node degree and connectivity of a wireless multihop network," in *Proc. ACM Symp. on Mobile Ad Hoc Netw. and Comp. (MobiHoc),* (Lausanne, Switzerland), June 2002.

13. O. Dousse, P. Thiran, and M. Hasler, "Connectivity in ad-hoc and hybrid networks," in *Proc. IEEE Infocom,* (New York), June 2002.

14. H. Hellbrück and S. Fischer, "Ansätze zu Analyse und Simulation von Ad–Hoc Netzwerken," in *Proc. German Workshop on Mobile Ad Hoc Networks (WMAN),* (Ulm, Germany), Mar. 2002.

15. B. Bollobás, *Modern Graph Theory.* Springer, 1998.

16. M. Matsumoto and T. Nishimura, "Mersenne twister: A 623-dimensionally equidistributed uniform pseudorandom number generator," *ACM Trans. on Modeling and Computer Simulation,* vol. 8, pp. 3–30, Jan. 1998.

17. N. A. C. Cressie, *Statistics for Spatial Data.* Wiley, 1991.

18. C. Bettstetter and O. Krause, "On border effects in modeling and simulation of wireless ad hoc networks," in *Proc. IEEE Intern. Conf. on Mobile & Wirel. Comm. Netw. (MWCN),* (Recife, Brazil), Aug. 2001.

19. E. Weisstein, ed., *E. Weisstein's World of Mathematics,* ch. Box-Muller Transformation. Wolfram Research, 2002.

20. C. Bettstetter and J. Zangl, "How to achieve a connected ad hoc network with homogeneous range assignment: An analytical study with consideration of border effects," in *Proc. IEEE Intern. Conf. on Mobile and Wireless Communication Networks (MWCN),* (Stockholm, Sweden), Sept. 2002.

Session Security/Management

A Flexible and Dynamic Access Control Policy Framework for an Active Networking Environment

A. Hess , G. Schäfer

Telecommunication Networks Group
Technische Universität Berlin, Germany

Abstract. To provide security for active networking nodes with respect to availability and controlled access the introduction of an access control mechanism and consequently a policy framework are mandatory. We follow the approach of a scenario-tailored runtime supervision of the service. During the development of the access control mechanism we strongly focused on keeping the mechanism as efficient as possible and to realize a modular design which allows to dynamically upgrade and configure the mechanism making use of the active networking technology itself while at the same time ensuring that mandatory security checks cannot be circumvented. Each service has to pass initial checks before it could be executed on an active node. Furthermore, also service-specific adaptive criterions could be included into the initial check. This paper discusses the corresponding flexible and dynamic access control policy framework and we also present results achieved with a first prototype realized for the active networking environment AMnet.

Keywords: active networks, security, policy, access control

1 Introduction

In this paper we present a security policy framework for an active networking environment which is flexible and dynamically configurable using the possibilities given through the underlying active networking infrastructure. Our approach bases on a scenario tailored runtime supervision [7] of the services whereas the supervision entities decide corresponding to access control policies whether to fulfill specific requests. According to [3] a policy makes clear, what is being protected and why. It states the responsibility for that protection and it provides a ground on which to interpret and resolve any later conflict.

In this report we do not precisely define how to express a policy but we recommend to follow the Principle of Least Privilege [14], which holds that each principal be accorded the minimum access needed to accomplish its task. Our approach provides the possibility to supply each active node and service with an individual, special-purpose access control policy. Active services may pose a threat, as the general prediction of code semantics is impossible [9]. Thus, the presented approach is a combination of origin verification and policy-based access control. Origin verification means, that only authenticated code could be executed on an active node, on which in turn an access control mechanism supervises the execution of the service. The access control mechanism decides corresponding to a policy whether a request for a resource or an operating system service respectively is authorized or not.

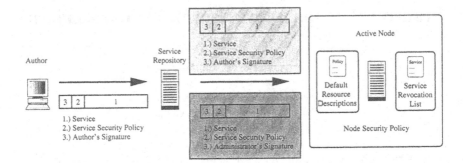

Fig. 1. The Transmission of a Service

For the development of the policy framework we posed the following requirements:

- An active node-specific protection: this requires the integration of a node security policy which can be configured dynamically at runtime.
- Service-specific supervision: this requires the integration of a service security policy.
- Polices must be easily extensible for future requirements due to:
  - new authorizations requirements
  - new known exploits, security holes
- Dynamic policy update in order to react on recognized security violations
- Possibility to execute untrusted / unreviewed services with a minimum set of privileges
- An efficient supervision: scenario-tailored runtime supervision
- Static and adaptive criterions in order to decide whether a service could execute on an active node
- Efficient policy management: the modification of a policy (e.g. adding or changing an entry of a service policy, etc.) should automatically propagate to the active nodes of a network in order to support policy updates for large networks.

Recapitulating, we state that our approach includes two different types of policies: a service security policy and a node security policy. In the following sections we will explain our approach in detail.

2 An Active Networking Environment

The active networking infrastructure consists of active nodes, a service repository (SR), a network provider and several users. An active node is able to execute services which are stored on the SR. If a new service is to be executed on an active node, the user / administrator is able to send the corresponding trigger signal to the active node, such that the active node downloads and installs the service. The installed service runs inside a so-called *execution environment (EE)* in user-space.

In figure 1 the transfer of a service between the host of the author and service repository and additionally, the transfer between service repository and active node is depicted. The transferred data consist as depicted of the service and the service security policy. Further on, regarding the transfer between service repository and active node the data are either signed by the author of the service or by the network administrator. A service security policy consists of a *resource and authorization description (RAD)*, a *trust label* and a *list of adaptive criterions (LAC)*. It is the responsibility of the network administrator to set the trust label and further on, to specify any required adaptive criterion (see section 3.2) for a service. If it is the case that the number of trust labels to be set by the network administrator is too big, the unreviewed services are handled as if they belong to the weakest trust category. The structure and functionality of the service security policy is discussed in detail in section 3.2.

Further on, the depicted active node in figure 1 is supplied with a node security policy, a *list of default resource and authorization descriptions (DRAD)* and a *service revocation list (SRL)*. The node security policy defines the security strategy of the active node, a DRAD specifies the limiting conditions for services of a specific trust label and the SRL is a listing of services which must not be executed on an active node.

3 The Policy Framework

In general a policy framework should protect the active nodes. It should detect misuse, attacks, bugs, etc. and afterwards itshould be able to react to the detected events. Our approach provides on the one hand a mechanism to configure the resources and authorizations which are available for services on an active node and on the other hand it provides also an mechanism to configure the resources and authorizations limits for a single service. Thus, the network provider could secure the execution of basic functions as routing tasks through the setting of reasonable authorization and resource limits on an active node (see also section 3.3). Further on, a mechanism is integrated to secure the execution of services which were not reviewed by the network administrator or which are labelled untrustworthy.

The policy framework consists of the following units:

- A service security policy, which consists of a resource and authorization description defined by the author of the service, a trust label and a list of adaptive criterions which are set by the network administrator.
- A node security policy which is defined by the network administrator and which specifies the security strategy of the active node.
- A list of default resource and authorization descriptions which are specified by the network administrator and each DRAD specifies the authorization and resource limits for services of specific trust label.
- A service revocation list, which is a listing of services which must not be executed on any active node and which is configured automatically by the active nodes and by the network administrator.

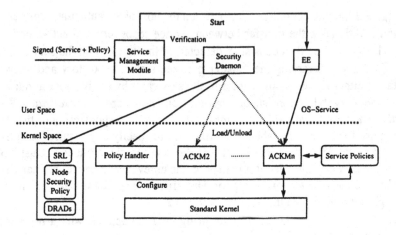

Fig. 2. Overview of the Architecture

3.1 The Policy Framework Architecture

In figure 2 the policy entities integrated into an active node are depicted. The policy framework consists of a *security daemon*, a *policy handler*, a set of *access control kernel modules (ACKM)*, an SRL, a node security policy, a list of DRADs and a database for the storage of the service security policies of the actual running services.

First we explain commonly used terms in the field of policies:

- Policy enforcement point (PEP) is the component that actually encounters the requests by services and is responsible for enforcement and execution of policy actions.
- policy decision point (PDP) is the component that is responsible for determining what actions are applicable to which services.

In our approach the functionality of PEP and PDP are realized together in so-called access control kernel modules. Each ACKM acts as PEP and PDP simultaneously for exactly one part of the service security policy, e.g. there is one ACKM for main memory requests, one for CPU cycles requests, etc. Our approach follows the goal of a scenario tailored supervision and through the setting of the trust label (see also section 3.2) the network administrator articulates his trust in a service or in other words he authorizes certain requests which could be posed by the service. Concluding, we do not want to supervise actions which the administrator labelled trustworthy and thus we follow the approach of a modular supervision of services. In figure 2 a security daemon is depicted. Security daemon and policy handler are the only two entities that must be running at any moment as they are responsible for the actual configuration of the policy framework structure. Before a service could be executed on an active node, security daemon and handler execute the initial check ($\Rightarrow$ is the service allowed to execute on that active node?) and afterwards they load / unload the required ACKMs. The initial check is depicted in detail in figure 3 and it consists of signature, SRL, node security policy, DRAD verification and the evaluation of the adaptive criterions. Node security policy (DRAD)

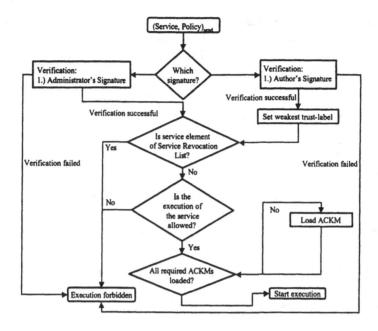

Fig. 3. The Initial Check

verification means a comparison between node security policy (DRAD) and service se-curity policy in order to decide whether to allow the execution of the service. Therefore, the service security policy must be a subset of the node security policy (DRAD). How the adaptive criterions are evaluated is described in detail in section 3.2. If all verifi-cations were successful, the security daemon and policy handler must take care about the required ACKMs. The security daemon is the only entity with the authorization to load / unload kernel modules and to modify the kernel variables as SRL, node security policy and DRAD. The procedure is described in more detail in section 3.6. Once all re-quired ACKMs are active the service could be started inside an execution environment as depicted in figure 2.

3.2 The Service Security Policy

A service security policy consists of two domains of responsibility. On the one hand there is the author who specifies the resource and authorization requirements for his service in order that the service could execute on an active node, but it is not said that the service obtains these. On the other hand the network provider specifies the supervision requirements for the execution of the service through the setting of the trust label and he has the possibility to specify an additional list of adaptive criterions for a service. Summarizing a service security policy consists of a RAD, a trust label and a list of adaptive criterions (LAC).

The Resource and Authorization Description Each service is supplied with a resource and authorization description which is specified by the author of the service as he is the person who knows best what kind and amount of resources and authorizations the service requires during its execution. The author describes in detail, what the service requires. In the following we give examples of required network authorizations:

- Specification of the resources to which access is required:
  - Network
- Specification of the quantity of required resource:
  - What bandwidth
- Specification of required parameters:
  - What kind of socket (RAW, DGRAM, STREAM, ...)
  - What port
  - Which destination addresses (it is also possible to define an address space through the usage of wild-cards)

The RAD is added to the service and then the author signs the service and RAD. Afterwards the signed data is transferred to the service repository. Now the signed data is in the area of responsibility of the network administrator (see also figure 1).

The Trust Label One question of interest is, under which supervision a service must execute? Therefore, we introduced the so-called trust label. Through the setting of a trust label the network provider is able to articulate his trust in a service ranging from completely untrustworthy to completely trustworthy. The ideal case is a service which is labelled completely trustworthy due to a long experience with the author or extensive testing of the service. A service with such a label does not require any runtime supervision.

Services with a trust label apart from completely trusted require runtime supervision. Besides the node security policy each active node is additionally supplied with a list of DRADs for partly / completely untrusted services which are defined by the network administrator. It depends on the strategy of the administrator if he defines one set of DRADs for all or groups of active nodes or if he defines an individual set for each active node. On each active node a DRAD for each trust label is present. A DRAD defines the limiting conditions (resources and authorizations) for services of a specific trust label. Summarizing we state that the trust label defines the supervision under which the service must execute and further it indicates the DRAD which specifies the limiting conditions for the service. Furthermore, a mechanism is provided by our approach to integrate dynamically a new trust label in order to provide a required intermediate trust label. If the security daemon receives a service which is supplied with an unknown trust label the security daemon contacts the service repository and downloads the DRAD corresponding to the unknown trust label.

Adaptive Criterions An adaptive criterion is a criterion which depends on a / set of changing condition(s). For the evaluation of an adaptive criterion a specified set of queries / calculations must be performed in order to know whether the criterion is fulfilled. An example for an adaptive criterion is an expiration date. This means that first the actual date must be evaluated and then, only if the expiration date is yet not reached the service could be executed on that active node. Another example is a performance test and only if the active node is performant enough the service could be executed. Or if two services could not execute on the same active node at the same time, this could be prevented through defining an adequate adaptive criterion and creating the corresponding active service.

Each adaptive criterion consists of input value(s) and an unique active service name which identifies the active service required for the evaluation of the adaptive criterion. This means the required input values and the unique name of the active service corresponding to the adaptive criterion are specified directly in the LAC. The security daemon depicted in figure 2 is responsible for the verification of the adaptive criterions. Whenever the download and installation of an active service for the evaluation of an adaptive criterion is required the security daemon initiates this. Then the service is fed with the corresponding input values and the adaptive criterion is evaluated. It must be mentioned that the main part of active services which are required for the evaluation of the most common adaptive criterions are already present on each active node and must not be downloaded from the service repository.

3.3 The Node Security Policy

The node security policy is used for the following aspects:

- Defining which resources and authorizations are generally available for the active services on that active node. Additionally, it also defines the complete quantity of each resource which could be maximally consumed by all actual running services on that active node.
- Part of the initial check: could the service be executed on that active node?
- Could be used for the creation of different quality of service nodes (see also below).

The node security policy is defined by the network administrator and could dynamically be changed at runtime including consequences for the actual running services. Through the definition of the node security policy the limiting conditions for the active services which could be executed on that active node are set.

The first task of the node security policy is the definition of resources and operating system services which are available to the services. Hence for each resource and operating system service the authorization could be given or negated. Additionally, upper limits for the resources which are available to the services in complete are defined. For example, an active node provides 500 MByte of main memory for the execution of services and furthermore, does not allow network access for any service whereas other active nodes could be configured differently. An active node located inside the Internet requires certainly another security strategy than an active node which is located inside an Intra-Net. For example only services originating from a specified list of authors or services with a specific trust label could be executed on a specific active node.

A component of the initial test (see also section 3.1) is the comparison of node security policy and service security policy. The service security policy must be a subset of the node security policy in order to allow the execution of the service.

Furthermore, a great degree of flexibility is gained through the integration of node security policies, as the network administrator specifies which services may be executed on which active nodes. Thus, the possibility is given to create quality of service domains through different sets of node security policies. For example inside a domain A only services of the highest trust label could be executed, this means that the services on these active nodes receive no supervision. Whereas inside a domain B services of all trust labels could be executed under a strict policy checking which requires fast hardware and produces higher costs but therefore, a higher availability is gained.

A third example could be "best effort" nodes, that perform only runtime supervision for network communications but not for other resources (main memory, CPU cycles, ...). This means, that it is granted that not any unauthorized service is able to send / receive any data besides the data stream it is acting upon and further on, no guarantee could be given that a specific service will execute with a specific performance guarantee on a best effort node as no further resource checking is performed.

3.4 The Default Resource and Authorization Descriptions

Each active node holds a list of DRADs and each DRAD specifies the authorization and resource limits for services of a specific trust label. Concluding for each trust label a DRAD is present. Further on, the DRAD list could be dynamically modified according to new circumstances which includes consequences for the running services. Thereby, the network administrator possesses the ability to change the limiting conditions for partly / completely untrusted services at runtime. The DRAD is also consulted during the initial test. Inside the node security policies the trust labels which are accepted by the active node are specified. Thus, if an active node allows principally the execution of services of trust label 1-3, it is still not said that all services of trust label 1-3 could be executed on that node. First a comparison between the RAD of the service and the DRAD belonging to the corresponding trust label must be performed and only if the RAD is a subset of the DRAD the service could be executed.

3.5 The Service Revocation List

Our approach includes also a reaction mechanism. Corresponding to the revocation lists that are known from certificates we integrated a service revocation list (SRL) in our framework. The SRL stores the services which never should be executed on an active node. Members of the SRL are services which tried to violate against the service security policy or services which the network administrator manually added. If on an active node a new service is inserted into the SRL, a mechanism is started which synchronizes the SRLs of all active nodes, thus that all SRLs are in the same state. After synchronization each active node verifies that the service that has been added to the SRL is not actually running on it. If yes, the service is instantly terminated. Additionally, the network administrator is able to add / delete (due to debugging) services manually to / from the SRL. In future work the reaction mechanism will be refined. A mechanism which classifies the violations against a policy into different offense levels will be implemented and further on, corresponding to the offense level of the violation the following reaction will differ.

3.6   The dynamic upgrading of Node Security Policy, DRAD and SRL

Node security policy, DRAD and SRL are realized in a manner that they can be configured dynamically at runtime according to changed circumstances. Furthermore, the elements are realized as structures which are stored in kernel space due to security and performance reasons. The security daemon is the only entity which is authorized to load kernel modules or to modify the mentioned kernel variables and therefore, a shared secret is established between security daemon and policy handler. The policy handler intercepts any user-space request to load a kernel module or to access a kernel variable and only if the security daemon (verification with the help of the shared secret) is the calling entity the request could be fulfilled. The shared secret thus establishes the mutual trust between security daemon and policy handler.

The configuration of an active node with its individual node security policy is possible through specifying its individual node name inside the node security policy. The security daemon compares the given node name with its own and only if they equal the node security policy could be updated. Of course, each transferred node security policy is digitally signed and supplied with a time stamp (version number) to prevent replay attacks. The dynamic upgrading of the node security policies in order to prepare the system for new authorization requirements is done in a similar manner as described above. The provision of new authorization requirements conducts into a new structure of node security policy, DRAD and requires a new ACKM for the supervision of the new policy entries. The modification of the RADs is done by the authors of the services which require at least one of the new authorizations. Whereas it is the responsibility of the network administrator to extend the node security policies and to realize the required ACKM. As described above, the network administrator adds the new authorization requirements to the actual node security policy and afterwards he updates it. If a service arrives at an active node with a service security policy in which authorizations are specified which the active node does not know the active node contacts the SR and verifies if there is a new node security policy for it. If yes, the new node security policy is downloaded and the initial check is executed. If not, the execution of the service is rejected.

Summerazing, we state that through the provision of the above explained mechanism new policies (node and service) respectively new authorization requirements could be easily integrated in an active networking environment.

3.7   Implementation and Measurements

In this section the measurements achieved with a first prototype for the active networking infrastructure AMnet [5] are discussed. AMnet provides a platform for rapid and flexible service creation and uses active nodes so-called AMnodes within the network for the execution of services.

Most common operating systems make a distinct differentiation between application and operating system. Each time a service requires an operating system service (e.g., to open a socket for communication) the service must send the proper system call to the kernel. The kernel checks the request of the process and then it decides whether to fulfill it or not. By inserting a loadable kernel module, it is possible to extend the functionality of the kernel. In our case, it is possible to introduce more detailed decision criteria in the kernel to determine whether the desired action is allowed or not.

The presented measurements focuses on the runtime supervision, the time spent on the initial check was left aside. The service used for the measurements created a socket. Afterwards it stepped into a loop of 1.000.000 cycles. In each loop cycle the service executed a *setsockopt()* command to change a socket option. This command was intercepted by the corresponding ACKM_Network. After intercepting a socket system call the security kernel module made a lookup in the local security database if the requesting service has got the authorization or not. We varied the number of stored security policies inside the corresponding database and the position of the security policy inside the database of the requesting process was uniformly distributed. The security policies are stored in an ordered array and to find the proper policy a binary search algorithm is executed. [1] Table 1 shows the results of our measurements. The first line of the table

Table 1. Overhead produced through the interception of system calls

Amount of service security policies	0	10	100	1000	10.000
overhead in [μs]	0.068	0.139	0.190	0.244	0.345
rel. overhead [%]	14.25	29.04	39.82	50.97	72.21

represents the number of service security policies stored inside the database. Thus, we see that for a number of zero policies, no lookup inside the database is required, we receive the overhead caused through the interception of the system call, which is about 0.068 μs. Additionally, we extended the number of service security policies stored in the database up to 10.000. The additional overhead which could be observed is caused through the lookup for the proper service security policy. The last line of the tables represents the relative overhead. It can be seen that an additionally overhead of 30 % is quickly reached.

4 Related Work

Application-dependent and special-purpose policies are increasingly important. Certainly Java [4, 11, 16] must be mentioned, which supports mobile code including policies. But the execution performance of services realized in Java is not efficient enough compared with other programming languages and thus not adequate for many networking services, whereas our approach supports all programming languages. The Naccio project of MIT [2] uses also the mechanisms provided by Java. Joust [6] is a Java active OS implemented in Scout [12] and provides a Java virtual machine for the execution of active services.

---

[1] The measurements were made with a Pentium III/800 machine running Linux 2.4.18 kernel and AMnet version 1 [17]

Regarding active networking projects, the Seraphim project [10, 13] must be mentioned. It follows the approach of dynamic policies. A dynamic policy is a program consisting of a set of guards and actions. For the realization so-called active capabilities are used, which are actually executable Java-byte-codes.

PLANet [8] is another active networking project. The project uses a type-safe, resource limited, functional programming language with dynamic type verification.

The key idea behind history-based access control [1] is to maintain a selective history of the access requests made by individual programs and to use this history to improve the differentiation between safe and potentially dangerous requests. Handlers are integrated to maintain the history, but the bigger the numbers of services which execute on an active node the bigger becomes the amount of data to be stored.

Enforceable policies by Schneider [15] are specified through the usage of a so-called Security Automata. But still there are difficulties in generating the security automata.

To our understanding Java seems not to be the language of choice for many active networking services, therefore we provide a mechanism which is applicable for any language. In addition, through the realization of the ACKMs, functions corresponding to the adaptive criterions and the node security policies as active networking service, the mechanism is easily extensible and can be upgraded.

5 Conclusions

The presented policy framework is flexible and provides mechanisms to react dynamically to changing circumstances which is a very important aspect considering the needs of a network. The framework includes two types of policies, with the node security policy dominating over the service security policy. Furthermore, services which have not been reviewed by the network administrator or which are labelled partly / completely untrusted could still be executed on active nodes, in addition, the modular approach provides a flexible mechanism to integrate easily new authorizations requirements.

As shown in section 3.7 the runtime supervision of services, although widely implemented in kernel space, could get expensive if a service executes a huge amount of system calls which are intercepted within a short period of time. Through the approach of a scenario-tailored supervision and through the possibility to create QoS active nodes the performance degradation caused through the runtime supervision could be minimized so that our approach allows to realize demand-driven access control for performance-critical active services. Furthermore, the supervision of access requests of active services in kernel space is highly efficient and additionally allows to control applications written in any programming language. Through the modular approach of Access Control Kernel Modules, node security policies and services belonging to an adaptive criterion which are realized as active networking services the possibility is given to refine a service or to integrate a completely new service into the infrastructure dynamically. Finally the policy framework is designed in a manner that it requires little maintenance work. If the structure of an element (node policy, DRAD, ...) of the policy framework must be changed this modification must be made only once. This allows for efficient policy management in order to support policy updates for large networks of active nodes.

Bibliography

[1] Guy Edjlali, Anurag Acharya, and Vipin Chaudhary. History-based access control for mobile code. In *ACM Conference on Computer and Communications Security*, pages 38–48, 1998.

[2] David Evans and Andrew Twyman. Flexible policy-directed code safety. In *IEEE Symposium on Security and Privacy*, pages 32–45, 1999.

[3] S. Garfinkel G. Spafford. *Practical UNIX & Internet Security*. O'Reilly, 1996.

[4] Li Gong. Java security: present and near future. *IEEE Micro*, 17(3):14–19, 1997.

[5] Till Harbaum, Anke Speer, Ralph Wittmann, and Martina Zitterbart. Amnet: Efficient heterogeneous group communication through rapid service creation.

[6] John J. Hartman, Peter A. Bigot, Patrick Bridges, Brady Montz, Rob Piltz, Oliver Spatscheck, Todd A. Proebsting, Larry L. Peterson, and Andy Bavier. Joust: A platform for liquid software. *Computer*, 32(4):50–56, 1999.

[7] A. Hess, M. Schoeller, G. Schaefer, M. Zitterbart, and A. Wolisz. A dynamic and flexible access control and resource monitoring mechanism for active nodes. In *Proc. of OpenArch 2002, Short Paper Session*, New York, USA, June 2002. IEEE.

[8] Michael W. Hicks, Jonathan T. Moore, D. Scott Alexander, Carl A. Gunter, and Scott Nettles. PLANet: An active internetwork. In *INFOCOM (3)*, pages 1124–1133, 1999.

[9] A. J. Kfoury, R. N. Moll, and M. A. Arbib. *A Programming Approach to Computability*. Springer, Berlin, 1986.

[10] Z. Liu, R. Campbell, and M. Mickunas. Securing the node of an active network, 2000.

[11] N. V. Mehta and K. R Sollins. Expanding and extending the security features of Java. In *7th Usenix Security Symposium*, pages 159–172, 1998.

[12] David Mosberger and Larry L. Peterson. Making paths explicit in the scout operating system. In *Operating Systems Design and Implementation*, pages 153–167, 1996.

[13] R. H. Campbell P. Naldurg and M. D. Mickunas. Developing dynamic security policies. 2002.

[14] Jerome H. Saltzer and Michael D. Schroeder. The protection of information in computer systems. *Proceedings of the IEEE*, 63(9):1278–1308, September 1975.

[15] Fred B. Schneider. Enforceable security policies. *Information and System Security*, 3(1):30–50, 2000.

[16] Dan S. Wallach, Dirk Balfanz, Drew Dean, and Edward W. Felten. Extensible security architectures for Java. In *16th Symposium on Operating Systems Principles*, pages 116–128, 1997.

[17] Ralph Wittmann and Martina Zitterbart. AMnet: Active multicasting network. In *COST 237 Workshop*, pages 154–164, 1997.

Dienstbeschreibung und –modellierung für ein SLA-fähiges Service-Management

Christian Mayerl

Arbeitsgruppe Lehrunterstützung der Fakultät für Informatik (ALFI)
Fakultät für Informatik, Universität Karlsruhe (TH), Postfach 6980, 76128 Karlsruhe
Telefon +49-721-608-6390, Fax +49-721-697760
mayerl@ira.uka.de

Sebastian Abeck, Mike Becker, Andreas Köppel, Oliver Mehl, Bruno Pauze

Forschungsgruppe Cooperation & Management (C&M)
Institut für Telematik, Universität Karlsruhe (TH), Zirkel 2, 76128 Karlsruhe
Telefon +49-721-608-6391, Fax +49-721-608-4046
{sebastian.abeck|mike.becker|andreas.koeppel|oliver.mehl|
bruno.pauze}@cooperation-management.de

Abstract. *Service Level Agreements* (SLAs) stellen die vertragliche Grundlage dafür dar, dass ein IT-Dienstleister im Auftrag eines Kunden i.d.R. verteilte IT-Systeme für die Anwender dieser Systeme betreibt. Ein SLA-fähiges Service-Management unterstützt den IT-Dienstleister, die in einem SLA getroffenen Vereinbarungen während des Betriebs der IT-Systeme zu gewährleisten. Es erfordert dabei ein sehr genaues Verständnis der IT-Dienste, die zum einen Gegenstand der Vereinbarung und zum anderen Gegenstand des IT-Managements sind. Der Beitrag zeigt auf, welche Aspekte in einer strukturierten Dienstbeschreibung auftreten müssen, damit SLAs vereinbart und eingehalten werden können. Die Dienstbeschreibung wird durch ein Dienstmodell formalisiert, das auf Basis des *Common Information Model* (CIM) erstellt wurde. Die Tragfähigkeit der vorgestellten Konzepte und Modelle wird anhand konkreter Beispiele aufgezeigt.

1 Einführung

Das Ziel, das ein IT-Dienstleister mit einer Managementlösung verfolgt, lässt sich wie folgt zusammenfassen: Der Dienstleister eines mittels Informationstechnologien (IT) bereitgestellten Dienstes muss durch das IT-Management sicherstellen, den Dienst in der von den Anwendern gewünschten Qualität zu erbringen. Inhärent müssen dabei die folgenden Fragen beantwortet werden:

- Wie definieren sich die vom Dienstleister bereitgestellten Dienste der IT-Systeme?
- Welche Funktionalitäten und Qualitäten werden vom Anwender gefordert?
- Wie lassen sich die zugesicherten Qualitätsvereinbarungen überwachen?

Im IT-Management werden die vom Kunden auszuwählenden Dienstqualitäten als Dienststufen oder *Service Levels* bezeichnet; die Vereinbarung von *Service Levels* im Rahmen der Bereitstellung eines IT-Systems nennt man dann *Service Level Agree-*

ment, kurz SLA ([1], [2], [3]). Die Notwendigkeit, für komplexe IT-Systeme binden-de vertragliche Vereinbarungen in Form von *Service Level Agreements* zwischen dem IT-Dienstleister (*Provider*) und seinen Kunden abzuschließen, ist heute unumstritten.

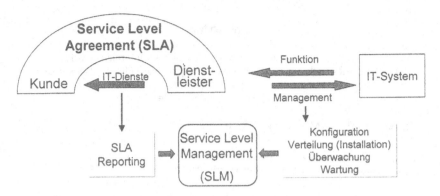

Abb. 1: *Service Level Agreement* und *Service Level Management*

In der Literatur [4] werden zahlreiche Gründe aufgeführt, die die Notwendigkeit von SLAs und das für deren Überwachung und Steuerung zuständige *Service Level Management* (SLM, siehe Abb. 1) aufzeigen. Zu nennen sind Kundenzufriedenheit, Erwartungsregulierung, Transparenz, Ressourcenregulierung und Marketing von IT-Diensten. Der Kunde möchte verstehen, was er für welche Leistung zu zahlen hat: *,The business wants to understand what it will pay and what it will get'* [5].

Das *Service Level Management* (SLM) umfasst nicht nur das SLA an sich, sondern auch eine Vielzahl an Managementfunktionen, wie z.B. die Messdatenaufnahme und die Aufstellung von Berechnungsmetriken zum Verdichten der Messwerte. Aus der Sicht des IT-Dienstleisters sind dabei das *Fault Management* und *Performance Management* [6] von besonderer Relevanz.

SLM wird in [7] wie folgt definiert: *'SLM is the disciplined, proactive methodology and procedures used to ensure that adequate levels of service are delivered to all IT users in accordance with business priorities and at acceptable cost'*.

Zur SLA-Erstellung wird zunächst ein grundsätzliches Verständnis von Diensten benötigt. Dienste sind die von IT-Dienstleistern den Anwendern bereitgestellten "Funktionen" und Leistungen, die in einem Dienstkatalog systematisch erfasst werden. Die für jeden Dienst definierten Diensteigenschaften (*service property*) sowie die zugehörigen Dienststufen (*service level*) bilden den Ausgangspunkt für einen Prozess, in dem die zu vereinbarenden SLAs mit den für einen Kunden relevanten SLA-Parametern (*SLA parameter*) in einem Dialog verhandelt und schrittweise dokumentiert werden.

Um den Prozess der SLA-Erstellung sinnvoll technisch unterstützen zu können, ist es notwendig, an dieser Stelle mit einer Formalisierung der Information zu beginnen. Ausgehend von der Dienstbeschreibung im Dienstkatalog über den Dienst in der SLA-Verhandlung hin zum vereinbarten Dienst im Rahmen der *Service-Level-*Überwachung stellt ein geeignetes Dienstmodell die notwendige Grundlage für eine effiziente Prozessunterstützung dar.

2 Aspekte der Dienstbeschreibung

Ausgehend von dem in der Informatik allgemein verwendeten Dienstbegriff erfolgt eine Konkretisierung auf den Dienst und der Dienstqualität als Gegenstand des Service-Managements und der *Service Level Agreements*.

2.1 Allgemeiner Dienstbegriff

Der Dienst beschreibt ein Leistungsangebot, das von einer Komponente (Dienstgeber oder Diensterbringer, *service provider*) einer anderen Komponente (Dienstnehmer, *service user*) an einer Dienst-Schnittstelle (*service interface*) bereitgestellt wird. Die Tele- und Rechnerkommunikation gehörte zu den ersten Bereichen, die in geschichteten Referenzmodellen [8], [9] den Dienstbegriff eingeführt und umfassend genutzt hat. Eine konsequente Weiterführung erfuhr der Dienstbegriff mit den Client-Server-Architekturen [10]; hierin übernimmt der Server die Rolle des Dienstgebers und der Client die des Dienstnehmers. Auf der Grundlage solcher Client-Server-Beziehungen wurde in verschiedenen *Middleware*-Ansätzen der Dienstbegriff weiterentwickelt. Ein neueres Konzept stellen in diesem Zusammenhang die auf W3C-Standards (*World Wide Web Consortium*) basierenden Web-Services dar.

2.2 Dienst im Kontext des Service-Managements

Die für die Erstellung von *Service Level Agreements* (SLAs) benötigten Dienstbeschreibungen unterscheiden sich von den oben genannten Diensten insofern, als dass die in SLAs beschriebenen Dienste als Vereinbarungen zwischen Personen bzw. Organisationen (und nicht zwischen Rechensystemen) gedacht sind. Es interessieren daher in einem SLA nur die vom Kunden als Endbenutzer eines IT-Systems in Anspruch genommenen Dienste, die auch als Ende-zu-Ende-Dienste (*end-to-end services*) bezeichnet werden. Zur Erbringung dieser Ende-zu-Ende-Dienste werden i.d.R. eine Vielzahl von technischen Diensten in Anspruch genommen, die von verteilten Rechnern und darauf laufenden Anwendungen erbracht werden. Zur Überwachung der vereinbarten Dienststufen der Ende-zu-Ende-Dienste muss vom SLM gerade dieser Dienste-Zusammenhang so genau wie möglich verfolgt werden.

Die von einem Dienstleister einem Kunden bereitgestellten Kerndienste [11] sind diejenigen Dienste, die der Kunde durch Nutzung des IT-Systems innerhalb seiner Geschäftsprozesse in Anspruch nimmt. Dementsprechend lassen sich Kerndienste entlang der allgemeinen Architektur eines IT-Systems in Kommunikations-, System- und Anwendungsdienste einteilen.

Um die Kerndienste ranken sich gewisse Zusatzdienste, die der Kunde zur Inanspruchnahme der Kerndienste je nach seinem Kenntnisstand benötigt und von einem IT-Dienstleister in Anspruch nehmen wird. Zu den Zusatzdiensten zählen Informations- und Schulungs-, Beratungs- und Planungsdienste sowie betriebliche Dienste.

2.3 Diensteigenschaften

Diensteigenschaften (*service properties*) lassen sich sowohl zu Kern- als auch zu Zusatzdiensten definieren, wobei hierdurch jeweils unterschiedliche Qualitätsaussagen getroffen werden:

- Diensteigenschaften zu **Kerndiensten** definieren die Qualität technischer Dienste von IT-Systemen. Für die Einhaltung der Dienstqualität sind Kennzahlen zu denjenigen IT-Komponenten zu erfassen, die an der Erbringung des jeweiligen Kerndienstes beteiligt sind.
- Diensteigenschaften zu **Zusatzdiensten** zielen auf die Qualität der Organisationseinheiten einer Betreiberorganisation und deren Kooperation untereinander ab. Die Zusatzdienste werden durch wohldefinierte Arbeitsprozesse erbracht, deren Qualität durch geeignete, messbare (Prozess-) Kennzahlen bestimmt werden.

Eine systematische Herleitung fundierter Diensteigenschaften führt zu der Frage, WIE die Dienstfunktionalitäten und –eigenschaften erbracht werden. Aus der Antwort auf diese Frage lassen sich die wichtigsten Diensteigenschaften ableiten. Diese sind:

- **Verfügbarkeit:** '*The most critical factor affecting end-user perception of service IT provides is system availability*' [12].
- **Wiederherstellungszeit:** Zeit, nach der ein ausgefallener Dienst spätestens wieder vom Anwender in Anspruch genommen werden kann.
- **Antwortzeit:** Zeitangabe, die höchstens zwischen Dienst-Inanspruchnahme und Auslieferung des Ergebnisses der Dienstausführung vergehen darf.
- **Durchsatz:** Menge der pro Zeiteinheit übertragenen bzw. verarbeiteten Daten.
- **Anzahl (aktiver) Benutzer:** Benutzeranzahl, die einen Dienst höchstens zur gleichen Zeit in Anspruch nehmen darf.

2.4 Dienststufen und Standard-Dienststufen

Die aufgelisteten Diensteigenschaften sind als Einheiten für die Definition der jeweiligen Dienstqualität zu verstehen, auf deren Grundlage mögliche Dienststufen (*service levels*) sowie vom Kunden gewünschte Soll-Größen festgelegt werden können.

Für jeden vom IT-Dienstleister angebotenen Dienst werden Dienststufen festgelegt, die vom Dienstleister angeboten werden und für die der Kunde entsprechend zu bezahlen hat. Bevor der Dienstleister in die häufig schwierige Verhandlung der Dienststufen mit einem individuellen Kunden tritt, kann und sollte er die von ihm im Dienstkatalog erfassten IT-Dienste im Hinblick auf die Dienststufen vorab analysieren und Folgendes für jeden Dienst festlegen:

- Auswahl der für alle Kunden relevanten Dienste und Diensteigenschaften
- Ermittlung der vom IT-Dienstleister unterstützten Dienststufen

- Zusammenstellen der Dienstbeschreibung in einem Dienstkatalog, aus dem der Kunde auswählen kann.

Diese vorab von einem Dienstleister ermittelten Dienststufen werden hier als Standard-Dienststufen bezeichnet. Durch die Festlegung von Standard-Dienststufen vor der Verhandlung mit einem Kunden umgeht der Dienstleister die Gefahr, eventuell Vereinbarungen zu treffen, die er gar nicht einhalten kann. Ziel des IT-Dienstleisters ist es, die Ausprägungen der Dienste zu standardisieren und dadurch deren Umsetzung im Betrieb zu optimieren.

3 Anwendungsdienste zu einem konkreten IT-System

Eine Präzisierung der Dienstbeschreibung und der im folgenden Abschnitt näher ausgeführten Dienstmodellierung soll anhand von exemplarisch ausgewählten Anwendungsdiensten eines bestehenden IT-Systems erfolgen. Dieses System mit der Bezeichnung ed.tec (educational.technology) ist ein Internet-basiertes *Content-Management*-System, das einen flexiblen Zugriff auf Wissensinhalte über das Internet realisiert und damit die Geschäftsprozesse eines Internet-basierten Wissenstransfers unterstützt.

Ein Dienstleister bietet Dienste auf der Grundlage des ed.tec-Systems an und tritt als so genannter *Application Service Provider* (ASP) auf. Die Anwendungsdienste lassen sich aus den auf den Teilsystemen ablaufenden Programmkomponenten (*components*) ermitteln. Zum besseren Verständnis der Qualitätsanforderungen der Anwender muss ein Dienst im Kontext des jeweiligen Geschäftsprozesses betrachtet werden. Die ed.tec-Architektur umfasst dabei Systemkomponenten zur Unterstützung des Autors, Dozenten und Lernenden im Szenario der Aus- und Weiterbildung. Anforderungen der einzelnen Rollen in den Geschäftsprozessen an die Qualität der Anwendungsdienste lassen sich unmittelbar auf die Komponenten von ed.tec abbilden.

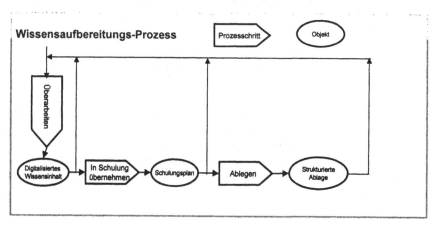

Abb. 2: Anwendungsdienste am Beispiel von ed.tec

Im Folgenden werden exemplarisch für einen der Geschäftsprozesse, den Wissens-aufbereitungsprozess, Qualitätsanforderungen an die Anwendungsdienste ableiten. Zur IT-Unterstützung der in Abb. 2 angegebenen Prozessschritte werden die folgenden Anwendungsdienste bereitgestellt:

- Inhalt_bearbeiten: Der Autor kann an seinem Autoren-Arbeitsplatz die von ihm für die Bearbeitung der Materialien benötigten Werkzeuge aufrufen und einsetzen. Die offensichtliche Verfeinerung hinsichtlich eines Anwendungsdienstes an dieser Stelle (z.B. Folieneditor_benutzen) würde zu einer unübersichtlichen Menge von Anwendungsdiensten führen. Aus diesem Grund werden gewisse Angaben als Diensteigenschaften (*service properties*) beschrieben.
- Schulungsplan_bearbeiten: Der Autor erhält mit diesem ed.tec-Anwendungsdienst die Möglichkeit, den Schulungsplan gemäß der von ihm erstellten Materialien fort-zuschreiben. Der Schulungsplan ist Teil der strukturierten Ablage.
- Inhalt_laden: Mit Hilfe dieses ed.tec-Anwendungsdienstes ist der Autor in der Lage, aus der strukturierten Ablage Inhalte zur (Wieder-) Verwendung innerhalb der von ihm aufbereiteten Schulung herunterzuladen (*download*) oder das von ihm erstellte Schulungsmaterial zum Zwecke der Verwendung durch andere Autoren, Dozenten oder Lernende hochzuladen (*upload*).

Ein analoges Vorgehen – ausgehend von den Geschäftsprozessen der Wissensver-mittlung und Wissensaneignung – lässt sich für die Anwendungsdienste angeben, die den Rollen des Dozenten und des Lernenden bereitzustellen sind.

Im Zusammenhang mit der Bereitstellung der IT-Dienste sind dem Kunden neben den Anwendungsdiensten außerdem gewisse Zusatzdienste anzubieten. Die Zusatz-dienste unterscheiden sich von den zu den Kerndiensten gehörenden Anwendungs-diensten dadurch, dass diese nicht unmittelbar durch die technischen Komponenten des IT-Systems sondern durch die personellen Ressourcen des IT-Dienstleisters er-bracht werden. Beispiele für Zusatzdienste im Zusammenhang mit dem hier betrach-teten Beispielsystem sind ed.tec-Benutzerschulung_abhalten, ed.tec-Testversion_bereitstellen, oder ed.tec-Benutzer_betreuen.

4 SLA-gerechte Modellierung von Diensten

Nach der strukturierten Dienstbeschreibung stellt sich die Frage, wie die oben ge-nannten SLA-Aspekte in angemessener Form modelliert werden können, um später im Rahmen des Service-Management weiterverarbeitet werden zu können.

Wie Abb. 3 zeigt, steht der Dienstkatalog zwischen IT-Dienstleister und potentiel-len Kunden und stellt die Grundlage für den SLA-Verhandlungsprozess dar. Das Ergebnis des erfolgreichen Verhandlungsprozesses ist das zwischen IT-Dienstleister und Kunde geschlossene SLA.

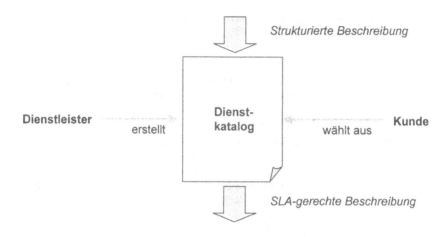

Abb. 3: Dienstkatalog

Aus der Sicht des Service-Managements stellt sich daher die zentrale Anforderung, den Dienstkatalog so zu gestalten, dass er nicht nur die Aufgabe der Präsentation von Diensten erfüllt, sondern auch als Grundlage für anschließende SLA-Verhandlungen genutzt werden kann. Der Kern des Ansatzes ist dabei ein Dienstmodell, auf dem der Dienstkatalog mit geeigneten Funktionen aufsetzen kann. Damit das Dienstmodell auch für die SLA-Verhandlungen geeignet ist, wird ein so genanntes SLA-gerechtes Dienstmodell angestrebt, das nicht nur während, sondern auch nach der SLA-Verhandlung zur Überwachung der SLA-Vereinbarungen im laufenden IT-Betrieb eingesetzt werden kann.

4.1 SLA-gerechtes Dienstmodell

Als Beschreibungssprache für das Dienstmodell wird die Modellierungssprache *Unified Modeling Language* (UML) verwendet. Das Modell setzt auf dem objektorientierten *Common Information Model* (CIM) auf. Abb. 4 zeigt das in CIM-konformer Beschreibung aufgestellte Dienstmodell [13]. Es setzt sich aus zwei Teilmodellen zusammen:

- Das **Definitionsmodell** (linke Seite in der Abbildung) repräsentiert die Beschreibung von Diensten mit sämtlichen Eigenschaften sowie möglichen Dienststufen und definiert damit die Strukturen für den Dienstkatalog.
- Das **SLA-Modell** (rechte Seite in der Abbildung) stellt den konkret mit einem Kunden vereinbarten Dienst im Rahmen eines *Service Level Agreements* dar.

340

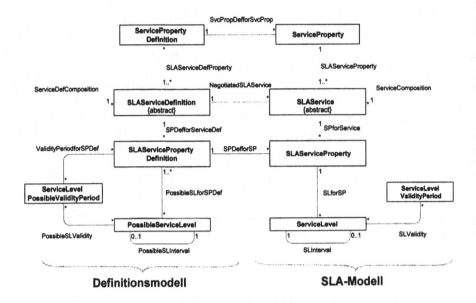

Definitionsmodell   SLA-Modell

Abb. 4: SLA-gerechtes Dienstmodell

Das Definitionsmodell als ein Teil des Dienstmodells hat den folgenden Aufbau: Die zentrale Klasse ist SLAServiceDefinition. Diese abstrakte Klasse ist durch die Aggregation von ServiceDefComposition in der Lage, hierarchische Strukturen von Diensten zu beschreiben, um so die Modularisierung von Diensten in Dienstmodule bzw. deren Komposition zu komplexeren Diensten zu ermöglichen. Auf jeder Hierarchiestufe des Dienstmodells kann ein Dienst durch (SLA-relevante) Diensteigenschaften (ServicePropertyDefinition für allgemeine und SLAServicePropertyDefinition für SLA-relevante Eigenschaften) spezifiziert werden. Die Klasse SLAServicePropertyDefinition wird dabei nicht direkt von der Klasse CIM_ManagedElement abgeleitet, sondern von einer Klasse mit dem Namen CIM_BaseMetricDefinition. Dadurch erbt von dieser Oberklasse SLAServicePropertyDefinition unter anderem die Eigenschaft Unit, in dem bereits bei der Definition einer Diensteigenschaft (*service property*) dessen Einheit hinsichtlich der späteren Messung festgelegt wird. Zur Beschreibung der möglichen Werte einer Dienststufe (*service level*) zu einer Diensteigenschaft dient die Klasse PossibleServiceLevel, die die vom IT-Dienstleister vordefinierten (Standard-) Dienststufen im Modell realisiert.

Das Definitionsmodell stellt eine allgemeine Beschreibungsform für beliebige Dienste dar. Da die Beschreibung aber dem SLA-Kontext gerecht werden soll – also ein SLA-gerechtes Dienstmodell erstellt werden soll –, wird das Definitionsmodell um ein SLA-Modell bestehend aus den im Folgenden beschriebenen weiteren Klassen erweitert. Bei Vereinbarungen von Dienststufen im Rahmen von SLAs ist die angebotene bzw. geforderte Qualität in einen zeitlichen Kontext zu stellen.

Die Klasse ServiceLevelPossibleValidityPeriod erlaubt die Einschränkung dieses zeitlichen Kontextes schon im Dienstkatalog bzw. Dienstmodell. Diese Klasse ist durch eine Assoziation mit der Klasse SLAServicePropertyDefinition verbunden und drückt aus, in welcher Zeit eine Diensteigenschaft gilt. Ein Beispiel hierfür wäre die Diensteigenschaft "Verfügbarkeit" des Zusatzdienstes edtec-Anwender_betreuen, die z.B. aufgrund tariflicher Bestimmungen nur von Mo. 6:00 Uhr bis Sa. 22:00 Uhr angeboten werden kann.

Die zeitlichen Einschränkungen für einzelne Dienststufen werden durch die Assoziation zu PossibleServiceLevel ausgedrückt. Ein konkretes Beispiel hierfür wäre die Diensteigenschaft "Wiederherstellungszeit" des Dienstes ed.tec-Inhalt_laden. So kann der Dienstleister – beispielsweise bedingt durch die Erreichbarkeit von Personal und Zulieferer – eine Standard-Dienststufe von 1 Stunde anbieten.

Für die kundenindividuelle Auswahl und den Abschluss von SLAs stehen den Definitionsklassen entsprechende SLA-Modellklassen zur Verfügung (siehe rechte Seite in Abb. 4). Das SLA-Modell definiert damit die Strukturen der mit den Kunden abgeschlossenen SLA-Verträge.

4.2 Instanziierung von Diensten aus dem Definitionsmodell

Bislang liefert das Dienstmodell eine Beschreibung der Dienste auf Klassenebene. Aus dem Definitionsmodell lassen sich konkrete Dienste, also Instanziierungen dieser Dienstbeschreibung, schrittweise entwickeln.

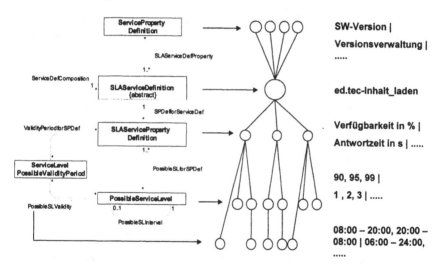

Abb. 5: Instanziierung eines ed.tec-Dienstes

Der Baum im mittleren Teil der Abb. 5 stellt eine Instanziierung des Definitionsmodells graphisch dar und zeigt (mit Ausnahme der Hierarchisierung der Dienste) die möglichen Verbindungen der einzelnen Objekte. Auf der rechten Seite des Baumes sind konkrete Beispiele für die Objekte im Zusammenhang mit dem ed.tec-System angegeben. Als Dienst wurde ed.tec-Inhalt_laden gewählt, für den exemplarisch Eigenschaften, Dienststufen und mögliche Zeitbereiche innerhalb des Dienstkatalogs aufgeführt werden.

4.3 Überführung der Dienstbeschreibung in das SLA

Im Rahmen der SLA-Verhandlungen wird der Kunde die von ihm gewünschten Dienste aus dem Dienstkatalog des IT-Dienstleisters auswählen und die Eigenschaften sowie Dienststufen gemäß seinen Anforderungen festlegen. Bezogen auf das Dienstmodell bedeutet dieser Vorgang, dass ein Dienst aus dem Definitionsmodell in das SLA-Modell überführt wird.

Die Überführung einer Dienstbeschreibung in ein SLA erfordert die Auswahl der relevanten Diensteigenschaften und Dienststufen und damit die Festlegung der SLA-Parameter. Der Vorgang wird im Folgenden zunächst nur anhand der Auswahl der Diensteigenschaften aufgezeigt. Ausgangspunkt ist der für das System aufgestellte Dienstkatalog, wobei für das hier behandelte Beispiel nur ein Ausschnitt der Autorenumgebung betrachtet wird.

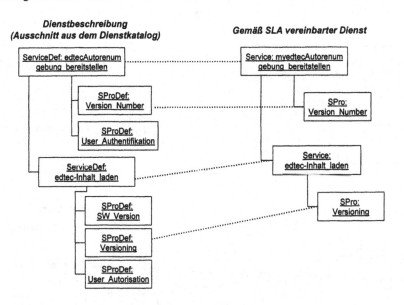

Abb. 6: Auswahl der relevanten Diensteigenschaften

Im Klassendiagramm in Abb. 6 ist ein Ausschnitt aus dem Definitionsmodell des Dienstes ed.tec-Autorenumgebung_bereitstellen dargestellt, der nur die Eigenschaften (*ServiceProperties*, SPro) des Dienstes zeigt. Auf der obersten Ebene der Komponentenhierarchie sind dem Dienst die Eigenschaften "Version" (Version_Number) und "Benutzerauthentifizierung" (User_Authentification) zugeordnet:

Mögliche Werte der Version_Number, durch die die verschiedenen Betriebssystem-Versionen des ed.tec-Systems bestimmt werden (z.B. Version für Linux/Unix-Clients oder für Clients mit Win9x-Betriebssystem).

Bei der User_Authentification sind folgende Alternativen möglich: Keine Authentifizierung, Authentifizierung auf Benutzername/Passwort-Basis sowie Zertifikats-basierte Authentifizierung.

Einen untergeordneten Dienst bildet der Dienst edtec-Inhalt_laden mit seinen Eigen-schaften "Version" (Version_Number), "Versionierungsverfahren" (Versioning) und einer „Benutzerautorisierung" (User_Autorisation). Für den Abschluss der SLAs wird jeweils nur eine Teilmenge der Diensteigenschaften ausgewählt und konkretisiert.

Die Auswahl der Dienststufen und damit die Festlegung der SLA-Parameter erfolgt analog. Hinsichtlich einer ausführlichen Beschreibung wird auf [13] verwiesen.

5 Erreichter Stand und weiteres Vorgehen

Im vorliegenden Beitrag lag der Schwerpunkt auf der Beschreibung und Modellie-rung von IT-Diensten mit dem Ziel, die Ergebnisse gezielt zur Unterstützung der SLA-Vereinbarung und der SLA-Überwachung im Rahmen des *Service Level Mana-gements* nutzen zu können [14]. Ein SLA-gerechtes Dienstmodell steht dabei im Zent-rum einer Lösung zum SLA-gerechten Service-Management.

Eine in Abb. 7 im Überblick dargestellte werkzeuggestützte Lösung wurde auf der Basis des erarbeiteten und hier beschriebenen Dienstmodells entwickelt. Die An-wendbarkeit der Konzepte und Werkzeuge wurde am Beispiel verschiedener konkre-ter IT-Systeme (u.a. SAP-CRM-System, *Customer Relationship Management*) im Rahmen von Projekten mit Industriepartnern erfolgreich erprobt.

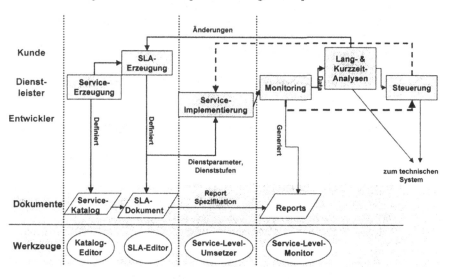

Abb. 7: Realisierte *Service-Management*-Lösung im Überblick

Zur Zeit wird das Ziel verfolgt, die bestehenden Werkzeug-Implementierungen als Web-Services zu realisieren [15] [16], um Teile der Service-Management-Funktionalität einfach und bequem dem Kunden oder weiteren Dienstleistern, die einen Teil der Dienstrealisierung erbringen, über das Web bereitstellen zu können. Eines der wichtigsten dabei zu lösenden konzeptionellen Probleme betrifft die Sicher-

344

heitsaspekte, da die in SLAs enthaltenen Angaben und die im *Service Level Management* anfallenden Managementinformationen hochgradig schützenswerte Daten darstellen.

Literaturverzeichnis

[1]   R. Sturm, W. Morris, and M. Jander, "The Heart of the Matter: Service Level Agreements," 2001.

[2]   ICS, "Service Delivery Management (http://www.ics.de/solutions/it_sdm.html)," 2001.

[3]   D. Shand, "Service-Level Agreements (http://www.computerworld.com/managementtopics/management/story/0,10 801,56572,00.html)," 2001.

[4]   R. Sturm, W. Morris, and M. Jander, *Foundations of Service Level Management*: SAMS Publishing, 2000.

[5]   C. Koch, "Service Level Agreements - Put IT in Writing," *CIO Magazine*, vol. November, 1998.

[6]   R. Sturm, "Service Level Management: The Big Picture (http://www.nextslm.org/sturm2.html)," 2001.

[7]   R. Sturm, W. Morris, and M. Jander, "What is Service Level Management (SLM)? (http://www.nextslm.org/slm1.html)," 2001.

[8]   ISO, "International Standardization Organization, Basic Reference Model, ISO 7498."

[9]   L. L. Peterson and B. S. Davie, *Computernetze - Ein modernes Lehrbuch*: dpunkt.verlag, 2000.

[10]   S. Abeck, G. Hillebrand, P. C. Lockemann, J. Schiller, and J. Seitz, *Verteilte Informationssysteme: Integration von Datenübertragungstechnik und Datenbanktechnik*: dpunkt.verlag, 2002.

[11]   H.-C. Hegering, S. Abeck, and B. Neumair, *Integrated Management of Networked Systems: Concepts, Architectures, and Their Operational Application*: Morgan Kaufmann Publishers, 1999.

[12]   R. Sturm, W. Morris, and M. Jander, "The Perception and Management of Service Levels (http://www.nextslm.org/slm2.html)," 2001.

[13]   B. Pauze, "Service Level Management for CRM 3.0," Universität Karlsruhe, 2002.

[14]   C. Mayerl, *Eine integrierte Dienstmanagement-Architektur für die qualitätsgesicherte Bereitstellung von Netz- und Systemdiensten*: Shaker Verlag, 2001.

[15]   U. Bettag, "Web-Services," *Informatik Spektrum*, vol. 24, 2001.

[16]   A. Krowczyk, C. Nagel, A. Banerjee, B. Maiani, T. Thangarathinam, A. Corera, T. Palmer, and C. Peiris, "C# Web Services: Building .NET Web Services with ASP.NET and .NET Remoting," *Wrox Press Ltd*, 2001.

Integrating Orthogonal Middleware Functionality in Components Using Interceptors

Christoph Pohl and Steffen Göbel

Technische Universität Dresden
Institut für Systemarchitektur, Lehrstuhl Rechnernetze
D-01062 Dresden, Germany
`pohl@rn.inf.tu-dresden.de, goebel@rn.inf.tu-dresden.de`

Abstract Current component platforms usually consider only a limited set of non-functional properties. Integration of these aspects is moreover handled in a rather static way. This article elaborates on possible uses of existing meta-programming facilities, notably interceptors, for custom integration of orthogonal middleware facilities. The concept is demonstrated with a concrete example of transparent client-side caching in Enterprise Java Beans. Further use cases exploiting the same principle to achieve adaptivity in the context of the COMQUAD project are presented in the second part.

1 Introduction

Today's middleware platforms like Enterprise Java Beans [5] follow a separation of concerns approach. Components are treated as black boxes; their business logic is opaque to the container's runtime environment. Middleware services are mostly integrated at deployment time, using declarative descriptors with meta-information about components' non-functional aspects. With common distributed component models like EJB, CORBA Components, Microsoft's COM+ and .NET [20], these aspects basically include transactional capabilities, persistence, synchronization, and security (authorization and encryption). Other aspects are not covered by their specifications and thus have to be integrated in vendor-specific ways. The authors already published on several of these non-functional aspects, like adaptation and caching [6, 18].

This article elaborates on how to seamlessly integrate these aspects with current component architectures, using *interceptors* as reflectional programming mechanism.

2 Related Work

Transparently adapting components' behavior is not a new idea: It actually dates back as early as 1982 when Smith published his thesis about reflection [19]. Although models have changed greatly since then, the basic concept is that components (programs) should have a notion about their current context and

346

(limited) control over their interpretative environment. This control is commonly referred to as *meta-programming*, i.e. programming at the abstract *meta-level* which is used to describe the executed code itself (classes, methods, etc.). *Meta-object protocols* (MOP) define interfaces to this meta-level.

According to [14], distributed systems are inherently predestined for reflectional programming, due to distribution transparency that is usually aimed at. Distribution itself can be viewed as a non-functional aspect that should ideally be separated from application logic by means of meta-programming mechanisms.

In distributed object-oriented systems, some sort of binding objects are typically employed as proxies to support location transparency. These proxies are often used as access points for meta-programming. For instance in the CORBA world, *smart proxies* have been developed as a simple meta-object protocol for altering behavior by intercepting calls from clients. Smart proxies provide better performance than *portable interceptors* as shown by [22], but they provide less flexibility and are not standardized by the Object Management Group[1]. Portable Interceptors have been in the focus of discussion for a few years and are now finally integrated in the OMG's CORBA standard [16]. Furthermore, smart proxy functionality can be implemented using interceptors[2], but not vice-versa.

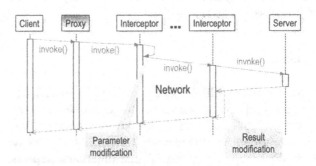

Figure 1. The principle of interceptors

The basic scheme of interceptors is shown in Fig. 1. On both client and server side, interceptors can be hooked into the control flow of (remote) operation calls, basically to add parameters and to augment results, but generally to alter virtually any property of a call's context, even its semantics. Interception may take place at different levels of call processing, hence there are request, message, object, and network-level interceptors. The OMG's standard [16] currently defines only request- and object-level interceptors; most of the others will surely follow.

Several recent publications [2, 21] leverage interceptors for building frameworks that more or less try to partly hide the complexity of meta-programming

---

[1] Some vendors like TAO [23], Inprise, and Iona adopted and pushed the development of smart proxies, but e.g. Iona is already discontinuing support for this feature.
[2] see [12]

or to add a higher abstraction level. Our goal is rather to pinpoint possible uses of basic mechanisms that already exist in current component platforms.

3 Approach

This section first presents how non-functional services have been integrated in available middleware using interceptors, instancing caching as a practical example. The second part elaborates on future prospects for further integrations in the field of adaptation.

3.1 Caching

While many existing distributed component-based applications follow a clear thin-client approach, fat clients still are eligible in certain scenarios with high user interactivity, e.g. e-Learning and collaborative multimedia. In these cases, the common issue "Either data must come to the process or the process must come to the data" can hardly be decided in the latter sense because this would require network round-trips upon every interaction. On the other hand, efficient client-side data access requires partial replication, which eliminates unnecessary network calls for already queried component attributes, to provide the appropriate locality of reference.

The authors already showed in previous publications [18] how caching functionality, a special form of partial replication, can be integrated using smart-proxy-like meta-programming techniques. This involved augmenting default (Java RMI) proxies. Unfortunately, deployment of modified component stubs proofed to be too complicated on most existing container (EJB) platforms because of the numerous providers' varying architectural concepts. For this reason, the current prototype is now based on an open-source EJB container's built-in facilities for reflectional programming.

Integration with interceptors in JBoss. JBoss [10] was chosen for being a vivid project with numerous cutting-edge software-architectural features, including a framework for request-level interceptors as introduced in Sec. 2. Client-side integration of these interceptors is shown in Fig. 2: Component proxies are transparently generated and instantiated using Java's Dynamic Reflection API. A ClientContainer passes each request through a chain of Interceptors, whose sequential order is determined by the bean provider or application assembler at deployment time. The last interceptor always hands the request to the appropriate InvokerProxy – JRMP in Fig. 2 for Java Remote Method Protocol – that finally calls the server. Server-side interceptors are stacked in a similar fashion. When a response returns from the server, it passes through the same interceptor chain in reverse order as already shown schematically in Fig. 1.

Even though CORBA Portable Interceptors are already part of Sun's Java 2 Standard Edition 1.4 and JBoss's IIOP provider JacORB [7], JBoss has not yet employed the CORBA API for integrating interceptors because it does not use

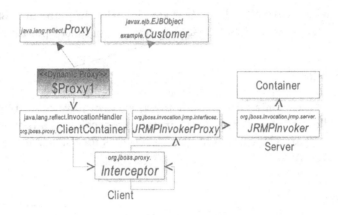

Figure 2. Interceptors in JBoss

IIOP but JRMP by default for performance reasons. Fortunately, org.jboss.-proxy.Interceptor's functionality can be viewed as a sub-set of org.omg.PortableInterceptor.Interceptor which should make future changes easy.

The integration of transparent client-side caching of component attributes basically relies on adding a CachingInterceptor to a component's jboss-container.xml descriptor during deployment as the second link in the client interceptor chain between Home- / EntityInterceptor and SecurityInterceptor. JBoss's interceptor API basically contains a method Object invoke(Invocation i) throws Throwable; where i contains all necessary information about the ongoing request, especially the component's identity, called method and parameters. Assuming that component attributes are typically exposed at an EJB's remote interface via Java-Beans-style getXyz() methods, this information is sufficient for attribute caching: The CachingInterceptor checks all Invocations i against its back-end and returns the request's response immediately if the result can be served by the local cache. Otherwise, returning responses from not yet cached invocations are automatically filed in the cache.

Cache back-end and multiple reference handling. Prototypically, the cache back-end was implemented using a simple Hashtable with component identity, method, and parameters as combined keys and results as values, i.e. $(i, m, \{p\}) \rightarrow r$. A more sophisticated version uses a *JCache*[3]-like API that caters for memory management, persistent caching etc. The basic granularity of cached data is per-attribute but these are members of identifiable components which enables collective invalidation of attributes.

As already elaborated in [18], *multiple reference handling* is also an important issue for caching services in distributed component middleware. Component

---

[3] Submitted Java Specification Request [3], similar to Oracle's *Object Caching Service for Java* (OCS4J).

references are typically passed around as marshaled objects (proxies / stubs) which makes it possible for a client to obtain a number of proxy objects for one and the same remote entity. This is counterproductive for memory consumption. `CachingInterceptors` have also be leveraged to support efficient multiple reference handling by checking all returned remote references, i.e. proxies, for duplicates in the local cache. As Sun's EJB specification [5] explicitly discourages direct equality checking between entities using `equals()` and `isIdentical()` may result in additional undesired remote calls, EJB handles[4] are held liable for component equality which is necessary for duplicate checking. Note that special attention must be paid when collections of proxies are returned, e.g. when accessing 1 : n relationships between entities. Corresponding accessor methods have to be tagged (see below) before generating caching code which ensures that every member of returned collections is checked for duplicates in the local cache.

UML and Computer-Aided Software Engineering. Simply caching every component attribute the same way is quite naive; some means of configurability would be appreciated. This can be accomplished by defining stereotypes according to the Unified Modeling Language (UML) [17] for tagging component attributes as shown in Fig. 3.

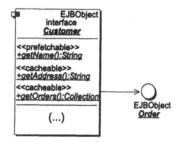

Figure 3. UML stereotypes for component attributes

Non-tagged attributes are considered *volatile* by default, i.e. their values are considered to be subject of frequent changes which makes them inappropriate for caching. The stereotype *cachable* denotes all attributes that usually change irregularly and *prefetchable* are frequently used attributes that should be transferred immediately. This is especially useful in combination with *Value Objects*[5].

The counterparts of stereotypes in Java source code are JavaDoc tags – special commands or attributes embedded in code comments which where originally intended for formatting purposes of API documentations. Thus, a stereotype $<< cacheable >>$ becomes a `/** @cacheable */` comment above an accessor

---

[4] JBoss's proxy implementations already transfer handles upon initialization, hence no additional network round-trips are needed.

[5] Introduced in [9], this pattern has become quite common for reducing network round-trips by bulk state transfer.

method. The auspicious code generation utility *XDoclet* [15] is used to evaluate these tags and create additional classes, adapt deployment descriptors etc. XDoclet follows the *one source approach*, i.e. one source file contains all necessary information about all supplementary classes, utilities, descriptors. It provides merge points in its generator templates for adding specific parts in descriptors or even for integrating custom templates capable of creating auxiliary classes.

Deployment. JBoss provides flexible ways for integrating custom deployers, i.e. server components capable of processing certain types of component archives, depending on file names, contained descriptors etc. This necessitates only the implementation of a `CachingDeployer` for scanning component archives comprising special caching descriptors. This deployer is integrated using JBoss's JCA[6] implementation and referenced by name from deployed components. Thus, component properties concerning cachability of attributes are dynamically installed in a client's runtime environment with the component's classes.

Synchronization and Consistency. Update synchronization is another important challenge for distributed caching systems. Most publications define graded consistency levels [11, 4] because guaranteed transactional consistency would require two phase locking (2PC) which would in turn entail additional network round-trips that were economized before with the introduction of caching.

The simplest solution are regular cache purges, automated by a background thread in the caching back-end that deletes cached objects after their expiration limit has been reached . Expiration limits are configurable via source code tags in the above described manner. Unfortunately, the *lag* until a given attribute update reaches the last client equals the defined expiration time in the worst case. This implies that expiration times have to be adapted to an application's least tolerable lag. On the other hand, much of caching's savings get spoiled if expiration times are much smaller than typical update cycles. Only heuristics lead to appropriate adjustments.

Consequentially, the authors currently experiment with more sophisticated update propagation algorithms. Instead of mixing the caching back-end's memory management strategy, e.g. least recently used (LRU), with consistency issues like expiration times, the caching interceptor should take care of these problems itself. Some means of multicast or publish-subscribe propagation seem to be at hand, where either modifying clients themselves notify other replicates (*write-through*) or let a component's originating server do so (*write-back*) [1]. Existing proposals like [11, 8, 13] are either intended for use in intranets or they simply abstract from underlying communication protocols. But today's typical network scenarios feature network address translation (NAT) devices, firewall configurations, and similar obstacles that make direct server-to-client connections, i.e. clients logically become server, difficult if not impossible. For this reason, protocols should preferably be client-initiated.

---

[6] *J2EE Connector Architecture*, see http://java.sun.com/j2ee/connector/.

A possible implementation of such a client-initiated protocol could regularly poll its leased component's servers with a list of component identities that would be replied with a list of update time stamps of these components which can be drawn on for cache invalidation. This performs poorly for large numbers of component references per client. So, a slightly better solution is to let clients send a list of name-value-pairs (*identity*, *timestamp*) to which servers reply only with a list of updated identities, as they also know the current timestamps for all identities. Directly replying with updated objects instead of their identities proofed to be less suitable. Anyway, a fast lookup facility for update timestamps is required for all of these solutions, e.g. a stateless session bean.

Updates can also be transferred selectively without having to initiate direct server-to-client connections by using either a JMS[7]-topic with clients as subscribers or a piggy-back approach as it is common for TCP acknowledgements. An additional server-side interceptor notices which component references are handed out to which clients, enabling it to keep track of necessary notifications. This solution is optimal in respect to bandwidth efficiency but it scales poorly on server side because of the tremendous overhead for state management of client-component-timestamp-relations.

Relations between components have already been mentioned above in the context of multiple reference handling, but they also become important in the connection with synchronization and consistency: Speaking in terms of UML [17], these relations can be categorized into *associations*, *aggregations*, and *compositions*. Especially the latter ones imply life-cycle-dependencies of their members, meaning that certain operations on one member affect the validity of the other member's cache. Up to now, such dependencies had to be analyzed manually; corresponding operations had to be tagged by hand. Ways of automating this tedious task are currently being worked on.

3.2 Adaptation

This section is to illustrate the use of interceptors in the context of the *COM-QUAD*[8] project. Component-based software engineering has become more and more important in the last few years. However, two important properties of modern distributed systems are not yet fully considered in existing concepts of component based systems:

- Quantitative properties such as network bandwidth or response time can neither be specified nor guaranteed in existing component models.
- Dynamic component adaptation is not explicitly supported. Components are rather relatively static constructs that are difficult to adapt to changing

---

[7] *Java Message Service API*, see http://java.sun.com/products/jms/. Although JBoss's own implementation JBossMQ (formerly spyderMQ) is not yet firewall-enabled, there already exist commercial tunneling solutions for JMS.

[8] *COM*ponents with *QU*antitative properties and *AD*aptivity. DFG-funded research group. See [6].

system and user environment. A possible classification of adaptational issues is shown in Tab. 1

Classification	Adaptation	Description	
Who?	User-driven	administrator	
(Trigger)	System-driven	container	
Where?	Parametric	within component	
	Structural	within application	
What for?	System-side		
	User-/application-side		
When?	Static	deploy-time	
	Dynamic	run-time	upon initialization
			during connection
How much?	(Overhead)	additionally needed time & resources	

Table 1. Classification of adaptation

The interplay of these two properties on changing quantitative properties of an application is especially important. The COMQUAD project aims at the development of a system architecture in conjunction with a development methodology supporting the composition of adaptable software from components with consideration of non-functional properties. Examples of non-functional properties are bandwidth, processing time, throughput, delay, jitter, and also security properties.

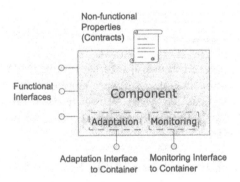

Figure 4. COMQUAD component model

In order to achieve these aims, the classic component model has been enhanced, consisting of interfaces and binary code with monitor and adaptation manager (cf. Fig. 4). The adaptation manager contains the logic for the dynamic reconfiguration of the component. It can be generated from a declarative description of the adaptation behavior or manually programmed by developers. The monitoring part of the component is necessary to observe the assured contracts at run-time. Meta-programming facilities like interceptors offer a conveniently simple way to obtain this information and make it available to the components. A component's container can transparently add appropriate interceptors at deploy-time or even upon initialization. The results of the monitoring are forwarded to the adaptation manager by the container in order to trigger the adaptation processes.

Monitoring. In the following we want to investigate which information can be gained by means of interceptors:

Invocation statistics. Statistical information about invocations includes frequencies of method calls and number of clients. These data are valid in a particular interval and they are required to monitor periodical tasks and to detect potential server overloads. The statistic belongs to component instances, component classes or the entire server. A monitoring interceptor has to maintain a table of invocation statistics for all component instances, component classes, and the entire server.

Data throughput. Data throughput is the amount of data transmitted by method invocations from client to server and back in a given interval. By means of the Java serialization mechanism an interceptor is able to obtain this value both at the client and the server. Furthermore, the data throughput can be divided into data of component instances, component classes, and the entire server.

Processing, response and delay times. The response time of a remote method invocation consists of the processing time of the method at the remote server, network transmission time, and the time for marshalling / unmarshalling parameters at client and server. These parameters are crucial in real-time applications. The processing time is measured by means of a server-side interceptor as the interval between forwarding a method invocation to a component instance and its completion. In a similar way, the response time is measured by a client-side interceptor.

The delay time of a remote method invocation is the interval between method calling by the client and starting method processing by the server. In contrast to response and processing time, this value is difficult to measure in a distributed environment without exactly synchronized clocks. At least it is possible to get good approximation. The difference between response time and processing time results in the time for sending and receiving method invocations over the network. If a constant network bandwidth is assumed, the ratio between sending time (another name for the delay time) and data size of sent parameters is the same as the ratio between the receiving time (transmission from server to client) and data size of return parameters. Hence, the delay time can be calculated.

Relocation of components. Interceptors can also be used to achieve transparent relocation of components at run-time which is an important adaptation mechanism. Components usually obtain references to other components by means of a name service (JNDI in case of EJB) at run-time and then store these references in a local variable for later usage. If a component is relocated to another server, all references from other components become invalid. To avoid this, an interceptor could forward a particular method invocation to the new location of the component, because all method invocations must pass an interceptor. Hence, all component relocations must be reported to the interceptor that maintains a table of old and new component references.

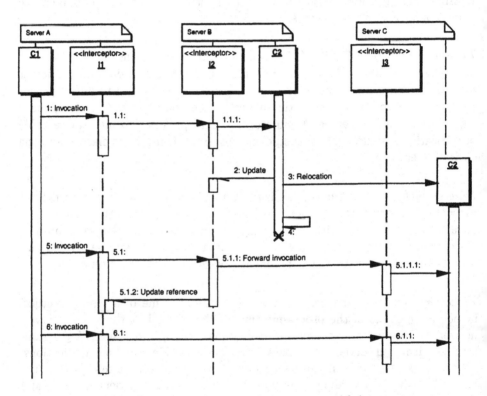

Figure 5. Transparent relocation of components with interceptors

A sequence diagram of a possible relocation scenario is depicted in Fig. 5. After relocation of component $C2$ from server B to server C, any method call to this component using an old reference is forwarded to the new location by interceptor $I2$. Obviously, this leads to a higher delay and response time for the client due to the additional step in the method call, but only for the first method call. Later on, the client interceptor of computer A redirects any further method invocations to $C2$ to the new location at server C. Prior to this, interceptor $I2$ sends a location update about component $C2$ to interceptor $I1$. The advantage of this solution is that every relocation of a component only requires one additional redirection. The processing time of the two interceptors at client and server can be disregarded in comparison to the network transmission time. As a drawback, local communication between components within one server must also pass through interceptors.

4 Conclusion

This article presented how non-functional aspects can be easily integrated in today's middleware platforms using existing meta-programming facilities, notably interceptors. Linking-up with software design and modeling facilities was demonstrated exemplary, as well as leveraging of code generation tools. An outlook was given to open issues the authors will tackle next, i.e. finding optimal cache synchronization strategies for given usage scenarios, automated component dependency analysis, and reference faulting mechanisms for more flexible cache memory management.

The second part elaborated on possible uses advanced component concepts in the *COMQUAD* project [6]. Especially for adaptational purposes, interceptors present appropriate ties for monitoring and relocation of components. Other synergies are currently being evaluated.

References

[1] Henri E. Bal, M. Frans Kaashoek, Andrew S. Tanenbaum, and Jack Jansen. Replication techniques for speeding up parallel applications on distributed systems. *Concurrency: Practice and Experience*, 4(5):337–355, August 1992.

[2] Gordon S. Blair, G. Coulson, P. Robin, and M. Papathomas. An architecture for next generation middleware. In *International Conference on Distributed Systems Platforms and Open Distributed Processing*, London, 1998. IFIP, Springer-Verlag.

[3] Jerry Bortvedt. JCache - Java Temporary Caching API. Java Specification Request #107, 19 March 2001.

[4] Gregory Chockler, Danny Dolev, Roy Friedman, and Roman Vitenberg. Implementing a caching service for distributed CORBA objects. In *Middleware'00*, pages 1–23, 2000.

[5] Linda G. DeMichiel, L. Ümit Yalčinalp, and Sanjeev Krishnan. *Enterprise JavaBeans Specification Version 2.0*. Sun Microsystems, final release edition, 14 August 2001.

[6] Technische Universität Dresden. COMponents with QUAntitative properties and ADaptivity (COMQUAD). Project homepage: http:// www.comquad.org/, August 2001. DFG research group.

[7] Freie Universität Berlin and Xtradyne Technologies AG. JacORB. Project homepage: http:// www.jacorb.org/.

[8] Arun Iyengar. Design and performance of a general-purpose software cache. In *Proceedings of the 18th IEEE International Performance Conference (IPCCC'99)*, 1999.

[9] Design patterns catalog. In *J2EE Design Patterns*. Sun Microsystems, 2001.

[10] JBoss Group. JBoss. Project homepage: http:// www.jboss.org/.

[11] Rammohan Kordale, Mustaque Ahamad, and Murthy V. Devarakonda. Object caching in a CORBA compliant system. *Computing Systems*, 9(4):377–404, 1996.

[12] Rainer Koster and Thorsten Kramp. Loadable smart proxies and native code-shipping for CORBA. In *Proceeding of the 3rd International IFIP/GI Working Conference, USM*, volume 1890, pages 202–213. Springer, 2000.

[13] Vijaykumar Krishnaswamy, Ivan B. Ganev, Jaideep M. Dharap, and Mustaque Ahamad. Distributed object implementations for interactive applications. In *Middleware 2000*, 2000.

[14] Jeff McAffer. Meta-level architecture support for distributed objects. In Gregor Kiczales, editor, *Proceedings of Reflection'96*, pages 39–62, 1996. Published before in IWOODS'95.

[15] Rickard Öberg, Andreas Schaefer, Ara Abrahamian, Aslak Hellesøy, Dmitri Colebatch, and Vincent Harcq. XDoclet. Project homepage: http:// xdo-clet.sourceforge.net/.

[16] Object Management Group. *CORBA Portable Interceptor Specification*, March 2001. ptc/01-03-04, formal/02-05-18.

[17] Object Management Group. *Unified Modeling Language, v1.4*, September 2001. formal/01-09-67.

[18] Christoph Pohl and Alexander Schill. Middleware support for transparent client-side caching. In Elke Pulvermüller, Isabelle Borne, Noury Bouraqadi, Pierre Cointe, and Uwe Assmann, editors, *European conference on Theory And Practice of Software ETAPS'02*, volume 65 of *Electronic Notes in Theoretical Computer Science*, Grenoble, France, April 2002. Elsevier Science Publishers. Software Composition Workshop.

[19] Brain Cantwell Smith. *Procedural Reflection in Programming Languages*. PhD thesis, Department of Electrical Engineering and Computer Science, MIT, Cambridge, Mass., February 1982.

[20] Clemens Szyperski. *Component Software: Beyond Object-Oriented Programming*. Addison-Wesley, November 1997.

[21] Eddy Truyen, Bart Vanhaute, Wouter Joosen, Pierre Verbaeten, and Bo Nørregaard Jørgensen. Dynamic and selective combination of extensions in component-based applications. In *International Conference on Software Engineering*, pages 233–242. IEEE, 2001.

[22] Nanbor Wang, Kirthika Parameswaran, Douglas Schmidt, and Ossama Othman. The design and performance of meta-programming mechanisms for object request broker middleware. In *6th USENIX Conference on Object-Oriented Technologies and Systems (COOTS'01)*, January 2001.

[23] Washington University, St. Louis and University of California, Irvine. Real-time CORBA with TAO. Project homepage: http:// www.cs.wustl.edu/ ~schmidt/ TAO.html.

Session Internet

Topology-Analysis of Pure Peer-to-Peer Networks

Rüdiger Schollmeier[1], Felix Hermann[1]

[1]Lehrstuhl für Kommunikationsnetze, Technische Universität München,
Arcisstr. 21, 80333 München, Germany
{Schollmeier, Hermaf}@lkn.ei.tum.de

Abstract. Recently Peer-to-Peer networking has gained considerable interest in the research community. Especially the architectural topics have been already strongly investigated, in order to find new architectures which try to improve the scalability of the classical pure Peer-to-Peer network topology, as e.g. of the Gnutella network. However, in this work we show, that in Peer-to-Peer networks the problem of the network growth and the resulting signalling load is not as high as generally expected in prior research. Therefore we present a topology analyzer, which analyzes the network topology from a single node's point of view. We do not employ a network crawler, because a network crawler does not return the network topology and the signalling load experienced by a single node. As a result, our measurements show clearly that the network grows much slower than commonly expected. Additionally we are able to verify our measurements by a theoretical estimation of the network topology growth.

1. Introduction

Peer-to-Peer Applications relying on a Pure Peer-to-Peer topology [9], like e.g. applications relying on the Gnutella protocol ([13], [14]) employ as a basic routing principle a simple flooding mechanism. The reason for the usage of flooding is, that the network is a highly dynamic network. Therefore routing, relying on fixed routing tables or fixed index-servers is hardly feasable. On the other hand, a flat routing scheme imposes a high signaling load on the network, caused by the forwarding mechanism of the flooding principle.

The traffic generated by Peer-to-Peer applications, based on a pure Peer-to-Peer network already consumes a significant amount of the available bandwidth capacity of some Internet Service Providers (ISP) ([17], [23], [24]). In the Deutsches Forschungsnetz (DFN) [19] 60 percent of the traffic within its network is generated by Peer-to-Peer applications [17].

This rising amount of traffic generated by Peer-to-Peer applications certainly also stems from the growing number of users [18], which are distributed all over the world, as illustrated by the map given in Figure 1. In this map the active nodes of the network are mapped to their geographical locations. Each of these nodes has an average of 3.4 connections, with the number of connection distributed according to a powerlaw distribution.

According to Ritter [4] such a network would not be scalable. The number of messages initiated by one message would grow exponentially with the number of hops, via which the message is forwarded. As outlined in [4] the reason for this is, that every participating node forwards any incoming message to every neighbor it is connected to, except the neighbor it received the message from. Further on Ritter bases his calculations on the assumption of a pure tree-structure of the network topology. This results in an exponential growth of the number of messages generated by one message, as shown in (1). If this would be true, any application based on a pure Peer-to-Peer network and used by more than a few hundred users, would be doomed to fail, as the necessary bandwidth would not be sufficient at the access level.

$$n_{cum\_ping} = n_c \cdot \frac{\left(n_c - 1\right)^{(h-1)}}{n_c - 2} \tag{1}$$

(n_c=average nr. of connections per node, h=hop count)

For this reason new network architectures are proposed in [20], [21] and [22], which introduce additional dynamic hierarchies, to reduce the signaling overhead.

However as indicated by the growing number of users [4] and by our theoretical considerations in [10], the expectation of a exponentially growing number of messages is not realistic. Further on it can be shown, that the probability for the establishment of a pure tree structure, is decreasing very fast and falls down to zero after a few number of hops (see Section 2). Thus the network must include some self limiting characteristics. Those restrict the number of available nodes and the traffic load imposed on any single node.

To explain this phenomenon in more detail, traffic issues have been analyzed in [8], [6], [7] and [12]. In these documents, the distribution of content, latencies and bottleneck bandwidths is measured, to analyze the traffic characteristics of a pure Peer-to-Peer network. However an explanation for the self limiting characteristics of a pure Peer-to-Peer network is not provided.

A first analytical approach to answer the question of the self limiting characteristics in Peer-to-Peer networks is provided by Annexstein et. al [1]. They study the impacts of short circuits within tree structured graphs. However as they concentrate on simulations and mathematical analyzations, they were not able to analyze the effects of short circiuting on active Peer-to-Peer networks as it is presented in this work.

Several measurement approaches to explain this phenomenon are suggested in [2], [3], [5] and [15]. However these measurement approaches, employ a network crawler, to determine the number of reachable hosts. From our point of view, this is not an accurate approach, as these measurements do not represent the network as it is perceived by a single, regular node. With a crawler parts of the network are taken into account which do not communicate with the node at all. Nodes which are out of a node's horizon are neither available to the node, nor put any additional messaging load on the node.

Therefore we implemented a network analyzer which only explores that part of a network, a node might experience. This is done by actively probing the network with signaling messages and analyzing the resulting responses from the network. With this tool we are able to verify the self limiting characteristics of pure Peer-to-Peer networks. These characteristics are additionally underlined by a theoretical evaluation of pure Peer-to-Peer networks in this work.

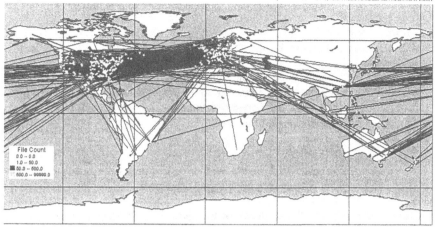

Figure 1 Map of the Gnutella Network, May 2002

This work is therefore organized as follows: In Section 2, we present an analytical consideration of the self limiting characteristics of a pure Peer-to-Peer network.. Afterwards we describe the experimental setup, and the network analyzer in Section 3. An evaluation of the measurements and a conclusion of this work and is given in Section 4.

2. Analytical consideration of the self limiting characteristics

As mentioned above Jordan Ritter [4] argues that the network model of the Gnutella network is based on a binary tree structure. As outlined in [4], the bandwidth usage in such a network would increase exponentially and therefore the Gnutella network could not scale. We argue that the proposed binary tree structure is not even close to the real network model that is existing. First of all the, the limited number of users in the network will lead to loops in the network when one after another user tries to join the Gnutella network with its client. Therefore the number of reachable nodes in the network should not grow exponentially.

Only in the case of a tree topology, the signaling load can grow exponentially with the number of hops over which the message is forwarded. For the estimation of this "tree" probability we use the following parameters:

- N_{all} : Total number of nodes, which are considered in our network

- n_c : Number of connections which are permitted on every node

- h : Hop-Count (number of hops over which the tree is established)

- $$N_{search}(h) = N_{search}(h-1) \cdot (n_c - 1) = n_c \cdot (n_c - 1)^{h-1} \qquad (2)$$

where $N_{search}(h)$ is the total number of nodes needed to establish a worst case tree up to hop h, and $N_{search}(h-1)$ is the total Number of nodes, each searching for (n_c-1) connections at hop h

$$N_{occ}(h) = 1 + n_c \cdot \frac{1-(n_c-1)^h}{2-n_c} \tag{3}$$

where $N_{occ}(h)$ is the total number of occupied nodes which are partly or fully connected to the tree established until hop h . Thus, these $N_{occ}(h)$ nodes can therefore not be used for the further establishment of the tree.

$$N_{free}(h) = N_{all} - N_{occ}(h) \tag{4}$$

where $N_{free}(h)$ is the number of free nodes, i.e. nodes which are not already connected to any other node.

Due to the mathematical complexity of the network establishment process in the simple Gnutella protocol, we are only able to compute a lower and an upper bound for the probability, that a tree is established. However the interval limited by the upper and the lower bound is very narrow, as it can be observed in and. The equations for the upper and the lower bound are given in (5) and in (6).

$$P_{Tree\_u}(h) = \prod_{i=0}^{N_{search}(h-1)-1} P_b(h,i+1) = \prod_{i=0}^{N_{search}(h-1)-1} \frac{N_{free}(h)-i}{\left[N_{free}(h)-i\right]+\left[N_{search}(h-1)-\left(\left\lfloor\frac{i}{n_c-1}\right\rfloor+1\right)\right]} \tag{5}$$

$$P_{Tree\_l}(h) = \prod_{i=0}^{N_{search}(h-1)-1} \frac{N_{free}(h)-i}{\left[N_{free}(h)-\frac{i}{n_c}\right]+\left[N_{search}(h-1)-\left(\left\lfloor\frac{i}{n_c-1}\right\rfloor+1\right)\right]} \tag{6}$$

According to the calculations outlined above we come to the conclusion that the probability for building a tree-structured Gnutella network is approaching zero rapidly after a certain number of hops. As illustrated by Figure 2 and Figure 3, the steepness of the decrease also depends on the total number of available nodes in the network. Thus the messaging load imposed on a node, is much smaller, than expected in [4].

Further on the loops, which occur randomly in the network lead also to less bandwidth consumption in the network. The reason therefore is that, according to the Gnutella protocol [13], any message which is received twice by one node is automatically killed and not forwarded any further. This means that the Gnutella network does scale. As a result of our analytical considerations, we can state, that the horizon of a single node accounting or the total number of reachable is significantly lower than a tree structure suggests. This fact is underlined by the measurements described in the following section.

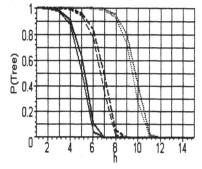

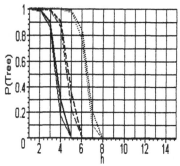

Figure 2 Upper and Lower bound of the probability for the establishment of a tree up to hop h for Nall=1.000 (solid), 10.000 (dashed) and 500.000(dotted) and nc=3

Figure 3 Upper and Lower bound of the probability for the establishment of a tree up to hop h for Nall= 1.000 (solid), 10.000 (dashed) and 500.000 (dotted) and nc=4

3. Topology-Measurements

In our experiment we measure the number of nodes that a single client can reach. In order to do so, we use the open-source Qtella client (http://www.qtella.org) employing the Gnutella network. Within this client we modify the implemented pong caching mechanism. The pong cache stores incoming pongs in a cache adding a time stamp and cleans this cache every 40 seconds using the time stamp to wipe out old entries.

Further on we change the class in which the pong entries are saved so it can also store query hits and pushes. With these modifications we are able to log the three messages in the Gnutella protocol containing IP addresses. All these messages contain a Time-to-Live (TTL) value, which is saved along with the rest of the data in the packets. Additionally we add a filter to the functions inserting the messages to the cache: before a new message is stored, the cache is checked and if the IP address is already in the cache, only the time stamp of the entry is updated.

To get as many messages as possible from the network, we initiate ping messages to all connected nodes and start queries for a set of expressions that are very likely to be found in the Gnutella network. This gives us a flood of incoming messages in response to the requests. All these messages are logged in the pong cache. After two minutes of measurements, the content of the pong cache is analyzed and logged to the local machine using the *syslog* mechanism of Linux. In detail we log the number of nodes that have sent replies separated by their TTL values. This is done for every connected node.

Additionally the TTL value for the messages sent by our client-application is adjustable but some experiments at the beginning showed that the best results can be obtained using a TTL of seven as suggested by the developers. The last line of each log entry stores the number of nodes that have been connected throughout the single experiment, since it is possible that a node disconnects during the measurement. It also saves the TTL value that has been set, since the modified client allows us to choose TTL values from 1 to 20. For the experiment we choose the proposed TTL value of 7.

The maximum number of connections of our analyzer is adjustable. It reaches from 3 connections to max 120 connections. The average number of connections that could be realized is slightly lower due to the frequent changes in the network structure.

The experiment is started by sending pings and queries to the connected nodes. Then the analyzer waits to coolect the responses of all the other clients partcipating in the network. After 2 minutes all received messages are written to syslog and the experiment is started again. The time period with which the pong cache of our Qtella client is "cleaned up" is set to 2 minutes as well. The duration of the measurements for each setting of the maximum number of connections has been conducted over a time frame of more than 24 hours. The motivation to measure with high numbers of direct connections of the analyzer is the fact. that in theory we should reach all available nodes in the Gnutella network at once, if enough direct connections can be established.

According to (7), it can be shown, that 32689 nodes can be reached, if n_{conn} (the number of direct connections) is set to a value of 100. 32689 also represented at the time of our measurements approximately the whole Gnutella network. In the equation we user an average number of connections of 3.4 which corresponds to the measurement results presented in [5]

$$N \quad = \sum_{T=1}^{t} n_{conn} \cdot (3.4-1)^{T-1} \tag{7}$$

Table 1 Number of reachable nodes in our measurements related to theoretical values

Number of direct connections (average)	Number of reachable nodes (in total)	Number of theoretically reachable nodes	Percentage related to the theoretical value of reachable nodes
1.29 Connections	223.73	421.62	53.06%
5.00 Connections	630.51	1634.00	38.59%
11.90 Connections	1247.65	3890.39	32.07%
17.84 Connections	1710.87	5832.88	29.33%
24.29 Connections	1912.20	7940.73	24.08%
40.76 Connections	2506.36	13323.94	18.81%

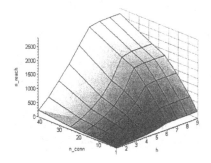
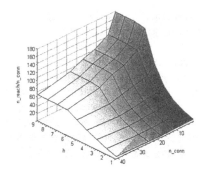

Figure 4 Total number of reachable nodes (n_reach) in dependence of the number of connections (n_conn) and the hop-count (h)

Figure 5 Total number of reachable nodes (n_reach) per number of connections in dependence of the number of connections (n_conn) and the hop-count (h)

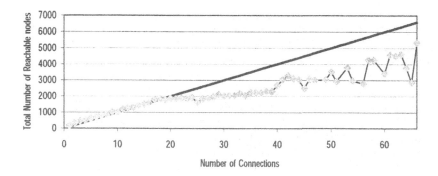

Figure 6 The total number of reachable nodes broken down on the numbers of connections of the client. The bold line represents the linear trend for the first numbers of connections.

As Figure 5 shows, the number of reachable nodes in the network is always significantly lower than the theoretical value of reachable nodes for a tree structured network with an average of 3.4 connections per nodes. To calculate the theoretical numbers of reachable nodes (7) is used.

In Table 1 the results of the measurements and the calculations according to (7) are given. It can be observed, that the values of the measurements are always significantly smaller than the calculated values. The reason therefore is the emergence of loops in the network. Due to details of the Gnutella protocol this leads to a reduced number of reachable nodes. The fourth column of Table 1 shows, that the number of reachable nodes is decreasing with an increasing number of connections of our analyzer. Since the number of total reachable nodes is raising this implies an increasing number of loops. This increase in the loops leads to less nodes being "visible" to our node in the network as Table 1 shows.

This phenomenon can also be observed in Figure 3, where the number of reachable nodes divided by the number of connections of our analyzer for every hop-value, ranging from 1 to 9 hops, is presented. In the case of a tree structure only an increase in the number of reachable nodes per connection along the h-axis should be observed. Along the n_conn –axes the number of reachable nodes should neither increase or decrease for a given hop-value. As it can be observed in Figure 4 the number of reachable nodes increases for decreasing values of the number of connections (n_conn), a tree structure can not be assumed for the topology of a pure Peer-to-Peer network.

In contrast, Figure 4 is a clear indication that loops establish within this network, as the number of reachable nodes is decreasing for growing numbers of connections of the analyzer. The reason is, if more connections are established an increasing number of nodes can be reached via several connections of the analyzer. Thus loops are established, as one node can be reached via several ways.

These loops lead to a significantly slower growth of the network, than expected, which can be observed in Figure 3 and Figure 7. Another interesting detail of Figure 3 is the saturation of the number of reachable nodes after approx 7 to 8 hops. From our point of view, this effect can be explained with tow reasons.

The first reason is, that already in a lot of nodes a so called TTL (Time-to Live)-cut is implemented. This means that any message which has been forwarded already via more than 7 hops is killed and not forwarded any further. Thus it may not possible to reach all nodes which are more than 7 hops away from our analyzer.

The second reason is, that after 7 hops the probability that new nodes can be found is already comparably small, as it is already indicated in Figure 2 and Figure 3. Thus after 7 hops additional connections to nodes to which our analyzer is already connected are established. As a result loops develop within the network, which limit the network growth significantly due to details of the Gnutella protocol.

In Figure 5 the graph of the total number of reachable nodes in dependence of the number of connections of the analyzer is given. The linear trend line in Figure 5 interpolates the first 20 values, since in this range a high number measurements could be taken. Due to the dynamics of the network, from about 30 connections onward less values could be measured. This results in more blurred results, as it can be observed on the right half of Figure 5. Analyzing the standard deviation for each of the measured values, it can be concluded, that these single results for higher numbers of connections are still in the range of the calculated standard deviation.

The most important result from our measurements is that there is no exponential growth in the number of reachable hosts in the Gnutella network as suggested by Ritter [4]. Additionally we find, that the number of reachable nodes in the network is not growing linearly with the hop distance. This is also a strong indicator, that such a pure Peer-to-Peer network can not be modeled with a tree topology.

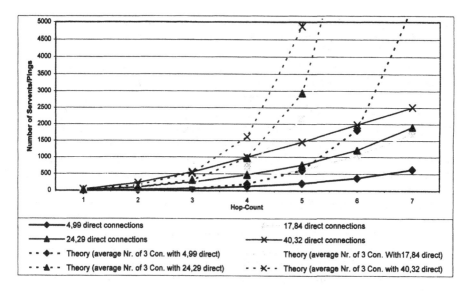

Figure 7 Comparison of the theoretical values and the measured values of the number of reachable nodes

4. Evaluation of the Measurements and Conclusion

The measurements achieved with our network analyzer, are quite remarkable, as it can be observed clearly, that the network grows much slower (see Figure 7 and Figure 5) than generally expected. In Figure 7 the resulting graphs of four measurements is given. The measurements presented in Figure 7 are done for four different values for the number of direct connections, i.e. an average of 4.99, 17.84, 24.29 and 40.32 direct connections. For comparison, the graphs for the theoretical values, according to a binary as they can be computed with (1) are also presented in Figure 7.

In Figure 7 the deviation between the theoretical value and the measured values is already significant in the area between 4 and 6 hops. After seven hops the deviation between the theoretical model of Ritter [4] and the measured values is already up to a several thousand nodes/pings. Thus it can certainly be stated, that the network grows much slower than generally expected.

This phenomenon of the restricted growth of the analyzed pure Peer-to-Peer network can be explained by two approaches. The first approach is a purely mathematical approach, as described in Section 0. In Figure 2 and Figure 3 the probability that a tree is established is decreasing rapidly after 4 to 6 hops. This fact is also reflected by Figure 7, which shows, as mentioned above the graphs of the network evolution, for different numbers of direct connections.

In all of the four cases a significant deviation of the measured values compared to the theoretical values can be observed also after 4 to 6 hops. This strong correlation between Figure 7 and Figure 2 is a strong indicator, that one reason for the limited horizon of a single node is certainly the mathematics presented in the first part of this work. This mathematics is based on the assumption of a limited network size, which leads to the rapidly decreasing tree probability. As result of this rapidly decreasing probability, the number of available nodes is decreasing too, as it can be observed in Figure 7.

The second reason for the restricted network growth is the spontaneous development of loops. A loop within a pure Peer-to-Peer network is established, e.g. when a node connects directly to a node to which it is already connected via another path. Such a loop thus short circuits the network [1]. Due to details of the Gnutella protocol [13] these short-circuits result in a shrinking total network size experienced by single node. Thus with every additional loop the number of reachable nodes per direct connection is decreases, i.e. the reciprocal of the number of reachable nodes per direct connection increases. This strong correlation can be observed in Figure 8. The minimum square fit straight line of both graphs have nearly the same slope, which shows the close proportionality between the reciprocal number of reachable nodes and the number of loops per connection.

With the mathematical approach combined with the measurements of our P2P-network analyzer, we are able to state and verify the reasons for the restricted network growth. Because of this restricted growth, the Peer-to-Peer network is divided into several clusters, which form self limiting groups. The network thus predicts its participants from unbearable and unnecessary traffic.

As a result the network and the load on the network scales much better than generally expected. Therefore hierarchical structures, as proposed in [20], [21] or [22] are not a must from our point of view, if the Peer-to-Peer network is used for common file sharing applications.

However if a Peer-to-Peer network should be used for tasks with significantly lower availability and redundancy, than in common file sharing applications, hierarchical architectures will be necessary. Otherwise the content or e.g. the user to whom a multimedia communication channel should be established, might not be found, if the demanded subject resides in another cluster.

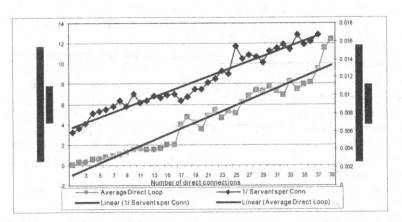

Figure 8 Correlation of the reciprocal number of nodes and the number of direct loops

References

[1]   F. S. Annexstein, K. A. Berman, M. A. Jovanovic. "Latency effects on reachability in large-scale peer-to-peer networks". Proceedings of the ACM Symposium on Parallel Algorithms and Architectures, pp.84-92. 2001

[2]   M. Ripeanu. "Peer-to-Peer Architecture Case Study: Gnutella Network". Technical Report, University of Chicago. TR-2001-26. 2001

[3]   M. Jovanovic, F.S. Annexstein, and K.A. Berman. "Scalability Issues in Large Peer-to-Peer Networks - A Case Study of Gnutella". Technical Report, University of Cincinnati, 2001.

[4]   J. Ritter, Why Gnutella Can not Scale. No, Really!. http://www.darkridge.com/~jpr5/doc/gnutela.html. 20.03.2002

[5]   M. Ripeanu, I. Foster. "Mapping the gnutella network". IEEE Internet Computing Journal. 6(1). 2002

[6]   K. Anderson, "Analysis of the traffic on the gnutella network" 2001, http://www-cse.ucsd.edu/classes/wi01/cse222/projects/reports/p2p-2.pdf. 14.05.02

[7]   S. Saroiu, P. K. Gummadi, S. D. Gribble. "A Measurement Study of Peer-to-Peer File Sharing Systems". Proceedings of Multimedia Computing and Networking 2002 (MMCN '02).2002.

[8]   E. P. Markatos, "Tracing a large-scale Peer to Peer System: an hour in the life of Gnutella". Proceedings of 2nd IEEE/ACM International Symposium on Cluster Computing and the Grid. 2002

[9]   R. Schollmeier. "A definition of Peer-to-Peer networking towards a delimitation against classical client server concepts". Proceedings of WATM-Eunice 2001. 2001

[10]   R. Schollmeier, G. Schollmeier. "Why Peer-to-Peer (P2P) Does Scale: An Analysis of Peer-to-Peer Traffic Patterns". IEEE International Conference on P2P Computing 2002, Linköping Sweden. September 2002.

[11]   K. Aberer, M. Punceva, M. Hauswirth, R. Schmidt. „Improving Data Access in P2P Systems". IEEE Internet Computing Journal. 6(1). 2002

[12]   E. Adar, B. A. Huberman. "Free riding on gnutella". Appeared in First Monday. 2000.

[13]   Gnutella Protocol Specification, version 0.4; available at http://www.clip2.com/GnutellaProtocol04.pdf, 20.03.2002

[14]   T. Klingberg, R.Manfredi. "Gnutella 0.6 RFC". June 2002, rfc-gnutella.sourceforge.net/draft.txt

[15]   L. Adamic, R. Lukose, A. Puniyani, B. Huberman, "Search in Power-Law Networks". Phys. Rev. E, 64 46135. 2001

[16]   B. Krishnamurthy, J. Wang, and Y. Xie. "Early Measurements of a Cluster-based Architecture for P2P Systems". Proceedings of SIGCOMM IMW 2001, California, pp. 105—109. 2001

[17]   G. Foest, R. Paffrath. "Peer-to-Peer (P2P) and beyond". DFN Mitteilungen 58-3. 2002

[18]   Limewire.com. "Current network size ".http://www.limewire.com/historical_size.html. 15.05.2002

[19]   Deutsches Forschungsnetz http://www.dfn.de. 18.05.02

[20] Stoica, R. Morris, D. Karger, M. F. Kaashoek, and H. Balakrishnan. "Chord: A scalable peer-to-peer lookup service for Internet applications". Technical Report TR-819, MIT, March 2001.

[21] I. T. Rowstron and P. Druschel. "Pastry: Scalable, Decentralized Object Location, and Routing for Large-Scale Peer-to-Peer Systems". Proceedings of the 18th IFIP/ACM International Conference on Distributed Systems Platforms (Middleware 2001). November 2001.

[22] Zhao, J. Kubiatowicz, and A. Joseph. Tapestry: An infrastructure for fault-tolerant wide-area location and routing. Technical Report UCB/CSD-01-1141, Computer Science Division, U. C. Berkeley, April 2001.

[23] Internet2 Netflow, Weekly Reports, Week of 20020826 http://netflow.internet2.edu/weekly/20020826, August 2002

[24] Aiko Pras, "Measuring Traffic on the Internet", IFIP WG6.7 Workshop and EUNICE Summer Scholl on Adaptable Networks and Teleservices, Norway, September 2002

On the Use of Passive Network Measurements for Modeling the Internet

Klaus Mochalski and Klaus Irmscher

University of Leipzig, Computer Science Department
{mochalski|irmscher}@informatik.uni-leipzig.de

Abstract. Many important discoveries in Internet research have been made on the basis of traces collected by passive measurement systems. However, the various difficulties involved in capturing a network traffic trace have resulted in a poor availability of high-quality traces. Furthermore, with the rapidly increasing data rates of today's Internet links, capturing a trace long enough to yield meaningful analysis results becomes more and more difficult. This paper emphasises the usefulness of passive measurements and outlines the methodology used to conduct them. We present three trace data sets to describe our analyses, among them a new trace captured at the University of Leipzig. We also show how packet traces can be used to support and evaluate Internet simulations.

1 Introduction

Passive measurements are a powerful tool for modeling Internet traffic. They produce a trace of the actual traffic on the measured link at a certain time. Such a trace can be seen as a snapshot of an Internet link. The achieved accuracy of a trace depends on the quality of a measurement. What exactly accuracy means and how to achieve it is discussed in this paper. Once a high-quality trace has been captured, it can be used for further analyses. This includes for instance verification of models of certain traffic classes, support and verification of simulations, and also very practical analyses like detection of denial of service attacks or misbehaving hosts and applications. Classical examples of discoveries made by trace analysis are, for instance, [10] and [11]. These works have greatly influenced subsequent research. Passive measurements will be especially useful to support current efforts toward Internet QoS support. They enable precise analyses of packet burst and delay behaviour—two important issues linked to QoS.

Capturing packet traces becomes more and more challenging with the increasing bandwidths of today's Internet. Different scalability issues have to be addressed including capturing speed during the actual measurement session, storage capabilities for longer traces, and processing power for offline analysis of trace data. In this paper we present the methodology we used to capture and analyse trace data sets at various locations—among them the Auckland-IV and VI [5] and the Leipzig-I [6] data sets.

The availability of specialised hardware to support Internet packet capturing turned out to be of crucial importance. Dag measurement cards [7] developed by the University of Waikato, Hamilton, New Zealand, have been used to collect these packet header traces. They provide high precision timestamps with clock synchronisation.

The rest of this paper is organised as follows: Section 2 gives a brief comparison of passive and active measurement techniques. Section 3 discusses various aspects of passive measurement methodology which have been applied to the Auckland and Leipzig measurements described in Sect. 4. Section 5 presents various analyses based on these data sets. We show how traces can be used to improve and evaluate network simulations. Section 6 discusses the results and concludes the paper.

2 Active vs. Passive Network Measurements

There are two forms of network measurements—active and passive.

Active measurements create and inject artificial packets into the network under observation. Later, these packets are intercepted and metrics based on their behaviour are calculated. The idea behind this technique is to use a well-defined sample to draw conclusions about the overall behaviour of a certain part of the network.

Passive measurements capture packets transmitted by applications running on network-attached devices over a network link. Usually, the arrival of each packet is earmarked with a timestamp. Storing all captured packets along with their timestamps in a trace file provides an accurate representation of network traffic.

The achievable measurement accuracy strongly depends on the accuracy of the timestamps supplied by the measurement system. While this applies to both active and passive measurements, it is a more important issue for the passive case. Since legacy hardware does not provide high-precision clocks and clock synchronisation to support accurate timestamps, specialised hardware has to be deployed in many cases. Section 3 provides further details about timestamping of network packets.

Active and passive measurements both have their specific advantages and disadvantages making them suitable for different purposes. One of the major drawbacks of active measurements is the potential interference of injected packets with normal network traffic. Depending on the network load and the amount of data transmitted by an active measurement platform, this could not only lead to a distortion of the very effects to be measured but also actually create an overload situation. This can pose a serious limitation as network measurements are especially interesting during periods of high load.

The passive approach does not have such a limitation. There is no interference of the measurement with network traffic. However, the above mentioned accuracy of passive measurements comes at a price. Each and every packet needs to be captured to gain a complete picture of a link's traffic behaviour. This imposes a serious scalability problem to passive measurements. With the Internet link capacities growing faster than other computer technologies such as CPU, memory, disk, and tape performance, it is just a matter of time until full network packet traces—even for short periods of time—become all but unfeasible. A thorough study of bandwidth requirements for passive measurements can be found in [1]. In this respect, active measurements scale much better because they often work with a data sample of negligible size in comparison to the overall traffic on a measured link. Section 3 discusses possible improvements of the poor scalability properties of passive measurements.

Safety and privacy are very important issues of any network measurement. Neither network operation nor user privacy should be adversely affected. The first aspect applies to active measurements as discussed in the last two paragraphs whereas user privacy is more of a concern for passive measurements. Active measurements generate their own data. Only these data are used for analyses, and user data remain untouched.

The situation is somewhat different for passive measurements. User data are intentionally captured and often stored for analysis purposes. This is one of the major sources of difficulties involved in conducting a passive measurement in an operational network. Most organisations running a network usually have strong objections to this kind of data collection. These privacy concerns have to be addressed by dropping any unnecessary data (e.g. any packet payload) and by anonymising IP addresses to prevent end user identification from the trace data. Section 3 describes how this is achieved for the Auckland and Leipzig data sets.

3 Passive Measurement Methodology

Timestamping is one of the central functions of a passive measurement system. To understand its importance, one has to be aware of the timescale at which events happen on a network link. With increasing link rates, requirements to timestamping precision rise proportionally. Table 1 gives an idea of timescales of different link technologies.

Table 1. Packet serialisation times for selected packet sizes and network technologies[2]

Packet size (bytes)	Link	Serialisation (in ns)
64	10BaseT	51,200
512	10BaseT	410,000
1500	10BaseT	1,200,000
64	100BaseTX	5,200
64	100BaseTX	520
53	OC3c	2,720
53	OC12c	675
53	OC48c	168

The simplest and cheapest approach to timestamping network packets is to use a standard PC equipped with a network interface card and to rely on the PC's clock facility along with a synchronisation package like NTP (Network Time Protocol). The disadvantage of this approach is the relatively low accuracy. NTP provides an accuracy within some milliseconds. Table 1 shows that this is by no means sufficient for today's high speed links.

The Dag network measurement cards developed by the University of Waikato [7] provide a solution to this problem. These cards are able to do packet capturing at full link rate for a wide variety of link layer technologies including Ethernet, ATM and Packet over Sonet (PoS). They are equipped with a high-quality clock which can be synchronised to UTC by feeding a PPS (pulse per second) signal into the cards using GPS (Global Positioning System) or CDMA (Code Division Multiple Access). The achievable clock accuracy is in the range of some 100 ns and is the basis for the timestamping process. More information about precision timestamping can be found in [2].

There are several approaches beside these two just mentioned which range in their timestamp accuracy somewhere in between. RIPE NCC, for instance, use GPS-conditioned PC clocks for their measurements [8]. Another approach is the utilisation of CPU cycles to improve the accuracy of the PC clock [9].

In Sect. 2, the scalability problem of passive measurements has been posed. There are several ways to improve the scalability properties of passive measurements. The most obvious one is to collect only a subset of the actual traffic on a link. This approach has two dimensions: first, instead of capturing complete packets, it is often sufficient to store only the packet header. The header contains most of the important information (e.g. IP addresses, port numbers, protocol information) needed for analyses. Second, filters can be applied to capture only certain classes–or flows–of packets.

All data sets presented in this paper are such packet header traces. They are stored in native Dag format [7] consisting of 64-byte records with a 64-bit timestamp at the beginning of each record and the rest used for the packet header. Depending on the link technology, each record stores at least the first 40 bytes of an IP packet thus including 20 bytes of IP header and 20 bytes of a possibly present TCP header (assuming no IP options).

A useful side effect of dropping packet payload is improved privacy. No user data are collected. However, there is still concern for the IP addresses which could be used to track an individual user's behaviour. This issue is addressed by an anonymisation scheme applied to a trace shortly after it has been captured. It basically performs an irreversible mapping of real IP addresses into an anonymous address range. The disadvantage of this anonymisation procedure is that it circumvents any analysis involving routing properties as these are lost with the change of IP addresses.

Packet filtering can be done based on different criteria. These criteria should be flexible enough to allow for different levels of flow granularity (e.g. TCP connections, application or host conversations). The specific filter properties depend on the intended analysis. However, once such a filtering decision has been made for a capturing session, any following analyses are limited to the collected sample. This may prove disadvantageous in case some unexpected results occur in the course of an analysis. The choice with the highest flexibility always is a full packet trace.

The challenge is to reduce the amount of collected data without compromising the purpose of a measurement. It is of central importance—both to the usefulness and the collected data volume of a measurement—where it is conducted. Network capacities in today's Internet are being deliberately over-provisioned. The Internet is a mesh of interconnected autonomous systems. The operator of each autonomous systems will design network resources in a way that there be virtually no data loss even during periods of extreme network utilisation. Problems are much more likely to arise at peering points between such autonomous systems. These interconnections are carefully rate-limited and their capacity is regulated by service level agreements and peering arrangements. This commercially motivated bandwidth reduction renders these points most likely for congestion-caused high packet delays and losses to occur. Our analysis presented in Sect. 5 will provide proof that this is indeed true.

These considerations make such points especially interesting for passive measurements. Moving a measurement point away from the Internet's core toward its edges means reducing the bandwidth that has to be handled. Furthermore, a peering point with a bandwidth reduction from OC48 speed to OC12 will likely display a similar behaviour as a point with a reduction from OC12 to OC3. With the scalability concerns of passive measurements in mind, it appears sensible to conduct a measurement at the lower speed link. It should then be possible to extrapolate the results to higher speed links.

In addition to the lossy data reduction described above, standard compression utilities (e.g. gzip) can be used to further reduce the amount of collected data. Tests with various traces have shown that gzip delivers the best trade-off between cost and efficiency. Depending on the data rate of the measured link and the performance of the measurement system, compression can either be done in real-time during the capturing session or afterwards. This has to be individually assessed for each measurement session.

Despite all these data reduction efforts, the amount of data collected in network traces is still huge. This calls for a means of automatic trace data processing. We have developed a set of tools [7] as part of the Dag software package to support a partially automated analysis of large data sets. This tool set has been used throughout the analyses of the data sets presented here.

4   The Auckland and Leipzig Data Sets

We have captured three different data sets at two locations—the University of Auckland, New Zealand (Fig. 1), and the University of Leipzig, Germany (Fig. 2). In both cases, the university's Internet access link has been instrumented on either side of the main Internet router, though only Auckland-VI is a multi-point measurement with taps on both sides being used to capture data. Auckland-IV and Leipzig-I were captured at the outer side of the router.

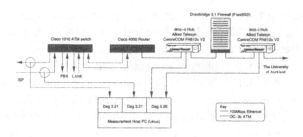

Fig. 1. Measurement configuration for the Auckland-IV and VI data sets

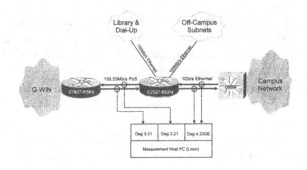

Fig. 2. Measurement configuration for the Leipzig-I data set

The ISP connection in Auckland is an OC3c ATM link with a 4.048 Mbit/s PVC. The University of Leipzig is connected to the German Research Network (G-WiN) via an OC3c PoS (Packet over Sonet) link running at 155.53 Mbit/s. Both campus networks are hooked to the router via an Ethernet connection running at 100 Mbit/s in Auckland and at 1 Gbit/s in Leipzig.

Instrumenting a university Internet access link means to exactly follow the principles for selecting an interesting monitoring point as proposed in Sect. 3. The disparity of link capacities on either side of the router induces heavy queuing of outgoing traffic with its adverse impact on the traffic behaviour. The analysis presented in Sect. 5 provides proof that this assumption is indeed true. It will be shown that the queuing delay added by the router renders any realtime application running over such a link without additional QoS functionality all but impossible.

Table 2 lists some statistical information about the traces. The Auckland data sets are available to the public [5].

Table 2. Trace data statistics

Data set	Duration (days)	Number of Packets (million)	File size (GB) Uncompressed	Compressed
Auckland-IV	45	3157	188	65
Auckland-VI	$4\frac{1}{2}$	3 * 312	50	18
Leipzig-I	$5\frac{1}{2}$	3800	226	113

The Auckland measurement system was equipped with three Dag measurement cards—two Dag 3.2 with OC3c/OC12c interface, one for each direction of the OC3c link, and one Dag 3.2E, a dual-port 10/100 Mbit/s Ethernet card, which was connected to the DMZ hubs (see Fig. 1). In Leipzig we used two Dag 3.21 with OC3c/OC12c interface to tap into the ISP link. Additionally, the measurement system is equipped with a Dag 4.22 with 1000Base-SX interface which hasn't been used for any measurements yet. However, we plan to capture a multi-point trace similar to Auckland-VI in Leipzig.

Clock synchronisation was provided by a Trimble Palisade GPS antenna in Auckland and a Trimble Acutime 2000 in Leipzig. The antennas were connected to the Dag cards ensuring that timestamping precision is within 600 ns to UTC at any time during the measurement session. Log files of the timekeeping process have been recorded for verification. In addition to these log files, the analyses did not reveal any timestamp inconsistencies (e.g. outliers) further reassuring the confidence in this data set.

5 Analysing Passive Traces

Analysing trace data is a time-consuming process. Table 2 gives an idea about what amounts of data have to be handled. We have developed a set of tools [7] written in C which take traces in Dag format as input and generate various statistics as text or graphics. Among them are programs to generate statistics about packet rate, bandwidth, application mix, and flow behaviour.

We have used these tools to generate comparable graphics about all three trace data sets. An examples is given in Fig. 3. A complete set of graphs can be found at the web sites [5] and [6].

We have also developed an algorithm to calculate one-way packet delays for multi-point measurements. It generates a 32-bit CRC over the whole packet header excluding IP TTL and checksum fields which will change when a packet passes a router. The CRC values of the trace captured at one point are stored in a hash table and matched against those of the trace taken at the second point. Multiple matches of a single packet are considered ambiguous and discarded from the analysis. Unmatched packets may occur for several reasons:

- cross traffic from untapped router interfaces
- packets sent to or originating from one of the router's interface IP addresses

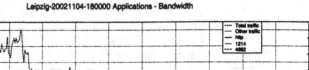

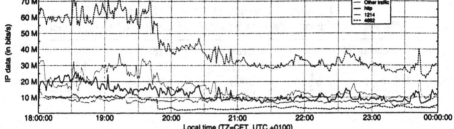

Fig. 3. Average bandwidth of incoming and outgoing traffic for a 6-hour period of Leipzig-I

- packets discarded due to filtering rules (e.g. firewall as for Auckland-VI, see Fig. 1)
- true packet loss due to link overload

Mismatches of the first two categories can easily be filtered out if the subnet addresses connected to the router and its interface addresses are known. However, this is only possible if the traces have not been anonymised as described in Sect. 3. Recognising missing packets from the second category is possible only if the firewall rules are known.

5.1 Analysing a Router's Behaviour

A router is basically a packet forwarding device with queues buffering packets. Watching all incoming and outgoing packets provides a complete view of a router's behaviour. That was done for the Auckland-VI data set. There are only two basic things which can happen to a packet passing a router—it gets forwarded with a certain delay, or it gets lost due to buffer congestion. A measurement configuration as deployed in Auckland and Leipzig (Fig. 1 and Fig. 2) can detect both.

The following paragraphs will outline the results of our delay analysis of the Auckland-VI data set to demonstrate the usefulness of such measurements. For a more complete discussion of this subject refer to [4].

During our analyses of the Auckland-VI data set we found scatter plots of the delay value distribution to be adequate visualisations of the router's behaviour. We applied a colouring scheme to reveal packet size dependencies of certain prevalent delay values. Five colour groups which represent packets of a certain size have been defined. The groups are different for ATM and Ethernet because the graphs show link layer size (i.e. multiple of 53 bytes for ATM, or Ethernet frame size). For ATM the groups are 53-106, 689, 1696, 159, 212-636, and 742-1643. For Ethernet they are 72, 602, 1526, 73-125, 126-601, 603-1525. Note that the first three groups respectively have been chosen to represent the typical IP packet sizes of 40, 576, and 1500 bytes. An analysis of packet size distribution of the trace revealed a strong prevalence of these packet sizes.

Figure 4 shows such scatter plots of the delay distribution with various clearly separated bands of different colours (i.e. different packet sizes). All bands for outbound packets and the bottom bands for inbound packets (below 0.4 ms) can be attributed to different serialisation times depending on packet size. The upper bands for outgoing traffic represent bursts of packets of the same size. Outgoing packet bursts arrive with up to 100 Mbit/s but can only be transmitted with 4.048 Mbit/s and thus have to be buffered. This only happens for outgoing packets which is the reason for the huge disparity of delay values for both direction. 99% of all inbound packets experience a delay of less than 0.53 ms, whereas for outbound traffic it is 82 ms—a difference of two orders of magnitude.

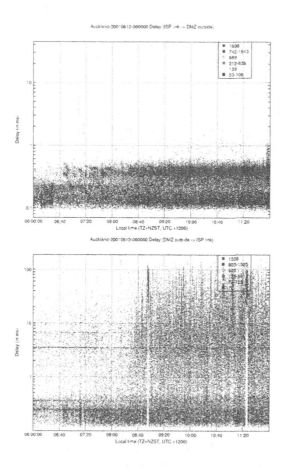

Fig. 4. Delay distribution of incoming (top) and outgoing packets at the University of Auckland on Tuesday, June 12, 6am-12pm

Apart from the horizontal banding, the plot of outbound packet delays reveals a number or periods during which the delay distribution seems distorted compared to general behaviour. Figure 4 shows two major incidents—one at about 8:55am, the second at about 11:25am—during which virtually no delay value is below about 30 ms. Considering that during normal operation a large proportion of delay values lies below 0.4 ms, this has to be taken seriously.

Our analysis revealed a plateau of SMTP traffic perfectly coinciding with the high-delay incidents. Interestingly, similarly high spikes of HTTP traffic do not have such a devastating impact on the overall delay. Checking the IP addresses has shown that a single host is responsible for this malicious behaviour. More about these anomalies can be found in [4].

5.2 Support and Evaluation of Network Simulations

The ultimate simulation is one based on real data. The main obstacle of many network simulation is that they use especially generated traffic based on a—possibly wrong—model of real traffic. Several influencing papers (e.g. [12]) have described the difficulties involved in conducting proper simulations of Internet traffic behaviour. Trace data collected by passive measurement system can provide a solution for at least a subset of these problems.

In [4] we presented a simple router simulation based on a leaky bucket model. This simulation takes a Dag trace file as its input and calculates a delay value for each packet based on buffer occupancy, which in turn depends on the burst behaviour of the input traffic.

The delay distribution calculated by such a simulation is visualised in Fig. 5. Its most obvious feature is the striking visual similarity to the real trace data (Fig. 4) which promises a good match of simulation and real world. The simulation is able to reproduce both, the horizontal banding due to packet queuing as well as the vertical patterns representing high-delay incidents as described in Sect. 5.1.

By using a trace file of the Auckland-VI data set, we can not only run a simulation based on real data but also evaluate its quality by checking simulated against observed delay values. This reveals some weaknesses of this simulation which are not obvious from the looks of Fig. 5. Only about 58% of all simulated values have an error of less than 20%. If we set the error threshold to 10%, the proportion of valid simulation values amounts to a mere 45%. Furthermore, the simulation predicts about 2,300 lost packets during a certain 6-hour interval. This value gets invalidated by the observed number of about 50,000 lost packets.

Although the router simulation largely fails, the comparison against the observed data reveals some useful hints at possible sources of its weaknesses which can be used to improve the simulation accuracy. By using real data for the simulation we can rule out an adverse influence by poor models used to generate test traffic. This allows to focus on the actual simulation instead of having to deal with proper test traffic generation. We plan to conduct a similar simulation based on traffic captured in Leipzig.

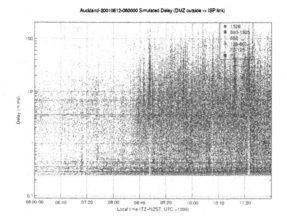

Fig. 5. Simulated delay distribution

5.3 Realtime Capabilities – An Outlook

All analyses described so far have one common disadvantage: they consume a significant amount of time in the order of some minutes up to hours for larger traces depending on the available computing resources. This fact renders such approaches unusable for network management purposes were immediate availability of information about network status is indispensable.

On the other hand, a passive measurement system equipped with Dag cards provides an undistorted view of the network traffic that few other solutions can match. That raises the question about possible realtime capabilities of such a system. We are currently planning on conducting a study about the kind and granularity of information that can be provided using such a passive measurement system.

6 Conclusion

This paper advocates the use of passive measurements as a modeling tool for today's still rapidly growing Internet. The specific advantages of passive over active measurements have been described. The key feature of passive measurements is the ability to provide a high-fidelity snapshot of real-world Internet behaviour. The importance of a thoughtful deployment of measurement systems has been discussed. Access and peering points have been identified as the most interesting monitoring points. Extending the measurement methodology by monitoring several points which maintain a traffic relation enables the analysis of packet delay and loss—key metrics when it comes to Internet quality of service. Such multi-point measurements can be conducted by instrumenting a single device (e.g. a router) or an end-to-end path.

We have presented several trace data sets to prove the usefulness of passive measurements. The Auckland-VI data set instrumented a router and a firewall at an Internet access link. This measurement confirms the presumption that a significant bandwidth reduction implies an adverse impact on the delay and jitter behaviour of real network traffic. Delay values ranging from below 0.2 ms up to about 200 ms have been observed. These results are of special interest if one seeks to implement QoS features to support real-time applications. The measurement methodology can easily be adopted to support QoS-specific analyses by taking into account different traffic classes.

We are planning to conduct subsequent measurements at the University of Leipzig. There will be a router instrumentation similar to Auckland-VI. This will put the results of Auckland-VI analyses into perspective and improve their value by allowing or ruling out generalisations. Furthermore, it is planned to conduct an end-to-end path measurement to focus on the user's perception of service quality. We will also explore the realtime capabilities of passive measurements.

References

1. Jörg Micheel, Hans-Werner Braun and Ian Graham: Storage and bandwidth requirements for passive Internet header traces, Workshop on Network-Related Data Management, Santa Barbara, California, USA, May 25th 2001
2. Jörg Micheel, Ian Graham and Stephen Donnelly: Precision Timestamping of Network Packets, Proceedings of the ACM SIGCOMM Internet Measurement Workshop, San Francisco, California, USA, November 1st/2nd 2001
3. Stephen Donnelly: High Precision Timing in Passive Measurements of Data Networks, PhD thesis, University of Waikato, June 12, 2002
4. Klaus Mochalski, Jörg Micheel and Stephen Donnelly: Packet Delay and Loss at the Auckland Internet Access Path, PAM2002 Passive and Active Measurement Workshop, Fort Collins, Colorado, USA, March, 25-26th, 2002
5. Waikato Internet Traffic Storage: http://wand.cs.waikato.ac.nz/wand/wits/
6. Leipzig Trace Archive: http://rnvs.informatik.uni-leipzig.de/ traces/
7. Web sites of Dag development at the University of Waikato and Endace Measurement Systems: http://dag.cs.waikato.ac.nz, http://www.endace.com
8. Maximo Alves, Luigi Corsello, Daniel Karrenberg, Cagdas Ögüt, Mark Santcroos, Reinhard Sojka, Henk Uijterwaal and René Wilhelm New: Measurements with the RIPE NCC Test Traffic Measurements Setup, PAM2002 Passive and Active Measurement Workshop, Fort Collins, Colorado, USA, March, 25-26th, 2002
9. Attila Pasztor, Darryl Veitch: PC Based Precision Timing Without GPS, ACM CLIOMETRICS 2002, June 15-19, 2002, Marina Del Rey, California, USA
10. Will E. Leland, Murad S. Taqqu, Walter Willinger, and Daniel V. Wilson: On the Self-Similar Nature of Ethernet Traffic, Proceedings ACM SIGCOMM 93, 13-17 September 1993
11. V. Paxson and S. Floyd: Wide-Area Traffic: The Failure of Poisson Modeling, IEEE/ACM Transactions on Networking, Vol. 3 No. 3, pp. 226-244, June 1995
12. S. Floyd and V. Paxson: Difficulties in Simulating the Internet, IEEE/ACM Transactions on Networking, Vol.9, No.4, pp. 392-403, August, 2001.

Modellierung und Konzeption eines verteilten Framework für personalisierte Onlinedienste

T. Specht, K-P. Fähnrich

Fraunhofer IAO
Nobelstr. 12
D-70569 Stuttgart
Thomas.Specht@iao.fhg.de

Die stetig zunehmende Verbreitung elektronischer Medien und Vertriebskanäle und die Kommerzialisierung des Internet verursachen eine Informationsflut, die manuell kaum noch zu bewältigen ist. Neben der Volltextsuche und den Internet-Suchmaschinen verspricht insbesondere die benutzerprofilabhängige Contentfilterung und –personalisierung eine deutliche Effizienzverbesserung bei der Informationssuche. Während für rein textbasierte Inhalte bereits prototypische Lösungen existieren [z.B. Rit01, QW00], befinden sich entsprechende Verfahren und Systeme für multimediale Streamingdaten, insbesondere Audio und Video, noch im Forschungsstadium. Dies gilt insbesondere im Hinblick auf die effektive Contentauswahl und –bereitstellung für mobile Endgeräte mit eingeschränkten grafischen und performancemäßigen Möglichkeiten.

Um nicht für jedes einzelne Endgerät eigene Anwendungen erstellen zu müssen, ist eine flexible und gut skalierbare Systemarchitektur mit strikter Trennung zwischen Datenhaltung, Anwendungslogik und grafischer Bedienoberfläche notwendig. Während die Mediendatenerfassung, -analyse und –personalisierung endgeräteunabhängig ist, müssen die grafischen Bedienoberflächen im Sinne einer anwenderfreundlichen und ergonomischen Lösung jeweils neu erstellt werden. Darüber hinaus erfordern die CI-Richtlinien der Diensteanbieter in der Regel ohnehin ein kundenspezifisches Layout.

Die vorliegende Arbeit beschreibt die Modellierung, Konzeption und prototypische Realisierung eines komponentenbasierten verteilten Framework zur effektiven Entwicklung und Evaluation neuer Personalisierungsansätze und –verfahren, insbesondere für multimediale und multimodale Onlinedienste[1]. Aufgrund der großen Datenmengen und wegen der rechenaufwändigen Algorithmen bei der Analyse und Klassifikation von Audio- und Videodaten wurde eine verteilte, lose gekoppelte Softwarearchitektur zugrunde gelegt. Bestehende Forschungsansätze lassen sich unabhängig von technologischen Parametern wie Programmiersprache, Betriebssystem oder Serverstandort als WebService einbinden. Zur Entkopplung der grafischen Bedienoberflächen sind sämtliche Funktionsmodule durch Fassaden gekapselt, sodass die Anpassung an neue stationäre oder mobile Endgeräte, der Aufbau neuer Dienste sowie die prototypische Entwicklung und Evaluation neuer Personalisierungsansätze durch den Framework sehr gut unterstützt wird. Bei Bedarf lassen sich einzelne Komponenten ohne große Eingriffe ins Gesamtsystem durch verbesserte Ansätze ersetzen.

---

[1] Wesentliche Impulse für diesen Beitrag stammen aus dem Fusionsprojekt PiAvida der Fraunhofer-Institute IAO, AIS, Fokus, IGD, IIS und IMK.

Vorgehensweise und Entwicklungsprozess

Aufgrund der hohen Komplexität des Framework für personalisierte Onlinedienste ist ein iterativer architekturgetriebener Entwicklungsprozess notwendig, der die parallele und weitgehend unabhängige Entwicklung der einzelnen Systemmodule ermöglicht. Während einzelne Module bereits als Forschungsprototyp vorliegen und konsequent weiter entwickelt werden, befinden sich andere noch im Spezifikationsstadium. Um die Unabhängigkeit der Module zu erhalten und aufwändige Portierungen auf andere Programmiersprachen, Datenbanken und Betriebssystemplattformen zu vermeiden, erfolgt eine lose Kopplung über Web Services ([W3C01], [W3C02]).

Als Entwicklungsprozess eignet sich aufgrund dieser Anforderungen hervorragend der von Jacobson, Booch und Rumbaugh entworfene Unified Software Development Process (UP), wie er in [JBR98] ausführlich beschrieben ist. Konsequenterweise wird als Softwaremodellierungssprache der weit verbreitete Standard Unified Modeling Language (UML) zugrunde gelegt, der ebenfalls von Jacobson, Booch und Rumbaugh (siehe JBR99]) spezifiziert wurde.

Gemäß dem Unified Process gliedert sich ein Softwareprojekt in die vier Phasen Inception, Elaboration, Construction und Transition, die sich ihrerseits in einzelne Iterationen zerlegen lassen. Innerhalb jeder Iteration erfolgen sowohl Anforderungsanalyse, Design, Implementierung als auch Test einer Teilkomponente des Gesamtsystems.

Inception-Phase

In der Inception-Phase wurden anhand von Anwendergesprächen, der Evaluation bestehender Onlinedienste sowie der gemeinsamen Diskussion aktueller Forschungsansätze zunächst die wesentlichen Top Level Use Cases des zu konzipierenden Framework für personalisierte Onlinedienste gesammelt und modelliert. Abbildung 1 gibt einen Überblick.

Darüber hinaus wurden in der Inception-Phase geeignete Softwaresysteme ausgewählt und evaluiert. Als tragfähig für den gesamten Framework hat sich folgende Lösung erwiesen:

- Bestehende Komponenten und Subsysteme werden in ihrer bisherigen Technologie weiter entwickelt und optimiert.
- Neu zu erstellende Komponenten werden in der Java Enterprise-Technologie J2EE (Enterprise Java Beans, Servlets, Java Server Pages) realisiert [Sha01]
- Als Application Server kommen das Open Source-Produkt JBoss [JBo02] und das kommerzielle Oracle OC4J [Ora02] zum Einsatz. Bei der Entwicklung wird darauf geachtet, keine proprietären Features dieser Application Server auszunutzen, um eine eventuelle Portierung auf andere J2EE-fähige Application-Server zu ermöglichen
- Als Datenbankserver kommt Oracle 9i zum Einsatz, wobei möglichst nur Standard-SQL eingesetzt werden soll, um später bei Bedarf die Datenbank austauschen zu können.
- Die Kopplung der einzelnen Subsysteme erfolgt lose nach dem SOAP/WSDL WebService-Standard [W3C01], [W3C02].

385

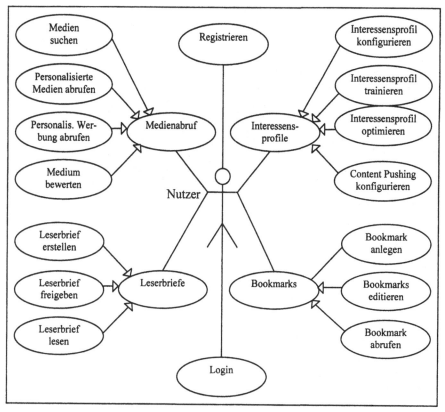

Abbildung 1: Use Cases des Framework für personalisierte Onlinedienste

Elaborationsphase

Hauptziele der Elaborationsphase sind die detaillierte Modellierung der wesentlichen Anforderungen an das Gesamtsystem sowie die Festlegung der Systemarchitektur. Anhand der Abbildung 2 werden nun die einzelnen Subsysteme kurz beschrieben. Externe Mediendatenquellen wie Nachrichtensender oder Filmstudios versorgen das System mit Audio- und Videodatenströmen. Nach einem zentralen Timestamping werden die Sprach-, Musik- und Videodaten zunächst separiert und getrennt voneinander analysiert. Ziel ist die Erkennung einzelner Beiträge (Segmente) in dem sequentiellen Datenstrom. Hinweise auf solche Segmentgrenzen liefern z.B. Szenenwechsel bei den Bilddaten, Sprecherwechsel bei den Sprachdaten, längere Redepausen oder ein eingespielter Jingle (kurze charakteristische Tonfolge).

386

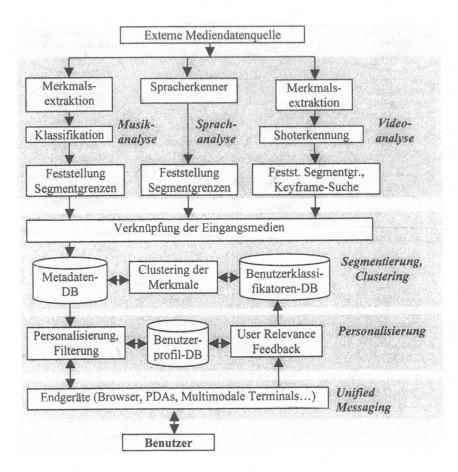

Abbildung 2: Systemarchitektur des Framework für personalisierte Onlinedienste

Des weiteren bestimmen die Analysemodule aus den Datenströmen charakteristische Merkmale, anhand derer eine inhaltliche Vorklassifikation stattfindet. Mögliche Analysekriterien sind z.B. bestimmte Schlagworte oder Silben in der gesprochenen Sprache oder Texteinblendungen in den Videodaten.

Zur Verbesserung der Segmentierungs- und Klassifikationsergebnisse werden im Segmentierungs- und Clusteringmodul die Einzelinformationen der drei Analysemodule verknüpft. Ergebnis ist die Zuordnung der einzelnen Multimediadaten zu Informationskategorien, z.B. nach dem IPTC-Standard[2] (siehe [IPTC02]).

---

[2] Die Top Level-Kategorien der insgesamt über 1000 Kategorien des IPTC-Standards sind: Kunst, Kultur und Unterhaltung; Justiz und Kriminalität; Katastrophen und Unglücke; Wirtschaft und Finanzen; Erziehung und Ausbildung; Umwelt; Medizin und Gesundheit; Vermischtes; Arbeit und Soziales; Freizeit und modernes Leben; Religion und Weltanschauung; Wissenschaft, Technik und Forschung; Gesellschaft und Bevölkerung; Sport; Krisen, Krieg und Konflikte; Wetter

Die extrahierten Metainformationen wie Datenquelle, Datum und Uhrzeit sowie die Einteilung in Kategorien werden in einer zentralen Metadaten-Datenbank gespeichert und dem Personalisierungsmodul zur Verfügung gestellt. Die eigentlichen Multimediadaten können an beliebiger Stelle im Internet abgelegt sein und werden per URL referenziert. Dadurch entsteht ein echt verteiltes System.

Die Personalisierung der Medien erfolgt durch Abgleich der im Benutzerinteressensprofil abgelegten präferierten Kategorien des Benutzers mit den Kategorien, die das Segmentierungs- und Clusteringmodul den einzelnen Medien zugeordnet hat[3]. Zur Optimierung der Benutzerinteressensprofile kann der Anwender die Nützlichkeit der ihm präsentierten Medien bewerten und so die künftige Auswahl der ihm übermittelten Inhalte beeinflussen („User Relevance Feedback").

Das Unified Messaging-System schließlich sorgt für die Anpassung der Darstellung an die technischen Fähigkeiten des jeweils eingesetzten Endgerätes. Soll ein neues Endgerät unterstützt werden, so beschränken sich die Anpassungen des Gesamtsystems weitgehend auf dieses Modul, während der Rest des gesamten Personalisierungsframework mehr oder weniger unverändert weiter genutzt werden kann. Die Erkennung des eingesetzten Endgerätetyps erfolgt in der Regel automatisch.

Construction-Phase

Stellvertretend für das Gesamtsystem wird an dieser Stelle das Personalisierungsmodul sowie dessen Schnittstellen zu den Nachbarsystemen „Segmentierung und Clusterung" sowie „Unified Messaging" näher beschrieben. Im Gegensatz zu den Analysemodulen und wichtigen Kernfunktionalitäten des Segmentierungs- und Clusteringmoduls erfolgte beim Personalisierungsmodul eine vollständige Neuentwicklung, sodass auf neueste technologische Entwicklungen und Standards zurückgegriffen werden konnte.

Als Grundgerüst dient ein Java 2 Enterprise-Edition-fähiger Applicationserver. Während in der frühen Inception-Phase noch der Oracle OC4J-Applicationserver zum Einsatz kam, wurde später auf das Open Source-Produkt JBoss umgestellt. Für OC4J sprach die sehr gute Integration in die Java-Entwicklungsumgebung Oracle JDeveloper und die gute Performance. Dem stand vor allem der Nachteil proprietärer Programmierschnittstellen zu den Java WebServices nach dem SOAP/WSDL-Standard entgegen.

Im Gegensatz dazu bietet der Open Source-Applicationserver JBoss eine standardisierte WebService-Schnittstelle, die frühzeitige Unterstützung neuester Standards und eine sehr gute Performance, allerdings mit dem Nachteil der weniger guten Integration in die Entwicklungsumgebung. Da das Entwicklungsteam des Unified Messaging-Systems mit JBoss ebenfalls bereits gute Erfahrungen gemacht hatte, erfolgte die Umstellung zu einem Zeitpunkt, an dem der Änderungsaufwand an den bereits realisierten Komponenten noch überschaubar war.

Abbildung 3 zeigt den Stand der Architektur des Personalisierungsmoduls Ende Oktober 2002.

---

[3] Für eine Übersicht der zugrunde liegenden Algorithmen siehe z.B. [BR99]

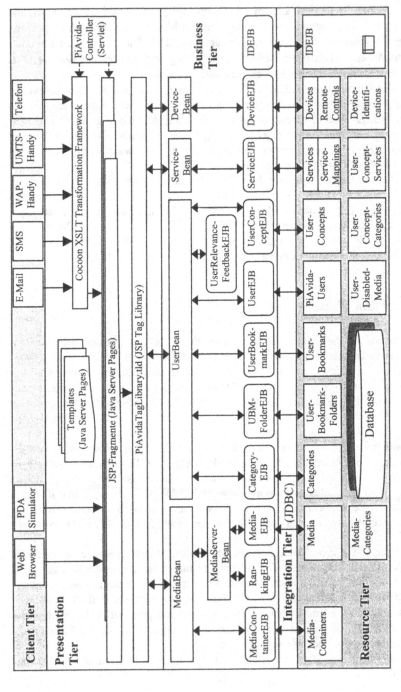

Abbildung 3: Architektur des Personalisierungsmoduls

Die **Resource Tier** beinhaltet die Datenbank des Personalisierungsmoduls. Als Datenbankserver kommt Oracle 9i zum Einsatz. Sämtliche Datenbankzugriffe erfolgen über die JDBC-Schnittstelle der **Integration Tier**. Um einen eventuellen Austausch des Datenbankservers gegen ein anderes Produkt (z.b. das OpenSource-Produkt mySql) zu einem späteren Zeitpunkt zu vereinfachen, wird soweit möglich auf ANSI-SQL gesetzt.

Im **Business Tier** kapselt zunächst eine Schicht von Entity Enterprise Java Beans (Entity EJB) die Datenbanktabellen des Resource Tier durch eine komponentenbasierte Schnittstelle. Aus Effizienzgründen werden dabei nur die wichtigsten Entities auf eine eigene EJB abgebildet, während der Zugriff auf Hilfstabellen möglichst in eine vorhandene EJB integriert wurde. So kapselt z.b. die *DeviceEJB* die Tabellen *Devices*, *RemoteControls* und *DeviceIdentifications*. Mit Ausnahme der IdEJB sind sämtliche Entity EJB vom Typ *bean managed persistence*, d.h. die Datenbankzugriffe erfolgen nicht durch den EJB Container, sondern die EJB selbst. Dem Vorteil der größeren Flexibilität der *bean managed persistence* gegenüber der *container managed persistence* steht der höhere Programmieraufwand nachteilig gegenüber. Die IdEJB ist ein datenbankserverunabhängiger Mechanismus zur automatischen Generierung eindeutiger Primärschlüssel und ist wegen ihrer Einfachheit vom Typ *container managed persistence*. Für sämtliche Entity EJB wird per Definition das Transaktionsmanagement vom EJB-Container abgewickelt.

Die UserRelevanceFeedbackEJB ist eine Session EJB und kapselt per Strategy-Designpattern (siehe GHV95) die austauschbaren Algorithmen des User Relevance Feedback[4].

Sämtliche EJB verfügen über die Möglichkeit, Value-Objekte an die darüber liegenden als Java Bean realisierten Fassadenobjekte (siehe [GHV95]) zu liefern, um die Komplexität der EJB von den höheren Schichten fernzuhalten. Die Fassadenobjekte folgen alle dem Singleton-Designpattern (siehe [GHV95]), um die Anzahl der Objekte im System möglichst gering zu halten und somit den Garbage-Collector zu entlasten.

Die Business Tier verfügt weiterhin. über die Schnittstelle des Personalisierungsmoduls (PM) zum Segmentierungs- und Clusteringmodul (SCM). Abbildung 4 zeigt den zugehörigen Ausschnitt des Business Tier im Detail. Während die Einordnung der Mediendaten in die Mediencontainerhierarchie durch das Personalisierungsmodul erfolgt, werden die Mediendaten inklusive ihrer Metadaten wie Datenquelle, Ersteller, Erstellungsdatum und –uhrzeit vom Segmentierungs- und Clusteringmodul verwaltet. Aus Effizienzgründen erfolgt keine Replikation der eigentlichen Medieninhalte (z.B. Videos) auf den Personalisierungsserver. Dadurch reduziert sich die SOAP/WSDL-Schnittstelle zwischen PM und SCM auf die Abfrage der zu einem Benutzerinteressensprofil passenden Medien (z.B. Videos) und Metadaten, siehe Abbildung 5.

---

[4] User Relevance Feedback ist ein Mechanismus zur automatischen Optimierung der Benutzerprofile. Der Benutzer kann zu jedem abgerufenen Medium eine Bewertung abgeben (explizites User Relevance Feedback), oder es können aus dem Abrufverhalten (z.B. vollständiges Abspielen eines Videos vs. Abbruch des Videos nach wenigen Sekunden) Rückschlüsse auf das Benutzerverhalten geschlossen werden (implizites User Relevance Feedback). In beiden Fällen ändert das User Relevance Feedback die Gewichtung im Benutzerinteressensprofil.

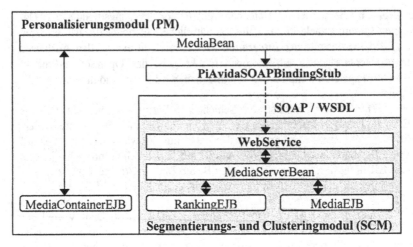

Abbildung 4: Schnittstelle des Personalisierungsmoduls zum Segmentierungs- und Clusteringmodul

Wie Praxistests gezeigt haben, macht sich die im Vergleich zu anderen Middlewarestandards wie CORBA oder RMI schlechtere Performance von SOAP/WSDL aufgrund der geringen übertragenen Datenmengen kaum bemerkbar. Der größte Vorteil von SOAP/WSDL über CORBA und RMI liegt in der Möglichkeit, sämtliche Remote-Datenübertragung über das HTTP-Protokoll und den standardisierten TCP-Port 80 abzuwickeln. Dadurch entfallen insbesondere die Konfigurationsarbeiten an eventuell vorhandenen Firewalls, da der Standardport 80 in der Regel ohnehin freigeschaltet ist. Tabelle 1 vergleicht die für diese Arbeit relevanten Eigenschaften gängiger Middlewarestandards.

	DCOM	RMI	CORBA	RMI over IIOP	SOAP/WSDL
Objektorientiert	ja	ja	ja	ja	ja
Programmiersprachneutral	ja	-	ja	(ja)	ja
Betriebssysteme	Windows	alle mit Java VM[5]	(alle)	alle mit Java VM	(alle)
Netzwerkbasisprotokoll	TCP/IP	TCP/IP	TCP/IP	TCP/IP	HTTP / TCP/IP
Übertragungsprotokoll	DCOM	RMI	IIOP	RMI /IIOP	SOAP / HTTP
Interfacedefinitionssprache	implizit	Java Interface	IDL[6]	Java Interface, IDL	WSDL
Performance	hoch	hoch	sehr hoch	hoch	gering
Kompatibilität der Produkte	hoch	hoch	mittel	mittel	mittel
Im J2SDKSE[7] enth.	-	ja	ja	ja	-
Im J2SDKEE[8] enth.	-	ja	ja	ja	ja

Tabelle 1: Relevante Eigenschaften gängiger Middlewarestandards

---

[5] Java Virtual Machine (Runtime Environment von Java)
[6] Interface Definition Language
[7] Java 2 Software Development Kit, Standard Edition
[8] Java 2 Software Development Kit, Enterprise Edition

```
/**
 * MediaServerBean.java
 * This file was auto-generated from WSDL by the Apache Axis Wsdl2java emitter.
 */
package de.fhg.piavida.media;

import de.fhg.piavida.category.SCategoryValue;
import de.fhg.piavida.category.WeightedCategoryCode;
import java.rmi.*;
import javax.ejb.*;

/**
 * This interface specifies the methods available via web service by the MediaServerBean located
 * at the Segmentation and Clustering Module (SCM).
 */
public interface MediaServerBeanInterface extends Remote
{
    /**
     * Get available media suitable to the given linear combination of categories and category weights.
     * @param theWeightedCategoryCodeArray Linear combination of weighted categories
     * @param maxCount Maximum number of categories to deliver
     */
    public RankedMediaId[] getAllMediaForCategoryVector(
        WeightedCategoryCode[] theWeightedCategoryCodeArray, long maxCount)
        throws RemoteException, FinderException;

    /**
     * Get all detail information for the specified media.
     * @param theMediaId Id of media to get detail information for
     */
    public MediaValue getMediaById(long theMediaId) throws RemoteException, FinderException;

    /**
     * Get array of all categories where the specified media is subscribed to
     * @param theMediaId Id of media to get subscribed categories for
     * @param maxCount Maximum number of categories to deliver
     */
    public SCategoryValue[] getSubscribedMediaCategoriesWithWeightOrderByWeight(
        long theMediaId, long maxCount) throws RemoteException, FinderException;
}
```

Abbildung 5: WebService-Schnittstelle zwischen PM und SCM

Im *Presentation Layer* werden dynamische Webseiten für den Client Tier generiert. Eine JSP Tag Library macht sämtliche Funktionalität der darunter liegenden Java-Bean-Fassadenobjekte in Form von Custom Tags verfügbar und entlastet den Designer der Bedienoberflächen von Programmierarbeiten. Der in dieser Arbeit beschriebene Framework definiert aktuell 92 Custom Tags innerhalb eines eigens dafür kreierten Namespace. Abbildung 6 zeigt anhand eines Sequenzdiagramms die wesentlichen Schritte bei der Nutzung eines Custom Tags zur Auflistung aller Benutzerinteressensprofile (intern als UserConcepts bezeichnet) mit aktuell verfügbarem personalisierten Content.

392

```
<%@include file="global.jsp" %>

<% String uid = (String)session.getAttribute("userid");

<p/>
<table border="3">
  <th><b></b><td>ID</td><td>Name</td></b></th>
  <pi:getUserConceptsWithMedia id="uc" uid="<%=uid%>">
    <tr>
      <td>
        <a href='<%="allMediaForUserConcept.jsp?ucid=" + uc.getId()%>'>show media</a>  
      <td><%= uc.getId() %></td>
      <td><%= uc.getName() %></td>
    </tr>
  </pi:getUserConceptsWithMedia>
</table>
</pi:getUser>
```

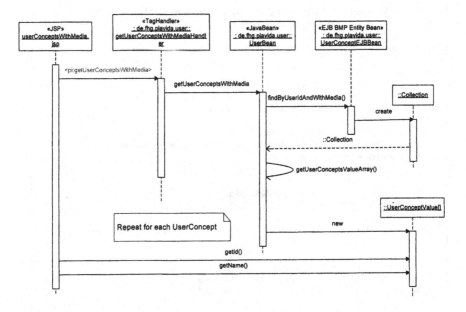

Abbildung 6: Sequenzdiagramm zur Auflistung aller Benutzerkonzepte mit passenden Medien

In den JSPs sowie den JSP Templates steckt das eigentliche Design der grafischen Bedienoberflächen. Während Webbrowser sowie der PDA-Simulator von den JSPs aus direkt mit speziell angepassten HTML-Seiten versorgt werden, läuft die Anbindung aller anderen Endgeräte über das Unified Messaging-Modul mit einem speziellen Transformations-Framework, der auf Cocoon und offenen Standards wie XHTML, XFORMS und SMIL basiert.

Der *Client Tier* besteht aus Endgeräten wie PDAs, Webbrowsern und Mobiltelefonen. Aufgrund deren sehr unterschiedlichen technischen Möglichkeiten muss jeweils eine gerätespezifische Anpassung der Bedienoberflächen durchgeführt werden. Diese Adaptionsarbeiten beschränken sich jedoch auf die Präsentationsschicht. Abbildung 7 zeigt beispielhaft einen personalisierten TV-Dienst auf einem simulierten PDA.

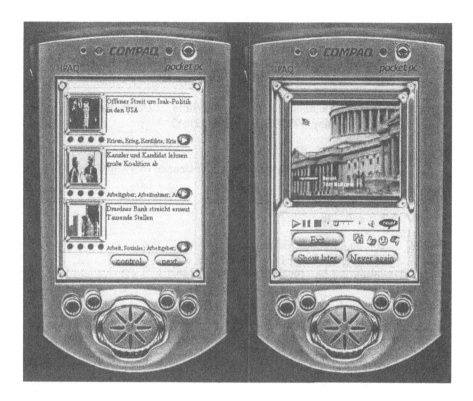

Abbildung 7: Beispiel für mit dem Framework realisierten personalisierten Dienst

Zusammenfassung und Ausblick

Im vorliegenden Beitrag wurde ein komponentenbasierter Framework für multimediale multimodale personalisierte Onlinedienste beschrieben. Die zugrunde liegende verteilte Systemarchitektur und die eingesetzten technischen Komponenten des Framework haben sich während der bisherigen Arbeiten als sehr tragfähig und stabil erwiesen. Das gilt insbesondere auch für die standortübergreifende SOAP/WSDL-Schnittstelle. Der durchgängige Einsatz von Internettechnologien ermöglicht die Erstellung und Portierung der Dienste auf jedes beliebige Endgerät mit XML-basierten Screen-Beschreibungssprachen

Während bislang als Zielsegment personalisierte B2C-Anwendungen im Vordergrund standen, zeichnet sich für zukünftige Erweiterungen ein hoher Bedarf in Richtung aufgaben- und rollenbezogener B2B-Anwendungen ab. Die dazu notwendigen konzeptionellen Erweiterungen, insbesondere die Zusammenfassung von Benutzern zu Benutzergruppen mit gleichartigen Aufgaben, lassen sich in einem nächsten Iterationsschritt nachträglich in den Framework integrieren.

394

Literatur

[BR99] Baeza-Yates, R.; Ribeiro-Neto, B.: Modern Information Retrieval
Addison-Wesley, 1999, ISBN: 0-201-39829-X

[GHV95] Gamma, E., Helm, R., Johnson, R., Vlissides, J.: Design Patterns
Addison-Wesley, 1995, ISBN: 0-201-633612

[IPTC02] IPTC Subject Codes
International Press Telecommunications Council (www.iptc.org)

[JBo02] JBoss Open Source Application Server
www.jboss.org

[JBR98] Jacobson, I., Booch, G., Rumbaugh, J.:
The Unified Software Development Process
Addison-Wesley, 1998, ISBN: 0-201-57169-2

[JBR99] Jacobson, I., Booch, G., Rumbaugh, J.:
The Unified Modeling Language User Guide
Addison-Wesley, 1999, ISBN: 0-201-57168-4

[Ora02] Oracle Technet
technet.oracle.com

[QW00] Quasthoff, U., Wolff, C.:
Adding Web Searches by Statistical Classification Tools,
ISI 2000, Darmstadt

[Rit01] Ritz, T.: Personalized information services- An Electronic Information
Commodity and its production
Proceedings of the 5th ICCC/IFIP Conference on Electronic Publishing
(ELPUB 2001) in Canterbury (UK), p.48-58

[Sha01] Shannon, B.:
Java 2 Platform Enterprise Edition Specification, V1.3
Sun microsystems (java.sun.com), 2001

[W3C01] M. Gudgin, M. Hadley, J-J. Moreau, and H. F. Nielsen:
SOAP Version 1.2 Part 1: Messaging Framework
World Wide Web Consortium, 17 December 2001.

[W3C02] E. Christensen, F. Curbera, G. Meredith, and S. Weerawarana:
Web Services Description Language (WSDL) 1.1
World Wide Web Consortium, 15 March 2002

Preisträger

Transaction-Based Intrusion Detection

Roland Büschkes

T-Mobile Deutschland GmbH
POB 300463
53184 Bonn, Germany
Roland.Bueschkes@t-mobile.de

Abstract. An *intrusion detection and response system* can build the core of a network monitoring and control architecture. However, not all intrusion detection techniques are necessarily suited to trigger reactive mechanisms.

A crucial point is the reliable determination of the actual state of the monitored network. If this state can not be determined reliably, it is not possible to appropriately react to any disturbances. Any reaction resulting from a misinterpretation of the current state can have severe consequences for the availability and security of the network. Especially, if this misinterpretation has been intentionally provoked by an attacker. In this paper, we discuss the analogy between intrusion detection and database management systems. The transaction concept is proposed as a possible foundation for a reliable state determination based on the detection of corresponding anomalies. In order to control the reactions to detected anomalies and to provide appropriate intrusion response capabilities techniques known from active databases are used.

1 Introduction

Modern tele and data communication networks provide users with all kinds of services. In the future, the variety of available services will increase, ultimately offering any service anytime and anywhere. But the growing range of available services also increases the complexity of the underlying networks. With this increasing complexity, it gets more and more difficult to detect, repulse and prevent abuse by in- and outsiders (see e.g. [Sch99]). Classical security mechanisms, like authentication and encryption, and security infrastructure components, like firewalls, can not provide complete security. Therefore, *intrusion detection* and *intrusion response systems* (IDS/IRS) have been introduced as an additional line of defence.

Current IDS use miscellaneous techniques to detect intrusions or intrusion attempts within a communication network. These techniques can be subdivided into two main categories, namely misuse and anomaly detection.

In this paper, we give an introduction to the theoretical foundations of *transaction-based anomaly detection*, a specific anomaly detection technique, which is based on the concept of database transactions.

A transaction-based IDS models protocol and process runs as transactions. While monitoring these transactions it checks whether the audit stream corresponds to an output schedule as it would have been generated by a database management system.

A detected anomaly is then forwarded to an IRS for further processing. In order to protect the monitored communication network the IRS has to provide appropriate countermeasures and to carefully control their execution. Continuing the analogy to database systems, techniques known from active databases are deployed for these tasks.

The paper is divided into five parts. After this introduction we discuss the theoretical foundations of our general anomaly detection model. Based on this model, section 3 introduces the concept of transaction-based anomaly detection. Subsequently, we present the basics of active database technology and our related intrusion response approach. The concluding section 5 summarises the results.

2 Intrusion Detection

An IDS can be used to monitor the users, processes and communication protocols within a communication network. And although these objects are quite different in their characteristics, the deployed intrusion detection techniques can be divided into two main categories, misuse and anomaly detection [Bac00].

2.1 Misuse Detection

Misuse detection tries to detect patterns of known attacks within the audit stream of a system, i.e. it identifies attacks directly. In order to do so it explicitly specifies attack patterns and monitors the audit stream for any occurrences of these patterns. Misuse detection is based on the assumption that the intersection between normal and intrusive behaviour is not negligible [Bac00]. The different techniques belonging to this category mainly differ with respect to the way of how the attack patterns are specified and detected. Typically, expert systems, state transition modelling or special languages are used [Bac00].

2.2 Anomaly Detection

Misuse detection, by explicitly describing the sequence of actions an attacker takes, is based on the specification of the undesirable or negative behaviour of users, processes and communication protocols. The dual approach is the specification of the desired or positive behaviour. Based on this normative specification of positive behaviour attacks are identified by observing deviations from the norm. Therefore, this technique is called anomaly detection. Anomaly detection is based on the assumption that the intersection between normal and intrusive behaviour is negligible or not present at all [Bac00]. Two general approaches exist to specify this positive behaviour:

1. Learning
2. Formal specification

The first approach, also known as profile-based anomaly detection, is suited for the monitoring of objects, which show a dynamic behaviour (e.g. users). It is often based on statistical methods or learning algorithms. The second approach, specification-based anomaly detection, is suited for the monitoring of objects, which show a static behaviour. It was first proposed by Calvin Ko [Ko96] and is based on the explicit formal specification of the positive object behaviour.

Policy

Default Permit	Misuse Detection	-	
Default Deny	Specification-based Anomaly Detection	Profile-based Anomaly Detection	
	Static	Dynamic	Object Behaviour

Table 1. Classification of intrusion detection techniques.

Tab. 1 summarises the different classes of intrusion detection techniques (see also [Lin99]).

2.3 The Model

In our intrusion detection model we focus on the monitoring of processes and protocols. The implementation of a process or a protocol is usually based on a corresponding specification [Hol91]. Both the specification and the implementation can be represented by *deterministic finite state machines* (DFSM)[HU79]. A DFSM $M = (Q, \Sigma, q_0, \delta, F)$ is an abstract machine consisting of a set of states Q (including the initial state q_0), a set of input events Σ and a state transition function δ. The transition function takes the current state and an input event and returns the next state. This next state is uniquely determined by a single input event. Some states may be designated as final states (the set F).

A state machine M accepts a language $\mathcal{L}(M) \subseteq \Sigma^*$, which is defined by $\mathcal{L}(M) = \{w \in \Sigma^* \mid \hat{\delta}(q_0, w) \in F\}$, with $\hat{\delta}$ being the extension of the state transition function δ from single input events to words w.

Based on this definition of a DFSM the specification and the implementation state machines are defined as follows:

Definition 1. *The representation of the specification of a process or a communication protocol as a deterministic finite state machine is called a* **specification DFSM** $M = (Q, \Sigma, q_0, \delta, F)$. *By definition, a specification DFSM M does not contain any design errors which could result in security breaches. Especially,* $|\mathcal{L}(M)| < \infty$ *holds. The representation of the corresponding implementation of a process or a communication protocol as a deterministic finite state machine is called an* **implementation DFSM** $M' = (Q', \Sigma', q_0, \delta', F')$.

Considering the assumptions made by the definition, it becomes obvious that the quality of the underlying specification clearly limits the quality of any specification-based anomaly detection approach. To ensure the necessary correctness properties, verification techniques like model checking [CGP99] can be used to analyse and improve the original process or protocol specification before deploying it for monitoring.

The requirement $|\mathcal{L}(M)| < \infty$ implies that the specification DFSM does not contain any cycles. If the original specification contains a cycle[1] the decision has to be taken whether the cycle is, from the viewpoint of the security policy, acceptable or not. Although transitions between a final state $q \in F$ and the initial state q_0 are generally acceptable, only single runs of the specification DFSM are considered in our model, i.e. $\forall q \in F\, \forall a \in \Sigma : \delta(q,a) =$ undefined.

It should also be noted that we do not assume the specification to be complete (partial transition function), i.e. it does not necessarily specify the behaviour for all possible combinations of states and inputs. In general, it only describes the expected input and the corresponding behaviour. The transition function of the implementation DFSM, however, is assumed to be total, i.e. the implementation reacts to all possible combinations of states and inputs.

For the following discussion, we assume that a suitable specification with the required properties is given.

For a correct transformation of the specification into an implementation $\mathcal{L}(M) = \mathcal{L}(M')$ should hold. But due to the implementation process an implementation usually does not exactly match its specification, i.e. $\mathcal{L}(M) \subseteq \mathcal{L}(M')$ holds[2]. Therefore, we additionally define a differential state machine:

Definition 2. *Given a specification DFSM M and an implementation DFSM M' the **differential state machine** M^Δ is defined to be the minimal DFSM such that $\mathcal{L}(M^\Delta) = \mathcal{L}(M') \setminus \mathcal{L}(M)$.*

At first sight, the differential DFSM simply models the difference between the specification and the implementation. But under the assumptions made above, this difference is actually what an attacker tries to exploit. Therefore, the differential DFSM also represents a model of possible anomalies and attacks against the implementation DFSM:

Definition 3. *Given a specification DFSM $M = (Q, \Sigma, q_0, \delta, F)$ and an implementation DFSM $M' = (Q', \Sigma', q_0, \delta', F')$ with $\mathcal{L}(M) \subseteq \mathcal{L}(M')$ a word α representing an **anomaly** corresponds to an accepting run of the differential DFSM M^Δ, i.e. $\alpha \in \mathcal{L}(M^\Delta)$. The set of anomalies $\mathfrak{A}$ is defined by $\mathfrak{A} = \mathcal{L}(M^\Delta)$.*

---

[1] The TCP specification e.g. is not cycle free. Considering its flow control procedure for a receiver announcing a window size of 0, a sender starts sending window probes until the receiver window opens up or either of the applications terminates. TCP itself does never give up sending window probes. This behaviour can potentially be used for a DoS attack.

[2] We assume that the implementation provides the functionality explicitly defined by the specification. This property of the implementation can usually be guaranteed by conventional software testing.

An attack can be defined as a special kind of anomaly:

Definition 4. *An **attack** corresponds to a word $\beta \in \mathcal{L}(M^{\Delta})$ and hence to an accepting run of the differential DFSM M^{Δ} resulting in a breach of the defined security policy.*

With $\mathfrak{B}$ denoting the set of attacks obviously $\mathfrak{B} \subseteq \mathfrak{A}$ holds, i.e. the set of attacks is a subset of the set of anomalies. Initially, we will not further differentiate between anomalies and attacks.

According to the defined model a misuse detection technique looks for specific words $w \in \mathcal{L}(M^{\Delta})$, i.e. the used attack patterns correspond to runs of the DFSM M^{Δ}. The problem is that M^{Δ} is usually not completely known. For this reason it is difficult to make a clear statement about the completeness of a misuse detection technique. To compound matters, a heterogeneous environment will include several vendor-specific implementation DFSMs M_i' and hence various differential DFSMs M_i^{Δ}.

Specification-based anomaly detection techniques do not rely on an explicit representation of M^{Δ} as they compare the behaviour of M' with the expected behaviour given by M. They do so, by checking whether $w \in \mathcal{L}(M)$ holds for an observed sequence of actions w or not. Consequently, the correctness and completeness properties of a specification-based anomaly detection technique are clearly defined, although not every deviation necessarily constitutes an attack. However, from a network monitoring and control perspective, even harmless anomalies are usually of interest, as they are a potential indication of error conditions or misconfigurations.

Thus, specification-based anomaly detection can have an advantage over misuse detection if M is known. For communication protocols and even for processes this is usually the case, because M is already given (e.g. by public protocol specification) or can be derived. The specification can also be issued by a *Trusted Third Party* (e.g. the responsible standardisation committee), additionally protecting the user from deliberately malicious protocol specifications and corresponding implementations.

But what kind of anomalies can actually appear during the run of an implementation DFSM? And how can these anomalies be detected? In the following section, we introduce a classification scheme for anomalies and attacks. It is based on the transaction concept and the related ACID properties, which have their origin in the field of database systems.

3 Transaction-based Anomaly Detection

For a database transaction the so-called ACID properties must hold [HR83, Vos94]:

1. Atomicity: All operations of a transaction must be completed, i.e. a transaction is treated as a single, indivisible unit.

2. Consistency: A transaction takes the system from one consistent state to another.
3. Isolation: Each transaction must be performed without interference with other transactions.
4. Durability: After a transaction has successfully been completed, all its results are saved in permanent storage.

3.1 Classification of Anomalies and Attacks

The ACID properties are also suited to classify anomalies and attacks related to processes and communication protocols:

Theorem 1. *With regard to a specification DFSM $M = (Q, \Sigma, q_0, \delta, F)$ the possible anomalies and attacks concerning an implementation DFSM $M' = (Q', \Sigma', q_0, \delta', F')$ can be classified according to the transaction properties of atomicity, consistency and isolation.*

Proof. Let M be a specification DFSM with $M = (Q, \Sigma, q_0, \delta, F)$. Q is a finite set of states with n denoting the length of the longest path from the initial state q_0 to a final state $q_i \in F$ ($n < |Q|$). Each state $q_i \in Q$ is described by a corresponding set of state variables $\{q_i.v_k | k = 1, \ldots, p\}$.

Let Σ be a finite input alphabet and δ a partial transition function with $\delta : Q \times \Sigma \dashrightarrow \Sigma$. The transition function does not allow ε-transitions. Further, let q_0 be the start state and $F \subseteq Q$ the set of final states.

Let M' be a corresponding implementation DFSM with $M' = (Q', \Sigma', q_0, \delta', F')$, which is supposed to implement M. Q' is a finite set of states with $|Q'| = m$. Each state $q_i' \in Q'$ is described by a corresponding set of state variables $\{q_i'.v_k | k = 1, \ldots, p\}$.

Let Σ' be a finite input alphabet and δ' a total transition function with $\delta' : Q' \times \Sigma' \to \Sigma'$. Further, let q_0 be a start state and $F' \subseteq Q'$ be the set of final states.

According to Def. 3 and Def. 4 respectively anomalies and attacks are characterised by reaching a final state of the differential DFSM $M^{\triangle}$, i.e. not reaching a final state of the specification DFSM M. Therefore, we take the word w, which represents a complete trace of a single run of the implementation DFSM M', and check whether $w \in \mathcal{L}(M)$ holds. Due to the structure of a state machine, two cases have to be distinguished, namely anomalies with regard to the transition function δ' and anomalies with regard to the state space Q' of the implementation DFSM M':

1. **Anomalies with regard to the transition function δ':** First, consider the possible inputs to the transition function $\delta' : Q' \times \Sigma' \to \Sigma'$ and the corresponding transitions of the specification DFSM M for a state q_i. The proof is given with respect to the number l of considered input actions and hence with respect to the prefixes of an input to the implementation DFSM. We distinguish two cases:

$l \leq n$: The proof is done by induction with regard to the number l of input actions.

  $l = 1$: A single input action corresponds to the input of a single symbol a or no input at all (denoted by ε). Concerning the possible transitions of the specification DFSM M from the initial state q_0 four cases have to be distinguished:

  1. $a \in \Sigma$ and $\delta(q_0, a)$ defined
  2. $a = \varepsilon$ and $\delta(q_0, \varepsilon)$ not defined
  3. $a \in \Sigma$ and $\delta(q_0, a)$ not defined
  4. $a \notin \Sigma$ and $\delta(q_0, a)$ not defined

  Obviously, a transition and therefore an accepting run ($\delta(q_0, a) \in F$) is only possible in the first case.

  In the second case no transition can be made by the specification DFSM M, because no input is provided. As a consequence, the prefix a can not be extended into a word w with $w \in \mathcal{L}(M)$, i.e. the transitions necessary to reach a final state will not be passed. This behaviour constitutes an anomaly, which represents a direct **violation of atomicity**.

  In the third and fourth case no transition can be made by the specification DFSM M either. The observed behaviours constitute anomalies, which both represent a direct **violation of consistency** as either the transition function is not defined for the given input or the input is invalid itself. Again, in both cases the prefix a can not be extended into a word w with $w \in \mathcal{L}(M)$.

  $l = i + 1$: For the inductive step a sequence of input actions with $l = i + 1$ ($l \leq n$) is considered. The word w resulting from this input sequence can be written as $w = w' a$, where w' is the prefix of w with $|w'| = i$, and there is a state q_i such that w' leads to q_i in M, i.e. $\hat{\delta}(q_0, w) = \delta(\hat{\delta}(q_0, w'), a) = \delta(q_i, a)$ with $\hat{\delta}(q_0, w') = q_i$.

  Now suppose that the antecedent of the implication is true for a particular choice of i and w'. The argument proceeds by the case analysis of the possible inputs a made in state q_i with regard to input action $i + 1$. This analysis is identical to the analysis for the case $l = 1$, with the exception that now instead of state q_0 state q_i has to be considered. Hence, the same conclusion holds.

This completes the proof of the induction step.

$l > n$: If $l > n$ holds, then the length of the sequence of input actions is bigger than the length of the longest path of the specification DFSM M. According to the Pumping Lemma a word $w \in \mathcal{L}(M)$ with $|w| > n$ can be split into three parts $w = xyz$, with x, y, z being words, $0 < |y| \leq n + 1$, and $xy^k z \in \mathcal{L}(M)$ for $k = 0, 1, 2, \ldots$ This contradicts the assumption made in Def. 1 and implies for $l \geq m$ that the implementation DFSM M' contains a cycle of input actions. If the specification DFSM does not contain a cycle, the first additional input with respect to the current path followed by the specification DFSM results in a **violation of consistency**.

If the specification DFSM contains a cycle, an attacker can prohibit the extension of the word $u = xy^k$ into a word v with $v \in \mathcal{L}(M)$ by repeatedly passing the cycle. This behaviour corresponds to the result for the first case ($l = 1, a = \varepsilon$). It constitutes an anomaly, which represents a direct **violation of atomicity.**

2. **Anomalies with regard to the state space Q':** Let the implementation DFSM M_x' be in state $q_{x_i}' \in Q_x'$, with the state q_{x_i}' being defined by state variables $\{q_{x_i}'.v_k | k = 1, \ldots, p\}$. Further consider an implementation DFSM M_y' in a state $q_{y_j}' \in Q_y'$, with the state q_{y_j}' being defined by state variables $\{q_{y_j}'.v_l | l = 1, \ldots, r\}$. Without restricting the universal validity of the proof, let the state variables $q_{x_i}'.v_s$ and $q_{y_j}'.v_t$ represent the same physical object (value in a database, file, etc.). If automaton M_y' performs a transition $\delta(q_{y_j}', a) = q_{y_{j+1}}'$, with $q_{y_j}'.v_t \neq q_{y_{j+1}}'.v_t$, then the corresponding state variable of automaton M_x' $q_{x_i}'.v_s$ becomes invalid. This can be interpreted as an implicit state transition of the implementation DFSM M_x' due to an indirect input a and therefore corresponds to a transition of the differential DFSM M_x^Δ. Hence, the prefix a can not be extended into a word w with $w \in \mathcal{L}(M_x)$. This is an anomaly, which represents a direct **violation of isolation.** $\square$

Hence, the ACID properties provide a suitable framework for the classification of anomalies and attacks. Instead of avoiding anomalies like a database management system does, an IDS can restrict itself to detecting anomalies.

This analogy is the basic idea of transaction-based anomaly detection. Transaction-based anomaly detection describes positive behaviour by the definition of transactions. A corresponding IDS receives an audit stream containing different protocol or process runs as its input and checks whether these runs satisfy the ACID properties, i.e., whether the audit stream corresponds to an output schedule as it would have been generated by a database management system.

3.2 Communication Transactions

The basis for the deployment of transaction-based anomaly detection is the definition of corresponding transactions for the monitored system domain.

In general, a transaction describes a state transformation $q_i \rightarrow q_j$, with q_i denoting the initial and q_j the final state. The transaction can be particularised with regard to intermediate reading and writing steps:

$$q_i \overset{p_1}{\Rightarrow} q_{k_1} \overset{p_2}{\Rightarrow} q_{k_2} \overset{p_3}{\Rightarrow} \ldots \overset{p_n}{\Rightarrow} q_j,$$

with $p_i \in \{r(x), w(x)\}$. But only the state transformation $q_i \rightarrow q_j$ has to satisfy the ACID properties.

For the access to persistent data (e.g. files) by processes this leads to a direct analogy. However, the analogy is less obvious for communication protocols.

Communication Model	Transaction	Subtransaction	Example
Connection-oriented	Connection	Connection Establishment	
		Data Transfer	TCP Connection
		Connection Termination	
Connection-less	Request/Reply	Request/Reply	Request	ICMP Request/Reply
		Reply	
	Event	Event	-	ICMP Error Message

Table 2. Communication models and transactions.

Due to the involvement of at least two communicating parties the run of a communication protocol is characterised by the consecutive execution of several subtransactions. These subtransactions imply a coordinated sequence of state changes and hence the progress of the protocol. In database theory the admissible sequences of states are specified by means of transitional and dynamic integrity constraints, while static integrity constraints describe the general state properties.

In the context of transaction-based anomaly detection these additional constraints regarding the admissible sequences of states are modelled by extended nested transactions. In case of a conventional nested transaction a transaction t_i is decomposed into subtransactions t_{ij}, which are executed in parallel. This nesting can be represented by a tree, in which only the top-level transaction t has to satisfy all four ACID properties. The subtransactions t_{ij} have to satisfy the properties of atomicity, consistency and isolation.

The extended model of *sequential nested transactions* is intended to meet the requirements of communication processes. The subtransactions t_{ij} are no longer executed in parallel $(t_{i1}||\ldots||t_{ik})$, but rather sequential $(t_{i1};\ldots;t_{ik})$. The execution sequence results from the front word of the tree, i.e. the labelling of the leafs read from left to right. Also in this case only the top-level transaction has to satisfy all four ACID properties.

Individual transactions can also be combined into a nested transaction on the process level. The admissible combinations of the individual transactions can be described by regular expressions and thus by finite state machines. Again, only individual, finite runs are considered, i.e. the use of the *-operator is restricted. Hence, a finite run corresponds to an individual sequential nested transaction.

For the TCP/IP protocol stack the three transaction types defined in Tab. 2 can be differentiated[3]. A connection-oriented, TCP-based communication is modelled by a sequential nested transaction. The connection is split into three subtransactions, namely connection establishment, data transfer and connection

---

[3] Multicast traffic is not taken into account.

termination. The connection establishment comprises three individual subtransactions, which correspond to the packets exchanged during TCP's 3-way handshake protocol.

Violation	Layer	Attack
Atomicity	TCP	SYN Flood
		SYN Scan
	Process Layer	Deadlock
Consistency	ICMP	Ping of Death
		Ping Sweep
	TCP	Null Scan
		Land Nuke
		FIN Scan
		SYN/ACK Scan
		SYN/FIN Scan
		RST Scan
		Xmas Tree Scan
	UDP	UDP Scan
	Application Layer	FTP Bounce
	Process Layer	Buffer Overflow
		Erroneous Parameter
Isolation	Process Layer	Race Condition

Table 3. Attack classification.

Tab. 3 classifies some popular attacks against the TCP/IP protocol stack
and the process layer according to the ACID properties. Other attacks can be
classified correspondingly.

It has to be taken into account that the given classification can be based on
different kinds of specifications. Besides the protocol and process specific constraints, the user can define additional restrictions. The TCP bounce attack for
example is based on legal protocol behaviour. However, it violates the consistency property, if the user further restricts the protocol specification and only
allows data channels between hosts, which have already established a control
channel.

By means of a corresponding extended finite state machine model it can be
checked at run-time whether a communication transaction satisfies the ACID
properties. A detected anomaly is then forwarded to an intrusion response system.

4   Intrusion Response

The ACID properties provide a direct classification of detected anomalies. Based
on this classification and complementary information from other sources like

network management, firewalls, etc. an intrusion response system can initiate appropriate and effective countermeasures.

But these countermeasures need to be carefully selected and controlled with regard to their effect and execution. Continuing the analogy to database management systems, the deployment of techniques used in the context of active databases stands to reason.

Active databases (see e.g. [PD98]) are able to respond to events, which arise internally to the database or from an external source. They differentiate between the *knowledge*, the *execution* and the *management model*. These basic models describe the actual active mechanisms, the concrete run-time strategy and collective properties of the active mechanisms like termination and confluence.

The knowledge model is based on *event-condition-action rules* (ECA rules), which are specified in the following form:

```
/* ECA Rule */
on event
if condition
do action
```

If an ECA rule is triggered by the occurrence of the defined event, the corresponding condition is evaluated in order to examine the context in which the event has taken place. Dependent on the result of this evaluation, the specified action is executed.

Based on ECA rules and the different considered information sources an *active IRS* can be defined as a tuple (S, E, R), where $S = \{s_1, s_2, \ldots, s_l\}$ denotes the set of monitored system components, $E = \{e_1, e_2, \ldots, e_m\}$ denotes the set of related events, and $R = \{r_1, r_2, \ldots, r_n\}$ denotes the set of ECA rules defined for S and E.

Due to the general objectives of an IRS the ECA rules will usually specify actions belonging to one of the following classes:

1. Corrective actions, i.e. repair of damage.
2. Preventive actions, i.e. prevention of further damage.
3. Forensic actions, i.e. collection of evidence.
4. Management actions, i.e. management of the monitoring and control architecture.

In the context of transaction-based intrusion detection the rules for the treatment of reported anomalies and for the re-establishment of the demanded system state can be further classified according to the violated transaction property, i.e. atomicity, consistency or isolation.

This allows a differentiated treatment of all reported anomalies. For example, by combining individual anomalies into composite events, it becomes possible to establish relationships between different protocol runs and to further classify detected anomalies in the sense of a misuse detection system. The according misuse detection capabilities can be embedded into the event and condition components of the active rules.

The theory of active databases provides the required techniques for these and
other tasks of an active IRS.

5 Conclusions

In this paper, we have discussed the analogy between intrusion detection and
database management systems. The theoretical concept of transactions, a key
component of database theory, obviously provides a suitable basis for anomaly
detection, resulting in the concept of transaction-based anomaly detection. This
specification-based anomaly detection technique logically combines several pro-
cess- and protocol-related actions into a transaction and checks whether the
transaction satisfies the ACID properties.

Any detected anomaly is forwarded to an intrusion response system, where
it triggers the processing of one or more ECA rules. The ECA rules take care
of the further classification and treatment of the anomaly. Thus again database
techniques are deployed for the design and implementation of an IRS as the
concept of ECA rules stems from the theory of active databases.

However, this paper has only given a general introduction to the basic idea
of transaction-based intrusion detection and response. For a more elaborate discussion of the related concepts and a detailed performance evaluation the reader
is referred to [Büs01].

References

[Bac00]   R. G. Bace. *Intrusion Detection*. Macmillan Technical Publishing, 2000.
[Büs01]   R. Büschkes. *Angriffserkennung in Kommunikationsnetzen*. PhD thesis,
          RWTH Aachen, 2001.
[CGP99]   E. M. Clarke, O. Grumberg, and D. Peled. *Model Checking*. MIT Press,
          1999.
[Hol91]   G. J. Holzmann. *Design and Validation of Computer Protocols*. Prentice-
          Hall, 1991.
[HR83]   T. Härder and A. Reuter. Principles of transaction-oriented database recov-
          ery. *Computing Surveys*, 15(4):287–317, 1983.
[HU79]   J. Hopcroft and J. Ullman. *Introduction to Automata Theory, Languages,
          and Computation*. Addison-Wesley, 1979.
[Ko96]   C. C. W. Ko. *Execution Monitoring of Security-Critical Programs in a Dis-
          tributed System: A Specification-Based Approach*. PhD thesis, University of
          California, Davis, 1996.
[Lin99]   U. Lindqvist. *On the Fundamentals of Analysis and Detection of Computer
          Misuse*. PhD thesis, Department of Computer Engineering, Chalmers Uni-
          versity of Technology, Göteborg, 1999.
[PD98]   N. W. Paton and O. Diaz. Introduction. In N. W. Paton, editor, *Active
          Rules in Database Systems*, pages 3–27. Springer, 1998.
[Sch99]   F. B. Schneider, editor. *Trust in cyberspace*. National Academy Press, 1999.
[Vos94]   G. Vossen. *Datenmodelle, Datenbanksprachen und Datenbank-Management-
          Systeme*. Addison-Wesley, 2nd edition, 1994.

Woven Convolutional Coding

Ralph Jordan**

Department of Telecommunications and Applied Information Theory,
University of Ulm, Albert-Einstein-Allee 43, D-89081 Ulm
ralph.jordan@e-technik.uni-ulm.de,
http://tait.e-technik.uni-ulm.de/~jordan

Abstract. Woven codes are a family of forward error correction codes. They are constructed by combining several convolutional codes in such a manner that the overall code is again a convolutional code. This is a tutorial paper dealing with design aspects of encoding and decoding woven codes.

Woven codes are the counterpart in convolutional coding to the classical product code in block coding. Analogous to the product distance of product block codes, woven codes can be constructed with a large free distance, i.e., with a large asymptotic coding gain. This is important for systems that are designed to operate at extremely small output bit error probabilities.

It is shown how to introduce additional permutation to the woven construction such that the lower bound on the free distance of the original construction is preserved. Randomly generated and designed convolutional permuters are considered. This enables us to design codes that achieve large coding gains at moderate bit error probabilities. In case of large permutation lengths, this allows us to design systems that operate at code rates close the theoretical limit.

1 Introduction

The discovery of *turbo coding* [1] in 1993 drew widespread attention among the coding community. After more than 40 years of research, these codes have been the first to enable reliable information transmission over the additive white Gaussian noise channel at code rates close to the channel capacity. Turbo codes are block codes. The encoder represents a parallel code concatenation of two component encoders. The information word and a permuted version of the information word are encoded with two component encoders and transmitted over the channel. The received word is alternately decoded whereby the two component decoders exchange information in consecutive decoding steps. After a certain number of decoding iterations, the estimated information sequence is output. A detailed description of parallel code concatenation and iterative decoding can be found in [3] and [2], respectively.

** This research was supported by the German research council Deutsche Forschungsgemeinschaft under Grant Bo 867/8.
The author now stays with EADS Ewation GmbH, Wörthstr. 84, D-89084 Ulm.

Turbo coding raised a storm of research activity and the concept of iterative decoding was successfully applied to a wide range of problems. It also led to the rediscovery of Gallagers' *low density codes* [4] and it turned out that turbo codes are from the same code family. Different turbo-like code construction have been suggested and investigated since, e.g., serially concatenated codes with permutation [5], repeat and accumulate codes [6], and woven codes [7].

This paper is devoted to woven convolutional coding. In Section 2, we introduce the various types of woven encoders and present the pipeline decoder. This is an iterative decoding method working in a sliding window. In Section 3, we consider design aspects of the woven construction. In particular, we study the asymptotic coding gain and the performance at code rates near capacity. We conclude with some remarks in Section 4.

2 Encoding and Decoding Woven Codes

2.1 Woven Convolutional Encoder

In [7], three related woven constructions were introduced, viz., woven codes with outer warp, woven codes with inner warp, and the twill. The corresponding woven encoders are depicted in Fig. 1-3. They can all be regarded as serial concatenations of two warps, both consisting of an array of parallel convolutional encoders. The outer warp input sequence u is de-multiplexed bit-wise to the outer encoder input sequences u_l^o, $1 \leq l \leq l_o$. The outer warp output sequence v^o is obtained by bit-wise multiplexing the encoder output sequences v_l^o, $1 \leq l \leq l_o$. Similarly, the inner warp input sequence u^i is de-multiplexed bit-wise to the inner encoder input sequences u_l^i, $1 \leq l \leq l_i$, and the inner encoder output sequences v_l^i, $1 \leq l \leq l_i$, are multiplexed bit-wise to the woven code sequence v. Here and

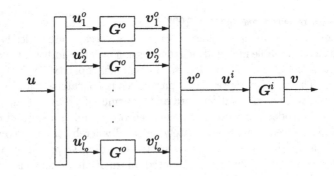

Fig. 1. Woven encoder with outer warp.

throughout this paper we assume that the outer (inner) warp consists of l_o (l_i)

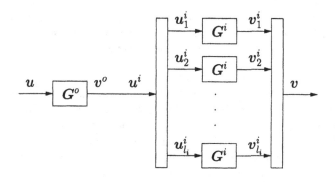

Fig. 2. Woven encoder with inner warp.

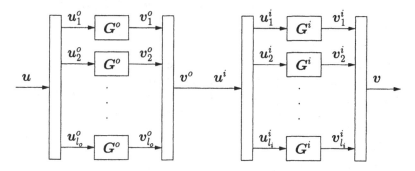

Fig. 3. Woven encoder of the twill.

identical rate $R_o = b_o/c_o$ $(R_i = b_i/c_i)$ convolutional encoders with generator matrix $G_o(D)$ $(G_i(D))$. The warps themselves represent rate $R_o = (b_o l_o)/(c_o l_o)$ and $R_i = (b_i l_i)/(c_i l_i)$ convolutional encoders. Hence, all three woven encoders represent a cascade of two convolutional encoders. The code dimensions

$$b \triangleq b_o l_o B_o \qquad (1)$$
$$c \triangleq c_i l_i B_i \qquad (2)$$

are obtained by *blocking* the outer and inner warp generator matrices with *blocking factors* $B_o = \text{lcm}(l_o c_o, l_i b_i)/(l_o c_o)$ and $B_i = \text{lcm}(l_o c_o, l_i b_i)/(l_i b_i)$ Blocking means that we regard sub-matrices of size $b_o B_o \times c_o B_o$ and $b_i B_i \times c_i B_i$ instead of sub-matrices of size $b_o \times c_o$ and $b_i \times c_i$ as the fundamental building blocks when deriving the generator matrices $G_o(D)$ and $G_i(D)$, respectively. The blocking factors are chosen such that the outer warp output sequence $v^o = v_0^o v_1^o \ldots$ and the inner warp input sequence $u^i = u_0^i u_1^i \ldots$ are sequences of the same tuple-size, i.e., we have $v_t^o = u_t^i$, where both tuples are binary and of size $b/R_o = c R_i$. Hence, the rate of a woven code is

$$R = b/c = R_o R_i. \qquad (3)$$

The constructions of woven codes with outer warp ($l_i = 1$) and inner warp ($l_o = 1$) are important special cases of the twill. We shall see later that the numbers l_o and l_i are important design parameter of the woven construction.

Additional Permutation The concept of convolutional permutation allows us to encode woven codes with additional permutation and thereby keeping the convolutional code structure of the overall code. In general, the permuter operates in between the outer warp and the inner warp, i.e., the inner warp input sequence u^i is a scrambled version of the outer warp output sequence v^o. The special case of rowwise permutation will be of particular importance in the sequel. Here we distinguish further between rowwise permutation in the outer warp and rowwise permutation in the inner warp. In the first case the sequences v_l^o, $1 \leq l \leq l_o$, are permuted, whereas in the latter case the sequences u^i, $1 \leq l \leq l_i$ are permuted.

2.2 Pipeline Decoding

In [8], iterative decoding of woven codes is described. The presented decoding scheme operates with a sliding window technique over the woven code sequence. This exploits the nature of convolutional codes as sequences and suits the concept of considering convolutional encoding and decoding as a continuous process.

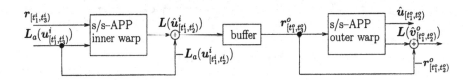

Fig. 4. The basic decoding step of the pipeline decoder.

Consider only one iteration. A segment of the received sequence is first decoded by the inner warp decoder. Then the output is passed to the outer warp decoder and used as input for the second decoding step. The outer and inner warp decoders consist of arrays of l_o and l_i window BCJR decoders [9], respectively. The two decoding steps are combined into a *basic decoding step* that represents one iteration in the decoding process, see Fig. 4. This basic decoding step is repeated I times by passing the soft-output of the outer decoder to the inner decoder that performs the next iteration. The different window sizes used in the decoding steps are $w_d^o = t_3^o - t_1^o$, $w_b^o = t_3^o - t_2^o$, $w_d^i = t_3^i - t_1^i$, and $w_b^i = t_3^i - t_2^i$. The size of the decision windows of the outer and inner decoder are the same, i.e.,

$$w_d = w_d^o = w_d^i. \tag{4}$$

Note that all window sizes are given in number of tuples of the considered sequences. Thus, the window sizes are the same for the woven code sequences, inner and outer warp sequences, and the component decoder sequences. In the following we denote the delay window size of the basic decoding step by

$$w_b = w_b^o + w_b^i. \tag{5}$$

In case of additional rowwise permutation we have

$$w_b = w_s + w_b^o + w_b^i \tag{6}$$

where w_s is a window size that is determines by the maximum permuter delay in the construction. After the decoding in the current window is finished, the input sequence segments are shifted by w_d tuples, we reinitialize, i.e., $t_j^i \leftarrow t_j^i + w_d$ and $t_j^o \leftarrow t_j^o + w_d$, and continue with the decoding in the new window.

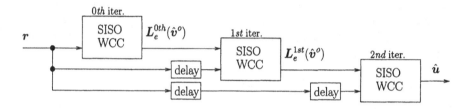

Fig. 5. Pipeline decoder performing three iterations.

In Fig. 5 we show a decoder consisting of three cascaded basic decoding steps. The first basic decoding step, denoted as the 0th iteration, is performed without a priori L-values at its input. The next two consecutive decoders take the extrinsic L-values of the previous decoder as its input a priori L-values. In general, the a priori L-values of the jth iteration are the extrinsic L-values of the $(j-1)$th iteration, that is, $L_a^{jth}(\hat{u}^i) = L_e^{(j-1)th}(\hat{v}^o)$.

Let us now consider decoding delays and the decoding complexity of the pipeline decoder. If the basic decoding steps are performed in parallel, then their sliding windows do not overlap and we have the delay

$$D_{\text{pipe}} = c(w_d + w_b)I. \tag{7}$$

If all basic decoding steps are done consecutively by starting with the 0th iteration, then the decoding delay can be reduced to

$$D_{\text{pipe}} = c(w_d + w_bI). \tag{8}$$

Once the pipeline decoder started to generate outputs, the delay between successively decoded segments of bw_d bits of the estimated information sequence $\hat{u}$ is

$$d_{\text{pipe}} = cw_d, \tag{9}$$

which can be considerably smaller than D_{pipe}. This leads to a smooth accumulation of the transmitted information at the receiver. The complexity of the pipeline decoder is

$$C_{\text{pipe}} = I f(w_d, w_b^o) C_{\text{BCJR}}(b_o, c_o, \mu_o) + I R_o^{-1} f(w_d, w_b^i) C_{\text{BCJR}}(b_i, c_i, \mu_i) \quad (10)$$

where $f(w_d, w_b) = 1 + w_b/(2w_d)$ and $C_{\text{BCJR}}(b, c, \mu)$ is the decoding complexity of the BCJR algorithm for a rate $R = b/c$ convolutional code with μ dimensional encoder state space.

3 Design Aspects of Woven Codes

3.1 Asymptotic Coding Gain

Consider a rate R convolutional code $\mathcal{C}$ is used to communicate over an additive white Gaussian noise (AWGN) channel with binary phase shift keying (BPSK) modulation and assume maximum-likelihood (ML) decoding is applied. Then, the asymptotic coding gain is given by [10]

$$\gamma = 10 \log_{10}(d_{\text{free}} R) \text{ dB}. \quad (11)$$

For high signal-to-noise ratios this is a rough estimate of the performance of a coded system representing the potential increase due to coding. Hence, large asymptotic coding gains are obtained by codes with a large free distance. In the following we study the free distance of various woven constructions with and without additional permutation.

The active distances are a family of distance measures that were introduced in [11] for binary convolutional codes. They can be used to describe the error correcting capability of the code and are very useful to study the distance properties of concatenated convolutional codes. In the case of the woven construction the active distances allow us to define two important parameters, viz., the sufficiently large number of outer encoders, l_o^*, and the sufficiently large number of inner encoders, l_i^*. They are given by

$$l_o^* \triangleq b_i \left(\lceil (2d_{\text{free}}^i - \beta^{b,i})/\alpha^i \rceil - 1 \right) \quad (12)$$

and

$$l_i^* \triangleq c_o \min \left\{ \lceil (d_{\text{free}}^o - \beta^{co})/\alpha^o \rceil, \ \lceil (d_{\text{free}}^o - \beta^{rco})/\alpha^o \rceil \right\} \quad (13)$$

where the parameters α^i, α^o, β^{bi}, β^{co}, and β^{rco} are given by the affine lower bounds on the active distances of the inner and outer encoder. In [12] an efficient and effective method can be found how to compute the active distances. Tables of l_o^* and l_i^* for a wide range of convolutional codes can be found in [8].

In the following theorem we summarize the statements on the free distance of various woven constructions considered in [7] and [8].

Theorem 1. *Let d_{free} be the free distance of a woven code with an outer warp of l_o encoders and an inner warp of l_i encoders. Then*

$$d_{\text{free}} \geq d_{\text{free}}^o d_{\text{free}}^i \tag{14}$$

where d_{free}^o and d_{free}^i denote the free distances of the outer and inner convolutional codes, respectively, if
(i) l_o and l_i are relatively prime and satisfy either

$$l_o \geq l_o^*, \tag{15}$$

or

$$l_i \geq l_i^*. \tag{16}$$

(ii) l_o and l_i are relatively prime and satisfy either (15), if random row-wise permutation is performed in the outer warp, or (16), if random row-wise permutation is performed in the inner warp.
(iii) $l_i = 1$ and the designed permutations in the outer warp satisfy

$$s_l \geq l_i^*, \tag{17}$$

and

$$t_l l_o \geq l_o^* \tag{18}$$

for $1 \leq l \leq l_o$.
(iv) $l_o = 1$ and the designed permutations in the inner warp satisfy

$$l_i s_l \geq l_i^*, \tag{19}$$

and

$$t_l \geq l_o^* \tag{20}$$

for $1 \leq l \leq l_i$.
(v) $l_o = 1$ and $l_i = 1$ and the designed permutation in between satisfies

$$s \geq l_i^*, \tag{21}$$

and

$$t \geq l_o^*. \tag{22}$$

The parameters s_l and t_l denote the separations of the lth permuter in the construction.

While part (i) of Theorem 1 is for woven codes without additional permutation, the underlying constructions in part (ii)-(v) employ additional rowwise permutation. Except for part (ii), which allows to apply random permutations, part (iii)-(v) use designed permutations.

Clearly, the separations (s_l, t_l) of the designed rowwise permutations in the outer warp, $1 \leq l \leq l_o$, respectively, in the inner warp, $1 \leq l \leq l_i$, play a decisive role in the design. A permuter with separation (s,t) reorders the input sequence such that any s consecutive input symbols appear in the output sequence parted by at least $t-1$ symbols. A randomly generated permutation will, in general, not have large separations. Moreover, it can be shown that, with high probability, it will have $t=1$ for all s.

In [13], separations are defined as parameters of a convolutional permutation. Additionally, a simple algebraic construction is presented that allows us to design a convolutional permuter with any given separation (s,t). It is shown that designed permuters exist that have a permutation delay δ satisfying $\delta \le st$. Small permutation delays are important to have small decoding delays.

3.2 Bit Error Probability at Code Rates near Capacity

Again, we consider the AWGN channel with binary input. The probability $P(r \mid v)$ of output r given input v is

$$
P(r \mid v) = \begin{cases} \frac{1}{\sqrt{\pi N_0}} e^{-\frac{(r-E_s)^2}{N_0}}, & v = 0 \\ \frac{1}{\sqrt{\pi N_0}} e^{-\frac{(r+E_s)^2}{N_0}}, & v = 1 \end{cases} \tag{23}
$$

where E_s is the signal energy and N_0 the half-sided spectral power density. Then E_s/N_0 is called the signal-to-noise ratio *per code symbol* and with $E_b = E_s/R$ we obtain E_b/N_0 which is called the signal-to-noise ratio *per information bit*. The capacity C of the AWGN channel is depicted in Fig. 6. The channel capacity is the smallest code rate that we can (theoretically) communicate reliable over the channel. From the strong version of Shannons' channel coding theo-

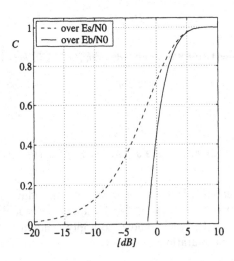

Fig. 6. Channel capacity of the AWGN channel with binary input.

rem, the error exponents of convolutional codes [14], we know that there exist convolutional codes of all rates $R < C$ that have an exponentially decreasing error probability with increasing memory m. When operating at rates R near channel capacity the error exponent becomes small and codes with large m are required to guarantee a certain error performance. Generally, for a given code rate R the complexity of ML decoding increases exponentially with the memory m. Hence, the fundamental problems in coding theory are on one hand to find "good" codes and on the other hand to develop decoding methods that can be realized with state-of-the-art hardware.

In the following we are interested in the bit error probability of woven constructions at code rates near capacity, i.e., in the performance of the code at low signal-to-noise ratios. This is in contrast to the previously considered asymptotic coding gain which determines the performance at high signal-to-noise ratios.

We can increase the memory of the woven code by increasing the maximum permutation delay $\delta = \max_l \delta_l$ in the construction. Since the decoding complexity of the pipeline decoder is determined by the decoding complexity of the component codes, increasing δ does not increase the decoding complexity. This enables us to generate woven codes with large memory and small decoding complexity. We notice that the pipeline decoder is not an ML decoder. However, it achieves an excellent performance.

Table 1. Comparison of rate $R = 1/2$ MS codes with rate $R = 1/2$ OFD codes.

	MS codes			OFD codes		
d_{free}	α	$G(D)$	m	α	$G(D)$	m
3	1	(2,3)	1	1	(2,3)	1
4	2/3	(6,7)	2	—	—	—
5	4/7	(14,15)	3	1/2	(5,7)	2
6	1/2	(15,17)	3	1/2	(15,17)	3
7	4/9	(70,65)	5	4/11	(23,35)	4
8	2/5	(76,65)	5	8/23	(53,75)	5
9	7/19	(122,157)	6	—	—	—
10	8/25	(135,163)	6	4/13	(133,171)	6

Simulations have shown that the slope α of the component codes plays an important role in the code design. The slope is a distance parameter that is derived from the active distances of the code. It essentially determines the error correcting capability. The lager α, the more errors can be corrected. In [12] a new family of convolutional codes, namely, the maximum slope (MS) codes, are introduced. MS codes have the largest slope among all convolutional codes of rate $R = b/c$ and free distance d_{free}. In Table 1 α and d_{free} of MS codes and optimum free distance (OFD) codes with memory $1 \leq m \leq 6$ are compared.

418

Notice, that the slope decreases as the memory increases!

Consider the serial cascade of a rate $R = 1/2$ MS code, a randomly generated permuter, and the rate $R = 1$ convolutional code with generator matrix $G(D) = 1/(1 + D)$. We terminate the MS code after $k = 10\,000$ encoded information bits and perform the random permutation over the complete block. Then the inner code is encoded and the code word is transmitted over an AWGN channel. Iterative decoding with 30 iterations is performed. In Fig. 7 the simulated bit error probability is shown for the MS codes of Table 1.

We notice that the construction performs the better the larger the slope of the component code. According to the capacity of the AWGN channel, see Fig. 6, we know that reliable transmission with rate $R = 1/2$ codes is possible at a signal to noise ratio E_b/N_0 of approximately 0 dB. The best performing code, i.e., the construction with the memory $m = 1$ MS code, has a bit error probabilities as low as 10^{-4} at about 1.2 dB from the theoretical limit. We mention that the corresponding decoding complexity is that of the BCJR decoder of a $m = 1$ convolutional code times the number of performed iteration!

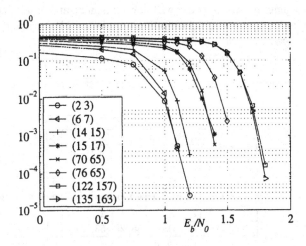

Fig. 7. Bit error probability of serially concatenated codes.

4 Concluding Remarks

In this paper, encoding and decoding aspects of woven codes were considered. Several woven constructions were presented. This, on one hand, enabled us to construct large free distances and, on the other hand, allowed us to apply additional permutation to realize large coding gains at code rates near capacity.

In future work it would be interesting to design permutations that achieve a free distance of serially cascaded codes or woven codes that is larger than the product distance. First results in this direction are presented in [15] and [16].

Another important application of the woven construction is unequal error protection. In [17], [18], and [19] the woven construction is shown to be well suited to generate convolutional codes that have unequal error protection.

Another interesting topic is woven coded modulation. Since the underlying codes are nonlinear, it becomes necessary to redefine the active distances for this case. A first approach in this direction can be found in [20].

Acknowledgment

Firstly, I would like to thank Martin Bossert for recognizing my interest in research and for giving me the opportunity to work in his group. He supported me in various ways, established the contact to other research groups, and gave me a high degree of academic freedom.

I would like to thank Viktor Zyablov for creating an inspiring academic atmosphere in our group. The numerous discussions with him helped me to gain a deeper understanding of coding theory. Without his guidance and support this work would not have been possible.

I am thankfully to Rolf Johannesson for inviting me several times to his research group in Lund University. Altogether I stayed 17 weeks in Lund and became good with his group. During this time I worked closest with Stefan Höst and learned a lot from him. With Rolf Johannesson it was exciting to discuss and solve difficult problems.

References

1. Berrou, C., Glavieux, A., Thitimasjshima, P.: Near Shannon Limit Error-Correcting Coding and Decoding: Turbo-codes (1). IEEE International Conference on Com., Geneva, Switzerland (1993)
2. Heegard, C., Wicker, S. B.: Turbo Coding. Kluwer Academic Publishers (1999)
3. Hagenauer, J., Offer, E., Papke, L.: Iterative Decoding of Binary Block Codes and Convolutional Codes. IEEE Trans. on Inform. Theory 42 (1996) 429–445
4. Gallager, R. G.: Low-Density Parity-Check Codes M.I.T. Press, Cambridge, Massachusetts (1963)
5. Benedetto, S., Montorsi, G.: Serial Concatenation of Interleaved Codes: Performance Analysis, Design, and Iterative Decoding. IEEE Trans. on Inform. Theory 44 (1998) 909–926
6. Divsalar, D., Jin, H., McEliece, R. J.: Coding theorems for 'turbo-like' codes. 36th Allerton Conference on Commun., Control, and Computing, USA (1998)
7. Höst, S., Johannesson, R., Zyablov, V.: Woven Convolutional Codes I: Encoder Properties. IEEE Trans. on Inform. Theory 48 (2002) 149–161
8. Jordan R., Höst S., Johannesson, R., Bossert, M., Zyablov, V.: Woven Convolutional Codes II: Decoding Aspects. IEEE Trans. on Inform. Theory submitted 2001
9. Bahl, L. R., Cocke, J., Jelinek, F., Raviv, J.: Optimal Decoding of Linear Codes for Minimum Symbol Error Rate. IEEE Trans. on Inform. Theory 20 (1974) 284–287

10. Johannesson, R., Zigangirov, K.: Fundamentals of Convolutional Coding. IEEE Press (1999)
11. Höst, S., Johannesson, R., Zigangirov, K., Zyablov, V.: Active Distances for Convolutional Codes. IEEE Trans. on Inform. Theory **45** (1999) 658–669
12. Jordan, R., Pavlouchkov, V., Zyablov, V.: Maximum Slope Convolutional Codes. IEEE Trans. on Inform. Theory submitted 2001
13. Jordan, R., Höst, S., Johannesson, R.: On the Construction of Convolutional Permuters with Large Separations. IEEE Trans. on Inform. Theory submitted 2002
14. Viterbi, A. J., Omura, J. K.: The Principles of Digital Communication and Coding. McGraw-Hill (1979)
15. Jordan, R., Johannesson, R., Bossert, M.: On Nested Convolutional Codes and Their Application to Woven Codes. IEEE Trans. on Inform. Theory accepted 2002
16. Hübner, A., Jordan, R., Grill, J.: On permuters with second order separations between cascaded convolutional encoders. IEEE Intern. Symposium on Inform. Theory, Lausanne, Switzerland (2002)
17. Zyablov, V., Jordan, R.: On Woven Convolutional Codes with outer Warp and Unequal Error Protection. European Trans. on Telecommun. submitted 2001
18. Jordan, R., Höst, S., Zyablov, V.: Woven convolutional codes and unequal error protection. IEEE Intern. Symposium on Inform. Theory, Washington, DC, USA (2001)
19. Pavlouchkov, V., Jordan, R., Zyablov, V.: Some simulation results for woven convolutional codes with outer warp and two-level unequal error protection. 4th ITG Conference on Source and Channel Coding, Berlin, Germany (2002)
20. Baumgartner, B., Jordan, R., Zyablov, Z., Bossert, M.: On Active Euclidean Distances for Trellis Coded Modulation. IEEE Intern. Symposium on Inform. Theory, Yokohama, Japan submitted 2002

Improving Performance
of SDH/SONET-WDM Multilayer Networks
Using Weighted Integrated Routing

Marc Necker

Institute of Communication Networks and Computer Engineering
University of Stuttgart
Pfaffenwaldring 47, D-70569 Stuttgart
necker@ind.uni-stuttgart.de

Abstract This work deals with routing schemes in SDH/SONET-WDM multilayer networks applying Synchronous Digital Hierarchy (SDH) or Synchronous Optical Network (SONET) on top of a dynamic photonic network in Wavelength Division Multiplex technology (WDM). The focus are integrated routing schemes which benefit from an integrated view of the SDH/SONET layer and the optical layer. Besides the comparison of known non-integrated and integrated methods, the new routing scheme *Weighted Integrated Routing (WIR)* is presented and its performance evaluated. In contrast to other known integrated routing schemes, *WIR* uses rating functions to evaluate different path alternatives and select the best route. In addition to the analysis of the different routing schemes, the dimensioning of network resources is treated.

1 Introduction

In optical networks, transmission rates have dramatically increased during the past years and dynamic provisioning of lightpaths will soon be available through an automated transport network control plane, e. g. ASTN [1]. Advanced node architectures which integrate electrical and optical layers will most likely be available in future systems. Assigning low-bandwidth electrical connections to high-speed optical lightpaths, also known as traffic grooming, is an important aspect in such networks, since small granularities are the major source of revenue for operators and provide service flexibility.

Routing on the electrical and optical layer is an essential component of every grooming strategy. Efficient transport of dynamic traffic demands of different granularities from the SONET/SDH hierarchy requires optimized multi layer routing and grooming algorithms [2]. *Non-integrated* routing schemes treat both layers separately while *integrated* schemes try to improve performance by combining both layers. Most approaches for integrated routing, e. g. [3] for SONET or [4] for IP, take advantage of complete knowledge about topology and occupancy of both layers, which is not supported by the overlay network model [5]. However, the overlay model is favored by operators as information on transport networks is very sensitive and should be kept secret.

In this paper, *Weighted Integrated Routing* is presented which solves the dynamic grooming problem without the need for gathering full state information of both layers. Instead, the routing instance probes the SDH/SONET layer and the WDM layer for different path alternatives. In addition, a method for dimensioning the number of transponders in multilayer nodes is introduced.

The structure of this paper is as follows: In section 2, the network model and fundamentals on traffic grooming are introduced. In section 3 the *Weighted Integrated Routing* scheme is explained, followed by a discussion of transponder dimensioning in section 4. Finally, selected results of the performance evaluation are presented in chapter 5.

2 Multilayer Grooming and Routing Options

The structure of a network node in the SDH/SONET-WDM network is shown in Fig. 1. On the optical layer, this model comprises an optical cross-connect (OXC), which is assumed to be non-blocking. Additionally, a certain number of wavelength converters allows for wavelength conversion without limitations. The electrical layer mainly consists of a non-blocking electronic cross-connect (EXC), which is able to switch electrical connections at arbitrary SDH/SONET granularities. The EXC thus allows for an effective grooming of electrical connections. The EXC and OXC are connected by z transponders and receivers, respectively. On the optical layer, a node is connected to its neighboring nodes with a total of w wavelengths in each direction.

In a centralized routing scheme, the routing control center (RCC) has to choose a path within the network for each connection request. It is therefore the

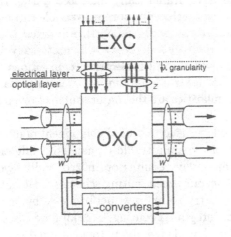

Figure 1. Multilayer node

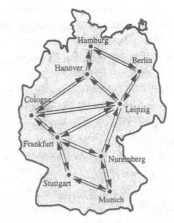

Figure 2. Network topology

RCC's responsibility to efficiently groom the connections. Four basic grooming options can be identified:

A **Single-hop grooming on existing lightpath:**
   The connection is assigned to one existing direct lightpath.
B **Multi-hop grooming on existing lightpaths:**
   Routing takes place on the electrical layer by using more than one existing lightpath and switching the connection in the EXCs of intermediate nodes.
C **Single-hop grooming on new lightpath:**
   A new lightpath is set up between the source and the destination node. The connection request is routed on the optical layer via this new lightpath.
D **Combined multi-hop grooming on new and existing lightpaths:**
   This is a combination of options A and C. The connection request can be routed on both the electrical and optical layer by using a series of existing and new lightpaths.

Non-integrated routing schemes are capable of grooming on either existing or new lightpaths. In contrast to that, integrated routing schemes have enough information to also perform the combined grooming described in D. As a reference, two different non-integrated routing schemes will be considered, namely *Prefer-Optical* and *PreferElectrical* (*TLRC* in [3]). Both schemes belong to the class of *overlay schemes* [5] and differ in the order they apply the different grooming policies until one succeeds. In *PreferOptical*, the options are applied in the order A-C-B, whereas in *PreferElectrical* the order is A-B-C.

3 Weighted Integrated Routing (WIR)

3.1 Basic Concept

In contrast to the non-integrated routing schemes, *WIR* explores the different grooming strategies in parallel, including combined grooming. This implies that in any case all grooming strategies are considered, whereas non-integrated routing schemes apply the grooming strategies in a particular order and interrupt their search once a grooming strategy delivers a valid path. In *WIR*, each possible path that results from a grooming strategy is rated according to a set of criteria representing the path cost. Finally, the path with the best rating is chosen to route the connection. The process of rating paths is described in detail in sections 3.2 and 3.3.

The ability of the routing scheme to perform combined grooming is an important design issue. On the one hand, the quality of the algorithm has a major influence on the performance of the routing scheme. On the other hand, it is much harder to find paths with combined grooming than applying grooming purely on the electrical or optical layer. Hence, it is a critical point in the design of the routing scheme to find an algorithm that delivers good combined grooming results at a reasonable complexity.

In [3], Zhu and Mukherjee use a reachability graph capturing all possible links for a given connection request between any two nodes for their proposed *SLRC*

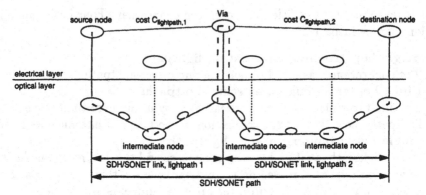

Figure 3. SDH/SONET path comprising two lightpaths

scheme. This approach has a constant high complexity. Here, an approach with variable complexity is presented. Combined grooming paths are searched along pre-calculated routes, for which the first N_{MaxAlt} shortest completely link disjoint paths from source to destination are used. On each of these pre-calculated routes, up to N_{MaxVias} intermediate nodes are allowed, in which the connection traverses the electrical layer. In the following, these nodes will also be referred to as *Vias*.

Fig. 3 illustrates how a connection might be switched within the network. In this example, the connection is routed along two lightpaths using one Via. A lightpath is represented as a logical link on the electrical layer and is also referred to as *SONET/SDH link*. The end-to-end path from source to destination node, on which the connection is routed, is termed *SONET/SDH path*. Eventually, any path alternative can be understood as an SDH/SONET path. Even a single lightpath is basically an SDH/SONET path comprising only one lightpath.

A route consisting of N hops has $N - 1$ vias. The *WIR* algorithm starts by selecting one intermediate node and rating all four possibilities for combined grooming with respect to that node (new–new, new–existing, existing–new, existing–existing). In this intermediate node, the connection traverses the EXC whereas it is kept on the optical layer in all other intermediate nodes. That is, the node is a Via. Afterwards, the remaining intermediate nodes are selected one after another to be a Via, and rating information is gathered for any of the four possibilities for combined grooming.

If $N > 2$, the algorithm additionally selects two intermediate nodes to be a via and rates all eight possibilities for combined grooming (new–new–new, new–new–existing, ...), eventually looking into all $\binom{N-1}{2}$ possibilities to select two intermediate nodes. Altogether, the search for combined grooming paths comprises all combinations of selecting up to N_{MaxVias} intermediate nodes. The total number M of tested path alternatives thus is:

$$M = \left(\sum_{i=1}^{N_{\text{MaxAlt}}} \sum_{n=1}^{N_{\text{MaxVias}}} \binom{N_i - 1}{n} \right), \tag{1}$$

with N_i being the number of lightpaths of the ith SDH/SONET path within the set of N_{MaxAlt} shortest completely link disjoint paths. The parameter N_{MaxVias} can dynamically be chosen for each connection request thus minimizing the algorithm's complexity (see below).

In contrast to other integrated routing schemes which require complete information of the electrical as well as the optical layer [3, 4], *WIR* separately probes rating information on different paths from both layers and selects a path based on a cost C. This is a significant advantage for network operators, who often want to hide network details from customers. Note that the RCC only needs rating information from each individual layer. Non-existing or blocked lightpath requests can be signaled with an infinitely high cost.

Rating the different path alternatives is an essential part of this routing scheme and ultimately determines its performance. The following sections present methods to rate single lightpaths, and to calculate the rating of SDH/SONET paths from the rating of the participating lightpaths.

3.2 Rating an SDH/SONET link

An SDH/SONET link occupies one transponder at the source node, one receiver at the destination node and one wavelength on each optical link of the lightpath. If necessary, wavelength converters are involved in intermediate nodes. Using the shortest path with N_{min} hops between each possible pair of nodes as a reference, the following two methods for calculating the cost $C_{\text{lightpath}}$ of a lightpath were defined:

– Calculation using absolute path length

$$C_{\text{lightpath}} = (N - N_{\text{min}}) \cdot W_{\text{OptHops}} + N_{\text{conv}} \cdot W_{\text{conv}} \;. \tag{2}$$

– Calculation using relative path length

$$C_{\text{lightpath}} = \left(\frac{N}{N_{\text{min}}} - 1 \right) \cdot W_{\text{OptHops}} + N_{\text{conv}} \cdot W_{\text{conv}} \;. \tag{3}$$

N is the number of hops in the lightpath and N_{conv} the number of occupied wavelength converters. W_{OptHops} and W_{conv} are weighting factors. The cost of the transponder at the source node and the receiver at the destination node are not considered, since these remain constant for every lightpath.

3.3 Rating of an SDH/SONET path

An SDH/SONET path comprises one or more lightpaths, which are connected on the electrical layer in the vias. The cost C_{el} of an SDH/SONET path is made up of the cost of the necessary transponders and receivers in the vias and the cost $C_{\text{lightpath,m}}$ of all participating lightpaths. Two methods which take into account the cost of these lightpaths were defined:

- **Mean value calculation**

The weighted mean value of the rating of all participating lightpaths is included in the rating of the SDH/SONET path:

$$C_{el} = N_Z \cdot W_{PTE} + \frac{W_{lightpath}}{N_{Vias} + 1} \cdot \sum_{m=1}^{N_{Vias}+1} C_{lightpath,m} \ . \tag{4}$$

- **Worst-Case calculation**

The weighted rating of the most expensive participating lightpath is included in the SDH/SONET path rating:

$$C_{el} = N_Z \cdot W_{PTE} + W_{lightpath} \cdot \max_m(C_{lightpath,m}) \ . \tag{5}$$

$N_{Vias}+1$ is the number of lightpaths an SDH/SONET path comprises. W_{PTE} is the weighting factor for the cost of the *Path Termination Equipment (PTE)*, i.e. lasers and diodes. Additionally, the weighting factor $W_{lightpath}$ allows for the weighting of all participating lightpaths.

In a practical implementation, the different grooming strategies will most likely be applied one after another instead of in parallel. If, for example, single-hop grooming on an existing lightpath delivers a path with a particular rating C', subsequent combined grooming makes sense only with $N_{MaxVias} = \lfloor \frac{C'}{W_{PTE}} \rfloor$. This property can be used to significantly lower the complexity of the algorithm by dynamically reducing the default value of $N_{MaxVias}$ for each connection request.

4 Transponder and Receiver Dimensioning

As mentioned before, the number of transponders or receivers z_k at each node k is a crucial design parameter of the system. If there are too few transponders, connections will already be blocked at the ingress or egress of the optical network. On the other hand, if there are too many transponders, resources (and thus money) will be wasted due to a low utilization of these units. Therefore, network planning has to precisely dimension the number of necessary transponders and receivers.

The traffic demand offered to the transponders at a multilayer node consists of three basic traffic types. 1. The major portion is the node traffic A_{node}, i.e. the traffic generated by users at that particular node. 2. The through traffic $A_{transit}$ describes the traffic switched by the EXC but not originating from or terminating at that node. 3. The virtual traffic $A_{virtual}$ describes unused capacity on a wavelength. For example, if there are only STM-1, 7-STM-1 (VC-4-7v [6]) and STM-16 connections in an SDH-network, a wavelength can be occupied by two 7-STM-1 connections. In this case, the wavelength does not have enough free capacity to handle another 7-STM-1 or STM-16 connection, but only to handle two more STM-1 connections. This free capacity (which is "invisible" to some connection requests) can be modeled as virtual traffic $A_{virtual}$. The total offered traffic at the transponders of node k thus is $A_{transp,k} = A_{node,k} + A_{transit,k} + A_{virtual,k}$.

A simple but effective method to dimension the transponders is based on the assumption that $A_{transit,i}$ and $A_{virtual,i}$ are small compared to $A_i = A_{node,i}$. Assume further that most of the blocked connections are STM-16 connections (i.e. connections requiring an entire wavelength). The transponders can then be dimensioned using the well known Erlang-B-formula with one Erlang corresponding to a wavelength:

$$B_{transp,k}(A_{transp,k}, z_k) = \frac{\frac{A_{transp,k}^{z_k}}{z_k!}}{\sum_{i=0}^{z_k} \frac{A_{transp,k}^i}{i!}} \ . \tag{6}$$

If the traffic $A_{transp,k}$ is known and the blocking probability $B_{transp,k}$ is given, one can calculate the number of transponders z_k numerically.

For any given network topology, the number of transponders and receivers is the major variable cost factor. Therefore, the *absolute cost* was defined as the sum of all transponders in the network, which allows to effectively compare the performance of different routing schemes. For convenience, the *relative cost* was introduced as the absolute cost normalized by the sum of all w_k at all nodes k, i.e. by the max. number of installable transponders. Since in our model the number of transponders equals the number of receivers at each node, only the transponders will be considered in the remainder of the paper.

Given a certain cost point, the transponders are distributed to the network nodes via the Erlang-B-formula, considering the offered traffic at each node. This is realized by an iterative algorithm, in which for each node k the individual offered traffic $A_{transp,k}$ is used. $B_{transp,k}$ is chosen equal for all nodes. In each iteration step, $B_{transp,k}$ is increased or decreased, until the desired cost point is reached. As a boundary condition, z_k may not exceed w_k at any node. That is, the actual number of transponders z_k is calculated from the number of transponders as delivered by the Erlang Erlang-B-formula $z_{k,Erlang}$ as:

$$z_k = \min(z_{k,Erlang}, w_k) \ . \tag{7}$$

5 Simulation Studies

In order to study the performance of the different routing schemes, an event driven simulation tool was developed using the simulation library developed at the Institute of Communication Engineering and Computer Architecture of the University of Stuttgart [7].

All simulation studies were performed using a fictitious 9-node network of Germany, the topology of which is shown in Fig. 2. This network was introduced and dimensioned for static traffic demands in [8] using a traffic model which is based on the population and distance of the different nodes [9]. All links contain a certain number of fibers each holding 8 wavelengths. The ratio of offered traffic load in the dynamic scenario and traffic load used for static dimensioning defines the *system load* chosen to be 70% for all presented studies. On the optical layer, the dynamic routing scheme ADR3 [8] is applied, while the electrical layer uses a Dijkstra algorithm to compute the shortest route online.

The presented results were obtained without wavelength converters at each node. The influence of wavelength converters has been studied in depth in various publications (e.g. [2, 10]) and a similar behavior can be expected in the presented environment. The weighting factors for *WIR* were set to 1, and a worst-case path rating with a lightpath rating using relative path length was used.

A traffic mix consisting of 80% STM-1, 15% Gigabit-Ethernet (referred to as 7-STM-1 and transported as VC-4-7v in SDH [6], but without diverse routing) and 5% STM-16 connection requests was used. The bandwidth of a wavelength was chosen to be STM-16. Connection requests arrive according to a Poisson process with exponential holding times.

Fig. 4 shows the blocking probability for different routing schemes. As a reference, the graph contains the performance of an opaque network with static point-to-point lightpath connections of adjacent nodes, which is only competitive at a relative cost of almost 100%. The non-integrated routing scheme *PreferOptical* outperforms the scheme *PreferElectrical* by almost one order of magnitude. The integrated *WIR* achieves a request blocking probability, which is about one order of magnitude below the best non-integrated scheme and slightly below SLRC. There is a noticeable bend in all curves at a cost of about 0.55. For a cost below 0.55, the request blocking probability is dominated by blocking at the transponders. For larger costs, there are sufficient transponders available and wavelength blocking dominates, i.e. it has no effect to further increase the number of transponders.

Fig. 5 shows the request blocking probability for different values of N_{MaxVias}. For $N_{\text{MaxVias}} = 0$, there is no possibility for combined grooming, i.e. the WIR scheme is basically degenerated to a non-integrated scheme. Still, WIR outperforms the non-integrated schemes due to the use of rating functions. Increasing N_{MaxVias} by one, which means including combined grooming at the lowest level,

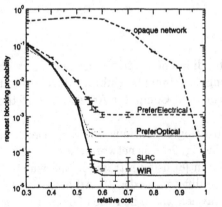

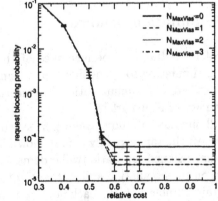

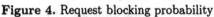

Figure 4. Request blocking probability   **Figure 5.** Influence of N_{MaxVias}

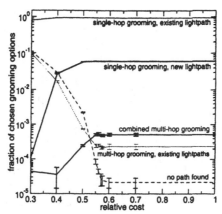

Figure 6. Path type distribution

lowers the request blocking probability by half an order of magnitude. Further increasing N_{MaxVias} gives diminishing returns. For all $N_{\text{MaxVias}} \geq 2$ the results are identical due to the limited path length in the Germany network. Not shown are the results when varying N_{MaxAlt}, since there is only a negligible difference in performance.

Interesting enough, combined grooming greatly improves system performance (compare Fig. 5). However, in the interesting cost range of above 0.55 it is only used for approximately 0.1% of all connection requests, as can be seen in Fig. 6. This picture shows the distribution of eventually selected grooming options. For low cost, an increased number of multi-hop paths on the SDH/SONET layer is chosen, whereas paths on the optical layer (i.e. setting up a new lightpath) become less frequently used. This is due to the lack of transponders at low cost, as the establishment of a new lightpath always requires a free transponder at the source and the destination node. For the same reason, combined grooming cannot be applied as often at low cost.

Several assumptions were made during the dimensioning of the transponders as described in section 4. Among others it was assumed that the through traffic in each node is negligible. To verify this hypothesis, the through traffic on the electrical layer $A_{\text{transit},k}$ was measured at each node and normalized by the offered traffic $A_{\text{node},k}$ at that node. The results can be seen in Fig. 7, which shows the normalized through traffic for each node and five different cost points (0.3, 0.4, ... , 0.7). For low cost there is a significant amount of through traffic present in each node. However, this portion quickly drops below 2% for all, and even below 0.1% for most of the nodes as cost increases. In the interesting cost range of 0.5 and above, the through traffic accounts for less than 2% at each node, which makes the assumption of $A_{\text{transit},k} \approx 0$ reasonable. It can also be observed that the through traffic expectedly is bigger in nodes which are located in the center of the network (labeled *transit nodes* in Fig. 7).

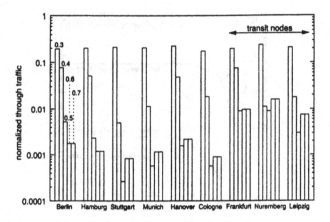

Figure 7. Normalized through traffic

In the course of dimensioning the transponders, another important assumption was that of only STM-16-connections being blocked. Fig. 8 shows the request blocking probability per connection request bandwidth for the two routing schemes *WIR* and *PureOptical*. Both routing schemes apparently favor connections with small granularities. This is obvious, since these connections can be routed more flexibly compared to connections that, for example, need an entire wavelength. For *PureOptical*, the blocking probability curves only differ by a scaling factor, whereas with *WIR* the blocking of STM-1- and 7-STM-1-connections is negligible for a relative cost of greater than 0.4. The reason for a virtually blocking-free behavior of the network for STM-1- and 7-STM-1-connections with *WIR* is that this routing scheme also allows for multi-hop grooming on the elec-

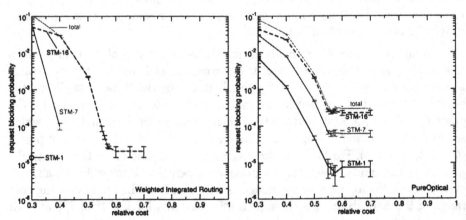

Figure 8. Request blocking probability per connection bandwidth

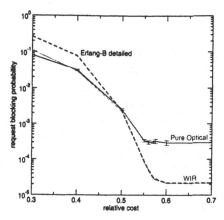

Figure 9. Lower limit of request blocking probability

trical layer and for combined multi-hop grooming, which makes it easy to find a path for connections with only small bandwidth demands.

It is desirable to predict the performance of a communication network before it is put into operation. In addition to the simulation studies, an analytical approach was taken to estimate the lower bound of the request blocking probability from the transponder blocking probability. Such an approach is likely to deliver a good estimate in the cost range of dominating transponder blocking. Using an iterative method with reduced load approximation, the request blocking probability caused by transponder blocking can be calculated for any node pair. These blocking probabilities are weighted with the corresponding traffic demand, delivering an estimate for the lower bound of the request blocking probability.

This estimate is shown in Fig. 9 (Erlang-B detailed). For the cost range of 0.5 and above, there is a good match between the estimate and the actual performance of the WIR-scheme. For lower cost, the estimate is not very accurate. The reason is that the presented Erlang-B-model does not take into account the different blocking behavior of different request granularities. In particular, the Erlang-B-model assumes a traffic mix of only STM-16-connections, resulting in a predicted request blocking probability which is too big at low cost.

It is astonishing that the estimate is even valid in the cost range where network blocking is expected to dominate. Further analysis leads to the insight that for a cost of 0.6 and above virtually all blocked connection requests originate from or end in small nodes at the edge of the network. The conclusion is that the optical layer of these nodes, i.e. the number of wavelengths w connecting the nodes, is underdimensioned. Since the number of transponders z might not exceed w, connection requests experience transponder blocking over the complete cost range if *WIR* is used. This interaction with network dimensioning is important and will be covered in future work.

6 Conclusion

This work presented a new integrated multilayer routing scheme with reasonable complexity that outperforms non-integrated and even more complex integrated schemes. A major advantage for operators is the fact that no full topology information of the optical layer is needed. Instead, a small interface between the Routing Control Center and the electrical as well as the optical layer for probing rating information and signalling new connection requests or connection teardowns is sufficient. Simulations showed that improved performance can be achieved even without the need for a full integrated view of the network.

Acknowledgement

This work is the result of a diploma thesis done under supervision of Prof. Kühn at the Institute of Communication Networks and Computer Engineering at the University of Stuttgart. The author would like to thank the thesis tutors Christoph Gauger and Stefan Bodamer for their excellent support and valuable discussions in the course of this thesis.

References

1. ITU-T G.astn Draft V.0.3, "Architecture for the Automatic Switched Transport Network (ASTN)"
2. E. Modiano: "Traffic Grooming in WDM Networks", IEEE Communications Magazine, Vol. 39, No. 7, July 2001, pp. 124–129
3. K. Zhu, B. Mukherjee: "On-Line Approaches for Provisioning Connections of Different Bandwidth Granularities in WDM Mesh Networks", Proceedings of the Optical Fiber Communication Conference (OFC 2002), Anaheim
4. M. Kodialam, T.V. Lakshman: "Integrated Dynamic IP and Wavelength Routing in IP over WDM Networks", Proceedings of the IEEE INFOCOM 2001, New York City, Vol. 1, pp. 358–366
5. B. Rajagopalan, D. Pendarakis, D. Saha, R.S. Ramamoorthy, K. Bala: "IP over Optical Networks: Architectural Aspects", IEEE Communications Magazine, Vol 38, No. 9, September 2000, pp. 94–102
6. ITU-T Rec. G.707/clause 11, "Network Node Interface for the Synchronous Digital Hierarchy (SDH)", 2000
7. Institute of Communication Networks and Computer Engineering: "IND Simulation Library", www.ind.uni-stuttgart.de/INDSimLib
8. J. Späth: "Dynamic routing and resource allocation in WDM transport networks", Computer Networks, Vol. 32, No. 5, 2000, pp. 519–538
9. M.J. O'Mahony, D. Simeonidou, A. Yu, J. Zhou: "The design of a European optical network", IEEE Journal of Lightwave Technology, Vol. 13, No. 5, pp. 817–828, May 1995
10. K.-C. Lee, V.O.K. Li: "Routing and Switching in a Wavelength Convertible Optical Network", Proceedings of the IEEE INFOCOM 1993, Vol. 2, pp. 578–585

Fluid-Flow-Ansätze zur analytischen Untersuchung eines Fair Queueing Bediensystems

Detlef Saß

Universität Stuttgart
Institut für Nachrichtenvermittlung und Datenverarbeitung
DSass@santiron.de

Zusammenfassung Um unterschiedliche Dienstgüten bei der Übertragung von Daten zu garantieren, muß der ankommende Datenstrom nach der verlangten Dienstgüte klassifiziert und in Warteschlangen isoliert werden. Außerdem muß eine Bediendisziplin vorhanden sein, die den aufgeteilten Datenstrom wieder entsprechend der Dienstgüten zusammenbringt und weitertransportiert. Es wird eine Bediendisziplin, erweitertes Prioritätenmodell, betrachtet, bei der jede Dienstgüteklasse eine Mindest-Bandbreite zur Verfügung hat. Dabei kann eine Dienstgüteklasse Bandbreite von der höherprioren Klasse leihen, wenn diese Klasse Bandbreite übrig hat. Dadurch kann eine effizientere Ausnutzung der Bandbreiten erreicht werden. Für diese Disziplin wird mit Hilfe der Fluid-Flow-Methode ein mathematisches Modell vorgestellt.

1   Einleitung

Im heutigen Zeitalter der Informationsgesellschaft wird die Welt in immer höherem Grade vernetzt. Dabei besteht die Idee Informationen jeglicher Art zwischen unterschiedlichsten Geräten und Orten auf einer möglichst einheitlichen Infrastruktur zu transportieren. Dies kann durch diensteintegrierenden Netze realisiert werden.

In diensteintegrierenden Netzen werden Informationen unterschiedlichster Dienstgüte gemeinsam transportiert. Um dennoch unterschiedliche Dienste anbieten zu können, warten Informationen in nach (Dienst-) Klassen isolierten Warteschlangen auf freiwerdende Resourcen. Ein Scheduler kontrolliert die Bedienung der Warteschlangen nach bestimmten Kriterien.

In dieser Arbeit wird ein sogenanntes *erweitertes Prioritätensystem* mathematisch beschrieben bei dem jede Klasse ein reservierte Mindestbandbreite zu Verfügung hat. Um statistisches Multiplexen zu ermöglichen, kann eine niederpriore Klasse Bandbreite von höherprioren Klassen leihen. Unter der Annahme, daß niederpriore Klassen ihre Mindestbandbreite eher ausnutzen werden, können höherpriore von niederprioren Klassen keine Bandbreite leihen. In Abb. 1 wird dies für den Spezialfall mit zwei Klassen dargestellt.

Dieses System erweitert das von Elwalid und Mitra in [3] vorgestellte Prioritätensystem um eine genauere Approximation der Verteilungsfunktionen

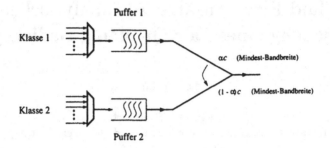

Abbildung 1. Grundmodell des erweiterten Prioritätenmodell

des Pufferinhalts und der Gewährung einer Mindest-Bandbreite der einzelnen Diestgüteklassen.

Das Papier ist wie folgt strukturiert. In Abschnitt 2 wird die Fluid Flow Methode aufgearbeitet. In Abschnitt 3 wird das erweiterte Prioritätenmodell erläutert und in Abschnitt 4 erfolgt eine Leistungsbewertung.

2 Fluid-Flow-Methode

Durch die Fluid-Flow-Methode kann ein FIFO-Modell (first-in-first-out Modell) analytisch beschrieben werden. Diese Methode wurde zuerst in [1] vorgestellt und danach durch viele weitere Veröffentlichungen weiterentwickelt.

Beim FIFO-Modell wird der ankommende Datenstrom in einen einzigen Puffer geleitet. In diesem werden die Daten nach ihrem zeitlichen Eintreffen eventuell zwischengespeichert und dann in dieser Reihenfolge abgearbeitet. Die Daten werden nur zwischengespeichert, wenn die ankommende Datenstromrate größer ist als die Bedienrate oder wenn sich bereits Daten im Puffer befinden.

Der entscheidende Ansatz bei der Fluid-Flow-Methode ist die Betrachtung des Datenverkehrs, wie der Name schon andeutet, als Flüssigkeitsströme. Dies bedeutet unter anderem, daß letztendlich nicht mehr die Datenpakete gezählt werden, sondern daß der Datenstrom als kontinuierlicher und gleichförmiger Fluß interpretiert wird. Vom mathematischen Standpunkt aus ist dies ein Übergang von einer diskreten Anschauung in eine stetige, kontinuierliche Anschauung. Der wesentliche Unterschied zur paketorientierten Anschauung ist der, daß sich der Datenstrom beliebig fein granulieren läßt. Damit kann erreicht werden, daß die Bedieneinheit nicht mehr mit einem einzelnen Datenpaket belegt bzw. blockiert ist, da die Bearbeitung jeweils an einer beliebigen Stelle stoppen und starten kann.

Hat der Quellprozeß Zustandsdauern die negativ-exponentiell verteilt sind, dann wird der Quellprozeß als *Markov Modulates Fluid Process* (kurz MMFP) bezeichnet. Entsprechend wird der Bedienprozeß als MMFP bezeichnet. Im folgenden wird der Bedienprozeß als Abflußprozeß bezeichnet, um deutlicher auf die Situation einzugehen, daß Flüssigkeitsprozesse betrachtet werden.

Die Fluid-Flow-Methode beschreibt das FIFO-Modell für eine große Puffer-größe sehr gut, da der Effekt, daß kurzfristig phasengleich Datenpakete ankommen können, durch einen genügend großen Puffer kompensiert werden kann.

Sei nun der Ankunftsprozeß ein Markov Modulates Fluid Process (MMFP) der durch die Übergangsratenmatrix M der Dimension $N+1$ und den Sende-ratenvektor r charakterisiert. Sei außerdem c die konstante Abflußrate mit dem der Puffer bedient wird.

Das ij-te Matrixelement $(M)_{ij}$ entspricht der Übergangsrate vom Zustand j in den Zustand i. Die Diagonalelemente der Matrix M müssen so gewählt werden, daß die Spaltensummen 0 ergeben.[1]

Sei $\pi_i(t, x)$ die Verteilungsfunktion des Pufferinhaltes des Systems zum Zeitpunkt t aus, wenn die Markov-Kette sich im Zustand i befindet, d.h.

$$\pi_i(t, x) := \mathrm{P}[\text{"Zustand zum Zeitpunkt } t\text{ "} = i \wedge$$
$$\text{"Pufferinhalt zum Zeitpunkt } t\text{ "} \leq x]. \tag{1}$$

Die zukünftige Entwicklung eines Markov-Prozesses hängt wegen der Eigenschaft der Gedächtnislosigkeit nur vom aktuellen Zustand ab, daraus ergibt sich der folgende grundlegende Lösungsansatz. Zur Bestimmung der Verteilungsfunktionen π_i ($i = 0, \ldots, N$) wird das System zum Zeitpunkt $t+\Delta t$ betrachtet und die Verteilungsfunktion zu diesem Zeitpunkt durch die Verteilungsfunktionen zum Zeitpunkt t ausgedrückt. Es können während der Zeitspanne $[t, t+\Delta t]$ für π_i zwei wesentliche Ereignisse geschehen. Es kann zum einen ein Zustandsübergang von irgendeinem Zustand in den Zustand i erfolgen oder es kann überhaupt kein Zustandsübergang geschehen. Somit ergibt sich der Ansatz

$$\pi_i(t+\Delta t, x) = \sum_{k=0, k \neq i}^{N} \pi_k(t, x - (r_k - c)\Delta t) M_{ik}\Delta t$$
$$+ \pi_i(t, x - (r_i - c)\Delta t)\left(1 - \sum_{k=0, k \neq i}^{N} M_{ki}\Delta t\right) \tag{2}$$
$$+ \mathrm{O}(\Delta t^2)$$

Nach geeigneten Umformungen und beim Grenzübergang $\Delta t \to 0$ und Zusammenfassung der Gleichungen in Matrixschreibweise ergibt sich folgende Gleichung

$$\frac{\partial}{\partial t}\boldsymbol{\pi}(t, x) + D\frac{\partial}{\partial x}\boldsymbol{\pi}(t, x) = M\boldsymbol{\pi}(t, x) \tag{3}$$

Wobei Matrix D als *Driftmatrix* bezeichnet wird und ist durch

$$D_{kj} := \begin{cases} r_k - c \text{ falls } k = j \\ 0 \qquad \text{sonst} \end{cases}. \tag{4}$$

---

[1] Die Matrix M ist eigentlich die transponierte Übergangsratenmatrix. Der Grund dafür liegt in der Links-Multiplikation der Matrix M in (5). Sie wird aber zur Erleichterung der Notation nur als Übergangsratenmatrix bezeichnet.

definiert. Die gemeinsame Verteilungsfunktion sei $\pi(t,x)$:=
$(\pi_0(t,x),\ldots,\pi_N(t,x))^T$.

Im stationären Fall, welcher für die weiteren Betrachtungen der wesentliche
ist, kann die partielle Ableitung nach t vernachlässigt werden. Bezeichne $\pi(x) :=$
$\lim_{t\to\infty}\pi(t,x)$, dann ergibt sich aus (3)

$$D\frac{\mathrm{d}}{\mathrm{d}x}\pi(x) = M\pi(x) \tag{5}$$

ein System von gewöhnlichen homogenen Differentialgleichungen erster Ordnung.

Dieses System kann durch die Berechnung der Eigenwerte z_i und Eigenvektoren φ_i der Matrix $D^{-1}M$ gelöst werden. Damit läßt sich die Lösung von (5)
in der Spektralform

$$\pi(x) = \sum_{i=0}^{N} a_i\, e^{z_i x}\, \varphi_i. \tag{6}$$

darstellen.

Der stationäre Zustandswahrscheinlichkeitsvektor $\omega := (\omega_0,\ldots,\omega_N)^T$, der
Eigenvektor zum Eigenwert $z_0 = 0$ ist, läßt sich aus der Normierungsbedingung
$\sum_i \omega_i = 1$ und den sogenannten "Gleichungen des statistischen Gleichgewichts
für stationäre Markov'sche Prozesse"

$$\sum_{j,j\neq i} M_{ji}\omega_i \overset{!}{=} \sum_{k,k\neq i} M_{ik}\omega_k \qquad (i=0,1,\ldots,N) \tag{7}$$

berechnen [10].

Die Zustände der Markov-Kette werden anhand des Vorzeichens der Driftwer-
te unterschieden. Die Zustände in denen die Senderate kleiner ist als die Abflußrate c werden als Unterlast-Zustände (Underload-Zustände, kurz *UL-Zustände*)
bezeichnet. Die Zustände, in denen dies nicht der Fall ist, werden als Überlast-
Zustände (Overload-Zustände, kurz *OL-Zustände*) bezeichnet.

Die Eigenwerte werden nach folgendem Schema indiziert

$$\underbrace{z_\tau \leq z_{\tau-1} \leq \cdots \leq z_1}_{\text{OL-Zustände}} < \underbrace{z_0 = 0 < z_{\tau+1} \leq \cdots \leq z_N}_{\text{UL-Zustände}}, \tag{8}$$

wobei τ der Anzahl der OL-Zustände entspricht.

Um die Koeffizienten a_i aus (6) berechnen zu können, müssen die Randbedingungen formuliert werden. Dazu wird angenommen, daß der Puffer die Kapazität
S hat.

Damit lauten die Randbedindungen

$$\pi_i(0) = 0 \qquad \text{für } i \text{ ist OL-Zustand.} \tag{9}$$
$$\pi_j(S) = \omega_j \qquad \text{für } j \text{ ist UL-Zustand.} \tag{10}$$

und bilden ein lineares Gleichungssystem der Dimension $N+1$.

Falls ein Wartesystem betrachtet werden soll, dies bedeutet ein System mit
unendlich großem Puffer ($S \to \infty$), dann vereinfachen sich die Randbedingungen
da die Koeffizienten $a_j = 0$ für $j = \tau+1,\ldots,N$ sind.

Werden nun mehrere verschiedene Quellen betrachtet, die in einen Puffer senden, dann kann mit Hilfe des Kronecker-Produktes und der Kronecker-Summe eine Ersatzquelle bestimmt werden. Mit dieser Ersatzquelle kann dann die Verteilungsfunktion berechnet werden. Seien die K Quellen durch (M_i, R_i) charakterisiert, wobei M_i die Übergangsratenmatrix und $R_i := \mathrm{diag}(r_i)$ Diagonalmatrix und r_i der Senderatenvektor ist, dann kann die Ersatzquelle durch (M, R), mit

$$M := M_1 \oplus M_2 \oplus \cdots \oplus M_K \qquad (11)$$

$$R := R_1 \oplus R_2 \oplus \cdots \oplus R_K, \qquad (12)$$

charakterisiert werden. Die stationären Zustandswahrscheinlichkeiten werden ebenfalls durch $\omega := \omega_1 \otimes \ldots \otimes \omega_K$ bestimmt bzw. durch (7) berechnet.

3 Erweitertes Prioritätenmodell

Beim erweiterten Prioritätenmodell soll jede Klasse eine vorher festgelegte Mindest-Bandbreite zur Verfügung haben. Die Summe über alle Mindest-Bandbreiten soll der Gesamtbandbreite entsprechen. Die Klassen sind nach ihrer Priorität absteigend sortiert. Die Daten einer Klasse werden (eventuell) in einem FIFO-Puffer zwischengespeichert.

Eine Klasse hat Bandbreite übrig, wenn der Puffer dieser Klasse leer ist und die Senderate der Klasse kleiner ist als ihre Mindest-Bandbreite. Dann wird die übrige Bandbreite der nächst-niederen Klasse zur Verfügung gestellt. Somit entsteht eine einseitige Kopplung in Richtung der niederprioren Klassen.

Das nachfolgende Modell unterscheidet sich von dem in [3] beschriebenen durch die Gewährung der Mindest-Bandbreite, einer unterschiedlichen Anwendung, Einbeziehen bzw. Lösen des modellierten Prozeß bzw. Gesamtsystems.

3.1 Ansatz und mathematisches Modell

Es wird ein System mit zwei Klassen betrachtet, da der wesentliche Ansatz und die wesentlichen Resultate bereits dadurch erklärt und entwickelt werden können.

Die Klasse i, ($i = 1, 2$), soll als Flüssigkeitsstrom (fluid process) interpretiert werden und soll durch das Paar Übergangsratenmatrix und Senderatenvektor

$$(M_i, r_i), \qquad (13)$$

welche die Dimension $N_i + 1$ haben, charakterisiert werden.

Eine andere anschauliche Darstellung dieses Systems, bei der die einseitige Kopplung besonders deutlich wird, ist in Abb. 2 abgebildet.

In dieser Abbildung wird ein Puffer als ein Gefäß ohne offensichtlichen Abfluß dargestellt. In dieses sendet die Klasse ihre Daten hinein und der eigentliche Abfluß ist ein Prozeß (mit einem Zustand) der die Daten hinausbefördert. Dies bedeutet, daß der Abflußprozeß als Quelle mit einer negative Senderate aufgefaßt wird. Die Unterscheidung Quelle oder Abfluß kann somit auf das Vorzeichen des Senderatenvektors reduziert werden. Dies ermöglicht eine flexiblere Sichtweise

438

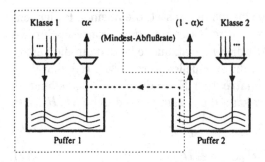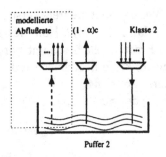

Abbildung 2. Alternative Darstellung einer einseitigen Kopplung (links) und Puffer 2 mit modellierter zusätzlicher Abflußrate (rechts)

bzw. Darstellung und eine vereinfachte Behandlung beim weiteren Vorgehen. Der gestrichelte Arm des Abflußprozesses von Puffer 1 soll die Abgabe der Abflußrate widerspiegeln.

Um die Verteilungsfunktion des Inhalts von Puffer 2 zu bestimmen, muß der gestrichelte Arm des Abflußprozesses von Puffer 1 in einer angemessenen Weise bei der Betrachtung Berücksichtigung finden. Diese muß das dynamische Verhalten der variablen zusätzlichen Abflußrate widerspiegeln, da wie in [13] zu finden ist, ein einfacher, undynamischer Ansatz nicht ausreicht. Dazu wird der gestrichelte Arm bzw. der Teil des Systems, welcher durch eine gestrichelte Linie umgrenzt ist, als ein weiterer Abflußprozeß für Puffer 2 modelliert. Dies ist durch einen weiteren Abflußprozeß in Abb. 2 dargestellt.

Der zusätzliche Abflußprozeß wird als MMFP interpretiert und geeignet modelliert. Damit kann der modellierte Abflußprozeß und der Abflußprozeß mit der konstanten Mindest-Abflußrate zu einem Prozeß überlagert werden. Dieses System kann dann mittels der Fluid-Flow-Methode, wie folgend erläutert, gelöst werden.

3.2 Modellierung des Abflußprozesses

Zur Modellierung des Abflußprozesses wird der Zustandsraum S der Klasse 1 in die zwei Bereiche Underload und Overload

$$S_{UL} := \{s \in S \mid (r_1)_s < \alpha c\} \tag{14}$$
$$S_{OL} := \{s \in S \mid (r_1)_s \geq \alpha c\}$$

partitioniert.

Die Zustandsübergänge der Klasse 1 innerhalb der Menge S_{UL} spiegeln das dynamische Verhalten der zusätzlichen Abflußrate wider. Wogegen die Zustandsübergänge der Klasse 1 aus der Menge S_{UL} in die Menge S_{OL} oder innerhalb der Menge S_{OL} keine Änderung der zusätzlichen Abflußrate bedeuten.

Die Modellierung soll anhand einer einfachen Markov-Kette plausibel gemacht werden. Sei Klasse 1 ein Geburts-Sterbe-Prozeß mit N_1+1 Zuständen, der durch

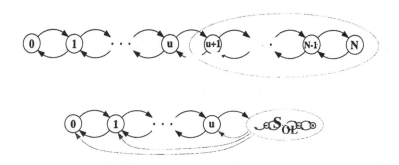

Abbildung 3. Zustandsdiagramm der Klasse 1 (oben) und der modellierten Abflußquelle (unten)

Überlagerung N_1 identischer, unabhängiger On-Off-Quellen entsteht. Sei Zustand u der größte UL-Zustand.

Die zu modellierende Abflußquelle soll die Dynamik der UL-Zustände $\{0, 1, \ldots, u\}$ widerspiegeln und werden deshalb in detaillierter Form einfließen. Wogegen die OL-Zustände zu einem Zustand s_{OL} zusammengefaßt werden. Es müssen allerdings zusätzliche Übergänge aus Zustand s_{OL} in $\{0, 1, \ldots, u\}$ bestimmt werden, da der Abarbeitung des noch gefüllten Puffer 1 Rechnung zu tragen ist, bevor Bandbreite abgegeben werden kann. Dies ist in Abb. 3 dargestellt.

Um UL-Zustände sehr detailliert einfließen zu lassen wird die Submatrix

$$M_{UL} := \{(M_1)_{ss'} \mid s, s' \in \mathcal{S}_{UL}\} \tag{15}$$

gebildet, welche die Übergangsraten innerhalb der Menge $\mathcal{S}_{UL}$ enthält. Die Diagonalelemente müssen allerdings so angepaßt werden, daß die Spaltensummen identisch 0 sind, damit M_{UL} einer Übergangsratenmatrix entspricht.

Sei $F(x) := (F_0(x), \ldots, F_{N_1}(x))^T$ die stationäre Verteilungsfunktion des Inhaltes von Puffer 1. Bezeichne $F_{UL}(x) := \{F_s(0) \mid s \in \mathcal{S}_{UL}\}$ den Teilvektor von $F(x)$, welcher nur die Komponenten der Verteilungsfunktion der UL-Zustände beinhaltet.

Die Situation, daß der Puffer 1 leer ist und leer bleibt, kann nur eintreten, wenn sich Klasse 1 in einem UL-Zustand befindet, der Puffer 1 leer ist und wenn nur Zustandsübergänge in weitere UL-Zustände geschehen. Die Wahrscheinlichkeit dieses obigen Ereignisses für die einzelnen UL-Zustände aus $\mathcal{S}_{UL}$ kann durch

$$q := \{q_s \mid s \in \mathcal{S}_{UL}\} := \frac{M_{UL}F_{UL}(0)}{\langle M_{UL}F_{UL}(0), 1 \rangle} \tag{16}$$

bestimmt werden. Das Skalarprodukt $\langle M_{UL}F_{UL}(0), 1 \rangle$ dient der Normierung.

Da die OL-Zustände für das dynamische Verhalten der Abgabe der übrigen Abflußrate kaum eine Rolle spielen, werden diese beim modellierten Abflußprozeß zu dem einen Zustand s_{OL} zusammengefaßt. Dazu muß die mittlere Zeitdauer bestimmt werden, bei der das System in der Situation verweilt in der keine Abflußrate übrig ist. Dies entspricht der mittleren Vollastdauer (mean busy period) der Klasse 1 und ist der Kehrwert der Übergangsrate, welche durch

$$\lambda_{s_{OL}} := -\frac{\langle M_{UL} F_{UL}(0), 1 \rangle}{1 - \langle F(0), 1 \rangle} \tag{17}$$

bestimmt werden kann.

Der modellierte Abflußprozeß läßt sich dann durch das Paar (M_{out}, r_{out}) aus Übergangsratenmatrix und Serverratenvektor charakterisieren. Diese werden wie folgt festgelegt. Sei d_{UL} die Dimension der Matrix M_{UL}. Dann haben die Matrix M_{out} und der Serverratenvektor r_{out} die Dimension $d_{out} := d_{UL} + 1$ und die Gestalt

$$M_{out} := \cdot \left[\begin{array}{c|c} M_{UL} - \text{diag}(a) & b \\ \hline a & -\lambda_{s_{OL}} \end{array} \right], \quad r_{out} := [\, r_{UL}, 0 \,] \tag{18}$$

Wobei $r_{UL} := \{(r_1)_s - \alpha c \mid s \in \mathcal{S}_{UL}\}$,

$$a_i := \sum_{k \in \mathcal{S}_{OL}} (M_1)_{ki} \quad i = 1, 2, \ldots, d_{UL} \tag{19}$$

die Gesamtrate aus dem UL-Zustand i in die OL-Zustände ist und

$$b_i := q_i \lambda_{s_{OL}} \quad i = 1, 2, \ldots, d_{UL}, \tag{20}$$

die Übergangsrate vom zusammengefaßten OL-Zustand s_{OL} in den UL-Zustand i ist. Für den stationären Zustandswahrscheinlichkeitsvektor des modellierten Abflußprozesses gilt $\omega_{out} = (F_{UL}(0), 1 - \langle F_{UL}(0), 1 \rangle)^T$, dieser hat die Dimension d_{out}. Es ist zu beachten, daß $F_{UL}(0)$ ein Vektor der Länge d_{UL} ist. Damit ist der zusätzliche Abflußprozeß für Puffer 2 vollständig beschrieben und die Verteilungsfunktion des Inhaltes von Puffer 2 kann mittels der Fluid-Flow-Methode bestimmt werden.

3.3 Bestimmung der Lösung

Sei π die Verteilungsfunktion des Inhaltes von Puffer 2. Um diese zu bestimmen wird die Fluid-Flow-Methode verwendet. Damit die Fluid-Flow-Methode angewendet werden kann, müssen einige Matrizen bzw. Vektoren definiert werden und Gleichungen aufgestellt werden. Dies wird nur in knapper Form geschehen, um sie an das in diesem Abschnitt betrachtete System anzupassen.

Dazu wird die Übergangsratenmatrix des Gesamtsystems, welches in Abb. 2 dargestellt ist, durch

$$M := M_2 \oplus M_{out} \tag{21}$$

bestimmt, welche die Dimension $(N_2+1)d_{out} =: N$ hat. Damit ist die Verteilungsfunktion $\pi(y) := (\pi_0(y), \ldots, \pi_{N-1}(y))^T$ durch das gewöhnliche Differentialgleichungssystem

$$D\frac{d}{dy}\pi(y) = M\pi(y) \tag{22}$$

bestimmbar. Dabei ist

$$D := \operatorname{diag}(r_2) \oplus (-\operatorname{diag}(r_{out})) \oplus (-(1-\alpha)c) \tag{23}$$

die Driftmatrix. Sie entsteht durch die Kronecker-Summe aus den Diagonalmatrizen der Senderate r_2 der Klasse 2, der modellierten Serverrate r_{out} und dem eigentlichen Abflußprozeß $(1-\alpha)c$.

Diese Vorgehensweise liefert für den Fall, daß der mittlere Drift

$$\omega^T D 1 < 0 \tag{24}$$

eine Lösung, wobei der Wahrscheinlichkeitsvektor ω ein (stehender) Vektor sein soll. Die Lösung kann durch die Spektraldarstellung

$$\pi(y) = \sum_i a_i e^{z_i x} \varphi_i \tag{25}$$

dargestellt werden. Wobei die Eigenwerte mit z_i und die zugehörigen Eigenvektoren mit φ_i bezeichnet worden sind. Die Koeffizienten werden durch die Randbedingungen, wie sie in Abschnitt 2 angegeben sind, bestimmt.

3.4 Verwendung der Lösung

Bei Betrachtung einer endlichen Größe von Puffer 2 werden alle N Eigenwerte bzw. Eigenvektoren betrachtet. Dieser Ansatz kann bei großer Puffergröße bzw. bei großen Eigenwerten zu numerischen Problemen führen. Diese Probleme können verringert werden, wenn der Puffer 2 als unendlich groß betrachtet wird und die Verlustwahrscheinlichkeit durch die Überschreitungswahrscheinlichkeit nach oben abgeschätzt wird. Die Überschreitungswahrscheinlichkeit wird durch

$$l(y) = 1 - \langle \pi(y), 1 \rangle \tag{26}$$

bestimmt.

Es können unter Umständen aber immer noch numerische Probleme auftreten, trotz der Betrachtung der nicht-positiven Eigenwerte, bei denen keine vernünftige Lösung zu bestimmen ist. Aus diesem Grund kann der Ansatz aus [3], welcher den dominanten (größten negativen) Eigenwert z_1 der Matrix $D^{-1}M$ und die Chernoff-Schranke L_0 verwendet, auf das hier betrachtete System übertragen werden. Diese soll im folgenden als ECDE-Approximation (extented Chernoff dominant eigenvalue) bezeichnet werden. Die Bestimmung der Chernoff-Schranke wird in [3], [13] erläutert. Damit kann die Überschreitungswahrscheinlichkeit durch

$$l(y) \leq L_0 e^{z_1 y} \tag{27}$$

abgeschätzt werden.

Der Ansatz für ein System mit zwei Klassen kann auf mehrere angewendet werden. Dazu werden die ersten beiden Klassen, entsprechend der Reihenfolge, wie die Klassen die übrige Abflußrate erhalten sollen, zuerst betrachtet. Dann wird nach obigem Ansatz der zusätzliche Abflußprozeß für die zweite Klasse aus der ersten Klasse modelliert. Dieser wird dann dazu verwendet, die Verteilungsfunktion des Pufferinhaltes der zweiten Klasse zu bestimmen. Der modellierte zusätzliche Abflußprozeß von der ersten Klasse und der konstante Abflußprozeß der zweiten Klasse werden aggregiert. Damit kann dann der zusätzliche Abflußprozeß der übrigen Abflußrate für die dritte Klasse modelliert werden. Dieses Verfahren wird rekursiv auf die noch verbleibenden Klassen angewendet. Dabei ensteht bei jeder Modellierung des zusätzlichen Abflußprozesses ein Fehler, welcher sich dementsprechend verstärkt und fortpflanzt. Dieser Sachverhalt wurde hier nicht untersucht, da in den meisten Fällen tatsächlich zwei verschiedene Klassen ausreichend sind [2].

4 Leistungsbewertung

Die oben beschriebene Approximationen wurde mit dem Programm MATLAB bzw. Octave numerisch bestimmt und mit den Simulationsdaten, welche durch die Simulationsumgebung SimLib des Insitutes für Nachrichtenvermittlung u. Datenverarbeitung der Universität Stuttgart [9] gewonnen wurden, verglichen.

Die Quellen einer Klasse wurden als identische, unabhängige On-Off-Quellen gewählt mit negativ-exponentiell verteilten Zustandszeiten mit Parameter μ_i, λ_i und Senderate h_i. Die Anzahl der Quellen je Klasse sind identisch.

Mit "Simulation Puffer 1" bzw. "Puffer 2" werden die Graphen der Überschreitungswahrscheinlichkeiten für den entsprechenden Puffer bezeichnet, welche durch die Simulation gewonnen worden sind.

Die beiden Approximationen der Überschreitungswahrscheinlichkeit wurden für (26) mit "Approximation des Puffer 2" und für (27) mit "ECDE Puffer 2", die Fluid-Flow-Lösung für Puffer 1 als "FFM Puffer 1", bezeichnet.

Diese Graphen sollen anhand Abb. 4 exemplarisch für eine Situation mit 20 Quellen je Klasse dargestellt werden.

Die ECDE-Approximation liefert eine konservative Abschätzung allerdings mit einer stärkeren Überschätzung der Überschreitungswahrscheinlichkeit des Puffer 2, da nur ein Eigenwert und die Chernoff-Schranke dort einfließen. Die oben ausführlicher beschriebene Approximation bei der alle (bzw. alle negativen) Eigenwerte einfließen liefert ein deutlich genaueres Ergebnis, allerdings liegt hier eine Unterschätzung der Überschreitungswahrscheinlichkeit vor. Diese ist allerdings eine deutlich geringere Abweichung als die Abweichung der ECDE-Approximation. Somit spiegelt die Approximation aus Abschnitt 3 genauer den Verlauf der Überschreitungswahrscheinlichkeit von Puffer 2 wider. Der bekannte Ansatz der Fluid-Flow-Methode aus [1] entspricht dem Graph "FFM Puffer 1", mit der erwarteten guten Übereinstimmung.

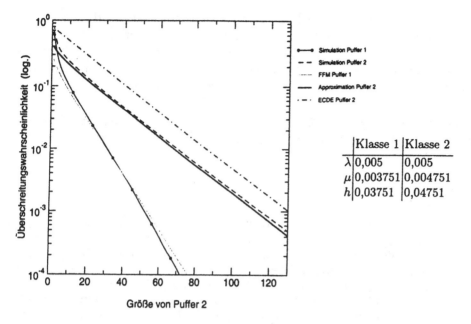

The following table appears within the figure:

	Klasse 1	Klasse 2
λ	0,005	0,005
μ	0,003751	0,004751
h	0,03751	0,04751

Abbildung 4. Verlustwahrscheinlichkeiten der Puffer ($\alpha = \frac{1}{2}$, 10^7 Pakete)

Der Grund weshalb bei der Approximation von Puffer 2 ein Unterschätzung zur Simulation vorliegt wurde noch nicht ausführlich genug untersucht. Es könnte zum einen sein, daß eventuell die Interpretation des Abflußprozeß von Puffer 1 als MMFP und die damit verbundene Gedächtnislosigkeit des Prozesses nicht vollständig die reale Situation widerspiegelt. Zum anderen könnten es numerische Ungenauigkeiten sein, da Gleichungssysteme gelöst worden sind bzw. Ähnlichkeitstransformationen zur Bestimmung der Eigenwerte durchgeführt worden sind. Vorallem aber, da die numerischen Ergebnisse von Puffer 1 verwendet werden müssen um den Abflußprozeß numerisch zu modellieren. Dieses wird dann wiederum zur Bestimmung der Fluid-Flow-Lösung verwendet.

5 Zusammenfaßung und Ausblick

Für die hier betrachtete Bediendisziplin wurde eine Approximation der Verteilungsfunktion für den Inhalt des gekoppelten Puffers, dies entpricht dem Puffer der sich Bandbreite ausleihen kann, bestimmt. Daraus läßt sich die Verlustwahrscheinlichkeit des Puffers und eine Abschätzung dieser bestimmen.

Die Abschätzung (27) ist eine robuste und numerisch schnell zu bestimmende Approximation. Dies erweitert das System aus [3] um die Gewährung einer Mindest-Bandbreite der einzelnen Klassen. Dieser Ansatz könnte zur Verbindungsannahmekontrolle (CAC) verwendet werden. Dieses CAC kann aufgrund der Gewährung der Mindest-Bandbreite unabhängig je Klasse durchgeführt werden.

Der Ansatz aus (26) liefert keine konservative, jedoch eine deutlich genauere, als die Approximation, welche nur den dominanten Eigenwert und die Chernoff-Schranke verwendet. Dies ist eine neue Approximation bzw. ein neuer Ansatz und wurde in [3] nicht betrachtet. Dieser Ansatz kann bei Dimensionierung- und Planungs- bzw. Designfragen Anwendung finden.

Acknowledgement Ich möchte meinen Betreuern Klaus Dolzer, Stefan Bodamer und Martin Lorang für Ihre Unterstüzung beim Estellen dieser Arbeit bzw. meiner Diplomarbeit danken.

Literatur

1. D. Anick, D. Mitra and M. Sondhi, *Stochastic theory of a data handling system with multiple sources*, Bell Sys, Tech. J., **61**,pp. 1871-1894, 1982
2. K. Dolzer, W. Payer and M. Eberspächer, *A simulation study on traffic aggregation in multi-services networks*, Proceedings of the IEEE Conference on High Performance Switching and Routing (ATM 2000), Heidelberg, June 2000, pp. 157-165
3. A. Elwalid and D. Mitra, *Analysis, approximation and admission control of a multiservice multiplexing system with priorities*, IEEE INFOCOMM 1995, pp. 463-473
4. A. Elwalid and D. Mitra, *Analysis and design of rate-based congestion control of high speed networks, I: stochastic fluid models, access regulation*, Queueing Systems **9**, pp. 29-64, 1991
5. A. Elwalid and D. Mitra, *Effective bandwidth of general Markovian traffic sources and admission control of high speed networks*, IEEE/ACM Trans. Networking **1**(3), pp. 329-343, 1993
6. M. Fiedler and H. Voss, *How to win the numerical battle against the finite buffer stochastic fluid flow model*, COST 257, 257TD(99)38, 1999
7. M. Fiedler and U. Krieger, *The fluid flow model with variable capacity*, COST 257, 257TD(00)18, 2000
8. L. Kleinrock, *Queueing systems, volume I: theory*, John Wiley and Sons, New York, London, Sydney, Toronto, 1975, ISBN 0-471-49111-X
9. IND, *Simulation Library (INDSimLib)*, www.ind.uni-stuttgart.de/INDSimLib
10. P. J. Kühn, *Teletraffic theory and engineering*, Vorlesungsskript, Institut für Nachrichtenvermittlung und Datenverarbeitung, Universität Stuttgart, Stuttgart 1999
11. H. Kröner, *Verkehrssteuerung in ATM-Netzen - Verfahren und verkehrstheoretische Analyse zur Zellpriorisierung und Verbindungsannahme*, 62. Bericht über verkehrstheoretische Arbeiten, Institut für Nachrichtenvermittlung und Datenverarbeitung, Universität Stuttgart, Stuttgart 1995
12. D. Mitra, *Stochastic theory of a fluid model of producer and consumer coupled by a buffer*, Advances in Applied Probability, **20**, pp. 646-676, 1988
13. D. Saß, *Fluid-Flow-Ansätze zur analytischen Untersuchung eines Fair Queueing Bediensystems*, Diplomarbeit Nr. 1676, Institut für Nachrichtenvermittlung und Datenverarbeitung, Universität Stuttgart, 2000
14. M. Schopp, *Analytische Behandlung allgemeiner Fluid-Flow-Modelle für ATM-Netze*, Diplomarbeit Nr. 1194, Institut für Nachrichtenvermittlung und Datenverarbeitung, Universität Stuttgart, 1992
15. T. Stern and A. Elwalid, *Analysis of separable markov-modulated rate model for information-handling systems*, Advances in Applied Probability, **23**, pp. 105-139, 1991

Autorenindex

Druck: Mercedes-Druck, Berlin
Verarbeitung: Stein+Lehmann, Berlin